# marketing

### SECOND EDITION

Greg ELLIOTT
Sharyn RUNDLE-THIELE
David WALLER

**WILEY**

John Wiley & Sons Australia, Ltd

Second edition published 2012 by
John Wiley & Sons Australia, Ltd
42 McDougall Street, Milton Qld 4064

First edition published 2010

Typeset in 10/12 pt ITC Velojovic LT

National Library of Australia
Cataloguing-in-Publication entry

| | |
|---|---|
| Author: | Elliott, Greg. |
| Title: | Marketing/Greg Elliott, Sharyn Rundle-Thiele, David Waller. |
| Edition: | 2nd edn. |
| ISBN: | 978 1 742 46721 4 (pbk.) |
| Notes: | Includes bibliographical references and index. |
| Subjects: | Marketing. |

Other Authors/Contributors: Rundle-Thiele, Sharyn. Waller, David.
Dewey Number: 658.8

*Cover images:* © Shutterstock/VikaSuh; Albachiaraa; Pavla Havlíková; grafica;
Kram78; DVARG; cg-art; Cristian Amoretti; Kuttly; Dora; mxz; Kraska, 2011.

Printed in China by
1010 Printing

10 9 8 7 6 5 4 3 2 1

# Brief contents

# Contents

## CHAPTER 5: Business buying behaviour — 145

## CHAPTER 13: International marketing — 457

# About the authors

## Professor Greg Elliott

Greg Elliott is Professor of Business (Marketing) and Associate Dean, International, in the Faculty of Business and Economics at Macquarie University, a position he has held since 2005. Prior to this, he was a Professor of Management in the Macquarie Graduate School of Management.

Greg has extensive experience in teaching marketing in Australia and overseas, and in course program management in South-East Asia. Before joining Macquarie University, he held academic appointments at the University of Technology, Sydney, the University of Western Australia and the University of Melbourne; and visiting appointments at Trinity College and University College, both in Dublin, Ireland.

Greg has published extensively in the academic marketing literature and his current research interests are in the fields of services marketing, financial services and international marketing. Prior to his academic career, Greg spent over a decade in the marketing research and marketing planning area of the banking industry. More recently, his consulting activities have been concentrated in the banking, financial services and professional services sectors.

## Associate Professor Sharyn Rundle-Thiele

Sharyn Rundle-Thiele is based in the Department of Marketing in the Griffith Business School, Griffith University. Her teaching experience includes introductory marketing, marketing management, market research and services marketing. In 2008 she received an Australian Learning and Teaching Council Award in recognition of her outstanding contribution to student learning.

Sharyn has published numerous papers in a diverse range of academic journals including the *European Journal of Marketing, Journal of Services Marketing, Journal of Consumer Behaviour, Journal of Product and Brand Management, Journal of Brand Management, Tourism Management, Journal of Retailing and Consumer Services, Business Horizons, Marketing Education Review* and the *International Journal of Bank Marketing*. Her most recent focus has been in the area of social marketing, and she is co-editor of the *Journal of Social Marketing* and the Treasurer of the Australian Association of Social Marketing.

Prior to her academic career, Sharyn worked in sales, management and marketing consultancy roles. Still actively involved with industry, she has worked on a host of marketing projects for leading Australian profit and not-for-profit companies. Her current projects include a social marketing intervention for alcohol in Year 10 school students (funded by the Queensland Catholic Education Commission and Griffith University) as well as a project to determine customer preferences, funded by the Mater Hospital. She has experience in implementing commercial marketing activities to a targeted audience in order to achieve social or profit goals. She loves to spend time with her three daughters, Dayle, Gabrielle and Rhianna. She also plays and coaches netball in an attempt to stay fit, and enjoys reading and travel.

## Dr David Waller

David Waller is a Senior Lecturer in the School of Marketing, University of Technology, Sydney. David received a Bachelor of Arts from the University of Sydney, a Master of Commerce from the University of NSW and a PhD from the University of Newcastle, Australia. He has over 20 years of experience teaching marketing subjects at several universities, including the University of Newcastle, the University of New South Wales and Charles Sturt University. He has taught offshore programs in Malaysia and China. Prior to his academic career, David worked in the film and banking industries.

His research has included projects on marketing communications, advertising agency–client relationships, controversial advertising, international advertising, marketing ethics and marketing education. He has published over 50 refereed journal articles in publications including the *Journal of Advertising, Journal of Advertising Research, European Journal of Marketing, Journal of Consumer Marketing, International Journal of Advertising* and the *Journal of Marketing Communications*. David has also authored or co-authored several books and workbooks that have been used in countries in the Asia–Pacific region, and is a regular presenter at local and international conferences.

# Applications at a glance

| Chapter | Opening case | Spotlight features |
|---|---|---|
| 1 Introduction to marketing | Everywhere you turn . . . | Amway and its ambassadors<br>Safe text<br>Just doing it<br>Wealthfarm<br>Consumed with happiness? |
| 2 The marketing environment and market analysis | Fast health? | In top gear<br>Up, up and away?<br>Let's get digital<br>The great Australian dream<br>Earth Hour |
| 3 Market research | Tuning in | So delicious the Italians want it back<br>What's the problem?<br>Phones net big spenders<br>Building donations through data |
| 4 Consumer behaviour | Gen Z: the new frontier | Tween celebrities<br>Online social networks<br>Pampered pets<br>Big decisions for little people |
| 5 Business buying behaviour | Global vision | The right chemical mix<br>Parallel imports<br>Flight turbulence<br>Brands and business buying decisions |
| 6 Markets: segmentation, targeting and positioning | The grey nomads | The money market<br>The Mambo evolution<br>An Intrepid adventure<br>Battle of the codes<br>Your choice of flights |
| 7 Product | Shooting star? | Toyota Hybrid Camry<br>Hungry Jack's gets 'angry'<br>The mobile battleground<br>iSnack 2.0<br>Running out of puff?<br>3D TV |

| | Closing case | | |
|---|---|---|---|
| Topic | Type of organisation | Type of market | Type of product |
| The 'Becky's not drinking' campaign | Government | Consumer | Idea |
| Youngcare and the donation landscape | Not-for-profit | Consumer and Business | Service |
| Hervey Bay leisure travellers | Government | Consumer and Business | Service |
| Time for a holiday | Government | Consumer | Service |
| The world of pharmaceutical marketing | MNC | Business | Goods |
| Online social intrusion (or target marketing)? | MNC | Consumer | Service |
| Apple iPad | MNC | Consumer and Business | Goods |

*continued*

| Chapter | Opening case | Spotlight features |
|---|---|---|
| 8  Price | Long way to the top | Great Wall, great value<br>Up in smoke<br>Black hole tunnels<br>The price of interest<br>Pricing by the book<br>Raising the bar? |
| 9  Promotion | Youi | Topical messages<br>Volkswagen Polo<br>Ahoy! An offensive ad<br>Killer' campaign against Nestlé<br>Good sports?<br>What do sales 'reps' do?<br>Sport, scandals and sponsorship |
| 10 Distribution (place) | Exporting flannel flowers | Gelatissimo<br>Toll Marine Logistics<br>Video on demand<br>Retail versus e-tail<br>CommSec: breaking the mould for broking<br>Costco |
| 11 Services marketing | The changing face of Australia Post | Ezypay<br>24/7 workout<br>Jumping the queue<br>Marketing a preventative cure for cancer |
| 12 Electronic marketing | Cradle Rock | Socially mobile<br>Illegal downloads<br>The devil in the eTail<br>Mobile marketing code of practice<br>Hidden Pizza |
| 13 International marketing | Boosting sales | East meets West<br>Westfield — an international retail empire<br>I still call Australia home?<br>Internationalising: a smart way to go? |
| 14 Marketing planning, implementation and evaluation | Bank bashing via Twitter | Keeping Cloncurry waterwise<br>Marketing sustainability<br>A well-deserved break<br>Drug driving |

| Closing case | | | |
|---|---|---|---|
| Topic | Type of organisation | Type of market | Type of product |
| Supermarket pricing: strategy versus tactics | SME/MNC | Consumer | Goods |
| The Resource Super Profits Tax | MNC | Business | Idea |
| Foodbank | Not-for-profit | Consumer and Business | Goods |
| Four is a crowd | MNC | Consumer and Business | Service |
| Tiger Beer — online and standing out from the crowd | MNC | Consumer | Goods |
| Subway in Japan | MNC | Consumer | Goods |
| Flight Centre — tracking customer experience and store performance | SME | Consumer and Business | Service |

# How to use this book

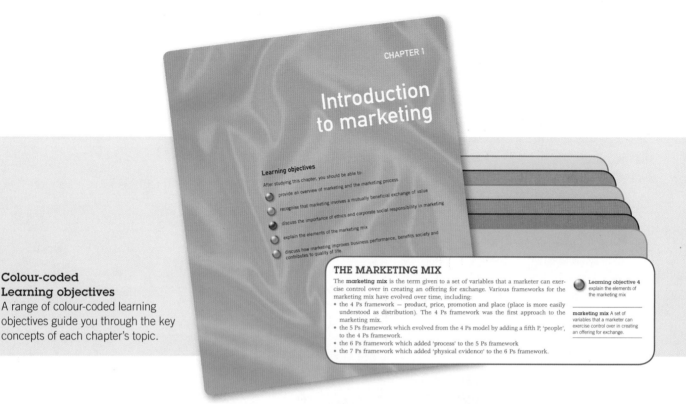

## Colour-coded Learning objectives

A range of colour-coded learning objectives guide you through the key concepts of each chapter's topic.

## Opening case/ Advanced activity

Each chapter opens with a real-world example, providing an overview of its theme and an opportunity for students to briefly reflect on their current level of understanding of the topic. This Opening case is revisited at the end of each chapter as an Advanced activity, where students are provided with the opportunity to demonstrate higher order thinking skills by applying key concepts that have been outlined in the chapter.

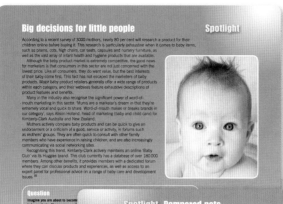

**Colour-coded Spotlights**

Throughout each chapter, several real-world examples are provided with accompanying applied questions. Each Spotlight is colour-coded to match its corresponding chapter learning objective.

---

## Concepts and applications check

**Learning objective 4** select specific target markets based on evaluation of potential market segments

4.1 Recall the most recent item of clothing that you purchased. Describe the market segment(s) at which you think it is targeted.

4.2 What factors should form the basis of an organisation's evaluation of potential market segments?

4.3 Choose a magazine that you read at least occasionally. List all of the possible market segments the magazine could target, and outline the competitive situation that the publication potentially faces in each. Which segment do you believe would be the most attractive for the magazine to target? Justify your answer.

**Colour-coded Concepts and applications check**

At several appropriate points throughout the chapter, questions and activities are provided to review and apply key concepts. These activities are colour-coded to match corresponding chapter learning objectives.

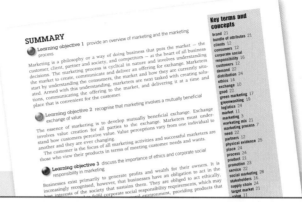

## Key terms and concepts
Key terms and concepts in each chapter are highlighted and defined in both the body text and the margin of each relevant page. A page reference for each is included in the end-of-chapter summary material. For ease of reference, key terms and concepts for all chapters are explained and page referenced in the end of book glossary.

### WHAT IS MARKETING?

Marketing is everywhere and much of what you do every day is in some way affected by it. Marketing is an evolving discipline and each marketer will have their own take on exactly what it is. Some people — mistakenly — think that marketing is selling; some that marketing is advertising; and some that it is making sure your business is listed at the top of every Google search that in some way relates to your product. No doubt, you already have your own ideas about what marketing is.

The most recent formal definition of **marketing** is:

the activity, set of institutions, and processes for creating, communicating, delivering and exchanging offerings that have value for customers, clients, partners and society at large.[2]

Figure 1.1 expands on this definition and begins to explain what each part of it means.

The definition refers to 'activity, set of institutions and processes', recognising the broad scope of marketing — that it is not just a function that exists as a 'marketing department' within an organisation.

**Learning objective 1**
provide an overview of marketing and the marketing process

**marketing** The activity, set of institutions and processes for creating, communicating, delivering and exchanging offerings that have value for customers, clients, partners and society at large.

## Colour-coded chapter summaries
A concise summary of each learning objective is provided at the end of each chapter.

### SUMMARY

 **Learning objective 1**  provide an overview of marketing and the marketing process

Marketing is a philosophy or a way of doing business that puts the market — the customer, client, partner and society, and competitors — at the heart of all business decisions. The marketing process is cyclical in nature and involves understanding the market to create, communicate and deliver an offering for exchange. Marketers start by understanding the consumers, the market and how they are currently situated. Armed with this understanding, marketers are next tasked with creating solutions, communicating the offering to the market, and delivering it at a time and place that is convenient for the customer.

 **Learning objective 2**  recognise that marketing involves a mutually beneficial exchange of value

The essence of marketing is to develop mutually beneficial exchange. Exchange involves value creation for all parties to the exchange. Marketers must understand how customers perceive value. Value perceptions vary from one individual to another and they are ever changing.

The customer is the focus of all marketing activities and successful marketers are those who view their products in terms of meeting customer needs and wants.

 **Learning objective 3**  discuss the importance of ethics and corporate social responsibility in marketing

Businesses exist primarily to generate profits and wealth for their owners. It is increasingly recognised, however, that businesses have an obligation to act in the best interests of the society that sustains them. They are obliged to act ethically, within the law, and to fulfil corporate social responsibility requirements, which may include philanthropy, protecting the natural environment, providing products that benefit society and generating employment and wealth.

## Supermarket pricing: strategy versus tactics

Coles and Woolworths dominate the Australian grocery industry, accounting for 80 per cent of the annual $90 billion national spend in this category between them. Two major supermarkets similarly dominate the New Zealand landscape (Progressive and Foodstuffs). By international standards, this is a relatively high level of market concentration. In the United Kingdom, for example, the *four* largest retailers between them have 65 per cent of the market. Interestingly, in the past decade, Britain's grocery prices have risen by 32.9 per cent, whereas Australia's and New Zealand's have increased by 41.3 per cent and 42.5 per cent respectively.

An analysis of supermarkets in Australia over the past decade provides an interesting insight into key factors influencing the price of groceries. In the past decade, the German-owned Aldi company has entered the market (and it is rumoured to be making plans to enter the New Zealand market in the future). Aldi currently has approximately 200 stores in Australia, predominantly in the more highly populated eastern states of Australia (New South Wales, Victoria and Queensland). This is compared to Coles and Woolworths, which both have approximately 700 stores spread across the country. Aldi supermarkets operate in a 'no-frills' warehouse fashion, with pallets of products parked in aisles rather than displayed on shelves, and minimal service provided to consumers. The chain also stocks a limited number of product lines (usually between 1000 and 2000; this is compared to the major supermarkets, which can stock up to 25 000 items), and competes aggressively on price.

Aldi's business model and associated cost structure enable it to operate from a cost base that Woolworths and Coles would find difficult, if not impossible, to match, especially at their higher current customer service levels.

**Case study**
At the end of each chapter, a case study is provided for more in-depth student analysis, further encouraging the application of key concepts to a real-life marketing situation.

APPENDIX

## Marketing plan

The following is an example of an actual marketing plan, which shows how the marketing planning process could be implemented. This model is a useful guide if you have to prepare a marketing plan.

### Marketing plan activity

Think of an organisation that you would like to be the focus of a marketing plan that you will prepare during this semester. Collect some background information on this organisation and its products (goods and/or services). Each week you will have the opportunity to develop and refine a draft of this plan as your marketing knowledge increases. By the end of the semester, by following the steps outlined in each chapter of the text, you will have developed a professional 'industry standard' marketing plan, and enhanced your practical marketing skills in the process.

A sample marketing plan has been included at the back of this book (see page 523) to give you an idea where this information fits in an overall marketing plan.

This marketing plan is based on a plan prepared by Brent and Carl Doherty and Cassandra Maw for adidas eyewear. Note that due to corporate confidentiality, some of the financial figures are not disclosed or have been changed. The authors would like to thank Brent, Carl and Cassandra for their permission to use the plan.

**Marketing plan activity/ Sample real-world marketing plan**
Students are encouraged to progressively develop a marketing plan for a product of their own choosing, via an activity at the end of each chapter. A real-world marketing plan is provided at the back of the book as an example to guide students through this process.

# Additional resources

This textbook is just one part of a total Introductory Marketing resource package. Additional resources are as follows.

**iStudy *Marketing***. This digital study guide contains a range of interactive modules and local videos to enhance student understanding and application of key marketing concepts.

**Wiley 'DeskTop' edition e-book**. A full electronic version of the text is available as a cheaper alternative to the printed text. The e-book runs on devices such as iPads, iPhones and computers.

**Blackboard, WebCT and Moodle** resources for *Marketing*, 2nd edition, are available for online teaching and learning designs supported by these systems. Your John Wiley & Sons representative can provide instructors with a demonstration of the rich resources available to enhance course delivery and student learning.

**PowerPoint teaching slides**, prepared by Lucy Miller, Macquarie University. These visually appealing PowerPoint presentations are an easy-to-use instructors' tool, bringing both marketing theory and real-world applications to the classroom. Numerous media slides featuring topical marketing-themed videos are provided to stimulate lecture or tutorial discussion and analysis of key marketing concepts.

**Video case studies**, prepared by Lucy Miller, Macquarie University. Local organisations and issues are featured, complete with accompanying student activities/thought-provoking questions that encourage the application of key marketing concepts.

**Instructor's test bank**, prepared by Lucy Miller, Macquarie University. The test bank provides an extensive range of multiple-choice questions to test student understanding, as well as short answer/mini-essay style questions to test higher order thinking skills. Questions are arranged by chapter learning objective and are identified as requiring factual, applied or conceptual knowledge. Each question includes a correct/suggested answer, a textbook page reference and a brief answer description.

**Instructor's Resource Guide**, prepared by Jannie Adamsen, Griffith University. The Instructor's Resource Guide offers a number of methods to facilitate course preparation and student assessment. Conveniently organised by chapter learning objective, these resources include suggested responses for in-chapter 'spotlight' questions; responses for in-chapter 'Concepts and applications check' questions; answers for end-of-chapter case study questions; and suggested responses for each end-of-chapter Advanced activity.

# Acknowledgements

The authors and publisher would like to thank the following copyright holders, organisations and individuals for their permission to reproduce copyright material in this book.

## Images

• © iStockphoto: **2** (middle left)/Dmitriy Shironosov; **25** (middle right)/Jacob Wackerhausen; **30** (middle left)/Gene Chutka; **146** (middle left)/manley099; **160** (top left)/Olga Demchishina; **256** (bottom left)/Joshua Hodge Photography; **293** (middle right)/mediaphotos; **331** (bottom right)/Sandra Gligorijevic; **388** (middle)/John Cowie; **388** (middle left)/Silvrshootr; **388** (middle right)/Dean Bertoncelj; **395** (middle left)/Alexander Raths; **395** (top middle)/monkeybusinessimages; **397** (bottom left)/Atid Kiattisaksiri; **397** (bottom middle)/Yu-Feng Chen; **397** (bottom right)/Gareth jago; **511** (bottom right)/Christian Wheatley; • © Shutterstock: **5** (bottom right)/Petoo; **56** (bottom left)/Elena Elisseeva; **74** (middle left)/Tim Tran; **94** (top left)/Yuri Arcurs; **112** (middle left)/Liv friis-larsen; **123** (middle right)/Ilya D. Gridnev; **126** (top left)/ssuaphotos; **139** (top right)/Melissa King; **152** (bottom left)/emin kuliyev; **206** (top left)/Adam Gregor; **267** (top right)/Igor Dutina; **346** (middle left)/MCL; **388** (top left)/Werner Heiber; **388** (top middle)/Anna Baburkina; **388** (top right)/Stephen Coburn; **389** (bottom right)/Monkey Business Images; • © Legacy Australia: **6** (bottom left); • © Getty Images: **7** (top right)/Bradley Kanaris; **20** (top left)/Bloomberg; **157** (middle right)/Bloomberg; **168** (top left)/Bloomberg; **173** (middle right)/Jb Reed/Bloomberg; **214** (middle left)/Rubberball; **231** (middle right)/Bloomberg; **245** (middle left)/Andrew Harrer/Bloomberg; **261** (middle right)/Bloomberg; **285** (top right)/Bryan Bedder; **309** (middle right)/Don Arnold; **333** (bottom right)/Kevork Djansezian; **341** (top right)/Tyler Stableford; **368** (bottom right)/Guang Niu; **368** (middle right)/Bloomberg; **369** (top right)/AFP/Omar Torres; **396** (middle left)/Mark Peterson; **415** FP/Torsten Blackwood; **441** (middle right) AFP/Ted Aljibe; **489** (top right)/Yoshikazu Tsuno; **497** (bottom right)/LGIS; **516** (middle left)/Doug Menuez/Photodisc; • © Amway: **9** (bottom right); • © Fairfax Photo Library: **13** (middle right)/Paul Harris; **39** Penny Bradfield; **42** (middle left)/Joe Armao; **178** (middle left)/Jason South; **277** (bottom right)/Erin Jonasson; **280** (bottom right)/Rebecca Hallas; **329** (top right)/James Brickwood; **378** (middle left)/The Age/Craig Abraham; **400** (bottom left)/Wolter Peeters; **408** (middle left)/Glenn Hunt; • © Chartered Institute of Marketing: **18** (top middle)/Triple Bottom Line taken from http://www.cim.co.uk/resources/ethics/home.aspx; • © Queensland Health: **34** (bottom left); • © Queensland Government: **35** (top right); • © Newspix: **46** (bottom left)/Grant Parker; **70** (top left)/News Ltd/*Quest Papers*; **105** (bottom left)/Sharyn Rosewarne; **115** (bottom right)/Stephen Cooper; **195** (middle right)/Calati Vince/News Ltd/3rd Party Managed Reproduction & Supply Rights; **201** (bottom right)/Stephen Cooper; **237** (middle right)/Dean Marzolla; **249** (middle right)/Brodie Campbell; **254** (bottom left)/AAP/EPA; **272** (middle left)/QNP; **303** (top right)/Parramatta/News Ltd/3rd Party Managed Reproduction & Supply Rights; **334** (middle right)/Justin Lloyd; **338** (top left)/Gregg Porteous; **367** (bottom right)/Paul Woodland; **373** (middle right)/News Ltd/Tracee Lea; **381** (bottom right)/Frank Violi; **410** (top left)/Steve Tanner/News Ltd/3rd Party Managed Reproduction & Supply Rights; **429** (bottom middle)/Andrew Ramadge; **457** (top left)/Brad Marsellos; **519** (middle right)/Bruce Long; • © Photolibrary: **50** (bottom left)/Photononstop/Till Jacket; • © AAP Image: **66** (top left)/WWF; **105** (middle left)/Steve Madden; **240** (middle left)/AFP Photo/HO/Australian Government; **248** (middle left)/Tracey Nearmy; **323** (middle right)/Gerald Herbert; **324** (bottom left)/Greenpeace, Sewell; **334** (middle)/Tracey Nearmy; **367** (middle right)/Paul Miller; **393** (top right)/Hilton Hotel Sydney; • © John Wiley & Sons, Australia: **81** (top right)/Renee Bryon; **84** (bottom left)/Renee Bryon; **132** (top left)/Renee Bryon; **174** (top left)/Renee Bryon; **239** (middle right)/Renee Bryon; **274** (middle left)/Renee Bryon; **276** (top left)/Renee Bryon; **289** (bottom right)/Renee Bryon; **326** (bottom left)/Renee Bryon; **363** (middle right)/Renee Bryon; **367** (middle right)/Renee Bryon;

**368** (middle right)/Renee Bryon; **368** (middle right)/Renee Bryon; **368** (top right)/Renee Bryon; **386** (top left)/Renee Bryon; **402** (top left)/Renee Bryon; **403** (bottom right)/Renee Bryon; **443** (top right)/Renee Bryon; • © Complete the Picture: **100** (top right)/Adapted from Complete the Picture Consulting Pty Ltd (2010), 'Mobile data survey — a global snapshot!, sample findings of PowerPoint presentation' co-published by Griffith University, Complete the Picture Consulting and mNet Group, Brisbane, p. 12; • © Globe International: **120** (bottom left); • © Linkedin: **124** (middle left); • © Jacqui Belesky: **134** (top left); • © Air Asia Berhad: **136** (middle left); • © Emma Knight: **142** (middle left); **242** (bottom left); • © Medicines Australia: **172** (bottom left); • © Corbis Australia: **181** (top right)/Andy Rain/epa; **197** (middle right)/Monalyn Gracia; **209** (bottom right)/Phil McCarten/Reuters; **232** (middle left)/Hannah Mason; **252** (middle left)/Boris Roessler/dpa; **464** (middle left)/Marianna Day Massey/ZUMA; • © Mambo Graphics Pty Ltd: **186** (middle left); • © Roy Morgan Research: **191** (middle left); **422** (bottom right); • © SRI Consulting Business: **192** (middle right)/SRI Consulting Business Intelligence (SRIC-BI) www.sric-bi.com/VALS; • © Toyota Australia: **221** (top right); • © Simon & Schuster, Inc: **226** (bottom middle)/Reprinted with the perfmission of The Free Press, a Division of Simon & Schuster Adult Publishing Group, from *Diffusion of Innovations*, fifth edition by Everett M. Rogers. © 1995, 2003 by Everett M. Rogers. © 1962, 1971, 1983 by The Free Press. All rights reserved; • © Palgrave Macmillan Ltd: **227** (middle bottom)/Schutte, H. & Ciarlante, D. (1998), *Consumer behaviour in Asia*, p. 77, MacMillan Press, London; • © Hungry Jack's: **228** (top left); • © Youi: **298** (top left); • © IKEA: **304** (middle right); **368** (bottom right); • © Volkswagen Australia: **310** (middle left); • © Department of Health & Ageing: **312** (top left); • © Chris Gray: **319** (top right); • © Gelatissimo Pty Ltd: **355** (top right); • © Toll Holdings Limited: **361** (top right)/Toll Group; • © Commonwealth Bank: **376** (top left); • © Ezypay: **391** (top right); • © McGraw Hill USA: **405** (middle left); • © Image Source: **407** (bottom right); • © New Zealand National Cervical: **411** (middle right)/New Zealand National Cervical Screening Programme, Ministry of Health, Wellington, New Zealand, www.cervicalscreening.govt.nz; • © Cradle Rock: **420** (middle left); • © Twitter: **424** (top left); **494** (middle left); • © realestate.com.au: **427** (middle right); Telstra: **432** (middle left)/Telstra Corporation Limited; **449** (bottom left)/® Registered trade mark of Telstra Corporation Limited. Sensis Pty Ltd has responsibility for production of Yellow Pages® directories and related products on behalf of Telstra Corporation Limited; • © Down Under Guys Gear Pty Ltd: **436** (bottom left); • © Drinkworks: **453** (bottom right); • © MAPgraphics: **468** (bottom right)/MAPgraphics Pty Ltd, Brisbane; **469** (top left)/MAPgraphics Pty Ltd, Brisbane; • © Transparency International: **473** (middle)/Adapted from Map 'Corruption perceptions index (CPI)' taken from http://www.icgg.org/downloads/CPI_2007_worldmap.jpg. Copyright 2007 Transparency International: the global coalition against corruption. Used with permission; • © Westfield Group: **475** (bottom left); **475** (bottom right); • © Richard Gould: **477** (bottom left); • © Gloria Jean's Coffees: **481** (middle right); • © Tourism New Zealand: **483** (bottom right); • © Ginger and Smart: **486** (top left); • © Townsville Queensland Solar: **505** (bottom right).

**Text**

• © Australian Marketing Institute: **15**/Australian Marketing Institute http://www.ami.org.au/bwWebsite/followon.aspx?PageID=5662; **514–15**; • © Nielsen Media Research: **127**; • © Interbrand: **167**; **233**; • © Paul Ellickson: **294**; • © AANA — Australian Association; **320**/Australian Association of National Advertisers; • © Department of Education: **331/32**/Department of Education, Employment and Workplace Relations; • © Cassandra Mow: **523–34**.

Every effort has been made to trace the ownership of copyright material. Information that will enable the publisher to rectify any error or omission in subsequent editions will be welcome. In such cases, please contact the Permissions Section of John Wiley & Sons Australia, Ltd.

## CHAPTER 1

# Introduction to marketing

## Learning objectives

After studying this chapter, you should be able to:

 provide an overview of marketing and the marketing process

 recognise that marketing involves a mutually beneficial exchange of value

 discuss the importance of ethics and corporate social responsibility in marketing

 explain the elements of the marketing mix

 discuss how marketing improves business performance, benefits society and contributes to quality of life.

# Everywhere you turn . . .

Marketing is everywhere. Take a look around and be amazed at how much marketing surrounds us every minute of the day. It might be advertisements heard on the radio as we wake up in the morning or it might be the billboards that we see as we pass by on our daily commute to university or work. Perhaps we try a new flavour of milk with our lunch or see a child who simply cannot live without the latest toy or the lollies on display at the supermarket checkout. We all need products in order to survive and most of us want products that make us happy. From the food you eat, to the clothes you wear, to the car you drive, and the media that you watch, marketing is everywhere.

Look around. How many brand names can you see? When you find yourself in a shopping centre or at an online shopping website, how many products do you have to choose

from? How many prices can you compare for the same or similar products? It seems marketing is with us — and marketers are talking to us — almost all of the time.

And from the marketer's perspective, customers and society have never talked back so much. Customers ask for customised or tailor-made products and a special deal on price; they want to be able to access products where and when they like; and they are more than willing to offer feedback on whether they are satisfied. Society as a whole is demanding that marketers work for the benefit of all of society and minimise any adverse effects of marketing activities. More than ever, marketing is becoming a discussion between marketers, customers and society that seeks to negotiate the best possible value for all the stakeholders in the marketing process.

## Question

Ask a friend to tell you what the word 'marketing' means to them. Write down and think about their definition of marketing.

# INTRODUCTION

Through accident or intent, the most successful businesses throughout history have been those built around and focused on making their customers happy — and doing it better than their competitors can. Every person, thing and process within a market-oriented organisation strives to create value for the organisation's customers. It is the creation of a mutually beneficial exchange of value between one party and another that is the purpose of all marketing efforts.

Recognising the importance of a market orientation to success, this chapter introduces the concept of marketing as a philosophy of how to do business. It explores the formal definition: 'the activity, set of institutions, and processes for creating, communicating, delivering and exchanging offerings that have value for customers, clients, partners and society at large'[1] and explains how this definition reflects the reality of marketing today.

A lot of people have the misconception that marketing is purely about selling. Marketing is most definitely *not* well described as 'the art of selling products to customers'. Not-for-profit organisations, community groups, governments and even individuals use marketing practices. For example, the Council of Australian Governments (COAG) Healthy Communities Initiative is an Australian government initiative that aims to reduce the prevalence of overweight and obesity within target populations. The target populations consist of individuals at high risk of developing chronic disease and who are not predominantly in the paid workforce. For more information about the campaign, go to www.healthyactive.gov.au.

Marketing, done well, is an approach to business that influences and informs every activity of the business or organisation. As you read through this chapter, think about how the ideas discussed can be applied to the things you encounter in your everyday life. You will realise that there are some common elements to each instance of marketing, such as product, price, promotion, place (distribution), people, processes and physical evidence. How these factors come together to provide a complete marketing experience is what differentiates one marketing effort from another, successful organisations from failed ones, and having loyal, satisfied customers from having no customers at all.

## WHAT IS MARKETING?

Marketing is everywhere and much of what you do every day is in some way affected by it. Marketing is an evolving discipline and each marketer will have their own take on exactly what it is. Some people — mistakenly — think that marketing is selling; some that marketing is advertising; and some that it is making sure your business is listed at the top of every Google search that in some way relates to your product. No doubt, you already have your own ideas about what marketing is.

The most recent formal definition of **marketing** is:

the activity, set of institutions, and processes for creating, communicating, delivering and exchanging offerings that have value for customers, clients, partners and society at large.[2]

Figure 1.1 (overleaf) expands on this definition and begins to explain what each part of it means.

The definition refers to 'activity, set of institutions and processes', recognising the broad scope of marketing — that it is not just a function that exists as a 'marketing department' within an organisation.

 **Learning objective 1**
provide an overview of marketing and the marketing process

**marketing** The activity, set of institutions and processes for creating, communicating, delivering and exchanging offerings that have value for customers, clients, partners and society at large.

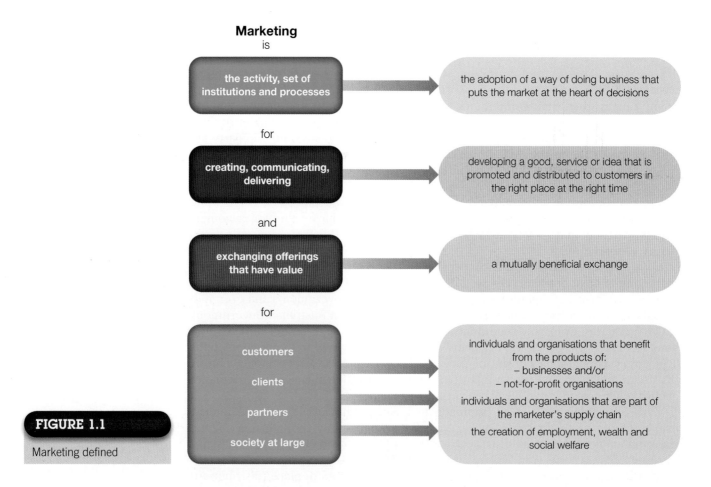

**Marketing**

is

the activity, set of institutions and processes → the adoption of a way of doing business that puts the market at the heart of decisions

for

creating, communicating, delivering → developing a good, service or idea that is promoted and distributed to customers in the right place at the right time

and

exchanging offerings that have value → a mutually beneficial exchange

for

customers
clients
partners
society at large
→ individuals and organisations that benefit from the products of:
– businesses and/or
– not-for-profit organisations
individuals and organisations that are part of the marketer's supply chain
the creation of employment, wealth and social welfare

**FIGURE 1.1**

Marketing defined

'Creating, communicating, delivering and exchanging offerings that have value' recognises that marketing must involve an exchange that benefits both the customer who buys the product (a good, service or idea) and the organisation that sells the product (a good, service or idea).

'Customers, clients, partners and society at large' recognises that organisations need to conduct their marketing in such a way as to provide mutual benefit, not just for the users of their products, but also for partners in the supply chain, and that marketers must consider their impact on society. Marketing brings many benefits to societies, including employment and the creation of wealth. With careful planning, some marketing activities can be good for customers, people in the supply chain and the environment. Consider McDonald's — one of many major coffee purchasers that changed their coffee buying practices in 2008. Today McDonald's only serves Fairtrade coffee. In order to prevent exploitation, Fairtrade coffee guarantees growers in developing countries a minimum price for their beans. Marketers must be aware of the impact their product has on society — and they must work towards minimising the negative impacts of their products and maximising the positive impacts. This is referred to as corporate social responsibility or sustainability. Corporate social responsibility is a commitment to behave in an ethical and responsible manner, to 'minimise the negative impacts and maximise the positive impacts'.[3]

Marketing is a relatively new discipline, which came into its own in the 1960s. Many of the ideas that underpin marketing theories draw on other disciplines, including psychology, sociology, economics and management. Many definitions of marketing have been proposed over the years and marketing, like any new discipline, continues to evolve today. Figure 1.2 describes how our understanding of marketing has changed in recent history.

## TRADE

Throughout history people have exchanged what they have for what they have wanted. While some core marketing ideas (such as mutually beneficial exchange) were at play, formal definitions of marketing did not exist.

## LATE 1800s/EARLY 1900s

As technology and infrastructure were developed and built, businesses were able to produce greater volumes of an ever-increasing range of products. Demand for these goods was strong. Marketing at this time could best be described by the concept of a 'production orientation'. Marketers' offerings were largely determined by *what could be made*, and what people bought was largely determined by what was available. This is summed up in the famous quotation of Henry Ford, 'Any customer can have a car painted any colour that he wants so long as it is black.' (Black paint dried faster than any other colour, so it was the most efficient colour to produce.)

## 1930s

As competition increased, companies could no longer rely on consumers to want and buy everything they could make. This led to the 'sales orientation', which focused on increasing profits through advertising and one-to-one selling. Consider the American Marketing Association marketing definition in 1935: 'Marketing is the performance of business activities that direct the flow of goods and services from producers to consumers.'[4]

## MID TO LATE 1900s

In the second half of the 20th century, customers had so many products to choose from that they could not buy them all. When they did want to buy a particular product, they could choose from many similar items. In a new era of increased competition, businesses realised that customers would not automatically buy any product that a business happened to devise. The approach to marketing changed to a 'market orientation' in which businesses worked to determine what potential customers wanted and then made products to suit. Marketing became mainstream business practice. Successful businesses in the late 1900s were those that adopted a market orientation throughout their operations and responded to the market's needs and wants.

## WHERE NOW/WHERE NEXT?

Today businesses are increasingly faced with not only satisfying customer wants but ensuring they are socially responsible corporate citizens. Businesses face well-informed customers with an enormous number of competing products vying for their attention. Marketers have broadened the concept of market orientation to view the market as not just their customers, but also broader society. This view is reflected in marketers' consideration of issues such as the sustainability of their products and the benefits their products might bring to society generally. This is known as a 'societal market orientation'. Examples of a societal market orientation in action include supermarkets offering to pack groceries in reusable bags, potato chip marketers developing chips cooked in lower-cholesterol oils, and health clinics offering free vaccinations. Companies with a societal market orientation have practices and policies that seek to minimise their negative impact on society and maximise their positive impact.

**FIGURE 1.2**

The evolution of marketing

As you study this book you will develop a deeper understanding of just what is meant by each component of the definition that we have described and, more importantly, *your own understanding* of what marketing is. Most importantly, though, you will understand that *for successful organisations marketing is a philosophy or a way of doing business*.

## The marketing approach to business

Marketing is an approach to business that puts the customer, client, partner and society at the heart of all business decisions. Marketing requires customers to be at the core of business thinking. Rather than asking which product should we offer, marketers who adopt marketing thinking ask which product would our customers value or like us to offer.

We are using the word 'business' in a broad sense. Remember that marketing is used by:

- small businesses and large multinational corporations
- businesses selling goods and businesses selling services
- for-profit and not-for-profit organisations
- private and public organisations, including governments.

As mentioned previously, it is important to recognise that marketing is not just about selling products to customers. In fact, for many organisations, that is not what marketing is about at all. Think about the following examples. They all involve marketing.

> FebFast is a national health and charity initiative that aims to reduce the impact of alcohol and other drugs on young Australians. It raises funds to support organisations working in the research, prevention and service delivery of alcohol and other drugs used by young people. Feb-Fast conducts a national education, awareness and fundraising campaign that invites people to sacrifice their alcohol consumption during February, and at the same time raise funds to support youth alcohol and other drug services. In recent years, more than 10 700 FebFasters have given up alcohol for one month, raising more than $1 700 000.[5]

> The Australian government maintains a website to attract tourists to Australia, providing them with an easy way to find and book activities and accommodation. By clicking on 'plan your holiday', for example, a series of itineraries are returned and potential visitors can explore a range of holiday options. Further, potential visitors can download a complete itinerary for a trip; search for and book their preferred type of accommodation; and gather information on other attractions, places to eat and so on. The website is one part of a broad strategy to attract tourists — the Australian government also uses television and print advertising under the tagline 'Share our story'.[6]

> In World War 1 General John Gellibrand made a promise to a dying mate that he would 'look after the missus and kids'. Over 90 years later, the organisation he founded is doing just that for more than 115 000 widows affected by some sort of military loss. Recently Legacy undertook a brand audit, which revealed that the organisation was not understood or seen as relevant to younger generations who had not been directly impacted by war. Historically, Legacy's relevance has been assured with older generations of Australians, who experienced World War 1 and World War 2 — wars in which the numbers of Australian casualties were severe. The findings of the brand audit have been used to reinvigorate the brand. Today Legacy increasingly focuses on younger families with loved ones serving in Afghanistan and Iraq. The organisation works with a tight $600 000 marketing budget to raise awareness and funds for the Legacy cause, through online channels, TV, radio, print and direct mail.[7]

Marketing is a science, a learning process and an art. Marketers need to learn what customers, clients, partners and society want. This is an ongoing process as customer preferences are continually evolving. Customers' needs and wants change with each product purchased, magazine read, conversation had or television program watched. Marketers must use information to maintain their understanding. Marketers must be creative and able to develop new ideas. Markets are cluttered and there are many options available to consumers. The best marketers are able to offer something that is unique or special to consumers.

> SKINS markets a range of apparel for athletes that enable, quicker recovery through muscle compression. Champion athletes are seen wearing the active wear with the SKINS brand emblazoned on it, thus increasing brand awareness and desirability among sports fans. Further, the technology that was initially designed for elite athletes eventually flows down to mass-market consumer products.

> The Gallery of Modern Art in Brisbane employs a person to survey patrons as they exit exhibitions. They ask patrons to rate the exhibition and facilities, why they came to the exhibition, how they found out about it, whether they visited the permanent art collection and whether they visited the gallery shop. This information is used to understand how the gallery can improve in the future.

## The marketing process

The **marketing process** involves understanding the market to create, communicate and deliver an offering for exchange. The marketing process is an ongoing cycle and often marketers will be undertaking multiple tasks simultaneously. However, when you start your first marketing job, you will have to start with 'understanding', and, for this reason, we will look at the marketing process sequentially. Marketers start by understanding the consumers, the market and how they are currently situated. This may involve undertaking some market research to gain insights into a problem the marketer currently faces or reviewing sales data to understand how the company is currently performing. Marketers need to undertake a situation assessment to understand how their company is positioned relative to the competition.

The understanding phase of the marketing process involves an analysis and assessment of the marketing environment and markets (local and/or international), as well as consumer and business buying behaviour. Marketers must start by understanding the situation they currently face, including both internal and external factors, in order to create a solution to meet the needs and wants of customers. Marketers use market research to understand consumer motivations, abilities and opportunities to act. For example, wine marketers can access market insight reports from a market research company, such as the Nielsen Company, in order to understand which wines they should range in their stores, how their wines should be branded and which consumers they should target with promotions. For example, a recent Nielsen report revealed that buyers of New Zealand wine are:
- more likely to be in their thirties
- more likely to live in metropolitan areas

**marketing process** A process that involves understanding the market to create, communicate and deliver an offering for exchange.

- more likely to have a household income of over A$100 000 per annum
- more likely to experiment within the wine category
- less likely to be brand loyal.[8]

Armed with this knowledge, marketers would understand that placing several varieties under one umbrella brand might be the best way to generate brand loyalty for New Zealand wines in Australia, and they could take steps to create, communicate and deliver such an offering to the market.

Let's take another example to illustrate the marketing process. Imagine that a food marketer, based on research and an understanding of current trends, determines that his company needs to create a new flavour of yoghurt in order to maintain or grow sales in this product category in the dairy aisles of supermarkets relative to competitors. Once testing and creation of the new flavour variant is complete, the food marketer needs to communicate the offering to the market. This could be achieved, perhaps, via mass media advertising and/or a point-of-sale campaign, in order to change the way a group of target customers think and purchase. The food marketer must constantly ensure their product is delivered and available at a time and place that is convenient for the customer. The new flavour yoghurt variant in this example has therefore progressed from the food marketer's initial understanding of market requirements through the production process and distribution chain — ultimately ending up on supermarket shelves, with target customers hopefully being fully aware of the new product offering. Marketers need to constantly monitor and understand their effectiveness in all aspects of this process, as this cycle is ongoing. Figure 1.3 visually represents these four broad components of the marketing process and the interrelationships between each.

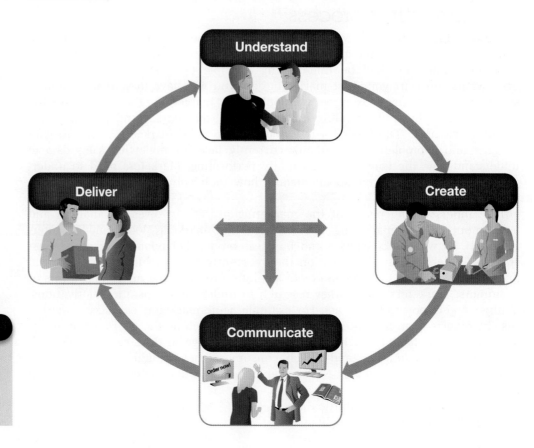

**FIGURE 1.3**

The marketing process involves understanding, creating, communicating and delivering an offering for exchange of value

It is important to note that delivery in the process outlined in figure 1.3 is also concerned with quality and satisfaction. Marketers need to ensure the offering (product, service or idea) satisfies the customer. Customers want products and brands that are reliable and services that fulfil promises. Many companies track quality to ensure they are delivering a product that is consistent, and which meets consumers' expectations. Marketers that are able to consistently satisfy their customers can build loyalty and, in turn, this can lead to word-of-mouth. It is commonly accepted in marketing that keeping customers loyal is cheaper than gaining new customers and that brands with a loyal base of customers have a value that is an asset for a company. For this reason, branding is studied by many marketing academics to understand how to build and maintain brands.

# Amway and its ambassadors Spotlight

Amway is one of the largest direct sellers in the world, with sales of more than US$8.2 billion. Founded in 1960, it has more than 3.5 million business owners distributing more than 450 health products in 80 countries. Amway prides itself on being a good corporate citizen. For example, Amway recently donated more than $450 000 to help disabled children ride modified bikes.

Amway started in Australia in 1970. Today it has 200 employees, with 100 000 people selling its products in Australia and New Zealand. Products are available in a wide range of categories, including beauty, jewellery, home essentials, accessories and gifts. Amway operates business centres in Sydney, Perth, Brisbane, Melbourne and Auckland. These centres allow people to go into a retail environment to learn more about Amway products.

Marketing is used by Amway to enable the company to provide better products, training and selling tools. For example, market research is performed to gain customer insights and to assist in developing the product range. In recent years, Amway has changed its product packaging in an attempt to freshen the brand and to provide global consistency. Amway has a multimillion dollar global marketing budget and invests heavily in advertising, training and online selling tools.

In recent years Amway has actively targeted its brand and product range to a younger audience. The company has done this to change a perception that it is all about soap and washing powders. Australian cricketing legend Adam Gilchrist and former Olympic swimmer Libby Trickett were signed up as ambassadors for Amway to promote its products. Gilchrist is the face of Amway's Nutriway range of vitamins, minerals and dietary supplements, while Trickett promotes its range of beauty products. In a recent Indian Premier League 20/20 cricket tournament, Amway set Gilchrist a target of hitting 25 'sixes' while he was batting. He hit 29! This promotion helped Amway to raise awareness for the Amway brand in many cricketing nations.[9]

## Question

Search Amway's website. In terms of what you have read in the chapter so far, how would you describe Amway's approach to business and the marketing process?

## Concepts and applications check

**Learning objective 1** provide an overview of marketing and the marketing process

**1.1** Find an example of marketing in action and analyse the extent to which you think the marketer has adopted 'marketing thinking'.

**1.2** Socially responsible companies must minimise the negative impacts and maximise the positive impacts of the products they sell. Describe the last purchase you made (or an instance where you chose not to buy a product) that was influenced by a company's stance on social responsibility.

**1.3** Find an example of a socially responsible company. Explain why you feel this company is socially responsible.

**1.4** Define marketing in your own words. How has your understanding of marketing changed after reviewing the first part of this chapter? How does your definition of marketing compare to the definition provided by your friend when you started reading the chapter?

**1.5** Explain how marketing can be used by not-for-profit organisations. Discuss an example in your answer.

# THE EXCHANGE OF VALUE

**Learning objective 2** recognise that marketing involves a mutually beneficial exchange of value

The aim of marketing is to develop mutually beneficial exchanges. Consider this example. A customer buys a 127 centimetre, 3D television for $3299. The retailer and manufacturer receive money for the purchase and clear one stock unit, which contributes to their profits. The customer receives their much-wanted television, which they hang on their wall at home. The customer enjoys better quality sound and picture and a more aesthetically pleasing television, along with many other benefits. Both parties have received a benefit and both parties had to give something up to receive something in return.

**exchange** The mutually beneficial transfer of offerings of value between the buyer and seller.

To be considered a successful marketing **exchange**, the transaction must satisfy the following conditions:

- two or more parties must participate, each with something of value desired by the other party
- all parties must benefit from the transaction
- the exchange must meet both parties' expectations (e.g. quality, price).

Once again, exchange can occur for all different types of organisations: large and small, for-profit and not-for-profit, and private and public. Consider the following examples of exchange:

> A farmer sells milk to a dairy goods company: the farmer receives 40 cents for each litre of milk produced, which is more than the cost of the land tax, feed, veterinary care, machinery, labour and other costs involved in producing the milk; the dairy goods company receives milk to process, bottle and package to sell for a profit to retailers.

> The Cancer Council Australia runs television advertisements encouraging people to protect their skin from sun damage. People become more aware that they should wear protective clothing when in the sun. The Cancer Council meets its objectives because more people are wearing protective clothing when in the sun. Long-term benefits will arise for society as the rate of skin cancer drops for the Australian population.

Both parties need to feel the exchange will leave them better off. Without this, exchange will not take place. Think about our first example again. The customer was quite happy to spend $3299 on a 127 centimetre, 3D television because the benefits received (3D picture, sound and aesthetics) outweighed the cost of purchasing the television. Further, the retailer only sold the television because it could make a profit that could be paid to the business's owners. Exchange is a value-creating process because it leaves both parties better off.

Like exchange, value is a core marketing concept. **Value** is a customer's overall assessment of the utility of an offering based on perceptions of what is received and what is given.[10] Some marketers view this simply as a ratio between quality and price. Another way to view value is as a comparison between what a customer gets and what a customer gives; in other words, the *benefits* a customer receives from a product in relation to its price.

The idea that value is a ratio between quality and price is a simple view of value to help you to understand the concept. Marketers know that the idea of value is more complicated. Value refers to the 'total offering'. This includes all aspects, from the reputation of the organisation to how the employees act, the features of the products, the after sales service, quality and price. Most companies have competitors and value is relative to the competition as the competing offerings influence how a customer perceives value. For example, say two different brands of diet yoghurt are available for purchase this week at Coles Online Supermarkets. Nestlé Diet Apricot Yoghurt 2 × 200 gram packs sell for $2.58 while Yoplait Forme Yogurt Banana Honey 2 × 175 gram packs sell for $2.91. It is likely that Nestlé will be perceived as offering more value with a cheaper price and larger pack size than Yoplait.

Value evolves continually. Value changes with each purchase, experience and conversation that a person has. For example, a student purchases a laptop online and tells her friend that by purchasing online she saved $100. Her friend had purchased the same model laptop at the recommended retail price at a department store near campus. She chose the department store because it was convenient and she does not have a credit card. While she was happy with her purchase at the time because it was quick and convenient, she no longer feels satisfied with her purchase because her perception of value has changed. Going back to the yoghurt example, the Nestlé yoghurt was on sale this week. It usually retails for $3.15. The Yoplait yoghurt may now be perceived to be better value.

Value means different things to different people. Value is unique for each individual.[11] Some customers perceive value when there is a low price while others perceive value when there is a balance between quality and price.[12] Going back to the flat screen television example used earlier, the customer paid $3299 for a 127 centimetre, 3D television. Another person might think that $3299 is an outrageous price for a television. It is clear then that value is a matter of individual perception. This is where marketing becomes a little more complicated, because marketers have to understand the perceptions of the market.

> **value** A customer's overall assessment of the utility of an offering based on perceptions of what is received and what is given.

## The market

A **market** is a group of customers with different needs and wants. Markets cover varying groups of customers from geographic markets (e.g. the Malaysian market), product markets (e.g. the smartphone market) and demographic markets (e.g. seniors), to name a few.

Markets can also cover different types of customers. Remember from our definition of marketing that marketing is aimed at 'customers, clients, partners and society at large'. The term 'customer' is used most frequently in this text to help you to better understand marketing because you are a customer. You are a customer who buys goods and services for your own and maybe others' use and you are already able to understand marketing from a customer's point of view. Our aim in this text is

> **market** A group of customers with heterogeneous needs and wants.

to teach you to understand marketing from a marketing organisation's or manager's point of view. While there are different groups that marketers cater to, the underlying principles of marketing remain the same.

Different marketers have to market to different groups. Some have to market to customers or consumers, others market to businesses or clients, while other marketers have to consider the needs and wants of society in general. The group that the marketer has to market to is the focus of all marketing activities.

Successful marketers are those who view their products in terms of meeting customer needs and wants. For example, a company that operates vending machines that serve hot drinks should view its business as one that quenches people's thirst, warms them when out on chilly winter nights and gives them a caffeine boost when they are feeling tired; not as a business that places machines on train station platforms and mixes lukewarm water with powdered flavouring in a cardboard cup.

We will now discuss each group — customers, clients, partners and society — in turn.

## Customers

**customers** People who purchase goods and services for their own or other people's use.

**consumers** People who use the good or service.

**Customers** are those people who purchase products for their own or someone else's use, while **consumers** are people who use the good or service. For example, a mother buys hair shampoo and conditioners for her own use. Her two children also use the hair shampoo and conditioner when they need to wash their hair. The children use or consume the products but they did not purchase them.

## Clients

**clients** 'Customers' of the products of not-for-profit organisations.

In the general sense, the word 'client' is often used as a synonym for 'customer', especially with regards to professional services such those provided by lawyers, accountants and architects. In the formal definition of marketing, however, **clients** refers specifically to 'customers' of not-for-profit organisations or social marketers (i.e. those seeking to encourage social changes), thus serving as a differentiator from customers of businesses. 'Customers' of Medicare, Centrelink or a public hospital and the viewers of anti-drug advertisements are all examples of clients.

## Partners

**partners** Organisations or individuals who are involved in the activities and processes for creating, communicating and delivering offerings for exchange.

**Partners** are organisations or individuals who are involved in the activities and processes for creating, communicating and delivering offerings for exchange. For example, a partner may be an advertising consultant who is hired to develop marketing communications to raise awareness for a sports club that wants to recruit new players for next year. A partner might be a supplier of raw materials or a retailer in the distribution channel. Thinking back to our flat screen television example, partners of the flat screen television manufacturer would include the retailer who sells the flat screen televisions to customers and the manufacturing company that supplies television screens to the television manufacturer. Marketers need to understand how their partnership will benefit the partner. For example, say a wine marketer wants retailers to stock their new wine. Before agreeing to stock the new range of wine, the retailer needs to be convinced by the wine marketer that including this wine in their product range will benefit their business.

## Society

Society is a body of individuals living as members of a community. A society is a highly structured system of human organisation for large-scale community living that normally furnishes protection, continuity, security and an identity for its members. Marketers must understand the needs of the societies in which they operate. For example, Toyota developed the Prius (a hybrid car that generates its own electrical power, thus reducing the amount of petrol it consumes) in response to growing concerns about the environmental impact of cars. Successful marketers demonstrate an awareness of community concern about the natural environment, responsible use of resources, sustainable practices and social equity. Studies suggest that companies that demonstrate social responsibility have higher profits and market capitalisation.[13]

## Safe text

Spotlight

Not only is marketing used to encourage you to buy goods and services; marketing is used to encourage people to undertake behaviours that benefit society. In Australia and around the world, chlamydia infection has been on the rise for several years. It is one of the most common sexually transmitted infections. In a recent year, nearly 60 000 cases of chlamydia were reported.[14] The highest infection rates are among people aged between 15 and 24. Research has found that although 61 per cent of teens rate their knowledge of sexual health issues as good or excellent, nearly half (45 per cent) of teens are not aware that they can be infected with chlamydia and have no symptoms.

Condoms are an effective preventative measure. Significantly, however, 43 per cent of sexually active students report using condoms only 'sometimes' when they have sex, while approximately one in ten sexually active students reported using the withdrawal method during their most recent sexual encounter. Research also shows that many young people are embarrassed to buy condoms, or they simply do not have the money to do so.

This understanding was used to develop a social marketing campaign, 'Txt 4 Free Condomz', by not-for-profit healthcare group Marie Stopes International. A low-budget campaign aimed at Australian males and females aged 15–24 was first launched in 2007 to coincide with Schoolies week. Direct marketing via a postcard drop, SMS marketing, online marketing, Schoolies event promotions and public relations initiatives were used to reach the target audience. In its first year, 1036 people texted at a cost of $0.55 to receive two free condoms in plain packaging. This increased to 1595 people in the second year of the campaign. In an effort to increase condom usage as a part of the annual Sexual Health Week activities, the campaign has since been expanded to target all sexually active Australians.[15]

### Question

Briefly explain the following core marketing concepts in relation to this campaign: the market, customers, consumers, clients, partners and society.

## Concepts and applications check

**Learning objective 2** recognise that marketing involves a mutually beneficial exchange of value

2.1 Provide three examples of products for which the customer may not necessarily be the consumer. Briefly outline how this would affect the marketing of each product.

2.2 In your own words, define 'value'.

2.3 Our perceptions of value are constantly changing. Describe the last time that your perception of value changed for a product. To answer this question you might want to describe the product or service that you have chosen, the factor(s) that led to your change in perception and how your perception changed.

2.4 You are applying for an internship with a marketing company. How is an internship mutually beneficial?

2.5 Go to an electronic goods website. Print a picture and the specifications of its newest product release (e.g. a tablet computer). Interview two people, showing them the information you have obtained and the picture. What are their perceptions of value? Compare and contrast the two opinions.

# ETHICS AND CORPORATE SOCIAL RESPONSIBILITY

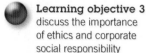

**Learning objective 3**
discuss the importance of ethics and corporate social responsibility in marketing

In the first two sections of this chapter, we have learned that a marketing transaction is an exchange of value that benefits the marketer, customers, clients, partners and/or society at large. Today's managers face volatile economic forces, differences in organisational and cultural values, cultural diversity among customers, rapidly changing technology, environmental issues and finite resources. These are global issues. Standards such as those published by the UK's Marketing and Sales Standards Setting Body (MSSSB) suggest that a principal activity that marketers must undertake is 'to ensure that an organization's strategies and policies are centered upon customers and an organization's corporate social responsibilities'.[16] As noted by the UK Chartered Institute of Marketing (CIM), marketers have a key role to play in shaping the sustainable agenda. Marketers are the employees that are closest to the customer, and much of the growing interest in social responsibility and sustainability is coming from consumers. Consumers want to know where a product is coming from and who made it. Consumers want to know what is behind the brand. In this section of the chapter we will explore these concepts in more detail.

The primary purpose of a business is to generate profits and long-term wealth for the owners. Businesses do, however, have many secondary purposes, including providing products and creating employment; and have many secondary stakeholders, including employees, customers and the community at large. Many organisations exist in which the profit motive is not the primary consideration. Public sector organisations and charities are examples of these.

For businesses, it has long been debated just where the balance should be between profit-motivated activities and secondary purposes — and whether it is appropriate to consider them 'secondary' at all. To explore this problem, we will look at ethics, law and corporate social responsibility.

## Ethics

**ethics** A set of moral principles that guide attitudes and behaviour.

**Ethics** refers to a set of moral principles that guide attitudes and behaviour. More simply, ethical behaviour involves doing what is 'right'. It is clear then that what is ethical cannot be summarised in a simple set of rules. Rather, ethics is subjective and depends on social, cultural and individual factors.

Many marketing decisions involve ethical issues, in which a choice must be made between multiple possible courses of action, which each involve different ethical, legal, social, economic and environmental considerations. Competing priorities are the source of many ethical dilemmas in business. Some of the most common that arise in marketing are truth in advertising, the marketing of products that may be dangerous or contribute to poor health, and engaging in fair competition with rival businesses.

Responsible businesses often implement a code of ethics or code of conduct to help govern their actions and guide the decisions of those who work in the business. The Australian Marketing Institute, a peak body representing marketers, has developed a code of conduct to guide marketing activities. The code is represented in figure 1.4.

**CODE OF PROFESSIONAL CONDUCT**
1. Members shall conduct their professional activities with respect for the public interest.
2. Members shall at all times act with integrity in dealing with clients or employers, past and present, with their fellow members and with the general public.
3. Members shall not intentionally disseminate false and misleading information, whether written, spoken or implied nor conceal any relevant fact. They have a duty to maintain truth, accuracy and good taste in advertising, sales promotion and all other aspects of marketing.
4. Members shall not represent conflicting or competing interests except with the express consent of those concerned given only after full disclosure of the facts to all interested parties.
5. Members, in performing services for a client or employer, shall not accept fees, commissions or any other valuable consideration in connection with those services from any other than their client or employer except with the consent (express or implied) of both.
6. Members shall refrain from knowingly associating with any enterprise which uses improper or illegal methods in obtaining business.
7. Members shall not intentionally injure the professional reputation or practice of another member.
8. If a member has evidence that another member has been guilty of unethical practices it shall be their duty to inform the Institute.
9. Members have a responsibility to continue the acquisition of professional skills in marketing and to encourage the development of these skills in those who are desirous of entry into, or continuing in, the profession of marketing management.
10. Members shall help to improve the body of knowledge of the profession by exchanging information and experience with fellow members and by applying their special skill and training for the benefit of others.
11. Members shall refrain from using their relationship with the Institute in such a manner as to state or imply an official accreditation or approval beyond the scope of membership of the Institute and its aims, rules and policies.
12. The use of the Institute's distinguishing letters must be confined to Institute activities, or the statement of name and business address on a card, letterhead and published articles.
13. Members shall co-operate with fellow members in upholding and enforcing the Code.

**FIGURE 1.4**

The Australian Marketing Institute code of professional conduct

Most marketing situations do not involve a simple choice between one ethical and one unethical path. The very nature of ethics is imprecise. In addition to codes of conduct and other guiding principles that a business may adopt, society imposes laws to govern the conduct of individual and organisational behaviour. The law's relationship to ethics is discussed next.

## Law

In addition to ethics, the way individuals and organisations conduct themselves in society is governed by law. Most law is derived from ethics, but it is quite possible to act unethically within the law, and — many would argue — to act illegally but nonetheless ethically. Laws represent society's attempt to ensure individuals and organisations act in a way that the society deems beneficial, or at least acceptable.

In Australia, business conduct is governed by numerous laws, including, for example, the Competition and Consumer Act (formerly the Trade Practices Act) and the Privacy Act. In addition, there are regulatory bodies at the state and federal levels; for example, the various state Offices of Fair Trading, and, federally, the Australian Competition and Consumer Commission. New Zealand has similar laws and regulatory bodies. The main New Zealand laws governing business conduct are the Sale of Goods Act, the Fair Trading Act, the Consumer Guarantees Act and the Commerce Act.[17] The New Zealand regulatory body equivalent to the Australian Competition and Consumer Commission is the Commerce Commission.[18]

# Corporate social responsibility

The concept of **corporate social responsibility** is simply that businesses have an obligation to act in the interests of the societies that sustain them. This is an overarching responsibility that affects all aspects of a business's operations and involves all of its **stakeholders**, including:

- *owners:* the business must generate long-term wealth by acting profitably and sustainably
- *employees:* businesses and not-for-profit organisations provide jobs that ensure wealth is shared among members of society, and provide employees with reasonable working conditions
- *customers (and clients):* the business must attract and retain customers by offering products of value
- *partners:* the business must act in such a way towards its partners that those partners can achieve their own business aims and meet their own corporate social responsibilities
- *government:* the business must abide by laws and regulations.

At the heart of corporate social responsibility is a business's obligation to act ethically, lawfully and in the best interests of all of its stakeholders, including the society — increasingly the global society — in which it operates. We should ask what motivates 'good corporate citizenship'. Is it to create benefits that ultimately serve the primary goal of generating profits and wealth, or is it a goal in its own right? We should also ask ourselves to what extent it matters.

Many businesses place a great deal of importance on being — and being seen to be — a 'good corporate citizen' and, increasingly, are devoting resources to ensure their operations act in the interests of all stakeholders. A business that meets its corporate social responsibilities can expect benefits from good public relations and the absence of restrictive regulations. After the devastating floods that hit Queensland in early 2011, as well as Cyclone Yasi in the north of the state, many businesses made generous financial contributions to assist with the rebuilding effort. Over $250 million was pledged to the Queensland Government's Disaster Relief Appeal. Some of the major corporate donations were from BHP Billiton ($11 million), Wesfarmers ($5 million), Flight Centre Limited (over $3.3 million), RACQ ($2 million), and XSTRATA Queensland ($2 million). The Commonwealth Bank pledged $1.35 million to the Disaster Relief Appeal as part of a $65 million flood assistance program for customers and the community. This corporate social responsibility program was set up to assist flood- and cyclone-affected people and local communities around the nation — including in affected regions in New South Wales and Victoria, in addition to in Queensland — in early 2011.[19]

Involvement with such activities can also help companies to attract high-quality employees — particularly high-quality younger employees. This is because individuals have come to ask not just what their employer can offer them, but also whether they can believe in what their employer does. Such activities extend philanthropic (i.e. giving) actions to make them of strategic benefit to the business — the voluntary acts benefit parts of society *and* benefit the business.

Conversely, a business that acts with disregard for its society can expect a customer backlash and the imposition of rules to force it to comply with society's expectations. This is demonstrated by the ongoing public debate about food advertising during children's television programming. Current regulation does not protect children from being bombarded with ads for junk food. Around 54 per cent of TV food ads aired between 6 am and 9 pm are for unhealthy foods. The volume of unhealthy food ads increases when children are most likely to be viewing television — early in evenings and on Saturday mornings. Australia has the world's highest rate of junk food advertising on children's television and one of the highest rates of childhood obesity.[20] The marketers of food aimed primarily or partly at children (a very broad range of products, including fruit juice, biscuits, hamburgers, pizza, muesli bars, lollies and bread) argue that it is important to advertise their products to their target market (which is not only the children, but also the likely purchaser — their parents or guardians). Some healthcare organisations, however, argue that advertising high-fat, high-calorie foods to children is a major contributor to the increasing rate of childhood obesity evident in most Western societies. Various organisations are, thus, lobbying governments to introduce regulations that restrict or ban the advertising of certain types of food during children's television broadcasts.

Most businesses have more power and resources than the customers and many of the other stakeholders with which they interact. As a result, the business tends to be the more powerful party in any marketing exchange. In a bid to create more of a level playing field and ensure consumers are not taken advantage of, various groups have been formed to play the role of consumer watchdogs or consumer advocates. The best known in Australia is CHOICE, which reviews and compares products, aims to educate consumers about their rights, and campaigns in consumers' interests. It publishes a magazine by the same name. In New Zealand, a similar organisation known as Consumer NZ acts on consumers' behalf. It publishes a magazine titled *Consumer*.

In recent years, the need to take a sustainable approach to the earth's resources, and particularly to the natural environment, has emerged as a major consideration for businesses trying to meet corporate social responsibility requirements. Organisations have responded by trying to minimise the environmental impact of their activities. Some ways they have done this include using recyclable or biodegradable packaging; using energy-efficient technologies; reducing waste and pollution; and developing products that either use renewable materials or are generally designed to better protect the environment, such as no-phosphate detergents and solar power. Marketers engaging in such activities can be said to be practising **green marketing**, which can be simply defined as the marketing of environmentally safe or beneficial products.

**green marketing** The marketing of environmentally safe or beneficial products.

A popular way of thinking about good corporate citizenship is the Triple Bottom Line, which is comprised of social, environmental and profit considerations. There are many avenues available for companies to increase their Triple Bottom Line, and some are outlined in figure 1.5.[21] Good corporate citizenship involves looking after the environment and employees; this approach, if taken, can assist a company to maintain or increase profits.

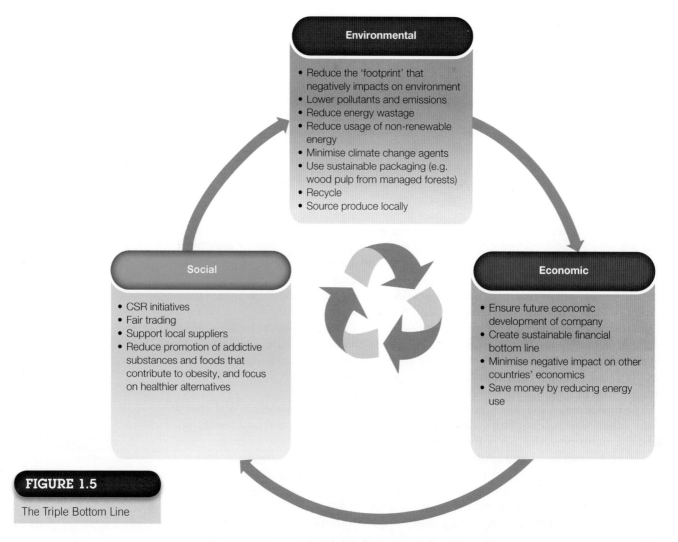

**FIGURE 1.5**

The Triple Bottom Line

A key issue faced by any manager in the twenty-first century is potential for corporate greed. Some executives are accused of being paid excessive amounts of money that are difficult to justify. Consider Westpac CEO Gail Kelly, who receives a salary package in excess of $10 million each year, or Commonwealth Bank CEO Ralph Norris, who earns in excess of $16 million each year.[22] These amounts of money are difficult for consumers to accept when they are faced with increasing fees on their banking accounts year in and year out. While it is acceptable to make profit as a return for the risk of investing capital in a business, companies need to operate in a transparent way to avoid consumer cynicism. Let's stay with banking for the moment. Interest rate movements by the Reserve Bank of Australia (or New Zealand) are usually the precursor to interest rate movements by the major banks in both countries. When banks such as the Commonwealth, NAB, Westpac or ANZ increase the interest rates on home loans by more than any increase announced by the Reserve Bank, there is usually a media and public outcry of corporate greed. The accusation is generally that the banks are putting profits and the interests of shareholders ahead of their borrowing customers.

Business models are built on constant growth, and it is this very model that is now being questioned in some quarters. From an economic perspective, the continual strive for greater efficiency is based on increasing production, profits and standards of living. But is it always realistic for businesses to expect to grow year in and year out? Can marketers increase prices each year to meet ever larger budget targets that are forced on them by managers who want more growth in profit? Can governments continue to raise taxes over time? Can you continue to gain more and more credit? The answer should be 'no', without a rising income! People generally have a fixed income level that, in time, rises with inflation or a job promotion. It is not possible for a person or a household to continually absorb more and more and more. There is a finite limit for consumption. Individuals are increasingly beginning to question companies and whether the values of their employer are consistent with what they want for their children, grandchildren and so forth. In order for future generations to live in the same style as we do today, traditional business practices and ways of thinking may need to be challenged to ensure that we can continue to survive — and indeed thrive — in a world of finite resources.

## Implementation

The idea that a business should act in such a way that it creates the most benefit possible for society is simple. Undertaking business activities in such a way as to ensure corporate social responsibilities are met can be complex. Once management decides to commit to a responsible way of conducting business, it should implement policies and processes that enable it. It should also seek to build a culture guided by ethics and consideration of all stakeholders. As discussed earlier, sometimes the policies and culture are embodied in a formal code of conduct.

A business must also ensure that it empowers its stakeholders to achieve the ideals included in its policies, processes and codes. For example, a business that commits that it will not exploit workers but then sets production targets that require excessive overtime is not meeting its corporate social responsibilities. A business must not send mixed messages, nor adopt codes or policies that are no more than public relations tools. Marketers are often accused by consumer rights groups of **greenwashing**. Greenwashing is the dissemination of questionable or potentially misleading information by an organisation in relation to its products, in order for the organisation and its products to be perceived as environmentally friendly. This practice should be avoided at all costs, and should not be confused with the concept of green marketing that was explained earlier.

**greenwashing** The dissemination of questionable or potentially misleading information by an organisation in relation to its products, in order for the organisation and its products to be perceived as environmentally friendly.

# Just doing it

# Spotlight

Nike was founded in Portland, Oregon, in the United States in 1964. By 1980 it had reached a 50 per cent market share in the US athletic shoe market. The term 'Just Do It' was first used in a Nike advertising campaign in 1988, and quickly became part of the vernacular of popular culture.

Sports stars and sweatshops were both associated with the Nike brand in recent decades. The footwear and clothing manufacturer had its reputation 'dragged through the mud' in the 1990s, when Canadian author Naomi Klein exposed its use of 'sweatshop' labour — including poor wages and working conditions — as part of its manufacturing operations in less developed countries. The revelations cast the company in an unfavourable light — reflecting a reality that was in stark contrast to the 'hip' brand the company had carefully constructed over time. Many consumers who had previously been willing to pay high amounts for Nike products (for instance, to pay $100 for basic jogging shoes), were now more reluctant to purchase the company's products. The strength of the iconic Nike brand had been called into question. Suddenly, the opinions of many of the company's ambassadors — most of whom were high-profile sportspeople — were less likely to sway consumers' opinions.

According to one *Harvard Business Review* paper, Nike once claimed, 'It's not our job to worry about other countries' labour conditions'. As a result of the claims leveraged by Klein, Nike became synonymous with the use of child labour in developing nations. This link, in turn, led to perceptions of an all-powerful and sinister corporation that cared only for profits, not people.

Considering its history, Nike has made impressive inroads in recent times — taking steps to make a more positive contribution to society. The company has prioritised corporate social responsibility

initiatives as a means of repairing its reputation. Nike is striving to achieve zero waste in its supply chain (i.e. to produce only products and materials that can be continuously reused). It is also increasing its use of environmentally preferred materials as a means of reducing the company's overall ecological blueprint. The company has formed partnerships that are designed to improve outcomes for people who are experiencing social disadvantage. For example, as a partner in the Grassroot Soccer program in Africa, Nike is helping to raise awareness about HIV/AIDS and to encourage children to use sport as an outlet for positive social change. At a macro level, the company is advocating for stricter energy and climate legislation in the United States. A recent report by Brand Finance puts Nike as the international benchmark for the apparel category in terms of corporate social responsibility. In a remarkable turnaround, Nike has certainly come a long way in its CSR journey.[23]

## Question

Examine Nike's latest corporate responsibility report which is available online at www.nikebiz.com. Find an example of a corporate social responsibility initiative for each of the following Nike stakeholders: owners, employees, customers, partners and government.

# Concepts and applications check

**Learning objective 3** discuss the importance of ethics and corporate social responsibility in marketing

**3.1** Distinguish between ethics and corporate social responsibility in the context of marketing.

**3.2** Discuss the relative pros and cons of self-regulation and formal government regulation in the context of ethical marketing.

**3.3** Visit the website of a business that you have dealings with (e.g. your university, your bank or your supermarket) and identify the key elements of its approach to corporate social responsibility.

**3.4** To what extent do you think businesses adopt corporate social responsibility as 'the right thing to do' versus seeking some type of public relations benefit? Find an example of a business undertaking some type of philanthropic activity. How might the business benefit from this activity?

**3.5** If a marketing campaign operates entirely within the law, has the marketing organisation necessarily fulfilled its obligations to its stakeholders?

# THE MARKETING MIX

The **marketing mix** is the term given to a set of variables that a marketer can exercise control over in creating an offering for exchange. Various frameworks for the marketing mix have evolved over time, including:

- the 4 Ps framework — product, price, promotion and place (place is more easily understood as distribution). The 4 Ps framework was the first approach to the marketing mix.
- the 5 Ps framework which evolved from the 4 Ps model by adding a fifth P, 'people', to the 4 Ps framework.
- the 6 Ps framework which added 'process' to the 5 Ps framework
- the 7 Ps framework which added 'physical evidence' to the 6 Ps framework.

To frame their thinking, marketers often choose to target certain types of customers. Markets are heterogeneous — they are made up of many different people with many different needs and wants. A **target market** is a group of customers with similar needs and wants. Not all customers in a target group will have exactly the same needs and wants but they are more similar than different. By narrowing their thinking to a target group, marketers can think about how they can best communicate, deliver and exchange their offerings with customers. For example, the target market of this book is first-year undergraduate marketing students. A business can also aim for multiple target markets. For example, Subaru targets different groups with various cars: its Outback range of station wagons is aimed at families and couples who value comfort, safety and life in the great outdoors, while its Impreza WRX STi hatch is aimed at performance car enthusiasts (with a lot of money).

Marketers cannot act with complete freedom in determining their marketing mix. They are governed by the costs of implementing the various marketing mix options, as well as the forces at play in the marketing environment. They are also governed by the people in their organisation. There is little point creating something that is simply not possible to implement.

We will now examine each of the elements of these various marketing mix frameworks. It is important to remember that marketing — whatever marketing mix framework you apply or consider — is ultimately about a total focus on servicing the needs and wants of the customer.

## Product

A **product** is anything offered to a market. It can be a good, a service, an idea or even a person. Marketers have to market goods such as batteries, milk and shoes. Marketers can market services such as hairdressing, legal representation, air travel and beauty therapy. Some marketers have to market ideas such as 'Quit' smoking while others have to market people such as celebrities and politicians.

Some products are branded and others are not. A **brand** is a collection of symbols such as a name, logo, slogan and design intended to create an image in the customer's mind that differentiates a product from competitors' products.

Products can be best understood as a 'bundle of attributes' that when exchanged have value for customers, clients or society. **Bundle of attributes** refers to the features and functions of a product, which benefit the customer. In the marketing mix, the product variable is concerned with creating an offering that anticipates and meets the needs and wants of customers.

**Learning objective 4**
explain the elements of the marketing mix

**marketing mix** A set of variables that a marketer can exercise control over in creating an offering for exchange.

**target market** A group of customers with similar needs and wants.

**product** A good, service or idea offered to the market for exchange.

**brand** A collection of symbols such as a name, logo, slogan and design intended to create an image in the customer's mind that differentiates a product from competitors' products.

**bundle of attributes** The features and functions of a product that benefit the customer.

To help you to understand what is meant by a bundle of attributes, think about a Nokia mobile telephone. It is a handset that is designed to look good. It has a battery, which means you can use the phone anywhere for a certain period of time. Features on the mobile phone might include SMS, MMS, MP3 and, of course, voice. These features mean you can talk to friends, send messages and photos to your friends, and listen to music. Some of the benefits that you receive from your mobile phone include staying connected with friends, the ability to communicate whenever and wherever you want, entertainment, and prestige if you own a new, up-market phone. The Nokia name might mean that you feel you have purchased a mobile phone that will be reliable.

Marketers understand that customers have needs and wants and this thinking is based on economics. You will study needs and wants in both economics and marketing. **Needs** are day-to-day survival requirements. People need food, shelter and clothing, personal growth and the social need of a sense of security. People also have wants. **Wants** are desires, and are not necessary for day-to-day survival. Wants cover products such as new television sets, iTunes playlists and perfume. Marketers provide products to satisfy customer needs and wants. People have unlimited wants and they do not have the resources to satisfy them all. They must therefore make a choice between competing alternatives. When a consumer has the ability (money) to buy something they want, the want is said to be a **demand**. Consumers choose among demands by finding the product that offers the most value in exchange for their money.

Products can also be categorised as either goods or services. **Goods** are physical (tangible) offerings that are capable of being delivered to a customer. The purchase of goods typically involves transfer of ownership from business to customer. You can see, smell, touch and sometimes taste goods. To buy a good you often become the owner of a good. You own the orange juice before you drink it. **Services** are intangible offerings. If you think about a hair cut or travel advice, you realise you cannot hold it; nor can you own it. You *experience* service. We will go into more detail about goods and services in chapters 7 and 11.

For exchange to occur, marketers must develop new products and modify their existing offerings so that they have value for customers, clients, partners and society at large. They must also know which products are not mutually beneficial. This means that marketers must be prepared to discontinue offerings because consumers no longer value them, because they are not profitable or because they have a negative impact on society. What is important to remember is that marketers need to understand value through a customer lens. Marketers need to understand where the value comes from. Does the value come from owning the offering, using the offering, or does the value come from both ownership and use of the offering? Consider any typical product. If you purchase it, do you get value simply by owning it? Do you get value from just sitting and looking at it? Your answer is likely to be no. You can only get value from *using* the product.

While this may sound simple it is often not applied well in practice. Too many marketers remain product rather than customer focused. It is important to understand that marketing thinking starts with the customer and ends with the customer. Marketers must consider offerings from a customer's point of view. For example, a marketer of the Master of Business Administration (MBA) course at your university should be able to tell graduates about the MBA (the offering) and importantly how the MBA can help them (how the offering has value for graduates); for example, by leading to a higher income.

**need** A day-to-day survival requirement: food, shelter and clothing.

**want** A desire, but not necessary for day-to-day survival.

**demand** A want that a consumer has the ability to satisfy.

**good** A physical (tangible) offering capable of being delivered to a customer.

**service** An intangible offering that does not involve ownership.

# Price

Price is the amount of money a business demands in exchange for its offerings. Pricing is a complex marketing decision that must take account of many factors, including:

- production, communication and distribution costs
- required profitability
- partners' requirements
- competitors' prices
- customers' willingness to pay.

Remember that marketing is about creating and exchanging offerings that have value for customers, clients, partners and society at large. While price plays an important role in value, it is not alone in creating value perceptions. Marketers need to understand the relationship between price and quality to understand value from a customer's point of view. They need to understand what customers would like to get and what they are prepared to give in return. For example, car marketers understand that customers are concerned about rising fuel costs and exhaust emissions and this is reducing their interest in buying larger cars. To overcome concerns about rising fuel costs, some car marketers offer customers one year of fuel for free, overcoming customer concerns about the expense of fuel.

Consider another pricing decision. In a brave move, alternative rock group Radiohead chose to make their *In Rainbows* album available for download from their website, giving fans the choice of how much to pay — or whether to pay at all. Essentially fans were able to decide just what the new album was worth to them (although they would not have heard the album until they had paid for it). This move helped Radiohead to gain a lot of publicity and media sources report that it helped them to gain $6–$10 million in sales, with 1.2 million people downloading the album from their website at an average of $8 per album.[24] This is reflective of a growing trend for value and the marketing mix to be negotiated more and more closely between marketers and customers. Price will be discussed in more detail in chapter 8.

# Promotion

**Promotion** describes the marketing activities that make potential customers, partners and society aware of and attracted to the business's offering. The product might be:

- *already established* — such as Fernwood, where the aim of promotion is to remind customers that Fernwood is a female-only fitness centre
- *modified* — such as a new variation of Coke, where the aim of promotion is to inform existing customers about the improvement or new variety and to attract potential new customers
- *new* — such as a new-release movie, where the aim is to make customers aware of the product for the first time
- *information or education* — such as advertisements designed to persuade youth not to take illegal drugs.

Promotion should not be thought of merely as advertising. While advertising is an important component of promotion, many organisations use other methods to promote products as well. For example, some businesses use loyalty schemes to try to encourage repeat business and word-of-mouth to gain new customers. Others may give away trial packets of new products when an existing customer makes a purchase of one of their other products. Promotional activities include such sales promotions, as well as personal selling efforts and public relations campaigns. Online

**promotion** The marketing activities that make potential customers, partners and society aware of and attracted to the business's offerings.

communications such as blogs, YouTube and Twitter are also used by marketers to increase awareness. Of course, there are many other interesting ways to communicate, including ambient forms of advertising such as a painting on a building or a display in a town square. Marketers have to think of ways to stand out in a cluttered market to raise awareness. Often, a combination of promotional methods is used, and in such cases it is crucial that they be carefully combined and coordinated to achieve a consistent message. Promotion will be discussed in detail in chapter 9.

## Distribution (place)

**distribution (or place)** The means of making the offering available to the customer at the right time and place.

**Distribution (or place)** refers to the means of making the offering available to the customer at the right time and place. It is largely a logistics function and marketers need to understand how logistics impact their ability to deliver a product at a time and place that suits customer needs or wants. The marketer must ensure products are available to the target market in the right amount and at the right time while managing the costs of making the products available. Such costs include inventory, storage and transport. Many businesses sell their products directly to the public through catalogues, a shop front or a website, but distribution, especially for larger businesses, usually also involves partners such as wholesalers and retailers. Technology, particularly the internet and associated communications innovations, has dramatically changed distribution, particularly for products that have been digitally enabled, such as recorded music. Not so long ago, the only option to purchase music was as a physical product on CD or vinyl. Now, consumers can download their favourite songs to a device such as an iPod. Nevertheless, physical distribution remains a key element in the marketing of many products. The science (or art) of ensuring products are in the right place at the right time in the right quantity is known as **logistics** and the various partners that contribute to the process make up what is called the **supply chain**. Distribution is discussed in more detail in chapter 10.

**logistics** That part of the marketing process concerned with supply and transport.

**supply chain** The parties involved in providing all of the raw materials and services that go in to getting a product to the market.

## People

Marketers must think about people, including employees and other customers. In the marketing framework, people refers to any person coming into contact with customers who can affect value for customers. For example, customer experiences with services are affected by the people who deliver the service. Think about the last time someone served you and they were not friendly. How did you feel? You would most likely have judged the offerings based on the employees you interacted with. Successful organisations that want to create and maintain a competitive advantage must recruit and retain the right staff. They must have the appropriate interpersonal skills, aptitude and knowledge to deliver offerings that customers value. Fellow customers can also affect the customer's service experience. For example, crowd behaviour at a sporting event or complaining customers who loudly voice their opinion can put off others who are waiting in a service queue.

You will study employee issues in human resources and management courses. The concepts studied in these courses are also important for marketers. For example, for services, highly motivated staff are important because in the customer's eyes they are inseparable from the total service.

## Process

**process** The systems used to create, communicate, deliver and exchange an offering.

**Process** refers to the systems used to create, communicate, deliver and exchange an offering. Marketers must understand the systems that are used to create, communicate and deliver offerings for exchange. This understanding is needed to understand how the systems affect value for customers. Imagine that you walk into Eagle Boys and order a Super Supremo pizza and it is handed to you three minutes later. What was the system that enabled such efficient service delivery? The motor registry mails out a vehicle registration renewal form about a month before a driver's registration expires. Efficient systems ensure the driver has time to budget for and pay their renewal. Processes can also be viewed more broadly to take into account almost everything the marketing organisation does, from market research to innovation to mailing out catalogues.

## Physical evidence

**Physical evidence** refers to the tangible cues, including the physical environment, that customers use to evaluate products, particularly services. Because services are intangible, it is difficult to assess their quality and suitability until they are consumed. Marketers can use physical evidence to reassure potential customers as to the quality of the service. Tangible cues should inspire confidence in the likely service product. Physical evidence includes architectural design, furniture, décor, shop fittings, colours, background music, staff uniforms, brochures, service or delivery vehicles and stationery.

**physical evidence** Tangible cues that can be used as a means to evaluate service quality prior to purchase.

# Wealthfarm                                    Spotlight

Wealthfarm (www.wealthfarm.com.au) is a team of professional financial planners, accountants, finance brokers and agents, whose aim is to work with customers to help them secure financial freedom and the lifestyle they seek. The company does this by taking the time to develop an understanding of each customer's current situation, needs and aspirations, and then assisting them to implement a tailored financial plan in order to achieve realistic goals. Wealthfarm's philosophy is based on achieving maximum financial returns for their customers with minimal risk. The company currently has in excess of $140 million in funds under management.

Developing ongoing relationships with customers is important to Wealthfarm. The company recognises that customers' life circumstances can change. Referrals from satisfied customers are also an important potential source of new business for the company. The company operates in an industry that has, at times, been plagued by sordid tales of 'fly by night' investment advisers. However, Wealthfarm prides itself on the fact that-was the third Australian financial planning organisation to be audited and accredited by SAI Global — and that it has demonstrated that its practices are fully compliant with international quality standards specifically set for the financial planning industry.

Wealthfarm seized opportunities during the global financial crisis to attract new clients wanting fresh investment advice, and the company expanded during this volatile period. According to the company's director, Nicholas Sinclair, when times are good people think they can plan for themselves, but when there is a financial crisis, companies such as Wealthfarm are inundated with enquiries. The decision to expand was made because, in terms of giving investment advice, it does not matter what the market does. What matters, rather, is how the financial planner responds.[25]

## Question

**Describe Wealthfarm's broad product offering (financial planning) in terms of a bundle of attributes that benefit customers. Refer to the difference between needs and wants in your answer.**

## Concepts and applications check

**Learning objective 4** explain the elements of the marketing mix

**4.1** Describe a car as a bundle of attributes.

**4.2** Think of a product (good or service) and analyse it in terms of as many of the elements of one of the marketing mix frameworks as possible.

**4.3** Find one example of an advertisement that is product focused and one example of an advertisement that is customer focused. Explain how the focus is evident.

**4.4** Using a job that you are currently or were previously employed in, describe one process. How could this process be improved to offer better value to customers?

# WHY STUDY MARKETING?

**Learning objective 5** discuss how marketing improves business performance, benefits society and contributes to quality of life

Marketing is an interesting and rapidly changing field that has an enormous influence on the world. Marketing improves business performance, benefits society and contributes to a higher quality of life. It can also be a rewarding career choice.

## Improve business performance

Since Theodore Levitt proposed a link between a market orientation and business survival in a paper called 'Marketing Myopia',[26] marketing has, indeed, become the driving force in many successful organisations. Firms with a market orientation perform better than firms without a market orientation.[27] Research shows that companies who have a well-defined marketing strategy perform better than companies that do not have a well-defined marketing strategy.[28]

A range of marketing practices have been linked to company performance. Specifically, research shows that companies using certain marketing practices have better profits, sales volumes, market share and return on investment when compared to their competitors. Organisations that undertake the following marketing practices perform better than companies that do not:

- conduct formal marketing planning
- undertake comprehensive situation analysis
- adopt a proactive approach to the future
- conduct frequent market research studies
- set more aggressive marketing objectives
- offer superior products and services at comparable or higher prices than their competitors
- introduce new ways of doing business
- innovate
- use a market intelligence gathering system to monitor changes in competitive and customer behaviour, technology and general trends.

You will be introduced to all of these key practices in this textbook. While the implementation of marketing practices has been linked to business performance, many companies do not implement these performance-enhancing marketing practices. Research shows that nearly half of all businesses in New Zealand undertake little or no formal marketing planning and over half attach little importance to a comprehensive situation analysis.[29] Market research is mainly outsourced.

The marketing department does not work in isolation in any organisation. The different business functions are closely interwoven to assist the organisation to reach its goals. For example:

- human resources is responsible for attracting, recruiting and retaining the right people to reach the organisation's objectives
- finance supports marketing with the funds required to achieve the organisation's objectives
- accounting provides marketing with some of the information (e.g. sales, costs) needed to analyse the current situation to inform strategy development
- logistics assists in delivering the offering to the customers.

In order to reach their goals, marketers must be able to work with all facets of an organisation. The foundation courses that you take in your business or commerce degree are interlinked in business practice. If you are fortunate enough to gain employment in an employer graduate program that provides experience in each area in your first 12 months, you will quickly gain an appreciation of the links between the different business disciplines.

Ultimately, every employee is a stakeholder in the success of their organisation. They influence its success by working toward providing value to the market — and its success or otherwise has consequences for both the individual and the organisation. A salesperson can only successfully sell products if the production department is focused on providing the salesperson with the right products at the right time. In a market-oriented organisation, the production department will be focused on doing just that. The production department can only service the sales force well if its suppliers provide raw materials of the right quality in the right quantity. By examining the relationships such as these that exist throughout organisations, it can be seen that the entire marketing effort is made up of numerous networks of internal and external stakeholders, all coordinated and focused on exchanging offerings that have value.

## Higher quality of life

Marketing is often criticised and is viewed negatively by many people. This is because marketing is a high-profile business function. Marketing creates, communicates and delivers an organisation's offering. Marketing does not achieve this alone and all other business functions are involved, from human resources, to accounting and finance, production, and logistics. Marketing often bears the brunt of criticism for bad company practices.

It is easy for people to criticise marketing and brands. As consumers we are exposed to advertisements every day, and some more credible than others. As consumers we see brands whenever we shop in a supermarket, pharmacy or clothing store. While marketing's role is to create, communicate and deliver offerings that have value for customers, consumers and a purchase are needed for exchange to take place. Marketers cannot buy products for their customers; they can only offer products that consumers may consider and purchase. While there is definitely bad practice, marketing is not an evil force. Let's take a brief look at how marketing has benefited society.

Marketing has helped to drive economic growth. Consumer demand is a key driver of economic growth and marketers play a role in stimulating consumer demand. Economic growth creates employment and wealth for the benefit of individuals and society as a whole. Marketing can play a role in improving people's quality of life through providing better or safer products and the promotion of consumer and social welfare. Consider McDonald's, which provides some healthy meal options today in response to public criticism linking fast-food restaurants to the obesity epidemic being experienced in many Western nations.

## Contribute to a better world

Marketing is often criticised for its role in stimulating excessive and often unnecessary consumption, and the consequent social issues that arise. The global financial crisis provided a stark reminder that sustainable models are required for business practice. The marketing discipline has much to offer to the social arena. Marketing seeks to understand what customers want, in order to deliver a solution that meets their needs and wants. Marketers make alternatives available for consumers to purchase. Marketing can, therefore, be viewed as part of the solution, rather than as the problem.

**social marketing**
A process that uses marketing principles and techniques to influence target audience behaviours that will benefit society, as well as the individual.

Indeed, many marketers work in the not-for-profit sector and/or in **social marketing**, where their work is directed towards social good. For example, there are more than 35 000 registered not-for-profit organisations in Australia that employ staff, many of whom are engaged in marketing activities or roles to raise funds and awareness for a host of worthy causes.[30] Central elements of social marketing include:

* behaviour–change as the benchmark for designing and evaluating interventions
* the development of attractive and motivational exchanges to encourage desired behaviours of the target audience
* formative research to understand the characteristics and the behaviours of the target audience
* the segmentation of the target audience to guide the development of intervention elements
* pre-testing and monitoring these elements during implementation (Andreasen, 2002).

## Be a better customer

By studying marketing you can become a better customer. By understanding the activities and processes for creating, communicating, and delivering offerings, you can make better decisions as to the relative value of products offered to you. For example, Aldi customers understand that products offered in Aldi supermarkets are cheaper than those offered by Woolworths or Coles because of Aldi's processes. Aldi's philosophy is that all people, wherever they live, should have the opportunity to buy everyday groceries of the highest quality at the lowest possible price. The products available for sale under the Aldi brand are manufactured by leading food manufacturers. Aldi keeps prices low by selling products under the Aldi brand wherever possible, and by limiting the product range to reduce costs associated with logistics. Other activities assist to achieve low prices.

Having studied marketing you will understand that companies that are serious about marketing welcome customer feedback. After studying marketing if you have a poor experience with a product or a service, you will know that by giving feedback you may help to persuade the marketer to do something to address your concerns, which may benefit yourself or other future customers.

## A rewarding career

Marketing can be a rewarding career path. Marketing offers a wide range of specialist areas including advertising, public relations, market research, product development, personal selling and market analysis. Marketers can work in the business sector or for not-for-profit organisations such as charities, governments and cultural institutions. Marketing skills are transferable overseas, and many marketing graduates travel and work abroad.

Marketers need good analytical, communication, and negotiation skills, and the power of persuasion. Those who want to work in a professional marketing position will usually also require a degree in marketing, or in a related area with a major in marketing. The recruitment process has lengthened, with many companies now asking candidates to make presentations as part of the interview process. There is a very competitive candidate market for marketing roles. Looking to the future, key areas with strong potential for growth include online marketing and digital marketing.[31] About 40 per cent of people employed in marketing in Australia and New Zealand are women. The average age is 40, which suggests marketing is a profession of younger people.[32]

The *Australian Graduate Survey* suggests half of all marketing degree graduates who secured a full-time sales or marketing position in Australia were being paid an average of $45 000 per year. With more experience, marketing managers can progressively expect to earn as much as $200 000 per year.[33] In New Zealand, depending on the industry and type of organisation (i.e. small- to medium-sized enterprise or larger multinational), the salary figures are generally comparable with those for similar roles in Australia. Product managers may earn up to $145 000 per year.[34] While marketing can be a lucrative career, it requires dedication and hard work. Marketers often have specific targets that must be met. The measurement of such targets involves 'marketing metrics'. Marketing metrics are discussed regularly throughout the text and in more detail in chapter 14. For example, a marketer responsible for an organisation's advertising strategy will need to achieve a certain level of brand awareness among the target market. A salesperson will usually have a specific level of sales revenue that they must meet. A production department will have quality and quantity standards that they must maintain.

## Marketing yourself

An understanding of marketing can assist you in your own life. When you apply for your next job you can apply the principles of marketing. Rather than simply telling your employer how good you are and the experience that you have (a product focus) you can tell your future employer how employing you will deliver value for them. You may do this by outlining successes achieved in recent marketing campaigns. For example, you might explain how a $1 investment in your marketing campaign returned $4 to the company, or how your marketing communications campaign increased customer enquiries by 50 per cent and sales volume by 20 per cent. The principles of marketing can help you to consider how you are unique from the other people who would be applying for the same job. Let's consider your first graduate job application. There are 300 students enrolled in your degree and 150 of them have the same major as you. There are also many other universities offering the same degree in your country and abroad. Everyone has a degree, 20 per cent of students have the same grades as you. There could be 300 people with the same degree and performance in their degree as you. How can you show that you are different? How can you make yourself stand out from the crowd? The principles of marketing teach you how to do this. Marketing thinking can help you. It is important that you keep evidence of success from now on.

## Spotlight  Consumed with happiness?

Many people in developed nations like Australia and New Zealand are seemingly addicted to consumption — to more food, bigger houses, extravagant home theatre systems, international travel, designer clothes, sports cars, and the list goes on. Previous generations could only have dreamed of many of the goods and services many people routinely enjoy today. On the surface, there appears to be no disputing that marketing has contributed to improved business performance, economic growth and a higher standard of living for most people. But are these the only metrics for success?

Consider the findings of one recent study. Despite being one of the most affluent countries in the world, with one of the highest standards of living, almost half of the richest 20 per cent of Australian households claimed they could not afford to buy everything they really need, even though they were quite willing to work long hours and go deep into debt to fund their desires.[35] Increased wealth and consumption has not necessarily brought happiness. Stress, obesity, marriage breakdowns and debt burdens are at record highs in our society.

The alternative to the apparent consumption craze, of course, is for individuals and households to 'downsize' — perhaps moving to a smaller house in a different area, and generally reducing the time spent chasing material possessions. This is a fate that some choose, but one that is forced upon others due to circumstance. For example, during the global financial crisis, many people around the world were forced to re-evaluate their priorities. The distinction between needs and wants is never as stark as during tough economic times, when job security and income levels are less assured. The irony is that during these very times, governments are encouraged by economists to introduce fiscal stimulus packages, encouraging people to spend in order to keep the economy growing and to protect employment.

### Question

Happiness, according to research, mainly depends on friendships, family and other relationships.[36] Why then have we put so much emphasis on consumption? Is marketing to blame?

## Concepts and applications check

**Learning objective 5**   discuss how marketing improves business performance, benefits society and contributes to quality of life

5.1   List the marketing activities that improve business performance.

5.2   Find and discuss an example that illustrates how marketing contributes to quality of life.

5.3   Think of a historical or contemporary successful product that demonstrates how marketers stimulate demand. Explain how they did it.

5.4   Marketing is often criticised and is viewed negatively by many people. What was your view of marketing prior to starting this course? Has your view changed? Why? Why not?

5.5   Using company annual reports, find an example of a company that has improved its business performance despite the challenges of the global economic crisis. Discuss how the company has used marketing to improve its performance. (*Note:* Annual reports or summaries are usually found in the investor section of corporate websites.)

# SUMMARY

 **Learning objective 1** provide an overview of marketing and the marketing process

Marketing is a philosophy or a way of doing business that puts the market — the customer, client, partner and society, and competitors — at the heart of all business decisions. The marketing process is cyclical in nature and involves understanding the market to create, communicate and deliver an offering for exchange. Marketers start by understanding the consumers, the market and how they are currently situated. Armed with this understanding, marketers are next tasked with creating solutions, communicating the offering to the market, and delivering it at a time and place that is convenient for the customer.

 **Learning objective 2** recognise that marketing involves a mutually beneficial exchange of value

The essence of marketing is to develop mutually beneficial exchange. Exchange involves value creation for all parties to the exchange. Marketers must understand how customers perceive value. Value perceptions vary from one individual to another and they are ever changing.

The customer is the focus of all marketing activities and successful marketers are those who view their products in terms of meeting customer needs and wants.

 **Learning objective 3** discuss the importance of ethics and corporate social responsibility in marketing

Businesses exist primarily to generate profits and wealth for their owners. It is increasingly recognised, however, that businesses have an obligation to act in the best interests of the society that sustains them. They are obliged to act ethically, within the law, and to fulfil corporate social responsibility requirements, which may include philanthropy, protecting the natural environment, providing products that benefit society and generating employment and wealth.

 **Learning objective 4** explain the elements of the marketing mix

The marketing mix describes the different elements that marketers need to consider. Many different frameworks have been used by marketing scholars to teach marketing and all have been designed to be memorable. Frameworks include the 4 Ps, 5 Ps, 6 Ps and 7 Ps.

A product is a bundle of attributes that when exchanged have value for customers, clients or society. A product can be a good, a service, an idea or even a person. Products cater to needs and wants. Needs are day-to-day survival requirements, while wants are desired but not required for survival.

Price is the amount of money a business demands in exchange for its offerings. Pricing is a complex marketing decision that must take account of many factors, including production, communication and distribution costs, required profitability, partners' requirements, competitors' prices, and customers' willingness to pay. Marketers need to understand the relationship between price and quality to understand value from a customer's point of view. Marketers need to understand what customers would like to receive and what they are prepared to give in return.

Distribution or place refers to the means of making the offering available to the target market at the right time and place while managing the costs of making the products available. Many businesses sell their products directly to the public, but distribution usually also involves partners such as wholesalers and retailers.

Promotion describes the marketing activities that make potential customers, partners and society aware of and attracted to the benefits of a business's products. The product might be already established, modified, new, or information designed to persuade. Promotional activities include advertising, direct selling, sales promotions and loyalty schemes.

In the marketing framework, 'people' refers to all the people that may come into contact with the customer and affect their experience of the product. Like the other factors, the people must be managed to maximise value for the customer.

Process refers to the systems used to create, communicate, deliver and exchange an offering.

Physical evidence refers to the tangible cues and physical environment a marketer can provide to help potential customers evaluate service quality.

 **Learning objective 5** discuss how marketing improves business performance, benefits society and contributes to quality of life

Organisations with a market orientation perform better than other organisations. Marketing creates employment and wealth for the benefit of individuals and society as a whole. It improves people's quality of life through better products and the promotion of consumer and social welfare. An understanding of marketing helps you make better decisions as to the relative value of products offered to you. Marketing can be a rewarding career path. While it can be lucrative work, it requires dedication and effort. Marketers need good analytical, communication, and negotiation skills, the power of persuasion, and often a tertiary qualification in marketing or a related discipline.

# The 'Becky's not drinking' campaign

Australia has a drinking problem. Alcohol currently costs the Australian community more than $10 billion per annum, through short- and long-term health consequences associated with alcohol use (e.g. hospitalisation and road crashes), along with additional support services that are required (e.g. alcohol dependency services and police). This means that every year over $500 in taxes for each and every Australian has to be spent on alcohol-related issues. Wouldn't you much rather have that money in your pocket? Guidelines provided by the National Health and Medical Research Council recommend that men and women aged 18 years and over drink no more than two standard drinks each day, and no more than five standard drinks within a 24-hour time period. Many Australians are drinking alcohol at levels that exceed these guidelines.

When compared to men, women are more vulnerable to both acute and chronic effects of alcohol misuse, because women's bodies are slower to process alcohol. The proportion of women that binge drink has been rising, and the frequency with which binge drinkers consume alcohol at dangerous levels is also rising. Based on the information that Queensland women aged 18–22 were consuming alcohol at long-term risky levels more often than their counterparts in other states, the Queensland Government took action: commissioning Redsuit Advertising to create a communications campaign aimed at reducing alcohol misuse by young women.

Following Redsuit Advertising's extensive research and communication campaign creation process, the Queensland Government launched a social marketing campaign designed to reduce risky drinking levels among Queensland women aged 18–22. Underpinned by market research, the 'Becky's not drinking' campaign moved away from the traditional 'negative consequences' approach practised by many government marketers (e.g. in play with the Australian government's 'Don't turn a night out into a nightmare' campaign) to deliver results that significantly exceeded stakeholder expectations.

The behavioural objectives for the campaign were to:
- maintain or increase the number of Queensland women aged 18–22 years who claim to have reduced the amount of alcohol they drink at any one time (goal was to achieve this objective for 35 per cent of the target market)
- maintain or increase the number of Queensland women aged 18–22 years who claim to have reduced the number of times they drink (goal was to achieve this objective for 38 per cent of the target market).

Existing research provided significant information relating to young women's alcohol consumption: where, when and at what levels they were drinking; their justification for drinking; and their levels of concern about drinking. But, it didn't give the full picture, and Redsuit Advertising decided to undertake additional market research to gain further insights into young Queensland women's lives.

Market research was undertaken by Redsuit Advertising to understand where alcohol fitted within young women's lives and lifestyles. This market research allowed Redsuit Advertising to paint a much more complete picture of the target market. The market research highlighted young women's desire to be in control, and it also emphasised the importance that young women place on sharing good times with friends. These were priorities that were used to great effect in the creative execution of the communication campaign.

The 'Becky's not drinking' campaign was based on three clear consumer insights.
1. The target market identified two areas of importance in their lives: (a) a strong desire to be in control; and (b) sharing quality time with friends. As they matured in their approach to drinking, young women were more likely to encounter internal conflict in relation to balancing these priorities. Redsuit Advertising's challenge was to address both of these priorities in the communication campaign, demonstrating how young women could satisfy one want without necessarily losing the other.
2. The second insight was an observation of how severely the maturation process was hampered by social and cultural influences that encouraged excessive drinking as a normal and desired behaviour for young women, and how sensitive to this pressure the 'reluctant drinkers' in the segment actually were. This sensitivity produced a barrier to behaviour change that was referred to

as a cultural hurdle. Barriers that needed to be overcome in the communication campaign related to questions such as:

- Am I ready to leave behind the fun and freedom of regularly getting drunk?
- Can I actually have a good time without getting smashed?
- Will I seem so sober and boring that nobody will notice me?
- How will my friends react if I stop getting drunk with them?
- Will I have to stop seeing some of my friends?
- Will I end up with no social life? Am I getting old before my time?

3. The third insight was developed following focus group testing of storyboards for advertisements based on negative consequences. There was a high level of agreement within the groups that these executions accurately depicted the downside of a night of excessive drinking. However, the researchers concluded that focus group endorsement of the messages actually meant that the messages had not gone far enough. The advertisements provided no new information, no replacement behaviour and no potential to take the target segment to the better place that they were seeking (a place where alcohol was an accompaniment to a good night out with friends, rather than the reason for it). Young women were already living with the short-term negative consequences of risky drinking every week, and they were not interested in the long-term consequences of their actions. As such, a consequence-based campaign would have merely restated what they already knew or had previously dismissed. So, unlike many other government health promotion campaigns (such as the Australian government's 'Don't turn a night out into a nightmare'), Redsuit Advertising decided to move away from focusing on either the short- or long-term health consequences of drinking, choosing to focus instead on the cultural and personal issues young women needed to address in order to reduce their drinking.

**Make up your own mind about drinking.**

For more information visit: www.health.qld.gov.au or call 1800 177 833

Queensland Government

In addition to giving consumer insights, the market research identified a range of environmental issues affecting drinking habits among young women in recent times. Excessive drinking was encouraged and considered normal among young women (and men). Young women had never had more access to beverages or outlets catering to their tastes. Young women have been encouraged to drink alcohol from an early age through the introduction of products (such as alcopops) that are designed to appeal to a younger palate. Consumption of pre-mixed, spirit-based beverages among female drinkers had increased from one in seven in 2000 to one in two in 2002. Compared to earlier decades, socialising had become more gender neutral, and young women were far more likely to gather at locations that, a generation earlier, may have been male domains. Licensed facilities valued their patronage and regularly geared their marketing towards young women. These trends were taking place amid continual increased spending by alcohol marketers; marketers who were determined to increase their market share through the promotion of alcohol as a key ingredient to any good night out. This environment resulted in attitudes that were very accepting of excessive drinking.

Pre-campaign research indicated that only three per cent of women aged 18–24 were concerned about the effects of drinking too heavily, and very few questioned the role of alcohol in society — or its impact on them. Alcohol was likely to be considered the driver of, or reason for, a good night out, rather than a harbinger of negative consequences. Young women were suspicious of messages from government authorities and did not want to be controlled — especially by politicians.

For the campaign, cinema and television advertising was produced, outdoor and point-of-sale material was displayed in and around licensed premises, and magazine advertising was used. The six-month campaign exceeded all expectations — with Redsuit Advertising bettering the behavioural objectives outlined at the start of the initiative:

- maintain or increase the number of Queensland women aged 18–22 years who claim to have reduced the amount of alcohol they drink at any one time (38 per cent achieved versus objective of 35 per cent)
- maintain or increase the number of Queensland women aged 18–22 years who claim to have reduced the number of times they drink (42 per cent achieved versus objective of 38 per cent).

This evidence was used by Redsuit Advertising to conclude that the communication campaign was successful. The aim to accelerate the maturation process had some effect: young women did not stop drinking; they did, however, reduce the number of drinks they were having. Many young women started to take control and to drink more responsibly.*

*The detailed information in this case was compiled with the assistance of Peter Cunningham, a partner at RedSuit Advertising.

## Questions

1. Describe the marketing process using the 'Becky's not drinking' campaign. You may wish to use the marketing framework presented in figure 1.3 to help with this.
2. Think about how you and your friends choose to drink or not drink alcohol. What else can a marketer do to slow alcohol consumption among young people, particularly among young women?

**Make up your own mind about drinking.**

## Advanced activity

Write down all of the marketing encounters that you have had today. Be thorough. You need to think about the activities and processes for creating, communicating, delivering and exchanging offerings that you have been exposed to, experienced and used today.

## Marketing plan activity

Think of an organisation that you would like to be the focus of a marketing plan that you will prepare during this semester. Collect some background information on this organisation and its products (goods and/or services). Each week you will have the opportunity to develop and refine a draft of this plan as your marketing knowledge increases. By the end of the semester, by following the steps outlined in each chapter of the text, you will have developed a professional 'industry standard' marketing plan, and enhanced your practical marketing skills in the process.

A sample marketing plan has been included at the back of this book (see page 523) to give you an idea where this information fits in an overall marketing plan.

## CHAPTER 2

# The marketing environment and market analysis

## Learning objectives

After studying this chapter, you should be able to:

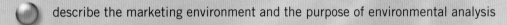 describe the marketing environment and the purpose of environmental analysis

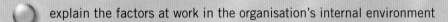 explain the factors at work in the organisation's internal environment

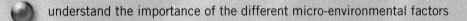 understand the importance of the different micro-environmental factors

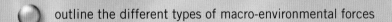 outline the different types of macro-environmental forces

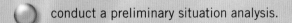 conduct a preliminary situation analysis.

# Fast health?

In a move that outraged obesity experts, McDonald's restaurants in New Zealand recently introduced four approved and branded Weight Watchers meals, including Chicken McNuggets.[1] Obesity experts suggest Weight Watchers certification will encourage more dieters to visit fast food restaurants, resulting in the sale of more high fat- and high salt-content burgers and chips. Weight Watchers, on the other hand, defended the decision, explaining that Weight Watchers certification is about providing more choices for people. Weight Watchers offers advice to people seeking to lose weight, and has devised a points plan that helps people to make better food choices.[2] Under the Weight Watchers system, foods are ranked based on their fat content and other nutritional factors, and participating dieters are supposed to stay within the daily limit.

A recent New Zealand national health survey found that 26.5 per cent of the New Zealand adult population is obese and a further 36.3 per cent is overweight. Almost 21 per cent of children aged two to 14 years are overweight and 8.3 per cent are obese.[3] The prevalence of obesity in Western societies generally is increasing to such an extent that it is now feared that life expectancies may fall for the first time in human history. Recent estimates in Australia suggest that 18 per cent of the adult population is obese and that more than 60 per cent of all Australians are overweight or obese. If current trends continue and forecasts are correct, three-quarters of today's teenagers will be overweight or obese by the time they turn 40.[4]

In Australia, McDonald's offers several items on its menu that have the Heart Foundation's 'Tick', which signifies they meet a reasonable standard of nutrition and health in terms of serving size, fat and salt levels, and vegetable/fibre content.

Obesity is a serious health concern and is strongly linked to health conditions including Type 2 diabetes, cardiovascular disease, some forms of cancer and arthritis. National governments have implemented various programs to try to reduce the incidence of obesity (and the health problems associated with it). For example, the Australian government committed $62 million to fight obesity as part of the National Preventative Health Strategy. Efforts such as this are leading to record levels of awareness of health, diet and exercise among the population. Takeaway food businesses such as McDonald's, which collectively serve almost three million meals to Australians and New Zealanders every day,[5] are responding to the increasing incidence and severity of obesity and to the growing public concern about healthy eating with their menu offerings.

## Questions

Survey at least ten people, asking each if they have eaten at McDonald's in the past month.
1. For those who have, ask the following:
   (a) Are they aware of any endorsement on McDonald's menu items (e.g. Weight Watchers or the Heart Foundation 'Tick')?
   (b) Have they ordered an item on the menu that is endorsed or would they consider doing so next time?
2. For those who haven't eaten at McDonald's in the past month, ask whether any healthy endorsement would make them more likely to eat at McDonald's, instead of at another takeaway food outlet, in the future?
3. Based on your results, is McDonald's encouraging any move to healthier meal alternatives?

# INTRODUCTION

In chapter 1 we learned that marketing is 'the activity, set of institutions, and processes for creating, communicating, delivering and exchanging offerings that have value for customers, clients, partners and society at large'.[6] Successful marketing must therefore be based on *understanding* the market. In addition to understanding the needs and wants of their customers and clients, marketers need to understand the wider environment in which they operate. They need to understand their products in light of what competitors currently offer and what they expect to offer in future. Marketers cannot expect to succeed by devising one strategy and sticking with it; nor will they succeed by simply copying a competitor.

In many ways, then, marketing can be likened to a game of sport. Like a sports team, organisations need to develop and implement a strategy to win, and they must be prepared to change their strategy to outfox their competition. Again like a sport, if you are ten points behind at half-time, there is little point carrying on with the same approach. If you are ten points ahead, you need to ensure you maintain and increase that margin. To achieve this, marketers need to understand and be attuned to their customers and society at large. Marketers need to plan and think of ways to stay one step ahead of the competition. Apple might be a good example of a company that can do this. Can you think of another?

As one means of staying ahead of the competition, marketers need to keep their 'fingers on the pulse'. To better meet customer needs — and to devise ways they can convince employees and/or partners to change if necessary — marketers need to understand both who they are competing with, and what barriers to change currently exist in their own organisation and in partner organisations.

This chapter is about understanding the environment in which organisations exist. In addition to their own internal environment, organisations operate within a micro environment (comprising the various players in the industry such as suppliers and competitors) and a macro environment (comprising broader forces such as social values and laws). Marketers must be able to analyse the environment in which they operate to obtain a comprehensive understanding of the situation they face. This understanding, together with management's objectives, is used by marketers to formulate a strategy to compete in the marketplace.

## THE MARKETING ENVIRONMENT

**Learning objective 1**
describe the marketing environment and the purpose of environmental analysis

___

**marketing environment** All of the internal and external forces that affect a marketer's ability to create, communicate, deliver and exchange offerings of value.

The **marketing environment** refers to all of the internal and external forces that affect a marketer's ability to create, communicate, deliver and exchange offerings of value. The factors and forces within the marketing environment can be classified as belonging to the internal environment, the micro environment, and the macro environment (see figure 2.1). The internal environment refers to the organisation itself and the factors that are directly controllable by the organisation. The micro environment comprises the forces and factors at play inside the industry in which the marketer operates. Micro-environmental factors affect all parties in the industry, including suppliers, distributors, customers and competitors. The macro environment comprises the larger-scale societal forces that influence not only the industry in which the marketer operates, but all industries. Macro-environmental factors include political forces, economic forces, sociocultural forces, technological forces and legal forces. This macro-environmental framework has been called the PESTL (for **p**olitical, **e**conomic, **s**ociocultural, **t**echnological, **l**egal) framework. Micro-environmental and macro-environmental forces are outside of the organisation and, while they can be influenced, they cannot be directly controlled.

Marketers seek to monitor, understand, respond to, and influence their environment. This is a complex task and encompasses all of marketing. **Environmental analysis** is an analytical approach that involves breaking the marketing environment into smaller parts to better understand it. This chapter introduces key considerations for an environmental analysis in order to provide you with insights into some of the things that effective marketers need to understand.

**environmental analysis**
A process that involves breaking the marketing environment into smaller parts in order to gain a better understanding of it.

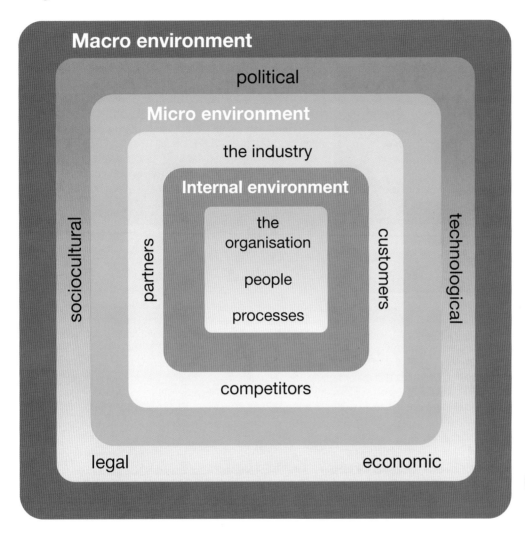

**FIGURE 2.1**

The marketing environment

In the course of your degree you may study economics, business law, management, logistics, human resources and other areas. Each subject is relevant to marketing. Studying these subjects will provide you with a more detailed understanding of each area. This will help you conduct an environmental analysis, which will in turn help you to build a more comprehensive picture of some of the environmental influences that marketers need to understand. The rest of this chapter provides an overview of the key considerations in the marketing environment. Successful marketers need a detailed understanding of each and every factor that we discuss. We will discuss the internal and external environments and conclude with an explanation of how to conduct a situation analysis of the organisation's overall marketing environment. The situation analysis and the organisation's objectives form the basis of marketing planning.

# Spotlight  In top gear

In recent years, the availability of more dedicated public bikeways, and concerns about fitness, the price of petrol and climate change have encouraged more commuters to leave their car at home and instead ride bikes to work. In Australia, bicycle sales have outstripped car sales for the past decade, with approximately 1.5 million bikes now being sold each year. More than two-thirds of these are imported bicycles.[7] Companies such as Sydney-based Cell Bikes have capitalised on these trends. Cell Bikes has a multimillion dollar turnover that grew by 70 per cent per year over a recent three-year period (at a time during which the economic downturn affected sales for many businesses).

Cell Bikes partners with manufacturers in China to develop bicycles to strict specifications, and imports these bikes into Australia. They have deliberately chosen a more upmarket product range — moving away from competitors like Kmart (who usually sell bikes in the $200 to $300 range). While still classifying their bikes as 'entry level' (under $1000), the average price of a bike at Cell Bikes is $800, and the company sells in excess of 5000 bikes each year.

About 40 per cent of Cell Bikes' revenue comes from online sales, but actual bike sales over the internet are rare. The majority of online sales are for accessories, such as helmets, gloves, lights, bags and bottles. The company also has a mechanical and repair unit to provide an additional revenue stream.

One challenge for the business is keeping abreast of fickle trends in cycling, due to the fact that the lead time for its orders from China is five months. A recent, sudden cyclist craze for fixed (single) gear bikes caught the company by surprise, forcing it to heavily discount its existing bulk stock of mountain bikes, which were falling out of fashion. Thankfully, a favourable exchange rate helped to cushion the company's profits during this price discounting period.

To help prevent this sort of situation happening in the future, Cell Bikes now polls its 13 000 e-newsletter subscribers to monitor trends. This feedback is used to plan the product range. With more bike paths being built in Sydney, Melbourne and Brisbane as a result of increased government infrastructure spending, there is plenty of potential for the business to expand interstate.[8]

## Questions

1. From the brief overview of the marketing environment provided in the chapter so far, outline some factors that you believe would particularly affect Cell Bikes. Categorise these factors as being part of Cell Bikes' internal, micro or macro environment.

2. Why would environmental analysis be useful for a company like Cell Bikes?

## Concepts and applications check

**Learning objective 1**  describe the marketing environment and the purpose of environmental analysis

1.1  Describe the factors in the marketing environment.

1.2  Which environmental factors can an organisation control or influence?

1.3  Name the five key forces in the PESTL model of the macro environment.

1.4  What is an environmental analysis and why is it important to marketing?

# INTERNAL ENVIRONMENT

The **internal environment** refers to the parts of the organisation, the people and the processes used to create, communicate, deliver and exchange offerings that have value. The internal environment is *directly controllable* by the organisation. A thorough understanding of the internal environment ensures that marketers understand the organisation's strengths and weaknesses. Strengths and weaknesses are internal factors that positively and negatively affect the organisation's ability to compete in the marketplace. Typically marketers seek to minimise weaknesses and maximise strengths.

As discussed in chapter 1, the most successful organisations are those with a market orientation. This means that all parts of the organisation are focused on creating and delivering value for the market. While this may seem simple, it is often very difficult in practice. Organisations consist of people, groups, departments and complex interrelationships. At times these can work against each other, rather than with each other. In reality, the internal environment of any organisation is affected by the personal and political natures of the people who make it up. It is important to be aware that as organisational complexity increases, so does the potential for conflict. Marketers need to understand the parts of the organisation and the processes that are in place. The main parts of a typical organisation include:

- *senior management* — responsible for making decisions about the overall objectives and strategy of the organisation
- *middle management* — typically responsible for a department or a geographic region. Middle management makes decisions about the overall objectives and strategy of the department or geographic region for which they have responsibility. Their aim is to make sure the objectives for their department or region are aligned with the objectives of the organisation as a whole.
- *functional departments* — organisations can be structured around functional departments and/or regions. If you are a business student you will study many of these functions during your degree. Functional departments may include:
  - marketing
  - sales
  - research and development
  - customer service
  - distribution/logistics
  - manufacturing
  - finance
  - human resources
  - administration.

  Functional department managers make decisions about the overall objectives and strategy of their department. Their aim is to make sure the objectives for their department are aligned with the broader objectives of the organisation and to manage their departments to ensure the departmental objectives are achieved.
- *employees* — employees are responsible for carrying out the work required to meet departmental objectives. Most corporations talk about their people being 'their most important asset'. Employees are also the 'face' of the organisation and marketers need to understand and manage the attitudes and behaviours of employees who come into contact with customers and clients.
- *external vendors* (*outsourcing*) — organisations often outsource functions and roles if they can be done more efficiently by specialist external providers. This represents a shift of the function from the internal environment to the micro environment

 **Learning objective 2**
explain the factors at work in the organisation's internal environment

**internal environment** The parts of the organisation, the people and the processes used to create, communicate, deliver and exchange offerings that have value. The organisation can directly control its internal environment.

and thus reduces the level of control. The organisation doing the outsourcing must, however, manage the service relationship with the external provider, and so outsourced functions still very much affect the organisation's internal environment. An organisation needs to ensure that the outsourced services remain consistent with its own objectives and do not adversely affect its market perception. This does not always occur, however, as Telstra discovered when one of its offshore information technology vendors, Satyam, was engulfed in a corporate fraud scandal. The India-based company overstated its cash reserves by $1 billion. The scandal, along with performance issues, led to the cancellation of Telstra's $32 million contract with the company.[9]

The structure of any organisation can be summarised in an 'organisation chart'. Most large organisations have a formal chart that illustrates the relationships between different parts of the organisation and the management hierarchy, but even the smallest businesses can be charted. Figure 2.2 is an extract of a typical example. An organisation chart can be a very useful tool to help analyse the internal environment. It gives an indication of the focus of the organisation's operations, how different areas relate to each other and where the power rests in the organisation.

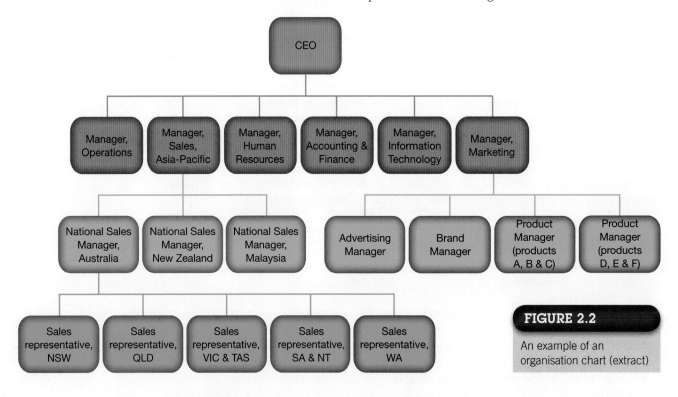

**FIGURE 2.2**

An example of an organisation chart (extract)

Marketers need to understand the objectives for each part of the organisation and how the objectives are being met. They need to understand whether the objectives align between the various parts of the organisation and whether the objectives are consistent with the overall marketing goals of the organisation. Employees are individuals and may perceive objectives differently. Consider the following case.[10] Senior management in two Australian financial institutions each decided to shift the emphasis of financial service staff from a *service* focus to a *sales* focus. Under this new strategy employees were given new titles. According to management, employees who previously had a service role were now called 'sales consultants' or 'sales officers'.

Employees resisted the management initiative, however, and continued to refer to themselves as 'customer service officers'. One employee commented:

> Basically I still think of myself as a customer service officer because I would rather service customers than sell them products. I think it is a much nicer title.

For many of the employees, their identification as caring service people had developed early in their careers and they were unwilling to make a transition from service to sales. Resistance to management's objectives from the employees would have reduced the ability of the organisation to meet its objectives.

To be successful, all of the parts of the internal environment should work together towards one common goal. This is most likely to occur when each person and department understands their contribution and the contribution of other departments. The marketing department is best positioned to understand what customers value. It is the marketing department's role to collaborate with the human resources department to ensure that all members within an organisation understand their role in creating, communicating, delivering and exchanging offerings that have value. It is then up to the other departments to use their own expertise to deliver that value.

With the increasing focus on a market orientation in many organisations, marketers have generally gained more influence and have been allocated more resources for their activities in recent decades. With this, however, has come an increasing expectation of results and an increasing need for marketers to be able to demonstrate and quantify their achievements. Marketing, like all other parts, processes and people in an organisation, must work to achieve the overall organisational objectives and must always demonstrate how it does so.

In many organisations, the severe squeeze on profits brought about by the global economic crisis resulted in tighter marketing budgets (particularly in the areas of new product development and advertising) and even more pressure for marketers to justify their organisation's investment in marketing. In general, during economic downturns, organisations tend to make drastic cuts to marketing budgets.[11] Marketing is viewed by many organisations largely as a cost, rather than as an investment. However, companies choosing to grow their marketing investment in economic downturns fare much better when economic recovery commences. Some companies were too swift to let staff go in the recent downturn in Australia, making it subsequently difficult to attract good staff when the economy recovered. Whatever the economic conditions, marketing can help influence consumer behaviour, set prices effectively, create value for marketing expenditure and take advantage of emerging opportunities.

It should be clear from the previous discussion that the internal environment is not an isolated entity. Much of what happens in an organisation's internal environment is affected by what happens in the less controllable external environment.

The **external environment** is concerned with things that are outside of the organisation. The external environment encompasses the people and processes that the organisation *cannot directly control*. Marketers can only seek to *influence* the external environment. For example, movie studios cannot prevent people from copying DVDs for their friends. They do, however, lobby governments to introduce legal penalties for doing so, and they include warnings about piracy on DVD packaging and on the DVD itself. Hence, they cannot control the factors in their external environment, but they do seek to influence them. The process of outsourcing (transferring an internal function to an external provider) has gone through waves of popularity over the past few decades. It represents a blurring of the line between the internal and external environment.

**external environment** The people and processes that are outside the organisation and cannot be directly controlled.

A thorough understanding of the external environment ensures that marketers understand the opportunities and threats that may arise. Opportunities and threats are external factors that positively and negatively affect the organisation's current and future ability to successfully serve the market. Typically marketers seek to make the most of the opportunities identified and minimise the threats arising in the external environment. The external environment includes the micro environment and the macro environment. We will look at each in turn to provide you with an understanding of the types of external factors that marketers need to understand.

## Spotlight Up, up and away?

Two-and-a-half hours prior to her scheduled departure time, a passenger went to an airline check-in desk at Brisbane Airport. She was intending to travel from Brisbane to Sydney, where she would connect with an international flight. The baggage allowance per passenger for the flight was 20 kilograms. An employee of the airline, Alison, weighed the passenger's bag and told her that because her suitcase weighed 28 kilograms, she had to go to the airline's cashier desk to pay an excess baggage fee. The passenger was not allowed to check the baggage in at this point. Alison pointed out the cashier's desk and instructed the passenger to pay the fee at this desk and then return to the check-in desk to receive her boarding pass and check in her baggage.

The passenger lined up at the designated cashier counter. However, another flight had been cancelled and more than 100 passengers were waiting in front of her in this queue, all of whom were trying to organise alternative flights. From the conversations overheard by the passenger, all other flights were fully booked. The passenger waited in this queue for over an hour. The queue did not move during this time. There was now one hour until her scheduled boarding time. The passenger was becoming increasingly worried that she would miss her domestic flight and, as a consequence, her connecting international flight.

The passenger went back to Alison and told her about the problem. The passenger asked if there was another way that the excess fee could be paid, as the queue was not moving. Alison told the passenger that there was no other way to pay the fee, and that she would simply have to pay at the cashier's desk. The passenger became angry at this stage. To ensure she could make her flight, the passenger decided to unpack her luggage, leaving non-essential items in an airport bin. The passenger then returned to Alison to have her bag weighed. The bag was within the limit and the passenger was given her boarding pass. The passenger told Alison that she would never fly with the airline again. She has since told numerous friends and family about her experience with this airline.

### Question

Imagine you are the marketing manager for this airline. What are some of the internal challenges you would face in integrating business units to create, communicate and deliver an offering that would have been more seamless for the passenger?

## Concepts and applications check

**Learning objective 2** explain the factors at work in the organisation's internal environment

2.1 Using an organisation that you (or a parent or friend) work in or have previously worked in as an example, identify areas of conflict that can arise in an organisation.

2.2 Think about a retail company that you have dealt with recently that sells services to consumers (e.g. a travel agency, bank or airline). Using its annual report to shareholders (usually available in the investor section of its corporate website), find its objectives for the next financial year. Were the behaviours of the staff who provided you with service consistent with management's objectives? If so, how were they consistent? If not, what improvements are needed for management's objectives to be reached?

2.3 Find an organisational chart and identify the areas of possible conflict that may arise from the structural organisation of the business. You should consider the number of different levels of management, the number of different departments and the number of employees in the organisation. How can marketers ensure that all employees understand their contribution and the contribution of other departments to providing value to customers and clients?

2.4 How does outsourcing affect the level of control a business has over its operations? Use an example to illustrate your answer.

# MICRO ENVIRONMENT

The **micro environment** consists of customers, clients, partners and competitors. Unlike, the internal environment, the micro environment is not directly controllable by the organisation. The organisation can, however, exert some influence on the customers, clients, partners, competitors and other parties that make up its industry. For example, a recent survey by CHOICE found that 60 per cent of Jetstar customers were satisfied with the airline. Jestar's customer relationship management has been overhauled and call centre practices have been changed, allowing the airline to cut complaint resolutions from 90 to ten days; also, instead of having to make a formal complaint in writing, customers can now do it over the phone. While Jetstar can't directly control a customer, it can influence satisfaction by improving its complaint handling procedures.[12]

In one way or another, all of the factors in the micro environment affect the marketer. In analysing the micro environment, marketers need to consider customers and clients; partners, including suppliers; and competitors. We will discuss each of these in turn next, and will look at how to conduct such an analysis later in the chapter.

**Learning objective 3**
understand the importance of the different micro-environmental factors

**micro environment** The forces within an organisation's industry that affect its ability to serve its customers and clients — target markets, partners and competitors.

## Customers and clients

Marketers must understand the current and future needs and wants of their target market. They must:
- understand what their customers value now
- be able to identify any changes in customer preferences
- be willing and able to respond to changes
- anticipate how needs and wants might change in the future
- be able to influence customer preferences.

Consider, for example, how the obesity epidemic (a macro-environmental factor) discussed at the start of the chapter has affected customers and clients (in the micro environment). Growing awareness of this issue will likely see some more individuals turning to exercise, healthy eating choices, or a combination of both to lose weight. Parents may become more conscious of the type of food they purchase and pack for their children's lunch. Marketers that can respond to these trends in order to satisfy changing consumer preferences will view this as an opportunity and tailor their marketing mix accordingly. Consumer behaviour is explained in detail in chapter 4.

In the business-to-business market (i.e. where businesses market their products to other businesses), marketers need to be similarly aware of the current and future needs of their target market. For example, changes in economic conditions (another macro-environmental factor), such as movements in interest rates, will likely have an impact on business investment and spending patterns. Astute marketers keep abreast of such developments, assess their likely impact and implement marketing strategies accordingly. Business-to-business marketing is explained in detail in chapter 5.

## Partners

Marketers need to understand their partners, how each partner's processes work and how their partnerships benefit each party. Partners include:

- *logistics firms.* Logistics is the term used to describe all the processes involved in distributing products; it includes storage and transport.
- *financiers.* Financiers provide financial services such as banking, loans and insurance, and the financial system's infrastructure facilitates electronic payment transactions with partners and customers.
- *advertising agencies.* Small businesses tend to devise their own advertisements, often with the help of the publication, radio station or other medium they are advertising with. Larger businesses can hire the services of advertising agencies. When they do so, they put an enormous amount of faith in the agency to attract the attention of potential customers and encourage them to actually engage in a marketing exchange with the organisation.
- *retailers.* Retailers are the businesses from which customers purchase goods and services. Many retailers, such as corner shops and supermarkets, sell mainly products made by others. Other businesses make and retail their products, particularly small boutique businesses, service businesses and businesses with an online shop.
- *wholesalers.* Wholesalers are an intermediary acting between the producer and the retailers to provide storage and distribution efficiencies to both.
- *suppliers.* Suppliers provide the resources that the organisation needs to make its products. Suppliers are a crucial business partner and they must be monitored for continuity of supply and price.

While the word 'partner' suggests a mutually beneficial relationship, there are also many risks involved in working with partners and often the balance of power between partners can be skewed towards one at the expense of the other. For example, Woolworths and Coles often sell Coca-Cola at a loss during price promotions. They do this because Coca-Cola specials draw customers to the store and these customers often then purchase other products as well. The Coca-Cola Company does not need to discount Coca-Cola in order to sell it and so does not offer a rebate to the supermarkets when they put it on special. This is rare in the food retailing business. Marketers need to know the missions and strategies of their partners. Ideally their strategies should be aligned and complementary. Marketers need to understand their partners' cost structure to enable them to price their offerings appropriately. Marketers need to understand how partners promote their offerings, if at all.

## Suppliers

Marketers need to know their existing and potential suppliers' costs, availability, time frames and planned innovations to determine how they can best create value. They also need to know and manage the risks involved in their dependency on their suppliers. Organisations need to be aware of and pre-empt any problems (e.g. labour strikes and stock shortages) with the supply of the resources they need to ensure they can fulfil demand. In summary, marketers must identify, assess, monitor and manage risks to supplies and risks to the price of supplies.

# Competitors

As stated in chapter 1, the most successful businesses throughout history have been those built around and focused on making their customers happy — and doing it better than their competitors can. To succeed, marketers must ensure their offerings provide their target market with greater value than their competitors' offerings. Marketers seek to understand their competitors' marketing mix, sales volumes, sales trends, market share, staffing, sales per employee and employment trends. They do this through casual and formal analysis, as we will describe later in the chapter.

Marketers exist in competitive markets and there are many different types of market competition. Table 2.1 summarises the types of competitive market and gives an example of each.

**TABLE 2.1** Types of competition

| Competitive structure | Description | Example |
|---|---|---|
| Pure competition | Numerous competitors offer undifferentiated products. No buyer or seller can exercise market power. | Markets for agricultural goods such as sugar and for financial securities such as shares are the closest real-world approximations to pure competition. In reality, pure competition does not exist. |
| Monopolistic competition | Numerous competitors offer products that are similar, prompting the competitors to strive to differentiate their product offering from others. | The market for laptop computers exhibits monopolistic competition. Acer, DELL, Apple, Toshiba and many others all sell versions of essentially similar products, though the products are differentiated by colour packaging, price, memory, processing speed and so on. |
| Oligopoly | A small number of competitors offer similar, but somewhat differentiated, products. There are significant barriers to new competitors entering the market. | The Australian supermarket industry is an example, with Coles and Woolworths selling over 75 per cent of all groceries in Australia. Smaller operators, such as Aldi and IGA, also exist. |
| Monopoly | There is only one supplier and there are substantial, potentially insurmountable, barriers to new entrants. | Many government services are essentially monopoly industries, such as the provision of roads and rail. These are maintained as monopolies when it is considered inefficient or somehow undesirable to have competition. This position can change, however, with some governments choosing to open up some of their monopoly markets to private competition (e.g. electricity supply in Queensland). |
| Monopsony | The market situation where there is only one buyer. | The federal government is the only buyer of fighter jets in Australia. |

When thinking about competition, marketers need to think broadly. There are many different levels of competition that marketers face. Table 2.2 summarises the different levels of competition and provides an example of each. While marketers often think in terms of brand competition, a broader definition of competition can place marketers in a better position to create, communicate, deliver and exchange offerings that have value.

**TABLE 2.2** Levels of competition

| Level of competition | Description | Example |
|---|---|---|
| Total budget competition | Consumers have limited financial resources and therefore must make choices about which products to consume and which to forgo. In this sense, organisations are competing against all alternative ways the consumer can engage in an exchange of value. | A university student would like to attend a concert and the tickets are $120. The concert is competing with all other possible uses of the student's $120 — refuelling the car, weekly rent, food and other bills, leaving it in the bank, and so on. |
| Generic competition | Consumers often have alternative ways to meet their product needs. The same want or need can be satisfied by quite different products. This is known as substitutability. | Sydney Buses competes with CityRail and Black and White Taxis for the business of consumers needing to get from A to B. Bus, train and taxi rides are quite different, but meet the same need. |
| Product competition | Some products are broadly similar, but have different benefits, features and prices that distinguish them from competing products. | Soft drinks, water, alcohol, coffee and juice are all beverages that people could purchase to drink. |
| Brand competition | Some products are very similar, offering the same benefits, features and price to the same target market. | Westpac, ANZ, the Commonwealth Bank and the National Australia Bank all offer savings accounts with similar minimum balances, interest rates, internet banking facilities, distribution of ATMs, fees and so on. There is not a lot to intrinsically distinguish these products from each other. This is in contrast to other options for investing savings, such as buying shares, debentures, real estate or artworks. |

# Spotlight Let's get digital

After six years of declining sales, the Australian recording industry recently experienced a welcome year of growth. Although sales of physical recorded music product (e.g. CDs and DVDs) continued to decline, digital sales managed to offset this decrease for the first time in many years. Commenting on the reversal of fortunes, Ed St John, the chairman of the Australian Recording Industry Association (ARIA) at the time, stated:

> We're pleased with the figures that we've seen today, but have a tremendous amount of work to do to stem the tide of illegal file-sharing, which continues to erode profits and hamper investment into the local industry. We remain hopeful that the internet service providers will work with us to address this pressing problem and help the growth of the legitimate market, something that will, of course, also be to their benefit.[13]

The music industry has been heavily impacted by illegal file-sharing technology in recent years, making it possible for pirated copies of recorded music to be downloaded for free online. There are over a million visits by Australians to file-sharing websites each year, and this figure is growing at annual rate of 30 per cent. According to

Music Industry Piracy Investigations, almost one in five Australians — and one in three children aged 14–17 — download music illegally.[14] A study by Quantum Research estimates that about one billion songs are downloaded illegally by Australians each year. If those songs were purchased through online stores, music industry revenue would soar by an additional $1.6 billion.[15]

In an environment where people can obtain music for free, music companies face the challenge of persuading people who are used to getting free music to become customers and pay. At present only about half of 14–24-year-olds agree that downloading music from file-sharing networks is stealing.[16] The music industry has also been actively lobbying internet service providers to switch off illegal downloading services. The television and film industries are similarly affected, and this issue is explored further in chapter 12.

---

## Question

**Imagine you are the marketing manager for a record company. From a marketing perspective, how would you attempt to influence:**

**(a) internet service providers**

**(b) customers.**

---

## Concepts and applications check

**Learning objective 3**  understand the importance of the different micro-environmental factors

**3.1**  What aspects of competitors' operations must an organisation understand as part of its micro-environmental analysis?

**3.2**  What risks are involved in a business partnership with suppliers?

**3.3**  An organisation cannot directly control its micro environment. It can, however, exert influence. Choose an organisation and describe five ways in which it could influence its micro environment.

**3.4**  Review the different levels of competition outlined in table 2.2. Imagine that you are the marketing manager for a wine bar. Outline two examples of competition that your wine bar faces for each level of competition outlined in table 2.2.

**3.5**  Imagine you are the marketing manager of a bank. Outline all of the micro-environmental factors that you should analyse when making marketing decisions for the business.

---

# THE MACRO ENVIRONMENT

The organisation itself and all of the forces within the micro environment operate within a larger environment known as the macro environment. The **macro environment** encompasses the factors outside of the industry that influence the survival of the organisation. In practice, the macro environment can be at any geographic level including local, state, country or regional (e.g. the Asia–Pacific or the European Union).

In some cases it is possible for marketers to *influence* macro-environmental factors. However, these factors will always remain beyond a marketer's *control*. For example, a company can lobby government to reduce the tax on wine but they cannot directly control the rate set by the government.

Failure to plan based on emerging trends can lead to business closure. Effective marketers continually monitor the environment, adapting and changing offers where necessary in response to changes in the macro environment.

Learning objective 4
outline the different types of macro-environmental forces

**macro environment** The factors outside of the industry that influence the survival of the company; these factors are not directly controllable by the organisation.

News services, business and investment media, libraries, the internet and industry associations are all avenues to inform marketers of developments in the macro environment. Key environmental factors that marketers need to consider when analysing the marketing environment include political, economic, sociocultural, technological and legal forces. (This view of the macro environment is commonly abbreviated to 'PESTL'.) The key considerations are summarised in figure 2.3 and each factor is discussed in the following sections.

**Political**

The political arena has a huge influence upon businesses and the spending power of consumers. Marketers must consider:

1. The stability of the political environment
2. The influence of government policy, laws and regulation
3. Government trade agreements such as ASEAN
4. Taxation and government rebate policies.

**Economic**

Marketers need to understand the economy in the short and long terms. Marketers must consider:

1. Interest rates, economic growth (gross domestic product) and consumer confidence
2. Income levels, savings, credit and spending levels
3. The level of inflation, employment and unemployment
4. Exchange rates and balance of trade.

**Sociocultural**

Social and cultural influences have a large influence on businesses. Marketers must understand:

1. Religion, culture, subcultures, values, attitudes and beliefs
2. Population trends including age, household size and composition, marriage and divorce trends, places lived, ethnicity and health.

**Technological**

Technology is vital for competitive advantage. Marketers must consider:

1. Whether offerings can be made more cheaply and to a better standard of quality using new technologies
2. Whether technology can be used to innovate
3. Whether distribution or communication can be improved using technology.

**Legal**

Marketers need to understand legal and regulatory influences such as:

1. Laws including the Competition and Consumer Act, The Privacy Act, The Spam Act, The Sale of Goods Act and the Prices Surveillance Act
2. Regulations from industry bodies such as the Advertising Standards Bureau.

**FIGURE 2.3**

The macro environment

Economic factors are the focus of economics courses and students intending to major in marketing should seek to take an introductory economics course if it is not a core degree requirement. An understanding of the political environment is also encouraged. Students intending to major in marketing should seek to take one course in politics and law to gain a broad understanding of the political and legal environments. Students choosing to continue in marketing studies will explore sociocultural factors in detail in consumer behaviour courses.

# Political forces

**Political forces** describe the influence of politics on marketing decisions. Politics is directly relevant to the marketing organisation through:

- lobbying for favourable treatment at the hands of the government
- lobbying for a 'light touch' approach to regulation
- the very large market that the government and its bureaucracy comprise
- the ability of political issues to affect efforts at international marketing.

Many organisations, particularly smaller ones, monitor political issues, but do not actively engage in politics. Larger organisations, or the bodies created to represent smaller ones, can engage directly in politics by seeking to influence lawmakers. Every time there is a federal election, the sources of large donations to one or other of the major political parties become headline stories in the media. Organisations can also campaign for legal or policy changes that can have a fundamental impact on their operating environment. The extensive changes to Australia's workplace relations system made by the federal government in recent years are an example of how political forces can change an organisation's operating environment.

It is worth noting too that political parties, governments and the public service themselves undertake a lot of marketing activities. For example, the federal government's Department of Foreign Affairs and Trade runs advertising campaigns and maintains its www.smarttraveller.com.au website to inform Australians travelling overseas about laws, customs, health issues and other matters that might affect their travel decisions.

**political forces** The influence of politics on marketing decisions.

# Economic forces

**Economic forces** refer to all of those factors that affect how much money people and organisations can spend and how they choose to spend it. The obvious components of this are income, prices, the level of savings, the level of debt and the availability of credit. Many of these factors are discussed in chapter 6, as they are fundamental defining characteristics of the market.

Economic forces and conditions can change quickly and dramatically, and marketers can find themselves facing a very different economic environment within a short period of time. Currency fluctuations, for example, affect the prices of exports and imports. A devaluation of the Australian dollar makes exports cheaper and imports more expensive. The reverse applies when the currency appreciates on international markets (i.e. exports become more expensive and imports cheaper). Interest rates are another economic force. Increases or decreases in interest rates can have a significant impact on both consumer and business confidence, and subsequent spending and investment patterns. The global financial crisis served to highlight an important aspect of the macro environment: it is made up of global forces that are beyond the control of any individual organisation or even government.

**economic forces** Those factors that affect how much people and organisations can spend and how they choose to spend it.

# Sociocultural forces

**Sociocultural forces** is a term used to describe the social and cultural factors that affect people's attitudes, beliefs, behaviours, preferences, customs and lifestyles. They comprehensively and pervasively influence the value people put on different product offerings. 'Demographics' describe statistics about a population. A population can be characterised by its demographic characteristics: age, gender, race, ethnicity, educational attainment, marital status, parental status and so on. These characteristics influence the behaviour of society as a whole and the individuals

**sociocultural forces** The social and cultural factors that affect people's attitudes, beliefs, behaviours, preferences, customs and lifestyles.

within it. Changes in demographic characteristics should be expected to result in changes in the behaviour of individual consumers and society generally. This topic is explored in detail in chapter 6.

One of the sociocultural themes to become a key issue for marketing organisations over the past couple of decades is the natural environment. Society (particularly the younger members of society) has become more and more concerned about the sustainability of humankind's lifestyle — the effect our activities have on the world that supports us. Think about how many issues related to the natural environment appear in the headlines every day: sustainability, corporate social responsibility, global warming, pollution, deforestation, salinity and carbon trading. Marketers need to be aware of these issues and society's expectations of how businesses and other organisations need to respond. Some marketing organisations have already capitalised on the growing environmental concern of society; others have responded to it; others are slow to respond and potentially risk destroying their businesses.

## Technological forces

It is important, when considering technological forces, not to fall into the trap of viewing technology just in terms of iPhones, satnavs and hybrid-electric cars. Rather, technology is a broad concept based on finding better ways to do things. That is, the electronic gadgetry of a satnav device is not really the technology; the technology is that a satnav is a better way (than a map) to navigate to your destination.

Technology is advancing at an unprecedented rate. Our daily lives are touched by technology almost all of the time. It is similarly common to be touched by technological *change*. Think about how often you change to a newer, better, brighter model of mobile phone (or at least how often you would like to). While email, Web 2.0, mobile phones, mobile internet and e-commerce are an everyday part of your life, they all represent major technological changes that your lecturers adapted to some years ago.

In a wired world, we are connected most of the time, be it to the internet via a PC, laptop or mobile phone, to our friends via Twitter, or to our work via a BlackBerry device. Never before have marketers been able to interact with the market as often, as intimately, and as extensively as they can today. For example, it is reasonably common today to receive follow-up phone calls, emails or text messages after making a major purchase decision, such as buying a new car.

Technology does not just change the expectations and behaviours of customers and clients. Technological change can have huge effects on how suppliers work. Today manufacturers, suppliers and distributors are likely to be in constant electronic exchange with marketing organisations, ensuring stock levels are automatically monitored and maintained, tracking goods in transit down to the nearest kilometre. Increasingly the customer can see how many goods are in stock or how long they will have to wait to have an item delivered. Consider the efficiencies brought about by electronic payment systems. How many more shoes can Mathers sell given a customer can whip out a credit card to purchase a pair that take their fancy, rather than have to go to a bank, fill out a paper form, stand in line and be handed some crumpled paper currency to carry back to the shop?

Technology, while enabling many advances, can also pose a threat to marketers. Kodak, long-established as a leading photography brand, suffered massive downsizing and its business was severely threatened by the advent of digital cameras in the 1990s. The mass market for photographic film disappeared in a few short years.

# Legal forces

**Laws** and **regulations** are intimately tied to politics. Elected officials and the bureaucracy that works for them are ultimately responsible for making legislation; that is, for creating and changing laws. Regulations are made under conditions established by legislation and tend to deal with more minor or more specific issues than legislation. They are by no means unimportant.

Laws and regulations govern what marketing organisations can and cannot legally do. They spell out their obligations to consumers, partners, suppliers, government authorities and society as a whole. The most significant laws and regulations fall into the following categories: privacy, fair trading, consumer safety, prices, contract terms and intellectual property.

In a bid to forestall legal regulation, many industries have adopted codes of conduct as a self-regulatory device. Self-regulation is usually cheaper, and more attuned to industry needs and actual practice. For example, Australian advertisers established the Advertising Standards Bureau to establish and uphold certain standards in advertising.

As mentioned earlier in the chapter when describing the impact of political forces on an organisation's macro environment, larger organisations (and industry lobby groups) can attempt to influence government lawmakers. A recent example of this occurred in 2011, when a group of high-profile Australian retailers (such as David Jones, Myer, Harvey Norman and Target) banded together in an orchestrated advertising campaign. This campaign was designed to highlight what Australian retailers perceived as an inequity in the market, where offshore retailers are not required by the Commonwealth Government to pay import duty or GST (goods and services tax) on sales to Australia under the value of $1000. The group of Australian retailers (which employ Australians and are required to pay 10 per cent GST on all purchases) argue that this inequity places them at a price disadvantage compared to offshore online retailers. The Commonwealth Government countered by saying it wouldn't be pressured into making a decision; while local consumer advocacy group CHOICE argued that the Australian retailers' campaign was motivated by self-interest, and would only result in higher prices for local consumers.[17]

# Macro-environmental complexity

There are numerous ways to view the macro environment. The PESTL framework we have outlined in this section of the chapter is just one. It is intended to help focus on some particular issues of importance for marketers, but it must be remembered that none of these factors act in isolation. Rather, they are all interdependent and a change in one will almost always have consequences for the others. For example, the development of internet technology created a need for new laws to regulate online conduct; an entire online economy developed; the provision of internet infrastructure and the regulation of internet content has become a major political issue; the nature of relationships and how people spend their days has been fundamentally changed by the online world.

Let's consider another example. Over the past two decades, the world as a whole has become more aware of the need to minimise the impact of human behaviour on the natural environment. Amid warnings from scientists of global warming, pollution, the exhaustion of fossil fuels and the extinction of flora and fauna species, individuals, businesses and governments have begun to give much more weight to the need for business activities to be responsible and sustainable. Options put forward to encourage such behaviour include proposals for emissions trading schemes and/or carbon taxes. Although New Zealand introduced a government-run emissions trading scheme in 2008, the potential introduction of one (or a carbon tax) in Australia has been the subject of considerable debate in recent years. Various political parties, business and industry lobby groups, and many in the general population, hold conflicting views. Emissions trading schemes and carbon tax proposals are designed to encourage market forces to reduce carbon pollution, which is one of the main contributors to global warming. Australians emit an average 18.75 tonnes per person of greenhouse gas emissions each year, while New Zealanders emit an average of 8.48 tonnes per person per year.[18]

Emissions trading schemes and carbon tax proposals are generally based on the theory that the price of products that generate more carbon pollution will increase as a result of the scheme/proposal, reducing demand; whereas carbon-friendly products will fall to be relatively low in price, increasing demand. Over time, those producers that are larger greenhouse gas emitters will be less able to compete in the market with those who can produce in a more carbon-friendly manner.

## Spotlight The great Australian dream

Australia has changed. Many older Australians will remember growing up on a large 'quarter-acre block' of land. This is now a distant memory, with blocks of land in many new housing estates becoming smaller and smaller over time. Changes to council regulations have enabled developers to maximise the number of housing lots they can market on their parcels of land. Yet, while block sizes in Australian cities are generally shrinking, new house sizes are growing — leaving minimal space between or around premises. The floor plan sizes of new homes in Australia have been getting larger and larger for many years. According to the Australian Bureau of Statistics, the average new Australian home in 1984–85 had about 150 square metres of floor space. A report by BIS Shrapnel quoted the 1999 floor space size as 228.1 square metres. Recent estimates show Australian homes are now averaging 253.1 square metres.

Despite declining yard space, Australians still spend more than $6 billion a year at garden retail centres. There are an estimated 20 000 garden-related businesses operating in Australia. About

3000 of these are production nurseries and about 6000 are garden retailers, with the remainder being related landscaping suppliers or garden service companies. Although smaller and less common than they once were, gardens are still seen by most Australians as having value, with 75 per cent of Newspoll survey respondents stating they believe plants around their home improve their health and add value to their home and lifestyle. The same survey indicated that 43 per cent of respondents grow herbs, 44 per cent tend to fruit trees and 63 per cent grow vegetables in their backyards.

These statistics are encouraging for the garden industry. However, the amount of time most working Australians have to do gardening work is lower than in previous generations, with current generations generally working longer hours in paid employment. Ironically, people are doing this, in some cases, to service high mortgages on their large homes![19]

### Question

Identify as many macro-environmental forces as possible that you believe would impact on the garden retail industry, and categorise them under the PESTL model.

## Concepts and applications check

**Learning objective 4** outline the different types of macro-environmental forces

**4.1** Identify five macro-economic factors and explain their relevance to marketers.

**4.2** You are a marketer for David Jones. Identify two macro-environmental trends that will affect your business in the next financial year.

**4.3** You are marketing large cars and understand that the trends towards environmentalism and smaller families are beginning to reduce demand for large cars. In addition, the global economic downturn has made people more likely to keep their current car rather than trade up to a new one. How would you respond to these environmental changes?

**4.4** Identify two major consumer laws in your country. Explain their relevance to marketers.

**4.5** The Australian Competition and Consumer Commission and the Commerce Commission are key regulatory bodies in Australia and New Zealand respectively. Choose one of these bodies and outline what they do and why marketers need to be aware of them.

**4.6** Choose a company that generates significant amounts of carbon emissions (e.g. a mineral processing company) and use the PESTL framework to analyse how a carbon emissions trading scheme will affect their marketing environment.

# SITUATION ANALYSIS AND MARKETING PLANNING

Before marketers can create an offering for exchange they must understand their current position or situation. **Situation analysis** involves assessing the current situation in order to clearly state where the company is now. Together with organisational objectives, situation analysis is used as the platform for **marketing planning**, as illustrated in figure 2.4.

 **Learning objective 5** conduct a preliminary situation analysis

**FIGURE 2.4**

Marketing planning

Consider the following example. A marketer is informed by top management that their objective for the next financial year is to achieve the number two position in terms of market share for a product that was launched 12 months ago (it is currently at number four out of six products in the market). Since the launch the product has achieved 17 per cent market share. To gain the number two position, the marketer needs to increase market share by a further 10 per cent, to achieve a total of 27 per cent market share. If successful, the marketer will receive bonuses. In practice, where competition exists, this is a difficult — but not impossible — objective to achieve. The marketer needs to gain a comprehensive understanding of the current situation, viewed through the eyes of customers, clients, partners and the society at large, in order to develop a marketing plan to reach the target.

Marketers need to be able to analyse their current situation, understanding not only their own business, but also their competitors' businesses and the marketing

**situation analysis** An analysis that involves identifying the key factors that will be used as a basis for the development of marketing strategy.

**marketing planning** An ongoing process that combines organisational objectives and situation analyses to formulate and maintain a marketing plan that moves the organisation from where it currently is to where it wants to be.

environment. As stated earlier, situation analysis leads to an assessment of where we are now. In addition to giving consideration to trends in the internal and external marketing environment, marketers must understand their past performance. Figure 2.5[20] outlines key factors that should be evaluated in a thorough situation analysis.

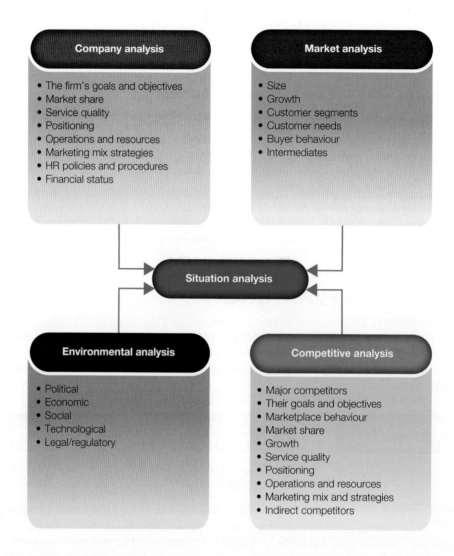

**Company analysis**

- The firm's goals and objectives
- Market share
- Service quality
- Positioning
- Operations and resources
- Marketing mix strategies
- HR policies and procedures
- Financial status

**Market analysis**

- Size
- Growth
- Customer segments
- Customer needs
- Buyer behaviour
- Intermediates

**Situation analysis**

**Environmental analysis**

- Political
- Economic
- Social
- Technological
- Legal/regulatory

**Competitive analysis**

- Major competitors
- Their goals and objectives
- Marketplace behaviour
- Market share
- Growth
- Service quality
- Positioning
- Operations and resources
- Marketing mix and strategies
- Indirect competitors

**FIGURE 2.5**

The situation analysis

As illustrated earlier in figure 2.4, the situation analysis, together with the organisation's objectives, should form the basis for developing the marketing plan. Essentially, a marketing plan communicates how marketers plan to get from the current situation to where top management thinks their company should be. Marketing plans are detailed documents, as can be seen by the example included as an appendix at the back of this book. Although the format and structure of marketing plans vary, the major components and types of information contained in a typical marketing plan are outlined in figure 2.6. At the end of each chapter in this text is an activity that allows you to gather information on a product for each of the major components of the marketing plan listed in figure 2.6. This will enable you to build a detailed marketing plan as you work through this textbook.

**FIGURE 2.6**

The marketing plan

# Executive summary

The executive summary provides a brief overview of the marketing plan. The purpose is to outline the main features of the marketing plan that will help the organisation to achieve its objectives. The executive summary is often the only part of a report that decision makers read, so it needs to effectively communicate the key issues.

# Introduction

Brief details on the internal environment of the organisation are provided in this section — its history, size, locations, number of employees, revenue, profitability and so on.

# Situation analysis

This is a more detailed section of the marketing plan. It includes a thorough analysis of the macro- and micro-environmental factors. This situation analysis will typically be synthesised into a capstone SWOT analysis for the organisation (an acronym for Strengths, Weaknesses, Opportunities and Threats). The SWOT analysis is explained in more detail later in this chapter, including via a visual representation in figure 2.8.

# Objectives

The organisation's overall objectives and mission statement are included in this section, along with the marketing objectives that are intended to help achieve the organisation's overall objectives. All objectives should be:

- **S**pecific
- **M**easurable
- **A**ctionable
- **R**easonable
- **T**imetabled.

# Target market

The marketing plan should contain a description of the organisation's target market segments, their characteristics and how the target market and market segments were selected. It is important that the description of the target market/segment is as specific as possible. For example, if it has been determined by the situation analysis that the target market is urban 25–30-year-old single males, this needs to be what is stated,

*(continued)*

**FIGURE 2.6**

*continued*

as opposed to a more general description such as 'young single men'. Information on how to effectively segment markets is contained in chapter 6 of this text.

## Marketing mix strategy

### Product

The product component of the strategy needs to be outlined, including an explanation of how the product offers value to the target market. A discussion of branding should also be included. While you might not include a total product concept analysis of the product in your marketing plan (see chapter 7 of this text), it may be a useful exercise to inform the product strategy that is outlined in the plan.

### Price

Pricing objectives (e.g. cash flow, positioning and market share) and the pricing method(s) used to determine prices for your product/s should be stated as part of the marketing mix strategy. Competitors' pricing should also be discussed. Pricing is discussed in chapter 8 of this text.

### Distribution (place)

Distribution is a further aspect of the marketing mix strategy that should be outlined in order to explain how the organisation's products will be available to customers where and when they want them. The distribution discussion should address the use of marketing intermediaries, if applicable. Chapter 9 of this text explains key distribution issues that need to be considered by organisations.

### Promotion

The promotion mix (advertising, public relations, sales promotions and personal selling) that the organisation wishes to pursue should be explained as part of its marketing strategy. Consideration should also be given to additional marketing communication options, such as guerrilla marketing, sponsorship and viral marketing, if appropriate for the organisation. Chapter 10 of this text explains the various elements of the promotion mix.

### People

For services products, a people strategy should be discussed as part of the marketing mix strategy, including how the organisation will address the specific service product characteristics of intangibility, inseparability, heterogeneity and perishability. These characteristics are explained in chapter 11. The people strategy should also outline how the organisation will ensure that its staff are technically competent, able to deliver high standards of customer service and able to promote products through personal selling.

**FIGURE 2.6**

*continued*

## Process

The systems and procedures, particularly for services products, that will be used to create the organisation's product offering should be discussed in the marketing plan.

## Physical evidence

For service products, the organisation should provide tangible cues as to the quality it offers. The organisation's physical evidence strategy may address issues such as shop fittings, background music and staff uniforms.

# Budget

It is important that the budgetary requirements of the marketing plan be outlined in detail, to demonstrate how the plan can be implemented with available resources.

# Implementation

How the marketing plan will be put into practice should be explained, including specific steps and milestones, as well as control mechanisms to ensure the implementation phase proceeds in accordance with the plan.

# Evaluation

The plan needs to outline specific metrics (e.g. return on investment, market share) that will be used to evaluate its success. These metrics can also be used by the organisation to inform both the refinement of the current plan if necessary and the development of future marketing plans.

# Conclusion/future recommendations

A brief summary/conclusion of the report should be provided, including recommendations for approval and/or action (e.g. that the marketing plan be accepted by senior management for implementation, in order to exploit market opportunities for growth).

## Marketing metrics

**Marketing metrics** are measures that are used to assess marketing performance. The Australian Marketing Institute offers a framework to guide marketers' choice of metrics. The framework's underlying principles are that metrics should be linked to strategy, and should include, as a minimum, four key elements: return on marketing investment, customer satisfaction, market share in targeted segments, and brand equity.

**marketing metrics** Measures that are used to assess marketing performance.

To give you an idea of the many different ways that marketers can measure performance, key marketing metrics are summarised in figure 2.7.[21]

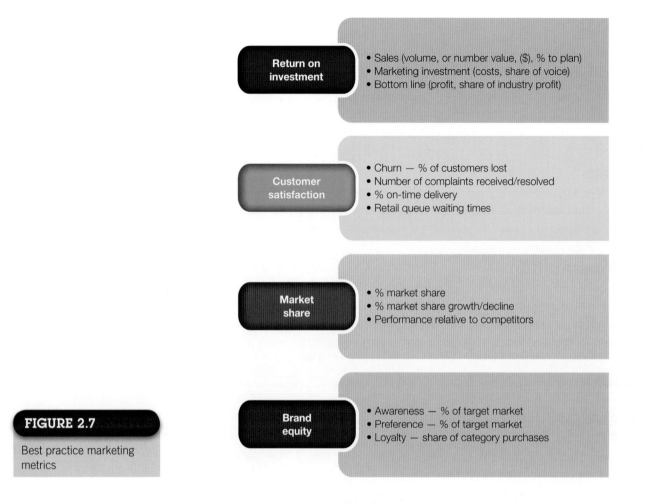

**FIGURE 2.7**

Best practice marketing metrics

**Return on investment**
- Sales (volume, or number value, ($), % to plan)
- Marketing investment (costs, share of voice)
- Bottom line (profit, share of industry profit)

**Customer satisfaction**
- Churn — % of customers lost
- Number of complaints received/resolved
- % on-time delivery
- Retail queue waiting times

**Market share**
- % market share
- % market share growth/decline
- Performance relative to competitors

**Brand equity**
- Awareness — % of target market
- Preference — % of target market
- Loyalty — share of category purchases

It is important to remember that there is no one best marketing metric. In practice, different strategies require different metrics and marketers need to select metrics accordingly. For example, Kellogg's objective was to revamp the way it used trade promotions in its overall marketing strategy. In trade promotions, manufacturers such as Kellogg's make payments known as rebates to grocers to display, advertise and offer reduced prices on certain products at specified times. Kellogg's knew almost nothing about the effectiveness of the thousands of sales promotions that took place in the supermarkets every year. The annual cost of Kellogg's trade promotions was $600 million. Using marketing metrics such as the sales uplift from the trade promotions, Kellogg's found that 59 per cent of its trade promotion events lost money for the company. Further, the profit generated by the other 41 per cent was almost entirely eaten away by the events that lost money.[22]

While the use of the sales promotion metric (sales uplift from the trade promotion) was ideal for Kellogg's purposes, it would not be relevant for others. Let's consider another example. A telecommunications company wanting to increase the profitability of its business customers would require a different metric. Telecommunications business customers include small- to medium-size businesses with up to 200 phone lines. A telecommunications company that wants to increase the profitability of its business customers can conduct an experiment where some customers are offered specially designed calling plans with unique pricing arrangements, while others are left the same. The success of this experiment can be tracked using two marketing metrics — the customer's 'change in spend' and the customer's 'churn rate' (proportion of customers choosing to change to another telecommunications company). Customers participating in the experiment can be compared to a control group of customers who are continuing to use existing calling plans. The change in spend and customer churn can help marketers to assess whether the specially designed calling plans increase the profitability of business customers.

Marketing metrics are vital for marketers. Marketers need to be able to articulate the return on investment for a host of reasons. First, the ability to articulate a return on investment can provide a solid rationale for *continued funding* for successful marketing programs — programs that might otherwise be cut if perceptions are that a program is too costly or is a large budget item. For example, a marketing director could potentially address or avert tough budget questions from a board of directors if they can demonstrate that their $3 million program contributed more than $6 million in sales. Second, return on marketing investment metrics can help marketers *allocate resources* where they are most effective. Third, marketers can build and share a *database of returns on investment* that should assist in evaluating the relative effectiveness of various programs.

Once marketers have gained a thorough understanding of their past performance they need to look forward. Marketers need to predict what they think is likely to occur in order to plan how they will compete in the market. A comprehensive understanding of the marketing environment is used to identify the key factors that are likely to impact in the foreseeable future.

## SWOT analysis

As we have explored earlier in this chapter, a multitude of factors are likely to impact a business. When marketers conduct a situation analysis, they will always find that there are more factors that need attention than they can possibly address within the constraints of the available time, money and other resources. Marketers need to be able to isolate the key, or most important, factors that need to be addressed to continue to compete effectively in the market. For example, while a garden nursery will identify that drought and government-imposed water restrictions will both have a large impact on its business, government-imposed water restrictions that do not allow people to water outdoor plants will have a more immediate impact. Marketers need to be able to prioritise or rank the factors to determine which factors will be used to inform their decision making. Factors included in a situation analysis are expected to have an immediate and sufficiently large impact on the business. A situation analysis must use insights from customers, partners, suppliers and other areas of the organisation.

Situation analysis involves identifying the key factors that will be used as a basis for the development of marketing strategy. Marketers must be able to understand the current opportunities that are available in the market, the main threats that business is facing and may face in the future, the strengths that the business can rely on and any weaknesses that may affect the business performance. Not surprisingly the method used to identify these factors is known as a **SWOT analysis**. SWOT is short for strengths, weaknesses, opportunities and threats.

**SWOT analysis** An analysis that identifies the strengths and weaknesses and the opportunities and threats in relation to an organisation.

**strengths** Those attributes of the organisation that help it achieve its objectives.

**weaknesses** Those attributes of the organisation that hinder it in trying to achieve its objectives.

**opportunities** Factors that are potentially helpful to achieving the organisation's objectives.

**threats** Factors that are potentially harmful to the organisation's efforts to achieve its objectives.

**Strengths** are those attributes of the organisation that help it achieve its objectives: competitive advantages and core competencies. **Weaknesses** are those attributes of the organisation that hinder it in trying to achieve its objectives. Strengths and weaknesses are considered to be internal factors and therefore directly controllable by the organisation. **Opportunities** are factors that are *potentially* helpful to achieving the organisation's objectives. Note the emphasis on the word 'potentially' in the previous sentence. Opportunities are only of benefit if the organisation responds effectively to them. Opportunities are factors that are beyond the organisation's direct control, though the organisation may be able to have some influence over them. **Threats** are factors that are potentially harmful to the organisation's efforts to achieve its objectives. Like opportunities, threats are beyond the organisation's direct control, but require an effective response by the organisation. Opportunities and threats can arise from many different factors in the organisation's environment.

A SWOT analysis is often used to help frame marketing thinking. A SWOT analysis can help marketers to identify ways to minimise the effect of weaknesses in their business, while maximising their strengths. Ideally, marketers will seek to match their strengths against market opportunities that result from competitors' weaknesses or voids. A potential framework for conducting a SWOT analysis, along with key factors to be considered, is outlined in figure 2.8.

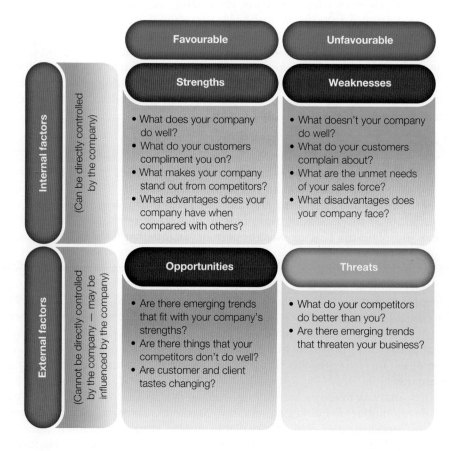

**FIGURE 2.8**

A potential framework for a SWOT analysis

Figure 2.9 shows a very basic example of a SWOT analysis for Hungry Jack's. This SWOT analysis, combined with an evaluation and understanding of the effectiveness of past marketing and business approaches, provides Hungry Jack's with the information it needs to consider possible actions. For example, given its strengths, Hungry Jack's could concentrate its marketing efforts behind core products, such as the Whopper® range, and core concepts, such as 'burger, fries and drinks'. However, given one of its identified threats is the trend towards light foods, it may also consider the possibility of adding more menu variety to cater for this trend. Further, the SWOT analysis identified an increased range of convenience foods for home use. Hungry Jacks could consider developing a range of ready-made meals for distribution through supermarket chains. These are just three possible responses to the strengths, weaknesses, opportunities and threats identified. There are many others that would need to be considered. Armed with this SWOT information, the organisation can begin to shape its marketing plan.

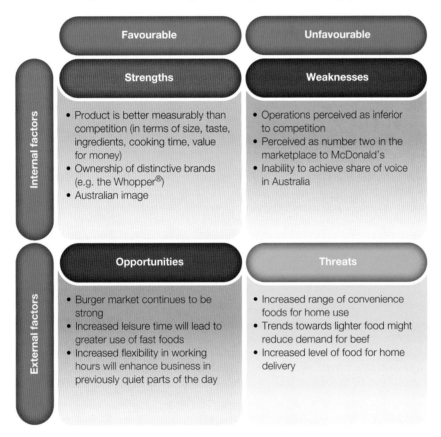

**FIGURE 2.9**

An example of a SWOT analysis for Hungry Jack's

# Earth Hour

Spotlight

Since the middle of the twentieth century, Australian temperatures have, on average, risen by about 1 degree, with an increase in the frequency of heat waves and a decrease in the number of frosts and cold days. Rainfall patterns have also changed. North-west Australia has seen an increase in rainfall over the last 50 years, while much of eastern Australia and south-west Australia have experienced a decline in rainfall, as well as droughts, for extended periods in many areas. In recent times, many areas in Australia that have previously been drought-affected have also been affected by severe flooding episodes. Climate change appears to be a global phenomenon, with many convinced that the carbon emissions of individuals and businesses are a major influence, rather than it being more of a natural phenomenon.

Earth Hour was conceived in a think tank involving Australian business and media leaders in response to the issue. The idea was to raise awareness in the broad community for the climate change cause, and to show people how they could contribute towards reducing carbon emissions in a very simple way — by turning off their lights. For the first Earth Hour event in 2007, 2.2 million individuals and more than 2000 businesses simultaneously turned off their lights for one hour in Sydney. Earth Hour has since become an annual, internationally coordinated sustainability event, with hundreds of millions of people across the world participating and showing their support for the event by switching their lights off. Global landmarks such as the Harbour Bridge in Sydney, the CN Tower in Toronto, the Golden Gate Bridge in San Francisco, and the Colosseum in Rome have all stood in darkness for the duration of an Earth Hour event. Online statistics within 24 hours of the 2010 event included:
- Nearly 75 million mentions of Earth Hour on Google
- Earth Hour being the number one worldwide trending topic on Twitter.
  While these statistics are impressive, and the event does reduce carbon emissions for an hour, the ultimate aim of Earth Hour is to change the thinking and behaviour of individuals and businesses around the world — so that carbon emissions can be minimised year round.[23]

## Questions

1. Use the information in this Spotlight, and any other necessary research, to develop a SWOT analysis for Earth Hour.
2. Earth Hour is a not-for-profit cause to promote awareness and behaviour change. What marketing metrics would you use to evaluate its effectiveness as a marketing campaign?

## Concepts and applications check

**Learning objective 5** conduct a preliminary situation analysis

5.1 You are a marketer responsible for encouraging people to use buses, rather than drive their cars, to the city's biggest sports stadium on event nights. You have enjoyed considerable success in this role, but you need to pinpoint the specific marketing tactics that brought more people out of their cars and on to public transport. What marketing metric will you use to understand which tactics were effective in achieving that goal?

5.2 You have a new employee in your marketing department and you need them to undertake a situation analysis. In your own words, explain to your new employee how they should approach a situation analysis.

5.3 Review the Hungry Jack's SWOT analysis in figure 2.9 and the surrounding discussion. Imagine you are the marketing manager for Hungry Jack's. How would you respond in order to effectively manage the identified strengths, weaknesses, opportunities and threats?

5.4 Choose a mobile phone service and analyse two of its competitors. What are their strengths and weaknesses?

# SUMMARY

 **Learning objective 1** describe the marketing environment and the purpose of environmental analysis

The marketing environment refers to all of the internal and external forces that affect a marketer's ability to create, communicate, deliver and exchange offerings of value. Marketers seek to understand, respond to, and influence their environment. They use environmental analysis to break the marketing environment into smaller parts in order to better understand it.

 **Learning objective 2** explain the factors at work in the organisation's internal environment

The internal environment refers to its parts, people and processes. An organisation is able to directly control the factors in its internal environment. A thorough understanding of the internal environment ensures that marketers understand the organisation's strengths and weaknesses, which positively and negatively affect the organisation's ability to compete in the marketplace.

Different parts of organisations often have different goals. The most successful organisations manage to align the goals of each part of the organisation to the overall market orientation of the business. This is most likely to occur when each person and department understands their contribution and the contribution of other departments.

 **Learning objective 3** understand the importance of the different micro-environmental factors

The micro environment consists of customers, clients, partners, competitors and other parties that make up the organisation's industry. The organisation cannot directly control its micro environment, but it can exert some influence over it.

Marketers must understand and respond to the current and future needs and wants of their target market. They must understand how each of their partners' processes work and how their partnerships benefit each party. They must also understand the risks involved in working with partners and the relative power balance between the organisation and each partner. Suppliers are a particularly crucial partner. Marketers must identify, assess, monitor and manage risks to supplies and risks to the price of supplies. To succeed, marketers must ensure their offerings provide their target market with greater value than their competitors' offerings. Thus, marketers seek to understand their competitors' marketing mix, sales volumes, sales trends, market share, staffing, sales per employee and employment trends. Marketers should analyse total budget competition, generic competition, product competition and brand competition.

 **Learning objective 4** outline the different types of macro-environmental forces

The macro environment encompasses uncontrollable factors outside of the industry: political, economic, sociocultural, technological and legal forces. Political forces describe the influence of politics on marketing decisions. Economic forces affect how much money people and organisations can spend and how they choose to spend it. Sociocultural forces affect people's attitudes, beliefs, behaviours, preferences, customs and lifestyles. Technological forces are those arising from the search for a better way to do things. Technology changes the expectations and behaviours of customers and clients as well as how organisations work with their partners and within society. Laws and regulations are closely tied to politics and establish the rules under which organisations must conduct their activities. The most significant laws and regulations for marketers are related to privacy, fair trading, consumer safety, prices, contract terms and intellectual property.

 **Learning objective 5** conduct a preliminary situation analysis

Situation analysis involves assessing an organisation's current position and situation. Together with organisational objectives, situation analysis is used as the platform for marketing planning. Essentially, a marketing plan communicates how marketers plan to get from the current situation to where senior management thinks their organisation should be.

Marketing metrics are used to measure current performance and the outcomes of past activities. A SWOT analysis is used to identify strengths (those attributes of the organisation that help it achieve its objectives), weaknesses (those attributes of the organisation that hinder it in trying to achieve its objectives), opportunities (factors that are potentially helpful to achieving the organisation's objectives) and threats (factors that are potentially harmful to the organisation's efforts to achieve its objectives).

# Youngcare and the donation landscape

There are over 40 000 charities operating in the not-for-profit sector in Australia. Total income generated by not-for-profit organisations in Australia is approximately $75 billion, with around 7.3 per cent of funds being in the health sector. The not-for-profit sector comprises just over 4 per cent of gross domestic product (about $43 billion), with nearly five million volunteers contributing a considerable amount of unpaid work. Volunteers contribute about $14.6 billion in unpaid work — an amount that is staggering to consider. Even with this support, demand means that not-for-profit organisations are often in need of more support — both in terms of financial aid and manpower — often in the form of volunteers — to help with managing operations.

Imagine this scenario. You are an 18 or 19 year old with a bright future ahead, and without warning you suffer a catastrophic accident or illness leaving you in need of permanent care. Despite the best efforts of family and friends, you realise your care needs are too great. Suddenly, you face the prospect of having to reside in aged care, simply because there are no alternatives.

This scenario is not unrealistic. Rather, it is a very real possibility. Offered no other alternative, 6500 young Australians are currently living in aged-care nursing homes, sharing a residence with people whose average age is 86 years. Being young is about having a lifetime ahead of you, yet aged care is designed for someone who is at the end of their life. The realities of aged care mean a young person will share a residence where the average age is 86 and the average life expectancy is just three years. More importantly, in most cases, their specific care needs will not be met and differ greatly to those of the elderly residents. For those young people living in aged care, statistics suggest that:

- 44 per cent will receive a visit from friends less than once a year
- 34 per cent will almost never participate in community-based activities, such as shopping
- 21 per cent will go outside the home less than once a month.

Countless other studies have demonstrated increased incidences of depression brought about by the social isolation that is involved when young people are forced to live in aged care.

In addition to considering such sobering facts, it is important to recognise that the family of a young person with 24/7 care needs also endures daily struggles. In addition to the thousands of young Australians who reside in aged care is a larger related group: a further 700 000 young Australians with high care needs are looked after at home by family and friends. The friends and family who care for young adults with high needs in a home context are also placed under considerable pressure and strain. About 70 per cent of all relationships involving the care of a young person with full-time care needs end in divorce. Further statistics reveal that:

- 56 per cent of carers are defined as moderately depressed
- 40 per cent of carers are found to be severely or extremely depressed
- carers have the lowest level of wellbeing of any group in society.

Fortunately, a not-for-profit organisation, Youngcare (www.youngcare.com.au) exists to provide hope, possibility and dignity for injured/high-care Australians. Youngcare is an organisation that is helping to take the strain off both young adults with high-care needs and the people that care about them — and for them. Formed in 2005, the organisation aims to raise awareness and funds to provide care, apartments and holiday/respite housing that can accommodate the needs of young people with serious injuries and high-care needs.

In an environmental context, Youngcare competes with other not-for-profit organisations in Australia for both funding and support. It is in competition with prominent local charities, including the Red Cross and the McGrath Foundation; as well as in competition with other not-for-profit organisations that don't have a charity focus (e.g. schools, sporting teams and community groups). The organisation also has less likely competitors. Making a contribution to a charity is a purchasing decision that consumers choose to make, just as they choose to spend money on other items and experiences (e.g. entertainment, food, travel and so on). A consumer may choose to buy a new item of clothing, or a trip to the theatre, rather than giving money to a charity. As such, not-for-profit organisations such as Youngcare have an array of indirect competitors in the marketplace.

There are many factors that influence people's donating behaviour. The research relating to donation behaviour has tended to focus on categorising the types of people who are likely to donate to charitable or educational institutions. Factors such as family wealth, marital status, number of dependents, age, gender and geographic regions have all been identified as variables that can influence donating behaviour. Research shows, for example, that:

- wealthier individuals give more money than poorer individuals
- women donate more time to charitable endeavours than do men
- people without children are more likely than people with children to leave a bequest.

During its first year of operation, Youngcare generated approximately $2 million. This amount equated to less than 1 per cent of the total funds donated nationwide to not-for-profit organisations in that year. In the following year, Youngcare increased its revenue by 156 per cent, securing $5.1 million of funding. Overall, this equated to an increase in the company's total share of donations relative to the donations received by other not-for-profit organisations around the country.

Increased awareness in the target market, as well as marketing efforts, were believed to be factors that contributed to Youngcare's reported increase in revenue. In recent years, Youngcare has been recognised with a major industry award from the Australian Marketing Institute for its marketing efforts. Youngcare promotes the message that it is 'committed to providing change and choice for young Australians with high care needs'. It won the major Australian Marketing Institute award for a campaign focused on the message that 'young people deserve young lives'. Speaking about the campaign, a judge at the Institute commented:

> Youngcare represents the true essence of not-for-profit brand marketing. With little budget and a very tight timeframe, they: understood their target market; had clear and definable objectives; created an innovative strategy that set about to achieve its objectives; executed that strategy with passion; were able to leverage third-party support to help it achieve its objectives; achieved outcomes in a time frame that were remarkable; and had a positive outcome for those in need.

Youngcare is continuing to monitor its marketing output to ensure that it communicates a message that is relevant for its target market. Today, the organisation is striving to meet various goals. It is:

- raising awareness for people with high-care needs
- securing support to fund its work (the organisation raises funds by organising various events, and also by allowing community supporters to organise funding initiatives)
- providing a helpline for people caring for young people with high-care needs
- providing an At-Home Care Grant Program to top-up government care funding for young people wishing to reside at home with loved ones
- continuing to build more accommodation facilities for young people in need
- undertaking further research about the issues faced by young adults with high needs living in different care settings.

In a short space of time, Youngcare has managed to build sets of apartments for young adults in Queensland. The organisation is aiming to build more apartments in Sydney, Melbourne and Brisbane in upcoming years. However, its organisational plans will be contingent on strategic marketing leading to increased public awareness about its objectives. Youngcare will be able to continue to make a difference in young Australians lives if it can secure ongoing funding and support from the wider Australian community.[24]

## Questions

1. Use your own research to supplement the information given in this case study. How have conditions in the economic environment affected donations to charities?
2. Conduct a situation analysis for Youngcare (or another charity of your choice) in your region.
3. Imagine you are the marketing manager for Youngcare (or another charity of your choice). How would you respond to the strengths, weaknesses, opportunities and threats you identified in question 2?

## Advanced activity

Name ten industries that will be affected by the obesity epidemic, which was outlined at the start of the chapter. Explain how each will be affected, and whether the epidemic is an opportunity and/or a threat for each industry.

## Marketing plan activity

Look back through the background information that you collected in week one for your chosen organisation and product. In terms of a preliminary situation analysis for your product, use figure 2.5 as a guide for questions that may help you identify the most important factors to consider. Conduct some additional research to identify more environmental (internal, micro environment and macro environment) factors that may affect your chosen organisation and product. Your aim is to develop a comprehensive list that will be further researched and refined as you develop your marketing plan.

Next use a SWOT analysis framework (see figure 2.8) to synthesise the information you compile. Make sure that you put factors into the correct category (strengths, weaknesses, opportunities and threats). Remember, strengths and weaknesses can be controlled by the company.

Finally, outline some preliminary marketing objectives that your marketing plan will be designed to achieve, using this initial situation analysis as a guide.

Typical components of a marketing plan have been included in this chapter (figure 2.6), and a sample marketing plan has been included at the back of this book (see page 523). These should give you an idea about where the information for this chapter's activity fits in an overall marketing plan.

## CHAPTER 3

# Market research

## Learning objectives

After studying this chapter, you should be able to:

 discuss the importance of market research as a basis for marketing decision making

 clearly define a research problem to guide a market research project, and prepare a research brief

 outline the issues in research design, including the role of primary and secondary data, and the uses of quantitative and qualitative research

 understand the key principles of data collection and analysis, and the subsequent reporting of market research findings to inform marketing decisions.

# Tuning in

Commercial Radio Australia Limited contracts market research company Nielsen to conduct radio audience surveys at regular intervals each year. These surveys are conducted in the capital cities of Sydney, Melbourne, Brisbane, Perth and Adelaide, as well as in areas such as the Gold Coast/Tweed, Newcastle, Wollongong and Canberra. Staggeringly, there are over 260 privately owned commercial radio stations in Australia, as well as more than 200 not-for-profit community stations and five national (Australian Broadcasting Corporation) stations. The ABC stations are owned and operated by the government.

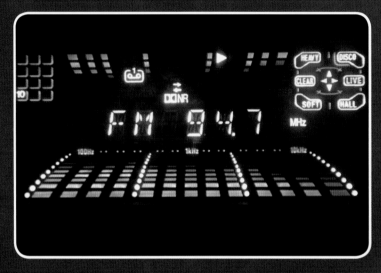

The results of these Nielsen radio surveys are known as 'the ratings'. The ratings provide an indication of each individual station's market share of radio listeners, as well as listener demographic profiles. In addition, other relevant information on radio listening behaviour can be obtained from these surveys, such as when, where and how people tune in to radio stations. Participants in the Nielsen radio surveys record their station listening over a seven-day period in a diary, with each day being broken up into 15-minute time slots across 24 hours. Each person aged over ten years in a participating household is eligible to have their results recorded in the survey. Household diary placements and collections are made by trained Nielsen staff.

The information in the survey diaries is subsequently compiled and eagerly awaited by a variety of radio industry stakeholders, including:

- individual radio stations (e.g. to assist with programming decisions, and as a basis for setting rates for selling station advertising time)

- advertising agencies (e.g. to assist with identifying the demographic profile of station audiences in order to effectively target radio advertising efforts for clients).[1]

## Question

Go online and find Nielsen's latest radio survey results. You should be able to access this information via Nielsen's site (www.au.nielsen.com) or a general online search. Pick a city or region and two different radio stations. From a marketing perspective, interpret the information in the survey for these two stations.

# INTRODUCTION

So far we have learned that successful marketing requires the marketer to *know* their market. Successful organisations put their customers' wants and needs at the heart of marketing and business decisions. To put it simply, in order to create, communicate, deliver and exchange offerings that have value for customers, clients, partners and society at large, marketers need to first understand what is of value. Market research is an essential component of *understanding* the market. It can be used for many things, including solving problems, identifying future opportunities and threats, generating ideas about how greater value can be offered to customers, determining how to create offerings, understanding how to communicate offerings and evaluating the effectiveness of marketing initiatives. Market research is used by marketers to stay in tune with their customers, clients, partners and society at large.

We start the chapter by discussing how market research is used in marketing for decision making. While there is no doubt that marketing managers make some decisions based on hunches or intuition, these decisions usually come from knowledge of the market. One of the most important sources of information is market research. We then consider how marketers define research problems. Clearly specified problems are needed to guide specific market research projects. In practice, market research is often outsourced and undertaken by research specialists. Marketers often need to provide a brief for market research agencies, and so we will provide an overview of the briefing process. We then continue to examine the processes that occur in a typical market research project.

Remember as you study the chapter that market research is only of value if the information it provides can contribute to improved performance.

## THE ROLE OF MARKET RESEARCH IN MARKETING DECISIONS

Every aspect of day-to-day marketing requires information. Market research generates much of the information and knowledge to enable marketers to make marketing decisions and develop marketing strategy. Formally defined, market research is a process that 'links the consumer, customer, clients, partners and public to the marketer through information — information used to identify and define marketing opportunities and problems; generate, refinc, and evaluate marketing actions; monitor marketing performance; and improve understanding of marketing as a process.'[2] In essence, **market research** is a business activity that discovers information of use in making marketing decisions.

Market research informs many different types of decisions, including decisions about:

- *market segmentation.* What is the segment's profile? What does each segment most value? Which segment should we target?
- *sales performance.* Why did we fail to meet our sales targets last financial year? How can we improve sales?
- *product.* What features should be included in our products? How should we package our product? How should we brand our product? How should we position our product?

 **Learning objective 1**
discuss the importance of market research as a basis for marketing decision making

**market research** A business activity that discovers information of use in making marketing decisions.

- *distribution.* What type of retailer should be used? What geographic region should we sell in? Should we sell directly to consumers online? How should we distribute products? What do our partners require?
- *promotion.* How much should we spend on advertising? In which media should advertising be placed? What advertising appeals should be used? Should we use sales promotions? When?
- *pricing.* What price should be charged? What response should be made to a competitor's pricing?
- *attitudes and behaviours.* What do our customers and clients think? What do our customers and clients know about our product? How do they feel about our competitors' products? What do they buy? When? Where? Who are our customers?[3]

This is by no means an exhaustive list of the types of issues that marketers face on a daily basis. In practice there are many more decisions. As you work your way through this textbook, you will be exposed to many of the issues that marketers must manage and it will become clear how important market research can be to marketing decisions. Figure 3.1 shows where market research sits in the overall marketing model.

**FIGURE 3.1**

Market research informs all aspects of the marketing process, with an organisation needing to thoroughly understand the needs and wants of its target market.

Figure 3.2[4] shows a market research project from Virgin Australia that discusses background information and research objectives for the company.

**BACKGROUND**

Colmar Brunton had been conducting brand tracking research with Virgin since 2006. Within a few years, a significant quantitative knowledge bank about consumer perceptions of the Virgin brands, the competitor brands and airline traveller behaviour in general was built. Virgin had evolved from a budget leisure carrier to a carrier that caters for both business and leisure travellers. Virgin had a need for greater flexibility in understanding market changes and influences. They wished to explore communications and brand issues in more depth to gain a deeper understanding of the changing market.

**RESEARCH OBJECTIVES**

- Identify the impact of marketing activity of Virgin and its competitors.
- Evaluate Virgin's advertising effectiveness.
- Understand the key impact of market events throughout the year.
- Identify broader market trends as they are happening.

**FIGURE 3.2**

Example of a market research project from Virgin Australia

## Marketing information systems

In addition to specific market research projects, organisations continuously collect data as part of everyday activities, such as sales, purchases, enquiries and accounting. Well-organised marketing organisations systematically collect and organise this information so that it can be used for future marketing decisions. The **marketing information system (MIS)** is the structure put in place to manage information gathered during the usual operations of the organisation. In large organisations, the MIS can comprise considerable infrastructure and dedicated staff. Think about a major telecommunications company like Telstra and the amount of information it has on the mobile phone transactions made by its customers. Australia Post conducts the Australian Lifestyle Survey. The survey is distributed to households all over Australia, and individuals who want to receive relevant offers and information provide their responses on a voluntary basis. Using the information obtained voluntarily from the survey results, a database of 4.4 million consumers is maintained by First Direct Solutions, a division of Australia Post. This information can be purchased by marketers wishing to target audiences for their campaigns.[5]

**marketing information system (MIS)** The structure put in place to manage information gathered during the usual operations of the organisation.

Marketing information systems play a vital role in linking the customer to the marketer. For example, Myer, a leading Australian department store, used its MIS to understand that for every $50 voucher given, $125 of sales result.[6] Armed with this knowledge, Myer could respond by promoting its gift vouchers more, particularly around traditional gift-giving times such as Christmas and Mothers' Day, in the expectation that gift recipients will then be drawn into the store and will make a substantial purchase.

In small organisations, the MIS — to be generous in our definition — might just be a file or notepad of observations. Regardless of the complexity or size of the MIS, it will feature information from internal records, market intelligence and market research, and some way of accessing and structuring that information so that it can be used to help make marketing decisions. Figure 3.3 shows the basic parts of an MIS.

Of course, just as market research is not always necessary or appropriate, not every marketing decision is made based on information stored in a MIS. Marketing managers also rely on intuition, insight and 'gut feel'. It is not an approach that can be wholly recommended, but is an important part of the reality of marketing. An MIS and market research can help support or invalidate such decisions.

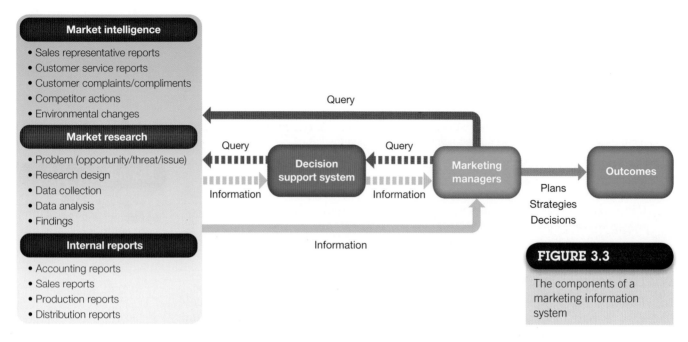

**Market intelligence**

- Sales representative reports
- Customer service reports
- Customer complaints/compliments
- Competitor actions
- Environmental changes

**Market research**

- Problem (opportunity/threat/issue)
- Research design
- Data collection
- Data analysis
- Findings

**Internal reports**

- Accounting reports
- Sales reports
- Production reports
- Distribution reports

Query

Query

Query

Information

Information

Information

Decision support system

Marketing managers

Outcomes

Plans
Strategies
Decisions

**FIGURE 3.3**

The components of a marketing information system

## Overview of the market research process

Market research involves five major components:
1. defining the research problem
2. designing the research methodology
3. collecting data in accordance with the research design
4. analysing data and drawing conclusions
5. presenting the results and making recommendations.

The stages in the market research process are designed, of course, to lead to marketing decisions; that is, market research should result in a course of action. In large organisations, a formal presentation of the findings and recommendations to senior management for approval is likely to be necessary before implementation. Upon implementation of any market research recommendations, careful monitoring is necessary to ensure the organisation's marketing goals are being achieved as a result.

Market research is an ongoing process and is constantly evolving. In practice, a market research project does not always occur in a strict sequence. At any point, new ideas or insights can occur that require a change in the project. For example, just the process of defining the purpose of the research can sometimes answer the question that is being asked; and in the data collection stage of the project, people being surveyed might offer a response that opens up new avenues for investigation that require the research to be redefined. It is important to understand the components of market research. However, it is also important to understand that the sequence can vary in individual market research projects. At every stage, the effectiveness of the market research process and how it is being conducted should be monitored and assessed, not just at the end.

## When market research is appropriate

The previous discussion makes it clear that market research is a valuable tool that is frequently used in day-to-day marketing. Before a marketer decides to use market research, some decisions must be made regarding the benefit of conducting the research. Marketers are faced with limited resources — a budget — that governs all activities.

Before undertaking a market research project, the following should be considered:[7]

- *relevance.* Market research must be able to address the problem at hand.
- *timing.* Market research is only of use if the information it generates can be analysed ahead of the time at which the marketing decision needs to be made. There is no point conducting market research if the information will not be used. Market research is often conducted under time pressure, arising from the need to make a prompt marketing decision; for example, when confronted by competitive pressures that require the marketing organisation to act quickly.
- *availability of resources.* Depending on the type of information needed, the market research process can consume considerable time and money. Larger organisations such as Virgin Blue and the Mater Hospital in Brisbane track brand health via engaging the services of professional market research companies. Virgin Blue (now Virgin Australia), for example, commissioned Colmar Brunton to monitor brand usage, loyalty and advocacy towards the Virgin Blue and Velocity brands. Such brand tracking studies cost approximately $250 000.[8] The Mater Hospital commission TNS to track brand awareness and brand image, collecting data in south-east Queensland each month. Market research should only be undertaken if it can provide reliable and valid results, which can occur only if adequate resources are devoted to the process. Results from rushed, poorly planned and executed research or research undertaken by people without the necessary skills will not truly reflect the market and will, in all likelihood, lead to poor marketing decisions.
- *need for new information.* Market research should not be conducted if the information needed is already available or the decision to be made does not require or will not benefit from the type of information that market research can provide.
- *cost–benefit analysis.* As with many business decisions, the costs of market research should be assessed against the resultant benefits. The decision to invest in market research can only be justified if the potential outcomes are more valuable. In considering whether market research should be conducted, the marketer must make a preliminary judgement about how valuable the research findings are likely to be.

## Ethics in market research

As we point out throughout this textbook, customers, clients, partners and society expect marketers to act ethically. Market researchers have an ethical responsibility to their clients or employers and to those who participate in the research (just as clients, employers and participants have an ethical responsibility to researchers).

The market research industry attempts to self-regulate its activities in Australia through the Australian Market and Social Research Society (AMSRS). The AMSRS has a detailed code of practice in place to govern the activities of market researchers. In New Zealand, the market research industry's peak body is called the Market Research Society of New Zealand (MRSNZ). The MRSNZ has a similar code of practice. The main principles of the codes are common to both countries and are outlined in figure 3.4. The full codes can be obtained from the AMSRS website at www.mrsa.com.au and the MRSNZ website at www.mrsnz.org.au.

The codes of practice are aimed at professional market researchers, but the principles apply to anyone who conducts market research. You should, of course, observe your ethical responsibilities when conducting market research in your future career, and this should start now as part of your marketing course. You have a duty to conduct research for university projects in an ethical manner and need to inform yourself about the requirements for conducting ethical market research.

**GENERAL RULES**
Research must be objective, based on scientific methods, and conducted in compliance with the law.

**RESPONSIBILITIES TO RESPONDENTS**
- Respondents' identities must not, without their consent, be revealed to anyone not directly involved in the market research project or used for any non-research purpose.
- Nobody shall be adversely affected or harmed as a direct result of participating in a market research study.
- Respondents must be able to check without difficulty the identity and good faith of researchers.
- Respondents' cooperation in a market research project is entirely voluntary at all stages; they must not be misled when being asked for their cooperation.
- No child under 14 years shall be interviewed without parents'/guardians'/responsible adults' consent.

**RESEARCHERS PROFESSIONAL RESPONSIBILITIES**
- Researchers must not, whether knowingly or negligently, act in any way that could bring discredit on the market research profession or lead to a loss of public confidence.
- Researchers must always strive to design research that is cost-efficient and of adequate quality, and then to carry this out.
- Researchers must not undertake non-research activities (e.g. telemarketing or list building) and research activities simultaneously.

**FIGURE 3.4**

Main principles of the AMSRS and MRSNZ codes of practice for market research

*Source:* AMSRS, www.mrsa.com.au; MRSNZ, www.mrsnz.org.au.

Many countries have professional associations with codes of practice for their market research industries. Many of the codes, including the Australian and New Zealand codes, are derived from the code of the World Association of Opinion and Marketing Research Professionals.[9]

So far we have looked at the use of market research in day-to-day marketing. In the next part of this chapter, we consider how marketers define research problems. This is followed with an overview of the briefing process, as marketers often need to provide a brief for market research agencies.

## Spotlight  So delicious the Italians want it back

La Famiglia Fine Foods (La Famiglia) produces and markets a range of garlic breads to supermarkets and the food service industry in Australia. La Famiglia was founded in 1993, and started with nine employees using second-hand equipment in a small manufacturing plant. Today, over 100 staff are employed in its plant, which is three times the size of the original plant. All equipment is custom built to ensure quality standards are maintained and products are produced quickly.

Bread categories have long experienced intense competition. Players such as supermarkets, convenience stores and bakeries have competed for a greater share of the bread market. The frozen bread category in supermarkets has helped supermarkets to win a larger share of the bread market from convenience stores and bakeries. In the early 2000s the success bread manufacturers had enjoyed in the chilled bread category stalled, when the large retailers (Coles and Woolworths) introduced their own brands. Large competitors commenced heavy price discounting in attempts to win market share and to continue to grow the frozen bread category.

La Famiglia decided to use market research in an attempt to grow its business. The results of its market research suggested that consumers perceived garlic bread to be an unhealthy product purchased by lazy people which had been popular in earlier decades.

La Famiglia used the consumer insights gained from conducting market research to reposition its garlic bread brand as a contemporary, quality offering that provided a convenient way to make family meals more special. The campaign focused on highlighting both its traditional recipe and the quality of the ingredients in the product, and built on a consumer perception that Italians appreciate and recognise flavoursome garlic bread because it is a famous Italian food item. The advertising campaign that followed helped La Famiglia to become the first competitor in the garlic bread category to attract premium profitability in three Australian states. The company doubled the size of its business in three years. The success of the integrated campaign titled 'La Famiglia. So delicious the Italians want it back' resulted in an increased trial of its garlic bread products and a very high trial-to-purchase conversion. La Famiglia has successfully repositioned its garlic bread as a 'contemporary, restaurant quality, convenient way to make a family meal more special'. Their success has been recognised by Woolworths, with La Famiglia winning a recent Supplier of the Year award.[10]

---

**Question**

Explain how market research informed La Famiglia's campaign development.

---

## Concepts and applications check

**Learning objective 1** discuss the importance of market research as a basis for marketing decision making

**1.1** Define 'market research' in your own words and list the major steps in a market research project.

**1.2** Outline ten examples of marketing decisions for a variety of products that are likely to require market research.

**1.3** What is the purpose of a marketing information system?

**1.4** Explain the importance of a cost–benefit analysis in the decision to undertake market research.

**1.5** Outline the market researcher's ethical responsibilities.

---

# DEFINING A MARKET RESEARCH PROBLEM

Marketers need all sorts of information to understand how they can better meet customer, client and society needs and wants to improve their marketing performance. Marketers use information to identify and define marketing opportunities and threats; generate, refine, and evaluate marketing actions; monitor marketing performance; and improve understanding of marketing as a process.[11]

Before starting a market research project, it is crucial to know — and be able to communicate — *precisely* what the purpose of the research is. The thing the market research is intended to address is often referred to as the **research problem**. A poorly defined research problem will lead to research that does not generate the information required to enable the marketing organisation to make marketing decisions.

**Learning objective 2** clearly define a research problem to guide a market research project, and prepare a research brief

**research problem**
The question that the market research project is intended to answer.

Usually there will be some trigger that prompts a market research project. For example, a home builder might notice that increasing numbers of prospective customers are asking about the environmental credentials of the builder's home designs. The builder might want to know whether it would be worthwhile to improve the environmental sustainability and performance of his or her houses. That seems a straightforward question, but it is important in the initial stage of the market research process to properly define what the research project is meant to find out. For example, what does 'worthwhile' mean? Does it mean of benefit to society generally, that it will create more business for the builder, that it will allow the builder to charge a higher margin, or that it will reduce or increase enquiries from the public if the builder includes the environmental aspects of his or her houses in advertising messages? The builder needs to know this and certainly needs to communicate it clearly to the market researcher. This step is about ensuring the research has a clear purpose and that the purpose is clearly defined. A clearly specified research problem will ensure that the research will actually answer the question asked of it.

In practice, as the research proceeds, the original questions asked may be redefined as further information comes to light or new questions or issues arise.

Once the purpose for the research is known, it is necessary to write a market research brief to specify the information needed. The next section provides an overview of the requirements for a market research brief.

# Preparing a market research brief

**market research brief** A set of instructions and requirements that generally states the research problem and the information required, and specifies the timeframe, budget and other conditions of the project.

A **market research brief** outlines the research problem and describes the specific information required from the market research project. A market research brief generally states the research problem and the information required, and specifies the timeframe, budget and other conditions of the project.

A typical market research brief will include the following:

- *executive summary*. An executive summary provides an overview of the market research brief. It outlines the research requirements and includes sufficient information to enable the reader to have a basic understanding of the proposed project. The executive summary is often the only part of a written document that senior managers read. It is important in obtaining approval for the research project from management and for enabling potential researchers to determine whether the project is a suitable one for them (and hence that they should read and consider the brief in full).
- *introduction*. The introduction explains why the research needs to be conducted and who is proposing the research.
- *background*. The background details the marketing problem that is currently faced, providing all known facts and referencing related research projects that are known to the organisation.
- *problem definition*. Effective research briefs clearly state the question that is to be addressed, including any objectives that have been set for the market research project. The information in the research brief is used by market researchers to design the research project. Taken together, the introduction, background and problem definition sections need to provide sufficient information to inform the research design.
- *time and budget*. The section on time and budget details the amount of money the marketer is able to spend on the market research project and when the results are needed. For complex market research projects, various milestones may be specified. It is also wise to include information on how contingencies are to be

handled (e.g. if an unforeseen issue arises during the research and needs further investigation).

- *reporting schedule.* The reporting schedule specifies the precise dates on which preliminary, interim and final reports are required. It may also include details about the format of the reports.
- *appendices.* Appendices may be included to provide additional detailed background information to further assist the design stage for the market research project.

Some research briefs include further details, such as the appropriate format for the research proposal, in-house resources that the researcher may be able to draw on, what selection criteria the organisation will use in choosing a market research provider and confidentiality requirements. Figure 3.5 shows an example of a typical market research brief. (This brief is relatively simple and short. In practice, many briefs are more detailed.)

**FIGURE 3.5**

A typical market research brief

## EXECUTIVE SUMMARY

### 1. Background
The XYZ cardiovascular business encompasses a broad range of medical devices used within healthcare specialties such as interventional cardiology and cardiac surgery. As the competitive environment continues to tighten and product differentiation becomes more challenging, the organisation must identify new areas of strategic advantage.

The consumers in these specialties in the Australian and New Zealand healthcare markets are mature, sophisticated and well educated. Growth expectations will be delivered by market share gains, rather than by an increase in clinical interventions. Within healthcare, both Australia and New Zealand are recognised as global leaders in new technology adoptions and clinical research, resulting in sophisticated and knowledgeable consumers in these markets. In addition, the competitive landscape is highly evolved and is served by companies with significant human resources. Messaging thus tends to be complex, in a space that is crowded and ultimately overloaded by information. These factors have contributed to the differentiation challenges faced by suppliers.

XYZ recognises that in order to gain market share, it needs to gain a higher level of understanding of its customers. To gain the necessary level of insight, XYZ will commission market research into the Australian and New Zealand cardiovascular market. Research outcomes will assist in the shaping of future sales and marketing initiatives, as well as messaging and customer activities. This will help XYZ to gain market share and to take business away from its competitors. This information will be used by the leadership group and the sales and marketing teams at the company.

### 2. Business and research objectives
The proposed research project can be categorised into three key areas: buyer behaviour; customer perceptions; and other market-influential factors. The research objectives have been identified as follows:
- to determine the key decision criteria when an implanting physician is selecting a medical device and the patient is 'on the table'
- to determine the market's perceptions of the major suppliers and rank the major suppliers against key attributes
- to determine the influence of other market factors, such as clinical data sources, conferences, speaker tours, training and education.

### 3. Target market
The research target audience has been defined by the following medical specialists:
- interventional cardiologists
- cardiothoracic surgeons.

*(continued)*

**FIGURE 3.5**

*(continued)*

A sample of customers from all three specialties should be gathered from a broad range of public and private institutions throughout Australia and New Zealand. The institutions should also represent the geographical (city and country) spread of these customers. XYZ will provide the names and email addresses of customers in the target market.

**4. Reporting requirements**

The reporting requirements for the research project are threefold, and include a top-line report, a PowerPoint presentation of the research outcomes and a final written report.

**5. Timing**

The expected timeframe for the research is as follows:
- scoping and preparation of the online survey to be completed by 15 November 2011
- online survey to be completed by 5 December 2011
- top-line report to be provided by 5 January 2012
- PowerPoint presentation and final written report to be delivered by 31 January 2012.

**6. Available budget**

We have allocated between $45 000 and $55 000 for the project.

It is important to realise that the market research brief will not necessarily propose a methodology or approach for the market research. Rather, it can communicate the marketer's needs to the market researcher, leaving the market researcher to bring their own expertise as to how to best obtain the information needed by the marketer. The more complex the research project, the more important this becomes. For example, international market research is often too complex and expensive to conduct in-house. International market research is research conducted in more than one country. The researcher encounters issues such as ensuring equivalence across different cultures and languages.

We have already detailed how marketers need to clearly communicate the research problem to help market research professionals design a market research project that can address the research problem at hand. An answer is only as good as the question asked. The more specific the problem, the more specific the answer will be.

## Spotlight What's the problem?

If you take a look at the roads heading into most capital cities at 8 am on any weekday morning, you will likely notice that traffic is barely moving. The same pattern is likely to be repeated around 5 pm each weekday afternoon. There may be a variety for reasons for this congestion — such as a rapidly growing population, inadequate public transport facilities and road systems, or consumers simply preferring to commute to work in their cars instead of exploring alternative options. The problem can be viewed a number of ways — as a population issue, a public transport issue, a road issue, a consumer behaviour issue, or a combination of all of these. Regardless of the cause (or causes), the problem needs an effective solution (or solutions).

City councils around the world grapple with various ideas that are proposed to reduce the number of commuter cars on busy inner city roads, such as:
- increasing the availability of public transport vehicles in peak hour

- increasing the number of dedicated public transport lanes on inner city roads during peak hour
- introducing inner city road toll charges during peak hour to discourage the number of cars driving on these roads at this time
- constructing tunnels to divert inner city traffic
- providing incentives for inner city businesses to adopt more flexible working hours for their staff.

Perth is one such city with traffic problems. The Royal Automobile Club (RAC) in Western Australia recently conducted a survey to gauge opinions and attitudes towards Perth's public transport system. Significantly, the survey found that 65 per cent of bus users and 59 per cent of train users had difficulties or concerns with their service. The most common complaints regarding bus services were 'service is not frequent enough' and 'poor connections', while the major issues identified with the train service in Perth were 'overcrowding' and 'lack of parking at train stations'.[12]

> ### Question
>
> Imagine you are the marketing manager for your City Council's bus service. Prepare an effective market research brief to gather information on how greater use of buses could be achieved to help alleviate your city's traffic congestion.

## Concepts and applications check

**Learning objective 2** clearly define a research problem to guide a market research project, and prepare a research brief

2.1 Why should marketers use a market research brief for a market research project?

2.2 What does a typical market research brief contain?

2.3 Using the example of the home builder discussed in this section of the chapter, discuss why research problems should be clearly defined.

2.4 Obtain a survey (e.g. look online or obtain a customer feedback form from a retail outlet). What research problem is likely to underpin this survey?

# KEY RESEARCH DESIGN ISSUES

There is a multitude of market research methods. The method used depends on the information required and the information already contained within the organisation. Different problems require different methods. The way that you frame your question will determine the type of method that will be needed to provide the information that you require; for example, research into a highly sensitive topic seeking to understand why consumers behave in the manner they do can only be obtained through interviews. In other instances, though, more than one method may be used to answer the chosen question. Let's consider a marketer who wants to understand the characteristics of people who shop at a particular shopping centre. This marketer could use observations, depth interviews, focus groups, surveys or secondary data (e.g. store scanner and customer loyalty card data) to address this research question. Marketers need to understand which techniques apply, and their strengths and limitations, in order to determine how best to design the research project to address the research problem at hand.

The **research design** must include a research question or hypothesis for testing and a description of the type(s) of research to be used.

 **Learning objective 3** outline the issues in research design, including the role of primary and secondary data, and the uses of quantitative and qualitative research

**research design** The detailed methodology created to guide the research project and answer the research question.

## Types of research

Market researchers conduct three different types of research:

1. **exploratory research**. Exploratory research, as its name suggests, is research intended to gather more information about a loosely defined problem.
2. **descriptive research**. Descriptive research is used to solve a particular and well-defined problem by clarifying the characteristics of certain phenomena.
3. **causal research**. Causal research assumes that a particular variable causes a specific outcome and then, by holding everything else constant, tests whether the variable does indeed effect that outcome.

The degree of knowledge about the research problem at hand affects the type and the amount of research that is required. *Exploratory research* is required when management is uncertain about what actions should be taken and has little knowledge about the research problem. Exploratory research is used in these situations to generate ideas to help management decide on an appropriate form of action and to increase management's knowledge. When management is aware of the problem but lacks some important piece of knowledge, *descriptive research* is undertaken. *Causal research* is used for sharply defined problems. In causal research, a hypothesis is generated for testing. A **hypothesis** is a tentative explanation that can be tested. The hypothesis is generated from existing knowledge and from expectations about what the research project will discover; for example, a marketer expects increased advertising expenditure to lead to greater brand awareness and conducts research to test their hypothesis.

More complex research projects may combine approaches. For example, a market research project might start with exploratory research to identify reasons for a fall in sales that has occurred for no apparent reason. After discovering possible reasons for the decline in sales, the market research project may continue by undertaking descriptive research to confirm which factors have contributed towards the decline in sales. An outcome may be that the packaging and advertising have contributed to the decrease in sales. Finally, causal research may be used to test whether consumers will buy more if the packaging is larger, and to determine which of two potential advertising campaigns will be more effective. The use of combined approaches is represented in figure 3.6.

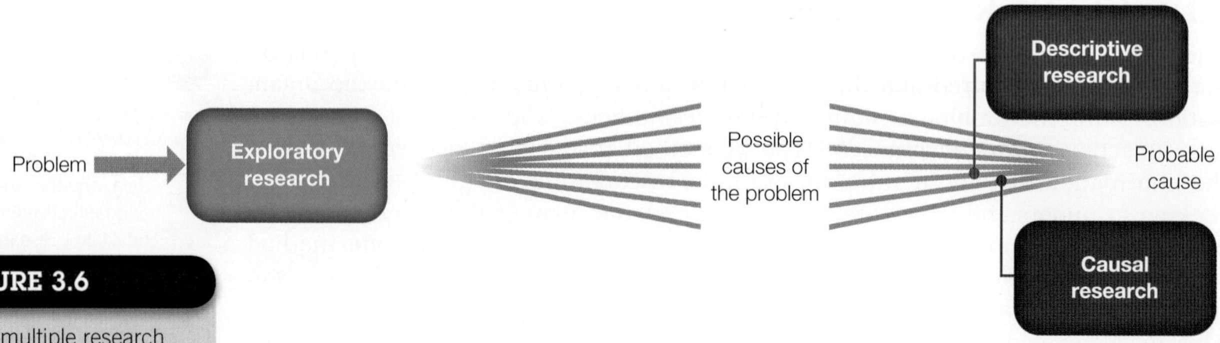

**exploratory research**
Research intended to gather more information about a loosely defined problem.

**descriptive research**
Research used to solve a particular and well-defined problem by clarifying the characteristics of certain phenomena.

**causal research** Research that assumes that a particular variable causes a specific outcome and then, by holding everything else constant, tests whether the variable does indeed effect that outcome.

**hypothesis** A tentative explanation that can be tested.

**FIGURE 3.6**

Using multiple research approaches for complex research problems

## Types of data

Two main types of data are available for marketers. Insights can be gained from information that is already available. This is termed secondary data. Where information is not already available or is not up to date, marketers will need to turn to primary data. We will now briefly consider these two types of data.

Secondary data are data that already exist. **Secondary data** comprise information originally gathered or recorded for some purpose other than to address the current market research problem. The information may be held by the organisation (e.g. sales records or customer profiles generated from business documents) as part of its MIS (discussed earlier), or by some external organisation (e.g. a market research company such as the Nielsen Company or a statistics organisation such as the Australian Bureau of Statistics or Statistics New Zealand).

**Primary data** are data observed or collected directly from respondents as part of the current market research project (e.g. responses given on a questionnaire). You may be wondering why we discussed secondary data first and primary data second — because it already exists, secondary data is cheaper, more quickly available and readily accessible, and often all that is required. Primary data only comes about through a dedicated market research effort. Marketers should always assess whether their research questions can use secondary data before embarking on primary data collection. With electronic records, the existence of large market research companies and the opportunity to obtain and share data provided by the internet, much contemporary market research now has the potential to come from secondary sources. In drawing on a secondary source, the researcher must be able to assure themselves that the source is trustworthy. This is particularly important in the online world, where published information may not have been obtained using valid techniques. Figure 3.7 lists some of the most useful sources of secondary data for the market researcher.

**secondary data** Data originally gathered or recorded for some purpose other than to address the current market research problem.

**primary data** Data collected specifically for the current market research project.

**FIGURE 3.7**

Secondary data sources

### GOVERNMENT AGENCIES AND INTERNATIONAL ORGANISATIONS

The governments of most countries have central statistics agencies that collect and analyse data for the use of the public service in making decisions in the best interests of the governance of the country. Much of the data collected by these agencies is available to the public, sometimes for free and sometimes at a cost. Examples include:

- Australian Bureau of Statistics, www.abs.gov.au
- Statistics New Zealand, www.stats.govt.nz
- Hong Kong Census and Statistics Department, www.censtatd.gov.hk
- Malaysia Statistics Department, www.statistics.gov.my
- Statistics Singapore, www.singstat.gov.sg

Most governments and many international organisations also have departments or agencies devoted to promoting industry. They undertake research or data collection for the express purpose of providing information to marketing and other organisations. Examples include:

- Austrade, www.austrade.gov.au
- New Zealand Trade and Enterprise, www.nzte.govt.nz
- MATRADE (Malaysia External Trade Development Corporation), www.matrade.gov.my
- SPRING Singapore (Standards, Productivity and Innovation Board), www.spring.gov.sg

A number of international bodies exist that collect enormous amounts of data as part of their activities. Examples include:

- Association of Southeast Asian Nations, www.aseansec.org
- International Market Research Information, www.imriresearch.com
- Organisation for Economic Co-operation and Development (OECD), www.oecd.org
- United Nations, www.un.org
- World Bank Group, www.worldbank.org
- World Trade Organization, www.wto.org

### MEDIA

The mass media (television, radio, newspapers, magazines) provide a wealth of information about all sorts of topics. Examples include:

- *BRW*, www.brw.com.au
- *B&T Weekly*, www.bandt.com.au
- *The Australian*, www.theaustralian.news.com.au
- *New Zealand Herald*, www.nzherald.co.nz
- *NZ Business*, www.nzbusiness.co.nz

### MARKET RESEARCH PROVIDERS

Market research is big business in itself. Australia's first market research study was undertaken by the J Walter Thompson advertising agency more than 80 years ago.

*(continued)*

Today, more than 300 businesses in Australia provide market research services.[13] Examples include:

- The Nielsen Company, http://au.acnielsen.com and http://nz.acnielsen.com
- Roy Morgan Research, www.roymorgan.com.au
- Euromonitor, www.euromonitor.com
- OzTAM, www.oztam.com.au
- IBISWorld, www.ibisworld.com.au
- Hitwise, www.hitwise.com
- Colmar Brunton Research, www.colmarbrunton.com
- TNS, http://www.tnsglobal.com/

**MARKETING INFORMATION SYSTEMS**

Efficient marketing organisations capture information from many sources within the organisation in order to inform later marketing decisions:

- raw data from sales reports
- processed data from sales reports (e.g. data filtered by region, season, salesperson, product type, customer characteristics, price)
- accounting information
- written reports by sales representatives and customer service officers.

**DATABASES**

Most organisations, often as part of the MIS, have databases holding vast quantities of information about their operations and market.

**INDUSTRY BODIES**

Most industries have a peak body that works in the interests of the industry and pools resources from members of the industry to conduct research and provide information for the benefit of the industry overall. This can be provided via the internet, directly upon request or through regular industry publications. Examples include:

- Association of Superannuation Funds of Australia
- Australian Pharmaceutical Manufacturers Association
- Internet Industry Association
- Seafood Services Australia.

**FIGURE 3.7**

*(continued)*

As discussed in relation to the MIS, the secondary data held needs to be structured and analysed if it is to be of use in addressing the research problem at hand. While large corporations and governments have long collected enormous amounts of *data*, it has only been in the past 20 years or so that technology has allowed databases to be quickly and efficiently interrogated to provide useful *information*. A technique known as 'data mining' involves processing large data sets to identify patterns and trends that would not be obvious or even discernible upon observation.

Despite the exponentially increasing amounts of information available, secondary data cannot always answer every marketing problem. In many cases it is necessary to collect primary data. Primary data collection tends to be more time-consuming, expensive and difficult than using secondary data. Sometimes marketing organisations, depending on the skills and resources they have available and the complexity of the market research project, undertake primary data collection themselves; others contract specialist research organisations such as Roy Morgan, the Nielsen Company or CoreData to undertake the research.

### Quantitative and qualitative research methods

There are two main types of research methods: qualitative research and quantitative research. Each methodological approach offers many alternatives for market researchers to use.

**quantitative research**
Research that collects information that can be represented numerically.

**Quantitative research** focuses on collecting data that can be represented numerically and analysed statistically. It often collects data by asking questions about 'how much', 'how many 'and 'how often', usually via online, telephone, mail or in-person surveys. Generally, if you respond to the researcher by providing a number, ticking a box, or circling an option in a list or scale, you are participating in quantitative research. Quantitative research is useful for:

- assessing market size
- identifying market segments
- predicting the success of proposed marketing campaigns
- finding out about customer perceptions of existing products.

Quantitative approaches are usually used for descriptive or causal research. Table 3.1 summarises some quantitative market research approaches: experimentation, observation and neuroscience. The chosen technique depends on the nature of what is being studied. For example, observation is used to study television viewing habits (a rating device in the person's home reports what the household was watching and when — or at least what the television was showing when it was on). Departments of main roads use observation to determine how many vehicles use particular roads at specific times of the day, using either automated counters or employing contractors to actually count if more specific details are required (such as the type of vehicle or number of passengers).

**TABLE 3.1** Quantitative research methods

| Method | Description | Major advantages | Major disadvantages |
|---|---|---|---|
| Experimentation | Manipulation of variables of interest while holding everything else constant in a bid to determine just what and how particular things affect behaviour. The variable of interest is known as the independent variable and the variable it influences is known as the dependent variable. | • Allows researchers to establish cause and effect<br>• Tracks actual behaviour rather than relying on consumers' self reports | • The artificial setting may not truly reflect real-life settings<br>• Variables other than the one being studied could be influencing the outcome |
| Observation | Studying people's behaviour and the circumstances surrounding it. | • Measures actual behaviour as opposed to intended or reported behaviour | • Can be expensive<br>• Results can be significantly affected by the subjectivity of the observer<br>• May provide 'shallow' data (e.g. it may reveal a lot of descriptive information, but little about the motivation or cause of observed behaviours) |
| Neuroscience | Techniques that show which parts of the brain are at work when people are exposed to different stimuli (e.g. an advertisement).[14] | • Objective rather than subjective | • Cannot explain 'how' a consumer thinks or what they remember<br>• The science is still evolving<br>• Very expensive<br>• Can be uncomfortable for respondents |

Unstimulated          Stimulated

Surveys are the most common quantitative research tool. Most survey techniques have similar characteristics. They rely on the research to formulate questions that can elicit a relatively closed answer. One of the major distinguishing features between different survey approaches is whether the research participant completes the survey themselves or whether it is administered by an interviewer (see table 3.2). This difference has important consequences for the survey results. For example, interviewer-led surveys can probe the participants for more information on their responses, but at the same time, the presence of an interviewer can influence the responses given and can make it difficult to get honest responses to questions about sensitive topics such as sex. All surveys are more or less prone to distortion because most people's reported behaviour does not precisely match their actual behaviour. For example, a study designed to compare the results of different research techniques found that consumers reported significantly different behaviour than their actual behaviour when it comes to buying alcoholic beverages. Among other differences, consumers said in interviews that they would spend more than ten minutes deciding which beverage to choose and reading labels and so on, whereas actual behaviour that was observed suggested they took less than three minutes to enter the store, find a drink, go to the counter, pay for it and leave.[15] The advantages and disadvantages of various survey methods are described in table 3.2.

**TABLE 3.2** Survey methods

| Method | Description | Major advantages | Major disadvantages | |
|---|---|---|---|---|
| **Interviewer-led survey** | | | | |
| Interviewer administered surveys | In-person survey administered by an interviewer, e.g. door-to-door, shopping centre. | • Comparatively high response rate <br> • Interviewer can ask more questions based on the responses given <br> • Props and visual aids can be used (when survey is conducted in-person) <br> • May be the best option for long or detailed surveys <br> • Speed | • Lack of anonymity can distort responses, e.g. respondents may be reluctant to honestly answer questions about sensitive topics <br> • There is potential for interviewer and respondent bias <br> • Comparatively expensive | |
| Telephone surveys | Administered by an interviewer over the telephone. | | | |
| **Self-response survey** | | | | |
| Mail surveys | A survey form is mailed to potential respondents along with instructions on how to complete and return the form. | • Comparatively cheap <br> • May provide a lot of information <br> • Suited to obtaining closed responses, e.g. yes/no <br> • Potential anonymity can lead to less respondent bias <br> • Wide geographic reach <br> • Convenient for respondents <br> • Speed of response (for online surveys) | • Poor response rate — easy for potential respondents to ignore <br> • Delay in receiving responses (for mail surveys) <br> • Email surveys may be intercepted by spam filters <br> • Poor response rate can lead to an unrepresentative sample | |
| Online surveys | Email or web-based surveys, completed and returned online. | | | |

**qualitative research** Research intended to obtain rich, deep and detailed information about the attitudes and emotions that underlie the behaviours that quantitative research identifies.

**Qualitative research** focuses on obtaining rich, deep and detailed information through techniques such as interviews and focus groups. Rather than identifying numerical patterns, qualitative research aims to get to the reasons behind behaviour. It looks to identify the attitudes and emotions that underlie the behaviours that quantitative research identifies. Qualitative research is particularly useful for investigating the reasons behind behaviours — it provides the 'why' that can be missing from the 'how much, how many, how often' questions answered by quantitative methods. Qualitative research is useful for:
• understanding customer needs
• evaluating potential new products

- testing promotional campaigns
- understanding customers.

Qualitative research approaches are usually used for exploratory research. Because they involve in-depth discussion, a skilled researcher can elicit detailed responses from participants. Table 3.3 summarises some qualitative market research approaches. The quality of data from the various approaches depends on the skill of the researcher. Conducting research via depth interviews and focus groups, in particular, is part-art and part-science. The best results are obtained by engaging highly skilled and experienced people to lead qualitative research.

**TABLE 3.3** Qualitative research methods

| Method | Description | Major advantages | Major disadvantages |
|---|---|---|---|
| Depth interview  | Researcher driven with questions to guide the interview. | • Elicits rich, deep and detailed information<br>• The interviewer can explore responses with further questioning to ensure as much information is gained from the process as possible | • Expensive<br>• Can be difficult to obtain participants<br>• Time-consuming<br>• Difficult to use for sensitive topics<br>• Interviewer can bias results<br>• Cannot necessarily generalise results |
| Focus group | A group of respondents are brought together, introduced to an idea, concept or product, and their interactions observed. | • Provides multiple perspectives<br>• Elicits rich, deep and detailed information<br>• Focus groups often give rise to responses or issues not foreseeable in survey design — the researcher/mediator can explore these issues by asking additional questions | • Expensive<br>• Can be difficult to obtain participants<br>• Time-consuming<br>• Group setting makes it difficult to use for sensitive topics<br>• Researcher/moderator can bias results<br>• Cannot necessarily generalise results |
| Observation  | Recorded notes describing actual events. | • Potentially higher insight into actual behaviour patterns<br>• Can be unobtrusive | • Expensive<br>• Time-consuming<br>• Can be difficult to implement ethically (e.g. privacy concerns) |

*(continued)*

**TABLE 3.3** *(continued)*

| Method | Description | Major advantages | Major disadvantages |
|---|---|---|---|
| Critical incident technique  | Respondents provide detailed information about a particular experience. | • May uncover issues not foreseeable by the researcher<br>• Minimises interviewer bias<br>• Potential to elicit rich information | • Relies on events being remembered and accurately reported |
| Thematic apperception/Cartoon tests  | The researcher provides a picture and the respondent tells a story. | • Projective — allows researcher to investigate sensitive issues | • Dependent on researcher's interpretation |
| Collages | The respondent assembles pictures that represent their thoughts or feelings. | • Potential for novel insights | • Dependent on researcher's interpretation |

In addition to deciding the appropriate method for a research project, the market researcher must decide on the participants. This is done through a process known as sampling.

## Sampling

**population** All of the things (often people) of interest to the researcher in the particular research project.

**sample** The group chosen for the study.

In market research the word **population** means all of the things (often people) of interest to the researcher in the particular research project. It is rarely possible to conduct market research directly on the entire population,[16] so market researchers try to study a smaller number of representative members of the population using a statistical principle known as sampling.

Sampling is the process of choosing members of the total population. The group chosen for the study is known as the **sample**. There are various approaches to sampling to try to achieve a sample that will give results that closely match the results that would be obtained were the entire population studied. The approaches can be broadly classified as probability sampling or non-probability sampling.

There are two main types of samples — probability and non-probability samples. **Probability sampling** ensures that every member of the population has a known chance of being selected in the sample that will be studied. Results obtained using probability sampling can be considered to represent the entire population. **Non-probability sampling** provides no way of knowing the chance of a particular member of the population being chosen as part of the sample. Samples obtained using non-probability samples are unlikely to be representative of the population. Non-probability samples can allow quicker data collection and hence lower costs. The main sample types are described in table 3.4.

**probability sampling**
A sampling approach in which every member of the population has a known chance of being selected in the sample that will be studied.

**non-probability sampling**
A sampling approach that provides no way of knowing the chance of a particular member of the population being chosen as part of the sample that will be studied.

**TABLE 3.4** Sampling methods

| Sample method | Type | Description | Example |
|---|---|---|---|
| Random sampling | Probability | Each member of a population has an equal opportunity of being selected for the sample. | If the population of interest is the members of your marketing course then a random sample would be every 10th student from an alphabetical list of all students. |
| Stratified sampling | Probability | The population is divided into different groups based on some characteristic (e.g. age, sex, home state) and then from each of those groups a random sample is chosen. Stratified sampling is used when you expect there to be variations in characteristics between groups within the population. | If you were conducting research on your marketing class to find out whether tutorials should be held during the middle of the day or in the evening, you might expect that opinions would differ between those members of the class that have children and those that do not. Therefore you could divide the class according to whether the members have children and then choose a sample from each group, thus ensuring that the opinions of population members with those characteristics are included in the sample. |
| Quota | Non-probability | Divides the population into groups based on a number of characteristics and then arbitrarily chooses participants from each group. The findings cannot be generalised. | A study seeks 50 female and 50 male participants. People are approached to participate in the study until the quota is reached. |
| Convenience | Non-probability | Participants are selected on the basis of convenience. The simplicity of this approach makes it a tempting option, but the findings cannot be generalised. | Fans at a cricket game are surveyed on their beverage preference. |

It is important to note that all market research involves some degree of error. Some of these errors arise from problems such as recording a response incorrectly or a poorly designed question. These types of errors are known as non-sampling errors. **Sampling error** is a measure of the extent to which the results from the sample differ from the results that would be obtained from the entire population. Because sampling error is directly related to the extent to which findings from a sample can be generalised to the population of interest, marketers must take steps to ensure that sampling error is minimised.

**sampling error** A measure of the extent to which the results from the sample differ from the results that would be obtained from the entire population.

# Spotlight  Phones net big spenders

The Mobile Data Survey is conducted annually and tracks user engagement with mobile phone data services globally. Each year Australian results are compared and contrasted with international Mobile Data Survey results (e.g. results from the United States, Taiwan, Eygpt, Japan, Korea and China). Online surveys are conducted to understand current mobile phone usage, along with sociodemographic data. In the most recent Australian component of the survey, banner advertisements inviting participants were placed on the websites for Bigpond, Virgin Mobile and Yahoo 7. Ten $100 vouchers were offered to encourage responses, and over 3800 people completed the associated questionnaire.

Key findings from the Australian component of the third Mobile Data Survey include that consumption of mobile data services among *existing users* has continued to grow as the true value of mobile data services among these consumers becomes better understood. Around one-third of current mobile data service users are willing to pay a monthly fee of more than $50 for unlimited data access. This is a significant shift, as the first Mobile Data Survey, held only two years earlier, revealed that no respondents were willing to pay more than $10 per month for unlimited access.

However, the most recent survey results show that the base level of mobile data users in Australia continues to hover around the 50 per cent mark, with 40 per cent of users owning smartphones. This is still higher than the US market results, which show 33 per cent of respondents use mobile data services, and only 20 per cent own a smartphone.

Dr Marisa Maio Mackay, a director of Complete the Picture Consulting, a research partner involved in conducting the Australian Mobile Data Survey, explains: 'The Australian Mobile industry may be trying to win over the next cohort of mobile data users, but it hasn't happened . . . yet! The base level of mobile data users has not shown real growth in the last year, but existing users of mobile data services continue to use an increasing number of services and appear to get real value from it, so it should only be a matter of time before even *more* Australians begin using mobile data services!' This is especially the case given the amount of money Australians are spending on their monthly phone bills. Around 70 per cent of Australians spend $30 or more per month on phone bills, with around one-third of Australians spending more than $60 per month.[17]

## Questions

1. Outline the research design used by the research partners in the Australian component of the Mobile Data Survey, and identify the type of data that would have been collected.

2. Outline the advantages and disadvantages of online surveys as they relate to the requirements of the Mobile Data Survey research project.

## Concepts and applications check

**Learning objective 3** outline the issues in research design, including the role of primary and secondary data, and the uses of quantitative and qualitative research

**3.1** A citizens' group interested in generating public and financial support for a new sports hall printed a questionnaire in local newspapers. Readers return the questionnaires by mail. How might such survey results be biased?

**3.2** Briefly explain the different types of primary research methods that market researchers can use, and categorise them as either qualitative or quantitative.

**3.3** How are probability sampling and non-probability sampling different? Explain in terms of the usability of the results.

**3.4** Neuroscience is increasing in popularity in market research. Find an example of a neuroscience study and prepare a summary of the study for class. Your summary should outline the research problem, the research design, the research findings and the conclusions drawn by the authors.

# DATA COLLECTION, ANALYSIS AND REPORTING

Data must be collected according to the methods specified in the research design. The goal of this part of the research process is to ensure the research design is properly followed, responses are recorded correctly and errors are not introduced.

The whole market research process needs to be managed according to project management principles to ensure the market research is delivered in accordance with the research brief, as well as on time and on budget; and provides value to the marketing organisation. The data collection process can be conducted in-house or it can be outsourced, with a market research or advertising agency taking on the responsibility of the data collection process (and often the analysis and reporting as well). A full discussion of project management is outside the scope of this textbook, but the basic principles are now briefly outlined.

**Learning objective 4**
understand the key principles of data collection and analysis, and the subsequent reporting of market research findings to inform marketing decisions

## Managing data collection

Given that time and financial resources are limited, budgeting and scheduling need to be planned and managed to ensure the most benefit is derived from the investment in market research. The market research project should proceed efficiently and effectively.

Budgets can be determined by estimating the likely actual cost of each phase of the project or determining the amount of time that each phase is likely to take and then applying a standard cost estimate to the hours. A market research project seeking to capture consumer preferences using an online questionnaire for a sample of 500 customers will cost around $20 000. A study involving 15 depth interviews and a 20-minute online questionnaire offering incentives for business professionals to participate will cost around $50 000. It is clear a market research project is a substantial investment.

During a project, some phases must be completed before others can begin. For example, researchers will often conduct depth interviews to generate items for a survey. The depth interview phase has to be completed prior to the implementation of the survey phase. Careful coordination and management are required to ensure each phase can proceed as planned.

It is important to note that the project must also be able to accommodate revisions as it proceeds. The market research process is not always a straightforward, linear path from start to finish:

- An initial survey of secondary data may prompt the marketing organisation to reassess the research problem definition.
- A focus group might similarly prompt a reassessment of the problem or suggest some other piece of data to analyse that was not included in the original brief.
- The initial data analysis might suggest some revision to the methodology for data collection requiring that part of the process to be reviewed.

All of this is part of the dynamic nature of market research. A research project that cannot or does not take the opportunity to refine itself when it is in progress is almost certain to result in less than optimal value.

A number of tools exist to help project managers maintain control of projects. The most commonly used are Gantt charts and the critical path method. Gantt charts are a visual representation of who is doing what and when. A simplified example is shown in figure 3.8. The critical path method involves dividing the research process into parts, estimating the time to complete each and arranging them so that a stage cannot proceed until all of the prerequisite parts are complete. This method is very useful for seeing the effect of a delay in one part of the project on the overall progress of the project.

| Task | Start | End | Time (days) | 22-Jan | 29-Jan | 5-Feb | 12-Feb | 19-Feb | 26-Feb | 5-Mar | 12-Mar | 19-Mar |
|------|-------|-----|-------------|--------|--------|-------|--------|--------|--------|-------|--------|--------|
| Prepare survey | 22-Jan | 24-Jan | 3 | ■ | | | | | | | | |
| Determine sample | 22-Jan | 25-Jan | 4 | ■ | | | | | | | | |
| Distribute survey | 29-Jan | 31-Jan | 3 | | ■ | | | | | | | |
| Receive responses | 5-Feb | 23-Feb | 15 | | | ■ | ■ | ■ | | | | |
| Filter responses | 12-Feb | 2-Mar | 15 | | | | ■ | ■ | ■ | | | |
| Analyse responses | 19-Feb | 9-Mar | 15 | | | | | ■ | ■ | ■ | | |
| Prepare report | 12-Mar | 16-Mar | 5 | | | | | | | | ■ | |
| Report findings | 19-Mar | 19-Mar | 1 | | | | | | | | | ■ |

**FIGURE 3.8**

A simplified Gantt chart (data collection, analysis, reporting)

Project management also assigns accountabilities for the various aspects of the market research project: who is responsible for what. If the market research project or part of it is outsourced, this aspect takes on extra importance and should be included in the contract.

# Data analysis

Once data has been collected, it needs to be filtered and organised. Depending on how the data was collected, it may be necessary to perform some quality control techniques to eliminate invalid data (e.g. where the interviewer recorded a response incorrectly or a respondent gave a nonsensical answer). Once cleaned up, the results need to be analysed. A wide range of analytical techniques are available and marketers need to understand which analytical techniques are appropriate for the data they have. They need to know how to condense a large pile of information into a more user-friendly form. A sound knowledge of data analysis is also essential if marketers are to properly evaluate and interpret the findings presented in market research reports. Without a working knowledge of data analysis, a marketer will not be capable of understanding if the analysis was appropriate and therefore if the findings and recommendations are valid. Market research, data analysis and business statistics courses will all help equip you with these essential skills.

The data analysis technique to be used will have been planned as part of the research design. For example, some methods require minimum sample sizes and this must be planned prior to data collection. As data is collected, a preliminary analysis can be conducted and the results of this analysis can be fed back into the ongoing data collection process, particularly if an unexpected issue or finding emerges that requires further probing.

Generally analysis will be quantitative or qualitative in nature. Both approaches can be applied to the same data in some cases.

## Quantitative analysis

Recall that quantitative research generates data that can be represented numerically. To be converted into knowledge that can be used to inform decision making, the quantitative data that has been collected must be analysed and understood.

Figure 3.9 is a perceptual map created from analysis of data collected in a study of surf brands Billabong, Quiksilver, Rusty and Roxy. A perceptual map is a two-dimensional diagram showing how competing brands relate to each other in terms of a range of factors. This perceptual map shows the interrelationships between various consumer perceptions and attributes of Billabong, Quiksilver, Rusty and Roxy. Such maps are constructed from a questionnaire in which respondents are asked to select which attributes apply to selected brands. For example, consumers might be asked to select which of Billabong, Quiksilver, Rusty and Roxy 'is about independence and individuality'. Respondents are able to select any number of the brands, including none or all brands for each attribute listed. In the perceptual map, the closer an attribute is to a brand, the closer consumers perceive that attribute to be associated with the brand. Conversely, the further away the attribute, the less it applies to the brand. When an attribute is situated between brands, then the brands cannot be differentiated based on that attribute.[18]

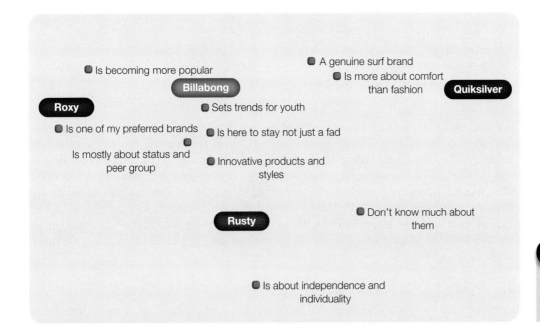

**FIGURE 3.9**

A perceptual map showing sample results from quantitative data analysis

Quantitative data is typically fed into software designed specifically for statistical analysis, such as SPSS,[19] or into more general purpose software that has at least some statistical analysis features such as Microsoft Excel. Software can analyse statistics based on one, two, or more variables (known respectively as univariate, bivariate and multivariate analysis), showing trends and patterns in the mass of data, often presenting them in easy to understand graphs, charts or tables. The analysis will support or refute the research hypothesis (or indeed it could be inconclusive). Even the most sophisticated statistical software will not generally identify patterns automatically. A skilled analyst needs to use the original research question to determine how to interrogate the data in order to identify patterns.

## Qualitative analysis

Qualitative data is not usually represented numerically. Indeed, the whole purpose of qualitative research is to gain richer and deeper information than can be obtained by quantitative techniques. Qualitative data will usually be in the form of interview transcripts, video recordings, observation record sheets and lengthy narrative responses to questions. Figure 3.10 shows qualitative data extracted from a transcript of a focus group that was part of a study on website design.

**Question: How do you find navigating the site?**

**Daniel:** The site shows what the department wants to tell me. The content I need to find is hard to get to. You get it eventually, but it's not intuitive.

**Maddy:** The site's not boring, as such, but it could be a lot better. Also, I don't know where to begin when I'm trying to find something. A lot of what is on the home page is just not relevant. It's also annoying that when you click a link it opens in the same window, so it's hard to get back to where I was.

**Raj:** You need to click through a dozen pages to find what you want. I'm not interested in trivia or irrelevant news. I don't use the site for that.

**Cheng:** The site is old-fashioned, with a lot of distracting things.

**Perry:** All the pages make you scroll. There's no shortcuts and no easy way to search. All the information you need is there . . . somewhere . . . but the organisation of it is terrible.

**Yasmin:** You shouldn't have to scroll down homepages at all. It should be clear what you want as soon as you get there.

**Cait:** It needs a better search facility.

**FIGURE 3.10**

Sample data from a focus group

Procedures such as reduction and coding are available to interpret and organise qualitative data to allow meaningful conclusions to be drawn. Researchers *reduce* qualitative data by categorising concepts and key variables in the study according to their properties or dimensions. *Coding* involves developing a series of propositions about the relationships between key concepts identified in the study. Diagrams are often used by researchers to illustrate relationships between key concepts in the study. It is important to remember, though, that treating qualitative data too much like quantitative data will lose much of the richness of information that makes qualitative data so valuable.

## Drawing conclusions

Once the data has been analysed and patterns or trends identified, conclusions must be drawn and recommendations made. The conclusions should state what the data has shown in terms of the original research question. For example, if a supermarket conducted research into how customers were likely to react to the introduction of a levy on plastic bags, the conclusion should state what the data suggests will be the reaction, such as:

- 40 per cent of customers will start bringing their own bags to use most or all of the time
- 20 per cent of customers will happily pay the levy
- 10 per cent of customers will switch to a supermarket that does not charge the levy
- 30 per cent of customers already use their own bags.

The set of conclusions from the data will suggest one or more courses of action. The alternatives will usually be formulated by drawing on more information than just that generated by the market research process. In the previous scenario, the possible courses of action include introducing a levy or not introducing it; setting the levy at cost or higher or lower than cost; and perhaps not offering plastic bags at all. The recommendations will need to draw on information about the cost of the bags, the existence of nearby competitors, the possibility of government regulation, and so on.

## Reporting the findings

Once data is analysed and conclusions drawn, the findings must be presented in a format that will enable the marketing decision makers to use the information. In practice this involves a written report and/or a presentation to the decision makers. Reporting should be concise and to the point. Market researchers often report the key findings in a PowerPoint presentation, with more detail provided in a formal written document.

The executive summary in the written report may well be the only part of the report that executives will read. A written report should include the detail of how the study was conducted and how the analysis was performed. This detail will be required by the person commissioning the market research. Decision makers might choose not to read that detail, but it must be available to them should they decide they want more background or a deeper understanding of how the conclusions or recommendations were reached.

A written research report should include:

- a *cover page*, noting the title of the study, the date the report was prepared, the marketing organisation, and the name of the researcher
- an *executive summary*, noting the research objectives, findings, conclusions and recommendations (an executive summary must summarise the entire report)
- a *table of contents*, enabling readers to easily find areas of interest in the report
- an *introduction* or *background* section, stating the marketing issue being studied and the research problem addressed by the project
- a *methodology* section, summarising the research plan, any variations from the plan in the implementation, and the rationale for the approach taken (a copy of the actual surveys, interview questions and so on should be included as an appendix)
- *findings*, which make up the main body of the report, supported by tables and graphics as required, and making clear how the research has answered the research questions
- a statement of *limitations*, so that the research findings can be assessed in context of any limitations that arose during the course of the research
- *conclusions* and *recommendations*, concisely stating what has been concluded from the findings and recommending possible courses of action
- *appendices*, to present detailed, often technical information.

An oral presentation of the written research report needs to be planned and delivered carefully. It is a mistake (and pointless) to simply read from the written research report. An oral presentation should focus on the main findings and recommendations, and the use of audiovisual aids (e.g. PowerPoint slides summarising key information and visuals) can help considerably in getting key messages across to the target audience. Audiovisual aids can also enhance the chances of audience message recall at a later date. Research has shown that audiences remember only about 30 per cent of what they hear and only about 20 per cent of what they see. However, retention of information rises to approximately 50 per cent of what they both hear *and* see.[20]

Care needs to be taken, though, that the use of audiovisual tools such as PowerPoint is not overdone in an oral presentation. Such slides should be used for impact and the effective presentation of information, not just for the sake of it. Figure 3.11[21] is a visual example that shows how research about smartphone use may be represented in PowerPoint slides.

## Summary

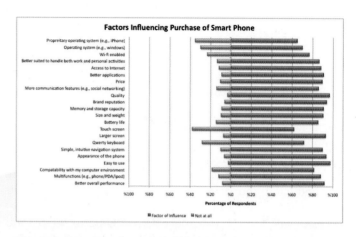

- All motivating factors contributed to the uptake of a smart phone (i.e., it is not the presence of a single factor alone).

- Phone quality, ease of use, appearance and screen size were some of the more important motivating factors in the decision to buy a smart phone.

- The presence of a touch screen, proprietary operating system (e.g., iPhone), operating system (e.g., windows), qwerty keyboard or being Wi-Fi enabled were least influential.

**FIGURE 3.11**

Mobile data survey

## Responding to the research problem

Earlier in the chapter, we noted that market research is usually undertaken to solve a problem — an issue, opportunity or threat that demands a response that requires information. Our discussion of market research would be incomplete if we did not consider the ultimate outcome of the market research process: marketing decisions that lead to marketing outcomes. Look back to figure 3.3 on page 78. An organisation that is using information effectively draws on the results of market research and all other sources of relevant information to make decisions that take the form of marketing plans and strategies. As discussed in chapters 1 and 2, these plans are then implemented by the various parts of the organisation to achieve the organisation's goals. The results are represented in figure 3.3 on page 78 as 'outcomes'.

Ideally, of course, the marketing outcomes align with the marketing goals of the organisation. An ideal market research project begins with an issue, discovers information about the issue, results in decisions about how to respond to the issue, and ultimately results in outcomes that match the marketing goals. For example, if the marketing 'problem' is 'How can we increase revenue by 8 per cent next financial year?', the ideal market research will discover how and the marketing outcome will indeed be 8 per cent revenue growth. Of course, the 'real world' issues facing organisations are far more complex than this simple statement suggests, and marketing outcomes are the results of a multitude of decisions taken within an organisation. High-quality market research helps makes these decisions better informed.

## Assessing the effectiveness of the market research

In order to create, communicate, deliver and exchange offerings that have value for customers, clients, partners and society at large, marketers need to understand their market. Without market research, marketers would face crucial decisions without the necessary knowledge. Those decisions would be an educated guess at best.

It is essential that marketers evaluate the effectiveness of each and every market research project that is undertaken. As with all aspects of marketing, those marketers engaged in market research need to be able to assess and demonstrate the effectiveness of their work in order to prove a return on investment. The ultimate test is whether the research answers the research problem and leads to decisions that contribute towards achieving the organisation's marketing goals. This will be captured by marketing metrics such as brand awareness, customer satisfaction and sales.

The market research process itself should also be measured for effectiveness. For example, as discussed in this chapter, market research projects have set objectives and specific resources allocated to them based on a cost–benefit analysis. Suitable measures of the effectiveness of the market research process include, therefore, whether the project was completed within the specified budgets and timelines, the quality of the information generated, the depth of the analysis, and whether senior management felt they could confidently make a decision based on the research findings.

# Building donations through data     Spotlight

Within two years of an Australian children's charity (called 'the Charity' here) joining a data cooperative offered by First Direct Solutions, two donor acquisition campaigns have been implemented. First Direct Solutions is a division of Australia Post, and its range of services include customer profiling and data management. Its data cooperative service works on the premise that members (including various charities) share 'privacy compliant' transactional data about their customers. (In the case of charities, for example, this may include general information on how much the average person donates, how old they are, and how often they donate.) This information is then made available to all members of the data cooperative (including other charities).

Upon becoming a member of a data cooperative offered by First Choice Solutions, 'the Charity' discovered useful insights, such as the fact that based on past donation data, certain female age groups are potentially more likely to donate to charitable causes. 'The Charity' responded by implementing two direct mail campaigns — one in each of the next two financial years:

1. A campaign was implemented in the first financial year targeting women aged 55 and over who were in a specific income bracket. The data cooperative's information revealed that such women had given an average charitable donation between $10 and $149 in the past.

2. In the second year, a campaign was implemented that targeted women aged 55 and over from selected 'potentially lucrative' postcodes in Queensland and New South Wales, based on past charitable donation data.

Existing donors to 'the Charity' were excluded from both campaigns. The two respective campaigns delivered the metrics shown in the table.[22]

| Campaign | Income raised | Cost of mailing | Average donation | Number of donations | Number mailed | Cost per donor | Response |
|---|---|---|---|---|---|---|---|
| Campaign 1 | $8 982 | $9 600 | $34.95 | 257 | 6 000 | $37.35 | 4.28% |
| Campaign 2 | $12 354 | $22 000 | $37.55 | 329 | 20 000 | $66.87 | 1.65% |

The data in the table indicates that the cost of mailing was greater than the revenue raised for both campaigns; however, significantly, 'the Charity' attracted 586 new, first-time donors. (Remember that existing donors to 'the Charity' were excluded from these two specific campaigns and their associated metrics.)

The challenge for 'the Charity' is in converting as many of these new donors as possible into regular donors, rather than them staying as 'one-off' donors. The increased brand awareness of 'the Charity' generated by the campaigns may lead to more long-term types of donation, such as bequests. Through the experience gained from these two campaigns and by analysing the data cooperative's collective information on the general characteristics of charitable donors, 'the Charity' now has a greater understanding about donor acquisition, retention and optimisation.

## Question

What role can a data cooperative service, such as the one utilised by 'the Charity', play in informing marketing decisions?

## Concepts and applications check

**Learning objective 4** understand the key principles of data collection and analysis, and the subsequent reporting of market research findings to inform marketing decisions

**4.1** Explain the key differences between the analysis of quantitative data and qualitative data.

**4.2** Briefly outline the main requirements of a market research report.

**4.3** Imagine you are a marketing manager for Billabong and you contracted Colmar Brunton to undertake the market research project described on page 97 and in figure 3.9. Interpret the results of the study.

**4.4** It is essential that marketers evaluate the effectiveness of market research projects they undertake or commission. Market research effectiveness awards are run annually by professional associations such as the Australian Market and Social Research Society (www.mrsa.com.au) and the Market Research Society of New Zealand (www.mrsnz.org.nz). Choose a winner from the most recent market research awards in your city, state or country. Briefly outline the case (using the research components presented in this chapter) and discuss why this is an example of effective market research.

# SUMMARY

 **Learning objective 1** discuss the importance of market research as a basis for marketing decision making

Market research links customers, clients, partners and society at large with the marketer through information. Information obtained from market research — along with information from other sources — is used to inform marketing decisions on a wide range of issues, including those that are fundamental to the organisation's marketing mix. The results of market research are fed into a marketing information system, which holds and organises all of the organisation's marketing information.

In deciding to undertake a market research project, the organisation should first consider whether the market research will be relevant, timely, feasible given available resources, necessary, and result in sufficient benefits to justify the costs.

Market research must be conducted ethically, respecting the rights of clients, employers and research participants.

 **Learning objective 2** clearly define a research problem to guide a market research project, and prepare a research brief

Before beginning a market research project, it is crucial to know precisely what the research is intended to achieve. The question that the research is intended to answer is known as the 'research problem'. As the research project proceeds and more information is gathered, the research problem may need to be redefined.

Whether the market research project is undertaken in-house or outsourced to a specialist provider, a market research brief should be prepared to guide the project. A market research brief specifies the research problem, the information required, the timeframe, the budget, and any other conditions relevant to the project.

 **Learning objective 3** outline the issues in research design, including the role of primary and secondary data, and the uses of quantitative and qualitative research

The research problem needs to be analysed in order to create a methodology that will provide an answer to the problem. This detailed methodology planned to answer the research problem is known as the 'research design'.

Depending on the nature of the research problem, market research usually takes the form of exploratory research, descriptive research or causal research. Exploratory research is intended to gather more information about a loosely defined problem. Descriptive research is used to solve well-defined problem by discovering more about certain phenomena. Causal research tests whether a particular variable affects a specific outcome.

Market research can draw on two types of data. Secondary data is data that already exists. Primary data is collected specifically for the purposes of the current research project.

Research methods can be broadly classified as quantitative research or qualitative research. Quantitative research collects data that can be represented numerically and analysed using statistical techniques. Experimentation, observation and neuroscience are among the quantitative research methods. The most commonly used quantitative research tool is the survey, which may be led by an interviewer or self-administered by the survey respondent.

Qualitative research obtains rich, deep and detailed information and is often used when the market researcher needs to know about the beliefs and attitudes that underlie observable behaviour. Interviews and focus groups are among the most

## Key terms and concepts

**causal research** 86
**descriptive research** 86
**exploratory research** 86
**hypothesis** 86
**market research** 75
**market research brief** 82
**marketing information system (MIS)** 77
**non-probability sampling** 93
**population** 92
**primary data** 87
**probability sampling** 93
**qualitative research** 90
**quantitative research** 88
**research design** 85
**research problem** 81
**sample** 92
**sampling error** 93
**secondary data** 87

commonly used qualitative research methods, but they are time-consuming and expensive.

Market research tries to find out about the population by studying a small part of it and then generalising the results. The smaller part is known as a 'sample'. Probability sampling ensures every member of a population has a known chance of being selected in the sample that will be studied. Non-probability sampling provides no way of knowing the chance of a particular member of the population being chosen as part of the sample.

 **Learning objective 4** understand the key principles of data collection and analysis, and the subsequent reporting of market research findings to inform marketing decisions

Once a research project has been designed, it must be implemented in compliance with the design. This requires careful project management. Data must be collected, filtered and organised so that it can be efficiently analysed. Quantitative data can be statistically manipulated to identify trends and patterns in the data. Qualitative data can be reduced to allow statistical analysis, but much of the rich detail can be lost. Often qualitative data analysis leads to further research in the form of quantitative research.

Data analysis allows conclusions to be drawn and recommendations formulated. The findings and recommendations of the market research project should be presented in a concise and clear manner. The underlying detail should also be provided to support the recommendations.

The recommendations ultimately lead to a marketing decision, which in turn will lead to marketing outcomes. Ideally, the outcomes are a successful response to the research problem that triggered the market research process.

# Hervey Bay leisure travellers

Tourism is Queensland's third largest export earner, and contributes significantly to the economic wellbeing of the state. The tourism industry is estimated to contribute $9.2 billion to the Queensland economy each year. The Fraser Coast offers visitors a variety of natural attractions, experiences and activities, including four-wheel-drive adventures, fishing, nature-based activities, and authentic country heritage and history experiences. Hervey Bay is situated on the Fraser Coast and is considered a gateway to Fraser Island — a world heritage area listed site that is famous for its dingoes, beautiful inland lakes and dramatic scenery.

Recently, it was decided that a comprehensive study should be undertaken for future tourism planning on the Fraser Coast. At the time of the study, there were 940 000 visitors to the region each year, with tourists spending about four million nights in the region. Of these visitors, about 751 000 were domestic tourists. Additionally, the region was receiving about 188 000 international visitors each year (about 20 per cent of all visitors to the region).

A survey was developed to understand the types of people that were choosing to visit Hervey Bay. Respondents were asked about their age, gender, travel party composition (TPC), income, location, trip purpose, length of stay, accommodation expenditure, activities expenditure, food and beverage expenditure, and motivations for travelling to Hervey Bay. Tourists at Hervey Bay were chosen as the sample for this study. Respondents needed to be over 18 and had to be planning to, or would have already spent, at least a night in the chosen destination. The visitors also needed to have made the choice to visit Hervey Bay for purposes other than business or work.

Some visitors who came to enjoy activities such as whale watching and beach camel rides at Hervey Bay

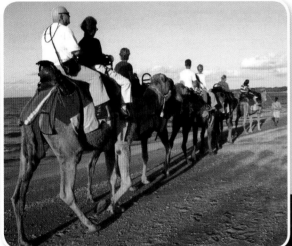

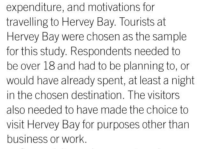

participated in a survey to measure their motivations for visiting the region. The results were used to help researchers map out future tourism initiatives for the Fraser Coast.

The survey was run over a seven-month period, with a monthly quota of 120 surveys per month. By using this design, seasonality was not a concern. This was because the data was collected during different seasons, catering to the high and low tourist times. Surveys were given out at a variety of popular locations to maximise heterogeneity. Surveys were collected at accommodation venues, including a caravan park, a backpacker hostel and a five-star resort; at a visitor information centre; and at various transport locations, such as a bus terminal, a ferry terminal and the airport. A minimum of eight responses were collected each month from every location to ensure that one location did not dominate the results.

A researcher was present to distribute and collect the survey. Several surveys were left in the lobby at the accommodation venues and in the main seating area of the visitor information centre. In these instances, approximately 20 surveys were completed, indicating a very low response rate without a researcher present. The time spent at each location to collect the responses varied. The researcher spent whole days at the accommodation venues to achieve the quota, whereas only one hour was necessary at the airport. In total, 84.9 per cent of tourists who were approached chose to complete the survey. Incomplete surveys (283 in total) were removed from the data analysis. Data collected in the survey were analysed using version 15.0 of SPSS (SPSS 2007).

A TwoStep® cluster analysis was the statistical technique used to reveal the tourist segments. Three Hervey Bay tourist segments were revealed in the survey: 'wealthy travellers', 'young Europeans' and 'long-stay travellers' (see tables 3.5 and 3.6). The information shown in bold in tables 3.5 and 3.6 shows the segments with the highest value ratings.

**TABLE 3.5** A comparison of the Hervey Bay tourist segments

|  |  | Wealthy travellers | Young Europeans | Long-stay travellers |
|---|---|---|---|---|
| **Segment size (people surveyed)** |  | **233** | 224 | 112 |
| **Segment (%)** |  | **40.9** | 39.4 | 19.7 |
| **Number of motivations (average)** |  | 5.8 | **6.2** | 5.5 |
| **Number of nights (average)** |  | 4.3 | 3.7 | **17.0** |
| **Age** | 18–24 | 6.9 | **39.7** | 10.7 |
|  | 25–34 | 29.2 | **48.7** | 3.6 |
|  | 35–44 | **21.5** | 7.6 | 17.0 |
|  | 45–54 | **24.0** | 3.1 | 17.9 |
|  | 55–64 | 12.9 | 0.9 | **32.1** |
|  | 65 and over | 5.6 | 0 | **18.8** |
| **Income** | less than $20 000 | 1.3 | **37.9** | 18.8 |
|  | $20 000–$39 999 | 8.8 | 15.6 | **23.2** |
|  | $40 000–$59 999 | 11.3 | 15.6 | **17.9** |
|  | $60 000–$79 999 | 12.1 | 10.7 | **17.9** |
|  | $80 000–$99 999 | **20.1** | 10.7 | 11.6 |
|  | $100 000 or more | **46.4** | 9.4 | 10.7 |

| | | Wealthy travellers | Young Europeans | Long-stay travellers |
|---|---|---|---|---|
| **Origin** | Europe | 21.5 | **70.5** | 0 |
| | New South Wales | **34.8** | 12.9 | 22.3 |
| | Queensland | 19.3 | 0.4 | **41.1** |
| | Victoria | 13.3 | 0 | **19.6** |
| | United States | 4.3 | **11.2** | 2.7 |
| | Australia (not specified) | 4.3 | 1.3 | **14.3** |
| | Asia–Pacific | 2.6 | **3.6** | 0 |
| **Daily accommodation expenditure** | less than $50 | 6.4 | 80.8 | **83.0** |
| | $50–$99 | 14.6 | **17.4** | 13.4 |
| | $100–$149 | **30.0** | 1.8 | 2.7 |
| | $150–$199 | **23.6** | 0 | 0 |
| | $200 or more | **25.3** | 0 | 0.9 |
| **Daily activities expenditure** | less than $50 | 19.3 | 36.6 | **72.3** |
| | $50–$99 | 24.9 | **33.5** | 21.4 |
| | $100–$149 | **24.5** | 16.1 | 4.5 |
| | $150–$199 | **15.9** | 6.3 | 0 |
| | $200 or more | **15.5** | 7.6 | 1.8 |
| **Daily food and beverages expenditure** | less than $50 | 8.6 | 78.6 | **79.5** |
| | $50–$99 | **42.5** | 19.6 | 17.9 |
| | $100–$149 | **33.0** | 1.3 | 1.8 |
| | $150–$199 | **6.4** | 0.4 | 0 |
| | $200 or more | **9.4** | 0 | 0.9 |
| **Travel party composition** | Couple | 42.5 | 28.1 | **50.9** |
| | Adult group | 18.5 | **51.8** | 8.0 |
| | Family | **34.3** | 2.7 | 14.3 |
| | By myself | 2.1 | 17.4 | **17.9** |
| | Other | 2.6 | 0 | **8.9** |

**TABLE 3.6** Tourist motivations

| | Wealthy travellers (%) | Young Europeans (%) | Long-stay travellers (%) |
|---|---|---|---|
| To go to a place where you have not been before | 50.2 | **77.7** | 25.0 |
| To rest and relax | 62.2 | 42.9 | **63.4** |
| To have fun | 44.6 | **68.3** | 35.7 |
| To go sightseeing | 51.5 | **62.9** | 31.3 |
| To see something different | 42.1 | **59.8** | 21.4 |
| To escape from your everyday lifestyle | 37.8 | **50.9** | 34.9 |
| To spend time with your partner | **35.6** | 26.3 | 22.3 |
| To experience a different culture | 12.9 | **45.5** | 6.3 |
| To participate in recreational activities | 22.7 | **25.9** | 8.9 |
| To be together with your family | 30.5 | 3.6 | **34.8** |
| To get away from the demands of home | **21.0** | 14.7 | 18.8 |
| The weather | 33.5 | 25.9 | **46.4** |
| It was recommended by someone | 24.0 | **35.3** | 15.2 |
| To experience a relaxed lifestyle | 21.5 | 6.7 | **36.6** |
| It is a convenient stop over point | 12.0 | **25.4** | 16.1 |
| The untouched nature | 17.6 | **19.2** | 10.7 |
| There's a variety of things to see and do | 15.0 | 5.8 | **19.6** |
| To go camping | 3.0 | 14.3 | **23.2** |
| It is a family orientated destination | 10.7 | 0.4 | **28.6** |
| The safe environment | 6.9 | 1.3 | **22.3** |
| The competitive price | **10.7** | 3.6 | 7.1 |
| The friendly locals | 4.7 | 2.7 | **18.8** |
| The luxury accommodation | **12.0** | 1.3 | 1.8 |

An analysis of these tables reveals that the 'wealthy travellers' segment was the largest of the three (40.9 per cent), just ahead of the 'young Europeans' segment (39.4 per cent). The majority of people in the 'wealthy travellers' segment earned over $100 000 a year and travelled from New South Wales. People in this segment were primarily aged between 25 and 54. These people generally travelled in a couple or as a family, and they stayed in the region for four nights on average. The people in this segment spent the most money in Hervey Bay, allocating over $100 for daily accommodation expenses and between $50 and $149 for daily activities and food and beverage costs. They had roughly four push motivations and one pull motivation. The most popular push motivation was 'to rest and relax', and 'the weather' pulled tourists most frequently to Hervey Bay. The key distinguishing features of the people in this segment were higher income and expenditure. These features led to the people in this segment being called the 'wealthy travellers'.

The 'young Europeans' segment was given its name because the overwhelming majority of European people in this segment in the survey were under 35 years of age. The people in this segment earned the least and travelled predominantly from Europe. They spent less per day when compared with people in the 'wealthy travellers' segment. Approximately half of the people in this segment travelled in adult groups. The people in this segment stayed for 3 to 5 nights on average. They had the most push motivations and the fewest pull motivations. 'It was recommended by someone' was the dominant pull motivation for the people in this segment, and 'to go to a place you have not been before' was the most popular push motivation.

The third segment in the survey, the 'long-stay travellers' segment, was the smallest segment. It represented approximately 20 per cent of the tourism data set. This segment was distinguishable based on a longer length of stay. The people in this segment were older, with more than half of the participants being over 55 years of age. The income of the people in this segment was evenly distributed across the six categories. This segment largely comprised of domestic travellers from Queensland. The people in this segment often travelled as part of a couple, and stayed for an average of 17 nights. They had the lowest number of push motivations and the highest number of pull motivations. Many of the people who were 'long-stay travellers' travelled 'to rest and relax', and were pulled by 'the weather' and 'to experience a relaxed lifestyle'.[23]

*This case was co-authored by Aaron Tkaczynski and Sharyn Rundle-Thiele.

## Questions

1. Explain the market research method used in this Hervey Bay tourist study.
   (a) What are its strengths?
   (b) What are its limitations?
2. Go online and find the website for a Hervey Bay tour operator. Choose one of the three segments identified in tables 3.5 and 3.6. Outline how the organisation appears to be targeting (or could potentially target) this segment.

### Advanced activity

Review the opening chapter example of the Nielsen radio ratings.
(a) Describe the research design for this type of survey in as much detail as possible, referring to concepts explained in the chapter.
(b) What are some data analysis, collection and reporting issues that Nielsen would need to be aware of in relation to their radio survey?

## Marketing plan activity

Market research is an important basis for marketing decision making. For the organisation you have chosen for your marketing plan (chapter 1), your SWOT, environmental and situational analyses (chapter 2) may have identified market research information that needs to be obtained. Clearly define your research problem(s) and prepare a simple market research brief(s) using figure 3.5 from the chapter as a guide.

Next, propose a methodology or approach for the market research. In the coming weeks, you will need to collect and analyse the information, making any necessary adjustments to your situation, environmental and SWOT analyses from chapter 2. You should also regularly reassess your preliminary marketing objectives and revise as required in light of the market research information you obtain.

This market research will be ongoing as you develop and refine your plan and progress on to target market analysis, marketing mix decisions and strategies in later chapters.

A sample marketing plan has been included at the back of this book (see page 523) to give you an idea where this information fits in an overall marketing plan.

## CHAPTER 4

# Consumer behaviour

## Learning objectives

After studying this chapter, you should be able to:

 explain why marketers require a thorough understanding of consumer behaviour and its major influences

 understand the major group factors that influence consumer behaviour

 analyse the major individual factors that influence consumer behaviour

 explain the general steps in the consumer decision-making process.

# Gen Z: the new frontier

Generation Z (defined as those born after 2001)[1] is the youngest demographic segment that marketers need to consider. Gen Z represents a unique target market. Some are still learning their 'ABCs' and are too short to even queue for thrill rides, while others are starting to think about high school. However, age is not a deterrent for Gen Z. While they are still young, this generation is following in the footsteps of tech-savvy Generation Y.

Gen Z are digital natives. As the children of Generation X, they are growing up in homes where a mobile phone isn't a novel concept — nor is it simply used for making phone calls. Their older siblings (or their parents) have taught them how to surf the web — and they use it to contact friends and to join online gaming networks. Gen Z is very familiar with Google, YouTube and other sites, such as the Cartoon Network website. Almost all of them have a computer at home, and they spend much more time online than children of previous generations. On a family holiday, Gen Z may be busy playing electronic games while their parents try to relax, and they aren't likely to be fazed by spending much of their time staring at a screen.

Despite having a selection of different mod-cons to choose from, Gen Z is still likely to watch plenty of television. The variety and scope offered by children's programming on cable networks, such as Foxtel, has led to the black box winning a special place in the hearts and minds of this generation. Channels such as Nickelodeon, Nickelodeon Junior, Kidzone, Disney and the Cartoon Network are proven Gen Z favourites. In a win for marketers, research suggests that this generation is receptive to television advertising. Additionally, Gen Z is less likely than older generations to multitask while watching the box. These factors make this cohort particularly appealing from a marketer's perspective.

With no cash flow to speak of, Gen Z has to defer to parents' wishes when it comes to making purchasing decisions. However, demographic and social trends are working in favour of Gen Z having greater purchasing power. The nuclear family of days gone by is being replaced by single-working-mother families, or families in which both parents are working to try to pay the bills. With increasingly absent parents, Gen Z has plenty of time to absorb marketing messages — and they are growing up fast. The same financial pressures that are leading to many parents having to return to work full-time can create added stress on the family. In a form of appeasement, Gen X is increasingly willing to swipe their credit cards at the request of their sweet, but sophisticated, offspring.[2]

## Question

What are the distinctive features of Gen Z and why are these important to marketers?

# INTRODUCTION

In chapter 1, we defined marketing and introduced the concept that those organisations that adopt a market orientation tend to be more successful than organisations that do not. In chapter 2, we looked at the marketing environment and how organisations can analyse it. Chapter 3 involved a more in-depth examination of how organisations go about understanding the environment, including the individuals and groups within it. By now we understand something about marketing, the marketing environment, and the individuals and organisations that make up the marketplace. This begs the question, 'How do we formulate a marketing mix to best serve our potential customers?' Clearly, we need to know the reasons behind the decisions consumers make — the what, why, how, when and where of their behaviours. This is the focus of our study of consumer behaviour.

Consider Gen Z, discussed on the previous page. Gen Z and the opportunities and challenges they present to modern marketers is just another instance of the social, economic and demographic changes that have swept across modern societies in recent years. For individual firms, such changes may have a positive, negative or neutral effect. The challenge to the marketer is to understand such changes, and how they might affect the firm's established business model — the products that it creates, how it communicates with the market, and the distribution channels through which buyers will access the product. The modern marketing concept suggests that the customer should be at the heart of the business. Consequently, understanding customers and their behaviour is at the heart of modern marketing.

In this chapter we will focus on *consumer* buying behaviour; not *business* buying behaviour. It is often assumed that consumer buying behaviour is different from, and perhaps less rational than, business (or industrial) buying behaviour. While this sweeping statement is difficult to test, it will be explored further in chapter 5 where we look at business buying behaviour in detail.

In this chapter, we will examine the influences on the buyer and how these influences might impact the buyer's choice of product category, brand, price, distribution outlet and their response to advertising messages. Taken together, the buyer's decision processes, their choices and how they manifest themselves in actual behaviours are known as consumer behaviour, the core topic of this chapter. The chapter explores a range of models of buyer behaviour, based on varying levels of consumer involvement.

## WHAT IS CONSUMER BEHAVIOUR?

To formulate a marketing mix that best serves our potential customers, we need to know the reasons behind the decisions consumers make. **Consumer behaviour** is the term used to describe the analysis of the behaviour of individuals and households who buy goods and services for personal consumption. As mentioned earlier, it is the what, why, how, when and where of consumers' behaviours.

Recall that the marketing mix refers to all the elements of the offering that the organisations makes to potential customers. An understanding of consumer behaviour informs every decision made about the marketing mix, including:
- what product attributes will appeal to customers
- how much value a product has for consumers and hence how much they will be willing to pay for it
- the likely response to various promotional options
- where the consumer is likely to want to purchase the offering
- what the consumer expects from dealing with the organisation.

 **Learning objective 1** explain why marketers require a thorough understanding of consumer behaviour and its major influences

**consumer behaviour** The analysis of the behaviour of individuals and households who buy goods and services for personal consumption.

Generally speaking, consumers purchase products to satisfy their needs and wants. These needs and wants vary in nature and the ways that consumers go about satisfying them varies as well. We can identify a range of consumer decision-making behaviour along a continuum from habitual decision-making behaviours at one end to extended decision-making behaviours at the other. For example, few consumers devote much time to choosing their next tube of toothpaste, but most consumers spend a lot of time deciding on a destination and itinerary for an overseas holiday. The ways in which consumers recognise their needs and wants, find out about how to satisfy them, choose among the options, and think and feel about their decision are subject to numerous influences.

## Influences on consumer behaviour

The range of factors that may influence a consumer is virtually limitless and studying them systematically is a mammoth task. The key to this task is to develop an awareness and sensitivity to the issues that may influence an organisation's target buyers. These influences may be:

- specific to a situation in which the consumer finds themself
- related to group (social or cultural) factors
- unique to the individual.

These broad categories of influences and some of the contributing factors are summarised in figure 4.1 and discussed in detail throughout this chapter.

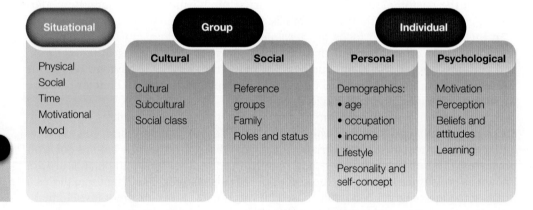

**FIGURE 4.1**

Factors influencing consumer behaviour

**situational influences**
The circumstances a consumer finds themself in when making purchasing decisions.

**Situational influences** on consumer behaviour are perhaps the easiest to understand. They are simply the circumstances consumers find themselves in when they are making purchasing decisions. Some circumstances prompt purchasing decisions; for example, a person who finds themself with a headache will often respond by purchasing Nurofen, Panadol or Herron Paracetamol. Situational influences can also prompt people to decide not to make a purchase; for example, a couple who decide at the last minute to go to their favourite restaurant for a romantic, candle-lit dinner may change their minds if they see that part of the dining area is being renovated.

The principal situational influences may be classified as:

- *physical* — the characteristics of the location in which the purchase decision is made (e.g. fashion retailers should install flattering lighting in the fitting rooms)
- *social* — the interactions with others at the time the purchase decision is made (e.g. asking your partner how you look in the pair of jeans you are trying on); not to be confused with social influences on consumer behaviour, discussed later in this chapter

- *time* — the time available for a purchase decision (e.g. a person who has left all of their Christmas shopping until Christmas Eve may not have the time to contemplate many options)
- *motivational* — the reasons for the purchase (e.g. a person choosing a book to give as a birthday present will make different decisions based on different rationales than a person choosing a book for themself)
- *mood* — the mood of a person at the time of the purchase decision (e.g. a person in a tired or emotional state may make a more impulsive decision).

In the following sections, we will turn our attention to the group and individual factors that influence consumption decisions.

# Tween celebrities Spotlight

They are too young for dating, but too old for toys. Such is the predicament of the tween market; a cohort comprising children aged six to 13 years of age.[3] Tweens are eager to develop a strong self image, and are happy to embrace behaviours that might be more typically expected of teenagers. As school students, tweens have a lot of time on their hands. When they don't have homework to do, tweens are busy watching television, seeing movies with friends, chatting online or listening to music. Because they are still developing their own self identities, tweens are receptive to the messages of marketers.

Several actors, singers and performers have focused on 'cashing in' on the tween market. Teenager Miley Cyrus rose to fame after playing the character of Miley Stewart/Hannah Montana on *Hannah Montana*, a show on the Disney Channel. With countless kids' and teen choice awards to her credit, Cyrus has established herself as a leading tween celebrity. In a recent year, she sold four million albums, generated US$86 million at the box office and secured a spot in *Forbes*' top 30 celebrities. For the same year, Cyrus recorded earnings of $25 million — an effort that wasn't hurt by her promoting everything from lunch boxes to sleeping bags to her devoted fan base.

Canadian singer Justin Bieber, a baby-faced teenager who rose to fame after his mother posted clips of him performing on YouTube, also has a huge tween following. Bieber-branded merchandise ranging from heart key rings to rubber bracelets, teddy bears, fake tattoos and collectable cards is available online. On his first major visit to Australia, Bieber created headlines when police cancelled his only performance because of safety concerns. Thousands of fans — most of whom were tween- and teen-aged girls — camped out at Circular Quay, Sydney, ahead of the event, and some fainted, while others were trampled on, before the show had begun. Presenter Grant Denyer said that even though *Sunrise*, the program that was hosting the concert, had hired the 'professionals who look after U2, Coldplay [and] Pink — the big acts' as a security force, it hadn't been enough to quell the mayhem. 'Even they weren't equipped and couldn't handle the Bieber fever', he said. The fact that a lot of the girls were not supervised was a factor that was also taken into consideration by police.

Tweens are reliant on pester power as a means of buying (or being given) what they want. Yet, with parents who are often cashed-up (thanks to many Gen X parents juggling careers with a family life), a willingness to 'pester' for what they want and a desire to fit in, tweens represent an important consumer segment.[4]

---

### Questions
1. Refer to figure 4.1 and outline the potential influences on consumer behaviour in the tween market.
2. What are the attractions and risks for marketers in responding to the emergence of this segment?

## Concepts and applications check

**Learning objective 1** explain why marketers require a thorough understanding of consumer behaviour and its major influences

**1.1** In your own words, define consumer behaviour.

**1.2** Recall four purchases you have made in the past month. Try to include goods and services in your list and, ideally, choose different types of product (e.g. having a haircut, buying petrol or some clothes, subscribing to a magazine). Add to your list the biggest purchase you have ever made. Describe how you made the decision to purchase each product. (Be specific — for example, you may have purchased new clothes because you had been invited to a party, but how did you actually make the decision about the clothes you ended up buying?)

**1.3** Ask a friend about what they have bought in the past week. Take some time to try to work out the reasons behind their purchases. Now ask them their reasons. How accurate were your assumptions?

**1.4** Describe an example of how each of the five situational influences on consumer behaviour has affected a purchase decision you have made.

# GROUP FACTORS

**Learning objective 2** understand the major group factors that influence consumer behaviour

People's purchasing decisions are profoundly affected by group factors. Group influences comprise social factors (the influence of other people) and cultural factors (the influence of the values, beliefs and customs of the person's community).

## Cultural factors

Cultural factors are those influences on behaviours that operate at the level of the whole society or of major groups within society. In studying cultural factors, we seek to understand how large social groups — and hence the individual members within them — behave. From a marketing perspective, this level of analysis corresponds with that of the mass market, in which the marketer is concerned with the behaviour of markets as a whole. The study of human behaviour at the cultural level has traditionally been the focus of sociology and anthropology, and a number of the key concepts used by marketers and behavioural researchers were originally discovered and studied by sociologists and anthropologists. Concepts such as social class are of interest to marketers where they can be demonstrated to explain or reliably predict buyer or consumer behaviour.

### Culture

**culture** The system of knowledge, beliefs, values, rituals and artefacts by which a society or other large group defines itself.

The broadest group influence on behaviour is arguably that of culture, although a precise definition of what constitutes 'culture' is perhaps debatable. For our purposes, we shall define **culture** as the system of knowledge, beliefs, values, rituals and artefacts by which a society or other large group defines itself. Clearly, from this definition, culture is multidimensional and includes both tangible and intangible elements:
- tangible elements include housing, clothing, food and artworks
- intangible elements include laws, beliefs, customs, education and institutions.

It is also important to recognise that culture operates at both the immediate experiential level — through such things as our tastes in food, music and entertainment — and at a deeper, and arguably more influential, level — through cultural values. While it is easy to appreciate the visible, tangible aspects of culture (such as products), this may lead to the more profound, influential and intangible aspects of culture being overlooked.

It has been popular over the past 20 years to argue that a global culture is emerging as a result of modern information and communications technology, as well as the influence of modern marketing, particularly through the creation of global brands. It must be recognised, however, that core cultural values are much more resistant to change than some would have us believe. Consumers the world over may wear similar clothes with familiar brands, drive the same cars and buy the same consumer electronics products, and want to live in similar, modern housing — however, at the level of core cultural values, they may differ markedly. Differences in national cultures have been measured by a number of researchers. Hofstede found that national cultures could be distinguished by variations across four dimensions that he described as follows:[5]

- **power distance** — the degree of inequality among people that is acceptable within a culture. Western societies tend to score low on 'power distance', reflecting their relatively egalitarian cultures, whereas Asian societies score high in 'power distance', reflecting the greater extent of social inequality and the traditions that maintain this.
- **uncertainty avoidance** — the extent to which people in a culture feel threatened by uncertainty and rely on mechanisms to reduce it.
- **individualism** — the extent to which people focus on their own goals over those of the group. Western societies are generally 'individualistic', whereas Asian societies are more 'collectivist'.
- **masculinity** — the extent to which traditionally masculine values (e.g. assertiveness, status and success) are valued over traditionally feminine values (e.g. solidarity, quality of life). Australia, New Zealand and the United Kingdom are examples of more 'masculine' cultures, while the Scandinavian countries and Thailand are examples of more 'feminine' (caring and nurturing) societies.

Follow-up research in Asia identified a fifth dimension:[6]

- **long-term orientation** — the extent to which a pragmatic, long-term orientation is valued over a short-term focus.

Figure 4.2 (overleaf) plots various countries' cultures on each dimension.[7]

Marketers must be sensitive to cultural differences among consumers and in workplaces when they seek to market their products overseas. They must not assume that consumers in foreign countries perceive their products and communication messages in the same way as they are seen in their home markets.

## Subcultures

Just as we can identify a national culture that exists across a society as a whole, so too we can identify distinctive subcultures that display differences from the dominant national culture along some of the key dimensions. A **subculture** is a group of individuals who differ on *some* dimensions from the culture in which they are immersed. Subcultures are usually identified based on differences in key demographic characteristics such as age, ethnicity, geographic location or religious affiliation. In this context, Australia displays a high level of **multiculturalism**, which reflects the ethnic, religious and geographic diversity of a high proportion of its resident population. Subcultures are important to marketers when their shopping and purchasing behaviour are significantly different from the remainder of the population, and they represent a distinct and commercially significant marketing opportunity. For example, Gen Z and their older siblings, Gen Y, represent a major marketing opportunity for telecommunications, information technology, entertainment, hospitality and fashion marketers. Similarly, Australia is famous worldwide for its beach and surf culture, which has spawned highly successful global surf brands such as Billabong and Rip Curl.

**power distance** The degree of inequality among people that is acceptable within a culture.

**uncertainty avoidance** The extent to which people in a culture feel threatened by uncertainty and rely on mechanisms to reduce it.

**individualism** The extent to which people focus on their own goals over those of the group.

**masculinity** The extent to which traditionally masculine values are valued over traditionally feminine values within a culture in Hofstede's cultural dimensions.

**long-term orientation** The extent to which a pragmatic, long-term orientation is valued over a short-term focus.

**subculture** A group of individuals who share common attitudes, values and behaviours that distinguish them from the broader culture in which they are immersed.

**multiculturalism** The existence of diverse cultures within a society.

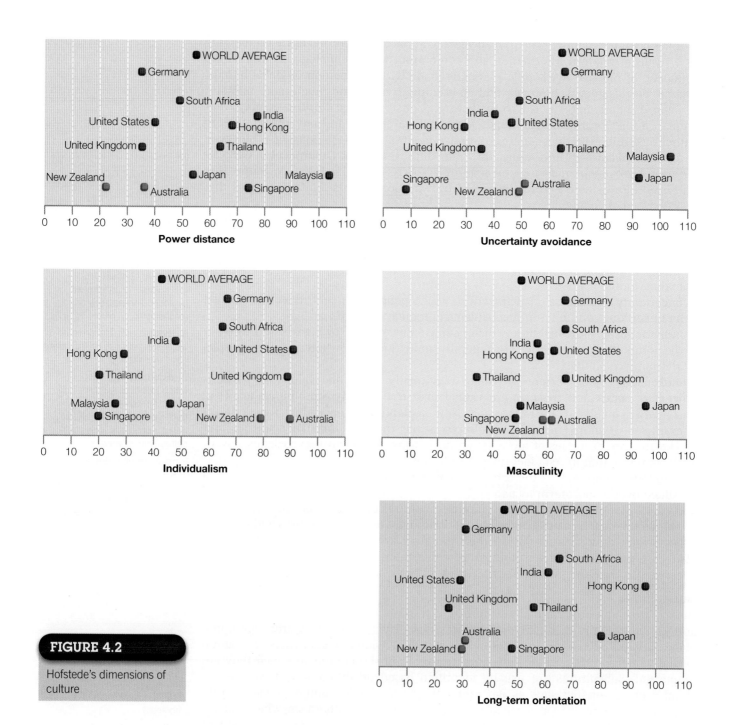

**FIGURE 4.2**

Hofstede's dimensions of culture

Within subcultures, members share common attitudes, values and behaviours that distinguish them from the broader culture. Relative to other subcultures, members may, for example, display clear preferences for specific clothing, entertainment and food. At the same time, it is worth remembering that subcultures are themselves subject to frequent change in response to changes in the broader society and in their internal membership. Nevertheless, subcultures can be very important to marketers, as they represent large potential market segments, often with distinctive preferences and behaviours and strong group loyalty. Astute marketers will always be on the lookout for changes in subcultures, or the emergence of new subcultures, which can create opportunities for new products and threats to existing product categories.

## Social class

Most societies exhibit a social hierarchy, organised into social classes. A **social class** comprises individuals of similar social rank within the hierarchy. Social ranking forms the basis of social prestige and respect. In Australia and New Zealand, the social class system is regarded as 'open' because individuals are able to move from one class to another relatively easily. In some other countries, perhaps most notably India, the system is relatively closed and it is difficult, if not impossible, for individuals to move to another social class. In Australia and New Zealand, an individual's social class is defined by values and lifestyles, but often rests on indicators such as income, occupation and education. In India, social class is based on tradition, history and cultural heritage. While discrimination on the basis of social class has been made illegal in India, it continues to have a pervasive influence, particularly outside the major cities.

In Australia and New Zealand, some aspects of consumer behaviour can be attributed to social class, but others are better attributed to specific underlying indicators of social class. For example, marketers would often be better served paying attention to the economic indicators of purchasing power such as income and perhaps occupation. For products such as entertainment, travel and cars, income is most important; whereas for products such as fashion, restaurants and real estate, occupation may be a more important determinant of purchasing behaviour.

For this reason, socioeconomic status can often be a useful concept for marketers studying consumer behaviour, where the primary focus is on 'purchasing power'. For example, marketers of high fashion, consumer durables, prestige products and many financial services will be more concerned with the ability of the target market to purchase. In this sense, it is income that is the primary concern, and not the source of income, which is implied in the social class construct. Conversely, social marketers often need to understand the behaviour of people at lower levels of socioeconomic status as this has been identified as a reliable predictor of individuals or groups who engage in high-risk social behaviours such as crime, violence, alcoholism, drug abuse and gambling.[8] Social marketers in the government and not-for-profit sectors will often use low socioeconomic status as a 'marker' and will target those groups in their service delivery and mass communication campaigns.

## Social factors

Studying consumer behaviour at the social level is concerned with developing an understanding of the behaviour of the individual within the group. This is the traditional domain of 'social psychology' and is focused on understanding how the group influences the behaviour of its individual members, typically through group pressures on the individual to conform with group norms. Such influences are known as social factors.

### Reference groups

A **reference group** is any group to which an individual looks for guidance as to what are appropriate values, attitudes or behaviours. The influence of reference groups is particularly strong when the individual lacks previous experience as a guide for behaviour, and where that behaviour carries a level of social risk. In a marketing context, if a consumer is contemplating purchasing a product for the first time, and where that product is socially conspicuous (e.g. clothing), the individual will often

**social class** A group comprising individuals of similar rank within the social hierarchy.

**reference group** Any group to which an individual looks for guidance.

**membership reference groups** Groups to which the individual belongs.

**aspirational reference groups** Groups to which the individual would like to belong.

**dissociative reference groups** Groups with which the individual does not wish to be associated or which the individual may wish to leave.

Several professional skateboarders and surfers promote Globe footwear. In addition to using opinion leaders to promote the brand, the company regularly sponsors surfing and skating contests as part of its marketing efforts to appeal to its target market.

look to the reference group to suggest and endorse the appropriate choice. Reference groups can be large or small, and an individual may be a member of several reference groups, depending upon the circumstances and the behaviours in question. For example, an individual may look to family, work or professional groups, sporting clubs, religious groups or civic organisations depending upon the particular behaviour or product category.

Three major types of reference groups have been identified:

- **membership reference groups** — groups to which the individual belongs. Individuals identify strongly with membership reference groups and take on the values, attitudes and behaviours that define members of the group. For example, an individual who considers themself an 'Emo' would adopt the characteristic appearance, clothing, attitudes and music of that group.
- **aspirational reference groups** — groups of which the individual would wish to be considered a member. The individual is likely to mimic the values, attitudes and behaviours of the aspirational group. Such groups can therefore become important role models and marketers may seek to have their products adopted by members of aspirational groups, especially where the product is new and socially conspicuous, such as fashion, information technology or drinks.
- **dissociative reference groups** — groups with which an individual does not wish to be associated or which the individual may wish to leave. An individual may not wish to be seen or to be known as a 'bogan' and so may choose to buy clothing, food and beverages which might set the individual apart.

A reference group can therefore help the individual in their purchase behaviour through suggesting information sources, the range of product alternatives and appropriate ways of evaluating and choosing between alternative products. For example, Globe footwear has become highly accepted among the surfing and skateboard community, reinforced by Globe's sponsorship of surfing and skateboard contests. Understanding the identity, dynamics, attitudes and purchase behaviour of such reference groups is a challenging task for market researchers since the groups are frequently difficult to identify; their group norms are often arcane; and their dynamics are constantly changing.

The extent to which a reference group influences purchase behaviour depends, in part, on the visibility or conspicuousness of the product and the familiarity of the purchase category. The purchase of highly visible products such as clothing, cars, information technology and beverages is often strongly influenced by reference groups. Reference groups can affect whether or not a person chooses to buy a product at all, to buy a particular product within a product category, or to buy a particular brand. For example, in certain reference groups, it is important both that you are buying a computer, *and* which brand of computer. At the same time, it is not important that you are buying a pair of shoes, but rather which brand of shoes you will buy. Equally, it may be important to some groups that you are air-conditioning your home, although the brand of air-conditioning may be unimportant.

### Opinion leaders

In many reference groups, some individuals have the role of opinion leader. These individuals will be consulted, formally or informally, as being reliable sources of information about the values, attitudes and behaviours of the group. An

**opinion leader** is a reference group member who provides relevant and influential advice about a specific topic of interest to group members. Opinion leaders are regarded by other group members as experts in a particular field or topic, such as politics, music, sport or community values. In a marketing context, opinion leaders often influence group members in relation to appropriate purchases of such products as technology, cars, houses, holidays, education, fashion, food and beverages. Marketers will often attempt to identify opinion leaders and to influence them in their product attitudes and purchase behaviour. For example, Microsoft might seek to identify elite computer gamers whose opinions on games and game consoles might be sought by other members of their reference group at school. At the same time, the concept of opinion leadership is often difficult to work with in practice because opinion leadership is typically situation- and product-specific. Within the same reference group, members may choose to consult different individuals for opinions on cars, information technology, sport or politics. An opinion leader, however, is likely to be of greatest influence in product categories where individuals are highly involved, but in which they lack knowledge, although they share the opinion leader's values and attitudes.

For example, beyond their undoubted altruistic credentials, community service clubs such as Rotary, Lions and Zonta are popular with members because of the opportunities they provide to network with local professionals, experts and dignitaries. Thus, most members of such groups would regard themselves as experts in their fields. They would expect to give and receive valued opinions and business contacts to and from other members, in professional fields such as real estate and property development, local government affairs, politics, information technology, law, economics, architecture and education, and in social pursuits such as golf, sailing and fine dining. Local professional service organisations might, therefore, target these organisations as a valuable source of clients and service providers. Similarly, medical practitioners will seek out their professional colleagues at regular meetings, and especially at annual conferences of various professional societies. Pharmaceutical companies seek to identify the opinion leaders in such groups by sponsoring research or conference sessions of recognised authorities in particular medical fields — such as cardiology, oncology and gastroenterology.

New products take time to develop popularity in the market. The way in which innovations are adopted can be described by the theory of diffusion of innovations.[9] The theory suggests that the influence of social groups on the decisions made by individuals determines the way in which new products and ideas are adopted. Innovations are introduced and used by 'innovators', who make up only 2.5 per cent of the total population. They do not generally influence the adoption of innovations by the rest of society. Rather, consumers known as 'early adopters', who represent about 13.5 per cent of the population, tend to drive widespread adoption. The early adopters group includes the opinion leaders. Adoption by the opinion leaders then drives adoption by the 'early majority', who adopt the innovation earlier than average. The 'late majority' adopts the innovation later than average, reflecting their sceptical nature. The last group to adopt is known as the 'laggards', who are driven by tradition.

The process is driven by social networks and communications. Because the role of the opinion leader is so important, the model suggests the existence of a *two-step flow of communication*: information can be directed to and focused on the opinion leader who, after adopting the innovation, will communicate the information to the broader population. From a marketing communications perspective, this model implies that it is not necessary to direct a marketing message to the entire population; rather it is more effective to address communication directly to the

**opinion leader** A reference group member who provides relevant and influential advice about a specific topic of interest to group members.

opinion leader in the hope that the idea will spread from them to the wider target population. The theory of diffusion of innovations is examined in more detail in chapter 7.

### Family

For most people, the social group with the most influence over their behaviour is the family. In particular, from a marketing perspective, the direct family — parents and siblings — teach the individual appropriate behaviours relating to purchasing and consuming products. This process starts when children are very young.

The stage of the family in the family life cycle is also an important influence on consumption behaviour. The **family life cycle** describes the stages through which most families pass. It is summarised in table 4.1. Of course, not all families fit the five stages in the family life cycle model, and the incidence of divorce and remarriage, single parents, and same-sex households are all significant and increasingly common alternative family arrangements. In this sense, it is perhaps misleading and dangerous to stereotype; nevertheless, marketers should be aware of traditional family patterns, and the significant alternative family groups.

**family life cycle** A series of characteristic stages through which most families pass.

**TABLE 4.1** The family life cycle

| Stage | | Description | Example of marketing consequences |
| --- | --- | --- | --- |
| Stage 1 | Young singles | Single person living apart from parents | Important target market for home furnishings, cars and entertainment products |
| Stage 2 | Young marrieds | Young married couple without children | Target market for new home construction, functional furniture and whitegoods |
| Stage 3 | Parenthood | A married couple with children at home | Heavy consumers of household products such as detergents, food and pharmaceuticals |
| Stage 4 | Post-parenthood | An old married couple with no children at home | Important buyers of luxury goods, packaged tours, investment products and health care products |
| Stage 5 | Dissolution | A single surviving spouse | Buyers with a focus on health, physical security and continuing financial independence. |

A further important way in which the family influences consumer behaviour is through the family decision-making roles and the influence of family members in decision making. While family roles are changing, family consumption decisions can still largely be categorised into four types:

- *autonomic decisions.* Most household products are typically purchased by either the husband or wife, including products such as the husband's clothing, furniture, cosmetics, pharmaceuticals, household appliances, cars and holidays.
- *wife-dominant decisions.* Although the role of women has changed significantly in the past two decades, women still make the majority of household purchasing decisions related to food, health care, laundry and bathroom products, children's clothing and kitchen products.
- *husband-dominant decisions.* A small range of products are traditionally purchased by men, including hardware and garage products, such as lawnmowers (although women represent the fastest growing market for many hardware products — typically those associated with home decoration, renovation and gardening).
- *syncratic decisions.* Some products are purchased by husband and wife acting jointly. Typically such decisions would be the major household purchasing decisions, such as purchasing a home and mortgage, a holiday, an entertainment product, childrens' education or another significant investment.

Note that 'wife-dominant' and 'husband-dominant' are traditional terms. The category refers to the adult female and male decision makers respectively.

Beyond these four decision patterns, different family members may play different roles in household purchase decision making, depending upon the nature of the product and the role expertise of individual family members. For example, the decision to purchase a broadband internet contract may be initiated by the children. The information search may be conducted by the older siblings, and the evaluation of alternatives may involve the entire family, while the actual purchase decision may be made by the father or mother.

Sometimes the role of children in purchasing decisions is a lot less civilised. The phenomenon of **pester power** can be a powerful influence on family consumption decisions. Pester power is the term used to describe children's influence over their parents' purchasing decisions. About one-quarter of parents take their children with them when they shop, so it is very common for children to be present when purchasing decisions are being made. The most common purchases made in response to pester power are fairly small (e.g. chips, biscuits and a preferred brand of toothpaste), but children can also influence or indeed initiate major purchases as well, such as gaming consoles, home swimming pools and holidays.

For marketers, children — even if they are not making the purchase — are a substantial target market. They are the focus of many advertising campaigns. The most successful advertisements targeted at children also include messages that appeal to parents. While the expression 'pester power' conjures images of children annoying their parents into giving in over a purchase, the term is widely used to include all child influence over purchasing.[10]

The important conclusion here is that a large proportion of household purchase decisions are not made solely by an individual. In these circumstances the dynamics of household decision making can be quite complex and vary according to the product category.

**pester power** The influence of children on their parents' purchasing decisions.

Children can have a powerful influence over their parents' purchasing decisions. What are the chances that this young girl's parents will give in to her request to buy a stuffed toy?

### Roles and status

Each individual in a society plays a number of roles, each of which entails a complex set of expectations — parent, child, neighbour, employee, employer, customer, friend, and so on. We understand that as part of our roles we are expected to engage in certain behaviours and actions. These roles may have a formal, even legal, definition, such as the role of parents or of officeholders in social or volunteer organisations. In other groups, individuals' roles may be less formally defined but may still be equally influential in the purchase decision. Such roles will frequently be based on perceived expertise, where the role is that of opinion leader (discussed earlier in the chapter). Again, this perception of expertise may be specific to a narrow product category, such as computers, music, food, wine, fashion or politics. Within the social group an individual may occupy multiple roles and roles may be shared among members of the group. Because such roles are difficult to generalise, it is equally difficult for marketers to identify in advance how the group will make its decisions, and who in the group would be most influential.

The influence of individuals within the decision-making social group will frequently be based on the perceived status of the individual, which reflects the position occupied by an individual in a notional hierarchy of group members. Such status can be based on a range of criteria, including formal role, age, length of group membership, technical competence, access to resources or social popularity. Under such circumstances, the usual challenges for the marketer are to identify group leaders and to seek to influence their behaviours, although the criteria for group leadership and the identity of group leaders remain as challenges. The combination of roles and status typically shape the *expectations* of group members, which exert an important influence on the buyer's final decision.

## Spotlight  Online social networks

The world of online social networking has grown exponentially in recent years, with advances in technology enabling sites such as LinkedIn, Facebook and Twitter to easily bring large numbers of like-minded people together as an identifiable group. In the online context, a social network is a community of people who share acquaintances, interests or activities and who want to expand their contacts of people with similar shared interests. These sites provide various ways for users to interact, including email and instant messaging. Social networking services include categorised directories (e.g. former school or university classmates), self-description pages to stay in touch with friends and recommender systems linked to trusted opinion leaders.

From the perspective of marketers, the appeal of social networking sites is that they facilitate the forming of readily identifiable groups of people who are likely to regularly communicate and to behave similarly. Individuals within these online social network groups also have the potential to influence the behaviour of others within the group. These days, an individual may be a member of several different social networks on both personal and professional levels. Many of the online social networks to which a person belongs are likely to reflect the 'offline' groups of people to which individuals feel they belong, or aspire to belong.

The majority of social networks have been created by individuals, but organisations are increasingly turning their attention to creating their own online social networks, in an attempt to harness their potential. For example, within months of launching its Facebook site, Tourism New Zealand had in excess of 100 000 members. Such a database provides a wealth of opportunities for an organisation, including the ability to directly communicate promotional campaigns with potential customers, or to conduct market research via cost-effective online focus groups.[11]

### Question

Think of an online social network to which you belong (or could belong to in the future). Identify how your membership of this group could potentially influence your own behaviour as a consumer.

## Concepts and applications check

**Learning objective 2** understand the major group factors that influence consumer behaviour

2.1 'In Australia and New Zealand, some aspects of consumer behaviour can be attributed to social class, but others are better attributed to specific underlying indicators of social class.' Discuss.

2.2 What are the three types of reference groups? For each, provide two examples of groups relevant to you.

2.3 Explain how opinion leaders influence group behaviours. Choose five products (ideally a mix of goods and services), and explain who you would consider an opinion leader in your decision to purchase each. Explain your choice.

2.4 Describe each of the five dimensions of culture according to Hofstede's model. Choose a product (a good or a service) and briefly explain the issues a marketer should address when marketing it in cultures at opposite extremes of the cultural dimensions.

2.5 Critique the four family decision-making types. Do they reflect your personal experiences?

2.6 Find an advertising campaign that is designed to invoke pester power. Analyse the campaign in terms of which elements are aimed at children and which elements are aimed at the purchaser (most likely a parent).

# INDIVIDUAL FACTORS

So far we have discussed how situational influences and group factors affect consumer behaviour. A third range of factors influence the consumer's behaviour and operate independently of social circumstances. These are known as individual factors and relate to personal and psychological characteristics. These factors can be measured for an individual and are presumed to differ significantly between individuals — in large part, they explain the individual's purchase process and final product choice.

**Learning objective 3**
analyse the major individual factors that influence consumer behaviour

## Personal characteristics

At the level of individual buyer or consumer, we can identify a range of personal characteristics that have been shown to exert a significant influence on consumers' choice processes and ultimate purchase decisions. These personal characteristics, in some ways, constitute an individual's *identity* and, in this sense, are objective and relatively stable. This stability is attractive to marketers in that these characteristics are relatively easy to observe and measure. They can therefore form the basis of ongoing marketing campaigns.

### Demographics

**Demographic factors** describe the general make-up of the population in terms of existing objective, measurable characteristics that are either assumed or demonstrated to be related to the purchase or consumption of products. In a strict sense, demographic characteristics do not *cause* shopping or choice behaviour, but rather they vary systematically and predictably with the observed behaviour. This, combined with their ready accessibility from organisations such as the Australian Bureau of Statistics and Statistics New Zealand, has made them reliable predictors of shopping behaviour. They are commonly used in the description and explanation of consumer behaviour.

**demographic factors** The vital and social characteristics of populations, such as age, education and income.

As a rule, demographic factors should always be used as part of the explanation for consumer behaviour. Their use enables marketers and researchers to establish the relationship between the causal explanation for behaviour and the likely observable distribution of that behaviour. For example, there is a strong, measurable relationship between the consumption of alcohol and age. While age alone does not explain the consumption of alcohol, a knowledge of age distribution of the population enables marketers to understand the likely incidence and geographic distribution of alcohol consumption, on the one hand, and of age-related alcohol abuse such as binge drinking, on the other. Aimed with this knowledge, marketers of alcoholic beverages can tailor their marketing efforts accordingly. Government bodies and health advocacy groups can also craft social marketing campaigns to best target those groups and individuals most likely to be at risk of alcohol misuse.

Similarly, occupation is a strong predictor of computer, mobile phone and internet usage. Marketers of these products seek to identify variations in occupational distribution across the population and across specific geographic markets. Likewise, in financial services markets, income is a leading indicator of customers' needs for sophisticated financial products such as investment funds, mortgage and investment loans, wealth management, and so on. Financial service organisations such as AMP find it profitable to target so-called 'high net worth individuals' who are always looking for better financial return for their investments, and lower costs and charges on their loans. While income does not strictly explain the demand for financial services products, it is a very reliable 'surrogate' or 'proxy' indicator of likely customer demand. Conversely, low income levels are a reliable indicator of demand for charity, emergency loans and financial counselling.

### Lifestyle

A person's lifestyle is defined by how they spend their time and how they interact with others. There may be a significant difference between an individual's *actual* lifestyle and their *preferred* lifestyle. For many of us, our *actual* lifestyle (which might involve work, study, shopping for groceries and the occasional party) is much more predictable and staid than our *preferred* lifestyle (which might involve glamour, excitement, travel and luxury yachts). Consumers regularly purchase products that play a role in their lifestyle. They also often purchase products to enhance or express their preferred lifestyle. Such products are *aspirational* in nature. Consumers often choose to express their preferred lifestyle through such products as fashion, motor vehicles, holidays, recreational equipment and activities, and entertainment. Marketers of lifestyle-oriented products should therefore devote considerable effort to understanding the preferred lifestyle of their target customers and how those lifestyles might be changing.

Consumers regularly make purchases that are aspirational and which reflect a preferred lifestyle. This girl's willingness to purchase expensive clothing and footwear may reflect a desire for glamour.

Lifestyle is partly a choice. For example, some people choose to spend their weekends surfing and their weekdays studying; others choose to work during the week and spend the weekend pursuing some creative hobby; and others choose to be politically active in their communities. Lifestyle is, however, also influenced by personality and demographic characteristics such as age, income and education. Lifestyle is typically measured through a lengthy series of questions, the outcome of which is frequently used in *psychographic* market segmentation (see chapter 6). Table 4.2 presents a psychographic market segmentation scheme from the Nielsen Company.[12]

### Personality

Personality is perhaps the most distinctive characteristic that defines an individual's behaviour, yet it is difficult to measure reliably. While it is relatively easy to describe someone's personality (with words such as 'positive', 'intense' or 'competitive'), attempts by researchers to establish a reliable relationship between personality and behaviour have met with limited success. We can define personality as the set of unique psychological characteristics and behavioural tendencies that characterise an individual. It is formed through a complex combination of genetics and experiences. While personality is relatively consistent and enduring, it does change throughout life in response to social and environmental influences and personal experiences.

**TABLE 4.2** PALS (Personal Aspiration Lifestyle Segments) psychographic data

**Balance seekers**

Representing 19 per cent of the population, they actively aspire to a balanced lifestyle, and are more likely to be middle-aged, with those in the workforce more likely to be found in managerial or professional roles.

- More likely to have a young family
- Lead healthy lifestyle
- Not too concerned about how others see them in terms of appearance
- Less attracted than most to new ideas and technology
- Only slightly motivated by success, but family very important — it's all about balance
- Medium to heavy viewers of commercial TV
- Medium to heavy listeners of commercial radio

**Health-conscious**

Representing 29 per cent of the population, their priorities are health and fitness. They avoid unhealthy foods and exercise regularly to maintain their fitness, although they are less likely to be concerned about their image. Definitely not early adopters of new technology.

- Heavily skewed to couples with no children
- All about healthy living, exercising and eating
- Least likely to try out new technology
- Less likely to be driven by success vs. other PAL segments
- Heavy commercial TV and pay-TV viewers
- Medium to heavy non-commercial TV viewers
- Light to medium use of the internet
- Print heavy (magazines/newspapers)

**Harmony seekers**

Representing 13 per cent of Australian consumers, these people are older; they have arrived and are now concerned about giving and sharing through community work. They are actively involved in hobbies and indulge in luxuries afforded by their achievements. They are not concerned about physical fitness or health, and are not quick to embrace new ideas or technology.

- Singles/couples, no children in the household
- Not particularly concerned about health
- Less likely to try to impress others
- Career and goals do not dominate their thinking
- Heavy viewers of commercial and non-commercial TV
- Heavy viewers of pay-TV
- Medium to heavy use of internet

**Individualistic**

Constituting 18 per cent of Australian consumers, these are 'me first' people who consider family a low priority. Life is really all about themselves; they are image and fashion conscious, heavily oriented to success and goal achievement. They are also big new technology, media and internet users.

- No children in the household; heavy skew towards singles
- Like to wear clothes noticed by others and be stylish
- Early adopters of new technology and new ideas
- Conscious about health
- Success and goal oriented
- Light commercial TV viewers
- Medium to heavy non-commercial TV viewers
- Heavy internet users
- Heavy cinema goers

**Fun seekers**

Representing 4 per cent of Australians, they are heavy consumers of commercial media and while responsible concerning family and financial security, they aspire to add more fun so as to improve their fairly structured lifestyles. Their escapist attitude makes them ideal candidates for holiday/entertainment and lifestyle improvement products and services.

- A sense of fun in their life is their main priority
- Skewed towards families with a heavy skew towards young families
- Like to look good and be fashionable
- Most likely to agree that technology/computers makes life easier; willing to try new products
- Medium commercial TV viewers
- Less likely to watch non-commercial TV
- Heavy listeners of commercial radio

**Success driven**

Representing 17 per cent of Australians, they consider their career a top priority, so success and visible signs of success are important to them. While families play a role in life, they are strongly oriented to personal goal achievement. They are early adopters of technology and new ideas and heavy consumers of media to stay in touch.

- Career is a top priority
- Very goal and success oriented
- Skewed towards families, especially older families
- Health is not on the forefront of their mind
- Very conscious regarding their image — strive always to look stylish
- Early adopters of technology and new ideas
- Light viewers of commercial and non-commercial TV
- Heavy internet users
- Heavy cinema goers

*Source:* The Nielsen Company

Marketers are interested in understanding those aspects of personality that are linked to an individual's purchasing behaviour. A number of measuring instruments exist to measure personality, but research has not adequately established consistent links between particular personality attributes and consumer behaviour. It is quite possible that the absence of proven links is more to do with the limitations of the research methods than with the absence of a link between personality and buying behaviour. Even without reliable scientific evidence, many marketers are convinced of the relationship between personality types and certain purchases and devote considerable resources to aiming marketing campaigns at particular personality types. For example, Lowes menswear's marketing campaigns are clearly aimed at the 'man's man' (or 'blokey bloke').

Often, as with lifestyle, individuals choose to purchase products as an expression of their personality. This is related to the individual's self-concept, which is a combination of how they see themselves and how they wish others to see them. Purchase decisions are both a cause and effect of self-concept. For some individuals, purchases related to self-concept are those that reflect things such as individual achievement and material success. Many would argue this is a driving factor behind the purchase of a Porsche sports car, besides the functional and other benefits the car provides. For other individuals, their self-concept may be tied to being socially and environmentally responsible and fashionable, prompting the purchase of a Vespa scooter, bed linen made from hemp, and canvas shoes. Self-concept, then, can be linked to most aspects of an individual's purchasing behaviour.

## Psychological characteristics

**Psychological characteristics** describe internal factors that shape the thinking, aspirations, expectations and behaviours of the individual. These characteristics are particular to the individual and independent of their situational and social circumstances.

### Motivation

The term **motivation** is used to describe the individual's internal drive to act to satisfy unfulfilled needs or achieve unmet goals. This internal force prompts behaviours that seek to move from an actual, current state to the desired state. Motivation is often made up of individual motives. A motive is specific to a particular drive, such as hunger. Behaviours are usually the result of a combination of motives.

While motivation is often specific to the individual and situation, some motives are consistent over time and across the population. For example, marketers can predict that consumers will be motivated by hunger at breakfast time and that breakfast will usually be within a range of a few hours for almost all of the population. Similarly, many people will feel a need for companionship and fun on Friday and Saturday nights and holidays in summer. Understanding motives presents an opportunity for marketers who wish to promote consumption of their products, and also to social marketers, who are interested in discouraging consumption; for example, the misuse of drugs, gambling or alcohol. The link between motivation and behaviour is direct, immediate and powerful. The challenge to marketers, however, is in being able to consistently identify the particular motives.

The most widely recognised theory of motivation is **Maslow's hierarchy of needs** which suggests that people seek to satisfy needs according to a hierarchy that places lower order needs before higher order needs. Only once lower order needs are met will an individual seek to satisfy higher level needs.[13] The hierarchy is shown in figure 4.3.

Lower order, physiological, needs are the most basic: food, water, shelter, clothing, sleep and sex. They are the fundamentals of survival. Marketers of fast food, drinks and condoms seek to capitalise on these needs. Once these needs are reasonably satisfied, then the need for physical and emotional safety and security will come to the

**psychological characteristics** Internal factors, independent of situational and social circumstances, that shape the thinking, aspirations, expectations and behaviours of the individual.

**motivation** An individual's internal drive to satisfy unfulfilled needs or achieve goals.

**Maslow's hierarchy of needs** A theory of motivation that suggests that people seek to satisfy needs according to a hierarchy that places lower order needs before higher order needs.

fore. Marketers of medical and property insurance are most commonly responding to these needs. In turn, once the individual feels safe and secure, social needs such as the desire for love, affection and belonging will be dominant. Marketers of holidays, internet dating sites, night clubs, entertainment, restaurants, champagne and perfume typically target these social needs, often by portraying that purchasing or patronising these products will bring popularity and social success. Social networking sites such as Twitter and Facebook also capitalise on individuals' social needs. Beyond social needs are the ego or esteem needs, which relate to self-esteem and the individual's need to be recognised and respected by others. Owning a prestige car, living in a ritzy suburb, holidaying in a luxurious resort, being a member of an exclusive club, or winning a recognised public award may all contribute to satisfying an individual's esteem needs. At the top of the hierarchy, self-actualisation needs refer to an individual's need for self-improvement, achievement and success. Individuals pursuing self-actualisation may choose to purchase services such as education, personal coaching, meditation and even yoga.

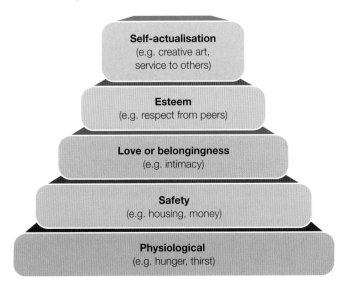

**FIGURE 4.3**

Motivation: Maslow's hierarchy of needs

Maslow's theory has been widely accepted, in part because of its logic and simplicity. It is particularly widely recognised and used to explain motivation in the workplace, and in understanding an individual's attitudes to their work and their employer. In marketing, the track record of Maslow's theory is perhaps less convincing. While the motives identified by Maslow are universal, it is the ordinal and hierarchical structure and logic of the model that are often criticised. The presumption that consumers will only pursue higher order needs when all their lower order needs are satisfied is clearly questionable. In practice, a consumer's behaviour, at any one time, is likely to be driven by a range of motives.

Motives are of immediate interest and importance to marketers, as they can explain the reasons for some key consumer behaviours, including:
• choosing to buy a particular product
• choosing to buy a particular brand
• being willing to pay a particular price
• preferring to shop through particular outlets.

Knowledge of these *patronage motives* is crucial to understanding and predicting consumer behaviour. For example, the marketers employed by a supermarket will seek to understand who from among their customers are motivated by location;

who are shopping for the lowest price; and who are motivated by convenience, the weekly shopping ritual or an enjoyable social experience.

## Perception

A widely held view in marketing is that 'perception is reality'. This recognises the central importance of perception in shaping a consumer's behaviour. It also acknowledges that there is an objective world of 'facts' and a subjective world of 'perceptions'. **Perception** is the psychological process that filters, organises and attributes meaning to external stimuli. Perception is particular to the individual, so, for example, a television commercial may be interpreted by viewers to mean something quite different to what the advertiser intended. Further, different viewers may perceive the commercial in different ways.

An individual is exposed to a potentially limitless array of stimuli via their senses — sight, hearing, touch, taste and smell. The first stage of the process of perception — filtering — enables the individual to deal with only those inputs that are relevant to their particular needs and circumstances. In this sense, perception is selective and produces:

- *selective exposure* — the tendency to actively seek out messages that are pleasant and agreeable and to avoid messages that are threatening or disagreeable. Consumers may, for example, actively shut out messages from political parties with which the individual disagrees.
- *selective attention* — the process by which an individual chooses to take in only those messages which are relevant to their needs. Some consumers will only be interested in particular brands; some only in price; some in appearance; and some in social acceptability. In these circumstances, messages that do not feature the particular brand, price, appearance or social success will be disregarded.
- *selective distortion* — an individual's tendency to perceive information which is inconsistent with existing beliefs or attitudes in such a way as to reduce the inconsistency. For example, an individual who idolises a sporting hero will seek to deny information which suggests the hero has been performing or behaving poorly.
- *selective retention* — the tendency to remember only that information which is consistent with other beliefs and which is relevant to an individual's needs. An individual will tend to remember information which supports prior beliefs and feelings and to forget information which is not consistent with these prior feelings. It is natural to 'only remember the good times' and marketers of 'heritage brands' such as Vegemite, Mortein, Heinz, and Johnnie Walker can capitalise on our selective retention of brand names.

The second stage in the process of perception involves organising new information and integrating it with existing knowledge. This process often involves connecting new information with existing memories via familiar expressions, sights and sounds. Advertisers often seek to capitalise on this process by leaving 'gaps' in their advertisements in a bid to have the audience connect the product on offer with positive information they already have in memory. Commercial slogans, such as Nike's 'Just do it', seek to link the brand with the context of the problem and the application of the product.

The ultimate outcome of the perceptual process is the assigning of meaning. In general, an individual will interpret new information in a way that is consistent with their expectations or with their existing knowledge or beliefs. Individuals strive for *cognitive consistency*, so messages that are unexpected or with which the individual disagrees are likely to be distorted or disregarded. An organisation that changes a familiar product, logo, package or taste does so at its peril, especially when the old product is highly recognised and regarded by loyal customers. Recently Kraft Foods launched Vegemite iSnack 2.0 after a campaign that

**perception** The psychological process that filters, organises and attributes meaning to external stimuli.

involved a public search for a new name.[14] To many, the initial suggestion of the campaign was that Kraft was launching a 'New Vegemite' and like Coca-Cola in the 1980s, the 'New Vegemite' would replace the iconic original recipe. This perception was false, as Kraft Foods never intended to modify the original Vegemite recipe. There was, however, a public backlash against Vegemite iSnack 2.0, with thousands of consumers complaining about the name on social networking websites such as Twitter (a website, Names That Are Better Than iSnack 2.0, was even launched). The furore, of course, created unprecedented publicity for, and interest in, the new product (and also renewed interest in the original product). When the new product was launched as Vegemite iSnack 2.0, the consumer interest, almost inevitably, resulted in a strong level of demand, as many consumers were driven by curiosity that was generated by the stage-managed publicity campaign. With 2.8 million jars sold between July and September 2009, the launch strategy clearly succeeded. (What is less clear is how many of the initially curious consumers were persuaded to repeat buy. Repeat purchase decisions were overwhelmingly driven by consumers' evaluation and approval, or disapproval, of the new taste.) In a response to the consumer backlash, Kraft Foods conducted online polling and a telephone survey that allowed the public to vote on an alternative name for the product. After tallying the votes of more than 30 000 Australians and New Zealanders, Kraft Foods announced that Vegemite iSnack 2.0 would be rebranded as Vegemite Cheesybite. This change generated even more publicity, and led to some consumers racing out to buy the remaining Vegemite iSnack 2.0 stock (because of a perception that the now limited-edition product might have some resale value in the future).[15] The Vegemite iSnack 2.0 controversy is discussed in further detail in chapter 7, where product branding is discussed.

Unless a product or package change is accompanied by an educational and promotional program that makes customers aware of the change and the reasons, valuable brand equity and customer loyalty may be lost. This consideration is one of the reasons organisations tend to maintain existing branding when they buy a portfolio of products from another company.

### Beliefs and attitudes

Beliefs and attitudes make up the 'mental map' that a consumer relies upon when making judgements about problems that require solutions (e.g. the need to purchase appropriate luggage for an extended overseas holiday) and products for which there are no readily apparent need (e.g. new high-technology products for which consumers do not generally perceive an immediate need). The mental map provides the context in which decisions are made. This positive, neutral or negative context has significant implications for marketing campaigns and initiatives trying to introduce new products or communication concepts.

Beliefs comprise descriptive or evaluative thoughts that an individual holds regarding their knowledge or assessment of a person, idea, product and so on. Beliefs may be based on objective knowledge, opinions or faith. They may be accurate or inaccurate. When they involve a judgemental or emotional component, they can form the basis of a strong *brand image.*

An attitude describes an individual's relatively stable and consistent thoughts, feelings and behaviours towards an object or idea. People hold attitudes regarding politics, ideas, food, clothing, art, music, religion, other people — in fact, almost everything. Attitudes, along with beliefs, therefore form the background against which new products or ideas are evaluated. Attitudes clearly relate to reputation, brand image and brand equity and negative attitudes can destroy reputation, brand image and brand equity, especially through negative *word-of-mouth.*

Apple is a brand that inspires significant brand loyalty among consumers.

Attitudes and beliefs display inertia — they do change, but usually only gradually. They also exist as a *gestalt* (i.e. as a sum total or configuration) and it is natural for individuals to strive for consistency in the pattern of their attitudes and beliefs. This instinct for consistency will often lead consumers to reject new ideas that are not consistent with their existing beliefs or attitudes. In this sense, new products need to overcome this instinctive defence against new ideas. *Brand loyalty* is a particular example of this generalised psychological tendency. Apple, for example, is a brand that inspires significant brand loyalty among many consumers, and the organisation has managed to capitalise on this via extending its product range from its initial offering of desktop computers to portable devices such as iPods, iPhones and iPads. Many loyal customers own multiple Apple products, and upgrade regularly as new models and versions become available.

The three components that make up an attitude are:
- the *cognitive* component, which comprises the person's awareness of and knowledge about the object or issue
- the *affective* component, which refers to feelings towards the object or issue
- the *behavioural* component, which reflects the individual's actions or intentions towards the object or issue.

It is important that marketing campaigns address all three components of attitudes in a strong and positive way. It is also too easy to create a campaign that changes just one component of an attitude. An advertising campaign that creates very high levels of awareness regarding a new product will leave the advertiser very disappointed if the cognitive change is not accompanied by an affective and, especially, behavioural change. Even some award-winning advertising campaigns suffer this fate.

To effectively manage attitudes towards an organisation's product, marketers need to use marketing metrics related to all elements of their marketing mix. Data for metrics related to issues such as brand awareness is commonly gathered through consumer surveys in which respondents indicate their degree of agreement with attitudinal statements about the organisation and its products. For example, a bank might ask its customers to indicate the extent to which they believe a bank is modern, friendly, efficient or ethical. *Tracking studies* ask the same set of questions regularly over an extended period, enabling organisations to measure long-term changes in consumer attitudes and to 'benchmark' these attitudes against competitors.

Because attitudes are relatively stable, it is difficult to change attitudes towards an organisation in the short term, especially when that company or brand is already very familiar. For example, Australia Post has succeeded in improving and updating its image, but this process has taken over 20 years. In so doing, they resisted the temptation to 'over promise and under deliver', a shortcoming common among long-established companies. Changing attitudes successfully therefore typically requires a heavy investment in information campaigns directed at all three aspects of attitudes, by creating high levels of awareness and positive images of the product or brand, and by offering customers or consumers a reason why they should try, buy or return to a brand.

### Learning

Learning is the process by which individuals acquire new knowledge and experience that they can apply to future problems, opportunities and behaviour. In the context of consumer behaviour, learning relates to acquiring knowledge about new products, ideas or problems that have some potential application to fulfilling a need or want. The topic of learning theories is as extensive as the theories are complex. In general, we can distinguish two major schools of learning theory:

- behavioural learning theories
- cognitive learning theories.

*Behavioural learning theories* stress the role of experience and repetition of behaviour. At the simplest level, 'classical conditioning', originally identified by Russian physiologist Ivan Pavlov, describes learning in which behaviour that results in a pleasant experience is likely to be repeated. If a brand can be consistently associated with a pleasant experience in the mind of the consumer over an extended period of time, then, eventually, the brand itself will provoke a pleasant experience. For example, Coca-Cola has established an indelible place in the minds of consumers by being regarded as synonymous with good times. In this way, drinking Coke itself comes to be regarded as the essence of good times. For classical conditioning to be effective, long-term repetition of a consistent, simple message is required. In this sense, response to advertising takes on the nature of a 'knee-jerk' reaction. Classical conditioning is therefore most relevant in *low-involvement* purchases; that is, where the product is relatively unimportant to the consumer and the cost of being wrong is equally minimal. With products like ice creams or soft drink, there is little risk involved, and the consumer is often willing to buy on the basis of 'trial and error'. Beyond classical conditioning, 'operant' or 'instrumental' conditioning, pioneered by American psychologist B.F. Skinner, is distinguished by the overt use of reward and punishment to stimulate appropriate behaviour. In behavioural learning, consumers learn from experience, frequently with very little deliberate thought or reflection. Nevertheless, learning occurs when the consumer associates a rewarding experience with the product. This rewarding experience is likely to be physiological in nature, such as through a rewarding taste, smell, sight or experience. Such immediate gratification can lead to long-term loyal consumption behaviour, such as among loyal beer drinkers, for whom the ritual of a cold beer after a hard day's work can become a lifelong habit. Beer brands such as VB (Victoria Bitter) have built their success on such operant conditioning.

In contrast, *cognitive learning theories* describe learning that takes place through rational problem solving, which emphasises the acquisition and processing of new information. As such, cognitive learning theories are generally more relevant in the case of complex problems for which the consumer needs to develop a rational solution. Cognitive learning theories therefore place a high reliance on the provision of information and guidance to enable the consumer to arrive at his or her desired solution. In cognitive learning theories, the emphasis is on reasoning (rather than experience), and so decision making is likely to be protracted, deliberate, rational and well informed. Cognitive learning is generally more relevant in *high-involvement* purchasing decisions, which are typically for high-cost, important and infrequent purchases that involve significant levels of risk for the consumer in the event of making a wrong decision. For example, the consumer decision regarding a new mortgage, superannuation or investment product, purchase of a new car or home, or choice of school or university are all typically high-involvement decisions with high level of attendant risk. Marketers of such products should seek to develop a dialogue with potential purchasers to provide them with adequate information and advice to enable or assist the buyer to arrive at a satisfactory resolution of the problem. Such purchases place a heavy emphasis on provision of information through such means as brochures, newspaper and magazine advertising, websites and personal selling.

# Spotlight Pampered pets

The pet industry in Australia is big business, with the most recent industry estimates claiming that 63 per cent of Australian households own a pet of some kind, and that total annual expenditure on pet-care products and associated services is $4.62 billion annually. The majority of pets owned by Australians are dogs and cats, but fish, birds, horses, rabbits, guinea pigs and other small animals are also popular pet choices. According to research conducted by the Australian Companion Animal Council (ACAC), the average dog and cat owner spends $746 and $583 respectively per annum on their pet. This includes food, veterinary bills and boarding costs.

Significantly, according to ACAC, although the number of dogs and cats in Australia is actually slowly declining, the amount of money being spent on them is increasing. It seems that Australian dogs and cats are increasingly being pampered, with owners prepared to spend significant sums of money on items such as luxury beds, kennels, gourmet foods, treats, rugs, quilts, vests, and an ever-increasing array of toys. Some owners take their 'pet pampering' efforts so far that they allow their pets to have free roaming rights both inside and outside – even if this means their pet, like this dog, gets to revel in the comfort of sleeping and lazing on their bed.

A number of reasons have been put forward to explain this phenomenon, including:
* couples choosing to have children later in life and treating their dog or cat as if it is their (future) first-born child
* couples not having children at all and viewing their dog or cat as a substitute
* the increase in single-person households, where pets may be purchased for companionship or safety reasons, and subsequently doted upon.

Numerous studies have shown that there are physical, mental and social benefits associated with pet ownership. For example, a pet such as a dog can encourage owner exercise, increase social interaction and generally make a person 'feel good' about themselves. To many pet owners, spending money on their beloved pets is the equivalent of spending money on themselves, their friends or their family.[16]

## Question

In terms of consumer behaviour, what 'individual factors' (i.e. personal and psychological characteristics) might help to explain the pampered pets phenomenon?

## Concepts and applications check

**Learning objective 3** analyse the major individual factors that influence consumer behaviour

**3.1** Briefly describe how your actual lifestyle and your preferred lifestyle differ. Identify which aspirational purchases you might make to express your preferred lifestyle.

**3.2** Critically discuss the PALS psychographic market segmentation scheme presented in table 4.2. Do you think it is a useful approach? What are its strengths and shortcomings?

**3.3** Discuss how accurately Maslow's hierarchy of needs reflects your own consumer decisions. Can you identify examples in your own life, the lives of your friends or through media reports where individuals appear to have chosen to satisfy a higher order need before lower order needs have been met? How do you explain this?

**3.4** Briefly explain the three stages in the process of perception. Choose an advertising campaign and analyse how it has taken into account the perceptual process of its target market.

**3.5** Research a marketing campaign that effectively appeals to the three components of attitude. Explain the appeal to each component.

# THE CONSUMER DECISION-MAKING PROCESS

Now that we have discussed the broad influences on the consumer, we will examine a general model of consumer decision-making behaviour. The **consumer decision-making process** involves five stages, illustrated in figure 4.4. These stages are typically present in all consumer buying decisions, but the relative importance and duration of each varies considerably from one decision to another.

**Learning objective 4**
explain the general steps in the consumer decision-making process

**consumer decision-making process** The process of need/want recognition, information search, evaluation of options, purchase and post-purchase evaluation that are common to most consumer buying decisions.

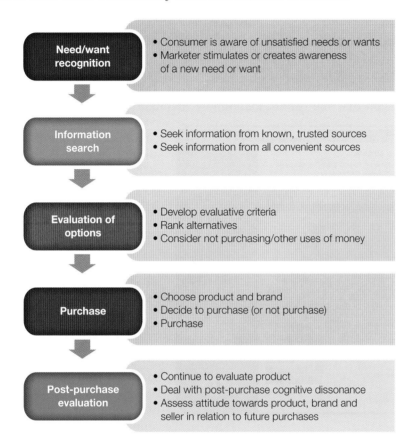

**Need/want recognition**
- Consumer is aware of unsatisfied needs or wants
- Marketer stimulates or creates awareness of a new need or want

**Information search**
- Seek information from known, trusted sources
- Seek information from all convenient sources

**Evaluation of options**
- Develop evaluative criteria
- Rank alternatives
- Consider not purchasing/other uses of money

**Purchase**
- Choose product and brand
- Decide to purchase (or not purchase)
- Purchase

**Post-purchase evaluation**
- Continue to evaluate product
- Deal with post-purchase cognitive dissonance
- Assess attitude towards product, brand and seller in relation to future purchases

**FIGURE 4.4**

The consumer decision-making process

Consumer decisions involve different levels of involvement. They can be categorised as follows along a continuum from habitual at one end to extended decision-making behaviours at the other:

- **Habitual decision making** involves little involvement with the purchase. Typically, the consumer minimises search and shopping efforts for purchases that are routine and habitual; for example, many supermarket and convenience store purchases.
- **Limited decision making** involves seeking limited information to evaluate options for infrequent purchases within familiar product categories such as clothing, books, music, inexpensive appliances and restaurants.
- **Extended decision making** involves full involvement with the purchase decision in a protracted, deliberate and detailed way. In such purchases, consumers will seek to gather comprehensive information concerning the nature of their need or want, the product category, the available brands, their relative merits and the specific details of the purchase. Such decision making is typical for high-involvement products, which are usually those that are high priced and infrequently purchased.

**habitual decision making**
Low-involvement purchasing decisions, usually involving small, routine, low-risk products.

**limited decision making**
Limited-involvement purchasing decisions, usually involving infrequently bought, but familiar, products.

**extended decision making**
High-involvement purchasing decisions involving high-price, high-risk and/or infrequent, unfamiliar products.

Examples include cars, prestige home furniture and decoration, holidays, home entertainment systems, new information technology, mortgages and investment products.

The level of involvement is fundamentally important to the type of marketing that will be effective. The following paragraphs describe each of the five stages of the decision-making process, recognising that the process can vary according to the nature of the product, the circumstances of the purchase and the individual consumers involved.

### Need/want recognition

Consider a jaded young professional lawyer or investment banker whose work has demanded long hours, punctuated by regular and 'impossible' deadlines and a personal responsibility for ambitious revenue and billings targets. She may arrive at the conclusion that she cannot indefinitely maintain this pace of living or normal personal relationships in these circumstances. She might become aware that she has become physically and emotionally run down, is lacking a close relationship partner, and needs a change or a break. The young professional has thus recognised a problem.

*Need/want recognition* typically occurs when a buyer becomes aware of a discrepancy between a desired state and the actual state. It can occur in a range of ways. Often, an individual, like our professional, will become aware of an unsatisfactory state of affairs such as poor physical or emotional wellbeing. Alternatively, marketers can stimulate recognition of the need or want by highlighting the incidence of the problem in the population; for example, loneliness or hypertension (high blood pressure). Marketers can use advertising, public information campaigns, salespeople or packaging to highlight the problem in the minds of the public. (Of course, such campaigns might also be partly responsible for adverse social consequences, such as the increasing incidence of depression and eating disorders. Marketers need to closely monitor the effects of such campaigns.) According to research by DoubleClick, awareness is driven principally by:

- websites in the travel sector
- direct mail in the credit card and retail banking sector
- internet ads in the mortgage and investment business
- print ads in the personal and home products sectors.[17]

### Information search

Having recognised the problem, the buyer searches for information about how to solve the problem. Our young professional will search for information that will help her overcome the problems of being tired and lonely. Typically, an information search will begin with the individual examining their knowledge and memory for appropriate solutions. The young professional may resolve to take a holiday in

AirAsia is one of several travel companies that generate much of their business online. The company has several social networking homepages, a main website that can be translated into several languages and a large database of customers who subscribe to receive email notifications of its promotions.

western Europe and, because she wants to retain her job position, she may conclude that an organised tour would enable her to make best use of the available leave time that she has. She might also resolve to later explore internet relationship and dating sites (unless, of course, she meets a suitable companion or partner in her travels).

Once this first stage of the information search has been done, decision makers look externally for more information. For example, if our young professional does not know of any suitable tours or tour operators, she will search for information from external sources, which may involve communication with friends, relatives or colleagues, use of an internet search engine or the reading of travel magazines. In engaging in an external search, the consumer will prefer sources that are reliable and efficient. In this sense, friends, family members and associates are the most highly valued sources, as the person trusts or respects them. This explains why 'word-of-mouth' is highly influential and so appealing to marketers, but is not easy to manage. On the other hand, the internet has become the most preferred information source for many categories of purchases such as expensive consumer durables and travel. In this case, the young professional searches local travel agents and the internet for a range of suitable tours to her preferred travel destinations. (Although she has travelled overseas before, she is more interested, on this occasion, in visiting more exotic and out of the way destinations.) She also discusses her professional and personal situation with her (mostly) female acquaintances to identify tour companies and destinations which might match her needs.

### Evaluation of options

A successful information search will usually yield a range of alternative solutions for consideration. For example, following her enquiries, the young professional may identify three tours that seem to match her requirements. To evaluate the options, the buyer uses a combination of objective criteria, such as price, and subjective criteria, such as style, image or feeling about a product. In the case of an organised ('package') tour, a critical consideration will be a judgement about the kinds of people who will be also be taking the same tour. These criteria will likely vary in importance. For example, destination, duration and the standard of hotel rooms may be more important to our young professional than price. From the range of evaluative criteria, the potential buyer rates and eventually ranks the alternative solutions. From her list of three tours, the young professional may reject one tour because it mostly stays at camping sites and youth hostels, or because the price does not include hotel breakfasts, side tours and/or evening meals.

Marketers can influence consumers' evaluations by presenting their products' features and benefits in a way that reflects consumers' needs and evaluative criteria, and hence influences their decision making. Marketers tend to feature those attributes of their products that are strongest and seek to convince the consumer that those features are the most important. In this way, marketers can shape the consumer's decision, particularly in unfamiliar needs, wants or product categories.

It is important to remember that the consumer is also considering completely different uses of their money. Because consumers have limited resources, not only will they compare a few different brands and styles when choosing a new dining room suite, for example, but they will also make a judgement as to whether a new dining room suite offers more value than other possible uses of their money, such as a holiday or just saving the money.

### Purchase

Once the evaluation of options is complete, the consumer moves to the purchase stage, in which the particular product and specific brand are chosen. It is important to recognise, of course, that the purchasing decision may, in fact, be to *not purchase*. At the purchase stage, our young professional may choose to purchase from a local travel agent after discussing her needs with a travel consultant. She may be influenced by the personal style, expertise or charm of the consultant. It is also likely that she will choose the tour package which offers the mix of destinations, attractions, facilities and inclusions that best meet her needs, is available over a suitable starting date and duration, and for which the price is reasonable. The actual purchase takes place when she chooses an individual tour and the travel agent accepts her credit card payment (which is linked to her frequent flyer card, and so she receives frequent flyer miles, which she regards as a minor but worthwhile bonus). Product availability (in the form of a suitable departure date and location) can often make a crucial difference at this stage, particularly when consumers are undecided between brands of packaged tours.

### Post-purchase evaluation

It is a common mistake for marketers to assume that the consumer decision-making process ends with the purchase. This is rarely the case for the consumer. After the purchase, the buyer continues to evaluate their purchase decision. In fact, once the purchase is made, the consumer is in a much better position to evaluate their choice. They continue to assess whether the product matched their expectations.

Our young professional, for example, is conscious that in choosing one tour, she has rejected other — possibly better — alternatives, and she needs to be reassured that she has made the right choice. She is also uncertain about her choice of travel destinations, and she is nervous, because a number of tour companies have 'folded' in the past, leaving members who have prepaid without a service. The young professional also needs to be reassured that she is receiving good value for money. Under such circumstances, like many buyers of expensive products, she may experience post-purchase or cognitive dissonance.

**Cognitive dissonance** occurs when a purchaser has second thoughts or doubts about the wisdom of the purchase. It is most probable when a person has recently purchased an expensive, high-involvement product, the features of which are shared with other acceptable alternatives. In these circumstances, there is a danger the buyer may feel they have made the wrong choice. Consequently, a buyer will actively seek out information from personal or commercial sources, which will reassure them about their decision.

In these circumstances, marketers may seek to communicate with their recent customers to ensure their experience has been satisfactory and they have no regrets. For this reason, car companies write to their new customers to receive feedback on the purchase experience and to provide evidence to customers that they have made a wise choice. In the case of the car companies, travel agents and tour companies, the objective in the post-purchase phase should be the same; that is, to ensure the customer is satisfied and is likely to continue the relationship by their loyalty to the tour company and the local travel agency when the consumer next purchases, or by recommending them to others who are contemplating travel. This forms the basis of a continuing, profitable customer relationship. Another strategy for reducing cognitive dissonance is the use of bonuses or rebates via redemption, which provide the consumer with additional value some time after the purchase. Apple regularly uses this approach, inviting buyers of its computers to send in a form and their barcode to receive cash back or a bonus product, such as an iPod.

**cognitive dissonance**
A purchaser's second thoughts or doubts about the wisdom of a purchase they have made.

# Big decisions for little people

According to a recent survey of 3000 mothers, nearly 80 per cent will research a product for their children online before buying it. This research is particularly exhaustive when it comes to baby items, such as prams, cots, high chairs, car seats, capsules and nursery furniture, as well as the vast array of infant health and hygiene products that are available.

Although the baby product market is extremely competitive, the good news for marketers is that consumers in this sector are not just concerned with the lowest price. Like all consumers, they do want value, but the best interests of their baby come first. This fact has not escaped the marketers of baby products. Major baby product retailers generally offer a wide range of products within each category, and their websites feature exhaustive descriptions of product features and benefits.

Many in the industry also recognise the significant power of word-of-mouth marketing in this sector. 'Mums are a marketer's dream in that they're extremely vocal and quick to share. Word-of-mouth makes or breaks brands in our category', says Alison Holland, head of marketing (baby and child care) for Kimberly-Clark Australia and New Zealand.

Mothers actively compare baby products and can be quick to give an endorsement or a criticism of a good, service or activity, in forums such as mothers' groups. They are often quick to consult with other family members who have experience in raising children, and are also increasingly communicating via social networking sites.

Recognising this trend, Kimberly-Clark actively maintains an online 'Baby Club' via its Huggies brand. This club currently has a database of over 180 000 members. Among other benefits, it provides members with a dedicated forum where they can discuss products and experiences, as well as access to an expert panel for professional advice on a range of baby care and development issues.[18]

## Question

Imagine you are about to become a mother or father for the first time and will need to purchase a range of baby products. Choose one product and explain how you would proceed through each of the steps in the consumer decision-making process outlined in figure 4.4.

## Concepts and applications check

**Learning objective 4** explain the general steps in the consumer decision-making process

**4.1** Briefly explain the five stages in the consumer decision-making process.

**4.2** Outline two examples of habitual, limited and extended purchasing decisions you have made.

**4.3** To what extent do you think 'need/want recognition' is generated internally versus externally? Explain your answer using a variety of examples.

**4.4** Imagine you are about to purchase a new smartphone (e.g. an iPhone or a BlackBerry). Explain how you would progress through the stages of the decision-making process. Which stages were more or less important?

**4.5** Choose a recent non-habitual purchase that you have made. Analyse the situational, group and individual factors that affected your decision-making process. Map the factors to each stage of the decision-making process. How important were the various factors to your decision?

# SUMMARY

 **Learning objective 1** explain why marketers require a thorough understanding of consumer behaviour and its major influences

'Consumer behaviour' is the study of the behaviour of individuals and households who buy products for personal consumption. It forms the basis of an understanding of the reasons behind the decisions consumers make, which is central to creating an effective marketing mix. Consumer behaviour is influenced by situational factors, group factors and individual factors.

Situational factors are simply the circumstances in which a person finds themselves when making a consumption decision. They relate to the influence of physical, social, time, motivational and mood factors.

 **Learning objective 2** understand the major group factors that influence consumer behaviour

Group factors comprise cultural influences and social influences. Cultural influences affect behaviours that operate at the level of the whole society or of major groups within society: culture, subculture and social class. Culture is the system of knowledge, beliefs, values, rituals and artefacts by which a society or other large group defines itself. National cultures can be described according to Hofstede's cultural dimensions: power distance, uncertainty avoidance, individualism, masculinity, and long-term orientation. A subculture is a group of individuals who share common attitudes, values and behaviours that distinguish them from the broader culture in which they are immersed. A social class is a grouping defined by similar social ranking within the social hierarchy.

Social influences are those that influence the individual to behave in a way that reflects group norms. A reference group is any group to which an individual looks for guidance, including membership, aspirational and dissociative reference groups. Within a reference group, some individuals take on the role of opinion leader on issues about which they are particularly knowledgeable. Opinion leaders are influential over other group members. Family influences are also important in consumer behaviour and many consumption decisions are traditionally made by particular members or combinations of members of the household.

 **Learning objective 3** analyse the major individual factors that influence consumer behaviour

Personal and psychological factors influence consumer behaviour independently of social circumstances. Personal characteristics include demographic, lifestyle and personality factors. Marketers consider all of them to have a close link to consumer behaviour, but it has proved notoriously difficult to demonstrate a reliable and predictable link between particular personal characteristics and consumer behaviour.

Psychological characteristics are internal factors that shape the thinking, aspirations, expectations and behaviours of the individual. They include motivation, which is the internal drive to satisfy unfulfilled needs. According to Maslow's hierarchy of needs, individuals, generally, try to satisfy lower order needs such as food and sleep ahead of higher order needs such as learning. Another psychological characteristic is perception, which describes how an individual filters, organises and attributes meaning to external stimuli, including marketing communications. Beliefs and attitudes are also an important personal influence on consumer behaviour, as they determine the context in which product evaluations are made. Effective marketing needs to appeal to the cognitive, affective and behavioural components of consumer attitudes. A final personal influence is the way in which an individual learns. Marketers can 'teach' individuals to have particular awareness of and attitudes towards their products using cognitive and behavioural learning approaches.

 **Learning objective 4** explain the general steps in the consumer decision-making process

The consumer decision-making process comprises need/want recognition, information search, evaluation of options, purchase, and post-purchase evaluation. These steps are common to most purchase decisions, but the extent to which each is used depends on the level of involvement in the purchase. Habitual purchases are made with little decision-making involvement; infrequent, but familiar, purchases are made with limited involvement; and rare, large or risky purchases are made with extensive involvement.

It is a common mistake for marketers to overlook the last stage of the decision-making process: post-purchase evaluation. It is after the purchase that the consumer can evaluate whether or not they made a wise choice. Effective marketers take steps to ensure they continue to build their relationship with consumers after the purchase to reduce cognitive dissonance (second thoughts about the purchase) and increase the likelihood of repeat purchase in the future.

# Time for a holiday

Many people spend considerable time thinking about holidays. This includes either daydreaming about a trip to an exotic destination, or actively researching and planning an itinerary for their next holiday. The potential sources of holiday information and advice are seemingly endless, whether from retail travel agents, accommodation providers, airlines, dedicated online forums or family and friends eager to pass on travel experiences.

In terms of the local tourism industry, there are two broad categories of tourists: domestic (i.e. Australians holidaying and travelling within Australia) and international (i.e. foreign visitors to Australia). Exchange rates have a significant impact on domestic tourism. When the Australian dollar appreciates on international markets, it becomes cheaper for Australians to travel abroad. It also becomes more expensive for international travellers to visit our shores. The situation is more favourable for the domestic tourism market when the Australian dollar depreciates and both of these trends are reversed. In the first decade of the twenty-first century, the Australian dollar fluctuated between a low of US$0.47 and a high of just over US$1.

Over the years, the industry has enjoyed peaks and troughs in terms of international visitors for other reasons as well. The high points have included surges during the 1980s and around major events, such as the Sydney Olympics in 2000. The low points, or periods when international tourist numbers to Australia have not been as strong, have coincided with significant international events, such as terrorist attacks, the outbreak of viruses such as severe acute respiratory syndrome (SARS) and the global financial crisis. Most recently, the global financial crisis and its aftermath have provided interesting insights into consumer behaviour in the tourism sector. Domestically, the mainstay of the tourism industry is the Baby Boomers (generally defined as people born in the post–World War II era, between 1945 and 1964). The Baby Boomers are generally in (or approaching) their retirement years. Prior to the global financial crisis, many in this age bracket had both the time and sufficient retirement funds to travel and 'see Australia'. However, the superannuation funds of many were hit hard by the crisis, with retirement savings generally being significantly eroded. Yet, despite this financial setback, many Baby Boomers still opted to travel, with a notable trend emerging: tourism operators reported a marked increase in bookings for budget and mid-range (3- and 4-star) accommodation, at the expense of the more luxurious (5-star) options usually favoured by this segment of the market. Although even cheaper options (such as tents and caravan parks) were also readily available, these were not as attractive, with many of this generation not prepared to 'rough it' to this extent on their travels.

Another significant pattern emerged in the business market for tourism in the immediate aftermath of the global financial crisis. The number of international conventions and conferences being held in Australia decreased significantly. This had major flow-on effects for the tourism industry. According to Sandra Chipcase, chief executive of the Melbourne Convention and Visitors Bureau, many delegates who attend conventions and conferences bring family or friends with them to go on tours to other parts of Australia; either immediately before or after the event they are attending. This is because they are generally 'higher net worth' individuals, and can therefore afford to do so. With less conferences and conventions as a result of the global financial crisis, this phenomenon occurred less frequently, and the local tourism industry was adversely affected.

In addition to the problems associated with the global financial crisis, domestic tourism also appears to have suffered with the rise of Generation Y in recent years (Generation Y are generally defined as being born between 1982 and 2000). Many of this generation favour an international holiday over a domestic one, with such trips almost seen as a 'right of passage' upon entering adulthood, and something to be undertaken as regularly as possible thereafter. The challenge for the local industry is in trying to persuade this generation to 'see Australia first', at a time in history when international destinations have never been more accessible to young people.

Domestic tourism has suffered in Australia in recent years for a variety of reasons. Many members of Generation Y prefer to take international holidays, with such trips almost being seen as a 'right of passage' upon entering adulthood.

A further potentially worrying trend for domestic tourism, both now and in the future, is that many Generation Z children appear to be growing up without the tradition of an annual local holiday — something almost taken for granted by generations before them. The pressures of modern working life, as well as job security fears at the height of the global financial crisis, have seen Australian workers accumulate a staggering 121 million days of unused annual leave. To put this figure into an individual perspective, one in four Australian full-time employees has accrued 25 days or more of annual leave, when the average annual leave entitlement for the majority of full-time Australian workers is only 20 days.

Many reasons have been put forward in an attempt to explain the apparent reluctance of contemporary Australian employees to take leave. One of the most common is that in today's fast-paced work environment, some employees fear that taking any more than a few days off or a week of leave at a time will result in an overloaded email inbox or desk in-tray when they return. And even a week of leave is hardly enough time to unwind, de-stress and really enjoy a holiday. Not all employees will have someone to cover their work while they are away on leave, particularly with many organisations currently operating on 'lean' staffing levels to maximise efficiency. Another reason advanced for the annual leave 'stockpiling' that is seemingly becoming entrenched in Australian workplace culture is consumer debt. In other words, the generally high mortgages and debt levels among contemporary households almost compel people to work increasingly long hours, overtime and even second jobs, just to keep up with loan repayments. In such circumstances, there may be no money left over to even consider a holiday, and no real incentive to take leave as a result.

However, such 'dedication' to work potentially comes at a cost. Work–life balance has become a popular catch cry in recent years among psychologists. 'Not taking leave can often be associated with an increased risk of "burnout" and stress-related problems', says Dr Peter Cotton, director of Psychology Services, Health Services Australia.

Bruce Ritchie, editor of *Men's Health* magazine, agrees, saying, 'There's nothing heroic about working ridiculous hours and going months without taking a break. Quite the opposite, there's a good chance such a crazy work ethic is making you less effective at work and less relaxed at home'.

Tourism Australia, the federal government agency responsible for the international and domestic marketing of Australia as a destination for leisure and business travel, views the information on Australia's unused employee leave as a major opportunity to grow the domestic tourism sector. In response, it has launched the 'No Leave, No Life' program. The aim of the program is to remind employees and employers of both the personal and professional benefits of taking annual leave, and to encourage the taking of that leave via Australian domestic holidays. It targets both employees and employers. The employer toolkit that is available as part of the campaign identifies practical and beneficial ways that employers can collectively reduce the estimated $33 billion in wages that have been accumulated as a result of annual leave stockpiling by employees.

It is not surprising that the federal government (via Tourism Australia) takes such an active interest in the tourism industry, considering the sector generates $86 billion in revenue annually, and is therefore a significant component of Australia's gross domestic product (GDP). In addition, nearly half a million Australian workers are employed in the tourism industry. In 2008 the federal government established a steering committee to conduct a far-reaching review of Australia's tourism sector, with the aim of using this committee's findings to inform the development of a national long-term tourism strategy. The review and its findings subsequently became known as 'The Jackson Report', so named after former Qantas chairwoman Margaret Jackson, the leader of the steering committee.

In terms of international tourists being attracted to Australia, the report identified that consumers in key overseas markets are increasingly focusing on climate change and environmental sustainability when making purchasing decisions for all products, including tourism. On these issues, the report concluded that an increased focus on Australia's natural environment, coupled with sustainable tourism activities (i.e. tourism activities that are economically, socioculturally and environmentally sustainable) would be vital to Australia's continued appeal as a travel destination. Heritage and cultural tourism is also a growth market internationally, with Australia again being well-positioned to capitalise on this trend, via both its unique landscape and its ability to offer Indigenous cultural experiences and attractions.

Ironically, given the importance of 3- and 4-star accommodation in cushioning the effects of the global financial crisis and its aftermath (as previously discussed), the report also identified this sector as a potential barrier to long-term tourism growth in Australia. The majority of Australia's 3- and 4-star properties were built between 1965 and 1980. When times were tough, consumers were prepared to downgrade or tolerate this. However, in better times, the report concluded that consumers will be more discerning in their holiday choices, and the standard of accommodation offered is a key factor in holiday decisions. Australia, it seems, must invest significantly in its tourism infrastructure, in order to remain competitive for both domestic and international tourists.[19]

## Questions

1. Using both the information in the case and your own knowledge and research, identify as many situational, group and individual factors as you can that could potentially impact on a person's holiday destination decision.
2. What trends or events have impacted most significantly on the behaviour of Australia's tourists (and potential tourists) in recent years, from both a domestic and an international viewpoint?
3. In terms of the consumer decision-making process, explain how a person choosing a holiday would potentially work through each of the steps. Be sure to identify any situational, individual or group factors that could influence each stage.

## Advanced activity

Having read this chapter, research and describe the likely group and individual influences on the consumer behaviour of Generation Z. Then, choose a product that is likely to appeal to this generation and outline how each of these influences could potentially impact on the consumer decision-making process.

## Marketing plan activity

Based on this chapter and the information you have been compiling for your chosen organisation's marketing plan in chapters 1 to 3 (situation analysis, SWOT analysis and any market research you have or will be conducting), outline the buying behaviour of potential purchasers of your product that you will need to understand.

Be as specific as you can at this stage in relation to the following, bearing in mind that you will be refining and revising this information as you gather market research and your marketing knowledge increases in subsequent chapters:
- the major group/sociocultural factors that may influence the buying behaviour of potential purchasers of your product
- the major individual — personal and psychological — factors that may influence the buying behaviour of potential purchasers of your product
- the level of involvement a potential purchaser may have with your product
- the stages of the decision-making process a potential purchaser may go through in relation to your product, including how much time and effort may be spent at each stage.

As with the marketing plan activities in previous chapters, the above analysis is likely to inform your overall and ongoing market research requirements. Such detailed analysis and understanding of consumer behaviour in relation to your chosen product will be crucial to the marketing strategies you will be developing in later chapters for your marketing plan.

A sample marketing plan has been included at the back of this book (see page 523) to give you an idea where this type of information fits in an overall marketing plan.

## CHAPTER 5

# Business buying behaviour

## Learning objectives

After studying this chapter, you should be able to:

- explain the characteristics of different types of business markets

- understand the major issues involved in marketing to business customers

- discuss the characteristics of demand in business markets

- analyse business buyer behaviour and decision making.

# Global vision

Opto Global is a South Australian company that commenced operations in the early 2000s. Its start-up funding included $5 million from venture capital investors, as well as a $1.2 million development grant from the federal government. The company designs, develops and distributes a range of precision ophthalmic equipment. Ophthalmology is the branch of medical science that deals with the anatomy, functions and diseases of the eye.

The target market for Opto Global's products are ophthalmologists, optometrists, hospitals and associated healthcare professionals. Its major products include prevention,

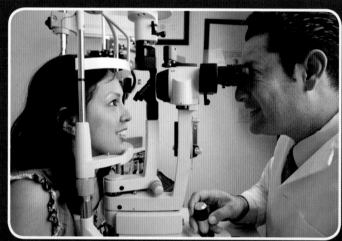

detection and treatment devices for the most common potential causes of blindness — glaucoma, cataracts and age-related eye degeneration. The company has a direct sales channel in Australia. It also markets its products to business consumers in more than 60 countries around the world, in regions such as Europe, the Middle East and Asia, via an extensive network of distributors. As part of the distribution arrangement, these international distributors are trained to install, operate, repair and maintain Opto Global's range of products. Almost all of the company's revenue (95 per cent) comes from overseas, due to the relatively small size of the local market, and its revenue has grown by 40 per cent per year on average since it was founded.

In an interview for *The Australian* highlighting the success of the company, entrepreneur and co-founder of Opto Global, Jairo Kerr Azevedo, explained: 'The primary objective is to increase market penetration of Opto-branded products by expanding the range to cater for all the equipment needs of ophthalmic surgeons around the world.' Mr Azevedo said gaining experience in different areas was essential to his preparation in the lead up to the launch of Opto Global. 'I always wanted to have a business in the technology field and I wanted to have had experience in many areas so I could develop that business well,' he said. 'I was working with international distributors; it gave me more experience.' It was through this experience that Mr Azevedo met his future business partner, who, with a background in sales, provided invaluable support with raising capital for the venture.

The medical technology field is characterised by intense competition, stringent legal and regulatory environments and long sales cycles. In particular, obtaining regulatory approval for products in the medical field can be a costly and time-consuming process. However, a positive indicator for Opto Global is that global demand for ophthalmology products is increasing. This increase is being driven by factors such as ageing populations, poor dietary habits and the opening up of large potential markets in India and China in recent times.

Opto Global's strategy is to develop or acquire technologies that they categorise as potentially being in a 'quick-to-market' state. The company develops its own prototypes before proceeding to commercialisation, via licensing manufacturers, as a means to produce such devices as part of a joint development program. Larger, multinational companies compete in the same industry as Opto Global. As such, the comparatively smaller company uses a niché positioning strategy: it focuses on establishing a market presence in developing countries that offer more relaxed regulatory conditions.[1]

# INTRODUCTION

The decision by an ophthalmic surgeon or a university medical or ophthalmology school to purchase state-of-the art instruments for the detection and treatment of eye diseases is, obviously, a long way removed from the decision of a patient to seek the best ophthalmic surgeon, and even further removed from the decision to purchase new glasses.

Business markets (also referred to as 'business-to-business' or 'B2B' markets) have distinctive characteristics that make them different from consumer markets. In particular, business markets frequently have a small number of large competitors. Purchases are often for large amounts. In such circumstances, it makes sense for sellers to seek to build close relationships with their business customers, which may extend to formal partnerships. Close relationships also help all parties to manage the inevitable fluctuations in demand that occur in business markets.

It is also worth noting that business markets are much larger in revenue terms than the consumer markets they service. This is partly explained by the fact that all business markets ultimately contribute to consumer markets. Consumer markets, however, represent only the last step in the value chain. All the earlier steps in the chain are, by definition, business-to-business transactions. It is true, therefore, that the majority of marketing jobs are involved with business-to-business markets.

In this chapter we will examine business markets and business buying decision processes. We will first examine different kinds of business markets and the suppliers that make up these markets. Next we will explore defining characteristics of business buying, such as the kinds of transactions, attributes and concerns of buyers, different methods of buying and the distinctive demand characteristics for products sold to business purchasers. Finally, we will examine models that can be used to analyse and understand business buying decisions.

## BUSINESS MARKETS

**Business markets** are made up of individuals or organisations that purchase products for one or more of the following three purposes:

1. to resell the product
2. to use the product in the production of other products
3. to use the product in their daily business operations.

The overall business market comprises four major categories:

1. reseller markets
2. producer markets
3. government markets
4. institutional markets.

The basic features of these markets are summarised in figure 5.1 and each is discussed in more detail in the following sections.

**Learning objective 1**
explain the characteristics of different types of business markets

**business markets** Individuals or organisations that purchase products for resale, use in the production of other products, or for use in their daily business operations.

**Business markets**

| Reseller markets | Producer markets | Government markets | Institutional markets |
|---|---|---|---|
| Intermediaries that buy products in order to sell or lease them to another party for profit | Business organisations and professionals who purchase products for use in the production of other products or in their daily business operations | Governments that buy and sell products to provide services for their citizens | Not-for-profit organisations |

Reseller markets: Wholesalers, Industrial distributors, Business professionals

Producer markets: Primary industries (agriculture and mining), Secondary industries (manufacturing), Business professionals

Government markets: Federal (Commonwealth), State (provincial), Local (municipal)

Institutional markets: Charities, Religious organisations, Clubs

**FIGURE 5.1**

Business markets

**reseller markets** The market of retailers, wholesalers and other intermediaries that buy products in order to sell or lease them to another party for profit.

# Reseller markets

**Reseller markets** comprise intermediaries, such as wholesalers and retailers, that buy products in order to sell or lease them to other parties for profit. Generally, the reseller does not make any substantial change to the products. For the most part they act, essentially, as a distribution mechanism. As we will see in chapter 10, the distribution of products usually involves various marketing intermediaries, including:

- *wholesalers*. Wholesalers purchase products from suppliers and producers for resale to other intermediaries, including retailers (and sometimes directly to organisational buyers and consumers).
- *industrial distributors*. Industrial distributors purchase products from producers and sell them on to organisational buyers (producers, governments and institutions).
- *retailers*. Retailers purchase products from suppliers, manufacturers or other intermediaries (including wholesalers) for resale to consumers.

Of course, some producers sell directly to consumers as well. For example, Daleys Fruit Tree Nursery supplies a wide range of fruit trees to nurseries, garden stores and hardware retailers in most of the mainland Australian states, but it also sells directly to the public at its site in Kyogle, New South Wales, and via mail order and its online store. Producers of fresh food and wine also commonly sell directly to consumers. Most producers, however, sell their products through intermediaries.

Resellers and producers share a common interest in developing successful partnership arrangements in which both parties' sales and profit objectives can be met. At the same time, the profit of both parties is ultimately derived from the price paid by the consumer, so each member of the partnership is essentially competing to maximise its share of the available profit. These circumstances lead to tough negotiations over price, volumes and other trading conditions. Both resellers and their suppliers seek to minimise ordering, transport and storage costs. Suppliers look to resellers to provide wide distribution, customer service and after-sales support services.

Purchasing, or 'procurement', is a crucial role in resellers' businesses. Larger resellers (and large retailers in particular) often employ specialist buyers to source suppliers and secure the best purchasing arrangements. The procurement role is becoming increasingly specialised as resellers source more and more supplies from offshore. Another important trend in recent years has been the growth in volume of products sold under retailers' own brands, such as Woolworths' 'Select' brand. This has placed the retailers in direct competition with their suppliers, and has the potential to fundamentally change the mix of manufacturers' and retailers' branded products in retail stores.

In Australia, the reseller markets are dominated by familiar large retail chains, such as Woolworths, Coles, Myer, David Jones, Harvey Norman and Bunnings. In New Zealand, the major retailers are The Warehouse, Farmers, New World, PAK'nSAVE, Woolworths, Countdown, Fresh Choice, Mitre 10, Placemakers, Harvey Norman, Noel Leemings, and Bond and Bond. With the growth in size and market power of the major retail chains, the importance of wholesalers has declined. Increasingly, large retailers buy directly from producers and sell directly to consumers, bypassing the wholesaler and other intermediaries.

On the demand side, resellers estimate the level of demand for a product in order to determine whether to deal in it, the likely volume and the appropriate resale price. The level of demand can vary significantly with the time of year (e.g. few bikinis are sold in winter in the southern parts of the country). Retailers have limited floor space to store and display products. To maximise the return on their investment in floor space, they assess the amount of space a product will need relative to its sales and profit potential — and relative to the sales and profit potential of other possible stock items. Retailers often charge suppliers for prized floor locations in supermarkets and department stores. At the same time, retailing and wholesaling profit margins can be very low. Making an acceptable profit relies on carefully managing costs and prices to achieve sufficient sales volumes and revenue.

## Producer markets

**Producer markets** — sometimes known as 'industrial markets' — are those in which business organisations and professionals purchase products for use in the production of other products or for use in their daily business operations. They operate across all sectors of the economy — primary, secondary and tertiary (services) industries. The following are all examples of transactions that take place in the producer markets:

**producer markets** The markets in which business organisations and professionals purchase products for use in the production of other products or in their daily business operations.

- buying raw materials to make other products (e.g. farmers purchase the right to pump water from rivers and underground aquifers in order to irrigate their crops)
- buying component parts to include in other products (e.g. a high-end racing bike manufacturer buys carbon fibre wheels from manufacturers such as 3 Sixty or X-treme)
- buying finished and semifinished items to produce other products (e.g. B&D purchases Colorbond® steel from BHP Billiton's BlueScope Steel to make roller doors)
- buying professional services to aid the production of other products (e.g. project home builders such as Coral Homes engage engineers and architects to design the houses they will build)

- buying office supplies to use in daily operations (e.g. a plumber buying a computer, MYOB accounting software, an inkjet printer and paper for invoices and other records).

The share of gross domestic product generated by manufacturing in Australia and New Zealand has been steadily declining for years as manufacturing has moved to lower-cost countries, especially in Asia. More recently, many service roles have also been 'offshored'. The highest profile example is call centre services for banks, insurers and telecommunications businesses. Other producer markets depend heavily on geographic proximity between producers and buyers, so in Australia and New Zealand most of the producer markets are centred in the major cities of Sydney, Melbourne and Auckland.

## Government markets

**government markets** The market for selling products to national (Commonwealth), state (provincial) and local (municipal) governments for use in providing services for citizens.

The purpose of government is to serve the will of the people. A significant part of this role is fulfilled through the provision of services, which can range from national security (through the defence force) to social welfare (through Centrelink in Australia or Work and Income in New Zealand) to the weekly rubbish collection. In order to provide these services, national (Commonwealth), state (provincial) and local (municipal) governments purchase an enormous volume of products in that part of the business markets known as the **government markets**. The government sector therefore represents a substantial provider and purchaser of goods and services, and governments are a major target for business marketers. Government spending accounts for hundreds of billions of dollars a year, funded by a complex system of taxation. In response to the onset of the global economic crisis, many governments increased their spending on major infrastructure projects in order to stimulate their economies and maintain employment, running up large budget deficits in the process.

The large scale and ongoing nature of many government projects often leads to the development of close and complex relationships between government agencies and their chief suppliers. In extreme cases, these relationships take on the characteristics of partnerships, where both parties are exposed to some financial uncertainties. For example, when a state government chooses to develop new transport infrastructure, the financial commitment may total billions of dollars, the planning period may be longer than ten years, and a successful outcome is certainly not always guaranteed (as many developers of toll roads have discovered over the past decade). In this sense, partnership relationships with government can take on the same risks and difficulties as those involved in commercial business-to-business marketing. Of course, some business with government is more conventional in nature; for example, ITW Fastex New Zealand supplies plastic buckles to the Australian Defence Force for use on military equipment.

Because governments have such an enormous responsibility for the wellbeing of their citizens, government markets are subject to extensive rules and regulations designed to ensure that government business is conducted ethically and legally. In particular, government purchases are closely monitored by government financial authorities, which are formally responsible for ensuring transparency and contestability so that the government achieves the best value for the taxpayer. These requirements often impose additional compliance costs on businesses seeking to sell to government. Aware of this, the government sector has been at the leading edge of the implementation of e-commerce and e-tendering, which have proved to be among the most efficient ways of guaranteeing that sellers have every opportunity of competing for sales to government, and that the taxpayer receives the best value. Purchases by government agencies above a threshold value are typically required to be made by public tender. Companies which aim to secure major contracts for the supply of capital goods, supplies and services to government need to invest significant time in preparing competitive tenders in which the successful bidder may not necessarily be the one with the lowest price. For example, several companies and consortia spent millions of dollars tendering to build and operate the Australian government's proposed national broadband network. Telstra's tender was ruled to be non-complying and therefore ineligible, and the other tenders, from groups including Acacia, Optus and Axia NetMedia, were *all* considered unsatisfactory. Instead, the Australian government established a government business enterprise, NBN Co Limited (known as NBN Co), to design, build and operate the network for a period of ten years, at an initial cost of up to A$43 billion.[2] The network will be built as a public–private partnership in which the Australian government will hold a 51 per cent share (with the remaining 49 per cent available to companies such as Telstra and Optus) and will operate the network for ten years after completion, before selling down their stake. Most recently, Telstra has agreed participate in the National Broadband Network rollout.[3]

Because of the time, cost and uncertainty involved in government tenders, many companies are reluctant to do business with government, regardless of the potential sales revenues. While not all government supply contracts are worth billions of dollars, the government represents a valuable commercial opportunity, both in terms of sales revenue and the prospect of a relatively stable supplier–customer relationship. Under these circumstances, it makes abundant business sense for organisations to invest the time and resources required to understand government purchasing procedures and to develop close working relationships with government.

## Institutional markets

There are many organisations that are neither public nor for-profit. Such organisations commonly have charitable or social objectives and include many schools, religious organisations and hospitals, as well as charities. The markets in which these organisations buy and sell products are known as **institutional markets**.

**institutional markets** Business markets in which non-public, not-for-profit organisations buy and sell products.

Non-public, not-for-profit organisations face many of the same marketing challenges confronting businesses, including recruiting members and publicising their activities and achievements. In essence, they compete with other community service organisations for 'market share'. Not-for-profit organisations also have different goals and fewer resources than commercial organisations. They often rely on volunteer members, public donations and bequests. Marketing to such organisations will often be less financially profitable, but overall the not-for-profit sector still comprises a very substantial market. In recent years, many organisations have recognised the financial opportunities in co-branding their organisations or their programs with commercial partners. For example, Scouts Australia has participated in co-branding activities with organisations such as Qantas, Woolworths and Dick Smith Foods. Under such circumstances, it is essential that both the non-profit and commercial organisations are seen to be combining for the benefit of their members and the community. As another co-branding example, Coles partners with the Cancer Council, donating the proceeds from the sales of a range of Daffodil Day merchandise. Coles also accepts customer donations on behalf of the Cancer Council. Since 1996 the Coles Group has raised in excess of $9 million for the cancer cause.[4]

# Spotlight The right chemical mix

The chemical industry is probably the largest industry that you know nothing about! The global chemical industry has an annual turnover of more than US$3 trillion and plays a major role in the conversion of a variety of liquids, solids and gases into a vast array of products. Chemicals are used to make a wide variety of consumer goods (such as cosmetics, soap and detergent), and there are countless chemical inputs to the agricultural (e.g. fertilisers), manufacturing (e.g. plastics) and construction (e.g. adhesives and sealants) industries. The majority of chemical sales are to the business, rather than the consumer, market.

| Rank | Company |
|------|---------|
| 1 | BASF |
| 2 | Dow Chemical |
| 3 | ExxonMobil |
| 4 | Bayer |
| 5 | Sinopec |
| 6 | LyondellBasell Industries |
| 7 | Shell |
| 8 | SABIC |
| 9 | Mitsubishi Chemical |
| 10 | DuPont |
| 11 | INEOS |
| 12 | Total |
| 13 | AkzoNobel |
| 14 | Evonik Industries |
| 15 | BP |

To illustrate the business-to-business (or 'industrial') nature of the chemical industry, consider the table with this Spotlight, which shows the 15 largest global chemical companies in terms of annual sales revenue for the twenty-first century.[5] Many of these companies are not 'household names', despite their multibillion dollar turnover: BASF, the world's leading chemical company in terms of annual sales revenue, views its core business as supplying chemicals to other organisations as an ingredient in the production of higher value products. Its product portfolio range includes basic chemicals, glues and electronic chemicals for the semiconductor and solar cell industries; solvents and plasticisers; and starting materials for products such as detergents, plastics, textile fibres, paints and pharmaceuticals.[6]

In marketing chemicals to business customers, two approaches are dominant. In 'bulk commodity' (i.e. undifferentiated) basic chemicals, dominant concerns to business buyers will most likely be price, delivery and conformance to standards. In the case of more specialised chemicals, buyers will likely place greater emphasis on the unique chemical formula, technical assistance in the application of the chemicals and the potential for technical partnerships in the development of 'next generation' chemicals. The chemical industry, therefore, represents a 'textbook case' of business-to-business markets: unlike the more typical, low-value, transactional focus of traditional consumer markets, it has a focus on building high-value, long-term relationships between suppliers and their customers.[7]

## Question

Refer to figure 5.1 and categorise the major type of business market that chemical companies would be most likely to target. Provide examples to justify your answer.

## Concepts and applications check

**Learning objective 1** explain the characteristics of different types of business markets

**1.1** Explain what is meant by the broad term 'business market'.

**1.2** Using an example for each, explain the four categories of business markets.

**1.3** Outline the similarities and differences of the marketing challenges faced by a not-for-profit organisation (such as a charity) compared with a commercial organisation.

**1.4** Research a recent decision that has been made in your city or state that provides an opportunity for a commercial organisation to supply the government with goods or services. Outline some organisations that could potentially capitalise on this marketing opportunity.

# MARKETING TO BUSINESS CUSTOMERS

Marketing to business customers is distinctly different to marketing to consumers. Some of the key differences are:

**Learning objective 2**
understand the major issues involved in marketing to business customers

- Many business market transactions are for very high-value purchases, particularly in the producer, government and institutional markets.
- Many business-to-business purchases involve high volumes and regular repeat purchases, particularly in the reseller markets.
- Price and other conditions of the sale are much more open to negotiation than is typical in consumer markets.
- There are far fewer buyers and sellers in business markets.
- Alternative products being considered for purchase are often subject to extensive formal evaluation, with decisions, particularly in the government and institutional markets, typically made by committees or subject to multiple levels of approvals.
- The relationships between buyers and sellers tend to be very long term and involve extensive after-sales support.
- Demand fluctuations have different drivers and consequences.

## High-value/high-volume purchases

Business purchasing decisions frequently involve very large sums of money (potentially billions of dollars) for high-value products or high-volume purchases. High-value products are relatively common in the producer, government and institutional business markets. For example, a regional area health service may purchase one magnetic resonance imaging (MRI) scanner for each of its five largest hospitals. An MRI scanner, depending on its specifications, costs between $1 million and $3.5 million, with a further $1 million required to cover installation costs. The expected life would be about seven to ten years, by which time the technology has progressed far enough that it is clinically unsound not to upgrade to a new model.

High-volume purchases are common in the reseller market. For example, an office stationery store would purchase dozens of reams of photocopier paper every week; a university would purchase hundreds. Supermarkets such as Safeway and New World, through centralised buying arrangements, would purchase thousands of packets of toilet paper every week. Because of the total value of their purchases, they can negotiate significant volume discounts on prices. Many producers and warehouses, in fact, are not set up to handle small purchases.

High-volume purchases are also relatively common in the producer market. For example, while a home handyman might need to purchase less than a hundred bricks to build a backyard barbecue, a project builder will typically expect to purchase millions of bricks from a single supplier over a year.

Of course, not all business-to-business transactions are high volume or high value. For example, a takeaway food store's purchase of a new milkshake maker is more akin to a consumer purchase than the high-value and high-volume purchases we have discussed.

## Price competition and negotiation

Prices directly affect business costs and, ultimately, profitability. As such, price is, of course, a dominant consideration when making business purchase decisions. This is especially the case when suppliers are selling comparable products. For example, car fleet purchases will often be based on prices for similar alternative products, such as the Holden Commodore and the Ford Falcon. In such circumstances, price competition will be intense and sellers' profit margins will be minimal.

Price is often much more open to negotiation than in consumer markets, particularly based on purchase volumes. For example, a university that purchases 1000 computers every year can negotiate a much lower unit price than a small accounting partnership that purchases one computer a year.

Beyond the initial purchase price, business purchasers consider other factors related to the lifetime cost of the purchase, including service costs, running costs and depreciation. Consideration of price also takes place in the context of other matters related to the purchase. For example, a purchase might take into account business image. This has been evident in the decision by a number of major companies and local councils to switch their car fleets from the traditional Holden Commodore and Ford Falcon to more environmentally friendly and economical cars, such as Toyota's best-selling Corolla, Camry, and 'hybrids' (Prius and Camry), Honda's Civic Hybrid, and European-made diesels as part of improving the public perception of their green credentials. Of course, there is also a price factor involved in this decision, with increasing petrol prices and the overall lower purchase and maintenance costs of smaller cars contributing to the decision, particularly in the context of organisational cost-cutting brought on by the global economic crisis.

## Number of buyers and sellers

There are far fewer buyers and sellers in business markets than in consumer markets. For example, the market for MRI scanners in Australia comprises the state departments of health and a handful of large private practices. The machines are sold by only a few companies, none of which are local: Siemens, Phillips Medical Systems and GE Medical.

The smaller number of buyers and sellers makes long-term and stable relationships crucial. The nature of these relationships is discussed shortly. The smaller number of players can also give some organisations enormous market power. For example, there are only a handful of large dairy product companies in Australia, which means dairy farmers have little negotiating power over the price they are paid for milk. Conversely, BlueScope, Smorgon and OneSteel are the only real options for businesses seeking steel for use in producing their own products.

Another consequence of the small number of buyers and sellers is that business markets tend to be concentrated in major centres such as Sydney, Melbourne and Auckland. This provides advantages and disadvantages to the buyers and sellers located in those markets and those located far from them. For example, a buyer located in a business market hub in Sydney may be able to access and deal with numerous suppliers, all competing for the buyer's custom. A buyer located in a regional area may have to actively seek suppliers and then is likely to face higher transport costs. This can affect their ability to compete against businesses located closer to their suppliers.

## Formal assessment of purchase alternatives

Business customers often demand extensive and detailed information about product features and specifications to ensure that the products fully meet the organisation's needs. Businesses use this information, along with price, distribution and promotional factors to more thoroughly and formally compare the relative strengths and weaknesses of alternatives. For example, the purchase of an MRI scanner would involve the comparison of hundreds of pages of technical data and a visit to an existing facility (possibly overseas).

The exhaustive evaluation that accompanies many business purchases has led to the assumption that business purchasing is more rational than consumer purchasing. However, the personal goals and opinions of procurement personnel tend to intrude on their decision making. While the image and reputation of business brands such as General Electric, IBM and Pfizer give them a strong advantage in the minds of business buyers, many purchasing agents make decisions based on how their choices will be perceived within their organisations. This has significant consequences for brand loyalty in business markets. Selling organisations therefore need to consider the professional roles *and* the personal motivations of the purchasing agents within customer organisations.

It is common in business markets for discussions and negotiations between buyers and sellers to take place over an extended period of time and to involve considerable marketing effort. For example, when a bank contemplates installing new computer equipment across its branch network, it will spend considerable time in researching its future needs, and the available and emerging technology, before clarifying its technical expectations and available investment. The final purchase decision is likely to be arrived at by a group of senior managers or, quite commonly, by a committee, usually involving several departments.

## Ongoing relationships

Organisational buyers and their suppliers often seek to develop very close and ongoing relationships. In some cases, this develops into a formal partnership or joint venture. For example, Sony and Ericsson have combined to develop and market new-generation mobile phone and communications technologies. To continue our MRI example, the buyer of an MRI scanner would typically enter a contract for maintenance and service worth about $200 000 a year and for consumables worth about $150 000 a year.

To ensure ongoing quality of products in long-standing purchasing arrangements, buyers and sellers often establish statements of minimum levels of performance, particularly in relation to high-volume and high-value purchases. These standards relate to both the products and the customer service provided. Failure to deliver to those standards can lead to penalties or termination of the supply arrangements. Long-term supply agreements are often best incorporated into 'preferred supplier' and 'preferred customer' arrangements that offer a degree of certainty to both parties.

The cost, volume, complexity and core importance of business purchases makes business buyers place especially high importance on the ongoing service they receive from suppliers. As in consumer markets, service often involves a warranty. There are often numerous additional aspects of 'after sales' service in business markets, including:

- transport
- just-in-time delivery
- returns
- repairs
- technical help desk support
- dedicated account and relationship managers.

Businesses often cannot carry out their operations if their suppliers fail to meet expectations. For example, a public swimming pool operator cannot open for business if it does not receive its order of chlorine. On a bigger scale, Rolls-Royce needs to ensure it can quickly supply airlines with spare jet engine parts and technical advice at every aircraft maintenance location around the world. As explained in chapter 2, businesses need to manage the risks associated with their suppliers and other partners. Stable, cooperative relationships are a key to managing these risks and, indeed, to containing the repercussions of any supply problems. Open communication, both interpersonally and using information and communication technologies, is a crucial concern of business. Today, real-time communication between suppliers and buyers via the internet is helping to lower costs to customers and to build closer relationships with suppliers. For example, Philips Australia and Philips New Zealand adopted a communication system that replaced paper-based procedures with an online claim validation, invoice and payment process.[8] These issues are discussed in more detail in chapter 10.

There are some limitations on the relationships that can be built. If an arrangement becomes so extensive as to be anti-competitive (i.e. it makes it unreasonably difficult for other competitors to operate), it could be deemed illegal. Competition is monitored in Australia and New Zealand by the Australian Competition and Consumer Commission, and the Commerce Commission,[9] respectively. For example, the Commerce Commission forced Real Estate Network to abandon an agreement that set minimum commissions payable between its members (comprising almost all real estate agents in Christchurch).[10] A particular problem occurs when businesses begin to exchange products and services, rather than conduct financial transactions.

## Demand characteristics

The demand characteristics in business markets are quite different to those in consumer markets. Because any particular product a business purchases is usually just one of many, businesses tend not to adjust their consumption of it in relation to price changes. Rather they pass the cost on to their customers or, over time, seek to identify substitute products. In business markets, demand is much more likely to be affected as a consequence of some change in demand of the buyer's products. For example, over the past several years, the consumer market has become much more sensitive to the use of battery cage hens to produce eggs. This has resulted in increasing demand for free range eggs. This change in the consumer market has a significant effect on demand in the business market for battery and free range eggs. Generally, changes in demand tend to be much more volatile in business markets than in consumer markets. A small change in the consumer demand for a business's product can lead to much greater changes in demand for the business's inputs. The demand characteristics found in business markets are discussed in more depth in the next section.

# Parallel imports

'Parallel importing' is the term given to the practice of a business sourcing its supply of a product internationally, and bypassing a locally licensed manufacturer or authorised distributor. The practice is made possible by manufacturers or distributors 'pricing to market'; in other words, charging different prices to customers in different markets. When manufacturers or distributors do this, they open up the possibility of distributors being able to 'onsell' their product in other more expensively priced international markets and still make a profit. At the same time, these distributors are 'undercutting' local manufacturers or distributors — making it hard for them to compete.

The primary attraction of parallel importing to the sourcing business is the potential ability to source the desired product internationally for a cheaper price. In Australia, parallel importing is legal in some industries, but not in others, based primarily on the federal government's cost–benefit analysis of the potential harm this practice may cause to the relevant local industry versus the consumer benefit of potentially lower product prices. Not surprisingly, the federal government is frequently being lobbied by various industry and consumer groups with their opposing viewpoints.

One such industry where parallel importing is legal in Australia is the liquor industry, and one company that is concerned by the practice is Foster's. Besides its locally produced brews, Foster's has a licensing agreement to distribute the popular international beer brands of Corona and Stella Artois in the Australian market. In return for paying a significant sum to the international owners of these two brands for distribution rights, sales of Corona and Stella Artois by Foster's in Australia enable it to generate an additional $80 million a year in profits.

Foster's appears to have a basis for its concerns, with industry estimates indicating that up to 20 per cent of foreign beer is sourced by local retailers, such as Dan Murphy's, through parallel importing. The practice also appears to have increased in recent years, with a stronger Australian dollar giving local retailers increased purchasing power in international markets.

Effectively, parallel importing is currently costing Foster's $20 million in profits per year. Foster's profits suffer every time a liquor retail chain or independent liquor store chooses to parallel import, and the return on its marketing and advertising efforts in relation to the international beer brands declines. However, proponents of parallel importing argue that the mere fact that the possibility for parallel importing exists helps to keep distributors, such as Foster's, 'on their toes' in terms of pricing. The Coles Group, which owns the 1st Choice Liquor Superstore retail chain, recently released a statement outlining its position. It stated: 'Coles is not a big user of parallel importing in the liquor market. We have a very good relationship with Foster's and have been able to secure Corona at equivalent prices to parallel imports, ensuring good value for our customers at 1st Choice.'

## Questions

1. Outline how Foster's marketing of beer to retailers would differ from the marketing of beer to consumers.
2. Imagine you are the marketing manager for Foster's. Prepare a case to put to an organisational buyer from a major national retail liquor chain to convince them to source their supplies of the Corona and Stella Artois brands locally, rather than via parallel importing.

## Concepts and applications check

**Learning objective 2** understand the major issues involved in marketing to business customers

2.1 Describe the key differences between business customers and households who purchase goods and services for personal consumption.

**2.2** Imagine you are the marketing manager for a company that markets PABX network telephone systems for large and medium-sized businesses. The company targets larger organisations (those it defines as having 50 office-based staff or more in one geographic location), as its most lucrative potential market. Outline some of the needs or concerns you think you may encounter from business buyers in such organisations, and how you would attempt to meet these from a business-to-business marketing perspective.

**2.3** Outline how the marketing mix may differ for a company that offers building supplies to each of the following markets:
  (i) home handymen for 'do-it-yourself' backyard projects
  (ii) professional building companies.

# CHARACTERISTICS OF BUSINESS DEMAND

**Learning objective 3**
discuss the characteristics of demand in business markets

As mentioned in the previous section, demand operates differently in business markets compared to consumer markets. Unlike typical demand for consumer products, demand for business products can display a range of distinctive characteristics that are now discussed.

## Derived demand

Consumers buy products for their own personal consumption. The demand for domestic refrigerators is determined purely by how many refrigerators consumers want to buy. The demand for thermal insulation in the business market depends on the demand for refrigerators in the consumer market. In turn, the demand for polyurethane foam in the business market depends on the demand for thermal insulation that will ultimately end up inside the door and walls of refrigerators. It is clear then that demand in business markets is **derived demand**. Derived demand has a 'knock on' (or even 'snowball') effect at all levels of the value chain. For example, if consumers change their purchasing habits in favour of Fairtrade coffee (i.e. coffee that is grown, harvested and traded under terms and conditions that are not exploitative of workers or developing economies), that change in demand will have immediate effects in supermarkets and coffee shops. Shortly thereafter, these effects will be felt by coffee wholesalers, and ultimately — hopefully — in sales of coffee by small farmers in countries such as Kenya, Papua New Guinea, Colombia and Brazil. Business buyers of coffee, such as Gloria Jean's and Dôme, therefore need to understand and respond to changing consumer tastes and preferences. Any number of similar examples of derived demand can be found. Micro-processor manufacturer Intel, for example, is dependent on demand in the consumer market for computers and games consoles.

**derived demand** Demand in business markets that is due to demand in consumer markets.

### Demand fluctuations

Business products are prone to fluctuating demand much more so than products in consumer markets. Consider the airline industry. While airlines may renew their fleets on average every 20 years, shorter-term demand for aircraft depends on the growth of airlines, which can be severely affected by fluctuations in the economy that cause changes in consumer air travel intentions. Airlines will usually place orders for aircraft for delivery up to ten years in the future, but they are prone to cancelling these orders when they sense a downturn in travel intentions, such as the downturn that occurred as the global financial crisis unfolded. In this way, even a small decline in consumer demand for air travel can lead to a massive fall in demand for new aircraft. Conversely, when demand for air travel subsequently recovers after an economic downturn, airlines seek new aircraft to ensure they can service increasing customer numbers.

A similar argument applies to most capital equipment, such as heavy transport machinery, mainframe computers, manufacturing facilities and medical equipment. Manufacturers of earthmoving equipment, such as Caterpillar and Komatsu, are subject to extreme fluctuations in demand. Business customers usually make purchase decisions based on expectations of long-run demand. When combined with the long economic life of such products and the volatility of demand, this results in purchase decisions occurring infrequently, and also being subject to reversal or deferment.

## Joint demand

Many business products, particularly in the producer market, use numerous components — and sometimes even thousands. This results in interdependent demand for multiple products. This situation is known as **joint demand**. In manufacturing operations, such as those that might be found in the computer industry, the dozens of components that are necessary to make the product are jointly demanded and all suppliers to the manufacturer need to be able to meet rigid production schedules. They are commonly also required to provide 'just in time' supply so that the manufacturer does not have to hold a large inventory of parts. Under these conditions, failure by one supplier, due to, say, a shortage of vital components or industrial action, can lead to the shutdown of a whole production process. For marketers, joint demand provides an opportunity to generate sales. For example, when Siemens installs an MRI machine in a hospital, it will also try to secure the maintenance and supplies contracts that are essential to keep the machine in service. In such circumstances, business buyers usually make purchasing decisions based on the total costs and benefits, rather than evaluating the individual items.

**joint demand** Interdependent demand for products that are used together in the production of another product.

## Pricing and demand

In many parts of the business market, demand is *inelastic*. **Inelastic demand** is an economic concept that describes demand that is relatively independent of price. In other words, a large change in price will result in only a small change in demand. Consider the computer industry. If the microprocessor in a laptop computer represents 10 per cent of the total production cost of the laptop, then even a 20 per cent rise in the cost of the microprocessor will result in only a 2 per cent rise in the cost of the finished product. Assuming this is passed on to the consumer, a $1500 laptop will rise in price to about $1530 and consumer demand for the laptop is unlikely to significantly change. Under these circumstances, it is unlikely that a computer manufacturer would immediately terminate a long-term relationship with its current supplier. It is, however, likely that such a price rise would have implications in the longer term, particularly if it is out of step with alternative suppliers. Similarly, a 10 per cent increase in the price of concrete will only have a minimal, if any, effect on the price of and demand for a finished home. At the same time, a 10 per cent increase in the price of concrete from the usual supplier is likely to lead a builder to obtain prices from competitive suppliers. Under these circumstances, the demand facing individual concrete suppliers will be highly elastic, especially since concrete is an undifferentiated commodity product. Generally speaking, *industry demand* tends to be price inelastic in business markets, while *company demand* can be highly elastic. Elasticity of demand is discussed in detail in chapter 8.

**inelastic demand** Demand that is relatively independent of price, a common characteristic of demand within industries in business markets.

# Spotlight Flight turbulence

French aircraft manufacturer Airbus delivered the first model of its long awaited A380 model to Singapore Airlines. The double-decker A380 model is the largest passenger aircraft in the world, with a seating capacity for up to 853 passengers. The attraction of such a large aircraft to major international airlines was immediate, with its potential seating capacity providing airlines with the potential opportunity to generate more passenger revenue per flight. Emirates and Qantas were other airlines that received A380 models to add to their existing fleets in the first year of its release.

In hindsight, the timing of the A380 model release was unfortunate for Airbus. Shortly after it was released, the global financial crisis began to adversely affect economies around the world. One of the first flow-on effects of the global financial crisis was a severe downturn in the number of flights; particularly the number of international flights. The phenomenon affected both the business and holiday travel sectors. The situation was further exacerbated around the same time by worldwide panic over the H1N1 influenza (swine flu) virus.

The demand for large, long-haul aircraft such as the A380 depends, to a large degree, on the level of demand for international tourism. As this fell away, airlines were forced to respond. For instance, Qantas cancelled 50 international flights over an eight-week period during this time, announced extensive job cuts to reduce its expenses, cut the price of fares to encourage travelling and — like many other airlines — cancelled or deferred orders of additional new aircraft with major manufacturers such as Boeing and Airbus. Boeing suffered 65 order cancellations in the first five months of 2009, while Airbus suffered 21 order cancellations. In total, the aircraft manufacturers went forward by just 11 orders in five months at the height of the global financial crisis, compared to 884 in the same period a year earlier.

While tourism volumes have recovered somewhat in more recent times, continuing macro-economic uncertainty and the possibility of a 'double-dip' recession in some of the world's major economies has resulted in continuing sluggish demand for long-haul aircraft. A recently placed bulk order for more A380 models by Emirates has gone some way, however, towards reviving the spirits of aircraft manufacturers. However, Airbus was further hampered by bad publicity associated with a series of mid-air engine incidents in their A380 aircraft in 2010. In Australia, Qantas temporarily grounded its entire fleet of six A380 models while engine issues were investigated.[11]

## Question

Describe the characteristics of demand for aircraft and whether this demand can best be classified as derived, joint or inelastic.

## Concepts and applications check

**Learning objective 3** discuss the characteristics of demand in business markets

**3.1** Explain the following aspects of business demand, using your own examples:
  (a) derived demand
  (b) joint demand
  (c) inelastic demand.

**3.2** Choose a product (a good or service) for which consumer demand tends to rise (or fall) depending on prevailing economic conditions. Trace the product back through the business market, using the concept of derived demand to explain how demand is affected at each stage of production.

**3.3** Find an example of a product for which a small increase in consumer demand could generate a large increase in business demand.

# BUSINESS BUYING BEHAVIOUR

Business buying behaviour shares some characteristics with consumer buying behaviour (discussed in chapter 4). Business buying behaviour, however, also has some unique characteristics that affect the buying decision process.

Business purchases take the form of a straight rebuy, a modified rebuy or a new task purchase. The form depends on the business's purpose for the purchase and reflects the level of involvement the business has with the purchase decision. The level of involvement is also reflected in the buying approach the business takes, which may involve some or all of negotiation, description, inspection or sampling.

A **straight rebuy** is typical of the majority of business purchases and occurs when buyers purchase the same products routinely from established vendors under already-established terms of sale, often through an automated or semi-automated ordering system. Businesses generally want straight rebuys to be efficient and convenient. For suppliers, straight rebuys can offer a relatively reliable source of income, provided they offer that convenience and efficiency. For example, Yellow Cabs and Black and White Cabs both try to become the preferred suppliers of taxi services to businesses. When this happens, the business adopts one service and, in return, the person booking the fare does not have to provide any details about the pick-up location. For many routine business purchases, the internet is proving to be a cost-effective medium. For example, a components supplier can go to TNT's website and book a courier to pick up products from their dispatch centre to freight them to business customers. Similar specialist e-business portals exist for many products. In Australia, almost 50 per cent of businesses place orders over the internet, while about 27 per cent or 193 000 businesses receive orders over the internet. These order placement numbers are growing at an annual rate of 15 per cent, while the revenue accompanying them is growing annually by more than 50 per cent. In New Zealand, 60 per cent of businesses place orders online, and 37 per cent of businesses receive orders online.[12]

Straight rebuys occur when a business has found a satisfactory product and its needs are stable. A change can be triggered by the development of new product features or the need for different performance characteristics from the product. In such an instance, the business chooses a similar, but not identical, product to one it has previously purchased. This is known as a **modified rebuy** and usually involves some degree of evaluation of alternative product options. For example, when it comes time for a police station to replace its photocopier, the station manager will usually evaluate a small range of alternative products from the current and other suppliers. The latest models are likely to have some additional features, such as faster copying speed and lower toner usage. Companies hoping to supply such equipment need to ensure that their brand is well known and that their sales staff make regular contact with existing and potential customers.

When a business identifies a new problem or introduces a new process or product, it will often need to make a purchase in a product category for the first time. This is known as a **new task purchase**. For example, when a newsagency makes the decision to offer a digital photo printing service, it is aiming to offer a completely new service in a new product category, with which it has no previous experience and no knowledge of the alternative products or suppliers. In installing a digital photo printing kiosk, the business will need to engage in an extended information search to develop an understanding of technical alternatives, product specifications, possible vendors and likely price, including consumables and servicing arrangements.

Each form of business purchase we have just described — straight rebuy, modified rebuy and new task purchase — involves a different level of engagement, which,

**Learning objective 4**
analyse business buyer behaviour and decision making

**straight rebuy** The low-engagement purchase of the same products as previously purchased from established vendors under established terms.

**modified rebuy** The purchase of a product that is similar, but not identical, to one a business has previously purchased, after evaluating a small range of alternatives.

**new task purchase** A first purchase in a product category in response to a new problem, process or product.

along with the complexity of the purchase, nature of the product and how crucial the product is to the purchasing business, affects how the business goes about making its purchasing decision. Typically, business purchasing decisions involve one or more of the following:

1. *negotiation.* Business purchases that involve large volumes of products, high-value products, infrequently purchased products or custom-built products are often subject to extensive negotiation between the buyer and the seller. For example, a business seeking to have a new warehouse built and fitted out would usually invite potential suppliers to submit bids on the tender for the warehouse. Based on the tender responses, the buyer may shortlist certain suppliers and then negotiate specific aspects of the deal with them, before making a decision on the successful tenderer and the exact specifications of the final purchase. In other cases, it may not be appropriate or possible for the buyer to specify their requirements in detail. This situation is common in the purchase of professional services such as architecture or management consulting. For these purchases, the buyer may prefer to evaluate the best proposal from potential suppliers and then negotiate further details, including price.

2. *description.* Some products can be described by a set of technical specifications and, given a level of trust between the buyer and seller, this may be sufficient to form the basis of a business purchase. For example, concrete can be ordered simply by specifying volume, strength and water content. Structural and reinforcing steel, used in construction, can be ordered by dimension and strength. Construction timber is ordered by botanical variety, dimensions and quality grade.

3. *inspection.* Some products do not lend themselves to description or specification. For example, a business looking to lease new office premises would always need to inspect the site, the facilities and the surrounds in order to properly evaluate what is on offer. As technology continues to advance, it is becoming increasingly possible to conduct a virtual inspection of products through complex multimedia presentations, often via the internet.

4. *sampling.* For high-volume, standardised purchases a sample of the product may be inspected or analysed. The sample is taken to be representative of the quality of the product. This method is appropriate for bulk purchases of commodities, such as sugar, or mass manufactured items, such as lightbulbs.

## The organisational buyer

In most organisations, business purchasing decisions are made by groups or must be approved by a number of levels in the organisational hierarchy. It is therefore appropriate to view most business buying as a group decision-making process. The groups and structures within an organisation that make business buying decisions are collectively known as the **buying centre**. Of course, in some organisations, particularly small businesses, purchasing decisions may be made solely by an individual — usually a manager or the proprietor. By contrast, in large organisations — and especially government organisations — large purchases may involve buying centres with dozens of people working on the purchase decision for months, or even years. For example, the purchase of defence equipment involves billions of dollars, years of development and extraordinary consequences. Suppliers of such products need to invest considerable time, people and financial resources to maximise their chances of success in a competitive purchasing process.

Marketers that wish to sell to organisations need to identify the buying centre. The various roles undertaken by members of the buying centre are:

- *initiators.* Initiators are those who recognise the need for the purchase. For example, a sales manager may decide that field sales representatives will be able

**buying centre** The groups and structures within an organisation that make business buying decisions.

to better serve their customers if they can access information and specifications from the company's website and intranet during sales visits. The manager may decide there is a need for each sales representative to have a wireless internet access service provided for their laptop.

- *users*. Users are those for whom the product is being purchased. To continue the example, if the business proceeds with the purchase of wireless internet access, then the field sales representatives will be the users. After a purchase has been made, users will be the ones who evaluate the product performance relative to expectations.
- *influencers*. Those who develop the product specification and who are responsible for formally evaluating alternatives. They are often technical experts. For example, information technology personnel will be involved in developing the specifications for the wireless internet access and evaluating the offerings by providers such as Telstra, Vodafone, Optus and Virgin.
- *deciders*. Deciders are those with the authority to make the final decision to purchase. For the wireless internet access, this could, for example, be the sales manager, their manager or the information technology manager, depending on how responsibilities and authorities are arranged within the organisation.
- *buyers*. Buyers are those in the organisation that ultimately make the purchase. They — in collaboration with the other members of the buying centre — choose between suppliers, deal with the seller, and negotiate purchase terms and conditions. For example, the buyer of the wireless internet access could be the sales manager, or a member of the information technology, administration, finance or office services teams. Buyers are often referred to as purchasing managers and, in some larger organisations, buyers are members of purchasing departments. In reseller markets, particularly among larger retailers, buyers perform an important marketing function and the buying role is highly specialised. In large department stores and supermarket chains, buyers will be responsible for product categories and will develop close relationships with a wide range of potential suppliers.
- *gatekeepers*. Gatekeepers are those who control information relevant to a purchasing decision. Gatekeepers can be very powerful in purchasing decisions and in organisations generally. For example, for complex purchases, businesses often have to rely on the advice of information technology specialists and engineers. The inability of people without specialist knowledge to interpret technical documentation makes gatekeepers important and influential. This role often overlaps with the buyer and influencer roles.

Each role may be undertaken by one person or several people, and some people may fulfil multiple roles. For example, it is relatively common for the buyer and decider to be the same person. The size, composition, degree of formality and structure of the buying centre will vary according to its size, market position, business activity, the volume and kinds of products being purchased and the company's structure and operational practices. In the cases of new task purchases, the buying centre is likely to be large, while routine repurchases are likely to be made by an individual.

The crucial tasks for the potential supplying organisation are to identify:
- those individuals who play the key roles, such as the decider and gatekeeper
- the stages in the decision process
- the criteria upon which the decision is likely to be made.

For supplier organisations, it is crucial to establish personal relationships with key members of the buying centre. Not all members will be accessible, but some typically are. In our example, at least some of the gatekeepers, buyers and influencers would likely be identifiable and accessible to a telecommunications services marketer. The marketer, of course, must determine the criteria upon which the ultimate purchase decision is likely to be based (how to go about this is discussed in detail in chapter 9).

## The business decision-making process

Broadly speaking, the business decision-making process involves the same basic stages as the consumer decision-making process, but for business purchases most stages are more protracted and formalised. The process is illustrated in figure 5.2.

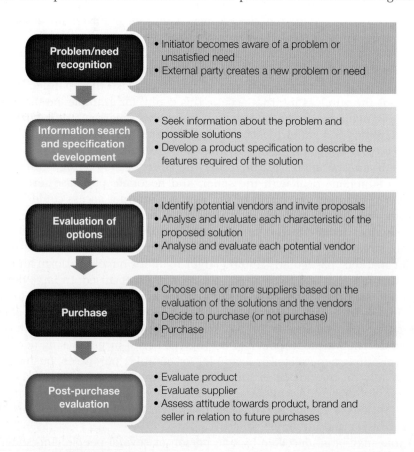

**FIGURE 5.2**

The business decision-making process

Just as the consumer decision-making process varies depending on the nature of the purchase (e.g. habitual purchases versus extended decision purchases), the business decision process, and the extent to which it follows this model, will vary between straight rebuys, modified rebuys and new task purchases.

### Problem/need recognition

Business purchase decisions begin when a problem or unfulfilled need is recognised. In the business buying centre model, the person who recognises the problem is known as the initiator. A problem or need may arise for any number of reasons. For example, a small manufacturer wishing to move into exporting may encounter a need for specialist consulting services or for an export agent. On a smaller scale, if an office photocopier runs out of toner, it triggers the need to purchase more toner. It is also common for problem/need recognition to be stimulated by changes in the company's external relationships with customers, distributors or suppliers.

For example, if a freight company decides to stop servicing a regional area, then the business will find itself needing a new freight service.

### Information search and specification development

The second stage of the business decision-making process involves seeking information on the problem/need and possible solutions, and formalising the product requirements. The product requirements are usually detailed in a written product specification. This is a distinguishing feature from the consumer information search process, in which consumers usually use less formal processes and are limited in their ability to demand customised solutions from potential suppliers.

This stage of the decision-making process requires extensive input from the members of the buying centre, especially the users and influencers, who are often best placed to describe how the product can meet their needs.

### Evaluation of options

Once the product specification has been developed, the buying centre searches for potential suppliers and specific product solutions. The buying centre may be aware of some possible suppliers through existing relationships or the promotional efforts of those and other suppliers. It can locate further possibilities through trade directories and the internet, which is particularly useful for identifying suppliers based abroad. The internet has led to the emergence of 'e-procurement' specialists, which are organisations that specialise in locating potential suppliers and facilitating relationships, production and delivery arrangements between purchasers in Australia and New Zealand and suppliers in countries such as China and India.

New task purchases are likely to involve extensive evaluation of potential suppliers and solutions. This will often involve inviting 'expressions of interest' or more formal proposals from potential suppliers. Government organisations often invite expressions of interest to help them identify panels of potential suppliers and, often, to help promote and support local businesses.

Once potential suppliers have been identified and details of their proposed offerings have been received, the purchasing organisation systematically analyses and evaluates all important aspects of the potential purchase, including materials, technological features, designs and customised features. Many organisations also formally analyse each potential supplier on characteristics such as price, delivery, product availability, resale value, reputation, reliability and compliance with government statutory requirements (e.g. employment practices and environmental safeguards). Potential vendors may be excluded under this process if there is any uncertainty regarding their ability to meet the required standards.

### Purchase

The detailed evaluation of suppliers and their offerings leads to a decision about whether to purchase, which product to purchase and which supplier to choose. It is common for businesses to choose multiple suppliers, with each providing some part of the total solution. For example, a business building a new e-commerce website may choose one business to create the information architecture of the site, another to build the software for the site and yet another to host the site. These choices are made based on the systematic analysis of each important aspect of the potential purchase that takes place in the previous step. Government organisations, in particular, often take this approach. Many businesses prefer to spread their purchasing over multiple parties to avoid becoming too dependent on any one supplier.

In this fourth stage of the business decision-making process, the chosen product is specified; delivery, pricing terms and conditions, and any post-sale servicing arrangements are explicitly agreed upon; and an order is placed.

## Post-purchase evaluation

Following purchase, the organisation — especially the users within the organisation — can fully evaluate whether the product fulfils expectations. For example, in the mobile internet access example discussed earlier, post-purchase evaluation would be based on speed, number of connection drop-outs and whether the actual coverage lived up to the promises of the vendor. Many capital equipment suppliers guarantee that the equipment will be operational a certain percentage of the time (e.g. that in any one period, a piece of machinery will be available and working 95 per cent of the time). Beyond conformance with technical requirements, a chosen product may not adequately solve the problem or satisfy the need that initiated the purchase decision. This is a common problem in purchase and implementation of computer software and hardware systems. If the performance of the product or of the supplier is below expectations, the business purchaser may choose to seek corrective action or compensation from the supplier. Alternatively, they may choose to search for a new supplier, particularly for recurrent or service product purchases. The results of the evaluation process become feedback and input in subsequent purchase cycles, both in terms of the product and the supplier.

# Environmental influences

Business purchasing decisions are influenced by the organisation's internal environment (the nature of the organisation, and the power structures and individuals within it) and the external environment (the micro environment and the macro environment) (see chapter 2).

## Internal environmental factors

Internal environmental factors can explain why each organisation may make different purchasing decisions in different ways. The key, closely related, organisational factors are:

* *the nature of the organisation* — its size, location, industry, objectives and resources. These characterstics are fundamental to the types of products the business will require.
* *the structure of the organisation and its buying centres* — how responsibilities and authorities are arranged within the organisation and, more specifically, the buying centres. The complexity of the buying centre, purchasing processes and organisational policy can influence an organisation's willingness and ability to respond to purchasing demands or opportunities. For the marketer, it is important to understand status, roles and the relative influence of members of the buying centre. While these may not be immediately obvious, successful business suppliers will usually devote significant time and resources to better understanding them and then building relationships with members of the buying centre.
* *the individuals within the organisation and its buying centre* — those personal characteristics of members of the buying centre that may affect their decisions, including their personality and status within the organisation. Marketers, generally, might expect younger members of the buying centre to be more technologically informed and more open to innovative products, but to encounter resistance from older members who might be more risk averse. Individual factors are a powerful influence on business purchasing decisions. They make developing trust and confidence between customers and suppliers — which is the key to success in long-term business-to-business relationships — extremely challenging.

## External environmental factors

As discussed in chapter 2, the external marketing environment includes the macro environment (political, economic, sociocultural, technological and legal forces) and the micro environment (the industry, customers and competitive situation). External environmental factors are not directly controllable by the organisation. This means there is a greater level of risk involved in decisions made in relation to the external environment. This can, in turn, lead to organisations deferring or avoiding business purchasing decisions, particularly in times of uncertainty. For example, the previous Spotlight highlighted that a perception or expectation of an economic downturn tends to cause airlines to defer or cancel purchase contracts. Sometimes decisions not to purchase can involve high penalty costs.

The recent decision of the New South Wales government to abandon the $5.3 billion Sydney Metro rail project, just months before work was due to start, is a case in point. The project was to construct a seven-kilometre underground rail line between Central Station and the city's inner-western suburbs. The cancellation was in response to widespread community anger from individuals and businesses that would have seen their properties and jobs affected by the line's construction. The project's extremely late cancellation put the New South Wales government in the position of having to offer substantial compensation payouts to construction and engineering businesses that had successfully tendered for the work and planned accordingly.[13]

Conversely, economic optimism, which follows after a period of sustained economic growth, may encourage organisations to make ambitious long-term purchasing decisions. Technological breakthroughs or improvements, such as the introduction of broadband and fibre-optic telecommunications technology, can also stimulate purchase decisions.

Competitors' actions are also, of course, crucial influences on how businesses may go about making purchasing decisions. For example, a business that sources components locally may decide to source them from a cheaper international supplier in order to remain competitive with other businesses that have already made the same decision.

# Brands and business buying decisions          Spotlight

The list of the world's top ten brands, published by Interbrand, contains few real surprises. Most of the companies listed in the table[14] are 'household' names, and are heavily involved in the consumer market. Perhaps one of the brands many consumers might be less familiar with is GE, which operates in both the business and consumer markets.

| Ranking | Brand | Brand value (US$ millions) |
| --- | --- | --- |
| 1 | Coca-Cola | 70452 |
| 2 | IBM | 64727 |
| 3 | Microsoft | 60895 |
| 4 | Google | 43557 |
| 5 | GE | 42808 |
| 6 | McDonald's | 33578 |
| 7 | Intel | 32015 |
| 8 | Nokia | 29495 |
| 9 | Disney | 28731 |
| 10 | HP | 26867 |

GE is a large and diverse technology-driven company. Its products and services include jet engines, power generation, financial services, water processing, oil and gas exploration, medical imaging and

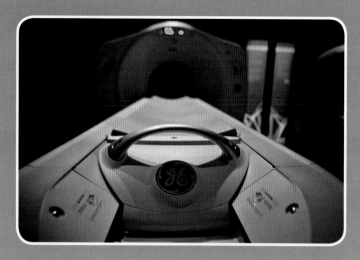

appliances. With origins springing from Thomas Edison and General Electric Company in 1890, technological innovation is thought of as part of the company's DNA.

Across the vast spectrum of its businesses, perhaps how GE may be best known to consumers is through its appliances and consumer finance activities (established to support the sales of its appliances). The remainder (and majority) of the company's activities occur far away from the gaze of consumers. This begs the question of how brands are actually valued in lists such as those complied by Interbrand, apart from the financial value of the corporation, and this is the subject of continuing academic debate.

In terms of buying decisions, the presumption is that business buyers are more 'rational' than consumers and, as a result, less susceptible to emotional brand triggers. Thus, does a hospital give preference to GE-branded diagnostic or imaging equipment; or does an airline prefer its aircraft to be fitted with GE engines; or does an electricity-generating company always specify GE turbines? It is difficult to respond to such hypothetical questions. However, on the basis of the Interbrand data, the old marketing adage that 'nobody was ever fired for buying IBM' (an even larger mega-brand for business buyers), probably also holds true for GE business customers.

## Question

Imagine you are the marketing manager for a competitor to GE, and are dealing with an organisational buyer. Referring to figure 5.2, consider how could you use your knowledge of the business decision-making process to guard against the organisational buyer's potential perception that 'nobody was ever fired for buying IBM (or GE)'?

## Concepts and applications check

**Learning objective 4** analyse business buyer behaviour and decision making

4.1 Describe business marketing situations that would best suit each of the following purchase methods:
   (a) negotiation
   (b) description
   (c) inspection
   (d) sampling.

4.2 Imagine you are the marketing manager for a telecommunications company that provides phone and internet services to the corporate sector and that you have business purchasers in each of the following three categories:
   (a) new task purchase
   (b) modified rebuy
   (c) straight rebuy.

   How would you tailor your marketing mix to suit each situation?

4.3 Explain the concept of a buying centre in the context of business marketing and outline the potential members of an organisation's buying centre.

4.4 What environmental influences may affect business buying decisions and which of these can potentially be influenced by marketers?

4.5 Draw up a summary table and list the major similarities and differences between business and consumer markets.

# SUMMARY

 **Learning objective 1** explain the characteristics of different types of business markets

The overall business market can be subdivided into reseller markets, producer markets, government markets and institutional markets. Reseller markets comprise marketing intermediaries that buy products in order to sell or lease them to another party for profit. Producer markets comprise businesses and professionals that purchase products for use in the production of other products, or in their daily business operations. Government markets comprise the markets made up of federal, state and local governments, which buy products for use in providing services for citizens. Institutional markets comprise non-public, not-for-profit organisations that buy and sell products.

 **Learning objective 2** understand the major issues involved in marketing to business customers

There are some fundamental differences in the characteristics of business markets compared to consumer markets. Many business market transactions are for very high-value purchases. Many business-to-business purchases involve high volumes and regular repeat purchases. Price and other conditions of the sale are often open to negotiation. There are far fewer buyers and sellers in business markets. Product alternatives are often subject to extensive formal evaluation, with decisions made by committees or subject to multiple levels of approvals. The relationships between buyers and sellers tend to be very long term and involve extensive after-sales support.

 **Learning objective 3** discuss the characteristics of demand in business markets

Demand in business markets is due to demand in consumer markets and so is known as 'derived demand'. Demand for business products tends to fluctuate much more than demand in consumer markets. Many products exchanged in business markets are used together in the production of another product. This creates a situation of joint demand, where demand for one product is the same as or directly related to the demand for another product. Because products in business markets are often just one of many used in the production of other products, demand for them tends to be relatively unresponsive to changes in price. This is known as inelastic demand. Demand tends to be relatively inelastic within an industry, but can be elastic in relation to individual companies.

 **Learning objective 4** analyse business buyer behaviour and decision making

Business purchases take the form of a straight rebuy, a modified rebuy or a new task purchase, each of which leads to different levels of engagement in the purchase decision-making process. Most business purchasing decisions are group decisions. The group of people involved in the decision is known as the buying centre. A buying centre is made up of initiators, users, influencers, deciders, buyers and gatekeepers. Marketers need to identify and understand the buying centre in target organisations and build relationships with those members of the buying centre who are accessible and influential. Marketers must also understand the stages in the buying centre's decision process and the criteria upon which the decision is likely to be made. The business purchasing decision-making process comprises five stages: problem/need

## Key terms and concepts

business markets  147
buying centre  162
derived demand  158
government markets  150
inelastic demand  159
institutional markets  151
joint demand  159
modified rebuy  161
new task purchase  161
producer markets  149
reseller markets  148
straight rebuy  161

recognition, information search and specification development, evaluation of options, purchase and post-purchase evaluation. The decision-making process is influenced by internal and external environmental factors, including the nature of the organisation, its structure and its people; political, economic, sociocultural, technological and legal forces; and the actions of competitors and customers.

# The world of pharmaceutical marketing

The pharmaceutical industry is one of the biggest sectors of the world economy, with annual sales in excess of US$800 billion. The industry is expected to experience solid growth in the next few years and be worth a staggering US$1.1 trillion by 2014. In addition to being one of the biggest sectors in the world economy, this industry is also very profitable.

The United States currently accounts for 38 per cent of the international industry, followed by Europe with 31 per cent market share. Asia, Africa and Australia combined accounted for only 12 per cent of the world market. Despite representing only a very small percentage of the world pharmaceutical market, the industry in Australia still contributes approximately A$8 billion to the national economy, and is responsible for keeping about 14 000 Australians employed. More than 260 million prescriptions were dispensed in community pharmacies in Australia in a recent year. The medicinal and pharmaceuticals sector recently became Australia's largest manufactured export sector, contributing over A$4.1 billion in annual export earnings. Australia is also a destination of choice for multinational companies that are conducting medical trials.

Macro-environmental conditions affect the industry, and several emerging trends are set to impact on the market over the next few years. For a start, different countries are recovering from the economic malaise brought on by the global financial crisis at different rates, which is affecting broader market conditions. IMS Health, a leading international pharmaceutical market research company, has flagged that the composition of the global pharmaceutical market is expected to shift strongly in upcoming years.

IMS Health lists 17 countries — identified as representing 'pharmerging' markets — which, due to factors including strong national economic growth and greater government (and private) healthcare funding, are beginning to represent a much larger proportion of the world pharmaceutical market. China, the leading pharmerging market is expected to have an additional US$40 billion in annual pharmaceutical sales within the next three years. Other pharmerging markets, including Brazil, Russia and India, are also expected to enjoy strong growth rates of between US$5–15 billion in annual sales over the same period. The other 13 pharmerging markets (including countries such as South Africa, Thailand, Romania and Egypt) are expected to have an additional US$1–5 billion in annual sales.

The world's major pharmaceutical companies enjoy considerable dominance in the industry, with the leading companies enjoying a generous market share and impressive sales results. The world's major pharmaceutical companies in a recent year are shown in the table that accompanies this case study.[15]

**TABLE 5.1** The world's top 15 pharmaceutical companies

| Rank | Company | Sales (US$ billions) | Location of head office |
|------|---------|----------------------|-------------------------|
| 1 | Pfizer | 41.7 | United States |
| 2 | Novartis | 36.7 | Switzerland |
| 3 | Sanofi-Aventis | 35.1 | France |
| 4 | GlaxoSmithKline | 34.3 | United Kingdom |
| 5 | AstraZeneca | 33.2 | United Kingdom/Sweden |
| 6 | Roche | 31.3 | Switzerland |
| 7 | Johnson & Johnson | 26.9 | United States |
| 8 | Merck & Co. | 25.0 | United States |
| 9 | Eli Lilly and Company | 19.6 | United States |
| 10 | Abbott | 19.4 | United States |
| 11 | Teva | 15.7 | Israel |

*(continued)*

**TABLE 5.1** *Continued*

| Rank | Company | Sales (US$ billions) | Location of head office |
|------|---------|----------------------|-------------------------|
| 12 | Bayer | 15.4 | Germany |
| 13 | Wyeth | 14.8 | United States |
| 14 | Amgen | 14.8 | United States |
| 15 | Boehringer | 14.6 | Japan |

The reason pharmaceutical companies generate such enormous sales is easily understood. Their products help people manage illness. However, just as the sales figures are impressive, the costs involved in developing new pharmaceutical products are staggering. Drug discovery and development can take decades and cost hundreds of millions of dollars. In a recent year, an estimated US$120 billion was spent on research and development for medicines worldwide. On a much smaller scale, the latest figures show that the Australian pharmaceutical industry currently spends just over A$1 billion annually on research and development.

Only a small portion of the total investment in drug research eventually leads to a marketable pharmaceutical product. For every 10 000 compounds that are tested for potential medical benefits, only five are clinically tested, and only one product reaches the market. Obtaining market approval from regulatory bodies such as the Therapeutic Goods Administration is a difficult and long process, involving years of closely controlled clinical trials. It is not uncommon for a pharmaceutical company to spend years developing a pharmaceutical product, only to discover some unacceptable side effect or risk factor in clinical trials when seeking market approval. This, at best, results in further development and trial costs; at worst, it can mean years of investment and work that generates no financial return at all.

When the total investment in research, development and trials is taken into account, the average cost of bringing a new drug to market is about US$1 billion. The average cost for a new biotechnology product is higher still. As for any innovative product, the developers of pharmaceuticals seek to protect their intellectual property in a new drug design by applying for a patent. The length of the development, trial and approval process, however, ensures that the patent period is already on its way to expiring by the time the company gets the opportunity to sell the pharmaceutical product for the first time. Once the patent expires, competitors are able to copy the pharmaceutical product's chemical formula and market their own branded or generic versions of the drug. It is, therefore, imperative that the company recoups its investment in the first five or so years after the product is introduced to the market. Clearly, there is enormous pressure to ensure that every new product does succeed in the marketplace. In a recent year, there were over 2950 medicines in development for various illnesses. The breakdown of medicines in development for this year is represented in figure 5.3.[16]

**FIGURE 5.3**

Medicines in development

Brain tumours: 58
Depression: 66
Antibiotics: 83
Female-only cancer: 163
Anxiety disorders: 38
Obstetric/gynecologic: 86
Pain management: 171
Thrombosis: 40
HIV/AIDS: 97
Childhood cancer: 25

Stroke: 22
Vaccines: 146
Dementia: 90
Cardiovascular: 250
Rare diseases: 303
Diabetes: 235
Multiple sclerosis: 46
Cancer: over 800
Genetic diseases: 36
Schizophrenia: 54
Infectious diseases: 33

The most marketable pharmaceutical products are, of course, the breakthrough drugs that introduce a treatment for a previously untreatable condition, or that substantially improve on the currently available treatment options. For such a product, demand is guaranteed. The best known breakthrough drug of the past 20 years is undoubtedly Pfizer's Viagra (or sildenafil citrate). Pfizer's researchers originally developed the drug as part of an effort to find a new treatment for high blood pressure and heart disease, but the product was eventually found to be an effective — and very marketable — treatment for erectile dysfunction. Sales exceed US$1 billion a year. Pfizer's patents on sildenafil citrate expire between 2011 and 2013 and it is likely to suffer a significant decline in sales as competitors release imitation products. This is the fate of most drug innovations.

The largest category of prescription pharmaceuticals are those that deal with heart conditions. The biggest selling drug in the world is Lipitor (or atorvastatin). Again, this is a Pfizer product. It alone accounts for more than 25 per cent of Pfizer's sales in dollar terms. In a recent year, there were nearly ten million prescriptions for Lipitor in the Australian pharmaceutical industry alone, and more than US$13 billion worth of sales of Lipitor were recorded globally. Pfizer lost its patent for Lipitor in 2011. When competitors enter the market with other-branded or generic versions of a pharmaceutical product, the developer of the drug can no longer charge a premium price. It can maintain a reasonable market share (due to being the established brand — people, including doctors, know 'Viagra', not 'sildenafil citrate'), but it cannot maintain the profit margin on the product.

With the loss of its patent for Lipitor, Pfizer risks losing the monopoly on sales that it has enjoyed with a flagship product offering. With a base in the United States (the economy for which was worst affected by the global financial crisis) Pfizer is already facing tough market conditions. As the market leader, Pfizer will need to think creatively in order to respond to the duel threats posed by the loss of some of its most profitable patents, and the rise of new, stronger competitors who are benefiting from the favourable conditions in the pharmerging markets.

## The promotion of pharmaceuticals

Having spent up to US$1 billion developing a pharmaceutical product, marketers need to implement effective promotional campaigns to ensure the investment is recouped and profits are generated. The marketing of pharmaceuticals is complicated by the heavy regulation that applies to the industry. Because misuse of pharmaceuticals can be dangerous — and indeed lethal — governments in every country apply strict rules to the marketing of drugs. For example, drugs are broadly classified into 'over-the-counter' drugs and 'prescription' drugs. Consumers may buy over-the-counter pharmaceuticals without a doctor's approval (though some, such as those containing pseudoephedrine, require identification to be presented in a bid to prevent illegal drug manufacturers from obtaining large quantities for use in producing amphetamines and other substances). Many prescription drugs, however, can only be sold to consumers who have obtained a doctor's prescription. Recent legislative changes in Australia mean that nurses and midwives are able to prescribe a specific range of medications that attract a subsidy under the Pharmaceutical Benefits Scheme (PBS). Another category of drugs can only be administered by doctors (e.g. strong painkillers that are not suitable for self-medication).

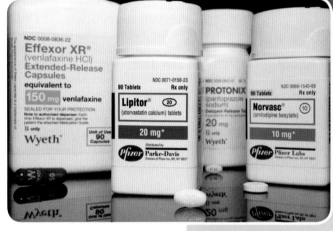

Pfizer, the world's number-one pharmaceutical company, lost its patent for Lipitor, the world's number-one selling drug, in 2011. The loss of the patent will affect the profitability of the brand, and along with other market factors, represents a challenge for Pfizer as it seeks to maintain its dominant market position.

In Australia it is illegal to advertise prescription drugs to consumers. Instead, pharmaceutical companies must promote prescription drugs to medical practitioners in the hope that they will (appropriately) prescribe the drug to patients. Some pharmaceutical companies have partly side-stepped the restrictions by running public advertisements on health issues (for which they have a treatment product) and encouraging people to ask their doctors about the treatment options. In New Zealand, on the other hand, pharmaceutical companies can advertise prescription medicines directly to the general public. This creates demand in that potential consumers become aware of the product and how it may help treat some health problem they may suffer. They can then enquire about the drug with their medical practitioner, who still ultimately decides whether or not a prescription for the drug is appropriate. Pharmaceutical companies also advertise their products in medical journals and other specialist publications.

Doctors are usually considered the most important players in pharmaceutical sales because they write the majority of the prescriptions that determine which drugs will be used by patients. Pharmaceutical companies generally employ sales people to market directly and personally to doctors. A medium-sized pharmaceutical company in Australia will have a sales force of dozens of representatives. The large companies have hundreds of representatives. Globally, the top pharmaceutical companies spend billions of dollars a year on sales representatives who deal personally with doctors. The management of such a large and important sales force that must deal with specialists (doctors) seeking technical information can be a challenge for pharmaceutical companies. Sales people need both scientific and technical knowledge of their products and strong skills in relationship marketing. Sales representatives for pharmaceutical companies often give medical practitioners free merchandise, as well as other giveaways, as a means of trying to keep their products in the forefront of their minds.

Pharmaceutical sales representatives take into account regulatory guidelines in their interactions with doctors and other medical professionals. For example, under the Code of Conduct Guidelines set out by Medicines Australia, which are used in conjunction with the Code of Conduct, revisions have been made restricting sales representatives to giving practitioners 'only items that are educational and/or directly related to the practice of medicine' as brand name reminders. This restriction means that pharmaceutical sales representatives can no longer give practitioners branded general-use items that can also be used in a home, car or social environment. The regulations also state that the value of any item with a pharmaceutical brand name reminder should not exceed $20.

Beyond marketing directly to doctors, pharmaceutical companies seek to employ word-of-mouth to opinion leaders, who may be able to influence physicians through their professional status. Pharmaceutical companies often engage opinion leaders early in the drug development process. Doctors acquire information through informal contacts with their colleagues, including social events, professional affiliations, common hospital affiliations, and common university medical school affiliations. Events sponsored by pharmaceutical companies are a common way for doctors to come into contact with opinion leaders.

## The pricing of pharmaceuticals

A perennial issue in the marketing of prescription pharmaceuticals in Australia is that of pricing and, in particular, the listing of a drug on the federal government's PBS. While many consumers are not aware of it, the price of pharmaceuticals is usually much more than they pay for them at a pharmacy. For example, pharmaceutical companies charge A$100 or more for a pack of contraceptive pills, but consumers pay only a small amount of the total cost. The rest is paid by the government under the PBS. Some pharmaceuticals cost tens of thousands of dollars, with this cost being met by the government. The total cost of the PBS to Australian taxpayers is very high. Consequently, the government is increasingly reluctant to list more drugs, especially very expensive drugs, on the PBS. This is often a controversial decision as it makes the drug unaffordable to those who would benefit from it. The government is also reluctant to list patented drugs if satisfactory alternatives are available. For pharmaceutical companies, when launching a new patented drug, the difficult question is whether or not to seek PBS listing. A PBS listing makes the drug available to a large market of consumers at a much lower retail price. A lack of PBS listing means the pharmaceutical company must charge the full price directly to the patient (of which only a fraction would be reimbursed by Medicare or private health insurers).

In a bid to control PBS costs, the federal government encourages medical practitioners and dispensing pharmacists to promote the availability of generic substitutes. To date, however, because the retail price is sometimes virtually the same, the majority of patients prefer the brand-named prescription drug over the equivalent generic drug, with the federal government meeting the extra cost.

### The consumer

The relationship between patients and their doctors has undergone fundamental change over the past few decades. Patients, armed with more information, particularly information garnered from websites, are more willing to suggest treatments to doctors and less willing to accept doctors' decisions without question. In some cases, consumers attempt to self-diagnose from information on the web. This may encourage some people to seek medical help for various conditions. It may also fundamentally change the relationship between doctors and their patients, with wide-ranging consequences for how pharmaceutical decisions are ultimately made.

The internet has also provided consumers with the ability to purchase pharmaceutical products online. Online pharmacies are able to dispatch products once a consumer sends them their prescription. The attraction of online pharmacies for consumers is lower prices (and occasionally, for some people, the ability to buy pharmaceutical products without dealing with a person face-to-face). Of course, the internet has also made it easier for consumers to buy drugs illegally or to obtain ingredients for home-made substances.

The pharmaceutical industry has clearly been a very healthy industry but, like our own health, it cannot be taken for granted.[17]

## Questions

1. Briefly discuss the main reasons for the historically high levels of profitability in the pharmaceutical industry.
2. What are the main differences between the over-the-counter and prescription pharmaceutical markets?
3. Why are patents so important in pharmaceutical marketing?
4. From a brief review of the internet and other published information sources, what are the major areas of public criticism of the pharmaceutical companies? How do the pharmaceutical companies defend themselves against such criticisms? Give an example.
5. How has the internet changed the pharmaceutical marketing environment?

## Advanced activity

Refer back to the Opto Global story at the start of the chapter. Now that you have a more detailed understanding about business-to-business markets after reading the chapter, describe the following in relation to Opto Global:
- the type of business market(s) in which the company competes
- likely characteristics of the market(s)
- the type of demand that is likely to exist for Opto Global's product (derived, joint, inelastic)
- how knowledge of the business decision-making process would be beneficial for Opto Global and its various international distributors.

## Marketing plan activity

For your marketing plan, consider whether your product has a business-to-business market. Some products have both a business-to-consumer and a business-to-business market, while others will be specifically aimed at one or the other. If your product has any business-to-business market potential you will need to research and analyse the following in relation to your marketing plan:

- the type(s) of business market(s) that exist or potentially exist for your product (e.g. reseller, producer, government or institutional markets)
- the needs of the business market(s) for your product identified in the first point and how your product meets those needs
- the factors that drive business demand for your product
- the ways in which buying decisions are made by potential business buyers of your product.

As with the marketing plan activities in previous chapters, this analysis is likely to inform your overall and ongoing market research requirements. Such detailed analysis and understanding of business buying behaviour, if relevant in relation to your chosen product, will be crucial to the marketing strategies you will be developing in later chapters for your marketing plan.'

A sample marketing plan has been included at the back of this book (see page 523) to give you an idea where this information fits in an overall marketing plan.

## CHAPTER 6

# Markets: segmentation, targeting and positioning

## Learning objectives

After studying this chapter, you should be able to:

 explain the broad concept of a 'market'

 understand the target marketing concept

 identify market segmentation variables for consumer and business markets, and develop market segment profiles

 select specific target markets based on evaluation of potential market segments

 understand how to effectively position an offering to a target market in relation to competitors, and develop an appropriate marketing mix.

# The grey nomads

They're back, and in increasing numbers. After a temporary decline during the global financial crisis, sales of caravans and motorhomes (or 'mobile roadblocks' as these vehicles are sometimes unkindly referred to by some other frustrated motorists), are once again on an upswing. So-called grey nomads have led this resurgence. This group of retirees has both the time to travel on extended holidays and the available superannuation funds to do so, particularly since the share market has recovered from the lows recorded in recent years.

According to the Recreational Vehicle Manufacturers Association of Australia, there are about 60 000 grey nomads throughout Australia. In Victoria alone, about 25 000 to 30 000 of these people leave the state and head north to chase a warmer climate in the winter months, returning home in spring. Recreational vehicles needed to tow caravans and motorhomes, such as the Nissan Patrol and the Mitsubishi Pajero, also benefit from any upswing in caravan and motorhome sales. Annual local production of such vehicles has doubled since 2000, and one contributor to this impressive statistic during this extended period has been the corresponding strong sales of caravans and motorhomes (even allowing for the temporary downturn in demand in recent years).

A range of both caravans and motorhomes are available — from budget to luxury models. Prices are about $250 000 for motorhomes at the upper end of the market, with appliances such as washing machines and dishwashers being standard in more expensive models. There are about 3000 caravan and recreational parks across Australia to cater for people who wish to travel this way. Although this number has declined by about 10 per cent over fifteen years, with large tracts of lucrative land previously occupied by parks being sold to developers, many parks that have remained have increased their service offerings. Indeed, facilities such as water slides, restaurants and movie rooms are not uncommon anymore, with the operators of many parks seeing families embarking on camping holidays as a lucrative market.[1]

## Question

Grey nomads represent a market segment that is, arguably, distinctively different from the retiree segment of past generations. In what ways do you think they are different?

# INTRODUCTION

The emergence of the grey nomad market segment represents the latest, and perhaps most visible, evidence of the changes brought about by the ageing population. While this group might be more conventionally described as comprising of active retirees, their accumulated wealth represents a very attractive opportunity. At the same time, their lifestyle choices are clearly distinctive, and their growing numbers will generate very significant market changes that will radiate throughout developed economies in the coming years. For all businesses, identifying potential customers and understanding the needs of those potential buyers is fundamental to market success.

We already know from chapters 4 and 5 that there are consumer markets (also known as business-to-consumer or B2C markets) and business markets (business-to-business or B2B markets). Consumer markets consist of households and individuals that buy products for private consumption. We are all members of consumer markets for an almost unlimited range of products that we use in our daily lives. Business markets consist of individuals and organisations that purchase products to resell, to use in production, or to use in business operations. In this chapter, we will explore this broad categorisation further and examine how we can better describe and segment the market. Because consumers and businesses have different needs, wants and demands, it is impossible for most organisations to successfully appeal to the entire market. Instead, the organisation typically identifies those parts of the total market to which it can offer the most value. Market segmentation enables the organisation to form a strategy for a group, or segment, that has common features, rather than try to market to everyone. The organisation makes use of its knowledge of these market segments to develop the most effective marketing mix for each. This approach is known as the target marketing concept and it is fundamental to marketing — identifying smaller, more targetable market segments, then tailoring the marketing mix to best appeal to those segments.

We discuss how businesses can best segment consumer and business markets for their particular purposes. Once the market has been segmented based on relevant variables, the organisation assesses the potential of each segment in order to decide which segments to target. We conclude the chapter with a discussion of how to position products relative to competitors in each target market.

## KNOWING THE MARKET

In chapter 1, we defined a **market** as a group of customers with heterogeneous needs and wants. This is a very broad definition. In chapters 4 and 5, we saw that the overall market could be broken down into consumer markets and business markets. Business markets could then, for example, be further broken down into reseller markets, producer markets, government markets and institutional markets.

These distinctions between markets are useful. As we shall come to understand as we work through this book, there are many marketing issues specific to organisations that market to consumers and those that market to particular types of organisations. Many organisations target both consumers and businesses, and usually apply different strategies to each sector. However, the concepts of the consumer market and the business market are so general that they can only be used in the broadest sense to help an organisation formulate a marketing strategy to target potential customers. Consumers and businesses vary considerably in their needs, wants and demands, and it is virtually impossible for an organisation to successfully appeal to every consumer or business.

To overcome this problem, the marketer seeks to identify and understand those parts of the total market to which it can offer the most value. The organisation then

 **Learning objective 1**
explain the broad concept of a 'market'

**market** A group of customers with heterogeneous needs and wants.

makes use of its knowledge of these market segments to develop the most effective marketing mix for each segment it chooses to target. This approach is known as the target marketing concept — identifying smaller, more targetable market segments, then tailoring the marketing mix to best appeal to those segments. This process involves understanding the organisation's micro environment (discussed in chapter 2) and will almost always draw on market research and existing market information (discussed in chapter 3). It also requires a thorough understanding of how buyers make purchasing decisions (chapters 4 and 5). Understanding the market is a fundamental prerequisite for effective marketing. In this chapter, we will develop our understanding from the broad view outlined above to a deeper, more specific understanding of target market segments. The understanding created by this detailed analysis is crucial to creating, communicating and delivering product offerings of value (see figure 6.1).

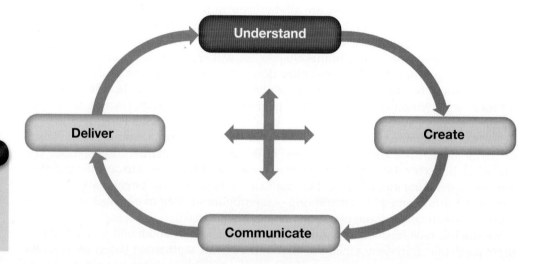

**FIGURE 6.1**

Understanding target market segments is crucial to creating, communicating and delivering product offerings of value

## Spotlight The money market

Banks are a good example of businesses that serve two broad, very large markets — the consumer market (e.g. via credit cards, and house and car loans), and the business market (e.g. via providing finance for business ventures). Both of these broad markets can easily be broken down further into smaller, identifiable groups of customers with similar needs and wants.

In recent times, both local- and foreign-owned banks with branches in Australia have increasingly come to recognise the lucrative opportunity posed by skilled migrants, and the need to tailor their offerings more specifically for this market. Since 2000, well over one million migrants have arrived in Australia, with more than 60 per cent classified as 'skilled'. Many are already high-net-worth individuals and, as such, are attractive potential customers for banks.

'When we look at the global needs of migrants, it is the service aspects that are the most difficult; arriving in a country and not having a bank account; not knowing who to speak to', says Graham Heunis, the head of personal finance for the Australian arm of the London headquartered HSBC Bank, which now has 26 branches spread across the major capital cities of Australia.

For one-sixth of Australia's current population, including the relatively recent migrant arrivals, English is not their first language. Most banks are now actively recruiting staff with the ability to speak two or more languages, and in most branches in the central business districts of Sydney and Melbourne banking product brochures are available in languages such as Hindi or Chinese.

The overseas-owned and headquartered banks, such as HSBC Bank and Arab Bank, have a major advantage over local Australian banks in terms of attracting many migrant customers — familiarity. On arrival, many migrants are unlikely to have ever heard of the 'big four' Australian banks — the Commonwealth Bank, Westpac, National Australia Bank and ANZ. The challenge for local banks is to successfully position themselves as viable and attractive alternatives.[2]

## Questions

1. Why do new migrants represent major opportunities for local banks?

2. What difficulties do you anticipate local banks might encounter in attracting new migrants as customers, and how could these potentially be overcome?

## Concepts and applications check

**Learning objective 1** explain the broad concept of a 'market'

1.1 Explain the difference between consumer markets and business markets.

1.2 Why is it unlikely that an organisation could successfully target an entire market with its offering?

1.3 Choose five products. For each, think of someone you know that might be an ideal target consumer for the product and someone who would be unlikely to be interested in the product, outlining your reasons in each case.

# TARGET MARKETING

There are various ways to view the market and the particular perspective an organisation takes has a pervasive influence on all of its marketing activities. Consider the following three different perspectives:

1. Buyers have common wants, needs and demands.
2. Buyers have unique wants, needs and demands.
3. The market contains subgroups — known as **market segments** — defined by similarities in regards to certain characteristics.

**Learning objective 2** understand the target marketing concept

**market segments** Subgroups within the total market that are relatively similar in regards to certain characteristics.

These perspectives suggest fundamentally different approaches to marketing. If all potential buyers are similar, then it should be possible to take an undifferentiated approach to the marketing mix; that is, the organisation makes the same offer to everyone. If all buyers have unique needs, then the organisation will be more successful if it differentiates its products to match the differences evident among potential customers.

If buyers differ, but have some shared characteristics, then it should be possible to use an undifferentiated marketing mix for any one group, while differentiating the offering between groups. In summary:

- The marketer can make an *undifferentiated* offer to the market as a whole (mass marketing).
- The marketer can make a *differentiated* offer to each individual buyer (one-to-one or customised marketing).
- The marketer can make an *undifferentiated* offer to groups of buyers with common wants or needs, but *differentiate* the offerings it makes to different groups.

Individuals and organisations in a market have different wants, needs and demands. The choice of marketing strategy typically involves a degree of compromise

between the necessity to respond to the particular desires of potential customers and the objective of achieving the lowest possible production and marketing costs. Hence, most marketers practise **target marketing** in identifying and responding to the needs, wants and demands of individual buyers or groups of buyers. Target marketing is based on three premises:
1. individual buyers or groups of buyers can be identified
2. sellers understand the needs of buyers
3. sellers will seek to shape their offer to meet the needs of target buyers.

Examination of these three premises shows that they reflect a market orientation, as discussed in chapter 1. They are important factors in understanding, creating, communicating and delivering offerings of value. The decision to address them through target marketing reflects the difference between a market orientation and a production orientation, as illustrated in figure 6.2.

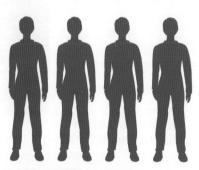 

**FIGURE 6.2**

Production-oriented and marketing-oriented views of the market

**Production-oriented organisations see everyone as basically similar and practise mass marketing.**

**Market-oriented organisations see everyone as different and practise target marketing.**

We will now discuss the key differences between mass marketing, one-to-one marketing and target marketing based on market segments, before moving on to a detailed discussion of the target marketing process. The different approaches to the market are illustrated in figure 6.3.

**FIGURE 6.3**

Three market strategies

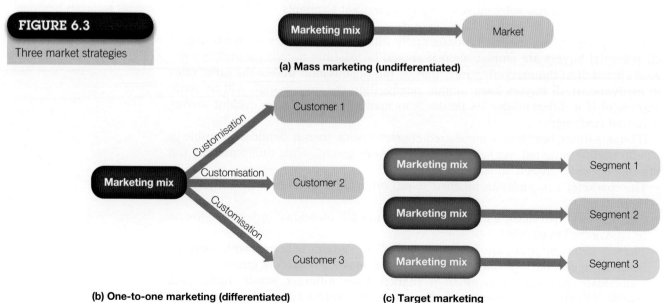

**Marketing mix** → Market

**(a) Mass marketing (undifferentiated)**

**Marketing mix** → Customisation → Customer 1
→ Customisation → Customer 2
→ Customisation → Customer 3

**(b) One-to-one marketing (differentiated)**

**Marketing mix** → Segment 1
**Marketing mix** → Segment 2
**Marketing mix** → Segment 3

**(c) Target marketing**

# Mass marketing

A *mass marketer* sees buyers as having common wants, needs and demands. Under such circumstances, it is possible to create, communicate and deliver a single product to meet the needs of most people in the market. This represents an undifferentiated approach to marketing. This undifferentiated offering, ideally, can be produced in large volumes and at a low cost per unit (by taking advantage of 'economies of scale'). The low unit cost makes it possible to sell at a low price, further expanding the market and driving costs lower again. In this way, organisations that practise mass marketing can capture very large markets at very low cost per unit, ensuring high levels of profitability. This strategy is characteristic of commodity products such as salt and of global mass market products such as blank CDs, bandages and pharmaceuticals. The market for government services also displays a high level of homogeneity, in that all citizens are entitled to a common, minimum level of service and benefits such as public transport. As long as all consumers have homogeneous needs, this model is extremely successful and profitable. However, it is common for markets to evolve as consumer preferences become increasingly diverse.

# One-to-one marketing

The *one-to-one marketer* seeks to appeal to each customer by providing a unique, customised offering that will meet their individual needs. In closely meeting their needs, the seller seeks to build a very close relationship with a customer in the expectation that the customer will reward them with loyalty and repeat purchasing, as well as positive word-of-mouth to friends and colleagues. Many small services businesses take a one-to-one marketing approach. For example, when a family engages an architect to design their new home, the architect will discuss their needs and preferences, study their land, assess their budget, and create and refine draft designs based on their feedback. A simpler example is a hairdresser who — usually — styles each customer's hair the way they want. One-to-one marketing is reasonably common in industrial business markets, where the size of purchases often dictates customisation of the marketing mix for each potential customer. A one-to-one approach often results in higher unit costs and a more restricted market. These conditions typically form the basis for a focus or niche strategy.

# Target marketing based on segments

Markets made up of buyers with diverse needs are said to be heterogeneous. Not everyone wants to dress the same, drive the same car, eat the same food or watch the same television shows. In this sense, most consumer markets can be said to be heterogeneous. Even so, most buyers or consumers can be grouped into segments: the segment has distinctive needs, but the members of the segment have similar needs.

The third marketing option — market segmentation — is the logical and common choice for many organisations that want to meet the needs of large numbers of customers more closely, but that lack the resources to address each customer as an individual. In choosing a market segmentation strategy, the focus of the organisation shifts from the individual buyer to the target market segment. The opportunity for the organisation becomes that of identifying groups of buyers (market segments) who have wants or needs in common that match well with the organisation's abilities. The key task of the organisation is to develop marketing programs to reach those market segments that have been identified, typically following marketing research. For many organisations, it is therefore common to view the target customers not as individuals, but as a market segment — and to design the organisation's offer to meet the needs of that market segment. Market segmentation forms the basis of the target marketing concept, implemented through the target marketing process.

When choosing target markets, the organisation will generally consider three factors:

1. *its own resources* — does the organisation have the financial, marketing and other resources required to cover the entire market?
2. *market demand* — do all customers look for the same attributes and benefits in the product?
3. *competition* — have competitors already segmented the market or are they selling to all buyers as a group?

With a **differentiated targeting strategy**, an organisation identifies a range of target market segments, covering the majority of the total market, and for each market segment develops a tailored marketing mix. This approach is favoured by most market leaders, which are able to serve almost all viable market segments with a product and offer designed specially to meet their needs. For example, Westpac offers a complete range of financial services designed to meet the needs of all consumer and business and government market segments. IBM offers computer hardware, software and consulting services for all business and consumer users. A market leadership position is often accompanied by premium prices in each market segment and product category, enabling high total revenues and profits. At the same time, it should be recognised that a differentiation strategy also entails higher costs. Achieving high profits through this strategy generally requires a combination of higher retail prices, high volume sales, strong market share and strong customer loyalty.

## Product and market specialisation

Small organisations with limited financial resources frequently adopt one of the following specialised approaches to target marketing:

- **product specialisation**, in which all efforts are concentrated on a single product range offered to a number of market segments. Nikon, for example, competes by concentrating solely on cameras. Stihl focuses on chain-saws.
- **market specialisation**, in which all efforts are concentrated on meeting a wide range of needs within a single market segment. For example, Elders provides a comprehensive range of goods and services to farmers. Similarly, credit unions provide a wide range of financial services to members who live in particular local communities or who are employed in particular industries. The differences between product specialisation and market specialisation are summarised in figure 6.4.
- **product–market specialisation**, in which the product and market specialisation approaches are combined to offer a single product to a single market segment. Micro businesses (e.g. local trades and professional services businesses) commonly adopt this approach. For example, restaurants will choose to offer a narrow menu, often based on a national cuisine, to a local market from a single location.

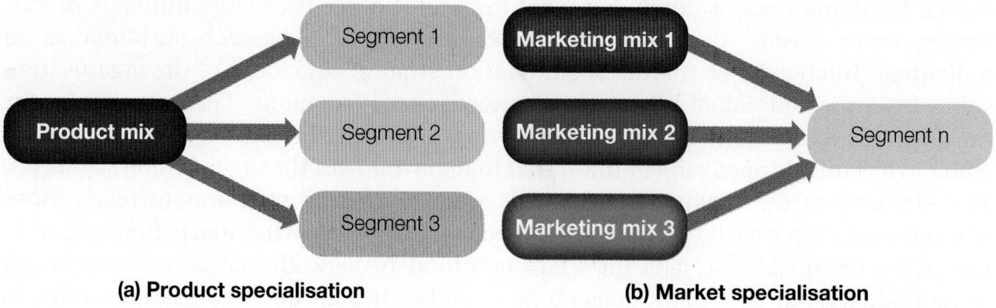

**differentiated targeting strategy** A marketing approach that involves developing a different marketing mix for each target market segment.

**product specialisation** A target marketing strategy in which all marketing efforts are concentrated on offering a single product range to a number of market segments.

**market specialisation** A target marketing strategy in which all marketing efforts are focused on meeting a wide range of needs within a particular market segment.

**product–market specialisation** A target marketing strategy in which marketing efforts are concentrated on offering a single product to a single market segment.

**FIGURE 6.4**

Product and market specialisation

(a) Product specialisation          (b) Market specialisation

Specialisation approaches usually only succeed if the following five conditions are met:

1. The market is characterised by a wide range of needs and product preferences.
2. Clear market segments, or product categories, are identifiable, each with its own distinctive preferences or characteristics.
3. The market is clearly divisible into segments so that each can be evaluated and compared.
4. Individual market segments, or product categories, are sufficiently large to represent profitable sales volume.
5. The organisation is able to reach individual market segments with a particular marketing offer and mix.

Organisations that pursue a specialisation strategy seek to establish a dominant position in their chosen *market niche*. Such organisations run the risk of putting all their eggs into one basket, but, if successful, they establish a strong, deep and long-lasting position. Such an approach enables an organisation to concentrate all its limited financial and other resources while achieving a strong market reputation and a secure position among its loyal customers. At the same time, such an approach clearly limits a company's growth potential in the longer term. This was the situation facing car maker Porsche when, in recent years, it expanded beyond its sports cars focus into the large four-wheel-drive market.

## The target marketing process

The target marketing process is a fundamental component of marketing strategy for any organisation. The process involves three main stages, with each requiring detailed analysis and decision making. This process is illustrated in figure 6.5 and is discussed in detail throughout the rest of the chapter.

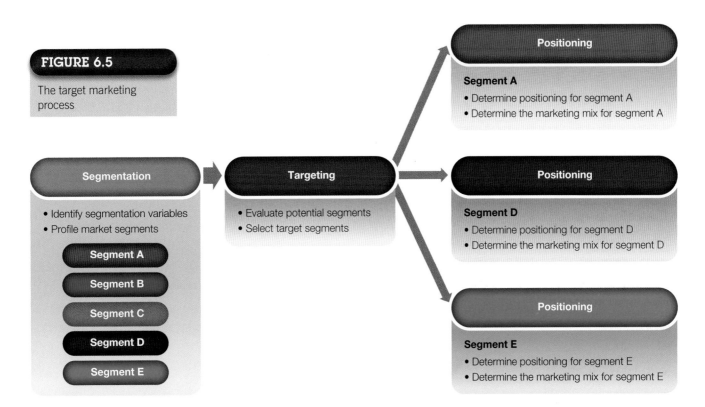

**FIGURE 6.5**

The target marketing process

## Spotlight The Mambo evolution

In the 1980s and 1990s clothing label Mambo was most well known for its quirky, irreverent (and, at times, controversial) designs and messages on T-shirts. These were generally marketed as 'arty surfwear' and targeted at this demographic. Such was the label's popularity among younger Australians that the Australian Olympic Committee even commissioned Mambo to design the casual 'Hawaiian-style' shirts worn by Australia's athletes at the Opening Ceremony for the 2000 Sydney Olympics.

In more recent years, Mambo has evolved into a mainstream brand. Nowhere is this more evident than in the recent agreement reached between Big W and Mambo for the discount retailer to stock Mambo's range of products. In addition to 'arty surfwear' clothing, Mambo's product range now includes items such as footwear, watches, sunglasses and scooters. On announcing the new distribution agreement, Mambo's managing director, Angus Mitchell, said that Big W would not stock 'controversial stuff', but that surf shops still would.

The decision by Mambo to sell through Big W is both momentous and risky. By moving to sell to 'mums and dads' at Big W, Mambo is clearly seeking to capture new and significantly larger market segments. At the same time, the new market segments dictate a new distribution channel, and will result in Mambo occupying a new position in the minds of consumers. The potential sales volume that Big W offers Mambo is undoubtedly attractive. However, the risk of alienating the existing surf shop clientele of the brand is a very real danger.

While Mambo will undoubtedly appeal to new market segments via its Big W distribution arrangement, the 'elephant in the room' is the question of whether or not the existing hard core, loyal Mambo customers will continue to pay a premium price for a brand that can also be bought at Big W. This risk is not new and the experience of Piping Hot and Golden Breed — two original, iconic surfing brands that are now sold at Big W or Kmart — is an ominous precedent. Neither brand is now regarded as representing trendy apparel. Of course, the same danger confronts any successful niche marketing company when it feels that it has outgrown its original market segment. The obvious solution is to add segments that do not clash with or 'cannibalise' existing customers, and to develop a differentiated targeting strategy. That is easier said than done. Mambo may find that to achieve this outcome, it needs to metaphorically add juggling to its existing repertoire of creative talents.[3]

### Questions

1. Why would Mambo be attracted to a 'discount department store' like Big W, rather than traditional and more upscale department stores like David Jones and Myer?

2. Explain how Mambo can adopt a differentiated targeting strategy and adjust its marketing mix in an attempt to successfully attract the two distinct target markets of:
   (a) 'mum and dad' shoppers at Big W
   (b) 'Surf shop' customers.

## Concepts and applications check

**Learning objective 2** understand the target marketing concept

2.1 Outline the difference between how mass marketers and one-to-one marketers would view a market.

2.2 In your own words, describe the concept of market segmentation.

2.3 Use an example to demonstrate your understanding of a differentiated targeting strategy.

2.4 Outline the three main stages of the target marketing process.

# MARKET SEGMENTATION

The first stage of the target marketing process is market segmentation. As shown in figure 6.6, there are two steps in the market segmentation phase: *identifying variables* that can be used to define meaningful market segments; and *profiling* the market segments so they can be assessed in the second stage of the target marketing process.

**Learning objective 3**
identify market segmentation variables for both consumer and business markets, and develop market segment profiles

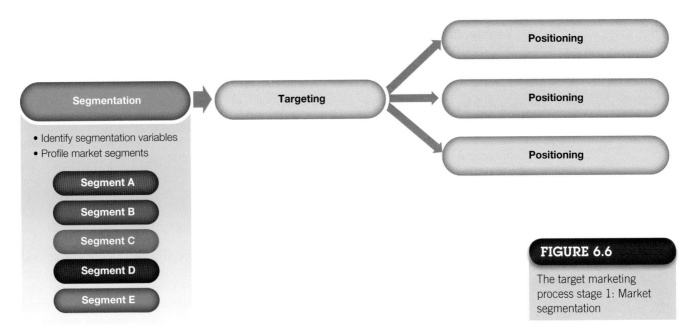

**FIGURE 6.6**

The target marketing process stage 1: Market segmentation

## Identify segmentation variables

The target marketing process aims to identify groups of buyers (market segments) who have wants or needs in common that are a good match with the organisation's ability to deliver products of value. This begs the question: On what bases can the total market be segmented? **Segmentation variables** are characteristics that buyers (i.e. individuals, groups or organisations) have in common and that might be closely related to their purchasing behaviour. Age, gender, income and occupation, for example, can all be linked to the purchase or consumption of particular products.

The key to effective segmentation is to choose segmentation variables that are:

- easy to measure and readily available (e.g. demographic data made available from the national census)
- linked closely to the purchase of the product in question (e.g. location may be an important segmentation variable in the purchase of snow sports equipment, such as skis and snowboards).

Market research plays a crucial role in the process of understanding the link between segmentation variables and consumers' purchasing behaviour. To be effective, market segmentation must be based on an in-depth, accurate and up-to-date understanding of the needs and buying behaviours of potential customers, and how those needs and behaviours might be changing.

Having identified appropriate segmentation variables, it is then important to understand how many possible segments an organisation might choose to pursue. An organisation cannot market to all potential customers, unless it is a market leader

**segmentation variables**
Characteristics that buyers have in common and that might be closely related to their purchasing behaviour.

with virtually limitless market coverage and marketing resources. Of course this is rare, and so market segmentation and target marketing typically involve organisations making difficult choices about which target markets to select (and which market segments to ignore).

For most organisations, therefore, the question is not whether or not to segment the market; it is — given that we *must* segment the market — which variables represent the best variables for identifying relevant target markets. The choice of segmentation variables is discussed in the rest of this section.

### Segmenting consumer markets

The range of possible variables for segmenting consumer markets is almost limitless. They fall into four broad categories: geographic, demographic, psychographic and behavioural variables.

### Geographic segmentation

**Geographic segmentation** is market segmentation based on geographic variables. Geographic variables are reliable predictors of customer needs and purchasing behaviours for a wide range of products. Useful geographic variables include:

- climate
- local population
- region
- topography
- urban, suburban and rural location.

Geographic segmentation is particularly relevant to a country that is both large and diverse, such as Australia. The islands of New Zealand also suit segmentation on this basis. Producers of building materials, for example, need to know how customers' needs and purchase behaviours differ by geographical *region* (e.g. deep wool carpets are less popular in beach towns). Similarly, purchase of certain product categories may depend upon the geographical terrain or topography of a given area. Toyota's LandCruiser is the preferred motor vehicle for those living in rugged inland and remote areas of Australia and Subaru built its early reputation in Australia among visitors and residents of the snow country.

The number of buyers or potential buyers in any given geographical area is an important measure of market potential. Targeting geographic areas with lots of potential customers also creates efficiencies in advertising and distribution, compared to areas with a smaller number of potential buyers. In the latter case, less intensive promotional media (e.g. direct mail) or less intensive distribution through agents may be more financially effective.

An emerging trend in segmentation is geo-demographics, which combines demographic variables and geographic variables to profile very small geographical areas (such as a suburb). Geo-demographic segments enable intense and specific targeting of small groups. Organisations such as Pacific Micromarketing have developed analysis tools based on publicly available data such as the census, which, when combined with proprietary analysis tools, enable them to produce precise profiles of the residents and businesses located in closely identified geographical areas. Such analyses are particularly useful to retail businesses that could choose to vary their product offerings based on the distinctive demographic characteristics of these areas. For the large supermarket chains, there is an opportunity to vary their product range based on the ethnic characteristics of the local customers. This may be necessary to compete with local retailers, such as delicatessens, that may have established market share based on their particular appeal to these ethnic market segments.

## Demographic segmentation

**Demographic segmentation** is market segmentation based on demographic variables, which are related to the vital and social characteristics of populations. They are the most commonly used variables for market segmentation. Consumer behaviour is often closely linked to demography, and ongoing studies by organisations such as the Australian Bureau of Statistics and Statistics New Zealand ensure demographic information is readily available, up-to-date and comprehensive. We will discuss a few of the demographic variables most frequently used by marketers to illustrate how they form the basis for market segmentation.

**demographic segmentation**
Market segmentation based on demographic variables, which are the vital and social characteristics of populations, such as age, education and income.

*Age* is one of the most commonly used segmentation variables and can be linked to the emergence of market segments such as Generation Y, Generation X and the grey nomads. It has become very popular to refer to different age bands in the population as a 'generation'. The most commonly used groupings are:

- *the Baby Boomer generation.* Baby Boomers were born in the prosperous years after World War II (1946–64) and are now beginning to retire from the workforce. Overall the Baby Boomers have been one of the most powerful generations: relatively wealthy; in positions of power in society, politics and the workplace — and willing and able to stay active as prominent members of society in their older years.
- *Generation X.* This term was coined by Douglas Copeland in his book, *Generation X*, to describe a group of self-indulgent slackers. The term has been redefined (by marketers!) to mean the people born between 1965 and 1980. Their formative years in Australia were during a period of high unemployment, high inflation and high interest rates. The generation is characterised by a strong work ethic, loyalty and quite a lot of frustration with Baby Boomers.
- *Generation Y.* This generation, born from 1980 to 2001 and sometimes also known as the 'Nintendo Generation', is characterised by comfort with technology; strong, almost tribal, friendships and loyalties; and high expectations in all spheres of their lives.
- *Generation Z.* This generation, born after 2001, was born digital. The internet, video games, mobile phones, wireless networks and friends they've never met are all second nature to Generation Z.

It is important that marketers remain aware that these classifications are broad, but they can be very useful. For example, television networks use age as a segmentation variable for their range of programs (e.g. *Law & Order* and *NCIS* are aimed at Generation X; *Better Homes and Gardens* and *Getaway* are aimed at Baby Boomers) and to identify opportunities for new formats such as reality television (aimed mainly at Generation Y).

*Ethnicity* is a useful segmentation variable for marketers of some products (e.g. food and travel during the Chinese New Year festival). Australia and New Zealand have ethnically diverse populations that present opportunities for marketers to identify direct links between ethnicity and the purchase of particular products. For example, descendants of European immigrants may still display strong loyalty and preferences for traditional wine and food from their native countries. Similarly, restaurant proprietors may target local consumers who share the same ethnic origins as the proprietor. At the same time, restaurateurs usually prefer to market to a larger, more diverse local population that includes customers who are attracted to the 'multicultural' experience.

*Household composition* is an umbrella variable that is influenced by a number of other demographic variables, including age, income, marital status and, often, ethnicity. Segmentation on such variables is complicated by the changes occurring in household composition, including increasing divorce rates, increasing numbers of single-parent households, increasing numbers of people choosing not to have children, and even trends such as friends sharing housing to make renting or buying a home more affordable. Household composition has profound effects on consumer behaviour. To varying extents, married couples live different lifestyles to single people; adults living with their parents spend their money differently to adults living in shared rental accommodation; and parents have needs for various services that are not so important for childless people. Household composition can be a particularly useful segmentation variable for marketers of financial services products, such as personal loans and mortgages, credit cards, and superannuation and investment products, all of which are closely linked to stages in people's lives.

*Income* is, of course, a strong determinant of what people can buy. Not only does it determine what they can afford to buy in absolute terms, but it is also significantly linked to the types of products they prefer. As discussed in chapter 4, many purchases are aspirational in nature — reflecting the lifestyle a person would like to have as much as the one they can actually afford. It is important that marketers do not make the mistake of simply targeting high-income earners — while they have more money to spend, marketers should be most concerned with identifying those market segments to which they can offer the most value.

*Sex* is another segmentation variable that has obvious implications for marketers of clothing, beverages, pharmaceuticals and magazines. For example, males constitute the heaviest consumers of beer. In contrast, females represent the heaviest users of 'alcopops'.

Of course, there are many other demographic variables that marketers can use for segmentation — occupation, level of education attained and so on. The appropriate demographic variables to use will vary depending on the type of product. While demographics are rarely advocated as the sole basis for market segmentation, there is a strong case for their use as part of the segmentation process: the data are freely available and, for many goods and services, demographics have proven to be reliable predictors of purchase and use. The need for consumption of government services such as health, education, police and social welfare are best predicted by demographics.

### Psychographic segmentation

Like demographic and geographic variables, psychographic (psychology plus demographics) variables are based on consumer characteristics. **Psychographic segmentation** is based on differences in:

- psychological traits (personality attributes and motives)
- key demographics
- lifestyles (the expression of the two former categories).

In contrast to using demographics (e.g. age, gender and education) alone to explain who consumers are, psychographics seeks to understand consumers by identifying their mind-sets and how they are expressed in their lifestyles. Psychographics combines insights of psychology with demographics to give a more precise description of consumer groups. People who share common demographics may lead very different lifestyles. Consider, for instance, 20-year-old women who have just completed their first year of university. It is easy to imagine that within this demographic group there are women who love university for the subjects they are studying, the realm of ideas they are being exposed to, and the satisfaction that self-discipline brings as they study instead of party. It is also easy to imagine there are other women in the same group who love university more for the parties and the heightened sense of stimulation than for the love of knowledge. Psychographics brings out differences like these that demographics miss. It is details like these, as well, that can make or break a marketing campaign.

Two psychographic segmentation models are the Roy Morgan Values Segments and VALS™ (see figures 6.7[4] and 6.8[5] respectively). VALS is owned and operated by

**psychographic segmentation** Market segmentation based on the psychographic variables of lifestyle, motives and personality attributes.

Strategic Business Insights (SBI, a spin-out of SRI International) in California. Advocates of psychographics believe that particular psychological traits (e.g. excitement-seeking, curiosity, achievement) in combination with key demographics are more powerful predictors of behaviour and lifestyle than demographics alone. For example, VALS Achievers share psychological traits of achievement, self-discipline, duty and responsibility, and lack traits of spontaneity, creativity and change for change's sake. Survey research, carried out year after year, confirms that people with these traits tend to buy particular products and services that enhance their productivity, serve as rewards for their hard work and demonstrate success to their peers. Achievers are likely to buy online-banking services, giant-screen televisions and domestic holidays.

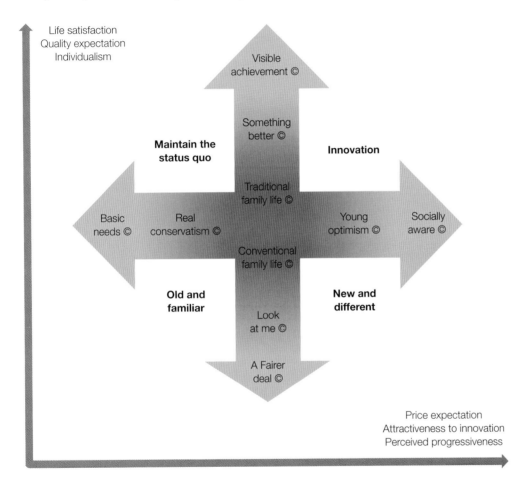

### FIGURE 6.7

Roy Morgan Values Segments™

The Roy Morgan Values Segments framework was used to discover the grey nomads, who emerged in response to the combined influences of the ageing of the Baby Boomer generation and their transition to retirement. The emergence of this segment has created, in turn, a boom for products and services — such as luxurious, recreational vehicles and internet-based communication — to suit an active but nomadic lifestyle.

Both VALS and Roy Morgan Values Segments are appealing to marketers, as they have been developed and proven across a wide range of product categories in various countries (e.g. SBI operates US VALS, Japan VALS and Venezuela VALS, and recently developed Dominican Republic VALS, all of which are based on the same principles, but optimised to the specific cultures).

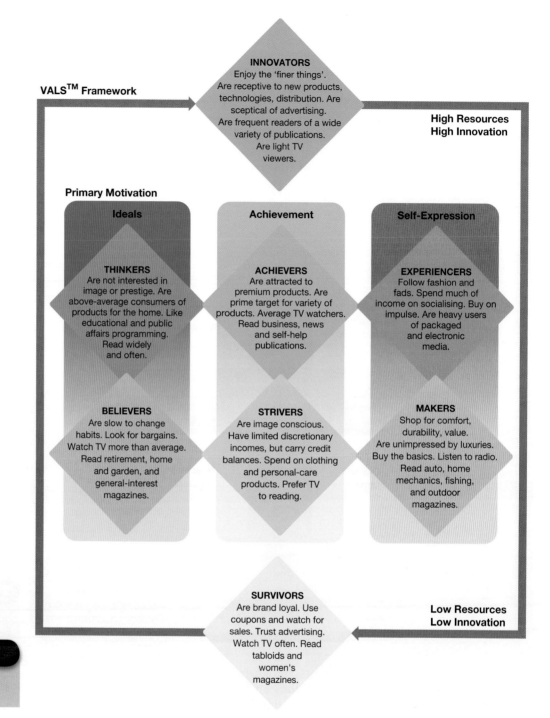

**VALS™ Framework**

**INNOVATORS**
Enjoy the 'finer things'.
Are receptive to new products,
technologies, distribution. Are
sceptical of advertising.
Are frequent readers of a wide
variety of publications.
Are light TV
viewers.

**High Resources
High Innovation**

**Primary Motivation**

**Ideals**

**Achievement**

**Self-Expression**

**THINKERS**
Are not interested in
image or prestige. Are
above-average consumers of
products for the home. Like
educational and public
affairs programming.
Read widely
and often.

**ACHIEVERS**
Are attracted to
premium products. Are
prime target for variety of
products. Average TV watchers.
Read business, news
and self-help
publications.

**EXPERIENCERS**
Follow fashion and
fads. Spend much of
income on socialising. Buy on
impulse. Are heavy users
of packaged
and electronic
media.

**BELIEVERS**
Are slow to change
habits. Look for bargains.
Watch TV more than average.
Read retirement, home
and garden, and
general-interest
magazines.

**STRIVERS**
Are image conscious.
Have limited discretionary
incomes, but carry credit
balances. Spend on clothing
and personal-care
products. Prefer TV
to reading.

**MAKERS**
Shop for comfort,
durability, value.
Are unimpressed by luxuries.
Buy the basics. Listen to radio.
Read auto, home
mechanics, fishing,
and outdoor
magazines.

**SURVIVORS**
Are brand loyal. Use
coupons and watch for
sales. Trust advertising.
Watch TV often. Read
tabloids and
women's
magazines.

**Low Resources
Low Innovation**

**FIGURE 6.8**

The VALS™ consumer
segments

While some psychographic systems suffer because they are conceptual in nature, do not reliably measure personality or do not effectively link relevant personality traits with consumer behaviour, other psychographic systems are grounded in empirical research and do effectively measure and link personality to purchase decisions. The VALS approach, for example, provides distinctive insights into purchases of particular products by conducting focus groups, surveys, and in-person interviews and then analysing the insights by each respondent's VALS type. An individual's VALS type is determined by their answers to a short list of attitude items and four demographics known as the 'VALS Questionnaire'. A recent study for an electric utility found one VALS type was open to paying extra dollars on their monthly bill to support development of renewable energy sources. Another VALS type with comparable demographics, including income, said, 'Absolutely not!' and was substantially less likely to even worry about global warming. Marketers with this insight will select a more focused target, will be able to isolate the features and benefits the target desires, and will develop communications that motivate the target to action.

### Behavioural segmentation

Geographic, demographic and psychographic segmentation are all based on 'consumer characteristics'. These consumer characteristics are relatively unchanging over time or between product categories. As such, they are reliable, but they may not provide the most useful insights or provide evidence of emerging trends in purchase behaviours or the consumption of particular products.

In contrast, **behavioural segmentation** is not based on consumer characteristics; rather, it is based on actual purchase and/or consumption behaviours, typically towards particular products. It is therefore likely to be a better indicator of market segments and their purchasing behaviour than segmentation based on generalised consumer characteristics. Behavioural variables include:

**behavioural segmentation**
Market segmentation based on actual purchase and/or consumption behaviours.

- benefit expectations
- brand loyalty
- occasion
- price sensitivity
- volume usage.

Segmentation based on *expected benefits* represents perhaps the most convincing basis for market segmentation, in that it is based upon the marketer's deep understanding of purchase and consumption motivations. It is a means to better understand *why* consumers purchase particular products and brands, and to base market segmentation around this understanding. Such an approach to segmentation is likely to prove rigorous, but time-consuming and expensive, as the consumer benefits sought for any particular purchase are likely to be specific to that particular product or product category. Effective benefit segmentation therefore generally requires thorough research among users of a product category, in order to understand underlying purchase and consumption motivations. Notwithstanding the additional time and expense required to develop benefit segmentation, there are good grounds for the belief that the effort is worthwhile, especially for marketers undertaking such segmentation for the first time. With additional experience, it may prove that less complex means of segmentation, such as using demographics, provide equivalent insights and guidance for less effort and at less cost.

*Occasion* is also an important segmentation variable in products such as entertainment, wine, travel and high-fashion. The assumption behind occasion-based segmentation is that it is the occasion that dictates the decision to purchase and the final choice of product. Wine purchasers may choose different wines based on the occasion for which it is purchased (e.g. as a gift, for the evening meal, for a celebration, or for 'cellaring'). For Chinese people around the world, the occasion of Chinese New Year represents a time of optimism, extravagance, gift giving, enjoyment and travel.

Segmentation based on *volume usage* seeks to identify heavy, medium and light users of a product category, helping an organisation identify and target the 20 per cent of buyers who typically account for up to 80 per cent of purchase volume or value. In this context, middle-aged males represent the biggest purchasers of high-end analogue watches. Notice, however, that this segment is also described in standard demographic terms, demonstrating that volume usage, by itself, is insufficient as a market segment descriptor.

The behavioural variables of brand loyalty and price sensitivity are complex topics and are discussed in detail in chapters 7 and 8 respectively.

### Segmenting business markets

Business markets are often characterised by a small number of buyers, each of which might display a very close relationship with the seller. Under such circumstances, traditional market segmentation variables may be less relevant, and 'customised' or 'one-to-one' marketing may be the best approach. For example, chartered accountants deal with their business clients personally and individually. Unisys works closely with its major banking clients to develop 'tailored solutions'. At the same time, many business markets do have a large number of buyers and market segmentation is a necessary approach to dealing with buyer diversity.

When a large organisation, such as Telstra, addresses itself to business markets, it is potentially dealing with all businesses in the country. It therefore needs to segment these businesses in a meaningful way to enable it to concentrate its marketing resources and maximise its marketing effectiveness. Under such circumstances, businesses of the size of Telstra and IBM will investigate how best to categorise their buyers in such a way that they have common product needs and are likely to respond in a common way to marketing programs. For example, Telstra could meaningfully segment its business market customers based on whether they are a small business, a medium-sized business, a large business or a multinational corporation. The organisation's size — in terms of employees or revenues — naturally affects its purchase volumes, purchasing procedures and the closeness of its relationship to the seller. Very large business customers will typically purchase directly from the seller and will expect advantageous volume, delivery and credit arrangements. They might have contracts with Telstra for thousands of landlines and mobiles, very large internet bandwidth and international roaming arrangements for some of their mobile services. Conversely, small business buyers may purchase through intermediaries and may be virtually indistinguishable from private buyers, with just a phone line, a couple of mobiles and a broadband internet connection. Officeworks, for example, does not distinguish between small business and retail consumer buyers in its retail stores.

Segmenting based on factors such as the size of the business customer is roughly equivalent to the demographic segmentation approaches that were described for consumer markets. Another 'demographic' type of approach in business markets relates to industry (sometimes known as vertical segments). IBM, for example, would identify different markets in education, health, manufacturing and distribution industry 'verticals'. Australian and New Zealand businesses seeking to segment their market in this way can access the Australian and New Zealand Standard Industrial Classification System (ANZSIC), which is produced by the Australian Bureau of Statistics and Statistics New Zealand. This system divides all business enterprises into 19 standard industry groups (e.g. manufacturing construction, transport and storage). These, in turn, are broken down further into 53 subdivisions. The subdivisions, again, are broken down into more specific categories. ANZSIC provides a comprehensive overview of the industry structure and participants. The information from ANZSIC can help an organisation to identify its potential customers and its competitors in terms of size, growth, profitability, sales and potential purchase activity. For example, polystyrene is used in a vast range of industrial applications in the manufacture of motor vehicles, toys, electronics, furniture, bedding and insulation. Each of these product applications typically represents major and distinct customer groups, each with their own purchase requirements and with varying needs for specialist technical support from their chemical suppliers. Segmentation based on the use of the product is therefore a useful approach in business markets. For example, a polystyrene manufacturer will treat car and car parts manufacturers, refrigerator and insulation manufacturers as separate segments.

One final commonly used method of segmentation in business markets is based on geography. In large countries such as Australia and geographically diverse countries such as Australia and New Zealand, geography can be highly relevant in business markets. For example, marketers of agricultural chemicals, fertilisers and pesticides would often segment the market according to the location of the buyer. Farmers —

the largest buyers of pesticides and herbicides — differ in their purchases according to location and climate, be they coastal, inland, dry, cold or tropical. Similarly, geographic location may be an important indicator of buyers in particular industries. For example, Caterpillar will focus much of its marketing of heavy mining equipment in Western Australia, Queensland and the Hunter region of New South Wales, as these are the country's primary mining areas.

> A commonly used method of segmentation in business markets is based on geography. Marketers of pesticides and herbicides, for example, need to consider the unique requirements of farmers — including the location and climate of their properties — in order to maximise the appeal of their products.

While the segmentation approaches we have described are commonly used, much of business-to-business marketing depends on individual relationships, and so it is necessary to develop a system for identifying individual potential customers. To enable an organisation to 'drill down' to the level of individual customers requires more detailed information. Commercial industrial directories provided by commercial organisations such as Compass contain information on individual companies, such as the name, industrial classification, address, phone number, types of products and annual sales, the names of chief executives and other details. This enables business marketers to isolate business customers and to develop targeted marketing campaigns to each individual potential business customer.

## Effective segmentation criteria

An almost limitless number of segments can be created using segmentation variables. It is crucial, of course, that the segments are of use in formulating a marketing approach. To ensure that segmentation is effective, the segments should be checked against the following criteria:

- *measurability*. The variables used to define the market segment must lend themselves to accurate measurement. Segmentation variables based on demographic variables are highly measurable and extensive data are available through commercial databases and organisations such as the Australian Bureau of Statistics and Statistics New Zealand. More abstract variables, such as personality, can be notoriously difficult to measure.

- *accessibility.* Segments must be able to be clearly identified, reached and served through distribution and communication channels. In this sense, opinion leaders are attractive to marketers but very difficult to identify and communicate with.
- *substantiality.* Market segments must be of sufficient size and purchasing power to make them a profitable target market. Ideally segments should be as large as possible, but still be homogeneous in their purchase preferences and behaviour. In this sense, market segments in New Zealand may not be viable in sales revenue terms, where they may be in a country like the United Kingdom. While manufacturing technology is advancing and mass customisation is increasingly possible, it is still true that aggregate sales volumes represent a vital constraint on industry profitability.
- *practicability.* Segments are only of use if marketing programs can be formulated to identify, communicate with and service those chosen market segments. Segmentation based on personality or psychological variables, while theoretically sound, might be incapable of successful implementation, particularly if no relevant and recent data are available. In particular, the chosen target markets should be large enough, clearly identifiable and able to be communicated with and distributed to in order to be viable.

## Profile market segments

**market segment profile**
A description of the typical potential customer in the market segment; that is, a description of the common variables shared by members of market segments and how the variables differ between market segments.

Having identified the range of ways in which market segments can be described, the next task is to develop a **market segment profile**. Such a profile describes the typical potential customer in the market segment; that is, it describes the common features shared by members of market segments and how they differ between market segments. Segment profiles will typically be described in terms of a number of segmentation variables. Individual segments will be uniquely described by a combination of segmentation variables, such as gender, age, occupation and lifestyle. With all the range of possible segmentation variables that can be used, it is usual for segments to be constructed in a multivariate and hierarchical fashion. For example, consider how the total market for athletic shoes in Australia could be segmented. A multivariate market segment profile within the overall athletic shoe market could be built as follows:

- segment initially on demographic grounds (e.g. people aged 7 to 12 years, 13 to 18 years, 19 to 30 years, 31 to 50 years, and over 50)
- then segment on usage variables (e.g. casual walkers, joggers, cross-trainers, serious amateur athletes, full-time elite athletes)
- as well as benefits (e.g. active, comfortable, supportive, durable, fashionable, performance enhancing).

As with this example, an important requirement of effective segmentation is to understand the target market segments completely: the insightful and creative marketer will know such target market segments implicitly — as if they were close friends. To develop such an intimate understanding of market segments will usually require comprehensive qualitative and quantitative market research (as discussed in chapter 3).

It is also important that market segments are sufficiently different from each other, so that a distinctive offer and message can be created for each target market segment without the risk of overlapping segments and/or sending confusing images and messages.

Having developed rich and vivid profiles of the range of possible market segments, it is important to determine how closely the organisation's current or potential product offerings might match the needs of these market segments. We will examine this next stage in the target marketing process in the next section.

# An Intrepid adventure

Intrepid Travel was founded in 1989 by Geoff Manchester and Darrell Wade, two friends and experienced backpackers. From its humble beginnings, the company has expanded to have more than 1000 employees in 12 countries. Currently about 70 000 travellers per year choose among the more than 400 trips that Intrepid offers to over 100 destinations across the globe.

In keeping with its 'backpacker' beginnings, the company's philosophy has always been to focus on offering tours and travel experiences that are 'off the beaten track'. Intrepid tours will often go to places that more traditional mainstream operators don't visit. Their preferred accommodation is also likely to include guesthouses and home stays in villages, in order to benefit local communities and also to offer travellers the chance for more 'real' cultural experiences in their chosen destinations.

It is not surprising, given its origins and philosophy, that Intrepid has always naturally attracted adventurous youth travellers. However, this can also be a negative association for the company.

'It's a difficulty (for us) that people see us as more youth oriented than we are', says co-founder and director, Peter Manchester. 'We like to talk about an attitude, rather than a demographic.'

Indeed, Intrepid has many clients in their forties, fifties and sixties, and has recently introduced a range of more 'comfortable' tour packages, which they describe as 'adventure travel with a soft landing'. The company also now offers tour packages specifically tailored to target markets such as families and gay/lesbian travellers. Carbon-offset trips have also been introduced, with an emphasis on minimising all transport, accommodation and waste emissions. Any assessed emissions on such trips are offset via Intrepid's purchase of carbon credits. For example, if a carbon-offset trip is assessed as emitting 1.3 kilograms of carbon dioxide per passenger, Intrepid purchases and surrenders 1.3 kilograms of carbon offset credits (representing a reduction in greenhouse gases of an equivalent volume).[6]

## Questions

1. Identify the market segmentation variables in evidence in Intrepid's tour offerings.
2. How can Intrepid position itself to overcome the general perception that it is primarily 'youth oriented'?

# Concepts and applications check

**Learning objective 3** Identify market segmentation variables for consumer and business markets, and develop market segment profiles

3.1 Briefly outline the major categories of segmentation variables in (a) consumer markets, and (b) business markets.

3.2 Why are behavioural variables a better indicator of purchasing behaviour than other consumer market segmentation variables?

3.3 Explain the four main criteria that can be used to assess whether an identified market segmentation scheme can be effectively implemented.

3.4 What is a market segment profile?

3.5 Choose a product (a good or service) and think of ten people that you know. Using your knowledge of those people, build a meaningful market segment profile based on appropriate segmentation variables relevant to the product you have chosen.

# MARKET TARGETING

**Learning objective 4**
select specific target markets based on evaluation of potential market segments

Having identified and described the range of possible market segments to which an organisation might direct its offer, the second stage in the process is that of market targeting (see figure 6.9). This stage involves a systematic examination of the range of possible market segments, their potential sales volume and revenues, and the relative ability of the organisation to satisfy the expectations of members of these market segments. This step also requires a close understanding of competitors, and how their offerings are seen by potential target market segments. In this context, it is important to realise that no company or brand can be all things to all people, especially when considering the vast array of potential customers and their diverse needs, wants and demands.

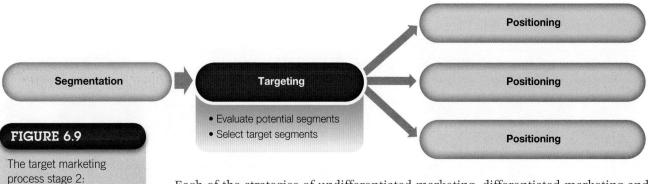

**FIGURE 6.9**

The target marketing process stage 2: Market targeting

Each of the strategies of undifferentiated marketing, differentiated marketing and specialised marketing (described in the second section of this chapter) offers advantages and disadvantages, which make the choice of target marketing strategy crucial for long-term survival and profitability. The choice of appropriate targeting strategy ultimately depends on:

- an understanding of the size and attractiveness of the market segments that have been identified
- the organisation's ability to service and compete for the chosen market segments.

We will discuss these issues over the following few pages.

## Evaluate potential segments

The evaluation of potential market segments involves detailed and rigorous analysis of sales potential, the competitive situation and cost structures. We will discuss each of these in turn.

### Sales potential

**Market potential** is the total volume of sales of a product category that all organisations in an industry are expected to sell in a specified period of time, assuming a specific level of marketing activity. For example, the market potential for new car sales in Australia is around one million cars a year. An organisation's **sales revenue** is equal to its total volume of sales multiplied by the average selling price. The total volume of sales is determined by the organisation's **market share**. For example, Toyota's market share is around 20 per cent. Therefore Toyota's total volume of sales will be about 200 000 units (20 per cent of one million) and its total sales revenue will be 200 000 multiplied by the average price of its cars.

While the overall sales and level of marketing activity for new cars (a well-established and well-defined product) can be predicted with some certainty, allowing for varying economic conditions, it can be difficult to determine the likely

**market potential** The total sales of a product category that all organisations in an industry are expected to sell in a specified period of time assuming a specific level of marketing activity.

**sales revenue** Total volume of sales multiplied by the average selling price.

**market share** The proportion of the total market held by the organisation.

marketing activity and sales relating to new products or product categories, such as apps for use with smartphones and tablet computer devices. Market size can be measured at several levels, including product category or geographical area. It is important, of course, that the organisation analyses the size of the market it can actually reach.

Company sales potential is an estimate of the *maximum* sales revenue and market share that an organisation can expect to achieve for a specific product. Several factors influence the organisation's ability to achieve its sales potential in a given market segment:

- the market potential (i.e. the maximum possible sales in the total market for a product category)
- the organisation's 'served market' (i.e. those segments of the market for which the organisation chooses to compete)
- the level of industry marketing activity, which directly influences the market potential
- the effectiveness of an organisation's promotional spending, which depends on the organisation's 'share of voice' (i.e. the organisation's promotional spending relative to total industry promotional spending) and the use of effective 'tactical' promotional spending designed to maximise impact.

As we saw earlier in this section, one approach to estimating sales potential is to look at total market size, current market share, planned marketing activities and environmental factors. For example, project home builders typically use Australian Bureau of Statistics data on the aggregate level of 'housing commencements' to estimate their likely market share, and then calculate the company sales potential. The use of historical data (and sometimes even current figures) in isolation can, however, be misleading. For example, the project home builder looking at housing construction data over the past several years will have seen dramatic fluctuations brought about by changes in interest rates, the unemployment rate and government first-home buyer grants and subsidies. Forecasting is a complex process subject to numerous uncertainties. Another approach to estimating sales potential is to examine individual parts of the market (e.g. sales territories), take into account the size or population of each territory and the organisation's relative share of total marketing activity, and then sum each territory's estimates to produce a sales figure for the total market.

## Competitive situation

Any estimate of sales potential must be conducted in the context of a thorough assessment of the organisation's competitive situation — the activities of competitors already in the marketplace and their relative market shares. This is usually done as part of a situation analysis, as described in chapter 2.

Without a competitive assessment, sales estimates can be misleadingly optimistic, especially where an organisation is entering an established competitive market. Under such circumstances, it is important to evaluate the level of competitive activity and the strengths and weaknesses of individual competitors before estimating the organisation's likely market share. To increase market share, it may be necessary to allocate a larger than normal promotional budget. It is safe to assume that competitors will take steps to defend their market shares when an organisation enters a new market. This can lead to promotional warfare, which can depress profits through higher costs and lower margins, even though sales volumes may be at the expected level.

## Cost structure

The organisation needs to consider the costs involved in creating, communicating and delivering an offering to meet the needs of each potential market segment.

Costs directly affect the price the organisation will need to charge for its products, its price competitiveness and its profitability given any particular sales volume. The organisation's cost structure includes production costs, administrative overheads and all associated promotion and distribution costs. Knowledge of sales potential, the competitive situation and the organisation's cost structure combine to give a good indication of expected profit. Of course, in many cases the organisation may decide that the financial returns do not outweigh the expected costs. When considering an organisation's cost structure, it is important to distinguish between fixed and variable costs. Fixed costs are constant, regardless of production and sales volumes. If they are high they serve as an 'entry barrier', and an organisation may choose *not* to enter a market even though revenue and volume expectations may be attractive.

## Select target markets

With a detailed evaluation of potential market segments based on sales potential, the competitive situation and the organisation's cost structures, the organisation can proceed to decide which market segments it will target and which it will disregard. Also, from an understanding of its chosen target market strategy (i.e. undifferentiated, differentiated or specialised) the organisation will now better understand how it needs to tailor its offer to best meet the needs of each segment. With an understanding of the opportunities and costs of serving each potential target market segment, the next stage is for the organisation to choose particular target market segments, recognising that this will require ignoring some market segments, which may not offer sufficient sales potential or for which the organisation may not be best equipped to compete.

Having identified a range of potential target market segments, the organisation needs to undertake a rigorous analysis to choose between the range of possible segments. If segmentation has been done effectively, then it is likely that there will be little overlap in the demands of key target markets. On the other hand, if the range of demands is relatively homogeneous, then the organisation may be able to cover several market segments with a single product offer and marketing mix. The organisation could use an undifferentiated approach, and in so doing capture larger sales volumes at lower incremental cost. However, such a position may leave the organisation vulnerable to attack by competitors that target each segment individually.

Assuming that several segments offer sufficient revenue opportunities, the organisation must decide which and how many of these segments to target. This decision will be based on the revenue opportunities identified in the previous step, together with an understanding of the organisation's resources and capabilities and the likely response of competitors. The size of the available market will be a prime consideration in deciding how many segments to target. Consider, for example, the rapidly growing energy drink category in Australia. Tackling mainstream brands such as Red Bull, V and Mother is an enormous challenge for new entrants in the market, but the identification of particular segments that are less well-served can provide a profitable niche for new competitors. This has been proven by entrants into the health-conscious beer drinking segments, including BlueTongue Brewery's Bondi Blonde. In New Zealand, boutique brewers have targeted particular segments to try to find a niche. For example, the Epic Brewing Company targets its pale ale at drinkers with a preference for a strongly flavoured beer and a rebellious image. Of course, once they do establish a successful niche, they should expect large competitors to introduce their own products targeting those segments.

Estimating market potential in each target market segment is important in determining whether the chosen target market strategy will lead to healthy sales volumes and sustainable profitability. This step requires estimation of market potential for individual market segments and, in this process, it is important that the organisation develops sales forecasts based on systematic, objective and reliable methods, and that the forecasts are sufficiently accurate. A range of methods are available, including market research (particularly surveys), analysis of historical trends, statistical analysis to identify underlying purchasing patterns, test marketing results, and indeed just the intuition of decision makers.

Selecting particular market segments, (and deciding to ignore others) is therefore at the heart of the marketing concept. The organisation is no longer referring to an individual buyer or the entire mass market — it is now a target market segment or segments (although the organisation may describe such target market segments as if they were individuals).

# Battle of the codes

The AFL has declared 'war', and it is targeting rugby league heartland. Rugby league has long been the pre-eminent winter football code in two Australian States — New South Wales and Queensland. However, these are the very states that the AFL has strategically earmarked for the expansion of its own code. When the AFL announced that it would be expanding its competition from 16 to 18 teams, it chose the Western Sydney area and the Gold Coast to be the respective bases for the two new clubs, despite bids for new teams from more traditional AFL strongholds, such as Tasmania.

News of their first major player signings subsequently shocked the Australian sporting landscape. Two high-profile National Rugby League players (Karmichael Hunt and Israel Folau) were offered and accepted million dollar deals to switch codes and play for the new Gold Coast and Greater Western Sydney AFL clubs respectively. Critics were quick to label these signings as marketing publicity stunts, and predicted that neither player would make an impact in the AFL.

The appeal of the Western Sydney and Gold Coast markets to the AFL is obvious. Sydney's population of more than 4.5 million people has historically only had one local team to support, the Sydney Swans. South-East Queensland is the fastest growing geographical area in Australia, and the Gold Coast is now Australia's sixth largest city, with a population of more than half a million people. Prior to the entry of the Gold Coast Suns in 2011, the AFL competition had only one Queensland-based AFL team, the Brisbane Lions. On the surface, these population statistics represent a huge potential market.

However, in terms of being quickly embraced and supported by their regions, history shows that it may not necessarily be a smooth ride for the two new AFL clubs. The Brisbane Lions (then known as the Brisbane Bears) ironically spent the first seven years of their existence based on the Gold Coast, and struggled for support before their eventual successful relocation to Brisbane in 1994. The Sydney Swans also struggled to initially gain support and an identity in the rugby league-oriented city in the early 1980s, with the club formerly being a Melbourne-based team that was subsequently relocated and renamed.

AFL administrators acknowledge that growing the sport in non-traditional areas is a challenge, but one worth taking with a long-term view. They are encouraged by the success of their popular Auskick program for children aged 5 to 12, which they have been working intensively in these markets for several years. The AFL is hoping that if AFL is the sport children first choose to play, it will be the one they continue to support and follow throughout their life.[7]

## Question

From a marketing perspective, evaluate the AFL's decision to target the Gold Coast and Western Sydney as expansion areas for its code.

## Concepts and applications check

**Learning objective 4** select specific target markets based on evaluation of potential market segments

**4.1** Recall the most recent item of clothing that you purchased. Describe the market segment(s) at which you think it is targeted.

**4.2** What factors should form the basis of an organisation's evaluation of potential market segments?

**4.3** Choose a magazine that you read at least occasionally. List all of the possible market segments the magazine could target, and outline the competitive situation that the publication potentially faces in each. Which segment do you believe would be the most attractive for the magazine to target? Justify your answer.

# POSITIONING

 **Learning objective 5** understand how to effectively position an offering to a target market in relation to competitors, and develop an appropriate marketing mix

**positioning** The way in which the market perceives an organisation, its products and its brands in relation to competing offerings.

The market targeting stage will provide organisations with a clear understanding of their best prospective market segments. The issue then arises as to the offer to be made to each segment, and how the organisation wants to be perceived by its target markets. The organisation must determine how its offer is 'positioned' in the minds of *each* of its target market segments and develop its marketing mix accordingly. **Positioning** describes how target markets perceive the organisation's offer relative to competing offers. It is how customers distinguish the organisation, its products and its brands from competitors when they are selecting from among the available alternatives. Notice that positioning is based on customer perceptions which may or may not closely correspond with the product's objective characteristics. For example, Penfold's Grange Hermitage wine is strongly positioned as Australia's premier wine in the minds of customers, even though some of its close competitors are judged above it from year to year. The important issue is how potential buyers *see* the brand, and this requires that the marketing organisation undertakes regular qualitative and quantitative market research to obtain an accurate understanding of the position it occupies in the minds of its target customers.

The organisation can pursue positioning to manage:
- how it, as a whole, is perceived relative to competitors in the minds of its stakeholder groups. Virgin, for example, seeks to position itself as the most friendly, casual and perhaps even 'irreverent' competitor across its range of businesses.
- how its brands are seen, typically focusing on distinguishing product attributes. For example, Apple focuses on simplicity, breakthrough design and the wide range of applications (apps) for its iPad.
- how the market distinguishes its offering from those of closely competitive brands. For example, Audi competes closely with BMW for the same target markets with closely comparable prices and product features.

Position is fundamentally important for organisations, because it describes how the organisation is perceived by the market, relative to its competitors on the attributes that customers regard as important in their decision making. In this way, positioning describes how customers make sense of the complex, crowded marketplace and make their brand choice decisions in an efficient way. Positioning enables buyers to take a 'shortcut' and arrive at decisions without an excessively complex or confusing process. When it is done successfully, positioning is generally based on simple propositions, with which customers agree and which can be easily retained in memory. In this sense, Qantas's positioning around the theme 'I still call Australia home' is believable, memorable and unique.

While communicating a product's attributes through advertising and other promotional campaigns is crucial in establishing an initial market position in the minds of target customers, it is important to understand that such promotion and communication can only attract 'first-time' buyers to the brand. Once customers have sampled the brand, the brand's positioning will subsequently depend very largely on the customer's experience of the brand. In this sense, the crucial question for positioning is 'Does the customer's experience match the promise?' It is easy for an organisation such as an airline or a bank to promise 'friendly and efficient service' in seeking to attract new customers. The crucial and more difficult question for the long term is whether or not the organisation's performance corresponds with its promise and its market positioning.

Positioning involves two steps: firstly, determining the position that the company wishes to occupy in the minds of buyers; and secondly, developing a marketing mix to reflect the expectations of the target market segment and which reflects that positioning. This is shown in figure 6.10.

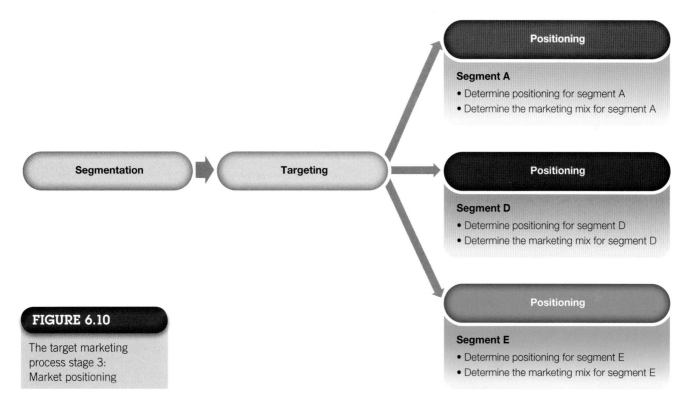

**FIGURE 6.10**

The target marketing process stage 3: Market positioning

## Determine positioning for each segment

To determine the appropriate positioning for its products, an organisation needs to undertake detailed market research to understand its current position in the minds of its target market segments. As outlined in chapter 3, a common technique for determining positioning is called *perceptual mapping* (see page 97), which produces two-dimensional maps showing how each of the competing brands relate to each other in terms of a range of product attributes. This, of course, assumes that consumers in the target segment are already familiar with the brand and its competitors and are able to subjectively or objectively compare them on attributes that they believe to be important. In a familiar product category like toothpaste, consumers will generally have little difficulty in describing how they distinguish between competing brands such as Colgate and Maclean's in terms of a range of attributes such as fresh breath, cavity protection, pleasant taste and suitability for sensitive gums. Under such conditions, familiar brands such as Colgate Total occupy clear and strong positions, which is paradoxically both a strength and a limitation. It represents a strength in that existing consumers are in no doubt about the benefits and features of the product. At the same time, such a strong position is difficult to change in the short term. Conversely, new brands in the market are better able to establish new positions based on new benefits as consumers develop awareness of newly discovered issues.

### Analysing current positioning

The process of establishing an organisation's current positioning is clearly of strategic importance and, as such, should be undertaken based on rigorous analysis and market research. The first step in determining the current positioning of a brand is to identify those product attributes that consumers use to distinguish between competing products or brands. For example, consumers differentiate between home and contents insurance products based on price and extent of coverage. Qualitative research methods such as focus group studies (see chapter 3) are commonly used to ascertain the relevant attributes.

Once the product attributes responsible for creating consumers' different perceptions have been identified, the organisation needs to assess how its own product or brand, and competitors' products or brands are positioned in relation to those attributes. This is typically done through quantitative survey research, using rating scales to establish how each competing brand scores on each of the product attributes within each of the target market segments. Based on the results of these rating scales, a perceptual map can be constructed. Figure 6.11 shows the perceptual map we developed for the Australian surfwear industry in chapter 3. The perceptual map shows how the different brands are currently positioned relative to each other on those attributes that consumers use to distinguish between their offerings.

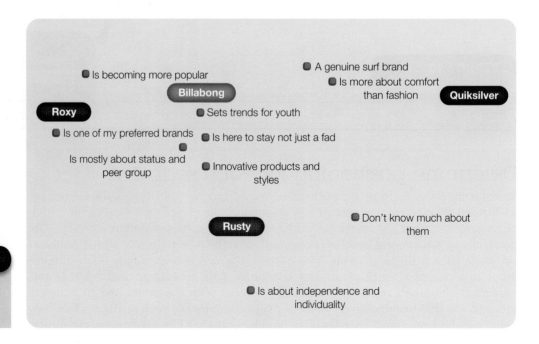

**FIGURE 6.11**

A perceptual map of the Australian surfwear industry, revisited

The next step is to devise some concept of the ideal position of the organisation's product or brand. This may need to be adjusted on the grounds of practicability — the desired position may not be attainable given the resources available.

Finally, the organisation needs to develop a plan to move to the desired position.

### Competitive positioning and repositioning

Refer back to figure 6.11. Having established its current position, Rusty, for example, might feel that its position as an individual and independent choice is holding it back from securing more market share. It might want to move towards a position related to peer status. For Rusty, the question would be 'How might we reposition?' One option would be to pay celebrities to wear the brand. Secondly, Rusty could change its advertising appeals to try to persuade the public that it is not so representative of independence. A further attribute which is not represented in this perceptual map, but which is present in almost all consumers' mental maps, is price. Generally price is relatively independent of other product attributes, and all competing brands will be evaluated on price (see chapter 8).

It should now be clear that positioning is fundamentally important in the marketing of individual brands and in the organisation's long-term competitive success. It should also be apparent that, once established, a competitive position should be protected and nurtured for the long term. This involves communicating a consistent message and delivering a consistent product over the long term. In this sense, positions should not be chopped and changed, but rather should be created, nurtured and consistently reinforced.

# Determine the marketing mix for each segment

With knowledge of the optimal, practicable positioning of our brand, the final step in the target marketing process is to determine an appropriate marketing mix for each target market segment. The marketing mix describes the entire offer the organisation makes to its target customers. The marketing mix for each segment should:

- be consistent with the desired positioning
- be internally consistent — each element of the marketing mix should be coordinated and supportive of the other elements
- be sustainable in the long term.

Developing the appropriate marketing mix for target market segments is the focus of the rest of this textbook and will be central to all of your work in marketing.

## Your choice of flights

Skytrax is an organisation that specialises in conducting market research for the air transport industry. In addition to specialist research projects that it undertakes individually for more than 200 commercial airlines that are its clients, Skytrax independently conducts a major international airline passenger survey each year. The results of this survey are widely reported in the global media.

More than 17 million air travellers from over 100 countries participated in a recent survey in which the performances of more than 200 international airlines were analysed by passengers. The survey analysed customer satisfaction with an airline on eight key criteria: value for money, cabin service, cabin comfort, in-flight entertainment, boarding/deplaning, on-board catering, check-in service and baggage service.

While naturally on a smaller scale than the Skytrax global surveys, the independent consumer advocacy group CHOICE also conducts passenger surveys on both domestic and international airlines each year in Australia. Customer satisfaction levels on a range of criteria are measured, including:

- baggage allowance
- check-in process
- cost
- food quality
- leg room
- in-flight service and entertainment
- redeeming frequent flyer points
- seat comfort
- timeliness of flights
- overall satisfaction.

### Question

Visit CHOICE's website (www.choice.com.au) and access the results of either their most recent domestic or international airline survey. Looking at the survey results for any two airlines of your own choice, describe:

(a) the current positioning of the two airlines in relation to their competition

(b) how each airline could potentially better position themselves against their competitors in the future.

## Concepts and applications check

**Learning objective 5** understand how to effectively position an offering to a target market in relation to competitors, and develop an appropriate marketing mix

5.1 Explain the concept of market positioning.

5.2 Choose five different products (goods or services) and list those attributes of each that would be used by consumers to distinguish between competing brands.

5.3 For the five products in question 5.2, describe the relative positioning of three different brands.

5.4 Why is it important for a marketer to take a long-term view of positioning and the marketing mix?

# SUMMARY

 **Learning objective 1** explain the broad concept of a 'market'

A market is a group of customers with heterogenous needs and wants. Marketers seek to identify and understand those parts of the market that they can offer the most value. These parts of the total market form the organisation's target market.

 **Learning objective 2** understand the target marketing concept

Market segments are subgroups within the total market that are relatively similar in regards to certain characteristics. Marketers can choose to make an undifferentiated offer to the market, to customise the offering for each individual customer, or to make offers that are tailored to the needs of market segments, but not further differentiated within each segment. Target marketing is an approach to marketing based on identifying, understanding and developing an offering for those segments of the total market that an organisation can best serve. Small organisations with limited resources often choose to specialise their offering to a particular market segment, focus on one product, or combine both approaches. The target marketing process involves market segmentation, market targeting and market positioning.

 **Learning objective 3** identify market segmentation variables for consumer and business markets, and develop market segment profiles

Market segmentation involves identifying variables that can be used to define meaningful market segments and then creating profiles of the market segments. The ideal market segmentation variables are those that are likely to be closely linked to purchasing behaviour. In consumer markets, geography, demographics, psychographics and behavioural variables are useful for segmentation. In business markets, organisation size, product use and geography are typically used. Whatever the segmentation variables, the defined segments should be measurable, accessible, substantial and practicable. Based on market segments, the marketer can develop a market segment profile, which is a description of the typical customer in the market segment in relation to their shared characteristics and the characteristics that distinguish them from other segments.

 **Learning objective 4** select specific target markets based on evaluation of potential market segments

Market targeting is the selection of target markets resulting from the evaluation of the market segments that have been identified. The choice of target markets will be made upon thorough assessment of the market segment's sales potential, the competitive situation in the market, and the organisation's cost structures. Once these factors are known for each segment, the most appealing segment or segments will emerge as the clear targets for the organisation's marketing strategy.

 **Learning objective 5** understand how to effectively position an offering to a target market in relation to competitors, and develop an appropriate marketing mix

Market positioning refers to how target markets perceive an organisation's offering in relation to its competitors' offerings. Market positioning is fundamental to how customers choose between competing products. Organisations may choose to undertake positioning at the company or brand level, or to focus on differences with close competitors. To implement a positioning strategy, the organisation must determine

## Key terms and concepts

behavioural
   segmentation 193
demographic
   segmentation 189
differentiated targeting
   strategy 184
geographic
   segmentation 188
market 179
market potential 198
market segment profile 196
market segments 181
market share 198
market specialisation 184
positioning 202
product specialisation 184
product–market
   specialisation 184
psychographic
   segmentation 190
sales revenue 198
segmentation variables 187
target marketing 182

how it wishes to be perceived by the market and then develop a marketing mix that will produce that perception. The first step in analysing positioning is to determine which product attributes consumers use to distinguish between competing offerings. The organisation then assesses how it and its competitors are positioned against those attributes. Once the current market position is known, the organisation can develop a concept of where it would like to be positioned. Finally, it must develop a plan to move to the desired position. The marketing mix developed for each target market segment must be fully consistent with the desired position.

# Online social intrusion (or target marketing)?

Market research is fundamental to understanding the market, and thus to successfully creating, communicating and delivering offerings of value to customers. Consumer information mined from the personal data provided by users of online social networking sites represents the next phase in the evolution of marketing thinking and practice in market segmentation and target marketing. The scope of the online social networking data mining task is potentially limitless, when you consider that sites such as Facebook and MySpace have become hugely popular in recent years, with millions of people creating accounts globally. Some people, however, view this form of data mining as an intrusion of privacy.

Along with the benefits of sharing their lives with others, users are becoming increasingly aware of the privacy issues associated with commercial data mining of the information they enter into their online profiles. In protest, over 32 000 users pledged their support for 'Quit Facebook Day' during 2010. Many ordinary websites, such as brand promotion sites and online shopping sites, inadvertently collect and store users' personal information. However, the information entered into online social networking site profiles is actively entered by users, many of whom are unaware of site privacy policies and potential privacy issues. Others are aware of the issues, but are unconcerned about the commercial usage of the data and the potential privacy risks, and choose to ignore the warnings. Users enthusiastically continue to push their intimate details out into the online world for all to see, contributing large amounts of personal data without fully understanding or comprehending what they are doing and the risks they are taking. The ability to share information, which is the key benefit of online social networking, is very closely linked to the potential abuse of this information.

Upon joining, online social networking site users need to provide information such as their name, email address, age and sex. They are then prompted to create a detailed profile including information, for example, on their hobbies, interests, affiliations, school or university, and musical tastes. Each time they enter 'status updates', upload photographs or videos, or join 'fan sites' they are entering more data into the system.

The task of data mining is used by marketers to identify consumer demographics, interests, preferences and purchasing behaviours. This data is then used to target advertising and promotional material to the individual site users. Clearly, providing individually tailored advertising and promotions will benefit advertisers and media owners (who can charge higher advertising rates). While the idea is not new (Google targets users with tailored advertising based on search queries), it is only recently that Facebook has begun to noticeably use the data it collects from users for commercial benefit.

Through the launch of Facebook Beacon (which has since been disbanded), Facebook was able to track the purchase behaviour of users on other external websites, and then used this information to provide personally targeted advertising on the Facebook site. Companies have exploited personal data for years, but this level of targeting was perceived by many as equating to intrusion. Some may argue that social networking sites should be free of advertising because they are social spaces; 'this is MySpace'. By tracking behaviour outside of the network, Facebook took a risk and subsequently faced criticism and negative repercussions from users, the media and others. The move allowed rival site MySpace to seize a high moral position, because it only uses data provided by members.

Other Australian businesses also invest heavily in data mining. The Woolworths Everyday Rewards loyalty card provides accurate, timely and insightful information to Woolworths on their customers. In this way, Woolworths knows who is buying what — when and how frequently, where, at what price, and in combination with which other products. In return for providing this information, the customer earns rewards and receives special offers. The major banks, especially NAB and Westpac, are arguably at the edge of world's best practice in their use of customer analytics to deliver tailored banking services to target segments and individual consumers. Similarly, Myer and David Jones have long histories of developing a close relationship with their customers. Myer's 'MYER one' loyalty program enables the retailer to link every sale to every customer member, benefiting from vastly improved knowledge of customers' shopping behaviours, which can be linked to the analysis of advertising, sales and merchandising campaigns. Arguably, the overall goal of this approach, like all customer relationship management initiatives, is to move closer to the corner store service, where customers and their preferences are known to them.

The increasingly commercial nature of online social networking sites is creating backlash from users. Noisy protests emanating from users (including 'Quit Facebook Day') and governments prompted Facebook management to update and simplify privacy settings, in a scrambling attempt to generate silence. The negative publicity could be highlighting a weakness with the site, inviting exploitation from rivals such as MySpace and Orkut. There is also the possibility that a new site will enter the market.

Online social networking sites were developed to allow and encourage users to share their lives with only their friends. This stand is arguably at odds with the companies' business models, which seek to profit from the information provided by users, either advertently or inadvertently. It is also at odds with many of the default privacy settings that mean users must actively opt out of sharing their personal information with 'everyone' and limit sharing to 'friends only'. Through the compilation of personal information, websites such as Facebook have the potential to generate huge profits. Personal information is a form of secondary market research data that can be sold to businesses. Businesses can use this data, for example, to effectively target specific market segments with tailored advertising and promotional offers. The information can also be used to monitor social trends and track usage behaviour.

Employers can use these sites to data mine for information about current and potential staff. But they also face the dilemma of whether or not to allow their employees to access these sites during working hours. They must choose between showing trust to develop loyalty, while risking a potential decline in productivity. Alternatively, staff could be encouraged to use online social networking sites to share company news and spread positive word-of-mouth and brand messages. Employees who are aware of the cost to the company of their unproductive behaviour are more likely to modify their behaviour.

Online social networking sites have also generated privacy and safety fears among school children, especially after the case of a Sydney teenager who was apparently killed by a man she met and befriended on Facebook. There are also an increasing number of cyber-bullying incidents being reported to police and by the media. In response to these incidents, the Australian government has created the online program 'Cybersmart Hero' to provide support for primary school children in dealing with online bullying. Primary school children, along with elderly users, are most at risk when using online social networking sites, according to online privacy experts.

Vulnerability stems from a lack of awareness of the privacy issues and from the propensity to disclose personal information. In a recent year, the fastest growing demographic of Facebook users was the over-55 age group, according to Facebook statistics. A lack of online knowledge and experience is also exposing younger and older users to identity fraud.

As users become increasingly aware of privacy issues and as the sites introduce changes to their privacy policies, the onus remains with users to actively take responsibility and control the information they provide for sharing. Information posted today has the real potential of coming back as a negative in the future. Only vigilance today can help ensure a secure future.

Many users claim that they log on to social networking sites to maintain friendships, find old school friends and even stalk their exes. However, online social networks foster vanity and ego development too: they are places where people talk about 'me'; where they create a profile of the trendiest, best looking, most attractive 'me' possible. Users post holiday photos, videos and status updates, hoping to make their friends both intrigued and slightly jealous. These profiles are 'me' marketing machines. They are personal PR machines for ordinary people. When individuals suffer the (mis)fortune of making the news media, online social networking sites are mined for information, photos and personal details. Then, suddenly, these sites become the targets of criticism about privacy. Alternatively, it has been argued that we are no longer private individuals, but rather people with publicly private identities.[8]

This case study was written by Lucy Miller from Macquarie University.

# Questions

1. How could Facebook users be divided using psychographic segmentation? Justify your answer using examples from the case study.
2. Which of the VALS consumer segments do most Facebook users fit into?
3. Behavioural segmentation is based on actual usage or consumption behaviours. List the relevant behaviours that could be used to segment Facebook users. Justify your answer with reference to the 'effective segmentation criteria'.
4. MySpace and Facebook have chosen to target different consumer markets. Discuss the positioning of each social networking site and create a perceptual map to demonstrate how they are positioned in the market.

## Advanced activity

The opening case at the start of the chapter highlighted the grey nomad consumer segment. Apart from caravans and motorhomes (and the recreational vehicles that are used to tow them), make a list of five other products that might be expected to experience a growth in demand from the grey nomad segment. Outline how you would position each of these products for this segment in relation to each of their major competitors.

## Marketing plan activity

Based on the information you have been compiling for your chosen organisation's marketing plan (from chapters 1 to 5 — the situation analysis, SWOT analysis, any market research you have or will be conducting, and your understanding of how consumers and/or businesses make purchasing decisions), identify your potential target market or markets. Be as specific as possible, outlining the following for each target market segment that you identify:
(a) demographic characteristics
(b) geographic characteristics
(c) psychographic characteristics
(d) behavioural characteristics.

Finally, analyse the needs of each target market segment, explaining the following.
(a) the current (and potential future) needs of each target market segment
(b) how your chosen organisation's current product offerings meet these needs (or will be able to be positioned to meet these needs)
(c) how competing product offerings currently meet these needs (or will likely be positioned in future to meet these needs).

  This needs analysis may require additional market research to be conducted and prompt you to modify the market research brief you prepared at the conclusion of chapter 3.

  A sample marketing plan has been included at the back of this book (see page 523) to give you an idea where this information fits in an overall marketing plan.

## CHAPTER 7

# Product

## Learning objectives

After studying this chapter, you should be able to:

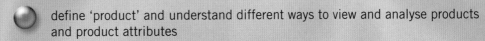 define 'product' and understand different ways to view and analyse products and product attributes

describe the product life cycle, new product development and the product adoption process

outline how an organisation can differentiate its products to obtain a competitive advantage

explain the value of branding and the major issues involved in brand management

describe the functional and marketing roles of packaging

explain key aspects of product management and positioning through the product life cycle.

# Shooting star?

*Guitar Hero* quickly became a billion-dollar product by combining two 'lame' activities to appeal to 'wannabe' rock stars — karaoke and air guitar. Players of the console game are required to strum on a plastic guitar, hitting five coloured plastic keys in time with dots that appear on screen, to simulate the chords played on classic rock songs. A quick search of YouTube reveals a vast array of video clips of *Guitar Hero* players either frenetically mimicking their favourite rock stars or displaying their own unique style.

The initial idea for *Guitar Hero* came from Japanese games publisher Konami's *Dance Dance Revolution*, a rhythm-based dance video game. Konami followed this with a guitar game called *GuitarFreaks*. The US distributor for Konami, RedOctane, subsequently approached a US software developer to create a new version of the game that would include a number of popular karaoke titles, and *Guitar Hero* was born. It was launched for PlayStation 2 in November 2005. Since then, regular sequels followed for each of the major gaming consoles (PlayStation, XBox and Wii), with enhanced musical capabilities and a variety of new songs for players to master.

The music industry's reaction to the evolution of *Guitar Hero* was an interesting phenomenon to monitor. In the initial two versions of the game, the vast majority of the songs included were not those of the original artists; rather, they were cover versions recorded by session musicians. As the success of the game grew, artists and record companies began to allow games developers unprecedented access to their original masters, so that they could be included instead of the cover versions. *Guitar Hero III* was such a success that record companies began seeing sales of previously stagnant old songs and albums increase significantly, almost overnight. Record companies and artists and their management became increasingly keen to have their songs included in each new version of *Guitar Hero* that was released.[1]

However, after the spectacular growth that was achieved with the early versions of *Guitar Hero*, sales began to significantly decline with the later versions. Critics attributed this, in part, to too many updated versions of both the *Guitar Hero* franchise and other similar games being released too quickly, oversaturating the market.

---

### Question

From a marketing perspective, could anything be done to reinvigorate *Guitar Hero*?

# INTRODUCTION

In chapters 4 and 5, we explored the reasons behind the purchasing decisions made by consumers and businesses, and how they go about making those decisions. Combined with the ability to divide the market into target segments, this information helps us begin to answer the question we posed at the start of chapter 6: 'How do we formulate the marketing mix to best serve our potential customers?' In this and the following chapters, we will examine the key components of the marketing mix — product, pricing, promotion and distribution (place) (as well as people, processes and physical evidence). Unlike factors in the micro environment and macro environment, the marketing mix can be directly controlled by the organisation.

We will first examine *product* decisions. As we learned in chapter 1, a product can be a good, service or idea. In this chapter, we will examine the broad decisions that need to be made about the product in the marketing mix. In chapter 11, we will look in more detail at some of the considerations demanded by the special nature of products that are services.

The product is, essentially, what the marketer takes to the market in an attempt to get consumers to buy or engage in some type of exchange, in order to achieve the organisation's objectives. A product can be relatively simple, like a potato chip, or much more complex, like an aircraft. It can even be a game that provides entertainment, like *Guitar Hero*. Developing, launching and positioning products can be difficult and uncertain. In this chapter we will be discussing what a product actually is, the types of products available, the product life cycle, branding, packaging, product development, management, and positioning. With this knowledge, the marketer is better placed to manage the product aspect of the marketing mix.

## PRODUCTS: GOODS, SERVICES AND IDEAS

In chapter 1, the marketing process was shown to comprise creating, communicating, delivering and exchanging offerings that have value for customers. A **product** is defined as a good, service or idea offered to the market for exchange. Clearly, *product* plays a vital role in the marketing process. Without a product, a marketer has nothing to offer. On the other side of the exchange, potential customers require products to satisfy functional, social and psychological needs, wants and demands. The core concept is that both parties must gain value from the exchange.

Goods are physical, tangible offerings that are capable of being delivered to a customer. Because it is tangible, you can see, touch, taste and smell a good (depending on what it is). The purchase of a good usually involves the transfer of ownership from marketer to customer; when the customer buys a good, they usually become the owner of the good. Examples of goods include toothpaste, shoes and cars. Services are intangible offerings to the market. As they are intangible, a service cannot be touched or tasted and does not involve ownership; instead, you *experience* a service. Hair cuts, legal representation and massages are all examples of services. An idea can also be offered to the market in the form of a concept, issue or philosophy. Ideas are often the products of community organisations, charities and political parties. Examples of ideas include Quit for Life; Slip, Slop, Slap; and Clean Up Australia.

## The total product concept

Products have many different features that can provide value for customers, clients, partners and society at large. In chapter 1 we described the features of a product

**Learning objective 1**
define 'product' and understand different ways to view and analyse products and product attributes

---

**product** A good, service or idea offered to the market for exchange.

---

as a 'bundle of attributes'. At the most basic level, marketers must ensure that the product attributes satisfy the needs and wants of potential buyers. It is this ability to satisfy a need or want that makes the product of value to potential customers. To make a product of more value than competing offerings, the marketer must take a more comprehensive view of the product. To understand how the product's value is perceived by potential customers, it is useful to describe the product in terms of its four levels: core product, expected product, augmented product and potential product. This view of the product is known as the **total product concept** and is illustrated in figure 7.1.

It is crucial for marketers to understand that when customers choose a product, they do not purchase some 'thing'; rather, they buy a solution to a problem. To revisit an example from chapter 1: A company that operates vending machines that serve hot drinks should view its business as one that quenches people's thirst, warms them when out on chilly winter nights and gives them a caffeine boost when they are feeling tired; not as a business that places machines on train station platforms and mixes lukewarm water with powdered flavouring in a cardboard cup. The total product concept is a way of viewing a product as the totality of value and benefits it provides to the customer. Products are offered to the market to be an answer to the customer's problem of an unsatisfied need or want.

**total product concept** A view of the product that describes the core product, expected product, augmented product and potential product in order to analyse how the product creates value for the customer.

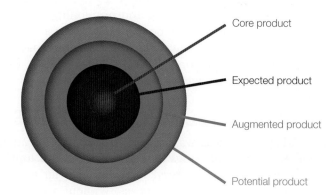

**FIGURE 7.1**

The total product concept

### The core product

The core product comprises the fundamental benefit that responds to the customer's problem of an unsatisfied need or want. So what is it that will satisfy a customer's need? What is the key benefit they want from a product? For a marketer, understanding these questions will greatly assist in providing the right product to the market, and make sure customers purchase from you and not a competitor. For a mobile phone, the core benefit is reliable, accessible communications; for a credit card, it is the ongoing provision of credit; for a hamburger, it is satisfaction of hunger. Regardless of other changes made to a product, the core product generally remains the same.

### The expected product

The expected product describes those attributes that actually deliver the benefit that forms the core product. They are the attributes that fulfil the customer's most basic expectations of the product. Marketers generally try to differentiate their offering using fundamental characteristics such as branding, packaging and quality standards at the expected product level.

## The augmented product

At the augmented product level, the product delivers a bundle of benefits that the buyer may not require as part of the basic fulfilment of their needs. The augmented product level enables marketers to significantly differentiate their offerings from those of competitors. It is often the augmented product features that form the main reason for choosing a particular brand. This can include support services, such as guarantees. For some mobile phone companies, augmented product features include access to music downloads. For a credit card, product augmentation may extend to loyalty programs and prestige (e.g. American Express has carefully ensured that its platinum card is considered highly prestigious). Over time, features that form part of the augmented product level can become so widely incorporated into the product that they become part of the expected product layer. Years ago, a loyalty program tied to a credit card was an augmented product feature, but as time passed and all competitors offered loyalty programs, the feature became part of the expected product.

## The potential product

The potential product comprises all possibilities that could become part of the expected or augmented product. This includes features that are being developed, planned or prototyped, as well as features that have not yet been conceived. Over time, many potential product features become part of the augmented product or even the expected product. For example, in the early days of mobile phones, SMS was an idea for a potential product feature. Within a few years, SMS capability became an augmented product feature and, ultimately, an expected product feature. Today, potential product features of a mobile phone could include digital television or Skype reception. A potential product for credit cards could be their use as a swipe card on public transport. Potential product features are attractive to marketers as they offer new ways to differentiate their product and increase the value for customers. Figure 7.2 shows how a product (a credit card) can be analysed using the total product concept.[2]

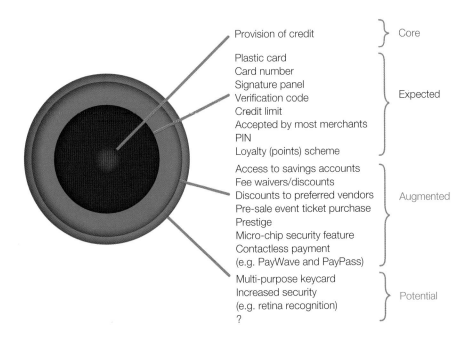

Provision of credit — Core

Plastic card
Card number
Signature panel
Verification code
Credit limit
Accepted by most merchants
PIN
Loyalty (points) scheme — Expected

Access to savings accounts
Fee waivers/discounts
Discounts to preferred vendors
Pre-sale event ticket purchase
Prestige
Micro-chip security feature
Contactless payment
(e.g. PayWave and PayPass) — Augmented

Multi-purpose keycard
Increased security
(e.g. retina recognition)
? — Potential

**FIGURE 7.2**

Analysing a credit card using the total product concept

# Product relationships

Many organisations produce multiple products or several different styles of a product. The relationships between the organisation's products can be described as follows:

- **product item** — a particular version of a product that can be differentiated from the organisation's other product items by characteristics such as brand, ingredients, style or price. For Bonds, a product item in their men's underwear range is Bonds Hipsters.
- **product line** — a set of closely related product items. The close relationship is usually in terms of end use, target market, technology or raw materials. Using the Bonds example, the product line for Bonds men's underwear includes trunks, Y-fronts, boxers and hipsters.
- **product mix** — the set of all products that an organisation makes available to customers. For Bonds, it is underwear, singlets, shorts, track suits, hoodie jackets, socks, and T-shirts, as part of their men's, women's and children's wear.[3] The product mix can be described by its width and depth. Product width refers to the number of product lines offered by a company. Product depth is the number of different products available in each product line.

# Product classification

Products can be classified into consumer products and business products according to the circumstances in which they are bought and their intended use. **Consumer products** are those products purchased by households and individuals for their own private consumption. **Business-to-business products** are those products purchased by individuals and organisations for use in the production of other products or for use in their daily business operations. Some products are both a consumer and a business product. Reflex photocopy paper, for example, can be purchased as a consumer product at a discount store to be used for a home inkjet printer, or as a business product from a wholesaler by the pallet to be used by an organisation's office printers and photocopiers.

The classification of products into consumer products and business-to-business products is a helpful first stage in understanding the different circumstances in which products are bought and the different uses customers have for them. It is useful, however, to develop the classification further as discussed in the following two sections of the chapter.

### Consumer products

It is useful to further subclassify consumer products into one or more of the following main categories:

- shopping products
- convenience products
- specialty products
- unsought products.

**Shopping products** are irregularly purchased items that involve moderate to high engagement with the decision-making process: consumers will often visit a number of stores, looking at the range and comparing items based on features, quality and price. Shopping products exhibit the following characteristics:

- they are expected to last a long time
- they are purchased relatively infrequently
- they are stocked by a small number of retail outlets
- they sell in low volumes
- they have reasonably large profit margins.

---

**product item** A particular version of a product.

**product line** A set of product items related by characteristics such as end use, target market, technology or raw materials.

**product mix** The set of all products that an organisation makes available to customers.

**consumer products** Those products purchased by households and individuals for their own private consumption.

**business-to-business products** Those products purchased by individuals and organisations for use in the production of other products or for use in their daily business operations.

**shopping products** Consumer products that involve moderate to high engagement in the decision-making process, in the purchase decision being based on consideration of features, quality and price.

Examples of shopping products include electrical appliances, furniture, cameras and clothing.

**Convenience products** also known as **fast-moving consumer goods**, are inexpensive, frequently purchased consumer products that are bought with little engagement in the decision-making process. Convenience products are usually available from a wide range of retailers, including supermarkets, corner stores and petrol stations. Being cheap, they usually depend on a high volume of sales to generate a reasonable profit. They are often self-service products and so packaging plays a major role in grabbing consumers' attention. Convenience products can be further broken down into three main categories:

- *staple products* — products that are bought and used by consumers regularly, such as milk, bread, rice and soap. Usually, there is not much promotion for branded staple products.
- *impulse products* — products that are bought with little planning, often purchased only after seeing the item at the retail store. Impulse products include magazines, chocolate and chewing gum. They are often positioned immediately next to the cash register in a store.
- *emergency products* — products that are bought when the product is needed in an 'emergency'; for example, an umbrella when you are caught in the rain or the services of an electrician if the power goes off.

**Specialty products** have unique characteristics that are highly desired by their buyers. The purchaser of a specialty product usually knows exactly what they want — they are not interested in comparing brands or considering alternatives. As such, consumers are willing to expend considerable effort to obtain specialty products. If someone is interested in purchasing a BMW car they will go to a BMW dealer and they will be prepared to travel some distance to get there if necessary. The main characteristics of specialty products are:

- they are pre-selected by the consumer
- there are no close substitutes or alternatives
- they are available in a limited number of outlets
- they are purchased infrequently
- they sell in low volumes
- they have high profit margins.

**Unsought products** are those goods or services that a consumer either:
(a) knows about but doesn't normally consider purchasing
(b) doesn't even know about.
A fundamental challenge for marketers with any product is to make consumers aware of the product's features and benefits, and the needs it satisfies. This is especially the case for unsought products, and marketing communication efforts are crucial.

For unsought products in category (a), a sudden, unexpected need may arise for consumers. For example, although most consumers will know that various home security products exist, it may take a spate of burglaries in their neighbourhood to prompt the consideration of purchasing such products. An actual break-in, of course, would prompt the engagement of police services. In such situations where unexpected needs arise, prior marketing communication efforts are likely to be crucial in order for a particular product or brand to be 'top of mind' for the consumer. For example, the consumer may be aware that 'Crimsafe' is a popular brand of home security products, due to concerted marketing communications efforts by the company over a number of years.

**convenience products (fast-moving consumer goods)** Inexpensive, frequently purchased consumer products that are bought with little engagement with the decision-making process.

**specialty products** Highly desired consumer products with unique characteristics that consumers will make considerable effort to obtain.

**unsought products** Goods or services that a consumer either knows about but doesn't normally consider purchasing, or doesn't even know about.

For unsought products in category (b), marketing communication is again crucial in terms of making consumers aware that the product is available, and that its features and benefits satisfy needs. Only then will demand for the product potentially be generated, in order for it to move out of the less desirable 'unsought' category and into one of the other consumer product classification categories (shopping, convenience or specialty).

In closing our discussion of consumer product classification categories, it is important to note that a product can be purchased as a different product class, depending on the customer's usual purchase behaviour or the reason for purchasing the item. For example, an umbrella may be especially purchased as a shopping product as a gift for someone, while an umbrella may also be bought as a convenience product if you are stuck outside in the rain.

### Business-to-business products

As we learned in chapters 5 and 6, not all products are intended for purchase by consumers. Business-to-business products are purchased by individuals and organisations for use in the production of other products or for use in their daily business operations. It is important not to confuse business-to-business products with the concept of business markets. Business markets include many transactions in which products are sold from one business to another for the purposes of then reselling to consumers. The fact the transaction takes place in business markets does not make the product a business-to-business product. It is the intention to use the product as part of business operations that defines business-to-business products. Business-to-business products can be classified into three categories: parts and materials, equipment, and supplies and services.

**parts and materials**
Business-to-business products that form part of the purchasing business's products.

**Parts and materials** are business-to-business products that form part of the purchasing business's products. They include:
- *raw materials* — unprocessed natural materials that are used in the production process to form part of the business's products. Raw materials can be farm products (e.g. fleece, used in the production of woollen yarn) or natural products (e.g. iron ore, used in the production of steel).
- *components* — processed items that form part of a business's product. Components are usually incorporated into the business's product through an assembly process. Components may be materials (e.g. yarn, used in the production of jackets) or parts (e.g. brakes, used in the production of bicycles).

**equipment** Capital equipment and accessory equipment used in the production of the business's products.

**Equipment** refers to those business-to-business products that are used in the production of the business's products. Equipment may be:
- *capital equipment* — installations such as buildings (e.g. offices, factories and warehouses) and machinery (e.g. generators, furnaces and conveyor belts)
- *accessory equipment* — smaller items that support the production of a product but that do not form part of the product (e.g. fork-lifts, drills, computers and filing cabinets).

**services and supplies**
Business-to-business products that are essential to business operations, but do not directly form part of the production process.

**Services and supplies** are business-to-business products that are essential to business operations, but that do not directly form part of the production process. Services and supplies include:
- *business services* — specialised services, such as financial, legal, market research and office cleaning services, that support the company's operations and are often provided by external suppliers, such as banks and solicitors
- *maintenance, repair and operating (MRO) supplies* — items that assist in the company's production and operations but do not form part of the product, including engine oil (for maintenance), rivets (for repair) and paper (for operations).

# Toyota Hybrid Camry

Cars have changed considerably since they were first mass produced by Henry Ford almost 100 years ago. With people generally becoming more environmentally aware in recent years, there has been a growing interest in hybrid cars that combine an electric and petrol powered engine. The cars are a relatively new product. As such, consumers who are interested in hybrid cars are likely to make considerable effort to find an authorised, reputable dealer. In particular, they will want the reassurance of knowing that they are dealing with people who have the technical knowledge to advise them on their purchase and provide after sales service.

The Hybrid Camry is the first commercially available hybrid vehicle (electronic/petrol powered) manufactured in Australia. The decision to make the Hybrid Camry in Australia came after Toyota experienced growth in demand for its internationally manufactured Prius model of hybrid car, and following subsequent discussions the company held with both the federal and Victorian governments. Toyota began manufacturing a hybrid version of the Camry sedan at its Altona plant in Melbourne from the beginning of 2010. The car utilises the technologically advanced hybrid technology, Hybrid Synergy Drive, to obtain peak driving performance, the best fuel economy and the lowest carbon dioxide emissions — and combines all of this with the comfort and reliability of Australia's most popular medium family car. It has become the first Australian-built car to obtain the maximum 5-star green environmental rating from the federal government.

All of the more than 200 Toyota dealerships in Australia have skilled sales and service staff with expert knowledge of the Hybrid Camry. In fact, before launching the car, Toyota sent 1000 dealers and sales staff to its Altona production plant to 'update their knowledge on the cutting-edge quality and features of Camry and Aurion and the vehicles' importance to Australia'. According to Toyota's senior executive director of sales and marketing, David Buttner, 'Through our sales personnel, our customers will know they have the option to back quality locally built products that contribute to the local automotive industry and economy.'

With a car that runs on around six litres of unleaded petrol to travel 100 kilometres, and is silent when idling, the motor car industry has certainly come a long way in the last 100 years.[4]

## Questions

1. Consumer products can be classified under four broad categories. Which of these does the Toyota Hybrid Camry fall under, and why?

2. Find out as much as you can about hybrid cars and then classify the features of this product under the four levels of the total product concept.

## Concepts and applications check

**Learning objective 1**   define 'product' and understand different ways to view and analyse products and product attributes

1.1   A product can be tangible, intangible or a combination of both. Give examples of tangible and intangible products.

1.2   Consumers give little thought to unsought products until the need for them suddenly arises. How would you market an unsought product? Illustrate your answer with an example.

1.3   How would you define the four levels of a product in the purchase of a mobile phone?

1.4   Using an example of your own, differentiate between an organisation's product line and its product mix.

1.5   Outline the three major types of business-to-business product.

# PRODUCT LIFE CYCLE

**Learning objective 2**
describe the product life cycle, new product development and the product adoption process

In the introduction to this chapter, we stated that the product is what the marketer takes to the market in an attempt to get consumers to buy or engage in some type of exchange, in order to achieve the organisation's objectives. Clearly products are central to the organisation's marketing mix. An organisation needs to be adept at developing new products and successfully launching them in to the marketplace. The products must then be effectively managed to ensure their ongoing profitability in the context of environmental changes, including technological changes, changes in fashion and the actions of competitors.

Just as people go through a life cycle, beginning with conception and ending with death (with many experiences in between), products, brands and, indeed, industries also go through a life cycle. The product life cycle has five stages: new product development, introduction, growth, maturity and decline. The way products progress through the life cycle varies with the product and the marketing environment.

We will begin by outlining the characteristics of each stage of the product life cycle and establishing the marketing challenges they present. We will then look in more detail at the development of new products and how those products are subsequently adopted in the marketplace. The last section of the chapter is devoted to explaining how marketers can manage various aspects of products throughout the product life cycle in order to achieve optimal profitability.

## Overview of the product life cycle

Very few products remain the same from their introduction through to their eventual removal from the marketplace. Think of your favourite movie. Though it is tempting to think of it as an unchanging product, chances are it has been repackaged several times on film, DVD, Blu-ray, and downloaded MP4 or games console format. There might be multiple versions — the original theatrical release and a director's cut; if it is an older movie, then it may have been digitally remastered, recoloured, or remixed for surround sound; and perhaps there have been sequels or spin-offs.

People usually make judgements about an individual's stage in life based on their age. Products, however, are not simply classified based on the number of years they have been in the market. For example, despite being around for thousands of years, bread would not be classed as being in the final stage of its life cycle. Rather, the stages in the product life cycle reflect the product's current place in the market and its sales and profitability, as shown in figure 7.3.

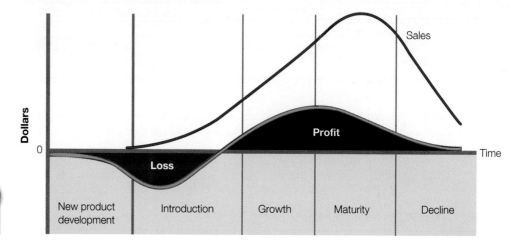

**FIGURE 7.3**

The product life cycle

The **product life cycle** (PLC) has five stages:

1. *new product development.* The first stage of a product's life cycle occurs when the organisation develops the idea, does research and prepares prototypes to pre-test the product. All of this, of course, occurs before the product becomes available to the market. During new product development, faults and problems can be eliminated and positive features can be refined and improved. New product development can involve substantial costs for a business and these are not offset by sales until later in the product life cycle. New production development will be discussed in greater detail in the following section.

2. *introduction.* This stage marks the first appearance of the product in the marketplace. The market is likely to know little or nothing about the product, and so the organisation must often make a considerable investment in promotional activities in order to build awareness of, and interest in, the product — in turn to trigger potential customers to evaluate, trial and purchase the new product. Even with a successfully launched product, there is often a lag between introduction and the building of substantial sales. Sales start at zero in the introduction stage and must offset promotional costs associated with the product launch and recoup the research and development costs incurred in the new product development stage. Only then does the product begin to generate profits.

3. *growth.* The growth stage sees increasing popularity, sales and profits. It depends, of course, on the product being welcomed by the marketplace and potential customers deciding to actually purchase the product. This is an exciting period for the organisation. At some point during this period, competitors enter the market with similar products, so while sales overall continue to increase, the rate of growth of a particular organisation's profits is likely to slow.

4. *maturity.* As competitors enter the market with similar products, the novelty of the product wears off, alternative — potentially superior — products become available, and the product's sales and profitability peak and start to fall. This occurs during the maturity stage of the product life cycle. In the maturity stage, the organisation must determine its future approach to the product. Organisations that want to continue in the market will often make some change to the marketing mix with the expectation that this will increase profits and move the product into a growth stage again. New strategies could be to change the product, lower the price, expand the distribution or differ the promotional activities. Alternatively, a marketer may decide to leave the market and allow the product to enter the decline stage.

5. *decline.* The decline stage of a product's life cycle sees sales and profits fall. New products may be entering, and there may be little interest in the current product. In the decline stage, the marketer must decide whether to reduce its investment in the product, drop the product from its product mix, or change the product and hope that it will enter a new growth stage. For products that the market perceives as old or of little interest, changes in the marketing mix, such as cuts in the price, will have little effect in increasing its sales. Eventually, a product left in the decline stage will be withdrawn from the market.

## New product development

No product or brand remains the same. Markets are in a perpetual state of change and organisations find it necessary to enhance the product characteristics or product mix to meet the changing needs of their customers. The first stage of the product life cycle involves new product development, commonly abbreviated to 'NPD'. This is a crucial time for the product as it is the stage at which the product benefits can be maximised and faults and problems minimised. Although research and development

**product life cycle**
The typical stages a product progresses through: new product development, introduction, growth, maturity and decline.

can be expensive, the organisation should make the appropriate investment. Achieving the organisation's goals depends on successful new products. A poor or unappealing product will fail to generate profits and may even damage the organisation's reputation and brand. According to one study, less than 3 per cent of new products survive on the market for more than five years.[5] Clearly, the new product development process is crucial to marketing success.

The new product development process sets out eight phases for introducing products:

1. *idea generation.* Idea generation is the phase in which ideas for new products are created. Most new product ideas are the result of a planned approach to generating innovations. The approach should be open to ideas from internal sources (employed scientists, engineers, marketers and so on) and external sources (customers, competitors and partners). Techniques specifically aimed at generating ideas, such as brainstorming and focus groups, are also a worthwhile investment. Of course, only a very small proportion of new product ideas become part of the organisation's product mix.

2. *screening.* No organisation has sufficient resources to pursue every product idea. Even if it was possible, it would not be a good approach to business. Instead, the organisation must undertake a screening process to eliminate those ideas that are not feasible, and to help identify the most promising of those that are. Screening may involve analysing the organisation's ability to produce the product, the target markets' potential interest, the market size, the product cost, the break-even point and so on. Any product idea that does not do well at this stage should be rejected. Screening is also an appropriate time for market researchers to look for what can best differentiate the product.

3. *concept evaluation.* Once a new product idea has passed the screening phase, it should be more thoroughly tested. The idea should be developed into a product concept that customers, management and other stakeholders can evaluate. The product concept is usually presented to potential customers as a description or drawing of various options for the product. This process is designed to determine whether the product could satisfy a customer need or want and to identify those attributes that could provide the most value to potential customers.

4. *marketing strategy.* A positive concept evaluation would suggest there is a market for the product. On this basis, management can start planning a marketing strategy. This includes describing the projected sales and profits, market positioning, potential target market, marketing mix strategies and long-term goals.

5. *business analysis.* Once the marketing strategy has been planned, the organisation should undertake a business analysis to determine whether the strategy will be a good fit with the company's current offerings and its overall business objectives. A business analysis reviews how the new product will affect the organisation's costs, sales and profit projections.

6. *product development.* If the business analysis finds the new product to be a good fit with the business's overall objectives, the next stage is to convert the product concept into an actual product. This often means developing a working prototype, along with additional investment in research and development to ensure the design, materials and so on will result in the optimum product.

7. *test marketing.* Once a prototype has been produced, the product should be tested in a market setting. Test marketing activities enable a 'real world' assessment of the entire marketing mix that supports the product. This is an important step before proceeding with full commercialisation. It is better to work out any

problems with the marketing mix in a smaller test market than to need to take corrective action nationwide.

8. *commercialisation*. If all has gone well for the previous phases, it is time to launch the new product into the market. Costs will be high at this stage, but, if the new product development process has been thorough, there is a solid chance that the new product will succeed.

## Product adoption process

Consumers have an enormous range of products and brands competing for their attention and their limited spending money. New products — whether a variation of an existing product or a totally new innovation — are regularly launched into the marketplace. *Most* of them fail. They do not achieve sufficient sales to survive.

To give an organisation the best chance of developing and marketing products that can succeed, marketers need to understand how a consumer perceives a new product, learns about it, and decides to adopt it. This typically entails five sequential stages, which form the **product adoption process**: awareness, interest, evaluation, trial, and adoption. The process is summarised in figure 7.4.

**product adoption process**
The sequential process of awareness, interest, evaluation, trial, and adoption through which a consumer decides to purchase a new product.

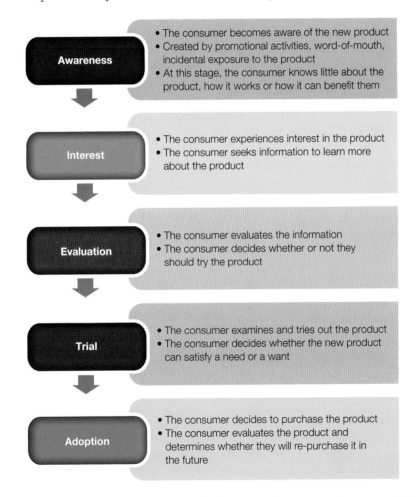

**FIGURE 7.4**

The product adoption process

The process appears relatively straightforward, but a product can fail at any stage. For example, without appropriate and targeted promotional activities, it is quite possible for consumers to never become aware of the existence of a product that could meet some want or need. Once a potential customer is aware of a new product, the product and its marketing must generate interest if the customer is to proceed further into the product adoption process. Similarly, if initial evaluation of the new product suggests it will not satisfy the potential customer's needs or wants better than their current product, then they will not consider trying it. An example is Sony's video delivery service, the Video Store, whereby by users of PlayStation 3 and the portable version, PSP, can rent or buy hundreds of movies online and watch them while they are downloading. This service, however, is competing with established video download services by Microsoft's Xbox 360, TiVo and Apple's iTunes store.[6]

For marketers, it is important to determine where potential customers are situated in the product adoption process and then aim to help them move to the next stage. This may take the form of promotional material that explains the product in detail and its advantages over competing products or activities, such as sampling, whereby potential customers are given a sample of the product to try.

### The diffusion of innovation

The launch of a product into the marketplace does not simply trigger all consumers to uniformly progress through the product adoption process. The behaviour of consumers in relation to the same product can vary a great deal. This is often a reflection of the individual's personality. Some people love new products and new technology. They want to be the first person they know to own it. Others have little interest in new products and prefer familiar things. They may take a long time to decide to investigate and purchase it. We introduced this concept in chapter 4 as the theory of **diffusion of innovations**.[7] The theory describes how innovations are adopted by the market over time and suggests that the influence of social groups on the decisions made by individuals determines the way in which new products and ideas are adopted. The adoption of innovations over time is shown in figure 7.5.

**diffusion of innovations**
The theory that social groups influence the decisions made by individuals in such a way that innovations are adopted by the market in a predictable pattern over time.

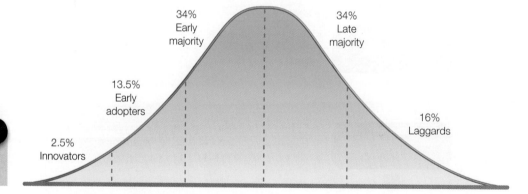

**FIGURE 7.5**

The adoption of innovations over time

The categories of product adopters shown in figure 7.5 are defined both by their product adoption behaviour and the characteristics that lead them to that behaviour:

- *innovators.* Innovators are the first adopters of new products. People in this group are usually adventurous, interested in new technology and ideas, and willing to take risks.
- *early adopters.* Early adopters are the next group to adopt. They are likely to be careful choosers of new products and are often opinion leaders, respected by peers and people in the other categories.

- *early majority.* The early majority tend to be more deliberate in their choice of new product and try to avoid taking risks. However, they usually adopt the new products before the average person.
- *late majority.* The late majority are more cautious and sceptical about new products and technologies but will eventually adopt the new product after most people have purchased it, and due to economic necessity or social pressure.
- *laggards.* Laggards are the last adopters. They are often wary of new products and ideas, and generally prefer products that are familiar.

The speed and pattern of market penetration for a new product innovation usually differ substantially between markets. New products that are successful in one country or region may not necessarily be successful in others. In chapter 4, which is about consumer behaviour, Hofstede's model of distinguishing cultures across different dimensions is outlined. In terms of the diffusion of innovation of new products in different cultures, research has shown that Hofstede's dimensions of uncertainty avoidance and individualism have the potential to significantly affect the rate of diffusion. Many consumers from Asian cultures, for example, display behaviour that is characteristic of uncertainty avoidance. These consumers are unlikely to take the social risk of being innovators. Instead, they are likely to display high social risk aversion in their purchasing decisions. In contrast, consumers from Western cultures are more likely to display high levels of individualism in their purchasing decisions. Figure 7.6 shows the shorter diffusion of innovation curve in Asia (compared with the curve in figure 7.5).

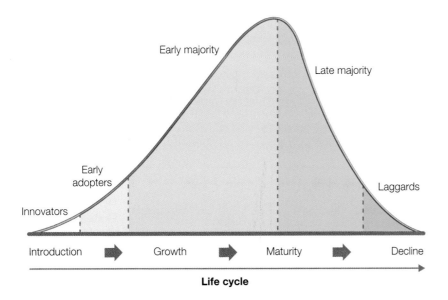

**FIGURE 7.6**

The diffusion of innovation curve in Asia

High versus low context is another factor that can influence the rate of diffusion. A low-context society is one that desires explicit information; whereas a high-context society relies more heavily on implicit and observed information from the environment. As such, consumers in high-context societies tend to gather information by observing how a product benefits other consumers, and consumers in low-context societies prefer to be given clear information about a product's benefits. The challenges of marketing new products to different cultures are explored further in chapter 13.

# Spotlight  Hungry Jack's gets 'angry'

Usually fast food companies have a set menu that is largely consistent across their stores, with the occasional new item 'for a limited time only'. McDonald's, for example, is known globally for its menu items like the Big Mac, French Fries, and the Happy Meal. When McDonald's introduced its range of Angus beef burgers in recent times, including the Mighty Angus and the Grand Angus burgers, it achieved considerable market success. The new product range became the most successful range that the organisation has released in Australia to date, and sparked a 'premium hamburger revolution'. Three months after the McDonald's launch, one of the fast food giant's rivals, Hungry Jack's, responded by introducing an Angry Angus burger.

The Hungry Jack's burger is available in either single or double patties. In addition to having an Angus high-quality beef patty (or patties), the burger includes bacon, cheese, salad and 'angry onions' that are fried and spiced.

Despite the similarities between their burger and the McDonald's Angus burger, Hungry Jack's denied that they were merely imitating their successful rival. A Hungry Jack's spokesperson says, 'It's been in planning for quite some time; the last thing we are doing is following McDonald's at all. In fact, Burger King, our ultimate franchisor, launched an Angus product about five years ago in the States, so we've been looking at creating our own version for a while.'

While consumers are willing to pay a premium price for an Angus burger, Angus cattle farmers are also very happy in the new interest in their product. Certified Australian Angus Beef chief executive Phil Morley says, 'Some would question whether we are bringing down the quality of the brand by supplying hamburger products, but I'd argue no. It's great brand awareness for Angus, as a premium, high-quality beef — and that can only help the product's image.'

With the two fast food giants fighting it out over their premium Angus offerings to put themselves into a growth market, one of them will still also be telling the public that 'The burgers are better at Hungry Jack's'.[8]

## Question

**'The fast food industry must constantly search for new product opportunities.' Briefly outline arguments both for and against this statement.**

---

## Concepts and applications check

**Learning objective 2**  describe the product life cycle, new product development and the product adoption process

2.1 Explain the stages of the product life cycle, using your own examples. In general terms, how would you suggest marketing strategies may differ depending on the stage of a product's life cycle?

2.2 Discuss how sales and profits change across the stages of the product life cycle.

2.3 Imagine you are marketing a new technology. How would an understanding of the new product adoption process assist in the development of your marketing strategies?

2.4 Briefly explain the phases for introducing new products.

2.5 According to one study, fewer than 3 per cent of new products last for more than five years in the marketplace. From a marketing perspective, why do you think this may be the case?

2.6 Using an example from your own experience, explain how you progressed through the stages in the product adoption process for a relatively new product. Under which category of product adopter would you be classified for this particular example?

---

# PRODUCT DIFFERENTIATION

As we discussed earlier, a product is a complex concept with a number of characteristics and attributes that can provide value to the customer and assist them in making their final purchase decision. The marketer, therefore, must decide on which product characteristics to include in the product offering that would best benefit and satisfy their customers' needs and wants *and* contribute to the organisation's objectives. Deciding on the right characteristics is not always an easy decision and it is recommended that marketers regularly undertake some type of market research to determine potential customers':

* desires in relation to the product category
* attitudes towards the product offering
* attitudes towards the product's features.

When making decisions about a product, it is important to decide on the characteristics that will make the product different to competitors' offerings. **Product differentiation** is the creation of products and product attributes that distinguish one product from another. If customers perceive there to be a difference between competing products, they will examine the specific product characteristics (as well as the other elements of the marketing mix) to assist them in making the final purchase choice. In terms of the product, most of the differentiating features are part of the augmented product layer of the total product concept. Some of the characteristics that customers may perceive to be differentiators include design, brand, image, style, quality and features. Any of these can potentially give the company a competitive advantage in the marketplace. These characteristics can also be used in the product's promotional activities to emphasise the value of the product and differentiate it from competitors. To better understand the creation of competitive advantage through product differentiation, let's look at some examples.

The Swedish furniture company IKEA focuses on simplicity and minimalism in its furniture designs. Most of its furniture is plastic or light-weight, laminated wood, held together by screws and other fasteners. It offers coordinated pieces that enable an entire room or house to be furnished. It also sells most of its furniture flat-packed. This lets IKEA keep more stock on hand and achieve cheaper prices, but requires customers to transport and assemble the furniture themselves. Contrast IKEA's product offering with another furniture company, Jimmy Possum. Jimmy Possum sells solid, handcrafted, fine furniture, made from handsome timbers using traditional techniques. Its products require careful upkeep, such as polishing and oiling to preserve the wood. While both companies sell dining tables that are the same at the core and expected product levels (see pages 216–17), the product attributes at the augmented product level are substantially differentiated in terms of appearance, quality, branding and positioning. In addition to product differences, they also vary significantly in terms of pricing, promotion and distribution.

Product attributes that serve to differentiate competing offerings are not always as dramatic as the difference between IKEA and Jimmy Possum. Consider Kiwibank, a bank operated by New Zealand Post. Kiwibank was established to compete with ANZ, ASB, BNZ, National Bank and Westpac, which have long dominated the New Zealand banking sector. It offers the standard range of services, such as savings accounts and loans, but Kiwibank has successfully differentiated its offerings through product attributes including New Zealand ownership, longer opening hours (including weekends at many branches), lower fees and interest rates, and innovative online banking services. In less than a decade, it has secured more than 15 per cent of the New Zealand population as customers.

**Learning objective 3**
outline how an organisation can differentiate its products to obtain a competitive advantage

**product differentiation**
The creation of products and product attributes that distinguish one product from another.

The 'Adopt a Pet' service of the Royal Society for the Prevention of Cruelty to Animals is differentiated from pet stores by not only the purpose of the service (in finding homes for abandoned or stray animals), but also the add-on services provided to the prospective pet owner, including an inspection of their home and yard to advise on how to make it most suitable for their new pet (as well as to ensure it meets basic requirements to have the pet). Warranties, installation, in-home training and free phone help lines are all examples of add-on services that some organisations use to differentiate their products from competitors. For some customers, certain extra services may be an essential product requirement. For example, those who are not computer literate may only choose to buy computer products that are backed with a reliable customer service help desk in a store or a toll free telephone support service. Apple has built a reputation on good after sales service and customer relations. Support does not necessarily mean a response to a problem; it can mean satisfactorily dealing with requests, complaints, suggestions and maintenance. Such services can encourage repeat purchases, positive 'word-of-mouth' promotion and customer loyalty.

Products can also be differentiated within an organisation's product mix; for example, when purchasing a new car, a luxury or sports model may include specific features (such as air-conditioning, air-bags and leather seats) that are not included in the base model. Of course, the luxury model will also feature a higher price. Similarly, the base model of a Dell computer is worth a certain amount of money; however, if you purchase it with a scanner/laser printer, high-quality speakers and a wide-screen monitor, then the price will be higher. Further into a product's life, such features are often added while the price remains unchanged. In this way, the marketer can maintain sales volumes, but will sacrifice some profit.

From these few examples, it should be clear that, in seeking a competitive advantage, organisations commonly differentiate their products based on design, quality, functionality and add-on services, as well as on the other elements of the marketing mix. These differences serve to create a unique value offering to the market and influence how the product is positioned (i.e. how customers perceive it relative to competing offerings). Product differentiation based on product attributes is intimately linked with product positioning. Consider power tools as an example. The German power tool manufacturer Bosch divides its product line and promotional efforts into a 'DIY enthusiast' sector and a 'professional' sector. The DIY line focuses on affordability and features that make the tools easier to use. The professional line focuses on durability (including the warranty offered) and power. Customers in each sector have significantly different definitions of the features, price and quality that constitute value. Bosch takes this a step further by offering several variations within each sector. For example, within the DIY line, it offers several models of jigsaw that vary on power, accessories (such as laser guides), aesthetics, size and packaging. Even a government-owned organisation like Australia Post, which is usually identified as a nationwide postal service, has been differentiating its services. With the growth of courier companies, and the rise in popularity of paying bills online, there has been a decline in its traditional businesses. In a recent year Australia Post expanded into the insurance market, offering car insurance. The organisation also has plans to expand into other areas, like travel, home and contents insurance.

Product differentiation must not be viewed as a static concept. Marketers usually modify, upgrade and reposition products during their life cycle to try to ensure their competitive advantage is maintained or improved. We will return to this concept in the last section of the chapter.

# The mobile battleground

In recent years, telecommunications companies have found it increasingly difficult to distinguish their product offerings from each other in the minds of consumers. The mobile phone device has emerged as a key battleground, particularly in the area of entertainment. As mobile phones have become web-enabled as a standard product feature, and with the increasing data capabilities and coverage of mobile phone networks, telecommunications companies have been able to offer an array of streamed video, music and games that their network subscribers can download on to their mobile handsets.

The rapid consumer uptake of smartphones, such as the Apple iPhone and the various Nokia and BlackBerry models now available, has opened up a range of opportunities for telecommunications network providers to differentiate their service offerings. For example, 3 promotes the option of subscription access to live cricket coverage as a feature to its mobile network customers. Similarly, Telstra provides its network users with the option of subscription access to Foxtel channels, while its subsidiary BigPond offers exclusive AFL and NRL content.

It seems the mobile phone is becoming as much of an entertainment device as it is a communication tool. Popular internet sites like Facebook and YouTube are increasingly being accessed via mobile phones. Network providers are competing aggressively with each other in terms of data download allowances in their various plans, including — in some cases — the unlimited use of social networking sites.

'The beauty of what we have done is that we have been able to grow revenue per customer and have grown the data side of the revenue, but it hasn't come at the expense of voice', says Telstra's executive director of mobility products, Ross Fielding.

Vodafone Australia's head of infotainment, Matthew Whittingham, also forecasts continued growth in data services and downloads. 'There are real signs of change in the way customers are using their mobile phones', he says.

Just how far telecommunications providers can take the online environment in differentiating their service offerings will be an interesting phenomenon to monitor in coming years.[9]

## Question

Go to the websites of any two of the major mobile phone network providers to compare and evaluate their mobile phone plans. Outline the extent of product differentiation that you can identify between the two providers.

---

## Concepts and applications check

**Learning objective 3**  outline how an organisation can differentiate its products to obtain a competitive advantage

**3.1**  For one type of product, explain the concept of product differentiation using examples other than those discussed in the chapter.

**3.2**  Prepare arguments for and against this statement: 'In today's highly competitive marketplace, developing a *sustainable* competitive advantage through product differentiation is impossible.'

# BRANDING

**Learning objective 4**
explain the value of
branding and the major
issues involved in
brand management

**brand** A collection of symbols
such as a name, logo, slogan
and design intended to create
an image in the customer's mind
that differentiates a product from
competitors' products.

**brand image** The set of beliefs
that a consumer has regarding a
particular brand.

The brand name can be one of the most important aspects in a customer's purchase decision. **Brand** refers to a collection of symbols, such as the name, logo, slogan and design, intended to create an image in the customer's mind that differentiates a product from competitors' products. A brand can identify one item, a family of items, or all the items of a seller. Brands play a particularly important role in high-involvement purchase decisions. Most consumers will prefer a well-known, reputed brand over a cheaper, unknown brand when making high-involvement purchases. For consumers, the brand helps speed up consumer purchases by identifying specific preferred products. The brand can provide a form of self-expression and status, as well as denote product quality. It can also arouse a collection of images in the customer's mind. **Brand image** is the set of beliefs that a consumer has regarding a particular brand. People can have a positive or negative brand image for a given brand, depending on things like past experience or word-of-mouth, which can substantially influence whether they would be willing to buy the product or not. When marketers make decisions about products, the decisions must relate to the product's brand and brand image.

## Brand name

The 'Qantas' brand
is one of the most
recognised in Australia,
with the core features
of the brand name and
the flying kangaroo
remaining relatively
consistent for decades.

Organisations with a well-known brand name are very protective of it and will be willing to spend large amounts of money ensuring it is not used or abused by other individuals or organisations. A brand name is part of a brand that can be spoken and can include words, letters and numbers. Coca Cola, IBM and 2Xist are all examples of brand names. The Nielsen Company's 'Top Brands' report has found Coca-Cola to be the number one grocery brand in Australia every year since it introduced the report.[10] A brand mark is the part of a brand not made up of words — it often consists of symbols or designs. McDonald's 'Golden Arches', Qantas's 'Flying Kangaroo' and the International Olympic Committee's 'Olympic Rings' are among the most recognisable brand marks.

Selecting a brand name is not easy, but it can make a crucial difference to the success of an organisation. A name that might sound good at first could give rise to unintended problems, particularly if you are going to sell your product in another country. For example, XXXX (pronounced 4X) is a beer from Queensland with a strong brand name in Australia, but in the UK the name XXXX is a brand of condoms. The ideal brand is distinctive, easily recognisable and relevant to the products it represents. Accordingly, brand recognition (both prompted and unprompted) is a key marketing metric.

Once the brand has been chosen, an organisation should guard its brand from misuse; for example, from competitors that might want to use it or a similar name. To protect the brand, an organisation can register it as a **trade mark** with the relevant body (e.g. IP Australia, or the Intellectual Property Office of New Zealand).[11] Once registered, organisations have legally enforceable rights to the exclusive use of the name. Applications to register trade marks are carefully assessed against numerous

**trade mark** A brand name
or brand mark that has been
legally registered so as to secure
exclusive use of the brand.

rules and guidelines. A brand should be chosen so that it can be protected easily; for example, it should be distinctive and consist of more than a description of the products.

# Brand equity

A well-known brand can be very valuable to an organisation in both financial and non-financial terms. Table 7.1 lists the ten most valuable brands in Australia.[12] The list was compiled by Interbrand based on financial factors, the importance of the brand in driving consumer selection, and the ability of the brand to drive future earnings through customer loyalty, retention and repurchasing.

**TABLE 7.1** The most valuable brands in Australia

| Rank | Brand | Sector | Brand value (A$ millions) |
| --- | --- | --- | --- |
| 1 | Telstra | Telecommunications | 9700 |
| 2 | Commonwealth Bank | Banking/Financial Services | 7100 |
| 3 | NAB | Banking/Financial Services | 5100 |
| 4 | Westpac | Banking/Financial Services | 4800 |
| 5 | Woolworths | Retail | 4600 |
| 6 | Macquarie Bank | Banking/Financial Services | 3200 |
| 7 | ANZ | Banking/Financial Services | 3100 |
| 8 | Billabong | Apparel | 2200 |
| 9 | St. George | Banking/Financial Services | 1900 |
| 10 | Harvey Norman | Retail | 1300 |

For marketers, the brand:
- identifies the organisation's products
- differentiates the organisation's products from competing products
- attracts customers
- helps introduce new products
- facilitates the promotion of same-brand products.

The value of a brand is found in the influence it has over purchase decisions. The *added value* that a brand gives a product is known as **brand equity**. All of the value in products arises from the choices that consumers make among those brands offered to them for purchase; brand equity is therefore a *consumer-based* concept.

**brand equity** The added value that a brand gives a product.

## Brand loyalty

The underlying factor in brand equity is brand loyalty. **Brand loyalty** exists when the customer:
- shows a highly favourable attitude toward a specific brand
- would prefer to buy a specific brand over any other brand in the market.

**brand loyalty** A customer's highly favourable attitude and purchasing behaviour towards a certain brand.

Brand-loyal customers are highly valued by organisations and represent a core segment for product sales. Some firms encourage brand loyalty by having a loyalty program, whereby customers are given an incentive to continue to make repeat purchases of a particular brand or product. For example, Gloria Jean's has a 'Frequent Sipper Club' card which entitles regular customers to a free drink after every ten purchased drinks. Brand loyalty exists on a continuum. At one end are fiercely loyal customers who will go to great lengths to obtain their preferred brand. They may be completely unwilling to accept a substitute. This degree of loyalty tends to be found for football codes and for specific clubs (i.e. brands) within each code. At the other end of the scale are consumers who have no brand preference for a particular product type. In such cases, purchasing decisions are likely to be based on other factors, such as price and convenience. In the middle are customers who prefer a particular brand, but will choose an alternative if their favourite is unavailable.

### Brand metrics

To measure the value of brands is extremely useful to organisations. Brand equity metrics include:

- brand assets (e.g. trade marks and patents)
- stock price analysis
- replacement cost
- brand attributes
- brand loyalty
- willingness-to-pay analysis.

High brand equity can be a valuable asset for a company and provide a strong competitive advantage.

## Brand strategies

When developing brands within a product mix, an organisation may decide to pursue the following possible strategies: individual brands, family brands or brand extension.

**Individual branding** uses a different brand on each product, giving each its own specific identity. Individual branding can:

- help position a product in the marketplace
- help reach a different market segment
- avoid confusion with existing branded products.

For example, Smith's Snackfood Company has a number of brands in addition to Smith's in its product mix, including Doritos, Twisties, Parker's, Nobby's, Red Rock Deli, Cheetos and Burger Rings, yet these are all known by their individual brand and not by the parent company name of Smith's. This does, for example, let Smith's build its Red Rock Deli brand around an image of sophisticated, adult flavours and textures, while building its Cheetos brand around a fun, rather unsophisticated, snack for children. Additionally, Smith's is owned by Frito-Lay Brands, itself in turn part of PepsiCo.[13] Goodman Fielder also pursues an individual branding strategy for its New Zealand bread products: Nature's Fresh, Vogel's Molenberg, Freya's, Country Split and Sunny Crust.[14]

**Family branding** uses the same brand on several of the organisation's products. A family branding strategy can be an effective way to introduce new products when a brand has an established reputation. The new product entering the market with the family brand connection will immediately benefit from the customer's existing association of that brand with quality or value. This can also assist in reducing the cost of promoting the new product. Pacific Brands' 'Bonds' is a well-known brand

---

**individual branding**
A branding approach in which each product is branded separately.

**family branding** A branding approach that uses the same brand on several of the organisation's products.

that has been used for a number of its products, including men's and women's underwear, track suits and shirts.

**Brand extension** gives an existing brand name to new product in a different category. For example, Redheads, a company that was only known for making matches, relaunched itself with an expansion into a range of BBQ products including firelighters, fuel, cleaners and scourers.[15] The Virgin Group has demonstrated one of the best uses of brand extension, with the same brand proving successful across music, air travel, mobile phones and credit cards. While using a well-known brand can have the advantages mentioned with family brands, it can also be a risky strategy. If the product extension is not successful, it may affect the image of the brand in general. Additionally, if the products are unrelated, there is potential for confusion or even rejection.

**brand extension** Giving an existing brand name to new product in a different category.

## Brand ownership

Brands may be owned by and identified with either the manufacturer or the reseller. Alternatively, in some cases, where branding is not a factor in the purchase decision, the seller may choose not to brand the product at all.

**Manufacturer brands** are owned by producers and are the most common type of brand. Products sold under manufacturer brands are clearly identified with the producer at the point of sale. As such, the producer is involved in the entire marketing process: production, pricing and distribution decisions, and promotional activities. The brand is an important asset to the producer, and brand loyalty is encouraged with customers. The Murray Goulburn Co-operative Co. Ltd, for example, manufactures cheese, butter and other dairy products branded as 'Devondale' in both consumer and business markets. In consumer markets, Devondale-branded products are available through supermarkets and convenience stores. In business markets, bulk Devondale-branded products are available directly from Murray Goulburn Co-operative's Devondale Foodservice division.

**manufacturer brands** Brands owned by producers and clearly identified with the product at the point of sale.

**Private label brands** are owned by resellers, such as wholesalers or retailers, and are not identified with the manufacturer. They are also known as private brands, dealer brands, house brands or store brands. Private label brands are becoming more popular as wholesalers and retailers seek increased exposure and increased turnover. Private label brands can provide better economies of scale through more efficient distribution and promotion. David Jones, for example, has the 'St James' and 'David Jones' brands, and Coles has its 'Farmland' and 'Savings' brands. Private label brands are often cheaper than similar products sold under manufacturer brands, but they usually enjoy little brand loyalty. The growing competition between manufacturer brands and private label brands has prompted the industry to dub it the 'battle of the brands'. While private label brands have a competitive advantage with distribution, the manufacturer brands have an advantage with brand reputation and image. Private label brands are often made by manufacturers that have their own manufacturer brands in the same product category. The underlying product is often very similar. Woolworths has been expanding its private label brands (Woolworths Fresh, Woolworths Select, Woolworths HomeBrand, Woolworths Organics and Woolworths Naytura) and substantially reducing the shelf space given to manufacturer brands.

**private label brands** Brands owned by resellers, such as wholesalers or retailers, and not identified with the manufacturer.

**Generic brands** are those products that only indicate the product category. These products do not promote a specific brand name, but state what the product is. They are sold in plain packaging at lower prices than branded items, and are usually found in supermarkets. They are also common in business markets, especially in relation to components parts and raw materials.

**generic brands** Products that only indicate the product category.

### Licensing

Some organisations want to avoid the time and expense of establishing their own special brand name. Such organisations can enter a **licensing** agreement to use the names and symbols of other brands for a fee. This has been a very successful strategy for some companies, especially where there is a clear marketing opportunity for two organisations to combine their relative abilities. For example, a toy manufacturer can become the licensee in a licensing agreement with the owners of the 'Star Wars' or 'The Simpsons' brand names and thus sell merchandise such as plush toys, figurines, clothes or school stationery branded with the licensor's brand. Successful licensing can benefit both parties greatly. The licensee capitalises on the brand equity of a brand it does not own and the licensor receives income from a product line it could not itself produce. Both parties also take risks. The licensee bears all financial costs if the product fails and the licensor risks its brand equity if the licensee's product is so poor as to damage the brand.

### Franchising

Gloria Jeans, New Zealand Natural, Michel's Patisserie, Sumo Salad, and Oporto are all well-known brands. They are also all franchises. Franchising has many parallels with licensing. In a franchise agreement, the franchisor permits the franchisee to use its business model, including products, brands, processes and suppliers, and to benefit from co-ordinated promotional activities. The franchisee pays fees to the franchisor, agrees to abide by the systems and rules set out in the franchise agreement and assumes the responsibility for the success of the individual franchise. The risk to the franchisor is similar to the risk involved in brand licensing. If the franchisee operates its business poorly, the entire franchise can suffer damage to its brand.

Franchising is a very popular business model. It provides franchisors a way to quickly expand their business without taking on all of the financing and risk responsibilities and it enables people who want to begin their own business to purchase an 'off-the-shelf' business model, which can greatly reduce the risk and effort involved in beginning a business.

### Co-branding

**Co-branding** is the use of two or more brand names on the same product. The use of co-branding has grown recently as organisations try to:

* capitalise on the brand equity of multiple brands
* improved the perceived value of a product
* maintain existing branding after another organisation's brands are acquired.

Domino's Pizza and *The Biggest Loser* is an example, forming an unlikely co-branding alliance in recent times to launch a 'Good Choice Range' of individual meals. Domino's introduced the co-branded meals, which each had less than 400 calories per serve, to capitalise on the popularity of *The Biggest Loser* television show and in recognition of the need to offer healthy eating options on its menu to attract more health-conscious consumers.[16] Often the co-branding is done by established brands and there is some complementary fit in the minds of consumers. Many credit card companies, for example, have teamed up with well-known retail, airline or charity partners so that purchases with the credit card benefit all parties involved. For example, the David

Jones American Express Credit Card has a rewards program in which cardholders receive 'Bonus Gift Points' when purchasing goods at David Jones or associated stores worldwide (including Selfridges, Harrods, Harvey Nichols, Nordstrom and Galeries Lafayette).

With any co-branding ventures, neither brand should lose their individual identities, although one may be the dominant brand. Co-branding can be source of competitive advantage in assisting the product to increase distribution, reputation and differentiation.

## iSnack 2.0 Spotlight

'What's in a name? That which we call a rose by any other name would smell as sweet', wrote William Shakespeare in *Romeo and Juliet*. Then again, Shakespeare was not a brand manager for a major organisation. As Kraft has discovered, a brand name is very important and a yeast extract by any other name can cause a lot of controversy.

Vegemite is an icon in Australia that has been eaten by children and adults since the 1920s. In a recent year, Kraft decided to add a new spread to the product line that combined cream cheese and Vegemite. To help publicise the new product, Kraft ran a national competition to name it. At first, Kraft launched the product for people to try with the words 'Name Me' on the label, accompanied by information about the naming competition. The product seemed popular, with almost three million 'Name Me' jars sold within months. In all, over 48 000 entries were received in the naming competition. The winner was iSnack 2.0, a name suggested by a 27-year-old Western Australian web designer, Dean Robbins. The name was publicly announced at an AFL Grand Final. It was claimed that the new brand name was chosen in an attempt to appeal to the young, internet-savvy generation that Kraft saw as a key underdeveloped market segment.

However, as outlined in chapter 4, there was significant consumer backlash against the iSnack 2.0 brand name, almost immediately after the product was launched. The wave of criticisms and complaints was especially strong via internet blog sites, Facebook and Twitter — presumably largely from the very demographic to which it was claimed the name was intended to appeal. Shortly afterwards, Kraft dumped the new name. Kraft's head of corporate affairs, Simon Talbot, said at the time, 'The new name has simply not resonated with Australians ... particularly the modern technical aspects associated with it.' He revealed that Kraft would clear their stock of about 500 000 iSnack2.0-labelled jars through supermarket shelves as quickly as possible, before changing to a new brand name. Ironically, the iSnack 2.0 jars quickly became collector's items.

Talbot further stated, 'I would think in Australian brand history this is unprecedented in terms of public demand for brand change ... [and] we've had teams of people working around the clock to turn this around in the space of a week. The bottom line is we've listened to the public and I think we have the respect of the Australian people to back down. We've moved as fast as we can.'

After some deliberation, it was decided that the new name of the product would be Vegemite Cheesybite. Cynics suggested the whole exercise had been a publicity stunt. Regardless of whether it was or not, the iSnack 2.0 experience provided a classic example of the importance of product branding.[17]

### Questions

**Kraft changed the brand name of its new cheesy-Vegemite spread after it first released it as iSnack2.0 due to public complaints.**

1. What do you think would have happened if the original brand name had been kept?
2. What are the risks of changing the brand name?

## Concepts and applications check

**Learning objective 4**  explain the value of branding and the major issues involved in brand management

**4.1**  How can a well-known brand name help a consumer make a purchase decision?

**4.2**  Write down the first ten brand names you can think of. What do you associate with each? Why do you think each one was more readily recalled than brands that do not appear on your list?

**4.3**  What is brand equity? How can this be good for a company wanting to expand its product mix?

**4.4**  Outline a situation where individual branding would be preferable to either family branding or brand extension branding.

**4.5**  Think of your own example of a co-branded product. What are the benefits for each organisation?

# PACKAGING

**Learning objective 5** describe the functional and marketing roles of packaging

Most products are sold in packaging — a bag, wrapper or container for the product. Many products need some kind of packaging to make them more convenient to store and use, and to protect them from waste, damage or spoilage. For example, it is difficult to imagine storing and selling lemon sherbet without packaging. As well as its functional features, packaging also plays an important role in promoting the product. It can gain people's attention at the retailer, make customers aware of the product and/or its contents, differentiate it from competitors' offerings and help build a particular message or image about the product. For example, Goodman Fielder in New Zealand was facing a mature market for bread. It decided to target new growth by introducing a new rustic style of bread packaged in brown paper, more closely aligned to what a customer would expect from a traditional local baker than from a supermarket shelf.[18]

For some products, the packaging may be more expensive than the cost to actually produce the product. This is the case for most perfumes and many food items. For other products, the distinct packaging is totally integrated into the product's brand image, which helps to differentiate it from the competitors' product. Many alcoholic drinks are packaged in distinctive bottles (e.g. Frangelico's bottle is shaped like a monk's robes, and Galliano's bottle is exceptionally tall). Packaging can also provide extra functionality to a product. For example, pump bottles of shampoo and moisturiser change the way the consumer uses the product compared to squeeze bottles. The snap-out nozzle design on sports drink bottles has added extra convenience for customers, particularly those who actually use the bottles during sporting activities, in that they no longer have to bother removing and replacing a screw-top cap. In summary, effective packaging should be designed to 'protect what it sells and to sell what it protects'.[19]

Packaging can become an important recognisable way for customers to identify a particular product, much like a brand. On the other hand, as a form of marketing tool, packaging can be changed. Marketers may want to change the package to:

- express to customers that the product has changed in some way, such as shape, size or ingredients
- update the style of package or logo to broaden the customer appeal
- emphasise certain elements to further differentiate it from the competition.

There are three main types of packaging:

1. The *primary package* holds the actual product, such as the curve-shaped plastic bottle for S.C. Johnson's Toilet Duck cleaning product.

2. The *secondary package* is the material used to hold or protect the product. It can be removed and discarded after purchase. For example, the seal on the Toilet Duck bottle that prevents the product leaking.

3. The *shipping package* is the packaging used to carry the product out of the factory, and through the channel of distribution (e.g. wholesalers and transporters), to the retailer. For example, several bottles of Toilet Duck are packed together in standard cardboard boxes that can be more easily and safely transported to retailers. Retailers then discard the boxes, placing the individual products on display on their shelves.

If a company wants to show that it is socially aware or eco-friendly, it can reduce the amount of secondary packaging that has to be thrown away, ensure that no dangerous or eco-damaging material is used in the packaging, or use recyclable bottles or containers. According to one international survey, 90 per cent of eco-aware consumers would be willing to give up an aspect of packaging if it meant it would help the environment. Of those surveyed, 49 per cent said they would give up packaging that makes the product easier to stack and store if it would help the environment. Consumers were less likely to give up packaging if it affected more crucial factors such as hygiene and protection.[20]

## Labelling

*Labelling* usually forms part of the package and provides identifying, promotional, legal and other information. This information can be an important factor in a customer's decision whether to purchase the particular product. At its most basic level, the label would identify the product and display the brand name. Labels can, however, provide a lot more useful information to the potential purchaser. For example, labels on cleaning products usually include instructions for use, as do labels on pharmaceuticals.

Packaging performs both functional and marketing roles.

Some of the information provided on labels is compulsory. For example, certain information must be presented on food labels under legal requirements monitored by the Australia New Zealand Food Standards Council (ANZFSC). Depending on the product category, some of the information required by legislation includes:

- brand name and logo
- product name
- size of packaging
- statement of quantity
- origin of goods
- name and address of packer or manufacturer
- representations
- nutritional information
- ingredients list
- use-by date or date of packaging
- bar code.

# Spotlight  Running out of puff?

Over the years the tightening of restrictions on the promotion of cigarettes left the packet as the only legal way for a manufacturer to promote its brands. However, the Australian government has mandated that tobacco companies use plain packaging on all packets from 1 July 2012. While the 'branding crackdown' is welcomed by anti-smoking advocates, the tobacco companies and some retailers are, not surprisingly, against the new legislation.

From 1 July 2012 cigarettes can only be sold in packets that have the current health warnings, and just the basic name and product information. This legislative change was based on recommendations from the National Preventative Health Taskforce. The aim is to make cigarettes less attractive to young people. It is claimed that 'colourful packaging cuts the shock value of graphic health warnings'. Ian Oliver, from Cancer Council Australia, says, 'Tobacco companies cleverly tailor product packaging to attract people to the pack and send a message to smokers about the personality of the consumer.'

However, according to Cathie Keogh, a spokeswoman from Imperial Tobacco Australia, 'Introducing plain packaging just takes away the ability of a consumer to identify our brand from another brand and that's of value to us.'

British American Tobacco Australia announced, 'We oppose plain packaging and we will defend the intellectual property which lies in that packaging. If that requires us to take legal action, then we would do so.'

The federal Health Minister at the time, Nicola Roxon, said 15 000 people a year were dying from tobacco-related illnesses, and that her father, a smoker, had died from cancer of the oesophagus. She said, 'If our action today can mean that any other child has their parents with them for a little longer, that'll be a good thing. And we don't make any apologies about taking this action.'

But, at the retail level, tobacconist Brent Hardie thinks that people will continue buying cigarettes. He says, 'It's like anything. If you enjoy something, you're going to continue to smoke . . . I don't really think it's the packaging that makes it attractive'.[21]

## Questions

1. What are some of the potential advantages and disadvantages of cigarettes being sold in plain packaging from the perspectives of each of the following:
   (a) the federal government
   (b) tobacco companies
   (c) cigarette smokers.
2. Do you believe plain packaging will help reduce the number of young people smoking cigarettes? Justify your answer.

## Concepts and applications check

**Learning objective 5** describe the functional and marketing roles of packaging

5.1 Using your own examples, outline the two main functions that product packaging can perform.

5.2 Analyse the type of information required on food product labels. How could a marketer use this information as part of their marketing strategy?

5.3 Explain the role that packaging plays in marketing strategies for products like perfumes.

# MANAGING PRODUCTS

The foregoing discussion makes it clear that product strategy is a central and complex part of the organisation's marketing mix. From the new product development process discussed earlier in this chapter through the remaining parts of the product life cycle, there are many decisions to be made which affect the success of the product and its contribution to the organisation's overall marketing objectives. As we emphasise throughout this book, these decisions are not simply made once and implemented; rather, product strategy consists of ongoing evaluation and responses to the changing marketing environment.

**Learning objective 6**
explain key aspects of product management and positioning through the product life cycle

## Approaches to management

We examined the internal environment of the marketing organisation in chapter 2. The internal environment includes the structure of the organisation — who is responsible for what. Decisions about how marketing is managed and how products are managed within an organisation can have a significant influence on the success of the organisation.

The traditional approach to organisational structure allocates different business functions to different groups within the business; for example, a human resources department, a sales department, a distribution department, a finance department, a production department and a marketing department. While such a structure can be appropriate for many businesses, the complexity of product development and management means specialists from across many areas of the business need to be involved. At the same time, managing the product may require coordination and cooperation across different business departments, which can be difficult to achieve in a traditional organisational structure.

A business may choose to employ one or more managers to take responsibility for the management of particular products or product lines, or the management of a particular brand within the organisation's portfolio of brands. The first is known as a product manager, and the second is known as a brand manager. With both approaches, the manager has the authority to coordinate aspects of the operation of various business departments. This approach is designed to ensure that the various areas of the business are all working toward achieving the organisation's ultimate marketing objectives.

Another alternative is to appoint a market manager who will be responsible for managing the marketing activities aimed at a particular part of the target market. For example:
- a car dealer may appoint a consumer market manager and a business market manager
- a motel chain may appoint a market manager to manage the marketing activities directed toward holidaymakers and another market manager to target business travellers and conferences
- a charitable institution may appoint one market manager to focus on corporate donations and another to focus on raising money from the general public.

Regardless of the organisational structure, the most important objective for the organisation is to ensure that all activities related to its products are coordinated across the organisation. Of course, a product cannot be seen as a simplistic, one-dimensional offering to the marketplace. There are many complex issues and decisions to be made relating to the product in the marketing mix. In later chapters we will be looking at pricing, promotion and distribution considerations. These must also all be managed in a coordinated way across the organisation. In other words, the organisation must have a marketing orientation.

# Managing products through the life cycle

We discussed new product development in some detail earlier in the chapter. We will briefly revisit this concept and look at its role in managing the organisation's product strategy as its products move through the product life cycle. Markets change constantly and organisations need to introduce new products and revise existing product characteristics to meet the needs of their customers and achieve the organisation's goals. New product development involves idea generation, screening, concept evaluation, marketing strategy, business analysis, product development, test marketing and commercialisation.

Some new product ideas are found by chance. Most are a logical or inspired response to some change in the marketing environment that brings about new opportunities or threats (including the products developed by competitors). For example, the past decade has been marked by ever-increasing public awareness of the potential threat of global warming. In response, numerous products have been developed that in all likelihood would not have had a viable market before. These include compact fluorescent lightbulbs, in-home electricity monitors and ethanol-based fuels. In addition to responding directly to changes in the marketing environment, organisations must develop new products to replace those that are nearing the end of their life cycle. Organisations cannot afford to have a product mix with many products in decline and few being introduced. The world's biggest oil companies are an example of organisations trying to avoid this situation. While BP is an organisation built on selling oil and petrol, it has been working for decades to expand into new areas with other energy products (such as solar energy panels).

By understanding the product life cycle, the marketer can determine which stage their product is in and decide on appropriate decisions for the next stage, be they related to packaging, pricing, advertising, positioning or some other element of the marketing mix. When a marketing manager uses the product life cycle concept, variations in the marketing mix will be timed to coordinate with the product's market situation and effort will not be wasted on unprofitable products. A well-timed change in strategy can move a product from the maturity stage back into a growth stage, resulting in a resurgence of sales and profits.

The release of a new film often generates intense interest in related merchandise, but the merchandise moves very quickly through the product life cycle.

If a product is seasonal in nature, then it may enter a natural decline stage: no matter what a marketing manager does in terms of advertising, the product will still decline in sales. For example, in the months after the football grand final, it is very difficult to sell team merchandise, because people become more interested in cricket and other summer sports. Further, some 'fad' products would have a short planned life cycle, as the product may only be intended to be sold for a short time; for example, Harry Potter merchandise proceeds very quickly through the product life cycle while a new Harry Potter film is screening at the cinema.

The product life cycle concept can also be used to analyse a *brand* in the marketplace. For example, while a product category as a whole may be in the growth or maturity phases of its life cycle, particular brands within the product category may be in the introductory or decline phases. This is most easily seen in relation to products subject to fashion, such as clothes.

Recall the idea of the 'augmented product' layer from our discussion of the total product concept earlier in the chapter. Branding is one of the key ways in which competing organisations differentiate their offerings at the augmented product level. Other approaches include product benefits, design, add-on services and packaging. The crucial aspect is to maintain a competitive advantage through the product life cycle. This is often done by modifying a product or creating a new variation of an existing product. While products created through such processes are thought of as 'new', the creation of a genuinely new product is relatively rare. Often the term 'new product development' is used to describe products that are not really new, but that are significantly different from the existing product they are based on. For example, Paul's Zymil milk is not a completely new product; rather, it is a variation on the existing product of milk — it has the lactose already broken down to aid digestion.[22] If a product is already in the market, an organisation can capitalise on the existing product and its knowledge of the market by modifying existing products or creating line extensions.

One or more characteristics of a product may be modified so that the resultant 'new' product supersedes the earlier one. This is frequently seen in high-technology products; for example, each generation of game console from Nintendo and Sony tends to supersede the previous one. Even if the older products remain, their popularity and sales decline because they are not as desirable as the new version. Product modifications usually improve the product's performance, convenience or versatility (e.g. the introduction of screw-tops for wine bottles), quality or durability (e.g. a seller of leather shoes could make Scotchguard treatment a standard feature of the product to better protect against scuffing and damage) or sensory appeal (e.g. the Mother energy drink's flavour was completely changed because the original flavour did not appeal to many customers; the change in flavour was promoted through a multimillion dollar advertising campaign).

Sometimes a variation or derivative of an existing product can be added to the product line, rather than superseding the original product. This is known as a **line extension**. The development of line extensions is a less risky and less expensive way to introduce a product. Line extensions are the most common form of 'new' product. A line extension product is, by definition, similar to existing products, but can focus on a different market segment or segment needs. For example, McDonald's introduction of the Angus line of burgers was aimed at a more upmarket segment that is willing to pay more for a premium McDonald's product. It is claimed that it increased profits by $2 million a week.[23]

**line extension** A new product that is closely related to an existing product in a product line.

Modifying a product or creating a line extension can breathe new life into an existing product. Even if the 'new' product does not enjoy the rapid growth of the introduction and growth phases of the life cycle, it can result in an existing product moving from maturity or decline back to the growth phase. In addition to modifying existing products to create new ones, repositioning can reinvigorate a product that is well into its life cycle.

## Repositioning

We introduced the concept of positioning in chapter 6. When making decisions about a product, the marketer must understand the current positioning of the product. **Product positioning** is the creation and maintenance of a certain perception of a product in the customers' minds in relation to competitors. The position is usually based on purchase criteria relevant to the customer's decision making, such as price, performance, quality and safety. For example, in the tea market, Twinings may be positioned at a higher price and quality than Lipton.

**product positioning** The way in which the market perceives a product in relation to competing offerings.

Operating in a market against a strong competitor can be daunting, but there are various positioning strategies an organisation can take. It can choose to compete head-to-head with the competitor. This may be appropriate if performance is similar and it is possible to compete with a lower price. This can be particularly effective during tough economic times, when consumers seek value for money. Alternatively, a company can position its products away from the competition. This approach is appropriate if there is a dominant feature that makes it stand out from the competition, and that can entice customers to purchase the product specifically for that feature. Such a strategy can use the information gained from market research activities of the type that inform the development of a perceptual map, such as that for the surfwear industry presented in figure 6.11.

For some organisations there may be the need to change an aspect of the marketing mix to reposition themselves in the market. This might be to stay relevant to the changing needs of customers, or in reaction to changes by a competitor. An organisation can physically change a product, its design, packaging or add-on services, and its price, distribution or promotional activities, in order to reposition it in the eyes of the customers. This can help rejuvenate an old image and expand into new markets, as seen by Adidas, which has repositioned from a shoe worn by athletes to a shoe worn by pop stars to become a cool brand for a whole new generation.[24] An achievement such as this can move a product from the maturity stage of the product life cycle back into a new phase of growth.

### Product obsolescence

Eventually products may become obsolete. Obsolescence may be either planned or unplanned. For example, most companies that market business software (e.g. Microsoft, Apple, Adobe and Sun) release a version of the software with the intention of replacing it after a year or two with an upgraded version that offers more features to the customer. This is known as planned obsolescence and enables the marketer to generate repeat business from the same customers. They need to be sure that the newer version offers enough value to prompt customers to upgrade. Another type of planned obsolescence relates to products that break down or wear out. While most products are created with a reasonable expectation of durability, this is often moderated by price considerations and so on. Unplanned obsolescence occurs when a product becomes superseded by another, often through technological or social change. For example, photographic film for consumer cameras has largely become obsolete due to the invention of digital cameras, although not all analogue cameras have ceased in the marketplace. The 'Diana' camera is a plastic-bodied box camera which uses 120 roll film. In the 1960s it was marketed as a cheap novelty item, but later the Diana model was used by photographers to take soft-focus, retro-style pictures. More recently, a niche market of young photographers and 'hipsters' has emerged, as new versions of the Diana camera have been made available by Lomography in different colours and styles.

Even if a product does not become obsolete, if it is in significant decline, it may be taking valuable resources away from other, more worthwhile, opportunities. It may not be worth trying (or indeed possible) to reposition the product in the market.

**product deletion** The process of removing a product from the product mix.

**Product deletion** is the process of eliminating a product from the product mix. Deleting a product may be a good business decision, but it can also disappoint or alienate some customers, and needs to be managed. It could damage sales of other products and product lines, as customers show their annoyance. On the other hand, product deletion should usually be the preferred option over trying to sell a failed or superseded product. For example, in 2008, JVC, the last manufacturer of stand-alone VHS video cassette recorders, ceased production, thereby bringing an end to the videotape era.[25]

# 3D TV

3D technology has been a huge success at cinemas, with films like *Alice in Wonderland*, *Avatar* and *Clash of the Titans* using the technology. With the launch of 3D TV, this technology is now also available in people's homes. Samsung was the first company to offer a range of 3D TVs for sale in Australia. They were quickly followed by Sony and Panasonic. The 2010 FIFA World Cup and NRL State of Origin series were the first major events to make use of the technology. More than twenty 2010 FIFA World Cup matches were filmed in 3D, including Australia's opening game of the tournament against Germany.

However, for the customer, there are some things that must be taken into account when purchasing a 3D TV. Viewers need special 3D glasses and have to sit in a particular position to get the full 3D effect. After the launch of the technology, there were various safety concerns about the use of 3D TVs. There have also been warnings on where in the house to place 3D TVs.

Still, Samsung were confident that the TVs would be a hit, with high levels of stock being shipped into the country to meet the initial demand. The cost of the first available models was about $2500, which came with two sets of special battery-powered glasses (valued at $100 each) in order to view programs in 3D.

Sony believes that 3D TVs will make up 10 per cent of its overall television sales relatively quickly. Movies on 3D Blu-ray discs have started hitting the market alongside the new TV sets, and game developers are flagging significant investments in 3D games for the future.[26]

## Questions

1. In terms of managing a product through the life cycle, outline how Samsung's marketing mix for 3D TVs is likely to change over time.
2. What might be the implications for its traditional range of TVs and how can this be managed?

## Concepts and applications check

**Learning objective 6** explain key aspects of product management and positioning through the product life cycle

**6.1** Outline the differences between functional manager, product manager, brand manager and market manager approaches and their consequences for product management.

**6.2** Why do you think most 'new' products are actually modified versions of existing products?

**6.3** Choose a product that is in the mature phase of its life cycle. Outline a product repositioning strategy for the product.

**6.4** Identify two products that have been deleted from the market over the past few years. Why did their marketers decide product deletion was appropriate?

# SUMMARY

 **Learning objective 1** define 'product' and understand different ways to view and analyse products and product attributes

A product is a good, service or idea offered to the market for exchange. It can be tangible, intangible or a combination of both. Marketers can better understand and analyse products using the total product concept, which describes four levels of a product: core product, expected product, augmented product, and potential product. Products can be classified as consumer products (products purchased by individuals to satisfy personal and household needs) and business products (products bought by an organisation to be used in its operations or in the production of its own products).

 **Learning objective 2** describe the product life cycle, new product development and the product adoption process

The concept of product life cycle proposes that a product passes through five stages: *new product development*, *introduction*, *growth*, *maturity* and *decline*. Products must be managed throughout the product life cycle to maximise their contribution to the organisation's marketing objectives.

New product development has eight stages: *idea generation*, *screening* (eliminating unviable ideas), *concept evaluation*, *marketing strategy*, *business analysis* (how the new product will affects costs, sales and profits), *product development*, *test marketing* and *commercialisation*.

The product adoption process describes the stages through which a potential customer passes, from first becoming aware of the new product right through to deciding to adopt, or buy, the product. In this process the consumer who accepts a new product passes through five stages: *awareness*, *interest*, *evaluation*, *trial* and *adoption*.

 **Learning objective 3** outline how an organisation can differentiate its products to obtain a competitive advantage

Product differentiation is the creation of products and product attributes that distinguish one product from another. Most of the differentiation of products occurs in the augmented product layer of the total product concept. Design, brand image, style, add-on services, quality and features are the major product attributes that can be used to differentiate offerings from competitors' products.

 **Learning objective 4** explain the value of branding and the major issues involved in brand management

*Brand* refers to a collection of symbols, such as the name, logo, slogan and design intended to create an image in the customer's mind that differentiates a product from competitors' products. Brands can play a major role in a consumer's choice of a product, particularly for high-involvement products, as a well-known brand with a good reputation will more likely be chosen than a cheaper, unknown brand. A brand can help speed up consumer decision making by identifying specific preferred products, and can provide a form of self-expression and status, as well as denoting product quality. *Brand equity* is broadly defined as the added value that a brand gives a product. It is underpinned by brand loyalty. Brand equity metrics include brand assets (e.g. trade marks and patents), stock price analysis, replacement cost, brand attributes, brand loyalty and willingness-to-pay analysis. A high brand equity can be a valuable asset for a company and provide a strong competitive advantage.

 **Learning objective 5** describe the functional and marketing roles of packaging

Packaging can be a very important part of a product. The main functions of a package are to protect the product and promote the product. Many products need some kind of packaging to make it more convenient to store and use while protecting it from waste, damage or spoilage. However, as well as its functional features, a package is also used as a marketing tool to gain people's attention at the retailer, make customers aware of the product and/or its contents, differentiate it from competitors' offerings and help build a particular message or image about the product. As a form of marketing tool, the package can be changed. Marketers may want to change the package to express to customers that the product has changed in some way such as in terms of shape or ingredients, update the style of package or logo to broaden the customer appeal, or emphasise certain elements to further differentiate it from the competition.

 **Learning objective 6** explain key aspects of product management and positioning through the product life cycle

Within an organisation, the marketing issues surrounding products can be managed through a functional approach or by using product managers, brand managers or market managers. The last three approaches are often better able to coordinate all of the activities across the organisation to ensure the product strategy is implemented well. In addition to introducing new products, an organisation can capitalise on existing products by modifying products or creating line extensions.

The organisation needs to manage the positioning of the product in the marketplace and it may sometimes be necessary to reposition the product during the product life cycle. Line extensions, product upgrades and repositioning can all help keep a product out of the decline phase. For some products, these approaches can move the product back in the life cycle to enjoy a new phase of growth.

Many products eventually become obsolete. A product in decline may be taking valuable resources from away from other opportunities. Product deletion is the process of eliminating a product from the product mix. Product deletion must be managed in such a way as to minimise discontent among customers of the deleted product. Otherwise the discontent can affect sales of continuing products.

# Apple iPad

Apple is a contemporary leader in new product development, with a number of successful new product launches in recent years, including the iPod, the iPod Touch, the iPhone and the iPad. The iPad was launched by Apple co-founder and CEO Steve Jobs at a special press conference. Apple started taking pre-orders for the iPad in March 2010 and the Wi-Fi version of the iPad went on sale in the United States in April of that year. The iPad was priced at a comparable level to a laptop computer, and over two million iPads were sold within two months of its release.

The iPad is a tablet computer, which is a cross between an iPhone Touch and a laptop, and is controlled by an LCD, scratch-resistant glass touchscreen, rather than a stylus, as with earlier tablet computers. It also runs various applications written for the iPhone and the iPod Touch, as well as applications written especially for the iPad, including e-book readers.

Apple's first tablet computer was the Newton MessagePad, which was introduced in 1993. The company re-entered the mobile computing market in 2007 with the iPhone, which included a camera and a mobile phone. By late 2009, the iPad's release had been rumoured and referred to as 'Apple's tablet', *iTablet* and *iSlate*. The iPad runs its own software, which can be downloaded from Apple's App Store, and software especially written by developers. It also comes with several applications, such as Safari, Mail, Photos, Video, YouTube, iPod, iTunes, App Store, iBooks, Maps, Notes, Calendar, Contacts and Spotlight Search.

Hundreds of Apple fans snapped up iPads within minutes of the product being released at the company's Sydney store. It was worth the wait for Rahul Koduri, who queued for 30 hours in chilly temperatures to be the first to buy the device in person in Australia.

The iPad has an optional iBooks application that can be downloaded from the App Store, which displays books and other ePub-format content downloaded from the iBookstore. The iBookstore is available in the United States. Many major book publishers, including Penguin Books, HarperCollins, Simon & Schuster and Macmillan, all publish books for the iPad. The iPad is in competition with similar products including Barnes & Noble's NOOK and Amazon's Kindle. However, iPad users don't need to access iBookstore to get the latest books. Major online bookstores often have their own apps and e-book readers that work on the iPad. A large range of magazines and newspapers are also available for the iPad.

Internationally, the iPad was simultaneously launched in Australia, Canada, France, Germany, Italy, Japan, Spain, Switzerland and the United Kingdom. The launch in Sydney was a big event. Some had waited in line for over 24 hours. The first person in the queue, Sydney resident Rahul Koduri, led a 30-hour vigil (beginning around 2 am on the Thursday before the Friday launch) in his quest to be the first person in Australia to own an iPad. The chilly Sydney weather — complete with wind and rain — wasn't enough to deter the fan, who was prepared with blankets, jumpers, chairs and a sleeping bag, and was offered coffee and an umbrella — as well as permission to use the Apple store's bathrooms if need be — during his long wait. There were around 300 people waiting at the George Street store by the time it opened, and Apple staff entertained customers with chants, claps and high-fives when they eventually entered the store. Michael Batty, the customer who was second in line, said, 'Last night was not fun, but we braved through it so we're all good now. There were quite a few intoxicated people wandering around, a lot of loud cars floating about, but we all [sort of] huddled in the bus shelter together when the rain came ... we shared a moment; it was beautiful.'

With the popularity of the new product, there were also concerns about deliveries arriving on time. According to a TNT driver writing on the MacTalk blog, there were 7800 iPads awaiting delivery in Sydney on the day of the launch. The blogger said that even with all leave cancelled and staff starting their day early — at 5 am — that 'there is no way we will be able to deliver that many in one day'.

Within a few months of the iPad launch in Australia, impressive sales of the product had been recorded. Analyst group Telsyte surveyed about 1000 consumers across all age groups, and identified that 300 000 tablet computers had been sold in Australia by September 2010 (less than six months after the initial launch). Almost all of these tablet computer sales were for iPads. The analyst group estimated that the national mobile application market had exceeded $100 million, and forecast that it would grow by up to one-third very quickly (within 12 months). Internationally, Apple sold nearly 15 million iPads between April and December 2010. This figure gave Apple a lion's share of the market, and equated to nearly $10 billion in revenue.

The consumer segments that were responsible for leading the initial charge to purchase iPads in Australia were early adopters and business executives. Gartner Australia research director Robin Simpson commented that the push by business executives to be among some of the first adopters of the technology reflected a unique consumer purchasing pattern. 'It's a top-down push which has never really happened before for a consumer technology', he said. 'Normally with a consumer technology you expect it to come from the bottom and get pushed up, but this time it's completely different.'

The research conducted suggested that consumers were likely to prefer using several 'must have' applications on their iPads. Email was considered by the majority of the consumers surveyed to be a 'must have' on their iPads, as were the ability to use the device to play music, get involved in social networking, do mobile banking, and use games and sports applications. In the initial six months after the device was released in Australia, consumers had begun to shift their social networking habits from computers to tablet and mobile computers, but were less likely to use their tablet computers as a substitute source for accessing news, sport and weather content.

Many initial reviews about the iPad were positive. Walt Mossberg from *The Wall Street Journal* called it a 'pretty close' laptop killer, while Tim Gideon from *PC Magazine* wrote, 'You have yourself a winner [that] will undoubtedly be a driving force in shaping the emerging tablet landscape.' However, not everyone was so impressed. Some critics argued that although the first iPad was meant to be a handheld device, its weight (around 730 grams) began to feel heavy if you were holding it for any length of time. There was also criticism of features like the file-sharing and printing abilities of the iPad, as well as criticism of its lack of a webcam facility (which limited the conferencing and social networking capabilities of the device). Other complaints included that it did not fold, and that the shape was awkward for fitting into a small bag. A major issue with the operating system of the initial model was that it could only run one application at a time. Apple countered this criticism by saying that it planned to release a multi-tasking format quickly. Stuart Kennedy, a writer at *The Australian*, summed up the iPad by saying, 'The iPad is great for reading electronic books, newspapers and periodicals and viewing photos. It's surprisingly good at playing games and just ok as a general-purpose productivity machine. The iPad is very much a work in progress.'

The popularity of the iPad has also seen other companies want to be associated with the technology. Budget airline Jetstar trialled renting iPads to passengers as its in-flight entertainment, with iPads being available for hire on selected routes. Jetstar's commercial executive head, David Koczkar, said, 'It's quite an amazing piece of technology and the sort of thing our customers will greatly appreciate. Our biggest fear is not being able to provide enough.' Other businesses quick to begin using iPads included restaurants, such as Sydney's Mundo Global Tapas and Melbourne's Pearl. While some restaurants created iPad menus, the restaurant team at two-hat restaurant Pearl created an original app that allowed patrons to view its vast wine list with ease.

With the introduction of iPad menus in some Australian restaurants, patrons can devour dinner with their eyes before taking a single bite.

In the third quarter of 2010, Apple had a staggering 93 per cent of the global tablet market. But, as is the case with most successful new products, it was soon facing competition. In the final three months of 2010, Apple secured only 73 per cent of the global tablet market. During 2010 and 2011, the release of a range of new competing tablets — including Samsung's Galaxy Tab, Dell's Streak 7, ViewSonic's ViewPad and Motorola's Xoom — reduced the dominance of the market leader.

With a desire to reclaim market share and an awareness of forecasts tipping a rapid increase in the size of the overall market, Apple soon launched the iPad 2. The model was lighter, thinner and faster than the original iPad, and was released to international acclaim. Some fans lined up in Sydney for more than 50 hours to purchase the product, with stock largely selling out around Australia within hours of the official launch. Similar initial sales results were recorded around the world, with one shopper reporting more than 3000 items being sold in a store in Paris in five hours, and supplies quickly selling out in London.

Despite forecasts of a trebling in the international tablet market, some analysts predicted the rush by competitors to launch alternative offerings could result in a 'bubble' in the market in the foreseeable future — with a risk of inventory supplies exceeding demand because of the sheer popularity of the Apple iPad. Considering Apple's focus on innovation and quickly releasing new models to the market, it is likely that it won't be too long before a new iPad model is making headlines.[27]

## Questions

1. Evaluate the iPad in terms of the total product concept.
2. What marketing strategies do (or could) Apple utilise to progress potential iPad consumers through the stages of the product adoption process?
3. Outline the advantages of Apple's branding strategy in relation to its range of successful new product launches in recent years.

## Advanced activity

Now that you have studied this chapter, re-read the opening feature on *Guitar Hero* and think about all the issues that relate to the concept of product (such as the total product concept, product life cycle, product differentiation and branding). Imagine you were in charge of making the decision whether or not to launch an updated version of *Guitar Hero* in the future. What issues would you take into account in making your decision?

## Marketing plan activity

Think about the product (good or service) for which you are preparing your marketing plan. What is the product? What are its main features? Why would the target market want to buy this product compared to the competition? Once you have thought about these questions, outline and evaluate potential product strategies that will likely meet the needs of the target market.

A sample marketing plan has been included at the back of this book (see page 523) to give you an idea where this information fits in an overall marketing plan.

## CHAPTER 8

# Price

## Learning objectives

After studying this chapter, you should be able to:

- understand the objectives that guide pricing strategies

- analyse demand to inform the development of an appropriate pricing strategy

- describe the principles of pricing based on cost and revenue analysis

- explain the role of competitive analysis in determining pricing

- appreciate the issues involved in pricing for business markets

- understand how to manage prices as part of the marketing mix.

# Long way to the top

Music promoters Michael Gudinski (The Frontier Touring Company), Garry Van Egmond (The Van Egmond Group) and Michael Coppel (Michael Coppel Presents) have been responsible for bringing major international recording artists to Australia for decades. In recent times, they have promoted the Australian concert tours of acts such as U2, AC/DC, Lady Gaga, Pink and Tom Jones, to name just a few. While the glamour of being a music promoter may be appealing, it is an inherently risky business. Tour costs and ticket pricing are major considerations for promoters. Even for a popular international act, simply booking them to perform a high number of concerts in Australia and selling a lot of tickets may not necessarily lead to a profitable tour for a promoter. 'You can do 10 shows, but if the last two lose money you're back to square one', says Coppel.

Shows have also become more elaborate and costly to stage over the years, and this has been reflected in ticket prices. U2's recent 360 Degrees tour, for example, reportedly cost $750 000 a day to keep on the road, with 120 trucks and 157 production crew required to transport and assemble the stage, sound, lighting and video equipment. Venues and international acts also generally have to be booked well in advance, and international artists usually want to be paid in US dollars, meaning the profits of local promoters are impacted by exchange rates when they price and sell tickets well in advance of the tour dates.

In today's concert ticket environment, prices can range from one to several hundred dollars, depending on the artist and the proximity of the seating to the stage. In

this context, it is hard to believe that when Gudinski entered the music business in the 1960s, the price of an album was much more than the price of a live concert ticket. In years gone by, artists would generally tour to promote their albums. Now, as revenue from album sales has evaporated due to issues such as internet music piracy, they will often release an album to promote a tour.

Music promoters are acutely aware of the importance of ticket pricing to profitability. Gudinski's Frontier Touring Company, for example, has recently significantly invested in web technology to enable it to sell tickets for the acts it promotes directly to concert-goers, bypassing 'the middleman' (in this case, specialist ticketing agencies).[1]

## Questions

1. What are some of the factors that affect concert ticket prices?
2. Evaluate the importance of ticket pricing for concert promoters in relation to the other elements of the marketing mix.

# INTRODUCTION

Price is a constant, fundamental concern in both consumer and business markets. We can distinguish between *price* (which can be influenced by economic factors such as the relationship between the supply of a product and demand) and *pricing* (which is a conscious, explicit management activity). In terms of the concert ticket price example at the start of the chapter, consumers may be prepared to pay a high *price* to see a popular international act live in concert because they may have limited opportunity to do so. This will be one factor tour promoters take into consideration in *pricing* the concert tickets, along with many others, such as the costs associated with staging the tour.

Price is a measure of value to both buyers and sellers. Buyers see price as a measure of the benefit they derive from the consumption of a product, whether it be a good, a service or an idea. Price also serves as a means for buyers to allocate their scarce financial resources between purchases. For example, a buyer may want a holiday and a new home entertainment system, but can only afford one or the other. To choose, buyers compare the prices and the utility or satisfaction derived from the alternative purchases.

Sellers need prices to cover their costs and provide sufficient profit margin to justify the risk they take by engaging in business activities. For example, a goods business will charge a price that covers the costs of developing, producing and supplying their products, and still provides a reasonable profit. Services businesses will charge a price based on several factors, including:

- the time involved in providing the service
- the time involved in obtaining a reasonable return for the years of specialised training undertaken by the service provider
- any standardised price levels prescribed by an industry professional body or government
- the customer's perception of the value of the service
- the customer's ability to pay.

It goes almost without saying that if a buyer and seller cannot agree on the value expressed in the price, the transaction is unlikely to proceed.

In this chapter, we will examine the role of price and pricing in the marketing mix, including a discussion of how demand, costs and competitors influence pricing strategy. We will also examine the issues involved in pricing for business markets. Finally, we will discuss how to manage prices as part of the overall marketing mix.

# PRICING OBJECTIVES

As we learned in chapter 1, the key to successful marketing lies in the creation of a mutually beneficial exchange of value between one party and another:

**Learning objective 1**
understand the objectives that guide pricing strategies

- For the *buyer*, the benefit is the satisfaction derived from the consumption or ownership of the product. In normal circumstances, a buyer will only engage in an exchange if that benefit is in excess of what they must give for the product.
- For the *seller*, the benefit is primarily the revenue derived from purchases. In normal circumstances, a seller will only engage in an exchange if that benefit is in excess of the cost of creating and delivering the product.

Price serves as a visible expression of the value of the product to be exchanged and enables buyers and sellers to negotiate and agree on that value.

In financial terms, this concept is straightforward. Someone buying a bag of apples pays a price of a few dollars. While an exchange of money and a product between the buyer and seller is the usual method, it is important to recognise that not all exchanges of value involve a financial transaction (and therefore not all involve a monetary price). Exchange may take place through *bartering* (the direct exchange of goods and services in payment for other goods and services). In this case, the goods and services given actually constitute the price. While it may seem old-fashioned, bartering remains common in many parts of the world and it is still an important method of exchange in business markets. In fact, the Bartercard business was established to help businesses trade goods and services. Its system works on 'points' earned and spent by members through the exchange of goods and services with other members. Its key advantage is that it removes the need to directly exchange one product for another. It also helps businesses administer their bartering activities, which can otherwise be complicated by tax and legal issues (discussed further later in the chapter).

When the product is an 'idea' rather than a good or service, the 'seller' is typically seeking to influence the opinions (e.g. through political campaign advertising) or the behaviours (e.g. through anti-smoking 'Quit' campaigns) of 'buyers'. The exchange of value may therefore occur in the *ideas* or *behaviours* exchanged by both parties. The astute social marketer will be mindful that, for the 'buyer', the required behaviour is the price of the transaction.

## Determining pricing objectives

The management of price is known as 'pricing'. Pricing objectives are derived from the organisation's marketing objectives, which are, in turn, based on the overall organisational objectives, as discussed in chapter 2. For example, Qantas established Jetstar with the aim of penetrating the holiday and family traveller markets through a relatively low-cost, 'low frills' service offering that would enable aggressive pricing. Qantas also operates its main business in the economy and holiday traveller market segments, but at significantly higher price points. Both Qantas and Jetstar need to ensure that, as far as possible, their pricing does not result in their competing directly for the same customers.

It can be tempting to dismiss the question of pricing objectives by simply assuming that pricing should aim to maximise profits. While this *is* a fundamental objective of all for-profit marketing activities, it does not help the marketer formulate specific strategies to achieve specific outcomes (it is also nearly impossible to achieve in practice). More specific pricing objectives tend to focus on various combinations of the following issues:

- profitability
- long-term prosperity
- market share
- positioning.

Pricing objectives guide the remainder of the pricing process. Pricing objectives (like all objectives) should be specific, measurable, actionable, reasonable and timetabled. The choice of pricing objectives adopted by a marketer will have immediate

Qantas operates its flagship carrier line and its 'low-frills' Jetstar business in the same market segments, but the dual businesses have different pricing objectives. As far as possible, Qantas needs to ensure that Jetstar is not in direct competition for its customers.

implications for the determination of prices. For example, the objective of a hotel to establish a high-quality, prestige image naturally implies setting prices at, or above, the top of the range for the industry. Conversely, an organisation which is new to a market, or is launching a new product, may set a low price in order to penetrate the market and achieve a reasonable sales volume. For example, when Czech car manufacturer Skoda entered the Australian market, it set prices in the mid-range of Japanese and Korean brands, and significantly below other European brands. An organisation must ensure that its pricing strategy serves all aspects of its marketing goals, both qualitatively (e.g. in communicating a high-quality image) and quantitatively (e.g. achieving market leadership in sales revenue). While raising the price might contribute to communicating a high-quality image, it may lead to a loss in total revenue (if there is a significant sales decline).

Organisations' objectives are, of course, complex and so any one organisation is likely to be pursuing multiple pricing objectives at the same time. Similarly, the particular mix of objectives is likely to change over time.

## Profitability

All for-profit organisations seek to make a profit to reward the business's owners for the risk they take in investing in the business. Profits are generated when total revenues exceed total costs. Thus, at the simplest level, on average prices must exceed costs over the long term.

The profit required to justify the investment in a particular product or project is known as the return on investment, or ROI, and it is a common basis for pricing decisions. For example, return on investment is used to determine the minimum acceptable level of profitability for new products, thus ensuring that the company invests its working capital in new products wisely. Of course, return on investment calculations can only be based on projections of sales revenue and associated costs. Nevertheless, they do provide an objective measure to guide pricing strategy.

Price and sales volume combine to form revenue, which is of course an integral component of profit. At the same time, price directly influences sales volume. In turn, sales volume influences costs (both in terms of the cost per unit sold and in the extent to which the organisation can achieve 'economies of scale' — in which the more units produced, the cheaper the production cost of each unit). Pricing is therefore directly and immediately linked to organisational profitability.

Price can be extraordinarily flexible in the short term. The active negotiation of price between buyers and sellers can make pricing a demanding, volatile and challenging activity. The minute-to-minute fluctuations in the prices of shares and other financial instruments provide a stark example of this. Beyond the volatility of pricing is the management of profit margins as the key to the long-term prosperity of the selling organisation. It is important to recognise that sales volume and satisfied customers alone do not guarantee profitability; pricing must reflect the long-term costs of production and distribution.

## Long-term prosperity

Ongoing survival is a fundamental goal of all businesses and brings a long-term perspective to the setting of pricing objectives. Well-run businesses put their survival ahead of short-term profit considerations. The rationale for this is simple: profitability over the long term leads to greater total wealth for business owners than does maximising short-term profits at the expense of the future of the business. For example, in an economic downturn in which consumers decrease their spending, many businesses lower their prices in order to ensure sales volumes are sufficient to generate enough cash flows for the business to meet its financial obligations, such as paying staff, meeting loan repayments and paying suppliers. A similar approach is taken to generating cash flow during potentially slow parts of the year (e.g. just after Christmas). At these times, major retailers promote annual and seasonal sales to stimulate higher than normal sales volumes. The risk in this approach is that customers learn to anticipate the annual sales and to defer their purchases until they can buy at reduced prices. This seems to be increasingly true of the regular seasonal sales.

During an economic downturn or recession, an organisation's pricing objective may simply be to generate enough cash flow for the organisation to survive, but at the same time astute marketers will be aware of the danger of beginning a downward spiral, leading to ever lower prices and margins. They must also be aware of the risk of long-term damage to the organisation's reputation and brands — consumers may begin to associate the brand with permanently low prices, which they may equate with low quality (see the discussion of positioning that follows shortly). This can create difficulties in raising prices again when the economy recovers. Pricing strategy during an economic downturn needs to take proper account of the need to maintain sales revenue and cash flow, and to remain price competitive in the short term, while at the same time ensuring that any price discounting is seen by customers as temporary and a genuine bargain. In this way, the company can protect the value of its brands and prepare to rebuild during an ensuing economic recovery.

### Market share

Pricing objectives may be formulated to achieve particular market share outcomes. Many businesses use aggressive pricing in an effort to increase or defend market share. Major car companies Toyota, Holden, Ford and Mazda use aggressive pricing to increase and defend market share in particular market categories, as well as overall market share. Higher sales volumes and market leadership generate a number of benefits for a business, including high levels of customer awareness and preference, and economies of scale in selling, marketing, distribution and administration. Increasing market share is, of course a legitimate business objective that can be achieved through pricing, but the pricing strategy must consider the effect on profit margins and the overall profitability of the business. For example, the low-cost airline operators have used aggressive pricing to grow sales volumes, but the approach has led to low profit margins.

### Positioning

Pricing is a fundamental tool of positioning (see chapters 6 and 7). Consumers often compare competing products based on price, and to some extent this assessment can occur relatively independently of some of the other elements of the marketing mix. Price is therefore crucial in how the organisation's offering is positioned in the minds of each of its target market segments.

Customers interpret price differently. The same price may convey quite different meanings to different customers. Marketers can therefore use price symbolically. Some customers are motivated by higher prices in the belief that such prices reflect higher quality. In some instances, as in the case of fine wines, quality may be difficult to judge accurately or objectively and so a high price may be used as a 'surrogate' measure of quality. Social marketers have come to learn that when information and

In some instances, as in the case of fine wines, quality may be difficult to judge accurately or objectively and so a high price may be used as a 'surrogate' measure of quality.

services are dispensed free of charge, consumers are likely to place a low value on them and may therefore be inclined to reject messages to change their behaviour. In other words, consumers are accustomed to equating value with a financial price; goods or services with no (or very low) prices are seen to have little value.

*Prestige pricing* involves setting prices high to convey an image of prestige, quality and exclusivity. As mentioned, this is also effective when consumers cannot objectively evaluate the quality of the product, and therefore use the high price as a proxy measure of high quality. This is the case with products such as pharmaceuticals (where consumers might regard high price as a measure of high potency and efficacy), rare wine, whisky and cognac, motor vehicles, *haute couture* and fine art. Prestige brands such as Chanel, Porsche, and Versace rarely advertise their prices at all, let alone advertise a price reduction. Organisations that have built their marketing strategy around high product quality and brand image will rarely, if ever, seek to compete on price. Such businesses invariably have higher cost structures, based on high development, manufacturing, marketing and selling costs, and expensive distribution channels. The prices they charge are also part of the product's appeal — customers would likely regard price cuts as contrary to the high-quality, prestige image. Such an approach can be difficult to sustain during an economic downturn, when consumers tend to search for value for money and avoid conspicuous consumption. In contrast, other customers will seek lower prices in the expectation that they will receive greater value. Organisations such as Aldi use pricing to create the perception of affordability and value for money in their supermarkets.

Rarely — if ever — will an organisation be in a position to make perfectly informed pricing decisions. As always, detailed understanding of the customer base is an important priority. This chapter will therefore discuss a range of issues, which will enable the sellers to make better informed pricing decisions, which complement the other elements of the organisation's marketing mix. No part of the marketing mix can be set in isolation from the other parts. Pricing needs to be consistent with the product, promotion and distribution strategies. In particular, it is essential that pricing does not undermine the positioning of the product in relation to its target market and competitors. The product itself, its relationship to other products in the mix, distribution, promotion and customer service must all work together. Marketers must ensure that the positioning achieved by their pricing is consistent with the positioning achieved by other elements of the marketing mix. For example, a high price cannot be matched with a product that is of low quality, that is distributed through discount stores or that is advertised through the newspaper classifieds. Only when the positioning achieved by the price is consistent with the rest of the marketing mix *and* the offering has been targeted at the correct market segment will consumers purchase the product in significant numbers.

Low prices may generate high sales volume, but may also conflict with a high-quality, differentiated positioning approach. Conversely, a high price may lead to a loss in sales volume and market share, and may be resisted by distribution partners. At the same time, frequent price cuts advertised by distribution partners will erode the perceived value and quality in the brand. Strong brands, such as Apple and Louis Vuitton, generally attract premium prices. Price and distribution channels are commonly linked, in that low-priced, high-volume products, such as bread, beverages and grocery products are sold through intensive convenient distribution, while high-price, high-margin specialty brands are sold through selective retail distribution. The organisation's partners in the distribution channel expect pricing to be managed in such a way that they can achieve reasonable profits from their participation. Pricing is also linked to promotion, in that bargain prices need to be widely advertised;

whereas premium prices are less likely to be featured in advertising copy. Similarly, higher-priced products tend to rely on personal selling, and complex pricing structures usually require detailed personal selling, whereas simple discount pricing can be promoted using mass media press, radio, television and in-store and internet promotions.

Marketers may be able to offer different versions of a product from budget to premium levels, with prices to match. For example, VW's Golf models range in price from $28 000 to $58 000.[2] This enables the organisation to appeal to customers across a range of price preferences. In addition, a *premium pricing* approach such as this may succeed in convincing consumers to trade up from cheaper alternatives to a premium model. This is an effective strategy when overall consumer confidence is strong and enables the marketer to de-emphasise price in initially attracting consumers. When consumer sentiment is weak, consumers tend to emphasise value, and premium pricing is unlikely to be effective.

## Not-for-profit pricing

While not-for-profit organisations, by definition, do not seek to make profits, they do generally seek a return on their activities and many charge for their products. Their pricing objectives may be to generate enough funds to sustain their activities (e.g. the fees and loan interest charged by credit unions are intended to simply cover the costs of supplying their service, including paying interest on deposits). Alternatively, a not-for-profit organisation may price its products in such a way as to make them appealing to their target market. For example, most public buses operate at a loss, but to charge passengers the full price necessary to cover costs would deter people from choosing public transport over private transport.

As mentioned earlier in the chapter, the price of a not-for-profit product may also be a change in attitude or behaviour among the target market (e.g. the price of 'buying' the 'Quit smoking' message is the effort the consumer must make to beat the habit of smoking).

## The legal environment

Regardless of the particular objectives adopted by an organisation, its approach to pricing must comply with various legal restrictions. Governments have always imposed laws and regulations on pricing in a bid to ensure that organisations do not take pricing measures that are against the public interest. All organisations are subject to laws and regulations when establishing prices. The areas subject to legal restrictions include essential services, misleading and deceptive conduct, price collusion, comparability of prices, clarity in pricing and price discrimination.

At various times, governments have chosen to intervene directly in markets to control prices for such services as hospital and medical care. In other instances, government approval is necessary when setting prices, such as for local government, water and electricity charges.

The Competition and Consumer Act (formerly the Trade Practices Act) in Australia and the Fair Trading Act in New Zealand prohibit misleading and deceptive advertising. For example, *comparison discounting* is the practice of explicitly quoting a discounted price and the regular higher price together. An organisation advertising a sale must base the advertised price savings on realistic, recent and comparable selling prices. Marketers using comparison discounting should also bear in mind that over the longer term there is a danger that the customers will not believe that the higher price is the regular price. The law also imposes restrictions on *bait pricing*, which involves establishing an artificially low price for one item in a product line to attract potential buyers, then trying to sell them a higher-priced item in the product line. Bait pricing is often implemented through advertisements such as 'Brand-name jeans for only $10'. While such an approach is legitimate if the retailer maintains sufficient stock of the low-priced product and is willing to sell it, *bait and switch* pricing is often illegal. Bait and switch pricing occurs when the seller has no intention of selling the lower-priced item and merely uses the 'bait' price as a pretext to lure shoppers into the store, after which to 'switch' them to the more normally priced items.

A number of government regulations and laws seek to prevent activities aimed at controlling or manipulating prices. The courts have, in recent years, ruled against major companies that have colluded to fix prices. For example, an Australian Competition and Consumer Commission investigation led to the charging of the late Richard Pratt, then chairman of packaging business Visy Industries, with price fixing, resulting in a $36 million fine. Visy and competitor Amcor have since faced lawsuits by aggrieved business customers such as Cadbury Schweppes.

A recent development in the regulation of the Australian market is the commitment by the federal government to mandate 'unit pricing' for products that are sold through supermarkets. This move was in response to a key recommendation made by the Australian Competition and Consumer Commission's inquiry into the competitiveness of retail grocery prices. Unit pricing requires product price tags to show the price per kilogram, litre or some other unit alongside the full retail price of the product, making it much easier for consumers to compare prices for competing products sold in varying quantities (e.g. a 400 gram bottle of tomato paste selling for $1.95 would be displayed as 49 cents per 100 grams, and a 425 gram bottle selling for $2.20 would be displayed as 52 cents per 100 grams). A number of retailers, including Aldi, moved to implement unit pricing ahead of any legal requirement.[3]

Unit pricing requires price tags of supermarket products to show the price per unit. In these examples, the price of each brand and size of cornflakes is shown per 100 grams. It is clear that the 1.5 kilogram pack of Brand One Cornflakes is the best value for money.

Amendments have also been made to the Competition and Consumer Act in recent years in an attempt to make price comparisons easier for consumers and to help them know the 'real' price of products. The 'clarity in pricing' amendment applies to the automotive, travel and tourism industries, and requires sellers to indicate the full price of the products. For example, traditionally, many car dealerships have advertised the base price of a car 'plus dealer delivery and on-road costs'. This is known as 'component pricing'. For an average car, dealer delivery and on-road costs can add more than 10 per cent to the actual drive-away price, so the clarity in pricing initiative should give consumers a much better idea of what they will need to pay. The car industry, on the other hand, has countered that different delivery costs to different regions, different state taxes, different competitive pressures at individual dealers and so on mean that a single all-inclusive price across the entire market is inappropriate. It is expected that advertising will move to a more local and regional basis. For example, Mercedes Benz removed pricing details from its website, advising potential customers to contact their local dealer instead. The clarity in pricing legislation does not make *captive pricing* illegal. Captive pricing involves offering a low entry price for a basic product, then charging more for desirable additional parts or functions. Car manufacturers often employ headline pricing for a basic model and then charge premium prices for commonly desired add-ons, such as air-conditioning. Photocopier manufacturers may set low initial purchase prices, then charge premium prices for toner cartridges. Captive pricing enables the marketer to extract a bigger sale than the headline price would suggest and, in the case of ongoing services and supplies, provide the manufacturer with a revenue stream. On the other hand, customers may feel exploited by captive pricing approaches.[4]

As we will read later in the chapter, it is common in business markets for buyers and sellers to negotiate on price. This is legitimate on a number of grounds. The Competition and Consumer Act in Australia and the Commerce Act in New Zealand do, however, make business-to-business *price discrimination* illegal. Price discrimination occurs when price differentials between business customers give one business customer an unfair advantage over another, thus reducing competition. Such price differentials can and do occur legally in a number of ways. In summary, price differentials are *legal* under the following circumstances:

- when they do not adversely affect competition
- when they arise because of differences in the costs of selling or transportation to various customers
- when they arise because a supplier has to cut its price to a particular buyer to meet a competitor's prices
- when they relate to volume discounts
- when they occur in consumer markets.

Price differentials are not illegal in the consumer markets, because consumers do not sell the product or use it in the production of some other product. Price differentials may thus arise between sales to individual consumers or to groups of consumers. For example, the practice of *secondary-market pricing* involves setting different prices for different target markets. Senior citizens are offered discounts by many retailers and service providers, based partly on their reduced capacity to pay. Apple charges university students a lower price for its products than it charges general consumers (in the hope of winning repeat purchase after the students graduate). Secondary-market pricing also enables the organisation to set prices that reflect the different costs involved in serving different markets. On the other hand, such an approach can involve ethical issues, administration complexities and, in the case of business markets, legal issues.

## Selecting the pricing method

Pricing is a key to profitability and it can be among the most complex decisions facing a marketer. Like all marketing decisions, pricing decisions should be based on an understanding of the customer. As we noted at the start of the chapter, successful marketing involves the creation of a mutually beneficial exchange of value between one party and another. It follows, then, that prices should reflect the value of the product to the customer. The customer's perception of value is determined by all of the factors in the marketing mix that go towards creating the organisation's offer. The value of the product to the customer places a ceiling on prices — potential customers will not usually give more than they receive. On the other hand, the organisation will forgo potential profits if it sets prices far below the value of the product. Of course, the value of any given product will be unique for each customer. The extent to which the market as a whole will buy products at a particular price is described by the economic concept of demand.

The organisation must also ensure it obtains value from the marketing exchange. The organisation's costs place a floor on prices — like customers, the organisation will not usually give more than it receives. Competing offerings are also crucial in pricing decisions. Competing offerings enable customers to compare the relative value of different purchase options. Organisations must therefore make pricing decisions that make their products competitive in the marketplace.

It is clear then that pricing decisions need to consider internal organisational factors and external environmental factors (which we discuss throughout this chapter). In the following sections of the chapter we will discuss the three major considerations of demand, costs and competition. The relative importance of demand, costs and competition issues will vary between organisations, markets, products, competitors and over time. While in theory it is impossible to set *optimal* prices across the three pricing dimensions (i.e. demand, costs and competition), in practice, it is important to seek a price which yields a *satisfactory* outcome (or compromise) across all three. That is, prices generally need to appeal to target customers, yield acceptable profit margins and provide a competitive market offer. Focusing solely on one dimension will almost certainly lead to unattractive, uncompetitive or unprofitable prices. In the final section of the chapter, we will examine how the marketing organisation can manage prices to ensure the marketing offer provides value to both the organisation and the customer.

# Great Wall, great value

The booming Australian market for light trucks and utilities recently became even more competitive, with the arrival of Chinese newcomer Great Wall Motors. Its entry level 'ute' model, priced at $17990 in Australia, dramatically undercut the established, mainly Japanese brands (such as Toyota's HiLux), by at least 20 per cent. Selling at this substantial price discount as a newcomer to the Australian market, Great Wall is relying on its value offer to attract mainly business customers as its most obvious target market segment (e.g. self-employed and small-business tradesmen).

In fact, the price is so low that the most immediate price competitors of the Great Wall entry level ute model will be three-year-old Japanese utes (which, in most cases, will have done three 'hard' years of use). The attraction of a new vehicle for the price of a well-worn second-hand vehicle is compelling. The Great Wall offer clearly relies on low price to offset any lack of brand awareness or perceived uncertainties surrounding the quality, durability and reliability of the unknown brand from a country previously unknown for quality motor vehicles.

The pricing strategy is an example of 'value in use' pricing. The retail price is based primarily on the benefits perceived by the customer, rather than the seller's costs. In business markets, the benefits are frequently long term (as will be the buyers' costs) and will include service, guarantees, reliability, low depreciation and brand image. In practice, different customers will assign different values and thus 'value in use' is likely to vary by market segments — ranging from the 'price-sensitive' to 'image conscious' segments.

While self-employed 'tradies' and farmers may find the value offer difficult to resist, other larger, more corporate business buyers (e.g. local councils, government departments and major construction companies) may be less likely to be swayed by the initial price alone and may continue to purchase established ute offerings. Over time, of course, Great Wall will hope that their price offer will be compelling even to large corporate bodies, especially after the brand develops a reputation for quality, reliability and value for money. For companies such as Toyota, a higher price for their ute models may be sustainable, at least in the shorter term. That brand image is important to some business buyers has long been recognised and goes some way towards explaining why, for example, IBM famously sustained a significant price premium over technically equivalent competitors' products during the 1960s.[5]

## Questions

1. In terms of the four broad pricing objectives outlined in the chapter, outline which appear to be being pursued by Great Wall Motors in the Australian market.

2. Imagine you are the marketing manager for the Toyota HiLux model. How would you respond to the threat posed by Great Wall Motors' ute model?

## Concepts and applications check

**Learning objective 1**  understand the objectives that guide pricing strategies

**1.1**  We are most familiar with the concept of monetary prices. Explain how goods, services, attitudes and behaviours can also be considered a price in certain circumstances.

**1.2**  Jetstar Airways is a low-priced subsidiary of Qantas. For each of the broad pricing objectives discussed, outline how the existence of Jetstar could potentially benefit the Qantas organisation as a whole.

**1.3**  Imagine you are a marketing manager in a fast-moving consumer goods company and your products are mainly sold through supermarkets. What impact would unit pricing have on your marketing strategy?

**1.4**  The Australian government has enacted legislation to promote 'clarity in pricing'. How does this legislation benefit consumers? Can you identify any downsides to this legislation for consumers or marketers?

**1.5**  Outline the circumstances in which price differentials are legal.

**1.6**  Explain the concept of value from both a customer's and an organisation's perspective.

# DEMAND CONSIDERATIONS

**Learning objective 2** analyse demand to inform the development of an appropriate pricing strategy

Demand exists when consumers are willing and able to buy a product. Demand for a product arises when it can fulfil an unsatisfied need or want of a consumer and is available at a price consumers are willing to pay. Demand can be affected by many factors, including economic conditions and associated consumer and business confidence. In good economic times when consumers generally have high job security, their confidence and spending on products can usually be expected to increase. Associated with this increased demand for products are usually either actual or expected increases in business profits and associated investment in their operations. Conversely, in economic downturns or recessions, such as the downturn experienced in economies around the world after the global financial crisis, consumer and business confidence and the associated demand and investment generally decrease. While price and value are always factors in any exchange between a buyer and seller, regardless of general economic conditions, price in particular is likely to be a more sensitive issue for buyers during downturn or recession periods.

It is important to remember that the broad demand trends outlined are general statements. The demand for some products will not significantly rise or fall according to economic conditions, and we will explore this concept in greater detail later in this section. Demand for some products may actually increase during an economic downturn. For example, for some products, consumers may switch from more expensive to cheaper brands.

Formally defined, demand is the relationship between the price of a particular product and the quantity of the product that consumers are willing to buy. Understanding the nature and extent of consumer demand for a product is central to the formulation of pricing strategy. Demand analysis is based on historical data and estimates of sales potential, price–volume relationships and price sensitivity. Such data shows the historical and likely future relationship between a product's price and the volume sold. These data can be used to construct the product's demand schedule and demand curve, which provide the theoretical foundation for the development of pricing strategy and tactics.

**Demand-based pricing** sets prices according to the level of aggregate or individual customer demand in the market. Demand-based pricing requires a thorough understanding of how demand is likely to be affected by changes in price for the product in question and an understanding of how consumers' sensitivity to prices varies over time, between customers and in different circumstances. Accommodation providers in the snow country, for example, charge higher prices during winter when they experience peak demand and can be confident of filling all of their rooms, and much lower prices during summer when there is no snow and tourist numbers are at a low. Similarly, at the individual consumer level, a car salesperson will seek to sell a car at the maximum price that they believe the customer is willing to pay. While demand analysis is based on the overall or aggregate demand in the target market, at the individual level, the organisation can implement *negotiated pricing*, in which the price is negotiated between the buyer and seller, thus more accurately reflecting the relative value to each party. This is common in consumer real estate and car purchases. It is extremely common in business markets, where prices are negotiated based on differences in the costs of selling or transportation to various customers, the need to match a competitor's prices for a particular buyer, or volume discounts.

The success of demand-based pricing depends on the organisation's ability to accurately forecast fluctuations in demand and to accurately predict consumers' price sensitivity.

**demand-based pricing** The influence of demand on pricing decisions.

## The demand schedule and demand curve

A **demand schedule** is simply a table that shows quantity demanded for a particular good at particular prices. An example is shown in table 8.1. If we plot the data, we obtain the graph presented in figure 8.1. This is known as the **demand curve**. For the vast majority of products, there is an inverse relationship between price and quantity sold; that is, as price rises, the quantity sold falls, and *vice versa*. Hence the demand curve has a downward, or negative, slope. For example, if Toyota advertises that it has cut $2000 from the recommended retail price of its Corolla model, it would confidently expect sales volumes to increase. If Jetstar advertises half price tickets, it would expect to sell significantly more tickets than at the usual price.

**demand schedule** A table showing quantity demanded for a particular good at particular prices.

**demand curve** A graph showing the relationship between price and volume sold.

**TABLE 8.1** A demand schedule for jet skis

| Price | Quantity demanded (per week) |
|-------|------------------------------|
| $16 000 | 80 |
| $18 000 | 64 |
| $20 000 | 52 |
| $22 000 | 44 |
| $24 000 | 36 |
| $26 000 | 28 |

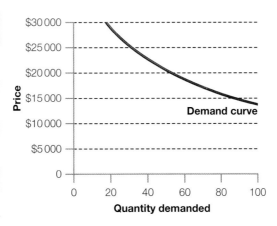

**FIGURE 8.1**

A demand curve for a product (jet skis)

As stated, the typical demand curve is downward sloping. *Prestige products* are an exception. Consumer behaviour in relation to prestige products is influenced by perceptions of status and exclusivity. For example, a Tag Heuer wristwatch may be beautifully designed and finely crafted, but most owners are just as interested in the prestige and exclusivity that comes from wearing a watch that costs several thousand dollars.

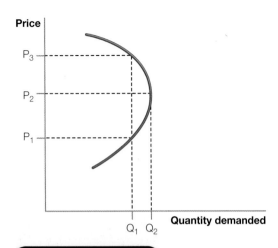

**FIGURE 8.2**

A demand curve for prestige products

In addition, it can be difficult for buyers to objectively evaluate the quality of a product (especially a service) and so they may use price as a surrogate indicator — a higher price signifies higher quality. As such, for some consumers, a high price makes a product more desirable and demand may actually *increase* at higher prices. A demand curve for prestige products is shown in figure 8.2. For a price increase from $P_1$ to $P_2$, the quantity demanded rises from $Q_1$ to $Q_2$. There are, however, limits on this pattern. In figure 8.2, prices above $P_2$ exceed the benefits of prestige and exclusivity conferred by ownership of the product and the demand curve reverts back to the traditional downward slope. At some point (shown as $P_3$), the quantity demanded will fall back to $Q_1$, the quantity demanded at $P_1$. For makers of prestige products such as fine wines, cognacs, rare whiskies, works of art and handmade Swiss watches, it makes sense to charge very high prices.

The relationship between price and quantity demanded shown on a demand curve is based on all else remaining constant. This condition (known as *ceteris paribus*) means the demand curve represents only changes in demand related to changes in price, without being confounded by other factors. A change in demand due to a change in price alone is known as a *movement along the demand curve*.

If some other factor changes, it will alter the relationship between price and quantity demanded and thus create a new demand curve. The demand curve for jet skis is shown again as $D_1$ in figure 8.3. Assume some non-price factor improves. This could be product attributes, promotional activities, distribution or some factor external to the marketing mix, such as consumer preferences, incomes, the size of the market, competitive conditions, consumer sentiment or the price of substitute products. An improvement in any of these factors creates a new demand curve, $D_2$, to the *right* of the initial demand curve. Notice in figure 8.3 that, with the *shift in the demand curve* from $D_1$ to $D_2$, the quantity sold at price $P_1$ increases from $Q_1$ to $Q_2$. A shift of the demand curve to the right means greater quantities will be demanded at all prices than was previously the case. A deterioration in a non-price factor, such as may occur with falling consumer sentiment during an economic downturn, will result in a shift in the demand curve to the left, meaning less will be demanded at all prices than before.

The relationship between price and quantity demanded can change in the short and long term. Short-term changes are known as fluctuations in demand. To the extent that these fluctuations can be predicted, they can be incorporated into the organisation's pricing strategy. For example, airlines and hotels have a reasonably accurate knowledge of the likely fluctuations in demand for their services on a daily and seasonal basis, and they are able to adjust their prices to ensure that they can sell the maximum number of 'seats' (in aircraft) and 'bed nights' (in hotels) respectively. Changes in demand for some products, such as fashion clothing, may be less predictable, and pricing such products may therefore be more problematic.

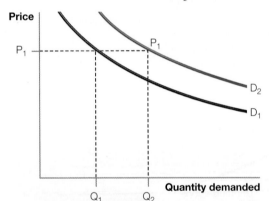

**FIGURE 8.3**

A shift in the demand curve

## Price elasticity of demand

**price elasticity of demand**
The sensitivity of quantity demanded to changes in price.

Our recent discussion emphasised that the quantity demanded is directly related to the price of the product. The sensitivity of the quantity demanded to changes in price is known as the **price elasticity of demand**. Only with a thorough understanding of the price elasticity of demand can a marketer effectively manage pricing.

The price elasticity of demand is a quantitative measure of the relationship between the size of a price change and the resultant size of the change in sales volume. In numerical terms, it is the percentage change in quantity demanded relative to a given percentage change in price:

$$\text{price elasticity of demand } (e_d) = \frac{\text{percentage change in quantity demanded}}{\text{percentage change in the price}}$$

Price elasticity of demand varies from product to product and industry to industry. Some of the principal influences on elasticity are the availability of substitute products, the price of the item relative to incomes, and whether the price change is perceived as temporary or permanent. If marketers can accurately estimate price elasticity of demand, then management of pricing is much more accurate and profitable:

- Demand is said to be **price elastic** if $e_d$ is greater than 1 (i.e. if the percentage change in the quantity demanded exceeds the percentage change in the price). For example, if a 10 per cent decrease in price leads to a 20 per cent increase in sales volume ($e_d = 20/10 = 2$), then demand is price elastic. In this situation, a change in price causes the opposite change in revenue, so it is generally logical to cut prices (i.e. a price reduction leads to an increase in revenue).

- Demand is said to be **price inelastic** if $e_d$ is less than 1 (i.e. if the percentage change in the quantity demanded is less than the percentage change in price). For example, if a 10 per cent decrease in price leads to only a 5 per cent increase in sales volume ($e_d = 5/10 = 0.5$), then demand is price inelastic. In this situation, a change in price causes the same directional change in revenue, so it is generally logical to increase prices (i.e. a price increase leads to a revenue increase).

Of course, while price elasticity of demand is the starting point for setting prices, it is also necessary to take account of the costs associated with varying sales volumes in order to calculate the impact of price changes on profits.

As can be seen overleaf in figure 8.4(a), a price elastic demand curve is relatively horizontal, illustrating that a small change in price leads to a proportionally larger change in volume. Figure 8.4(b; also overleaf) shows that a price inelastic demand curve is relatively vertical, illustrating that a large change in price leads to a proportionally smaller change in quantity.

Demand for discretionary products such as cinema tickets and confectionery, for example, is usually relatively elastic, and a price fall from $P_1$ to $P_2$ results in a proportionally larger volume increase, from $Q_1$ to $Q_2$ as shown in figure 8.4(a) overleaf. In contrast, demand for the basic necessities of modern life such as water, electricity and petrol is relatively inelastic. In figure 8.4(b) overleaf, a price rise from $P_1$ to $P_2$ results in a proportionally smaller fall in quantity demanded, from $Q_1$ to $Q_2$. It may seem natural for the producers of water, electricity and petrol to raise the price at every opportunity, but other factors such as competition, consumer criticism and government regulation can work to prevent this.

Knowledge of the price elasticity of demand is potentially invaluable in managing prices. Estimating price elasticity of demand or price sensitivity is fundamental to establishing pricing strategy and ongoing price management. By assessing the target market's price sensitivity, the marketer is in a better position to manage price in relation to the other elements of the organisation's offer. Accurately estimating price elasticity, however, is very difficult. In addition, the assumption that all factors other than price are known and remain equal is rarely valid. Price sensitivity will vary from buyer to buyer, product to product, market to market, and over time. Nevertheless, organisations should examine the historical relationship between changes in prices (with adjustments for any inflation) and sales volumes, as this will provide the basis for any assumed or explicit understanding of price elasticity of demand.

**price elastic** Demand for which price elasticity is greater than 1 (i.e. the percentage change in quantity demanded exceeds the percentage change in price).

**price inelastic** Demand for which price elasticity is less than 1 (i.e. the percentage change in quantity demanded is less than the percentage change in price).

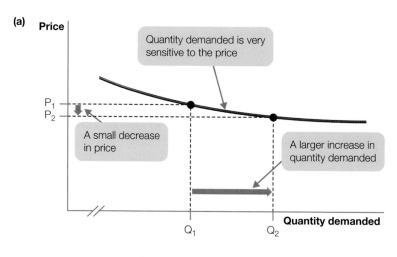

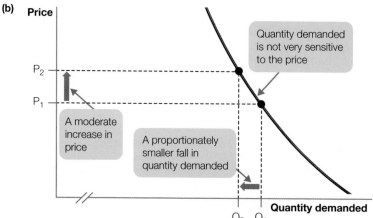

**FIGURE 8.4**

Comparing price elasticity of demand: (a) price elastic demand (b) price inelastic demand

In this section, we examined the relationship between price and demand and how pricing decisions could be made based on an analysis of the price elasticity of demand. We also noted, however, that other factors play an important role in pricing decisions. We will discuss these factors in the following pages and return to them in the last section of the chapter when we look at how the organisation integrates all of the various influences in order to construct a pricing strategy.

## Spotlight Up in smoke

Tobacco smoking is the single most preventable cause of ill health and death in Australia, contributing to more hospitalisations and deaths than alcohol and other illicit drugs combined. The social costs in terms of associated health care are enormous. Smoking increases a person's risk of developing cancer, especially lung cancer, and is also a major risk factor for a range of other serious diseases and conditions — including stroke, coronary heart disease and peripheral vascular disease.

The most recent statistics show that despite the known health risks, around 2.9 million Australians — one in every six people aged 14 years and over — smoke daily. While smoking rates have been declining in recent decades in Australia, alarmingly, more than 43 000 children still start the addictive habit each year. Many vulnerable groups in society are also more likely to smoke — including the unemployed, people unable to work and people who live in lower socioeconomic areas. Indigenous Australians are also more likely to smoke than other Australians.

The Australian government's National Preventative Health Task Force, along with the World Health Organization and the World Bank, recommend price increases as one of the most important measures a government can take to reduce tobacco consumption in a society. It is argued that price increases not only encourage existing smokers to quit (or even reduce the daily quantity of cigarettes they smoke), but also provide a barrier against young people taking up smoking in the first place. According to the National Preventative Health Task Force, teenage smokers are up to eight times more responsive to price increases than smokers aged in their late 20s.

Governments can have a significant impact on the price of cigarettes, as they place an excise tax on the sale of the product. A recent Australian Institute of Health and Welfare survey found that around two-thirds of Australians support increasing the tax on tobacco in order to:

- discourage smoking
- fund health education programs
- contribute to smoking-related treatment costs.

In 2010 the Australian government raised the excise on all tobacco products by 25 per cent, though this was well short of the National Preventative Health Task Force's recommended increase of 68 per cent. The government's overall target is to reduce the smoking rate to 10 per cent of the Australian population by 2018, through a combination of price increases, education campaigns, and the introduction of plain packaging (discussed earlier in chapter 7).[6]

## Questions

1. Evaluate the Australian government's pricing strategy in relation to the concept of price elasticity of demand.

2. Assume the Australian government's pricing strategy is successful and contributes to reaching the 2018 target. Construct a demand curve to reflect this (for the purposes of constructing the diagram, ignore the impact of education campaigns and plain packaging in reducing smoking statistics).

## Concepts and applications check

**Learning objective 2** analyse demand to inform the development of an appropriate pricing strategy

2.1 Explain the typical demand curve, including the relationship between price and sales, in your own words.

2.2 Using your knowledge of consumer behaviour, how would you explain a 'backward sloping' demand curve that can occur for some prestige products?

2.3 Would price competition be an effective strategy for a product whose demand could be categorised as inelastic? Justify your answer.

2.4 List five products with elastic demand and five with inelastic demand.

# COST AND REVENUE ANALYSIS

Profits represent the difference between total revenues and total costs. Profitability and prosperity require that, on average, over the long term, revenues exceed costs. To effectively manage pricing based on costs, organisations must understand the composition of their total costs. The cost mix includes *fixed costs*, which do not vary

**Learning objective 3**
describe the principles of pricing based on cost and revenue analysis

with changes in output, and *variable costs*, which do vary with changes in output. Variable costs may also be viewed in terms of *marginal costs*, which is simply the variable cost expressed in terms of the cost per extra unit of production. Some costs may be shared across different products and these are known, logically enough, as *shared costs*. Shared costs may include advertising, selling, distribution, and research and development.

**price floor** A minimum price that must be charged to cover costs.

Costs establish a **price floor**, below which prices are not sustainable for a for-profit organisation. Even though a business may sell at a loss for a short period of time (e.g. to generate cash flow, attract customers to trial a new product or achieve some other pricing objective), it cannot maintain such an approach. During an economic downturn, organisations need to closely manage their costs as their prices come under pressure from intense competition and softening consumer demand.

As products approach the maturity phase of the product life cycle (see chapter 7), it can become difficult to increase sales volumes and so pressure mounts to lower prices, which requires a lowering of costs. The need to lower costs is one of the reasons behind the trend to 'offshore' various aspects of production to lower-cost countries, including China, India, Malaysia and Mexico.

To properly manage pricing, it is necessary to develop a detailed understanding of the relationships between price, demand and costs, and the resultant link to profits. In the absence of such an understanding, organisations that pursue sales volume and market share as pricing objectives may find themselves unprofitable. This is a common mistake made by low-cost operators. They may achieve their sales and market share goals, but the failure to cover their costs will force them out of business, or at least force them to revise their pricing. On the other hand, pricing a small number of key, high-volume products below the usual retail price, near or below cost can be an effective way to encourage trial purchases and quickly establish market share. If priced near cost, a product is called a **price leader**; if priced below cost, it is called a **loss leader**. Such pricing is designed to attract customers into the store (to generate 'store traffic') and make the organisation's pricing more competitive. Within the supermarket, department store and restaurant sectors in which it is most used, the organisation expects that customers drawn to the store will also purchase other products to offset any loss of margins in the price leader products.

**price leader** A high-volume product priced near cost to attract customers into the store, where it is expected they will buy other, normally priced, products.

**loss leader** A high-volume product priced below cost to attract customers into the store, where it is expected they will buy other, normally priced, products.

Price-sensitive, value-conscious customers can force retailers and service providers to provide enhanced value, often at unchanged or even lower prices. For example, the supermarket business in Australia and New Zealand operates on very small profit margins (frequently less than 5 per cent). In these circumstances, it is crucial for marketers to understand the relationship between retail prices, sales volume, costs and, ultimately, profits. Economics provides marketers with two useful approaches to understanding these relationships: break-even analysis and marginal analysis.

## Break-even analysis

**break-even analysis** An analysis designed to estimate the volume of unit sales required to cover total costs.

A **break-even analysis** determines the volume of unit sales at which total costs equals total revenue. This is known as the 'break-even point'. Estimating the break-even point is a crucial starting point for pricing, especially for new products. Obviously, if the expected sales volume will not meet the break-even point over the life of a product, then the product should not be launched. Break-even analysis can be conducted for a specific period, a project or the life of a product.

A break-even analysis requires an understanding of total costs and total revenues. As we learned earlier, total costs comprise:

* *fixed costs* — costs that do not vary with changes in the volume of production or sales; for example, office rent payments (sometimes referred to as *overheads*)

- *variable costs* — costs that vary directly with changes in the volume of production or sales; for example, money paid for raw materials, packaging and sales commissions.

Assume that a small snowboard manufacturer has fixed costs of $80 000 a year (including rent, insurance and ongoing magazine advertisements) and variable costs of $250 per snowboard manufactured and sold (including raw materials, labour, packaging and transport). We can plot these costs on a break-even chart, as shown in blue in figure 8.5. It can be seen that if 100 snowboards are manufactured and sold, total costs are:

$$\$80\,000 \text{ (fixed costs)} + 100 \times \$250 \text{ (variable costs)} = \$105\,000$$

For 500 snowboards, total costs are $205 000 (i.e. $80 000 × 500 × $250) and so on. Total revenue is the product of:
- *total sales volume* — the number of units sold
- *unit price* — the price charged per unit.

Assume our snowboard manufacturer sells its snowboards for $450. This is plotted in green on the break-even chart in figure 8.5 (see overleaf). It can be seen that eventually the total revenue line and the total cost line meet. This is the break-even point. For this example, the break-even point is at 400 units (when total costs and total revenues equal $180 000). For volumes below 400 units, the snowboard manufacturer's total costs exceed its total revenues. At such volumes it will make a loss (or be 'in the red'). Beyond 400 units, the snowboard manufacturer will be profitable (or be 'in the black').

The break-even point can also be derived mathematically using the equation:

$$\text{break-even point (volume)} = \frac{\text{fixed costs}}{\text{price per unit} - \text{variable costs per unit}}$$

For the snowboard example:

$$\text{break-even point (volume)} = \frac{\$80\,000}{\$450 - \$250}$$

$$= \frac{\$80\,000}{\$200}$$

$$= 400 \text{ units}$$

The difference between the price and the variable cost per unit is known as 'contribution margin'. In the snowboard example, the contribution margin is $450 − $250 = $200. The contribution margin is the amount per unit sold that contributes to offsetting the fixed costs and, once the break-even point has been reached, contributes to profits. (Prior to the break-even point, the gap between the revenue line and total cost line represents losses; after the break-even point, the gap represents profits). In the break-even chart and the equation, we have assumed a price of $450, but the chart and equation allow the marketer to examine different possible prices and volumes. In the chart, the price is represented by the slope of the revenue line. Higher prices result in a steeper line and thus a lower break-even volume; lower prices result in a flatter line and thus a higher break-even volume.

Break-even analysis is therefore the starting point to understanding the relationship between costs and selling price. In using break-even analysis, it is important to test the price and volume sensitivity to ensure that the break-even volume is feasible (i.e. price is not set so high that it will deter sales volume; nor is it set so low that the required sales volume can never be achieved).

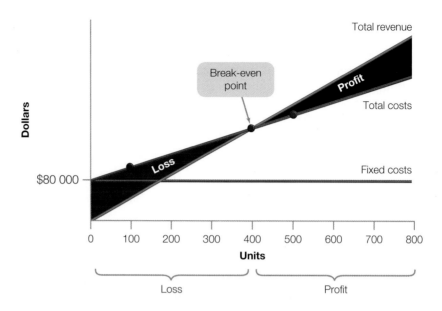

FIGURE 8.5

A break-even chart

While break-even analysis is undoubtedly important, and relatively easy to calculate, it is also important to recognise that break-even analysis is focused only on establishing the volume of sales necessary to cover costs. There is no guarantee that this volume can, or will, be sold. The focus is therefore solely on breaking even; and not on establishing desirable or attainable sales objectives.

## Marginal analysis

**marginal analysis** An analysis designed to determine the effect on costs and revenue when an organisation produces and sells one more unit of product.

**Marginal analysis** is concerned with understanding the effect on costs and revenue when a company produces and sells one more unit of product. As long as the additional revenue earned from selling one more unit exceeds the cost of supplying that additional unit, then that single sale contributes positively to the organisation's profits. Conversely, if the marginal cost to supply one more unit exceeds the marginal revenue, then that sale is unprofitable and total profits decline. As such, marginal analysis allows the organisation to identify the combination of price and output that will maximise total profit.

Marginal analysis can be useful in pricing individual units of output or to individual buyers. For example, it can be used in pricing individually negotiated sales or supply transactions, such as when a car manufacturer or distributor agrees to supply a government department.

To undertake marginal analysis, an organisation needs to understand and evaluate its costs and revenues. Costs must be examined in terms of:

- *average cost*. Average cost is the total cost divided by volume of production. The average cost for a product initially falls as production is increased and economies of scale are realised; eventually, however, average cost increases as production exceeds the maximum volume at which it is most efficient.
- *marginal cost*. Marginal cost represents the cost to produce and sell *one more unit* of output. Just as for average costs, marginal costs initially decline with increases in output, but eventually rise.

Revenues must be examined in terms of:

- *average revenue*. Average revenue is the total revenue divided by unit sales volume.
- *marginal revenue*. Marginal revenue is the revenue obtained by selling *one more unit* of the product.

Profit is maximised by selling the quantity at which marginal cost *equals* marginal revenue. Before this point (i.e. where marginal cost is less than marginal revenue), the organisation can increase its profits by selling more units. Beyond this point (i.e. where marginal cost *exceeds* marginal revenue), each additional unit sold actually incurs a loss for the business.

Clearly, marginal analysis is potentially very useful. Such an analysis, however, requires detailed data on actual and estimated costs and revenues at all volumes and prices. Marginal analysis is therefore difficult to implement precisely. A further challenge in this sort of analysis is that it is even more difficult to estimate marginal cost and marginal revenue when launching new products, before costs and demand patterns have been clearly established.

Nevertheless, marginal analysis is a useful tool to assist in pricing decisions, especially in industries characterised by high fixed and low variable (and marginal) costs, such as hotels, airlines, telecommunications, education and mass entertainment. In these industries, it is important for organisations to maximise their revenue by ensuring that each unit of output is actually sold. For example, for an airline to fly a plane from Auckland to Sydney, it involves a large fixed cost and only a small marginal cost per passenger. It is important, therefore, that pricing is set to fill as many vacant seats on the aircraft as possible, so long as marginal revenue exceeds the marginal cost. With entertainment products like concert tickets, a key to such pricing is to ensure that each customer pays the highest price that they are willing to pay and that individual customers do not establish a 'black market', which occurs, for example, when concert tickets are illegally 'scalped'. There are also potential ethical implications in the assumption that all customers will be prepared to pay the maximum price, and also that individual customers may pay very different prices for the same product.

## Pricing based on costs

Pricing approaches based on costs are concerned primarily with achieving target profit margins and aggregate profits. In **cost-based pricing**, the selling organisation adds a percentage or dollar amount to the cost of the product. The amount added is the organisation's profit. Cost-based pricing approaches are usually either cost-plus pricing or markup pricing.

**cost-based pricing**
An approach to pricing in which a percentage or dollar amount is added to the cost of the product in order to determine its selling price.

*Cost-plus pricing* is often used when it is difficult or impossible to determine the costs of the product until it has been made or completed. This is often the case for large, complex projects such as roads, defence equipment and information technology installations. In such cases, the seller adds their required profit margin as a dollar amount or percentage to the costs once the project is complete. The disadvantage for the buyer, of course, is that they cannot be assured of the final price they will pay.

*Markup pricing* is used by wholesalers and retailers and involves adding a percentage of their purchase cost to determine the resale price. The more parties there are in the chain between producer and consumer, the more times markup is added to the product. Markup percentages are usually fairly similar, if not standardised, within a particular retail sector. For example, markup on food and groceries is about 10–20 per cent, and markup on high fashion is about 100 per cent. Most retailers adopt a consistent markup for ease of administration. Markup can be expressed in two ways: *percentage of cost* and *percentage of selling price* (or 'margin'). If a retailer buys a pair of jeans for $75 and sells them for $150, the markup ($75) expressed as a percentage of cost ($75) is 100 per cent. The markup ($75) expressed as a percentage of selling price ($150) is 50 per cent.

Cost-based pricing using a markup is attractive in its simplicity and its guarantee that all units sold will be profitable. However, there is no guarantee that a cost-based pricing approach will result in a price which is competitive and which customers are willing to pay.

**Black hole tunnels**

Constructing a tunnel to ease city traffic congestion is a massive infrastructure project. Governments typically partially or fully outsource the construction, ownership and operation of such projects to private enterprise. In recent times, the financial success of these ventures has been abysmal. Ineffective toll pricing and ambitious traffic volume forecasting have led to high-profile receiverships, with operators discovering that they couldn't generate enough revenue to break even, much less run a profitable venture. Consider the sobering statistics that are represented in the table with this Spotlight.

| Tunnel (year of opening) | Construction cost | Initial forecast for daily traffic | Actual daily traffic, Year 1 | Outcome for initial operator |
| --- | --- | --- | --- | --- |
| Cross City, Sydney (2005) | $900 million plus | 90 000 | 30 000 | Cross City Motorway placed into receivership (2006) |
| Lane Cove, Sydney (2007) | $1.6 billion | More than 100 000 | 55 435 | Connector Motorways placed into receivership (2010) |
| Clem7, Brisbane (2010) | $3 billion | 60 000 | 22 000 | RiverCity Motorway reported a $1.67 billion loss (30 June 2010) and was soon placed into receivership (2011) |

After an initial free month to encourage drivers to use the tunnel, the operators of Brisbane's Clem7 (RiverCity Motorway) set an initial 'special toll price' for cars of $2.95, with plans to increase the toll after three months to $4.28. This was the 'standard' toll on which the company had based their initial tunnel traffic estimates and revenue forecasts. However, as the traffic volumes continued to fall well short of forecasts, and in a desperate bid to increase volume, the operators indefinitely slashed the toll even further to $2 per car. 'Our decision to reduce tolls is in response to feedback from Brisbane motorists that they are more likely to use the tunnel if the toll is set at $2', said Fran Cleary, chief executive of the Clem7 operator, RiverCity Motorway.

In November 2010, the company increased the toll for the tunnel from $2 to $3 per car, with similar increases in fees for other vehicle types. In an open letter, Mr Cleary said that even though the volume of trips had increased by 35 per cent, the discounts could not continue. In February 2011, RiverCity Motorway was placed in receivership, owing $1.3 billion to a syndicate of 24 banks. In March 2011, it was announced that tolls for the Clem7 would increase again — rising to $3.95 per car in April 2011.[7]

### Question

Imagine you are the marketing manager for RiverCity Motorway and evaluate the pricing strategy for the Clem7 tunnel. How would you attempt to increase traffic volume?

## Concepts and applications check

**Learning objective 3** describe the principles of pricing based on cost and revenue analysis

**3.1** Generally, costs establish a price floor. Explain why prices may sometimes be set below cost.

**3.2** Under what circumstances would a 'loss leader' pricing strategy be appropriate for an organisation?

**3.3** Explain break-even analysis, using your own example.

**3.4** 'Marginal analysis is especially relevant for organisations with high fixed costs and low variable costs.' Prepare an argument to support this statement.

## COMPETITION CONSIDERATIONS

Organisations that engage in price competition seek to match or better their competitors' prices. Price competition usually emerges when competitors' offerings are not significantly differentiated in the minds of consumers. In this situation, consumers naturally seek the lowest price. They will readily switch suppliers, often for minimal savings. While all markets will contain price-sensitive customers (usually in the vicinity of 25 to 30 per cent of customers), it is usually difficult to build a long-term sustainable strategy based on targeting these customers, unless the organisation has a sustainably lower cost structure. Price competition is undesirable from a seller's point of view, unless the seller has a cost advantage. A cost advantage arises when the organisation is the lowest cost supplier in the industry. It can arise through:

**Learning objective 4** explain the role of competitive analysis in determining pricing

- *economies of scale in purchasing.* For example, Bunnings hardware advertises that it will refund in full, plus add 10 per cent of the purchase price, if it fails to match the price of its competitors (under specified conditions). For Bunnings to make such an offer, it needs to be confident that it is the lowest cost supplier, which is plausible, given its sales volumes and its economies of scale. Given its lowest cost position, Bunnings is still likely to be the most profitable — even if its competitors' match its prices.
- *low-cost production, often based on the country of origin.* For example, the Korean car manufacturer Hyundai (which also owns Kia) has enjoyed lower costs than its European, Australian or Japanese competitors. Previously, this position enabled Hyundai and Kia to achieve a strong share of the new car market based on price competition. The emergence of Chinese manufacturers was expected to be one factor threatening Korean manufacturers' cost advantage. Hyundai has more recently repositioned its brand, creating differentiation with a premium dimension, rather than heavily emphasising price. Today, the company differentiates its brand on the basis of design, safety and quality — as well as affordability. It promoted its first hybrid car, the 2011 Hyundai Sonata Hybrid, on the basis of quality, describing the model as a 'hybrid in a tuxedo'.[8]

Approaches to pricing based on competition are appropriate in highly competitive markets in which consumers base their purchasing decisions primarily on price. Competition-based pricing involves setting prices based on the prices charged by competitors or on the likely response of competitors to the organisation's prices. **Competition-based pricing** serves to ensure that an organisation maintains its sales volumes and market share, but it does not guarantee profitability. Supermarkets, hardware stores, electronics retailers and discount department stores all rely on competition-based pricing.

Businesses using competition-based pricing can choose to set their prices at a level above, the same as, or below the prices charged by their main competitors,

**competition-based pricing** An approach to pricing based on the prices charged by competitors or on the likely response of competitors to the organisation's prices.

depending on the other aspects of the marketing mix. The major supermarket chains, for example, closely scrutinise the prices charged by their main competitors, especially on high-volume items such as milk, bread, laundry detergent and soft drinks. Companies adopting competition-based pricing must also decide whether they should 'lag' or 'lead' the market in price changes. An organisation that 'leads the market going up' or 'lags the market coming down' can improve its profit margins relative to the competition.

Price competition can result in price volatility, as is the case in petrol retailing, where prices can move more than 10 per cent in a day. If one organisation seeks to achieve an advantage through lower prices, it is inevitable that competitors will respond quickly. Under such circumstances, 'price wars' can break out. If they continue for a substantial period of time, they may ultimately force weaker competitors from the market. Price competition is therefore a difficult strategy to sustain over the long term unless an organisation enjoys clear market or cost advantages. For other organisations, the lack of a cost advantage usually implies that price competition should only be initiated in very rare cases, and then for only brief periods. The entry of Woolworths and Coles into the petrol retailing market in Australia has made it difficult for independent operators to survive, as they are less able to sustain low prices.

The entry of Woolworths and Coles into the petrol retailing market in Australia has made it difficult for independent operators to survive, as they are less able to sustain low prices.

In developed economies such as those of Australia and New Zealand, long-term price competition can thus create oligopolies in which the market is dominated by a small number of large suppliers, each selling similar products. In Australia and New Zealand, the markets for steel, banking, petrol, concrete and air travel are oligopolistic, and any price cuts initiated by one organisation are usually matched immediately by competitors. Organisations that find themselves competing within oligopolies are therefore forced to compete on a non-price basis by emphasising their differentiation in such aspects as brand image, customer service and distribution channels.

## Understanding competitors' pricing

A business should almost always consider prices set by its competitors, although the importance of competitors' prices will vary with the number and intensity of competitors in a market and with the degree of perceived uniqueness of the business's products. In price-sensitive industries (e.g. the supermarket, liquor and petrol sectors), organisations monitor their competitors' prices on a daily or even more frequent basis. In responding to competitors' prices, a business can choose to price above or below them, or to closely match their prices.

The likely response of competitors to the organisation's pricing will in part be determined by the competitive structure of the industry. Within the Australian and New Zealand marketplaces, there is a growing tendency towards greater levels of economic concentration; that is, where particular industry sectors are dominated by fewer, but larger players (e.g. in the banking sector through acquisitions such as Westpac's purchase of St George). As discussed in chapter 2, under such circumstances, *oligopolies* may arise in which there are only a small number of large players selling a relatively undifferentiated product. This is true in banking, airlines, petrol retail, and steel and concrete production. In such industries, any price move by one company is likely to be reflected quickly in the pricing of its competitors. In particular, if a business lowers its prices, its competitors will quickly lower theirs. On the other hand, if one business raises its prices, competitors may take the opportunity to raise theirs as well; if they do not, the first business is likely to be forced to lower its prices again, as it will not be competitive. It is clear, then, that there is very little likelihood of securing a competitive advantage through price competition in an oligopoly. Organisations in oligopolies tend to compete on a non-price basis through variables such as service quality, customer relationships or branding.

An organisation that operates as a *monopoly* (traditionally gas and electricity suppliers and telecommunications companies) can, by definition, determine price without regard for competition. This suggests monopoly organisations have considerable ability to maximise profits through pricing since, regardless of price, consumers have no alternative supplier. However, to exploit their monopoly position in this way will invite government intervention. Governments are intolerant of monopoly actions, including pricing, that are against the overall public interest. Government-owned monopolies, such as bus and rail operators, often price products below cost to encourage their use and to ensure the community can access them. For example, most public health care is provided well below cost. Government-owned monopolies might also choose to set high prices in order to limit demand for scarce resources such as parking spaces in beachside tourist towns (thus encouraging people to walk or use public transport).

At the other end of the scale, in a *perfectly competitive* market, a large number of buyers and sellers sell undifferentiated (commodity) products, such as fruit and vegetables, wheat, flour and rice. Under such market conditions, the individual seller has no control over the price. The lowest price a seller is willing to sell for becomes the market price at which all of the products are bought and sold. Organisations operating in such perfectly competitive markets are therefore 'price takers' and, under such circumstances, the individual business should endeavour to find some way to differentiate its products. For example, the growers of Sunkist oranges have successfully created a brand for an otherwise undifferentiated product. The brand has a reputation for high-quality, flavoursome oranges and Sunkist growers enjoy global market leadership and higher than average prices as a result.

Organisations operating in markets characterised as *monopolistic competition* have numerous competitors, whose product offerings are differentiated by design, quality brand image and product features. To the extent that a company's product is perceived to be unique, the organisation enjoys considerable flexibility in its prices. In general, however, organisations operating in monopolistic competition will seek to differentiate themselves and to compete on factors other than price. In this sense, the existence of intense price competition is evidence of the lack of meaningful product differentiation.

The extent to which consumers base their decisions on price comparisons between competitors is influenced by purchasing costs, including time, travel and inconvenience, and their ability to actually compare prices. Some organisations provide a price guarantee to their customers that they will beat competitors' advertised prices. Some online stores can charge higher prices and delivery charges because of the convenience they provide. The internet has also made price comparisons much easier for consumers. They can 'visit' multiple outlets without leaving their home or use an online service such as WebJet (for airfares) and iSelect (for private health insurance) to find the cheapest price for their desired product. The state motoring organisations such as NRMA, RACQ and RACV also monitor and publish fuel prices on their websites.

In competitive industries, it is important to develop a close understanding of competitors' prices and how competitors are likely to react to the organisation's prices or price changes. In highly price-sensitive sectors such as supermarkets, systematically checking on the prices of competitors is a daily activity. In the business-to-business markets, it can be very difficult to establish competitors' prices, since they are unlikely to be published publicly and unlikely to be disclosed by customers. In many markets, prices are negotiated and the final price may not be publicly declared. In other markets, major customers can negotiate purchases at extremely advantageous terms, especially when they purchase in large volumes. Such prices may not be available to competitors, and therefore large intermediaries have a distinct advantage in reselling these products. For example, electronic retailers such as Harvey Norman and Bing Lee compete to secure advantageous purchase prices from their suppliers, which they can pass on to their retail customers. Under such circumstances, retailers do not compete directly item by item, but rather seek to draw in-store traffic through low 'headline prices'.

In some markets, major customers can negotiate purchases on extremely good terms, especially when they purchase in large volumes. Harvey Norman uses this strategy and passes on advantageous prices to its retail customers.

This hints at the importance of also understanding competitors' costs, of which the 'buy price' is the basis of profit margin and the competitor's willingness and ability to cut price. By understanding individual competitors' fixed and variable costs, it is possible to anticipate the competitor's likely response to the organisation's price or to price changes. In general, competitors with higher fixed and lower variable costs will find it difficult to lower their prices to defend their market share from any loss in sales volume. Conversely, competitors with lower fixed and higher variable costs will suffer and fight to defend any loss in profit margins. How competitors' costs and prices are affected by the organisation's prices can vary from indifference through to aggressive price wars to defend market shares. The organisation therefore needs to clearly analyse the likely response of competitors to its pricing strategy or tactical pricing decisions. In particular, the marketer should avoid provoking a competitive retaliation by larger competitors.

## Alternatives to competing on price

As explained in chapter 2, marketing strategies need to be based on a thorough understanding of the competitive environment. In general, most organisations seek to compete using a strategy of 'differentiation', which emphasises the uniqueness of the organisation's products. To the extent that the organisation's products are perceived to be unique, the organisation can distance itself from direct price competition and thus charge higher prices. Organisations with a strategy of differentiation focus on product attributes such as uniqueness, quality, brand, image or service. When it is feasible, non-price competition is clearly preferable to price competition as it gives the organisation greater power to decide on the profit margin per unit sold.

For most organisations, non-price competition should form the basis of the competitive strategy. Organisations that engage in non-price competition focus on differentiating their offer from competitors' offers through product, promotion and distribution factors. It is not feasible for organisations to totally ignore the prices charged by their competitors, but the greater the extent to which they can achieve uniqueness, or at least the perception of uniqueness in the minds of consumers, the greater the freedom they will have in setting prices.

A strategy of non-price competition requires the organisation to develop in customers a preference for the organisation's products based on factors other than price. To be effective, the organisation must successfully differentiate itself from competitors by the provision of unique product attributes such as:

- product quality (e.g. Lexus)
- innovation (e.g. Apple)
- brand image (e.g. Mont Blanc)
- styling (e.g. Bang & Olufsen)
- customer service (e.g. Singapore Airlines)
- distribution coverage (e.g. Commonwealth Bank)
- local convenience (e.g. Baker's Delight).

Ideally, competitive strategy should be based on differentiation which is substantial, recognised and valued by customers, and which cannot be easily replicated by competitors. This enables an organisation to build loyalty among its customers and that loyalty can, to a certain extent, insulate the organisation from the price offers of its competitors. For example, Bob McTavish was an early pioneer of surfing in Australia. Forty years later, McTavish Longboards, which are priced at a premium, remain a board of choice, particularly among older surfers.

Pricing can also be used to promote stability in the marketplace. Pricing for stability places a greater emphasis on non-price competition among industry participants. When an organisation is satisfied with its position in the market, it can use pricing to maintain market share, achieving price and competitive stability, maintain a favourable market image, or preserve existing relationships with customers and partners. Stability can be an important pricing objective for a market leader, as it can reinforce its market position while minimising costs. At the same time, smaller market competitors may choose to pursue stability to avoid provoking price wars or the competitive attentions of a market leader.

# The price of interest

Interest rates on loans, mortgages and overdrafts can be regarded as the principal pricing tool available to banks (another tool, though comparatively less substantial in terms of raising revenue, is the fees charged on banking transactions and other services). Imagine a couple who take out a typical first home mortgage of $300 000, with fortnightly repayments to be made over a 25-year term. If the variable interest rate averages 7.5 per cent over that 25-year period, and the loan runs the full term, the couple will pay $364 712 just in interest!

Each home loan a bank signs with customers is therefore an extremely lucrative piece of long-term revenue, and competition among banks for home loan business is fierce. Prices (i.e. interest rates) are at the forefront of this battle. In the past two decades, 'non-bank' lenders, such as Aussie Home Loans, have also aggressively entered the home loan market, with their founder John Symond's catchcry 'At Aussie, we'll save you' becoming a familiar refrain.

Banks (and non-bank lenders) generally offer very attractive introductory home loan interest rates, such as discounts off standard variable or fixed rates for the first six or 12 months, or sometimes even for the first two or three years, in order to entice prospective home loan customers to sign with them. The rationale for this from the lenders' point of view is simple. The chances of a customer remaining with a lender for the duration of their mortgage are relatively high. Because

of this, the lender offers an initial discount as a means to attract a customer's home loan business — and maximise the probability that the customer will decide to do business with them.

Of course, interest rates move over time, and existing home loan customers who have variable, rather than fixed, interest rates are subject to rises and falls in their rate. Even something as seemingly small as a 0.25 per cent interest rate rise will add $14 699 in interest repayments over the duration of a 25-year, $300 000 home loan.

Although they aren't the only determinant of interest rate rises (as many lenders source funds offshore), banks and other lenders actively monitor movement in the official rates set by the Reserve Bank of Australia. At times, lenders may raise their rates by more or less than corresponding Reserve Bank movements. In raising their rate by more, a lender can potentially generate more revenue (though it runs the risk of potential negative publicity in the media and leaves itself more vulnerable to competitors). Conversely, a lender may choose to be aggressive and pass on less than an official Reserve Bank rate increase to their loan customers. This is generally done by a lender in the hope that the competitive goodwill generated will attract sufficient new customers to offset any loss in revenue incurred through not passing on the full rate increase to existing customers.[9]

## Question

**Describe the competitive structure of the home loan industry and analyse how competition-based pricing applies to this market.**

---

## Concepts and applications check

**Learning objective 4** explain the role of competitive analysis in determining pricing

**4.1** What are some risks for an organisation in engaging in price competition?

**4.2** Explain how the competitive structure of an industry can impact on price.

**4.3** Provide an example of a product where price competition is an effective marketing strategy, and justify your answer.

**4.4** Explain why most organisations would prefer to engage in non-price competition.

---

# BUSINESS-TO-BUSINESS PRICING

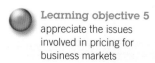

**Learning objective 5** appreciate the issues involved in pricing for business markets

As we learned in chapter 5, business markets consist of individuals and organisations that purchase products for use in the production of other products, for use in their daily business operations, or for resale. In the first two circumstances, a seller is often dealing directly with the end user of the product; for example, an office equipment manufacturer often deals directly with organisational purchasers. In the case of resale, however, the seller may be distributing via intermediaries such as agents, brokers, wholesalers and/or retailers; for example, another office equipment manufacturer may choose to distribute their products via retail outlets. Regardless of the size and complexity of the distribution channel, the factors of demand, costs and competition discussed in this chapter are common to both consumer and business markets.

Business-to-business marketing relationships between suppliers and organisational buyers tend to be close, long-term and formal in nature. This leads to pricing practices that are more formal than those in consumer markets. At the same time, pricing is more complex in the business markets — differences in the size of purchases, the frequency of purchases, geographic factors, costs involved in warehousing and transport, and other considerations often require sellers to adjust prices for individual customers and individual transactions. Thus, price is often much more open to negotiation than in the consumer market, particularly based on purchase volumes. For example, a hospital that purchases 10 000 boxes of latex gloves every year can negotiate a much lower unit price than a small veterinary practice that purchases 50 boxes a year. Business purchasers are also more likely than private consumers to consider lifetime costs involved in a purchase; for example, service costs, running costs and depreciation.

## Pricing for intermediaries

Organisations will only choose to deal with intermediaries who can add value to the organisation's offering. There can be many steps involved between the producer and the consumer. Figure 8.6 shows a typical distribution channel for a consumer product. The transactions between producer, agent/broker, wholesaler and retailer are all business-to-business transactions and involve business-to-business pricing decisions.

**FIGURE 8.6**

Intermediaries in the distribution chain for consumer products

Figure 8.7 shows a typical distribution channel for a business-to-business product that will be used in business operations or as an input to some other product (and will not be resold to consumers). All of the transactions in figure 8.7 involve business-to-business exchanges and therefore business-to-business pricing.

As we will see in chapter 10, the distribution channel may comprise one, some or all of these intermediaries. For example, the operator of a fishing trawler might use a fishermen's cooperative to sell their catch to wholesalers, who in turn sell to retailers, who finally sell to consumers. An electrician on the other hand might deal directly with a landlord or via the landlord's managing agent.

**FIGURE 8.7**

Intermediaries in the distribution chain for business-to-business products

Most producers recommend a final retail price or 'list price' that consumers should pay, but each intermediary needs to make a profit. To ensure the profitable operation of the various partners involved in getting products from the producer to the consumer or organisational buyer, various discounts apply to transactions in the business markets:

- *functional discounts.* Functional (or trade) discounts are a percentage reduction off the list price and are provided by suppliers to marketing intermediaries or business customers in return for the various functions they perform such as retailing, transport and providing credit (see chapter 10). The trade discount forms the basis of the intermediary's profit margin and needs to be competitive with the discounts offered by alternative suppliers.
- *quantity discounts.* Quantity discounts are provided to business customers that purchase large volumes. Quantity discounts are funded by the economies of scale that the seller achieves by supplying in bulk quantities. Quantity discounts can be based on single transactions (non-cumulative discounts) or on the total purchase volume in a specified period (cumulative discounts). Cumulative discounts are sometimes paid as a rebate — an amount of money refunded to the customer based on the purchase volume in the specified period. Quantity discounts result in larger customers receiving lower prices. Cumulative quantity discounts encourage customers to build an ongoing relationship with one supplier rather than to spread their business across suppliers.
- *seasonal discounts.* Seasonal discounts are provided to buyers who purchase products outside the peak selling period of the year. Such discounts are designed

to smooth sales, inventory and distribution costs across the year. For example, hotels and conference venues offer seasonal discounts in off-peak and 'shoulder' periods when bookings would otherwise be low.

- *cash discounts.* Cash discounts are offered to customers who pay promptly and who thus save the supplier time and money in managing and collecting accounts receivable. Discounts are based on cash payments made within the stated time. For example, '2/10 net 60' means a 2 per cent discount will be applied if the account is paid within 10 days; the total balance is due within 60 days; and beyond 60 days interest or penalties may be charged.

## Pricing for distribution

The costs of shipping products can vary greatly, particularly in a geographically large country such as Australia. Transporting cartons of frozen fish from one side of Darwin to the other is obviously much cheaper than transporting the same cartons to Launceston or an international market. Businesses deal with these issues through a **geographic pricing** strategy, which includes price differentials that reflect the different costs involved in selling to buyers in different locations.

A seller may charge:

- a 'freight on board destination' price (abbreviated to FOB destination), which means the seller has built the transport costs in to the price
- a 'freight on board origin' (FOB origin) price, which means the price excludes the delivery costs, which must then be met by the buyer.

The more complex the price differentials built in to a geographic pricing strategy, the more difficult and expensive it is to administer. Some organisations simply adopt uniform geographic pricing in which the transport costs for all buyers are averaged out and built in to the price charged to all customers. A level of sophistication can be added to this approach to devise zone pricing, in which price differentials are charged based on geographical regions (e.g. the states of Australia). For example, customers in South Australia may be required to pay higher transport costs from a supplier in Sydney than customers in Victoria.

**geographic pricing** A pricing strategy that includes price differentials based on those costs that vary with distance between the buyer and seller.

This model has come under threat in recent times with the advent of electronic books that consumers can download directly to laptop computers and also to other devices, such as iPads. It is now possible for consumers who know what they want to download free software applications and an electronic book version (often supplied direct from the publisher) for an increasing array of titles. The attraction of this model for consumers and publishers is the potential for cheaper prices. As opposed to physical books, there are no printing, warehousing or distribution costs for electronic books, and if publishers set up online shopping cart facilities for the purchase of e-books, there is theoretically no need for the hefty intermediary margin traditionally necessary to enable book retailers to stock and sell publisher's products. Of course, this new distribution and pricing model assumes that consumers largely know what books they want, and are prepared to read them on an electronic device.

### Question

**Imagine you are the marketing manager for a major publishing house, and are preparing for a meeting with the marketing manager of a major retail book franchise, such as Dymocks, to discuss pricing terms. Outline the potential disadvantages of reducing the retailer's margin in light of the new e-book pricing environment.**

## Concepts and applications check

**Learning objective 5** appreciate the issues involved in pricing for business markets

5.1 Why might a business marketer be prepared to offer a trade discount?

5.2 Provide your own examples of a product or industry in which the following price discounting methods may be an effective business-to-business pricing strategy:
(a) quantity discount
(b) seasonal discount.

5.3 Prepare an argument for and against this statement: 'Marketing intermediaries increase the price of products to consumers.'

## PRICE MANAGEMENT

**Learning objective 6**
understand how to manage prices as part of the marketing mix

Having considered both the underlying economic principles of pricing and the range of issues which an organisation should consider when developing its pricing strategy, our attention now turns to the important issue of determining and managing prices.

The attitudes and likely behaviours of customers are clearly at the heart of all marketing decisions. For marketers, a crucial question is 'How do our current and target customers perceive our price?' Customer perceptions are of course subjective and particular to each individual, but it is important that marketers try to match pricing as closely as possible to customers' expectations. Prices above customers' expectations will result in the loss of potential sales — and all other marketing activities will have been wasted. Prices below customers' expectations sacrifice revenue and profits, as well as potentially destroying the product's image and the organisation's brand equity.

### The psychology of pricing

Consumer purchasing behaviour is usually based on a rational evaluation of value. The relative importance of price varies between individual consumers, however. For example, consumers who are particularly price conscious may concern themselves primarily with price when making purchasing decisions. Other consumers, however, may be more concerned with prestige; for them, price is only relevant in so far as it contributes to that sense of prestige. An important indicator of the importance of price in consumers' purchasing decisions is the perceived uniqueness or differentiation of the product. For example, Apple has enjoyed considerable success with its iPod, iPhone and iPad products by creating the perception that its products are technologically advanced, very user-friendly and uniquely styled. This perception enables Apple to charge premium prices, while maintaining very high levels of customer satisfaction and loyalty.

Different market segments will have varying levels of sensitivity to price. For example, David Jones customers will respond differently to price changes than Kmart customers. In general, however, it can be assumed that a proportion of consumers in many markets can be characterised as 'price shoppers' and businesses need to decide if these customers will be included in their target markets. While all customers will ultimately be concerned with value, what customers regard as value is personal and, at times, idiosyncratic. Some customers will regard value in terms of low price, while others will see value as high quality at reasonable prices. At the same time, these perceptions will vary across product categories, and over time, especially over economic cycles between booms and recession.

## Customer value perceptions

Customers' attitudes to price can be extremely variable and predicting customers' responses to particular prices can prove difficult. All customers will have a notional price range or specific price in mind when contemplating a purchase. When the retail price falls outside that price range, buyers might experience 'price tag shock'. Some approaches to pricing attempt to influence how buyers perceive prices. The seller may, for instance, implement pricing based on 'trigger points'; that is, prices at which buyers' resistance is appreciably lower. For example, a product priced at just under $100 (even $99.95) may psychologically be significantly more attractive than a price of just over $100 (e.g. $104.95) to certain market segments. Specific forms of psychological pricing that attempt to manage customers' perceptions of value are summarised in table 8.2.

**TABLE 8.2** Managing customers' perceptions of value and price

| Approach | Description | Example | Advantages | Disadvantages |
|---|---|---|---|---|
| Odd–even pricing | Pricing based on the theory that odd prices are perceived as significantly cheaper than even prices | Prices are often set to $19.95 or $99.95 rather than $20 or $100 respectively | Manages customers' perceptions of price and value | Research on the effectiveness of this technique is inconclusive |
| | The use of idiosyncratic prices to attract attention and create the perception that the price is discounted to the lowest amount possible | Prices such as $17.58 are unusual | | |
| Reference pricing | Pricing a product at a moderate level and positioning it next to a more expensive model | 'Upsize' deals at fast food restaurants<br><br>Real estate agents frequently show buyers properties outside their price range before showing the most suitable property | The customer may use the higher price as a relevant comparison; that is, as an external reference price<br><br>The customer may choose to 'trade up' to the more expensive product | Upsize deals have drawn criticism from health groups for contributing to obesity |

| Approach | Description | Example | Advantages | Disadvantages |
|---|---|---|---|---|
| *Multiple-unit pricing* | Multiple units of a product are sold for a single price, usually significantly lower per unit than the individual price | Ice creams are sold in six-packs in supermarkets<br><br>Batteries are offered in a range of pack sizes, from single batteries to several dozen<br><br>Wine and beer are available per case or per carton respectively | Customers save by buying at a low unit price<br><br>Customers benefit from convenient bulk packaging<br><br>Retailers gain from higher aggregate sales<br><br>Consumption of products may increase, due to the ready availability of the product at home | Margin per product may be lower |
| *Bundle pricing* | Selling a combination of complementary products for a single price, which is less than the sum of the individual product prices | Fast food 'meal deals'<br><br>'Run out' deals on cars, in which the manufacturers bundle popular combinations of extras at a lower incremental price than if the extras were purchased separately | Offers extra value to the customer<br><br>Can increase the overall sale | May undermine pricing of unbundled products |

As explained at the start of this chapter, customers assess value by comparing expected product benefits with the price. Of course, this is often difficult to do prior to purchase. Customers thus often use *reference prices* to help them form an impression of value and price. For familiar products such as beer, soft drinks and petrol, consumers have clear expectations about an acceptable price range based on past experience. In other words, they have an **internal reference price** for the product. For less familiar products, however, consumers are more likely to rely on an **external reference price**, such as a comparison price provided by retailers, advertisers or salespersons. For example, during a stocktake sale, a retailer may claim that the usual price for an LCD television is $3995, but is on sale now for $2495. It is important that manufacturers and retailers ensure that this external reference price is realistic; otherwise potential buyers will reject the message. Consumers' reference prices are also influenced by their most recent purchases and their expectations of prices in the future. For example, buyers of imported products such as most cars and premium electronic equipment may base their reference prices and purchases on the likely future exchange rate. Consumers will also consider their purchasing costs including time, travel, inconvenience and uncertainty.

**internal reference price**
The price expected by consumers, largely based upon their actual experience with the product.

**external reference price**
A price comparison provided by the manufacturer or retailer.

As discussed earlier, a marketing exchange is unlikely to take place unless both parties gain value from it. In some cases, however, one party may feel it has no choice; for example, a person who loses their job and cannot meet their mortgage repayments may have to sell their house and accept whatever price they can get for it. Even in less drastic circumstances, a person seeking to sell their home may be forced to accept less than they had hoped for if they want to complete the transaction. In such circumstances, where sellers feel they have little choice but to sell at the offered price, they will experience dissatisfaction in the sale and will try to avoid engaging in a similar transaction in future. Similar dissatisfaction can arise whenever a purchaser or seller feels they have not benefited from the marketing exchange. Such dissatisfaction is highly unlikely to result in lasting relationships between buyers and sellers.

For many organisations, it can be advantageous to set prices for groups of products rather than to set a price for each individual product. This approach is known as **product-line pricing**. It ensures consistency in pricing over a product line, while enabling the prices of individual products to be adjusted to meet the needs of particular market segments. For example, when Sony prices its Bravia LCD televisions, there are clear price steps between different sizes of screens and different levels of features. Sony is therefore able to cover the entire spectrum from entry-level to high-end products, and to provide a progressive transition to enable customers to consider taking the next step up in price. An example of product-line pricing is setting a limited number of prices for selected groups or lines of merchandise. This approach is known as *price lining*. For example, a computer retailer may sell notebook computers in three price ranges: $1000, $1500 and $2000. Such an approach reduces the importance of price differences factor in consumer decisions once the price *range* is chosen. It emphasises factors other than price.

## Pricing throughout the product life cycle

Pricing decisions should be systematic and rigorous, following a methodical and logical process that ensures all relevant issues and options are considered. It should be noted, however, that pricing is not an exact science. Many pricing decisions will be made without going through a formal sequence of steps. Even when a formal process is followed, a marketer should not expect to derive *the* optimal or 'correct' price. Rather, pricing in practice usually involves a trade-off between the competing and conflicting considerations of the organisation's costs (and its profit objectives), the activities of competitors, and the attitudes and price sensitivity of customers. In this sense, pricing could be argued to be 'an exercise in compromise'.

With an understanding of customer perceptions of value, demand, costs and competition, the organisation must identify its preferred pricing tactics in order to implement pricing. In addition to providing a path for implementing pricing, pricing tactics allow the organisation to manage its responses to situational opportunities and threats, such as unexpected fluctuations in industry supply (e.g. worldwide fluctuations in supplies of oil, food, minerals or raw materials) or the unexpected behaviour of competitors (e.g. when a competitor 'dumps' product in the local market).

### Pricing new products

Setting the initial price for the launch of a new product is a crucial aspect of product life cycle strategy (see chapter 7). While prices can be adjusted after a product launch, the initial launch price can fundamentally influence the success of the entire marketing strategy. In settling the launch price, beyond considering the cost of manufacture and supply and the need to recover the investment in research and development, the marketer should consider consumers' likely response to the new product, its perceived uniqueness and the likelihood that competitors will follow into the market (i.e. the organisation needs to consider value, demand, costs and competition). Two broad pricing strategies for new products are penetration pricing and price skimming.

**Penetration pricing** uses a low price in order to gain maximum sales volume, rapid market share and turnover of a new product. The low price also encourages consumers to at least trial the product. Penetration pricing is commonly used in grocery product launches. The low-price, high-volume strategy may also serve to deter competitors from launching similar products.

**Price skimming** involves charging the highest price that customers who most desire the product are willing to pay. Over time, the price is lowered to bring in larger numbers of buyers, again at the highest prices that these buyers are willing to pay. Price skimming allows an organisation to generate cash flow quickly to offset product development and launch costs. Price skimming also serves to temporarily limit demand, enabling the organisation to better balance demand with limited supply capacity. Both Sony and Microsoft adopt price skimming strategies when they respectively launch their most recent PlayStation and Xbox game consoles. The high prices and higher margins produced by price skimming may attract competitors, who will seek to replicate or undercut prices charged by the innovator businesses. There is also a risk that the organisation will damage its relationship with its most loyal customers by always charging them higher prices as they rush to buy newly released products.

Developing an appropriate pricing approach for new products is complex, especially given the response of customers and competitors cannot be entirely predicted. Nevertheless, in general terms, if demand for the new product is expected to be inelastic, then it is logical to initially employ a high-price, low-volume price skimming strategy. Conversely, if demand for the new product is expected to be elastic, then a low-price, high-volume market penetration strategy is advisable. Which of these two demand conditions applies can, of course, vary, although it is likely that genuinely innovative high-value products (such as the latest generation televisions or computers) are more suited to price skimming. Conversely, high-volume, low-value consumer non-durables such as food and grocery products are more suited to penetration pricing.

Companies such as Sony and Microsoft use price skimming strategies to maximise the profitability of their games consoles throughout the product life cycle. These consumers, shown here at an Xbox 360 launch, will pay a higher price because they have a strong desire to own the new console soon after its release.

## Pricing established products

An organisation may choose to charge each customer the same price. This approach is simple to administer and avoids the need to negotiate with customers, but it also ignores the different value that the product represents for each customer and the different price sensitivity that each customer may have toward the product. In doing so, it may result in lost revenue from customers who cannot afford the set price and from those who would be willing to pay a higher price.

**Differential pricing** is the practice of charging different buyers different prices for the same product. For differential pricing to be effective, the organisation must be able to:

- identify market segments that have different price sensitivities
- administer the differential pricing in such a way as to avoid confusing or antagonising customers
- prevent the development of a 'black market', in which low-paying customers resell the product to customers who would have been charged a higher price by the organisation.

**differential pricing** The practice of charging different buyers different prices for the same product.

A common approach to differential pricing is to use discounts to vary the price of a product over time. For example, an organisation may offer *periodic discounts* by temporarily reducing prices for Christmas sales, post-Christmas sales, 'cheap Tuesdays' or some other predictable occasion. Periodic discounting can attract customers and help manage demand fluctuations, but it can also lead to customers deferring purchases until discounts are offered. A related approach is *special-event pricing.* This approach links discounted prices across an organisation's entire product range with some special or seasonal event, such as the Olympics or New Year's Day. Special-event pricing is designed to increase total sales volumes. Such a campaign requires the pricing strategy to be combined with promotion. Such an approach is called **promotional pricing**. Special event pricing typically requires intensive advertising, discount pricing and special arrangements such as extended trading hours, entertainment or other attractions.

**promotional pricing** The combination of a pricing approach with a promotional campaign.

The danger in linking special pricing to regularly occurring events — as with any approach to periodic discounting — is that customers may become conditioned to such special occasions, and may defer their regular purchasing patterns in anticipation of the lower prices. To overcome this last problem, an organisation may prefer *random discounting* in which temporary price reductions are implemented in an unpredictable fashion. Some of the major supermarket chains randomly discount products on a daily basis. Such an approach creates a consumer perception that at least some products are always on special, but they are not able to reliably predict when any particular product will be available for a lower price. Some organisations avoid discounting altogether, instead adopting *everyday low prices (EDLP)*. Such an approach forgoes the advantages of differential pricing through discounts, but offers easier administration, more predictable sales volumes and lower promotional costs.

Differential pricing is extremely common in business markets. For example, a business buying a motor vehicle will usually pay substantially less than a private consumer for the same car. Further, a seller is likely to charge a lower price if an organisation buys a large fleet of vehicles or has a long-term established relationship with the seller. Differential pricing may also be implemented through *trade-in allowances*, which are discounts based on a customer returning used products when buying new products. Trade-in allowances are used when second-hand products maintain considerable value (e.g. motor vehicles in consumer markets and office equipment in business markets). In business-to-business pricing, a seller may offer a *promotional allowance* discount to customers and intermediaries in return for participating in marketing campaigns.

Regardless of the approach, differential pricing must be implemented in such a way that it does not contravene the price discrimination provisions of the Competition and Consumer Act in Australia or the Commerce Act in New Zealand. In general, price discrimination is illegal in business markets if it limits competition, although differential pricing can be justified on a number of grounds, including differences in costs in serving different customers, or in cutting prices to meet competition.

## Setting and managing the final price

Consideration of all of the issues discussed in this chapter will indicate a price for the organisation's product and how that price may be implemented. Once implemented, the price must always be monitored in relation to all of the factors we have discussed in this chapter. All of these factors can change over time. In addition, it is essential that the final price should be perceived by potential customers as consistent with all elements of the organisation's offer, so that consumers believe they are receiving fair value for the price.

Pricing is perhaps the most flexible element of the marketing mix. Airlines for example, maintain a highly complex array of prices, even though they sell, at most, only a few classes of seats. Individual airline passengers will pay differing prices depending upon the class of seat, the flight, the day of the week, and month of the year, the method of booking and method of payment — for thousands of seats, every day. In addition, the internet has made prices more visible, more flexible and, consequently, more competitive than ever before. This flexibility ensures that pricing is the most dynamic element of the marketing mix and its direct relationship to profitability makes its effective management an essential marketing capability.

There are, however, some regulations that restrict pricing, and organisations must be mindful that their pricing practices are in accordance with these. We have already discussed price discrimination earlier in the chapter. Additionally, the Competition and Consumer Act in Australia and the Commerce Act in New Zealand prohibit manufacturers from forcing their distributors and retailers from reselling the product at a particular price (this illegal practice is known as *resale price maintenance*).

From the discussion in this chapter, it should be clear that price management is a dynamic area of marketing. Franchise businesses can face special advantages and disadvantages in pricing. In some franchises, the franchisor sets prices that are to be consistently applied across the franchises in order to maintain a consistent customer experience and to facilitate the use of standardised national or regional price advertising. The disadvantage to the franchisor and franchisee is that pricing may not reflect local conditions, which may be important across the entire range of factors discussed in this chapter.

Table 8.3 summarises the various specific pricing tactics explored in this chapter.

**TABLE 8.3** Pricing tactics — a summary

| Tactic | Description | Example | Advantages | Disadvantages |
|---|---|---|---|---|
| *Prestige pricing* (p. 257) | Setting prices high to convey an image of prestige, quality and exclusivity | Pharmaceuticals (where consumers might regard high price as a measure of high potency and efficacy), rare wine, whisky and cognac, motor vehicles, *haute couture* and fine art | Effective when consumers cannot objectively evaluate the quality of the product, and therefore use the high price as a proxy measure of high quality | Can be difficult to sustain during an economic downturn |
| *Comparison discounting* (p. 258) | Quoting a discounted price and the regular higher price together | A stocktake sale | Attract customers | Legal restrictions — must be a genuine comparison<br><br>Customers may be sceptical about whether the 'usual price' is authentic |
| *Periodic discounting* (pp. 285–6) | Temporarily reducing prices on a predictable, regular or periodic basis | Christmas sales<br>Post-Christmas sales<br>Cheap Tuesdays | Attract customers<br>Smooth demand | Customers may defer purchases in expectation of a discount at a known future time<br><br>Usually requires extra promotional efforts |
| *Random discounting* (p. 286) | Temporarily reducing prices in a pattern which is difficult for consumers to predict | Major supermarket chains randomly discount different products on a daily basis | Consumers cannot predict when discounts will apply to particular products<br><br>Preserves average retail margins<br><br>Creates a consumer perception that something is always on special | Difficult to administer<br><br>May not attract additional customers |
| *Bait pricing* (p. 258) | Establishing an artificially low price for one item in a product line to attract potential buyers, then trying to sell them a higher-priced item in the product line | Advertisements such as 'Brand-name jeans for only $10' | Attracts customers<br><br>Legitimate if the retailer maintains sufficient stock of the low-priced product and is willing to sell it | *Bait and switch* approaches are unethical and in some circumstances illegal. Bait and switch pricing occurs when the seller has no intention of selling the lower-priced item and merely uses the 'bait' price as a pretext to lure shoppers into the store, after which to 'switch' them to the more normally priced items<br><br>Customers may feel manipulated |

*(continued)*

**TABLE 8.3** (*continued*)

| Tactic | Description | Example | Advantages | Disadvantages |
|---|---|---|---|---|
| *Captive pricing* (p. 259) | Offering a low entry price for a basic product to attract consumers, then charging more for desirable or necessary additional parts or functions | Car manufacturers frequently employ headline pricing for the basic model, and charge premium prices for desirable options such as air-conditioning and side-curtain air bags<br><br>Photocopier manufacturers set low initial purchase or lease prices, then charge premium prices for toner cartridges | Enables marketer to extract a bigger sale than the headline price suggests<br><br>Makes it easier for customers to make the initial purchase<br><br>In the case of ongoing services and supplies, provides manufacturer a revenue stream | Customers may feel exploited |
| *Negotiated pricing* (p. 263) | Negotiation of the selling price between buyer and seller | In the consumer markets, cars and real estate purchase prices<br><br>In the business markets, prices are negotiated based on differences in the costs of selling or transportation to various customers, the need to match a competitor's prices for a particular buyer, or volume discounts | Price can more accurately reflect the relative value to the buyer and seller | Difficult and time-consuming to administer |
| *Secondary-market pricing* (p. 260) | Setting different prices for different target markets | Senior citizen discounts<br><br>Apple charges university students a lower price for its products than it charges general consumers (in the hope of winning repeat purchase after the students graduate)<br><br>Higher prices charged in rural and remote areas | Makes product affordable to a greater range of customers<br><br>Enables prices to reflect different costs involved in serving different markets | Ethical issues<br><br>More complex to administer |
| *Price lining* (p. 284) | Setting a limited number of prices for selected groups or lines of merchandise | A computer retailer may sell notebook computers in three price ranges: $1000, $1500 and $2000 | Price differences become less of a factor in consumer decisions once the price *range* is chosen<br><br>Emphasises factors other than price | Limited flexibility in setting prices |
| *Premium pricing* (p. 258) | Offering different versions of a product from budget to premium levels, with prices to match | VW's Golf models range in price from $28 000 to $57 000 | Higher profits from the premium model<br><br>In times of strong consumer confidence, it is an effective form of non-price competition | Relies on the willingness of consumers to 'trade up' from cheaper alternatives<br><br>Unattractive when consumer sentiment is weak, as consumers emphasise value for money |

| Tactic | Description | Example | Advantages | Disadvantages |
| --- | --- | --- | --- | --- |
| *Value-based pricing* (pp. 281–3) | Attempts to manage customers' perceptions of value versus price | Odd–even pricing<br><br>Reference pricing<br><br>Multiple-unit pricing<br><br>Bundle pricing | May increase the perceived value of one product relative to another<br><br>May offer a saving to consumers<br><br>May result in higher levels of consumption | Research on the effectiveness of some of these techniques is inconclusive<br><br>Margin per product may be lower<br><br>May undermine products not priced on one of these approaches |
| *Everyday low prices (EDLP)* (p. 286) | Setting a low and relatively fixed price for products | Used by supermarkets and packaged goods retailers such as hardware chains | Easy to administer<br><br>Predictability of sales volumes<br><br>Lower transport and stock holding costs | Lower average price over the long term<br><br>Customers have grown to expect discounts |
| *Price leader* (p. 268) | A high-volume product priced near cost | Supermarkets often discount some products to use as price leaders | Attracts customers into the store, where they may buy other, normally priced products | Low profit on price leader products<br><br>Customers may not purchase anything else |
| *Loss leader* (p. 268) | A high-volume product priced below cost | Supermarkets often discount some products to use as loss leaders | Attract customers into the store, where they may buy other, normally priced products | Financial loss on loss leader products<br><br>Customers may not purchase anything else |

# Raising the bar?

Confectionery giant Mars Snackfood Australia recently came under fire in the media when it was revealed it had reduced the size of its highest selling snack, the standard-sized Mars Bar, by 11.6 per cent, while keeping the price of the bar the same. To put this reduction into perspective, 30 million Mars Bars are sold in Australia each year, and the reduction in size could potentially save Mars 210 000 kilograms of chocolate, caramel and nougat ingredients annually. Similar size reductions occurred across their entire range of more than 90 products (including Milky Way, Maltesers and Snickers), with the price of one-third of these now reduced-size products also remaining the same.

The general manager for Mars Snackfood Australia, Peter West, publicly defended the company's actions, claiming that the reduction in size of Mars products was a direct response to the obesity debate and the fact that the company's bars contain too many calories. 'Big food is an issue — the portion size that people are eating, whether the muffin you buy, or the cake, or when you go to a restaurant, the size of the plate in front of you. We want to make sure we sell our portions in the right size.'

He also pointed out that although one-third of Mars' product range had reduced in weight but held price, two-thirds of their range had had both a size *and* a price reduction. He said, 'Across our entire range, the net impact of these changes was the equivalent of a price rise of 1.7 per cent. As a company, we had to decide between two options:

- Passing on a 2 per cent price rise to our consumers
- Reduce the weight of our range with a maintained and/or reduced price.'[10]

**Question**

The decision by Mars to decrease the size of its chocolate bars can be viewed as a price rise 'in disguise'. From a marketing point of view, outline the advantages and disadvantages of the product range pricing decision that Mars has made.

## Concepts and applications check

**Learning objective 6**  understand how to manage prices as part of the marketing mix

**6.1**  Outline some ways in which a marketer can influence a customer's perception of price.

**6.2**  Explain the difference between price skimming and penetration pricing, using an example to illustrate when each pricing strategy would be appropriate.

**6.3**  Choose a product and outline one or more pricing tactics from table 8.3 that could form the basis of an effective pricing strategy. Justify your answer.

# SUMMARY

 **Learning objective 1** understand the objectives that guide pricing strategies

Price is a visible expression of the value of the product to be exchanged and enables buyers and sellers to negotiate and agree on that value. Pricing objectives are derived from the organisation's broader marketing objectives. Pricing objectives tend to focus on the issues of profitability, long-term prosperity, market share and positioning. The pricing strategy and specific tactics an organisation chooses must comply with laws and regulations that govern issues such as misleading and deceptive conduct, price collusion, comparability of prices, clarity in pricing and price discrimination. Ultimately, pricing decisions must be based on an understanding of demand, costs and competition in order to deliver value to the customer and the marketer.

 **Learning objective 2** analyse demand to inform the development of an appropriate pricing strategy

Demand is the relationship between the price of a particular product and the quantity of the product that consumers are willing to buy. Demand analysis is based on historical data, estimates of sales potential, and estimates of price–volume relationships and price sensitivity. The data enable the marketer to construct a demand curve. The traditional demand curve slopes downwards, indicating that as prices rise, quantity sold falls, and vice versa. Prestige products have a unique demand curve in which, up to a threshold point, increasing prices actually increases demand due to the perceived quality, prestige and exclusivity conveyed by the product's price. The sensitivity of consumer demand to price changes is known as the price elasticity of demand. In instances of price elastic demand, a particular percentage change in price will cause a greater percentage change in quantity demanded. In price inelastic demand, a particular percentage change in price will cause a smaller percentage change in quantity demanded.

 **Learning objective 3** describe the principles of pricing based on cost and revenue analysis

Costs determine a price floor, below which the business cannot survive in the long term. It is crucial for marketers to understand the relationship between retail prices, sales volume, costs and ultimately profits. Break-even analysis estimates the volume of unit sales required to cover total costs. Marginal analysis determines the effect on costs and revenue when an organisation produces and sells one more unit of product. Cost-based pricing involves adding a percentage or dollar amount to the cost of a product in order to determine its selling price. Cost-plus pricing is used by producers when it is difficult to determine the costs of the product until it has been completed. In such cases, the seller adds their required profit margin as a dollar amount or percentage to the costs once the project is complete. Markup pricing is used by wholesalers and retailers and involves adding a percentage of their purchase cost to determine the resale price.

 **Learning objective 4** explain the role of competitive analysis in determining pricing

Price competition usually emerges when competitors' offerings are not significantly differentiated in the minds of consumers. Price competition is undesirable from a seller's point of view, unless the seller has a cost advantage through economies of scale in purchasing or low-cost production. Competition-based pricing is based on the prices charged by competitors or on the likely response of competitors to the organisation's prices. When it is feasible, competition on factors other than price is preferable as it gives the organisation greater power to decide on the profit margin per unit sold. Most organisations seek to compete using a strategy of 'differentiation', which emphasises the uniqueness of the organisation's products in terms of product quality, innovation, brand image, customer service, distribution coverage and local convenience.

 **Learning objective 5** appreciate the issues involved in pricing for business markets

Business-to-business marketing relationships tend to be close, long-term and formal. This leads to more formal pricing practices than those in consumer markets. At the same time, pricing is more complex in business markets — differences in the size of purchases, the frequency of purchases, costs involved in transport and other considerations often require sellers to adjust prices for individual customers and individual transactions.

 **Learning objective 6** understand how to manage prices as part of the marketing mix

Customer perceptions are subjective and particular to each individual, but it is important that marketers match pricing as closely as possible to customers' expectations. These expectations are based partly on the customer's internal and external reference prices. Tactics such as odd–even pricing, reference pricing, multiple-unit pricing and bundle pricing can be used to manage customer perceptions of value. In launching a new product, an organisation may choose a penetration pricing or price skimming strategy to maximise volume or margin respectively. For established products, an organisation may seek to implement differential pricing or promotional pricing. Pricing should always be consistent with the other elements of the marketing mix.

# Supermarket pricing: strategy versus tactics

Coles and Woolworths dominate the Australian grocery industry, accounting for 80 per cent of the annual $90 billion national spend in this category between them. Two major supermarkets similarly dominate the New Zealand landscape (Progressive and Foodstuffs). By international standards, this is a relatively high level of market concentration. In the United Kingdom, for example, the *four* largest retailers between them have 65 per cent of the market. Interestingly, in the past decade, Britain's grocery prices have risen by 32.9 per cent, whereas Australia's and New Zealand's have increased by 41.3 per cent and 42.5 per cent respectively.

An analysis of supermarkets in Australia over the past decade provides an interesting insight into key factors influencing the price of groceries. In the past decade, the German-owned Aldi company has entered the market (and it is rumoured to be making plans to enter the New Zealand market in the future). Aldi currently has approximately 200 stores in Australia, predominantly in the more highly populated eastern states of Australia (New South Wales, Victoria and Queensland). By comparison, Coles and Woolworths both have approximately 700 stores spread across the country. Aldi supermarkets operate in a 'no-frills' warehouse fashion, with pallets of products parked in aisles rather than displayed on shelves, and minimal service provided to consumers. The chain also stocks a limited number of product lines (usually between 1000 and 2000; this is compared to the major supermarkets, which can stock up to 25 000 items), and competes aggressively on price.

Aldi's business model and associated cost structure enable it to operate from a cost base that Woolworths and Coles would find difficult, if not impossible, to match, especially at their higher current customer service levels. According to an Aldi spokesperson, 'We can keep our prices low because we run a lean and efficient business, and concentrate on selling a select range of exclusive brand products. We don't spend money on expensive brand marketing campaigns, customer loyalty programs or merchandising and point-of-sale displays'.

The average Australian household spends about 12 per cent of its income on groceries, and a recent supermarket price survey by CHOICE provided the following interesting, if unsurprising, conclusions:

- The intensity of supermarket competition in a geographic area has a major impact on the price consumers pay for groceries in that area, particularly in the presence of an Aldi store.
- Even when specials are included, there is almost no difference in the average price of a basket of groceries at Coles and Woolworths.
- Smaller independent operators such as IGA and Foodworks are more expensive than Coles or Woolworths.

Further to CHOICE's findings, a recent Australian Competition and Consumer Commission (ACCC) inquiry into supermarket pricing also found that consumers pay less at Coles and Woolworths supermarkets when there is an Aldi store located within a one kilometre radius. The statistics showed, for example, that compared to customers who shopped at a Coles store with no Aldi competitor within five kilometres, customers paid 5.1 per cent less for comparable products if they shopped at a Coles store situated within one kilometre of an Aldi store.

While these findings showed that the presence of an Aldi store in an area was beneficial to local consumers in terms of lower prices, it must be remembered that the overall national price effect of Aldi being in the market is limited by its comparatively low number of stores. As such, the

A 'no-frills' approach to doing business ensures that Aldi customers can generally put more grocery items in their trolleys for the same money that consumers might otherwise spend at Coles or Woolworths.

competitive price benefits that Aldi may bring are not felt by all shoppers in all regions and states. The effects are further diluted by Aldi's comparatively limited product range, compared to the ranges offered by Coles and Woolworths.

In a significant development after the ACCC inquiry, Coles recently announced the introduction of a uniform pricing policy across its network of stores. Key details of Coles' uniform pricing model announcement included:

- 8000 grocery products (including meat, seafood, dairy, deli and bakery items) to be priced at uniform levels across Coles supermarkets nationally
- the remaining 17 000 products in Coles' range (including fruit and vegetables) to be matched to the lowest prices in each state.

Significantly, Aldi had introduced a uniform pricing policy in Australia two years earlier. It is believed Coles' move was in response to customer criticisms of differential pricing between Coles stores that were just a few kilometres apart (identified in the CHOICE and ACCC studies), and also to ward off any potential predatory pricing allegations.

Woolworths is progressively rolling out a similar uniform pricing strategy. While this move to uniform pricing will largely remove the suburb-by-suburb price differentials between individual company stores (which, on the basis of the recent CHOICE and ACCC studies, seemed dependent on the existence or otherwise of a competing Aldi store in the area), the broader pricing strategy of Coles and Woolworths remains an interesting (and, at times, paradoxical) phenomenon to observe.

Academic research on supermarket pricing is comparatively rare, but research that is published is strongly consistent with the CHOICE and ACCC findings. In addition, in arguably the most rigorous and widely cited study to date, a finding, consistent with the recent Australian experience, was that rather than choosing a pricing strategy that distinguishes them from their rivals, supermarkets generally choose matching strategies. (See the article 'Supermarket pricing strategies' co-authored by US academics Paul Ellickson and Sanjog Misra, which should be available online.) This finding is in direct contrast to existing theoretical models that view pricing strategy as a form of competitive differentiation.

The authors of this study contended that:

> Most supermarket firms choose to position themselves by offering either everyday low prices (EDLP) across several items or offering temporary price reductions (promotions) on a limited range of items ... In many retail industries, pricing strategy can be characterised as a choice between offering relatively stable prices across a wide range of products (often called everyday low pricing) or emphasising deep and frequent discounts on a smaller set of goods (referred to as promotional or PROMO pricing). Although Wal-Mart did not invent the concept of everyday low pricing, the successful use of everyday low pricing (EDLP) was a primary factor in their rapid rise to the top of the Fortune 500, spawning a legion of followers selling everything from toys (Toys 'R' Us) to building supplies (Home Depot). In the 1980s, it appeared that the success and rapid diffusion of the EDLP strategy could spell the end of promotions throughout much of retail. However, by the late 1990s, the penetration of EDLP had slowed, leaving a healthy mix of firms following both strategies, and several others employing a mixture of the two.

In their recent histories, Woolworths and Coles have both dabbled in EDLP which, at least conceptually, offers attractions to the supermarkets in terms of more stable retail prices, with fewer and less extreme peaks and troughs in prices and sales volume. This, in turn, leads to more stable and predictable inventory levels and lower resultant handling costs. Consumers are said to benefit from lower prices (on average, over time), especially when they compare the costs of their total weekly shopping bills. Of course, supermarket shoppers continue to be attracted to headline-grabbing 'promo pricing' offers, and even when Woolworths, for example, publicly promotes its 'everyday low prices', it also aggressively promotes its weekly specials — especially those for regular high-volume sellers such as bananas, bread and soft drinks. Ironically, this effectively undermines its message.

On Australia Day 2011, Coles announced it was slashing the price of its generic milk to $1 a litre and supporting the price drop with a new 'Down Down' point-of-sale and advertising campaign. The move — made despite an estimated loss of $30 million in profit — signalled the start of a new aggressive pricing battle between Coles and Woolworths. This was soon dubbed the 'milk wars'. Woolworths matched Coles' $1 a litre generic milk offering, and smaller competitors including Aldi and Franklins were also pressured to follow suit. Consumers supported the price drop at supermarket checkouts, and national consumption of milk increased by nearly 2 per cent in just two months. This figure meant that Australians were on track to drink an additional 40 million litres of milk a year if the sales results continued.

Despite this, the milk wars caused considerable controversy. Farmers and milk processors were furious about increased pressure in the supply chain, and the real risk of the loss-leading pricing strategy devastating the viability of the Australian dairy industry — if it continued over the longer term. A senate inquiry was also called to scrutinise supermarket pricing strategies. Prior to slashing the price of its generic milk, Coles had begun heavily discounting products including Sanitarium Weet Bix, Moro Extra Virgin Olive Oil and Handee Ultra Paper Towel in 2010. In March 2011, Australia's biggest brewer, Foster's, also halted deliveries to Coles- and Woolworths-operated alcohol retailers on the basis that they were selling cartons of their products, including VB, Carlton Draught, Pure Blonde and Crown Lager, below cost. 'We have done so to protect the brand equity — the image of our brands — and we don't do this lightly,' a spokesperson for Foster's explained.

During the senate inquiry, data collected by an independent agency suggested a link between bowser petrol prices and Coles' ongoing 'Down Down' discounting campaign. It showed that there was an increased gap in petrol prices offered at Coles Express and Woolworths' Caltex petrol outlets at crucial points in the Coles campaign, such as when it first slashed its milk prices. Although a spokesperson for Coles Express rejected the allegations, Senator Nick Xenophon said that the figures 'clearly' showed Coles' petrol was consistently more expensive than petrol sold at other outlets. 'This is what happens when the supermarket chains also own petrol stations and bottle shops,' he said. 'Coles and Woolies have too much market power and that means they can use this discounting to squeeze out other competitors.'[11]

## Questions

1. Explain how the oligopolistic market structure of the grocery industry in Australia impacts upon pricing.
2. The CHOICE and ACCC evidence suggests that Aldi has a measurable impact on supermarket prices, especially in those areas surrounding Aldi shops. Under the more uniform pricing model that both Coles and Woolworths have implemented, how should these large supermarket companies respond to Aldi's pricing in the long term?
3. How does 'promo-pricing' conflict with EDLP, and what are the potential ramifications of it?
4. Who do you think are the real winners and losers in Australia's recent milk wars?

## Advanced activity

Research the current concert ticket pricing environment. Imagine you are a music promoter and choose both a high-profile international act and a local band that could potentially tour your city. Compare and contrast the likely issues you will need to consider for pricing concert tickets for both scenarios. In your analysis, outline the similarities and differences in terms of the following:

(a) pricing objectives
(b) demand considerations (including the concept of elasticity)
(c) cost considerations
(d) competition considerations (including different ways your target market may be able to potentially spend their entertainment dollar)
(e) business-to-business pricing (e.g. a direct ticket distribution model versus the use of intermediaries)
(f) the psychology of pricing.

## Marketing plan activity

For your marketing plan, consider the following four pricing issues in relation to your chosen product:

1. Is the industry predominantly characterised by price competition or other forms of competition?
2. Is your product demand elastic or inelastic? If elastic, construct a demand curve for it at varying prices, based on realistic sales estimates. You may need to conduct some market research to determine this.
3. Outline what would be the main internal and external influences on your pricing decision.
4. Explain how you would determine prices based on the seven-step model for setting prices. For each step, explain and give examples of specific issues that would need to be considered in making pricing decisions for your product.

A sample marketing plan has been included at the back of this book (page 523) to give you an idea where this information fits in an overall marketing plan.

## CHAPTER 9

# Promotion

## Learning objectives

After studying this chapter, you should be able to:

- explain promotion (marketing communication) and its role in the marketing mix

- understand the integrated marketing communications approach to marketing promotion and the major elements of the promotion mix

- describe different types of advertising and the steps in creating an advertising campaign

- outline the role of public relations in promotion

- explain how sales promotion activities can be used

- understand the nature of personal selling

- discuss a range of marketing communication options additional to the traditional promotion mix.

# Youi

Generally insurance is a boring topic, especially to younger people, even though they may have to take out insurance policies on their car or home. The insurance industry has traditionally been dominated by local companies like GIO, Insurance Australia Group (IAG) and Suncorp. However, a new company, Youi, has caused a stir since entering the car and home insurance market in 2008. The company has undertaken a major multimedia awareness campaign including television, radio, outdoor and digital, with price differentiation being a major message. One television advertisement, 'Ridiculous assumptions', features three traditional-looking insurance company men laughing and making assumptions about how a woman drives her car. Then a young, cool Youi employee enters and actually asks the woman how she uses her car, pointing out that Youi does not make assumptions, but instead tailors its products to ensure customers get the best possible price.

Primarily targeting Gen Y, Youi's outdoor campaign has involved buses, trams and billboards. For example, Monash University in Melbourne was surrounded by towering billboard advertisements with the tagline 'Smarter car insurance that saves you money'. According to Bernard Salt, a leading social commentator and adviser on consumer, cultural and demographic trends, 'Youi insurance ads are very Gen Y-focused — the ads are very cool, very edgy, very of the moment — and it speaks to and connects with the new generation, but it's selling insurance'.

In addition to its focus on price in its promotional messages, Youi is broadening its appeal to demonstrate that it also understands the importance of providing good service to its policyholders. When Melbourne was hit by a major storm, causing millions of dollars worth of damage to cars and homes, the company was quick to respond. Within weeks, Youi created a series of radio advertisements that highlighted its speedy response in processing its customers' policy claims, including testimonials from satisfied customers. Brendon Dyer, head of marketing, said at the time, 'We have already processed hundreds of claims in Melbourne since the storms hit, so this advertising is about letting consumers know that, at Youi, cheaper premiums don't mean poor service.'

Although Youi generated a net loss of $13 million in its first year of operating in Australia, its aggressive promotional campaign is increasing brand awareness and growing its customer base. This is a concern for established companies in the competitive insurance industry.[1]

## Question

Briefly outline how Youi insurance used different media and messages to communicate to the target audience for its campaigns. Which one (or combination) of these media do you believe would be most effective for this type of market entry campaign? Justify your answer.

# INTRODUCTION

The last two chapters have looked at the concepts of product and price. This chapter will focus on another part of the traditional marketing mix: promotion (or marketing communications). Promotion is a fundamental part of marketing that is designed to make consumers aware of products. Imagine for a moment a world without marketing promotions: you would not know where your favourite band is playing, when they release their new CD, what is on television tomorrow, what options are available for places to eat, what health symptoms require a visit to a doctor and so on.

Promotion is an extremely important part of the marketing mix. After all, no-one will rush to buy your product if they don't know it exists! It is crucial to effectively and efficiently communicate your message about your product to the marketplace. Remember that a product can be a good, service or idea. In fact, promotion is often the main element of the marketing mix for 'ideas'. For example, when the federal government runs a multimillion dollar advertising campaign on television to discourage young people from using drugs such as ice, it is essentially promoting the idea that drugs are detrimental to health (and illegal). Promotion is often worked out after other parts of the marketing mix, and part of the message sent by the promotion can be that we are selling the 'right' product, at the 'right' price, at the 'right' place — thereby sending messages about other parts of the marketing mix.

Think about how Youi insurance has used marketing communications activities to encourage young people to consider them when buying insurance. There is a particular image that Youi wants to associate with the them. In this chapter we will first discuss what promotion (marketing communications) is, and then relate it to integrated marketing communications, or IMC. Each part of the promotion mix will be discussed, and finally we will look at some special topics in promotion.

## WHAT IS PROMOTION?

**Promotion** is the creation and maintenance of communication with target markets. In marketing, promotion is usually thought of as comprising a strategic mix of advertising, public relations, sales promotions and personal selling. As promotion is basically about communicating a message to the marketplace, a term for promotion that is growing in popularity is 'marketing communication'. Further, when carefully combined and coordinated to achieve a consistent and effective message, the promotional approach is known as integrated marketing communications (IMC). Much of this chapter is dedicated to explaining IMC. The idea behind IMC is that the planning of each part of the promotion mix — advertising, public relations, sales promotions and personal selling — should not be done in isolation; rather, strategies should be planned so that they work together to achieve greater clarity and consistency, and a better overall result. When everything is working effectively, other elements, such as word-of-mouth communication, can have a strong influence on consumers in some product markets (especially in relation to services such as movies, restaurants, doctors and accountants, but also in relation to some products, such as books). These other elements also need to be managed by the marketing organisation.

**Learning objective 1**
explain promotion (marketing communication) and its role in the marketing mix

**promotion** The marketing activities that make potential customers, partners and society aware of and attracted to the business's offerings.

## A model of communication

Given that promotion is about communicating with target markets, it is important to discuss how communication works. The model presented in figure 9.1 describes the communication process: a message is encoded and sent by a sender or source, via a message channel or medium, to a receiver or target audience, who decodes the message and responds by some form of feedback.[2] Anything that interferes with the effectiveness of the communication process is referred to as 'noise'. The communication process is also influenced by the 'fields of experience'; that is, what the participants in the communication process know about each other and how that influences the way they encode and decode messages.

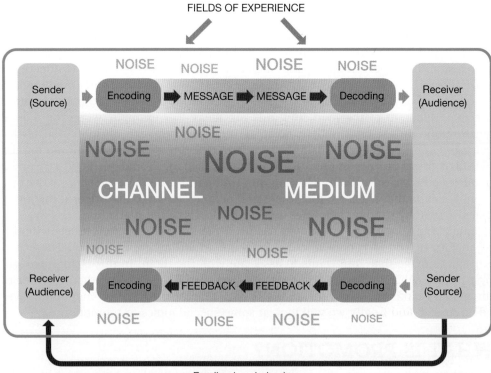

**FIGURE 9.1**

A model of communication

Many researchers have analysed communication processes, building on the basic communication model, examining different aspects of the process and applying it to different situations, from interpersonal communication to mass communication. Nevertheless, the basic ideas of 'sender', 'message', 'receiver' and 'feedback' remain constant.

As shown in figure 9.1, the sender initiates the communication message. In many situations this would involve an individual, but in the case of promotion it is an organisation intending to communicate a specific message about its market offering. The sender aims to ensure that a clear and concise message is developed, which is then sent to the target audience (and possibly the marketplace in general) through advertising or other promotional activities. It is important that all activities involved with communicating to the target audience are coordinated and consistent. Any inconsistency or incongruity involved in the communication process could result in sending mixed messages, which could affect the successful transmission of the message.

The planned message is then encoded for the target audience. There is a possibility that the encoding of the intended message results in a message that is in some way different to what was planned. Encoding is done by the use of words (a script in the case of broadcast media and copy in print media), music (such as jingles), and many other verbal and non-verbal communication cues.

The message channel can vary depending on the type of communication being undertaken and the target audience. Message channels include the various mass media, such as television, radio, newspapers and magazines. For example, the media choice for a product aimed at young people could be a television commercial during 'The Simpsons'; the choice for a product aimed at young girls could be a half-page advertisement in *Dolly* magazine.

At times, the message channel may not encode the message correctly. This is especially true when the marketing organisation does not control the message channel. For example, when using a public relations approach, such as issuing a press release, it is up to news media to interpret, present and relay that information to the target audience. While organisations attempt to prepare comprehensive press materials, there is no guarantee that the information will get 'passed on' in the desired way. The media's editorial independence not only means they cannot be controlled, but each intermediary may present the same information in a different way. Even when the firm does control the message channel, such as with paid advertisements, there are sometimes problems. This can occur when organisations advertise internationally, with the intended message sometimes being 'concussed' in the encoding process due to mistranslations. Communication is only 'successful' if it passes on the undistorted message to those intended to receive it.

The target audience can include potential and past customers. In a complex marketplace, it is virtually impossible to perfectly target a particular group without members of other groups also receiving the message. One message may be designed to relay different messages to each group or the same message can be targeted at multiple groups. For example, the Minerals Council of Australia's campaign against a proposed super profits mining tax had two different targets. The Council wanted to communicate to the general public that the proposed tax was a bad idea. In so doing, they were trying to pressure the government to show that the Council is a strong lobby group and that the proposed tax should not go ahead. This particular campaign is analysed in detail in the case study at the end of this chapter.

While organisations can provide broad-based communication, the information designed for Target A may, in fact, distort the message designed for Target B. For example, when trying to attract guests, a hotel may promote (communicate) that it has a 'wild' nightlife. While this information may be appropriate for the young singles market, it may discourage family holidaymakers from staying there. Communication targeting each group specifically may be more effective than using mass communications and reduces the risk of distortion of the message.

Of course, just as the way that the sender encodes the message can result in the 'wrong' message being sent, the way in which the receiver or audience decodes the message is subject to their individual characteristics and circumstances. One of the results of this is that different audience members can interpret the 'same' message in quite different ways, or even just subtly different ways.

Once the message has been received, to complete the flow of communication the receiver responds in the form of feedback. Feedback may be in the form of behaviour or communication. If it is via communication, then that communication is subject to the same processes we have described for the original message. The extent to which the market communicates with marketers through feedback has increased enormously over the past few years, due to the opportunities offered by information and communications technology. The behavioural response from the receiver can depend on the type of communication originally sent and the objective of the communication. For example, if the objective is to change the behaviour of customers, then a mechanism should be introduced to measure the change in customers' behaviour. Likewise, if the managerial objective is to increase sales, the feedback to be measured is whether there has been an increase in sales during the time of the communication or promotional campaign.

It is very important for management to implement a control mechanism and keep track of all feedback to determine whether the communication being sent is successful. Monitoring feedback is a complex process, not only requiring a company to monitor changes in sales (i.e. customer feedback), but also including monitoring media, publicity and editorials related to organisational activities (e.g. using a company such as Media Monitors). Unwanted responses from the receivers may indicate that there should be some correction of the original message being communicated.

The messages sent and received in the communication process may be distorted by 'noise'. Noise is any factor that creates a barrier to communication. Measures such as creating interesting advertisements may be needed to decrease the effect of noise. Noise may also be produced by negative or sceptical attitudes towards promotional activities. For example, many people believe promotion encourages inappropriate and excessive consumption by constantly exposing people to products they do not need. For target market members with this critical attitude, there will be significant 'noise' affecting the marketer's message.

## Objectives of promotion

The main objective of promotion is to support the organisation's overall marketing objectives. Promotional activities do this by influencing the consumer and business decision-making processes that were discussed in chapters 4 and 5. This involves influencing the target market's (existing and potential customers) awareness, attitudes and behaviours towards the organisation's offerings (existing and new products).

In competitive marketplaces, promotion aims to demonstrate that the features and benefits of the organisation's products offer more value than competing offerings. The organisation tries to persuade potential customers to trial its product through persuasive information or perhaps by providing a sample of the product. For example, *Gardening Australia* magazine sometimes has a Dilmah teabag or Mr Fothergills seed packet attached to the front cover as a strong inducement for its readers to try the products of the businesses that advertise within the magazine. Many fashion magazines give away sample cosmetics for the same reason.

Marketing communications aimed at existing customers reinforce the product or brand and encourage repeat purchases or the purchase of other products offered by the organisation. For example, Coca-Cola is the number one brand name in the world and does not need to advertise to say that it is a carbonated cola drink, but it advertises to make sure that awareness is maintained and that it translates into sales. Some seasonal products need promotional campaigns that refresh awareness; for example, swimwear manufacturers, such as Tiger Lily, start to promote their products in late winter and spring as they have been largely out of mind during the colder seasons. Loyalty programs are another common approach to retaining existing customers. For example, in promotions such as the Qantas Frequent Flyer program and the petrol discount vouchers offered by the major supermarkets, the more a consumer engages with one brand, product or company, the more they are 'rewarded' with discounts, gifts and special offers.

For a genuinely new product that is unfamiliar to the market, the marketer will first need to create demand for the product itself, rather than its brand specifically.

For example, when it introduced its Blu-ray player, Sony focused on promoting the concept of the Blu-ray technology more than promoting the brand itself. New product innovations are often a prompt for promotional efforts designed to make the most of a competitive advantage. Being first to market with some innovation gives what is known as a first mover advantage. Once successfully built, competitors can find it very difficult to overcome a business's first mover advantage. Promoting the product rather than the brand is not limited to new products. Surfwear company Quiksilver, like most of the surfwear companies, promotes surfing as a sport and a lifestyle, believing that increasing the popularity of surfing generally and building an association between the surfing lifestyle and its brand will flow through to more demand for its products. The promotional efforts run by industry associations are also aimed at creating demand for a particular type of product. For example, Seafood Services Australia promotes eating seafood two to three times a week, thus promoting seafood as a product.

In addition to promoting products, marketing communications can be designed to increase general awareness about and goodwill towards an organisation. These efforts usually involve some degree of philanthropy. When such promotional efforts are actually tied to the purchase of a product, they become part of what is known as **cause-related marketing**. Brands like Meadow Lea, Kit Kat, Dunlop Volleys, and QantasLink have been associated with connecting with the National Breast Cancer Foundation and the 'pink ribbon', and have all achieved sales spikes as a result.[3] Cause-related marketing can be a very powerful promotional tool — many consumers, buying a largely substitutable product, will opt for the one that supports a good cause.

**cause-related marketing**
Philanthropic activities tied to the purchase of a product.

Sponsorship is another way that a business can build awareness and positive associations with its products. For example, Qantas sponsors the Australian Rugby Union's Wallabies and Red Bull sponsors the Red Bull Air Race. As these examples suggest, the sponsoring brand or product does not necessarily have to directly relate to the sport or event being sponsored (indeed alcohol and, in the past, cigarettes were often associated with sport, though they are detrimental to performance) — it is the overall association that counts. Westpac sponsors search and rescue helicopters in Australia and New Zealand. Search and rescue is in no way directly related to Westpac's core business — banking and financial services — but its sponsorship of the helicopters exposes its brands to the community and associates it with a good cause. Sponsorship is discussed in more detail later in the chapter.

Effective promotional efforts can increase the level of support offered by retailers. For example, making a product highly desirable through effective advertising will often lead to the product featuring more prominently in shelf displays in retail stores and the more intense direct selling of the product by retail staff. This is a win–win situation for the product manufacturer and the reseller as both experiences increase sales. Such campaigns are often carefully coordinated and the parties share in the cost of some advertising activities, known as cooperative advertising.

Regardless of the specific objectives of marketing communications, the implementation of promotional activities should be consistent with the rest of the marketing mix and different elements of the promotional mix must be consistent with each other.

Westpac's sponsorship of search and rescue helicopters associates the company with a good cause.

After a rapid challenge against incumbent Kevin Rudd, Julia Gillard became Australia's 27th Prime Minister, and the first woman to hold the position. Predictably there were thousands of words written about the historic event the next day. In a quickly arranged show of creativity by the advertising industry, newspapers also featured thousands of dollars worth of advertising the next day, capitalising on this topical story. Some examples included:

- 'Yes Julia . . . chicks rule.' (Nandos)
- 'Taking a break?' with a picture of Kevin Rudd. (Jetstar)
- 'The leader in cleaning up party spills.' (Viva paper towels)
- 'Kevin, here's a cabinet that won't let you down.' (Ikea)
- 'Support for our new Prime Minister.' (Nurofen)

# Kevin, here's a cabinet that won't let you down.

$599
HEMNES
glass-door
cabinet

IKEA®
Love your home

© Inter IKEA Systems B.V. 2010. www.IKEA.com.au

These are all examples of 'topical advertising', where advertisers take advantage of a current event or issue to get the attention of potential customers — often using humour as a hook. In addition to being clever, current and relevant, they can also generate extra publicity in their own right. For example, they can quickly become the focus of talkback radio segments, and/or become viral by being spread online via social networks, due to their timeliness, creativity or controversial nature.

Another example of topical advertising surrounded the Sydney dust storms. In a spectacular 'once in a lifetime' show of nature, the city of Sydney literally had thousands of tonnes of dust dumped on it. Advertisements that were circulating the next day included:

- 'How do you get red dust out of white pants? Time to call your mum?' (Telstra)
- 'Now that the dust has settled, enjoy a streak-free shine.' (Windex)
- 'A little dirt isn't the end of the world.' (OMO)
- 'Great for stains. And dust storms.' (Napisan)
- 'We see the world in orange. We wanted you to see it that way too. We're sorry about the dust.' (Bankwest)

There were also ads for Subaru, Viva Glass and Mirror Wipes and Visa that related to the dust storm. Even a spokesperson for Tourism NT claimed that it was part of the Northern Territory 'get ceNTred' campaign via 'bringing the red centre to Sydney'. It is evident that while many in Sydney turned up to work late the next day or even took the day off, some of the creative people at advertising agencies were obviously working overtime.

Sporting events like the Olympics, a grand final or a test series can also attract topical advertising. Some companies even have topical advertisements as part of their normal advertising strategy. Nandos, for example, have regularly run topical advertisements in recent years that have mentioned the current state of the economy; as well as ads about issues concerning competitors, politicians and even refugees. Wherever there are newsworthy events — whether political, natural or sporting-related — creative minds also see an opportunity for topical advertisements.[4]

## Questions

1. Why do you think companies would spend money on advertising messages with such a short lifespan? In your answer, refer to the communication model in figure 9.1.

2. Identify an example other than those listed of a company that has undertaken this type of promotional activity. What do you believe was the company's main promotional objective with the campaign?

## Concepts and applications check

**Learning objective 1** explain promotion (marketing communication) and its role in the marketing mix

1.1  What is meant by 'promotion'? How do marketing communication activities assist the other elements of the marketing mix in an organisation's marketing strategy?

1.2  How does the model of communication help in explaining how an advertisement works? Analyse a current advertising campaign in your answer.

1.3  What are the main objectives of promotion? Provide an example of a campaign that would appear to have awareness as its objective.

1.4  Using an example of your own, explain why an organisation may aim to create demand for a product type rather than its specific brand.

## INTEGRATED MARKETING COMMUNICATIONS

Just as the different elements of the marketing mix need to be carefully coordinated to achieve the best possible effect, promotional efforts also need to be constructed to maximise the return on what is often a large investment. **Integrated marketing communications (IMC)** is the term given to the coordination of promotional efforts to maximise the communication effect.

The goal of IMC is to consistently send the most effective possible message to the target market. The four main components of IMC are advertising, public relations, sales promotion and personal selling. As you will discover in this chapter, these categories overlap and some promotional activities do not fall neatly into any of the main components. Nevertheless, they provide us with a useful framework for analysing and designing IMC.

As advertising, public relations, sales promotion and personal selling approaches have become more sophisticated, personalised, targeted and specialised, they have also become more expensive. In response, management in marketing organisations has placed greater emphasis on evaluating marketing efforts and demonstrating the return achieved on the investment in promotion. The best return on promotional efforts is achieved when there is a high degree of consistency, and hence synergy, across the four areas of promotion. This possible high return on promotional efforts has led to the growing popularity of IMC approaches.

## The promotion mix

Various combinations of promotional methods are used to promote a specific product (good, service or idea). The four main elements of a promotion mix — advertising, public relations, sales promotion and personal selling — are discussed in detail in the following sections of this chapter, but first we will provide an overview of the relative strengths and weaknesses of each to provide a basis for understanding how to establish, monitor and adjust the appropriate promotion mix.

### Advertising

Advertising is the transmission of paid messages about an organisation, brand or product to a mass audience. Advertising is a big business, worth over $12 billion a year in Australia, with many large organisations spending millions each year on traditional media advertising. Tables 9.1 and 9.2 list the top advertisers in Australia and New Zealand respectively, while tables 9.3[5] and 9.4[6] show the corresponding media expenditure for each country.

 **Learning objective 2** understand the integrated marketing communications approach to marketing promotion and the major elements of the promotion mix

**integrated marketing communications (IMC)** The coordination of promotional efforts to maximise the communication effect.

The main benefit of advertising is the ability it offers to reach a lot of people at a relatively low cost per person. While advertising is expensive, its ability to reach a lot of people makes it cost effective based on price per exposure. It is also possible to aim advertising at particular target markets by choosing appropriate media. For example, high-end watch companies tend to advertise in *GQ* and *BRW*, whereas makers of baby formula tend to advertise in *New Idea*. The choice of the right media can add to the brand image of the product, so if a perfume advertises in *Vogue* or *Harper's Bazaar* it is perceived as a high-quality product.

The main limitations of advertising are the difficulties in measuring its effectiveness (one of the most famous quotes in advertising, attributed to US retail pioneer John Wanamaker, is that 'Half the money I spend on advertising is wasted; the trouble is I don't know which half'). Because of its mass market approach, there is very limited presentation and personalisation of the marketing message carried by advertising. TV commercials are often only 30 seconds in length, which can limit the content presented. Even the most sophisticated personalisation approaches in direct mail usually do little more than include the reader's name along with a standard message.

**TABLE 9.1** Top 10 advertisers — Australia

| Rank | Advertiser group/ Advertiser | Annual expenditure A$ (millions) | Key brands |
|---|---|---|---|
| 1 | Wesfarmers | 225–230 | Coles supermarkets, Kmart, Target, Officeworks, Liquorland |
| 2 | Telstra | 160–165 | Telstra Corp Ltd, Trading Post Group, Universal Publishers |
| 3 | Harvey Holdings | 135–140 | Harvey Norman, Domayne |
| 4 | Woolworths Limited | 135–140 | Woolworths supermarkets, Big W, Dick Smith |
| 5 | Commonwealth Government | 115–120 | Defence, Health & Ageing, Medibank Private, Environment & Water Resources |
| 6 | Nestlé/L'Oreal | 115–120 | Nestlé Australia, L'Oreal Australia, Uncle Tobys, Jenny Craig |
| 7 | NSW Government | 95–100 | NSW Lotteries, Cancer Institute, Roads & Traffic Authority, Health, Tourism, Commerce |
| 8 | Victorian Government | 95–100 | Transport Accident Commission, Transport, Sustainability & Environment |
| 9 | Toyota Motor Corporation | 80–85 | Toyota, Lexus |
| 10 | Suncorp Group | 80–85 | AAMI, GIO, APIA, Suncorp, Shannons |

*Source:* Nielsen Media; 'Australia's Top Advertisers' AdNews 27 March 2009

**TABLE 9.2** Top 10 advertisers — New Zealand

| Rank | Advertiser group/Advertiser | Annual expenditure NZ$ (millions) |
|---|---|---|
| 1 | Foodstuffs NZ | 54.4 |
| 2 | Progressive Enterprises | 53.5 |
| 3 | The Warehouse | 51.5 |
| 4 | Harvey Norman | 51.1 |
| 5 | Telecom Corp of NZ | 40.4 |
| 6 | Noel Leeming Group | 38.1 |
| 7 | Reckitt Benckiser NZ | 38.1 |
| 8 | Unilever Australasia | 36.6 |
| 9 | NZ Lotteries Commission | 35.3 |
| 10 | Mitre 10 NZ | 32.4 |

*Source:* Nielsen Media Advertising Information Services 2009

| TABLE 9.3 Advertising by media sector — Australia | |
|---|---|
| **Sector** | **Annual expenditure A$ (millions)** |
| Free-to-air TV | 3 245 |
| Metropolitan/national daily newspapers (including inserted magazines) | 3 030 |
| Internet | 2 115 |
| Magazines | 1 300 |
| Radio | 980 |
| Outdoor | 420 |
| Pay TV | 360 |
| Cinema | 98 |
| **Total** | **12 548** |

*Source:* Australian Financial Review, 16 November 2009

| TABLE 9.4 Advertising by media sector — New Zealand | |
|---|---|
| **Sector** | **Annual expenditure NZ$ (millions)** |
| Newspapers | 623 |
| Television | 570 |
| Radio | 236 |
| Magazines | 217 |
| Interactive | 214 |
| Outdoor | 68 |
| Unaddressed mail | 58 |
| Addressed mail | 53 |
| Cinema | 6 |
| **Total** | **2 045** |

*Source:* Advertising Standards Authority, NZ 2009

## Public relations

Public relations refers to communications aimed at creating and maintaining relationships between the marketing organisation and its stakeholders. Stakeholders include customers, suppliers, owners, employees, media, financial institutions and those in the immediate and wider environment. Effective public relations are created when the public relations messages are timely, engaging, accurate and in the public interest.

The main benefits of public relations promotions are credibility (as public relations efforts do not appear to be advertising), the significant word-of-mouth communications that can result, their low or no cost nature, and their effectiveness in combating negative perceptions or events. For example, McDonald's runs the annual McHappy Day, one of Australia's longest running charity days, which raises over $2 million for Ronald McDonald House Charities (RMHC). More than 800 celebrities and local VIPs donned aprons and took drive-thru orders at close to 800 McDonald's restaurants across Australia, including Kylie Gillies, the host of *The Morning Show* on Channel Seven, and *Home and Away* cast members, who adopted a store on Sydney's Northern Beaches.[7]

Public relations strategies have some limitations, however, including that many efforts are seen by the news media as attempts to obtain free advertising and are thus rejected. This can result in poor exposure of the organisation's public relations message. Another limitation is that a marketing-savvy public is increasingly cynical about the motivations of businesses when they involve themselves in activities other than the direct marketing of their products. Many consumers, rightly or wrongly, now view sponsorship of a concert as an effort to sell something, rather than as a philanthropic effort to bring the arts to the public. Nevertheless, the consumers are still exposed to the marketer's message and branding.

## Sales promotion

Sales promotions offer extra value to resellers, salespeople and consumers in a bid to increase sales. They are often used on an irregular basis to smooth demand. For example, businesses that install home air-conditioning offer sales promotions (such as price discounts, a bonus remote control or free ceiling insulation) in winter in hot areas and in summer in cold areas.

The main benefits of sales promotions are to smooth out sales in periods of low demand and to facilitate retailer support. While sales promotions targeted at consumers are familiar and obvious, many sales promotions are aimed at the resellers and salespeople, rewarding them for selling the company's products or particular volumes of products. Motor dealers almost universally get bonus payments from car manufacturers based on exceeding certain threshold levels in sales each month or quarter. This is why car buyers can often negotiate a better price on a car towards the end of a month or quarter than right at the start of a new trading period. If you go into a mower store, you might find the staff wearing shirts with Stihl branding or Honda branding, even though the store sells both brands (and others besides). This is both a promotion aimed at the salespeople and at customers who go into the store.

The main limitations of sales promotions are that they can lose effectiveness if overused (in particular, customers can come to expect some bonus or price discount and simply wait en masse for a promotion to begin before they buy a product), they are easily copied (particularly price discounts and bonus offers), and the public is becoming increasingly cynical about whether they offer any real value or whether they just highlight that the usual price and conditions under which a product is purchased has a great deal of extra margin built in.

### Personal selling

Personal selling refers to personal communication efforts that seek to persuade consumers to buy products. Certain industries or types of products tend to favour personal selling as a promotional activity, such as expensive, high-involvement or industrial products.

Personal selling benefits include that the message can be very specifically and personally tailored to the individual consumer — thus having greater influence than less personal advertising, sales promotions and public relations strategies. Personal selling also enables the marketing message to be adjusted based on feedback given by the target of the selling effort.

Personal selling also has limitations, including that it is expensive and has a limited reach. During personal selling, the potential customer consumes all of the salesperson's time and effort. Personal selling is labour intensive and time consuming. Additionally, as consumers become more and more educated and informed — often having done considerable research online before entering a store — efforts at personal selling are viewed with increasing cynicism. At its worst, the customer can know much more about the product they are interested in than does the salesperson.

## Integrating promotion mix elements

Armed with a basic understanding of each component of the promotion mix and some of their relative strengths and weaknesses, we will now consider how they are chosen and combined to form an effective IMC strategy. The most effective choice and mix of promotion elements will vary with the specific goals of the marketing effort, individual product characteristics, individual target market characteristics, the nature of the marketing organisation itself, and the resources and budget available to the marketer.

All marketing organisations have different promotional needs and finite financial and other resources, and so must choose from competing options in the promotion mix. Marketing organisations with very large promotion budgets will usually use multiple promotional strategies, while those with smaller budgets will rely on fewer and simpler strategies, often executed on a smaller scale (e.g. advertising in the free local newspaper or sponsoring the local under-10s cricket team as opposed to advertising on television and sponsoring the Olympic swim team).

Consider the promotions mix of the Myer department store:

- advertising through expensive large, glossy catalogues delivered by mail and inserted in newspapers (and available online); television commercials, multiple-page newspaper and magazine advertisements; website
- sales promotions, including offering 'sales' (discounts on normal pricing), interest-free credit terms (pay nothing for 3 months), and bonus products (e.g. two shirts for the price of one)
- personal selling in-store by staff working on commission in departments run as independent businesses
- public relations by hosting book signings, fashion shows and product launches in selected stores; for example, with Jennifer Hawkins, Jamie Oliver, Harry Kewell and the Bondi Rescue team.

Contrast this with a smaller operator such as a Rivers store:

- advertising through television and radio commercials, small advertisements in newspapers; and a website
- sales promotions, including offering 'sales'
- personal selling in-store by expert staff

and a very small operator such as local dress shop:

- advertising through the Yellow Pages and a website
- personal selling in-store by expert staff.

The appropriate promotion mix is likely to change over time as each of those characteristics changes and as the effectiveness or otherwise of the current promotional mix is evaluated. Formulating an appropriate promotion mix can be a complex undertaking. In the case of franchises, franchisors usually hand most of the promotion mix to the franchisees. This concentrates the strategic work and ensures a consistent promotional message. It does, however, limit franchisees from responding to local conditions.

### Pull policies and push policies

In addition to choosing a mix of promotional tools, marketing organisations must choose whether to primarily aim their promotions at consumers or at marketing partners such as retailers, or both. A **pull policy** is an approach in which the producer promotes its product to consumers, usually through advertising and sales promotion, which then generates demand upward through the marketing distribution channel. For example, the consumer becomes interested in a product through the producer's television advertisement and then enquires at a retailer. The retailer asks its suppliers about the product and the suppliers seek out the producer. By contrast, a **push policy** is an approach in which the product is promoted to the next organisation down the marketing distribution channel. For example, a producer promotes its

**pull policy** An approach in which a product is promoted to consumers to create demand upward through the marketing distribution channel.

**push policy** An approach in which a product is promoted to the next organisation down the marketing distribution channel.

product to a wholesaler, which in turn promotes the product to a retailer, who finally promotes the product to consumers. Of course, many products are promoted via both techniques. Additionally, producers and retailers may undertake a cooperative advertising campaign where both the producer and the retailer are promoting the product to its target market.

Often the guide to which strategy to use is based on discovering where the consumer decides on obtaining more information or buying the product. For example, if the consumer is more likely only to think about purchasing the product at the retail outlet, a push strategy would be favoured; whereas, if consumers are more likely to think about the product independently (i.e. away from the store environment), a pull strategy may be more appropriate. Elements of a pull strategy are often evident in producers' websites.

## Spotlight Volkswagen Polo

When car manufacturers promote a small car model, they often portray it as a car for women. Volkswagen (VW) changed this traditional approach when the company launched its redesigned 'Polo' with a campaign based around the creative idea: 'For dedicated followers of no one.' VW Australia's general manager of marketing, Jutta Friese, said: 'We're targeting the Polo more to young males. In

other car maker's ads [for city cars], it's always women going shopping. The new Polo is not a girly car. VW doesn't do girly, trendy cars. You only have to look at the car's body colours — there's no pink or what we call "nail polish" colours.' Although she adds, 'There are no big signs [in the Polo ads] saying: "Not for women. Men only!" We're not going to eliminate females with this car.'

The marketing communication campaign includes cinema, television, digital and print media. Targeting young male customers who see themselves as drivers who do not feel the need to follow others by latching onto the latest trends, the television commercial depicts four young males driving along in a Polo and heading to a nightclub. The three passengers continually change their appearance with different beards, moustaches and hairstyles, while the driver keeps to his same hairstyle and look, thereby keeping to the 'For dedicated followers of no-one' theme.

In addition to the television commercial, an innovative interactive website was created which allows users to choose their own pathway to explore the new Polo, and to watch interviews with other 'dedicated followers of no-one'. These people include pyrotechnics expert Allan Spiegel, interior designer Paul Kelly, aerialist and trapeze artist Tammi Dawson and the Flipsters (the young design duo behind the innovative 'Flipster' shoes). The online campaign is also supported by an extensive digital media platform including online banners and social media marketing. Print advertising, direct marketing and outdoor billboards also complement both the television commercial and online promotional activities.[8]

### Questions

1. Describe the extent to which VW's 'For dedicated followers of no-one' could be described as an integrated marketing communications campaign.
2. Are there any other promotional mix elements that could effectively be utilised in an integrated marketing communications campaign for the Polo?

## Concepts and applications check

2.1 Explain what is meant by the term 'integrated marketing communications' and the advantages of an IMC campaign for a company. How can a company combine promotional mix elements to achieve more communication impact?

2.2 Analyse the major elements of the promotion mix, explaining the advantages and limitations of each.

2.3 Outline how each major element of the promotion mix could be used in an integrated marketing communication campaign for a product of your own choosing.

2.4 How can knowing about 'pull' and 'push' marketing channel strategies assist in planning promotional campaigns? Describe some 'push' examples at a retail outlet of your own choosing.

# ADVERTISING

You are already familiar with advertising. Almost every time you watch television, read a magazine, listen to the radio, drive along a highway or visit a website, you are targeted by advertising. Formally, **advertising** is the paid promotion of a business, product or brand to a mass audience. It can involve the traditional mass media — television, radio, newspapers and magazines — or other media such as billboards, direct mail, the internet, email, SMS, and displays and signs on trucks, buses and taxis. We are again using 'products' in a broad sense that includes 'ideas'. Political parties, charities, medical research institutes and celebrities are among the enormous range of 'non-business' organisations and individuals that use advertising to promote their product, idea, message and themselves.

Advertising can be designed to promote either a product or an organisation. Product advertising includes advertisements for goods and services such as Vegemite or a seven-day sailing holiday in the Whitsundays. Product advertising usually aims to demonstrate the features and benefits of the product and to promote the product or group of products above competitors' products. When this is taken a step further and the advertisement specifically compares products with a competitor's products, it is known as comparative advertising. Comparative advertising can be particularly useful in winning market share from a relatively established strong competitor. It is often used in low-value items such as groceries and in particularly competitive sectors such as the automotive and housing industries. It is, however, subject to legal restrictions (essentially the advertiser must be truthful in their comparisons) and is in fact illegal in some countries, principally in Asia.

Organisational or institutional advertising is aimed at promoting ideas and images. Banks, insurance companies and travel centres often use this type of advertising to promote the nature of the service you can expect (e.g. short queues, experienced and friendly staff) rather than specific products you can buy. Insurer AAMI takes this to an extreme, personifying its name by featuring a charming call centre worker called 'Amy' in its advertising. Such advertising can also be combined with public relations campaigns to foster a particular image of the organisation or for it to push its agenda. Trade unions, employer groups, political parties and many other organisations often use this type of advertising. In the case of governments, advertising is sometimes used to persuade the public to act in a particular way (e.g. to

**Learning objective 3** describe different types of advertising and the steps in creating an advertising campaign

**advertising** Paid promotion of a business, product or brand to a mass audience.

**INSOMNIA, MEMORY LOSS OR PSYCHOLOGICAL PROBLEMS.**

**ECSTASY. FACE FACTS.**

For help or information, call **1800 250 015**
or visit **australia.gov.au/drugs**

NATIONAL DRUGS CAMPAIGN  Authorised by the Australian Government, Capital Hill, Canberra.  **Australian Government**

Truth (some side effects of ecstasy use) and fear (the reinforcement of a photo of a disturbed young female) are used in this advertisement to communicate the message that ecstasy use is dangerous.

report suspicious behaviour that might be linked to terrorism, 'Be Alert — Not Alarmed', or to obey road rules). The Commonwealth Government used this type of advertising as part of its National Drugs Campaign.

# Creating an advertising campaign

Within the IMC strategy, the overall advertising plan is known as the advertising campaign. Putting together an effective advertising campaign can be relatively straightforward, consisting of a block advertisement in the classified pages of the local newspaper, signage on a store and a Yellow Pages entry, or unimaginably complex, with customised television spots in multiple countries, interactive context-sensitive advertisements on websites that link to a more extensive product website, signage at major sporting events and product placement in Hollywood films. Any decisions about advertising should be made in the context of an IMC approach. This will help determine whether advertising is the appropriate promotional approach, how much of the budget it should get and what it needs to do to complement the other promotional approaches used. The more complex and ambitious the campaign, the more likely it is the marketing organisation will engage the services of a specialist advertising agency to assist in the creation, production or placement of an advertising campaign.

The key steps in creating an advertising campaign are:
- understand the market environment
- know the target market (audience)
- set specific objectives
- create the message strategy
- allocate resources
- select media
- produce the advertisement
- place the advertisement
- evaluate the campaign.

We will discuss each of these in turn in the following sections.

### Understand the market environment

Marketing organisations should not view advertising in isolation, so before major decisions are made on the advertising campaign it is important to review the marketing environment. Emerging issues in the marketing environment may affect the advertising campaign. If they are not anticipated, changes in the marketing environment, such as a new technology launched by a competitor, can make a campaign ineffective. An understanding of the market environment can be built by preparing, or reviewing, a situation analysis. This briefly reviews the success or otherwise of the organisation's current marketing mix and presents an analysis of the various internal and external factors which will influence how the firm will undertake its planned campaign. Some of the internal issues include a marketing mix analysis and company analysis, to assess the organisation's current marketing position. The external factors may include a customer analysis, competitor analysis and a macro-environmental analysis (which refers to the various uncontrollable factors that can affect how marketing and promotion activities are undertaken). A macro-environmental analysis examines political, economic, social, technological and legal factors (see chapter 2).

## Know the target market (audience)

A solid knowledge of the target market underpins all of the decisions to be made in formulating an advertising campaign (and indeed any marketing effort). Simply, if you are sending a message, it is important to know about who you are sending the message to. The marketing organisation must identify its target market, existing customers, potential customers, or both. It must then analyse the target market to determine what choice of advertising is most likely to reach and persuade the members of that market, or the specific target audience for the message.

Identifying the target market includes researching:

- demographic factors (such as age, income, education)
- its geographic location
- consumer attitudes
- the current level of knowledge of the organisation and its products.

Marketing organisations that run advertising campaigns that are not built on knowledge of the target market set themselves up to fail. Consider the target market for the following range of products and messages. As you do, think about how important it is to the success of each to reach the right target market with the right message:

- Absolut Raspberri Vodka (a sweet, fizzy raspberry-flavoured alcoholic vodka drink) — The target market is young (20 to 29) females looking for alcoholic beverages that are easier to drink and more feminine and 'fun' than the traditional spirits, beer and wine. They are available in multi-packs aimed at both home/party drinking and at single-bottle drinking in clubs.
- The New South Wales Teachers Union (the trade union of public school teachers in NSW) — The federation has two target markets: (1) public school and TAFE full-time, part-time, casual and unemployed teachers, to which it advertises itself, its mission and its services; (2) stakeholders in school and TAFE education, such as parents, students, the NSW Department of Education (i.e. the employer), the Federal Department of Education, the wider community, textbook publishers and so on.
- Cervical cancer screening — The target market is sexually active women, as well as health professionals who have a direct role in promoting screening to women.
- The Big Day Out music festival — The target market is music lovers generally, and in particular younger people with an interest in popular and alternative music.
- Sumo Salad outlets — The target market is semi-health conscious shoppers in major shopping centres and workers from businesses located near to shopping centres. Quick salads and healthy rolls have become fast foods of interest to young women in particular.

## Set specific objectives

A marketing organisation contemplating an advertising campaign will probably know the overall aim of the campaign — often simply to increase sales — but a successful advertising campaign needs to be based on narrower specific communication objectives that will help contribute to the broader overall goal. For example, if Cancer Council Australia wants to increase the percentage of women who have regular pap smears, its more specific advertising objectives might be any or all of: to increase the percentage by 15 per cent; to raise awareness among the general community about the disease; to raise awareness about the role of screening; to encourage safe sex to reduce the risk of contracting HPV (a virus that increases the risk of contracting cervical cancer); to let women know who to contact to arrange testing; to inform healthcare workers about their role; or to reach populations with known low rates of screening (e.g. Indigenous peoples). Once the objectives are more precisely defined, the next steps in planning the campaign can be taken.

Specific objectives also facilitate evaluation of the campaign once it is under way. The more specific the objective, the more measurable its achievement will be. For example, the success or otherwise of a Cancer Council Australia campaign to increase screening rates can be measured by comparing screening rates before and after the advertising campaign.

Not all advertising campaigns are designed to immediately increase sales. Some are designed simply to improve brand awareness or positive attitudes towards the marketing organisation. Others may be designed to start a word-of-mouth or viral marketing campaign, and pass on advertisements or websites to family or friends. Television stations sometimes use this approach with teaser campaigns, by showing abstract representations of a new show without giving any details, which generates discussions of what the show is or is about.

### Create the message strategy

The creation of the main message or issue to be presented in the advertising campaign is intimately linked to knowledge of the target market and to the specific objectives of the advertising campaign. To check that the message strategy is on target and likely to be effective, many organisations pre-test their campaigns using focus groups before committing any further resources.

For example, participation by famers in conservation programs is vital for achieving many environment goals, but there are different types of famers and some can be difficult to contact, or are not interested in being informed or participating in relevant programs. One study analysed the different farmer, or landholder, groups and analysed the types of messages and media that are most effective for reaching landholders. This includes the importance of channels involving personal contact for reaching lower sociodemographic mainstream farmers, together with messages linked to how programs will have economic benefits for their farms; for smaller hobby farmers, more general media was recommended with more information-based messages; and for absentee landowners, the importance of reaching farm managers was identified.[9]

### Allocate resources

A marketing organisation will determine a budget for its advertising campaign based on its financial and other resources, the objectives of the campaign and what it expects the return on the investment to be (which should be achievement of the objectives). The marketing organisation also needs to allocate human resources and time to the advertising campaign. It is difficult to predict the success of an advertising campaign so there is never an answer to 'What is the right amount of time and money to spend?' Instead, ensuring it remains within the resources it has available, a business can choose to:

- match its competitors' advertising expenditure
- set a certain percentage of sales or revenues aside for advertising (sometimes based on the previous year's figures)
- make an educated guess
- work backwards from the objectives to determine what will be required to produce the appropriate advertising, then calculate the cost of all of those tasks (which may then require revision of the plan if the cost is beyond the organisation's means).

### Select media

Marketing organisations can choose among a variety of media, each with their own special characteristics. Table 9.5 outlines the advantages and disadvantages of the principal media options.

**TABLE 9.5** Advertising media options

| Media | Subtype | Advantages | Disadvantages |
|---|---|---|---|
| Television | Free-to-air | Mass audience (in the millions)<br>Low cost per person reached<br>Advertising content can be presented as part of the program | Very expensive to produce and air in total<br>Carries a lot of advertising competing for attention of viewers<br>Viewers increasingly immune to advertising or using technology to skip ads<br>Impossible to customise message |
| | Cable/satellite | Large audience, or a specialised or niche audience, depending on the station<br>Advertising content can be presented as part of the program | Very expensive to produce and air<br>Viewers increasingly immune to advertising or using technology to skip ads<br>Impossible to customise message |
| | Community | Cheap total cost to air<br>Audience open to alternative products<br>Advertising content can be presented as part of the program | Can be expensive to produce<br>Small audience<br>Low production values<br>Impossible to customise message |
| Radio | AM/FM | Mass audience<br>Potentially low production costs<br>Advertising content can be presented as part of the program | Radio is often played while doing some other activity, so attention may be low |
| Internet | Brand or product website | Can be cheap to produce<br>Easily updated<br>No competing messages on site<br>Can be tailored/interactive | Need to attract audience to website |
| | Company website | Can be cheap to produce<br>Easily updated<br>No competing messages on site<br>Can be tailored/interactive | Need to attract audience to website<br>Website often performs multiple other purposes, e.g. information for shareholders |
| | Advertising on other sites | Can be cheap<br>Can reach a large audience<br>Can be tailored/interactive | Difficult to measure effectiveness (even with technology)<br>Often presented alongside competitors<br>Cannot control context |
| | Search engine optimisation | Requires constant vigilance/ monitoring/refinement<br>Can reach a large, specific audience | Public and search engine operator resistance to search engine optimisation tactics<br>Difficult to measure effectiveness (even with technology) |
| Email | Subscription newsletters | Cheap<br>Specific, opt-in audience | Very easy to ignore<br>Very difficult to measure effectiveness |
| | Spam | Very cheap<br>Very large potential audience | Very easy to ignore<br>Spamming is illegal in Australia |

*(continued)*

**TABLE 9.5** (*continued*)

| Media | Subtype | Advantages | Disadvantages |
|---|---|---|---|
| **Newspaper** | **Major metropolitan daily and weekend** | Large audience, mostly geographically concentrated<br><br>Can change message daily<br><br>Relatively cheap | Very short life (time reader is on the page)<br><br>Easy for reader to ignore |
| | **Regional** | Geographically concentrated audience<br><br>Can change message daily<br><br>Cheap | Very short life<br><br>Easy for reader to ignore |
| | **Community weekly** | Geographically concentrated audience<br><br>Can change message weekly<br><br>Cheap<br><br>Readers often specifically consult these newspapers to find ads for services, local events etc. | Short life (often a week — readers retain the paper for the weekly television guide)<br><br>Easy for reader to ignore or discard entire publication<br><br>Usually low production values |
| **Magazine** | **Consumer** | Large audience, often with particular demographic features<br><br>High production values<br><br>Prestige<br><br>Reasonably long life (magazines are retained and revisited over days, weeks or longer) | Expensive<br><br>Easy for reader to ignore (competing for attention with competitors and content) |
| | **Niche** | Audience has an inherent interest in products related to the magazine's focus<br><br>Prestige<br><br>Long life (often read over weeks and retained indefinitely) | Can be expensive<br><br>Almost certainly appear next to competitors' ads |
| | **Business/trade/ professional** | Very specific audience with an inherent interest in products related to the magazine's focus | Can be expensive<br><br>Almost certainly appear next to competitors' ads |
| **Direct mail** | **Letters** | High level of control over circulation<br><br>Personalised appeals<br><br>Can be combined with sales promotions, coupons and samples | Expensive<br><br>Easily discarded<br><br>Can generate ill will |
| | **Catalogues/ brochures** | High level of control over circulation<br><br>Often considered away from competitors' advertising | Expensive<br><br>Easily discarded<br><br>Seen as damaging to environment |
| **Public signage** | **Public transport and taxis** | Cheap<br><br>Potentially large audience | Easy to ignore<br><br>Not prestigious |
| | **Billboards** | Cheap<br><br>'Always on' when people are passing by<br><br>Can be used near store to draw customers | Not prestigious<br><br>Easy to ignore<br><br>Subject to complaints about visual pollution/driver distraction |
| | **Shop signage** | Cheap<br><br>'Always on' when people are passing by | Only visible to people in immediate vicinity |

Two of the most important considerations in choosing media are reach and frequency. **Reach** measures what proportion of the target audience is exposed to the advertisement at least once. **Frequency** measures how many times each target market member is exposed to the advertisement. Reach and frequency should be considered in terms of each media option as well as the combination of media chosen.

In selecting the media, the marketing organisation will often start with a broad plan and gradually narrow it down until they have selected particular media to use. For example, they might begin with the idea that they should publish print advertisements and eventually reach the conclusion on the specific media vehicle, such as advertising in *Burke's Backyard* magazine.

It seems a reasonable assumption that advertising online would be the most environmentally friendly approach. In fact, a survey by outdoor advertiser Ooh Media found that 54 per cent of media buyers did indeed believe this to be so. However, in reality, advertising online generates more carbon emissions than any other advertising medium. Ooh Media's billboards and shopping centre signs use lots of PVC plastic and consume large amounts of electricity, prompting the company to initiate a program to try to reduce the amount of carbon dioxide related to its products. One move was to introduce LED floodlights to replace existing lighting, which would save 2600 tonnes of carbon dioxide a year — the equivalent of taking 500 cars off the road. The company also moved to green power — offered by electricity companies and representing electricity that is generated sustainably.[10]

While direct mail might seem old-fashioned, Australia Post has reported that direct mail is growing. According to Australia Post mail marketing manager Mark Roberts, 'It is not cool, but it works'. Roy Morgan Research has found that 80 per cent of promotional mail is read, filed or passed on (only 20 per cent being completely discarded).[11]

In addition to choosing media, marketing organisations need to choose how long to advertise for and when to run or place the advertisements. This is a complex task and aims to maximise the exposure of the message and the effectiveness of the message. If the advertisement runs for too long, however, it can become annoying and the message impact may 'wear out', making the campaign ineffective.

## Produce the advertisement

In creating and producing an advertisement, the marketing organisation must create content (based on the message strategy) and then work out how best to present that content. Small organisations with limited resources may undertake the decisions and creative processes themselves. Sometimes their chosen media may be able to provide advertisement design services (this is particularly common for radio stations and newspapers). For large-scale advertising campaigns, it is common to engage the services of an advertising agency. The creative services required to produce an advertisement may include copy writing, graphic design, illustration, scripting and photography. In addition to the creative aspects of the advertising campaign, some advertising agencies provide full advertising services, including market research, pre-testing and media placement. The obvious advantage of engaging an advertising agency is access to specialist expertise. The disadvantages include the cost and some loss of control. Some of the highest profile advertising agencies operating in Australia and New Zealand are Mojo; Saatchi and Saatchi; Singleton, Ogilvy & Mather; Adcorp; and TMP Worldwide.

Advertisements should aim first to grab the potential customer's attention. They then aim to create a need or want in the customer, present the features and benefits of the product and invite the customer to purchase the product.

**reach** The proportion of the target audience exposed to the advertisement at least once.

**frequency** The number of times each target market member is exposed to the advertisement.

### Place the advertisement

The implementation of the advertising campaign involves the buying and placement of media space and time (i.e. securing television advertising spots or column space in newspapers and magazines according to the desired schedule), dedicating people and other resources to ensuring the campaign proceeds (e.g. appointing someone to liaise with Australia Post for direct mail campaigns), and monitoring the effectiveness of the campaign so that it can be improved based on initial feedback. In some cases, an advertising campaign might be ended early if it receives a negative response. In others, it may receive such a good initial response that it is run less often. Carlton & United did this with its well-known 'Big ad' advertisements promoting Carlton Draught beer — after its web-based campaign was so successful, it cut back significantly on the planned television time for the advertisement. In others, the advertisement itself might be changed (e.g. if it pushes the boundaries of public taste too far and elicits complaints).

### Evaluate the campaign

Advertising campaigns can be evaluated before (pre-tests), during and after (post-tests) the campaign is run. Just like Hollywood movies, many advertisements are trialled before general release to determine whether they will be well received. Based on feedback from the participants in the 'advanced screening', the advertisement may be revised. As mentioned in relation to the message strategy, focus groups are often used by advertising agencies to test different concepts, creative techniques, audience comprehension and attitudes towards the advertisement.

During the campaign, its effectiveness can be monitored by measuring changes in sales and enquiry levels, and any extra publicity generated by the campaign (e.g. some advertisements, especially controversial ones, are discussed on radio and television programs). Where multiple media are used, the relative effectiveness of each can be compared. For example, it is possible to count exactly how many people exposed to an advertisement on a newspaper's website actually click through to the advertiser's website. After the campaign, its effectiveness can still be measured through changes in sales and enquiry levels, as well as by conducting market research to assess the level of attention or awareness, such as brand recognition or brand recall, the advertisement generated and whether it changed consumers' behaviour. Advertising agencies often undertake evaluation of the campaigns they run for clients in order to demonstrate the return on their clients' (usually considerable) investment.

Marketing organisations need to be careful in attributing any or all changes in customer behaviour during an advertising campaign to the advertisements. There are always confounding factors such as changing seasons, the acts of competitors and changes in economic conditions and audience sentiment.

## Legal issues in advertising

While the advertising sector is largely self-regulating, there are a number of legal restrictions on what can be advertised and how. The main regulatory issues relate to the need to be truthful and honest in all forms of advertising and promotion, and come under the jurisdiction of the key provisions of the Competition and Consumer Act in Australia and the Fair Trading Act in New Zealand.

While some promotions undoubtedly stretch the truth or add 'puffery' (exaggeration), outright lying is not only illegal, but damaging to customer relationships. The promotion of therapeutic goods is highly regulated. One recent high-profile example was for the promotion of wristbands that would allegedly improve flexibility, balance and strength. The distributors of the product in Australia claimed that the hologram discs in the silicone wristbands would improve the wearer's brain function, muscle response, stamina, oxygen uptake, recovery and flexibility. They recruited some high-profile athletes, such as rugby league player Benji Marshall, to wear the wristbands as paid product ambassadors. Millions of dollars worth of the bands were sold in the Australian market before the Therapeutic Goods Complaints Resolution Panel investigated and found that there was no scientific basis to any of the advertising claims made by the distributors. They were ordered to remove any such statements from their website, which the company subsequently did amid bad publicity for their product.[12] The Australian Competition and Consumer Commission (ACCC) also ordered the distributors (Power Balance Australia) to refund all customers who felt they had been misled by the supposed benefits of the wristbands. At the height of their popularity, the wristbands had been sold to consumers for $60 each. Announcing this decision, ACCC Chairman Graham Samuel also stated: 'When a product is heavily promoted, sold at major sporting stores and worn by celebrities, consumers tend to give a certain legitimacy to the product and the representations being made.' Samuel further warned that retailers who continued to sell the product in their stores with either misleading point-of-sale advertising or packaging would also be leaving themselves exposed to potential action from the ACCC.[13]

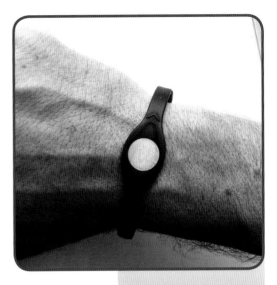

The distributors of silicone wristbands in Australia were found to have misled consumers in their advertising claims.

As mentioned earlier, the advertising industry also attempts to self-regulate. Figure 9.2 (overleaf) presents the Code of Ethics of the Australian Association of National Advertisers.[14] New Zealand's Advertising Standards Authority is a similar organisation with a similar code of ethics.[15] Advanced Medical Institute had a novel response to the Advertising Standards Bureau's ruling against its 'Want longer lasting sex?' billboards. The business kept its advertisements, but plastered a 'censored' sign over the word 'sex' on its 140 billboards around Australia.

Some industry bodies have guidelines for their members, such as for the alcohol, health and financial sectors. Recently, there has been growing pressure for greater regulation of advertising. For example, in recent years there have been growing calls for junk and snack food advertisements to be banned or at least strictly limited during children's programming. A parliamentary inquiry into obesity recommended that research be commissioned into this issue, but that self-regulation should be maintained rather than pursuing legal regulation of advertising food during children's programming. In response, parts of the fast food industry undertook to self-regulate their advertising aimed at children. It is a matter of contention how much children are able to correctly distinguish between editorial and advertising content.[16]

Subliminal advertising on television is banned by the Australian Communications and Media Authority's Commercial Television Industry Code of Practice. Subliminal advertising is a technique that flashes images momentarily on a screen. The idea is that the image is at the edges of people's perceptive abilities. They subconsciously process the image without registering that they have seen it. Channel 10 was found guilty of breaching this aspect of the code during an Aria Awards broadcast. Channel 10 broadcast single-frame images of the logos of the broadcast sponsors — Chupa Chups, Big W, Olay, Telstra, BigPond, KFC and Toyota. It argued that the presentation was just in keeping with the rapid-cut nature of the broadcast, but its argument failed and it was ordered by the Australian Communications and Media Authority to educate its production staff about the issue to avoid any similar incidents in the future.[17]

## AANA CODE OF ETHICS

This Code has been adopted by the AANA as part of advertising and marketing self-regulation. The object of this Code is to ensure that advertisements are legal, decent, honest and truthful and that they have been prepared with a sense of obligation to the consumer and society and fair sense of responsibility to competitors.

### 1. SECTION 1

1.1 Advertising or Marketing Communications shall comply with Commonwealth law and the law of the relevant State or Territory.

1.2 Advertising or Marketing Communications shall not be misleading or deceptive or be likely to mislead or deceive.

1.3 Advertising or Marketing Communications shall not contain a misrepresentation, which is likely to cause damage to the business or goodwill of a competitor.

1.4 Advertising or Marketing Communications shall not exploit community concerns in relation to protecting the environment by presenting or portraying distinctions in products or services advertised in a misleading way or in a way which implies a benefit to the environment which the product or services do not have.

1.5 Advertising or Marketing Communications shall not make claims about the Australian origin or content of products advertised in a manner which is misleading.

### 2. SECTION 2

2.1 Advertising or Marketing Communications shall not portray people or depict material in a way which discriminates against or vilifies a person or section of the community on account of race, ethnicity, nationality, sex, age, sexual preference, religion, disability or political belief.

2.2 Advertising or Marketing Communications shall not present or portray violence unless it is justifiable in the context of the product or service advertised.

2.3 Advertising or Marketing Communications shall treat sex, sexuality and nudity with sensitivity to the relevant audience and, where appropriate, the relevant programme time zone.

2.4 Advertising or Marketing Communications to Children shall comply with the AANA's Code of Advertising & Marketing Communications to Children and section 2.6 of this Code shall not apply to advertisements to which AANA's Code of Advertising & Marketing Communications to Children applies.

2.5 Advertising or Marketing Communications shall only use language which is appropriate in the circumstances and strong or obscene language shall be avoided.

2.6 Advertising or Marketing Communications shall not depict material contrary to Prevailing Community Standards on health and safety.

2.7 Advertising or Marketing Communications for motor vehicles shall comply with the Federal Chamber of Automotive Industries Code of Practice relating to Advertising for Motor Vehicles and section 2.6 of this Code shall not apply to advertising or marketing communications to which the Federal Chamber of Automotive Industries Code of Practice applies.

2.8 Advertising or Marketing Communications for food or beverage products shall comply with the AANA Food & Beverages Advertising & Marketing Communications Code as well as to the provisions of this Code.

## FIGURE 9.2

The Code of Ethics of the Australian Association of National Advertisers

# Ahoy! An offensive ad

While some companies have a deliberate strategy to show controversial images, such as Calvin Klein, other companies claim they unintentionally run advertisements that may offend some people. This was the defence used by Nautilus Marine Boat Insurance in relation to complaints over one of their print advertisements. In the advertisement, which appeared in an insurance industry magazine, there was a picture of the Nautilus sales team and, at the top, an image of a crowded commuter boat in Asia, with the text 'there's boat people . . . and there's boat people'.

The advertisement received complaints to the Advertising Standards Bureau by people who felt that the image was of a boat of refugees and was offensive 'to illegal immigrants, and to anyone who understands or sympathises with the plight of people who are forced to enter Australia'.

In its response, the company said:

We are a company that promotes our expertise to insurance intermediaries for their clients' boating insurance needs. The inference in the complaint is a long way from the intention of the advert. The intention expressed to our intermediaries is that we know boats.

As for the perception of an image of a boat of refugees, the company pointed out that:

The people on the boat show no signs of distress and it is clear that it is a commuter boat. They are well dressed, obviously commuting, including one with a bicycle in hand and others with shopping bags. The image and text is directly related to a style of boat. There is a wide variety of marine craft worldwide and this style of craft and number of occupants aboard would not be uncommon for a variety of uses in many regions. There is nothing in the advert that discriminates or vilifies a person or section or the community . . . there is no reference to any particular person/s or region . . . We do, however, see how this could be misconstrued and voluntary elected not to continue with the advert post the publication edition the complaint was received from.

The Advertising Standards Bureau considered this case and found that the advertisement was in breach of section 2.1 of the AANA Code, and upheld the complaint. In their determination, the Advertising Standards Bureau stated that:

the terminology 'boat people' is a negative term and that the image of Asian people juxtaposed with the images of the staff of the advertiser, in the context of the term 'boat people', created a negative and degrading impression of Asian people.[18]

> ### Question
> Refer back to the key steps in creating an advertising campaign and identify where Nautilus appears to have gone wrong.

## Concepts and applications check

**Learning objective 3** describe different types of advertising and the steps in creating an advertising campaign

**3.1** Not-for-profit organisations, such as charities, often run advertising campaigns. How might their campaigns differ from those run by commercial organisations?

**3.2** Think of a product and describe how it could be promoted using comparative advertising.

**3.3** Briefly explain each of the key steps in creating an advertising campaign.

**3.4** Choose two advertising media options outlined in table 9.5 (e.g. television versus the internet). Outline the advantages that each advertising media option has over the other.

**3.5** Explain how the effectiveness of an advertising campaign can be measured.

# PUBLIC RELATIONS

**Learning objective 4**
outline the role of public relations in promotion

**public relations** Promotional efforts designed to build and sustain good relations between an organisation and its stakeholders.

**Public relations** is a term used to describe promotional efforts designed to build and sustain good relations between an organisation and its stakeholders. Stakeholders include customers, employees, neighbours, shareholders, regulators, governments, competitors, the media and society in general. In contrast to advertising, which often promotes products, brands or the organisation through direct paid communications in the media, public relations uses written materials, sponsorships, giveaways, good deeds and other ways to generate positive publicity and goodwill toward the organisation. Public relations is also used reactively to counter poor publicity (e.g. when a business is accused of being an environmental polluter, they may embark on a public relations campaign to 'set the record straight' or to show the benefits of the business that offset its negative environmental impact) or as a part of crisis management.

For example, Shine Lawyers is a legal firm that specialise in plaintiff litigation and employ over 250 full-time staff with 17 offices nationally. They employed the PR company BBS to manage the promotional visit of Erin Brockovich to Australia, in which she would announce her partnership with Shine Lawyers to take on the tough cases and help right the wrongs for everyday Australians. To do this, a media itinerary was developed, with the aim of generating further publicity. This included numerous TV, radio and print interviews, press releases, school visits and so on. The result was more than $15 million worth of media coverage during the five-day visit[19]

## Approaches and methods

**publicity** Unpaid exposure in the media.

One of the most effective public relations outcomes is publicity. **Publicity** is the exposure a marketing organisation receives when it obtains free coverage in the media. Positive coverage is preferred, but many marketers adhere to the old idea that 'any publicity is good publicity'. Apart from the obvious advantage that it is free, publicity is also often better received by the public, which is increasingly sceptical about and tired of advertising. Publicity seems to have an implicit endorsement of the news organisations that carry the story.

Organisations can generate publicity by promoting something newsworthy to news media. This is most often done with a media release — a short article written in news format and sent to news organisations. Some news organisations, particularly smaller ones, will simply publish many of the media releases sent to them. Others are choosy and some will not use media releases as a source of articles. A media release is most likely to lead to positive publicity if the content is of genuine public interest. For example, pharmaceutical companies can generate publicity by issuing news releases about breakthroughs in medical treatments; many organisations can generate publicity by making a donation to charity or offering some community service. In the aftermath of the Victorian bushfire crisis, many businesses donated money, goods and services to the aid and recovery efforts.

A related approach is to call a press conference, which is essentially the same strategy on a grander scale, where media reporters are invited to attend a presentation involving a speech, written materials, demonstrations and the opportunity for questions and photos. This approach is often used to generate publicity for sporting events; for example, in the lead up to and during the Australian Open, Tennis Australia arranges press conferences with star players, issues articles, media releases and background information about the tournament and players, provides photos for media to use and makes several staff available to respond to media enquiries. Press conferences are also one of the basic tools of the trade for politicians.

Besides publicity, marketing organisations can generate good public relations through written communications directly with stakeholders. For example, public companies send annual reports and other reports to their shareholders, which provide them with financial and non-financial information, such as the company's corporate social responsibility activities. Schools give newsletters to students to take home to their parents or guardians, which outline successes in the school.

One of the highest-profile public relations tools is sponsorship. This is covered in more detail later in the chapter. Briefly, sponsorship is a paid association with an event or person. For example, Sanitarium sponsors Australia's state cricket competition, the Sheffield Shield, via its Weet-Bix breakfast cereal brand. On a smaller scale, local businesses might sponsor school fetes by donating prizes.

A further public relations tool is the involvement of the company in charitable donations or acts. Many businesses donate to charity or a 'good cause' and usually receive a public thank you and a certificate they can display at their premises. Businesses may also receive publicity for their charitable work, such as McDonald's McHappy Day events.

Another major role of public relations, apart from proactively presenting good news stories, is to be reactive, countering negative publicity or managing a crisis. This can be extraordinarily complex. Think about trying to run the public relations campaign for:

- BP's oil spill in the Gulf of Mexico
- Jetstar when it was going through a series of customer service mishaps
- the AFL during a series of incidents involving players related to sex, drugs and violence.

Even a highly successful company such as Apple is not immune from negative publicity surrounding new product launches. The company experienced this when it launched the iPhone 4 in 2010. This particular iPhone model had its antenna on the outside of the phone in a stainless steel band. When held a certain way (in what became known as 'the death grip'), the phone's signal and reception capabilities were diminished, increasing the likelihood of dropped calls. Within weeks, and after several hundred complaints, Apple CEO Steve Jobs called a press conference to announce that Apple would give

BP was forced into a public relations 'crisis control mode' after one of its oil rigs exploded in the Gulf of Mexico in 2010, creating the largest marine oil spill in history. In the first 16 weeks after the disaster, the company paid nearly $400 million in compensation payments. Such claims and the associated clean up operation are ongoing, with the environmental impact of the spill likely to be felt for years to come.[20]

away free bumpers (cases that wrap around the rim of the phone) in order to prevent this problem from occurring on the iPhone 4. He further stated that customers who are still not satisfied could return the phones for a full refund. He said, 'We are human and we make mistakes sometimes', while still extolling the many virtues of the product.[21]

# Public relations as a profession

Public relations professionals, whether employed in a specialist public relations business or within a department of some organisation, may undertake any or all of the following activities:

- organisation of publicity campaigns
- organisation of special events
- publishing
- investor and financial relations
- government relations (lobbying)

- media liaison
- crisis management.[22]

Many organisations and individuals use public relations specialists to manage their publicity. This is particularly the case among celebrities and public identities, whose publicists have the dual role of ensuring regular positive media attention while minimising negative press. For example, the Markson Sparks organisation manages public relations for Ky Hurst, Catriona Rowntree, Pauline Hanson and Richard Wilkins, among many others.

Given the complexity of running a public relations campaign to deal with an incident, marketing organisations should prepare contingency plans and materials so they can make a response quickly and efficiently. Managers and others in the organisation who may be called on to comment publicly should all be advised as to the business's position on various issues so that they can provide a consistent message to the media. Many organisations do have predetermined policies and procedures to get their message into the news as quickly as possible. Police and other emergency services in particular have dedicated public relations offices to deal with the incidents — positive, negative and neutral — that they are inevitably involved in.

## Spotlight 'Killer' campaign against Nestlé

Crisis management is an important part of effective corporate public relations. However, companies are not always prepared for negative publicity. The public relations team at the world's largest food company, Nestlé, went into damage control after a social media campaign led by environmental organisation Greenpeace went viral on the internet.

The campaign, known as the 'Kit Kat killer' campaign, was launched via a video on YouTube, and compared eating Kit Kats to munching on bloodied orang-utans. The vivid association was used to highlight Nestlé's relationship with Sinar Mas, a palm oil and paper supplier, as well as its relationship with Cargill, a palm oil supplier that purchases from Sinar Mas. Greenpeace has repeatedly caught Sinar Mas destroying precious rainforest areas in Indonesia that are home to many orang-utans, as well as a source of livelihood for many local communities.

The graphic imagery shown in the footage caught the eye of YouTube followers, quickly receiving more than a million views. The controversy surrounding the video — and its subsequent popularity — only increased with an attempt by Nestlé to have it removed from the site. This decision led to Greenpeace encouraging supporters to share their thoughts by posting protests on Nestlé's Facebook fan page, and to adjust their profile photos to show modified versions of the Kit Kat logo (e.g. uploading an updated logo that read 'Killer' instead of 'Kit Kat'). Many thousands of fans of the page that had previously been exposed to more favourable comments were soon made aware of the issue, with feedback such as 'Start taking some responsibility for where you source your ingredients . . . and just maybe we will forgive you', showing the extent of the backlash.

The administrator for the page inflamed the negative consumer sentiment further by writing: 'We welcome your comments, but please don't post using an altered version of any of our logos as your profile pic — they will be deleted.' The company's attempt to control consumer sentiment and to edit profiles only fuelled the backlash, and created a sense of people not having a chance to freely express their views. Scott Rhodie, a director of a digital public relations agency, House Party, noted that it was obvious Nestlé did not have a 'crisis communications plan' in place. He argued the company had ignored the rules of social media. 'If you are in that space you have to respect it. The moment you start pulling down comments you lose that respect', said Mr Rhodie.

In an about-face, Nestlé executives met several times with Greenpeace campaigners and made a commitment to stop buying palm oil from companies owning or managing farms or plantations associated with rainforest destruction. The commitment will apply to Sinar Mas, as well as to Cargill. As part of the arrangement, Nestlé has partnered with a non-profit organisation, The Forest Trust, and will review its supply chain for palm oil use and audit suppliers for evidence of illegal activity. An update on the company's Facebook page read, 'Social media: as you can see, we're learning as we go'.[23]

### Questions

1. How could Nestlé have handled the situation better from a public relations perspective?
2. What measures could Nestlé put in place that they could implement in the event of a future public relations crisis?

---

## Concepts and applications check

**Learning objective 4** outline the role of public relations in promotion

**4.1** What are some examples of public relations activities?

**4.2** Prepare a marketing argument for and against this statement: 'Any publicity is good publicity.'

**4.3** What steps can companies take to counter the effects of negative publicity and/or manage a crisis?

**4.4** Steve Jobs from Apple has been described as a 'master of PR'. Why do you think he would be described in this way? What activities does Apple undertake to generate publicity?

---

## SALES PROMOTION

**Sales promotions** are short-term activities that are designed to encourage consumers to purchase a product or encourage resellers to stock and sell a product. Sales promotions offer some extra benefit or incentive above and beyond the intrinsic value of the product (e.g. a bonus product with the purchase, a discount on the price or the opportunity to trial the product). Sales promotions are often used in combination with advertising. After all, the sales promotion can only be an effective inducement if people know about it.

**Learning objective 5** explain how sales promotion activities can be used

**sales promotions** Short-term incentives to encourage purchase of a product by either resellers or consumers.

The choice of sales promotion approach will be based on consideration of:
- other elements of the promotional mix
- the characteristics of the product
- the characteristics of the target market
- whether the promotion is aimed at resellers, the business market or consumers.

## Consumer sales promotions

Sales promotion methods aimed at the consumer include:
- free samples
- premium offers
- loyalty programs
- contests
- coupons
- discounts

- rebates
- point of purchase promotions
- event sponsorships.

We will discuss each of these in turn.

### Free samples

Free samples are just that: a sample of a product provided for free to consumers so they can experience the benefits and features of the product without having to commit to a purchase. Homemaker magazines often have a one-use sample of shampoo or laundry powder included. Trade shows often give free samples to both consumers and resellers. Time-limited software downloads are also an example of a free sample sales promotion. Free samples remove any monetary disincentive to trial a product. Once the potential customer has tried the product, they are in a better position to decide whether to purchase.

### Premium offers

**premium offers** Bonus products given for free or sold at a heavily discounted price when another product is purchased.

**Premium offers** are somewhat similar to free samples, but are given as a bonus for purchasing a product. Sometimes they are free; other times they are at a substantial discount to the usual price. For example, JB HiFi recently gave away free *Dr Who* mouse pads and collector cars with purchases of the latest DVD box set of the *Dr Who* television series. JB Hi-Fi also has bonus gifts of free ink cartridges with particular printers sold.

Many premium offers are on a much smaller scale. For example, booksellers often give away a bonus cheap paperback book with the purchase of a full-price book. Some butchers give away a free kilo of sausages with any purchase of meat over a certain value.

### Loyalty programs

**loyalty programs** Schemes that reward customers based on the amount they spend.

**Loyalty programs** are designed to encourage repeat purchases by rewarding consumers based on the amount they spend. The rewards can be discounts, vouchers, free gifts and so on.

MyerOne and Woolworths' Everyday Rewards cards, and Qantas Frequent Flyer points attached to credit cards are two well-known examples. Every purchase at Myer contributes two Shopping Credits for every dollar spent, and when 2000 Shopping Credits are earned, consumers receive a $20 gift card that can be redeemed at Myer. Frequent flyer points were originally conceived to reward those who travelled regularly with airlines. The more kilometres they travelled, the more points they would accumulate — eventually having enough to qualify for a free flight. Over time, these schemes evolved to the point that in addition to points for kilometres flown, points were awarded for all purchases on co-branded credit cards (with bonus points for purchases at affiliated businesses) and could be redeemed for a host of products, not just flights.

Loyalty programs can be very effective in creating customer loyalty as customers look to accumulate enough points to get something for free. On the other hand, there is from time to time a backlash against loyalty programs that require the consumer to spend an enormous amount of money in a limited time period to obtain a product of relatively little value.

## Contests

One of the most common examples of contests asks potential customers to 'Tell us in 25 words or less why you would like to win [insert product name]'. This is a clever promotion, as only people who want the product will be motivated to enter (so they are potential customers), and the contest requires the entrants to think about and articulate the benefits of the product to them (this is an aim of all promotional efforts). Contests and games like this can thus be an effective way to promote product benefits to consumers. A less involving promotion along similar lines is a sweepstake, which is simply a prize draw based on luck. In addition to encouraging consumers to think about the products that are offered as prizes, sweepstakes and contests can help marketing organisations build a database of the contact details of the members of their target market.

## Coupons

Coupons are vouchers that offer consumers a discount price on a product or service. They are commonly used by the major takeaway pizza chains where presentation of the voucher results in cheaper pizzas or a 'meal deal'. Coupons often have some conditions attached, as well as an expiry date. They may be distributed by direct mail, printed within some publication, available to print from a website or printed on the back of supermarket dockets (e.g. 'Shop-A-Docket'). Some businesses compile coupons from different businesses into booklets and distribute these through the mail.

## Discounts

Discount offers provide a certain amount off the regular price. The major supermarket chains offer fuel discounts on purchase of a certain value of groceries. This encourages grocery purchases at the supermarket, encourages fuel purchase at company-owned or co-branded petrol outlets, and is often teamed with a further discount if the customer buys goods other than fuel at the petrol station.

## Rebates

Rebates are the return of some of the purchase price to consumers upon presentation of proof of purchase. To the consumer they result in a similar price to a discount, but they offer several advantages to the marketer over discounts:

- any regret or second thoughts the consumer might experience after purchase is softened by the receipt of cash
- the consumer needs to apply for the refund and usually has to give up some personal information (e.g. phone number, address) when making the application
- some consumers will not bother to claim the refund (whereas no consumers turn down a discount and ask to pay full price).

A special type of rebate is offered by governments when they want to encourage the purchase of particular products. For example, in Australia governments at various times have offered rebates on such items as rainwater tanks, LPG-fuelled cars, private health insurance, child care and land care. This benefits both consumers, who in effect get a discount, and marketers, who can expect higher demand from the lower effective price and the other promotional activities the government undertakes to encourage consumption. In some instances, especially with rainwater tanks, it can be possible to make a purchase at no net cost.

## Point of purchase promotions

Point of purchase promotions include signage and displays in stores and free product trials or demonstrations in stores. Most stores have displays in their windows, behind the counter, on walls and on display throughout the store. Bakeries can probably count the aroma of freshly baked warm bread as a point of purchase promotion!

Many retailers use in-store demonstrations. The cosmetics departments in the large department stores are typical examples where customers can trial products (in fact, on a slow day, it can be difficult to get through the department without being perfumed!). Many liquor sellers offer free tastings of wine, often in combination with a discount price, on Friday evenings. Finally, many supermarkets have taste test displays set up during busy times to enable consumers to try a small sample of a new product for free. Such approaches, particularly with cosmetics, can be expensive, but the potential customer often feels obliged to make a purchase after receiving something for free.

### Event sponsorships

Sponsorship is an approach to promotion that we cover in more detail later in the chapter. One aspect of event sponsorship that can be classified as a form of sales promotion could be an exclusive merchandise deal, whereby the sponsor has sole rights to sell products at the venue. This can include merchandise specifically related to the event (e.g. concert programs, T-shirts, souvenirs) or unrelated products such as food and drinks. Sponsorship usually crosses over with advertising and public relations as well.

## Trade sales promotions

Trade sales promotions are aimed at business purchasers and are run by producers or industries to present products to business customers. Major examples are *conventions and trade shows*. In addition to having a captive audience of decision makers with an inherent interest in the products being presented, products can be demonstrated and much goodwill can be created, particularly if expenses are met, meals are provided and free products are given away. In particular, most people who attend a trade show or convention will depart with free, branded notepads, pens, coffee mugs, caps and T-shirts. These are known as promotional products.

*Sales contests* offer rewards to marketing intermediaries that sell a certain level or sell the most of a particular product in a particular timeframe. The rewards can be quite significant and may be cash prizes, overseas holidays and other desirable gifts. Sales contests are only effective when the thresholds to receive a reward are achievable and the delivery of the reward is very clearly tied to the achievement of the threshold. Sales contests can be both a business-to-business approach and a trade sales promotion approach.

Trade sales promotions aim to persuade wholesalers and retailers to stock and market particular products. They are not aimed at consumers. As such they are push policy methods. They are often run in conjunction with promotions aimed at consumers. The marketer generates consumer demand and ensures the retailers and other intermediaries are in a position to capitalise on it. Trade sales promotion methods include:

* *trade allowances*. These aim to encourage marketing intermediaries to stock and push the marketer's products. They essentially give marketing intermediaries price discounts, refunds or contributions towards promotional efforts in return for stocking and promoting a producer's products.
* *gifts and premium money*. These are simply free merchandise or monetary rewards given to resellers once they purchase and/or sell a particular volume of product.
* *cooperative advertising*. Cooperative advertising shares the media costs between manufacturers and retailers for advertising the manufacturer's products.
* *dealer listings*. These involve the manufacturer promoting the retailers that carry their products, thus influencing retailers to stock the products, building traffic at the retail level, and encouraging consumers to shop at participating dealers.

# Good sports?

In 2010 Coles supermarkets ran a two-month 'Sports for schools' campaign that was launched by Australian Olympic legend Cathy Freeman. The promotional material associated with the campaign also featured several high-profile Australian athletes who were competing in the Delhi Commonwealth Games at around the same time. In essence, participating primary or high schools could sign up for the 'Sports for schools' program, and for every $10 that a family associated with a particular school spent at Coles during the two month period, that school would accrue a one-point voucher towards a variety of sporting equipment.

Coles provided schools with a catalogue of over 300 sporting items that were available to be redeemed during the program, with each item requiring a certain number of voucher points to be accrued for the school to be eligible to receive the item. Participating schools were encouraged to promote the Coles 'Sports for schools' program in their school newsletters, and were also given promotional banners to display at their school gates to encourage maximum school community support.

As part of its publicity for the campaign, Coles maintained that they were helping to 'get all Aussie kids more active at school and were investing in our sporting champions of the future'. Critics of the scheme argued that the amount a school community needed to spend at Coles in order to be eligible to redeem equipment under the program was exorbitant. For example, in order to receive a Sherrin AFL football, an item which typically retails for around $140 at sporting goods stores, a school community needed to acquire a total of 2605 Coles 'Sports for schools' voucher points. This equated to the school community needing to spend a total of $26 050 at Coles supermarkets during the program, just to receive this one item alone.

However, others defended the Coles campaign, claiming that it was valid in an environment where government funding is tight and schools are increasingly looking to the private sector for the funding of resources. It was further argued that shopping is a spending activity that every family has to undertake on a weekly basis anyway, and on this basis the requirements should be considered reasonable.[24]

## Question

Provide a marketing argument both for and against the Coles 'Sports for schools' campaign.

---

## Concepts and applications check

**Learning objective 5**  explain how sales promotion activities can be used

5.1  Briefly explain the major types of consumer sales promotion activities. What factors would make a company choose one activity over the others?

5.2  Think of an example of a sales promotion that you have you seen recently. Describe it and explain whether you thought it was an effective form of promotion.

5.3  Provide arguments for and against this statement: 'Loyalty programs rip off consumers.'

5.4  Provide examples of trade sales promotions. How can trade promotions assist an organisation's sales when they are not aimed at the final customer?

---

# PERSONAL SELLING

Personal selling, as the name suggests, is the use of personal communication with consumers to persuade them to buy products. Personal selling is the most expensive form of promotion as it requires the full dedication of a salesperson, or sales representative, to a customer. It does, however, have strong advantages over the impersonal forms of promotion — in particular that the salesperson can tailor the promotion to the customer's needs, adjusting the promotion as they receive feedback from the customer.

**Learning objective 6**
understand the nature of personal selling

# A model of personal selling

Many marketing organisations use a sales model to manage the personal selling process. Such a model gives salespeople a defined approach to use. There are many differing models, but in this chapter we will look at one: INPLCF, which stands for Information, Needs, Product, Leverage, Commitment/close, Follow-up.

## Information

Gathering information includes developing a list of potential customers, a process known as prospecting. For some organisations, this might involve market research; for others — many of those in retail — it is just the people who walk into the store. In non-retail situations, salespeople develop a list of potential customers using some predetermined set of criteria (e.g. those who live in a particular area or those with an income in excess of a particular amount). Once the potential customers are identified, further information is sought and analysed about each prospect. Using this analysis, prospects are further narrowed down to those that will actually be approached. Upon approaching the potential customer, the information-gathering process continues as the salesperson tries to discover the particular needs of the prospect.

## Needs

Identifying the individual customer's specific needs is the most often overlooked and most poorly performed part of personal selling. Many salespeople move straight into a product presentation without first finding out what the potential customer wants or needs from the product. This puts the salesperson at a disadvantage as they do not know which benefits, features and strengths of the product to promote to the potential customer. In finding out the needs of the customer, the salesperson should begin to build a relationship with the customer. As part of this, the salesperson will discover more about the customer's wants and needs. Armed with that knowledge, the salesperson can begin to analyse how best to choose and present a product to match the customer's needs. They should also be able to pre-empt likely or possible objections.

## Product

Once the salesperson knows what the customer's needs are, they should present the product in such a way as to highlight how the product features match those needs. They should be able to stimulate interest in the product and hold interest in the product. This may involve a formal product presentation and opportunity for touching, holding or using the product. In a business-to-business environment, it might involve a group presentation.

## Leverage

In presenting the product, the salesperson should highlight comparative and competitive advantages. There will usually be some objections or hesitations from the customer. In overcoming them, the salesperson should treat objections as requests for further information. If the needs analysis has been performed well, it should be possible to anticipate likely objections and to have responses prepared.

## Commitment or close

Commitment or 'close the sale' is the stage in the selling process when the salesperson asks the prospect to buy the product. It is important that salespeople do not rush to this stage. To maximise the chance of a successful sale, the salesperson should have taken every opportunity to identify the needs of the customer and to have presented the product in such a way that those needs are best met. They should have properly addressed any objections.

### Follow-up

Customer loyalty and repeat business can be encouraged by following up with customers. Follow-up should determine if the delivery and setup of the order was completed to the customer's satisfaction. Follow-up also helps reduce post–purchase dissonance (the feeling that many purchasers develop that they have spent too much, bought the wrong product, or are not finding the product all that they thought it would be). Like needs identification, many salespeople under-use follow-up, instead concentrating their efforts almost exclusively on trying to generate the next sale with a new prospect. Such an approach can be problematic, particularly for organisations that are dependent on both repeat and new business. In such cases, a careful balance is necessary between a salesperson's focus on the follow-up and servicing of existing customers versus chasing new business leads.

## Managing a sales force

Salespeople are the public face of a business. They are crucial — at times defining — to the customer's experience of interacting with the business, and determine not only whether the customer makes a purchase, but whether they will repurchase in the future and initiate positive or negative word-of-mouth about their experiences. As such, retailers and/or sales managers need to both choose salespeople carefully and manage them effectively.

While a topic as broad as managing a sales force could fill many books on its own, the following are the key tasks that a sales manager will likely need to undertake:
- establish sales force objectives and targets
- determine the appropriate size and location of the sales force
- recruit and train salespeople
- assist salespeople to effectively manage their time
- monitor and motivate performance
- compensate salespeople (usually comprising a base salary plus a commission or bonus scheme designed to motivate them by offering rewards based on results).

- carry out formal presentations of products using videos and other training aids, attend promotional markets and organise product displays
- work on telemarketing campaigns
- plan to meet sales targets and budgets
- use e-business technology.

Personal requirements for sales reps include:
- enjoy working with people
- friendly and confident manner with a pleasant personality
- able to work without direct supervision
- able to clearly present product and service information
- good personal presentation
- excellent communication skills.

## Question

Refer to the INPLCF sales model of personal selling and compare it to the sales representative job description provided by DEEWR. As comprehensively as possible, itemise the major tasks performed by a sales representative and the related skills required into the six categories of the INPLCF model.

## Concepts and applications check

**Learning objective 6** understand the nature of personal selling

**6.1** Not all organisations use personal selling as part of their IMC campaign. What types of industries and products are suited to a focus on personal selling in their promotional mix? Why, for example, would pharmaceutical companies spend a lot of effort on personal selling?

**6.2** Briefly describe each of the steps in the personal selling process and relate it to the marketing of an industrial product.

**6.3** 'Sales people are all talk.' How could a professional salesperson disprove this statement by following the steps in the personal selling process?

**6.4** Think of the last time you had an encounter with a salesperson. Analyse their performance and how it could have been improved in relation to the steps in the personal selling process.

**6.5** Briefly explain the major aspects of a sales manager's role.

# ADDITIONAL FORMS OF PROMOTION

**Learning objective 7** discuss a range of marketing communication options additional to the traditional promotion mix

In addition to the major elements of the promotional mix that we have discussed (advertising, public relations, sales promotion and personal selling), there are a number of other methods that can be utilised by an organisation. Some of these are well established, while others are still in their early stages. Many of the newer approaches have emerged as marketers try to ensure promotional activities are effective. We will examine these before looking at some of the challenges that marketing organisations face in managing promotion as part of the marketing mix.

## Ambush marketing

**ambush marketing** The presentation of marketing messages at an event that is sponsored by an unrelated business or a competitor.

**Ambush marketing** is the presentation of marketing messages at an event that is sponsored by an unrelated business or even a competitor. Ambush marketing is legal and can be extremely successful.

Advertising company Messages On Hold's use of ambush marketing for self-promotion at televised sporting and celebrity events has been so extensive and successful that the ABC's *Media Watch* program described the company as the world leader in ambush marketing. In one stunt, the company sent a staff member to a cricket test match with a life-size cardboard cut-out of former cricketer Shane Warne wearing a Messages On Hold-branded T-shirt and big hand. During his decorated cricket career, Warne had become infamous for several embarrassing incidents involving mobile phones. Although Warne was actually a paid spokesperson for the organisation, the Messages on Hold employee was subsequently fined $100 for advertising at the ground without a permit.[26] Compared to the value of the publicity the stunt generated for Messages on Hold, the fine was obviously a paltry sum.

The Olympics, one of the biggest televised events on a global scale, is often a target for ambush marketers, and they are often rewarded by considerable success. Several years prior to the event, organisers of the 2012 London Olympic Games took the precaution of pre-booking almost all of the city's billboard space for the duration of the Games. The London Olympic Games and Paralympic Games Act 2006 created the London Olympic Association Right (LOAR), giving Games' organisers the power to grant licences to authorised sponsors to use the symbols, words and logos of the event, as well as preventing any advertisement or merchandise with a combination of words and symbols that could create an unauthorised association with the Games. Fines of up to £20 000 were put in place should companies break these rules.[27] Strategies by 'non-sponsors' to connect to the Games can build the impression in consumers' minds that the company has an official link with the Olympics.

While the Olympics organisers pursue and prosecute companies that illegally use trade-marked imagery like the Olympic rings, there is little they can do to prevent a company sponsoring or portraying an individual Olympic athlete or team. The Sydney Olympics sponsors suffered these problems. Qantas arranged endorsements by successful athletes, including two of the major local stars of the Games, Cathy Freeman and Ian Thorpe — overshadowing the Olympic sponsor airline, Ansett. Another high-profile example of ambush marketing occurred at a recent AFL grand final, when Holden flew a blimp over the MCG, even though the official sponsor was Toyota.[28] Even legitimate sponsorship deals can have unwanted results. For example, at the Beijing Olympics Nike had the rights to outfit the Chinese Olympic team in the clothes they wore while competing, but Adidas had the right to outfit any Chinese team member who won an Olympic medal at the medal presentation — essentially forcing winning athletes to don a top layer of clothes before accepting their medals.[29] Marketers considering sponsoring events need to take steps to defend themselves against ambush marketing, including assessing whether the risk is worth it.

Another major international sporting event that is vulnerable to ambush marketing is the FIFA World Cup, held every four years. In the 2010 event held in South Africa, during the Netherlands vs Denmark match, 36 young women wearing orange mini dresses associated with the Dutch brewer Bavaria entered the stands and attracted a lot of attention from the crowd. Authorities proceeded to eject the women, with two people being arrested for organising 'unlawful commercial activities'. The World

In an act of ambush marketing, young women associated with the Dutch brewer Bavaria wore orange mini dresses to attract attention at the 2010 FIFA World Cup.

Cup's authorised beer was Budweiser, and the company had paid millions for the privilege of exclusive representation during the competition.

# Product placement

**product placement** The paid inclusion of products in movies, television shows, video games, songs and books.

**Product placement** is the paid inclusion of products in movies, television shows, video games, songs and books. The product is portrayed or mentioned in context as part of the story line of the show, usually in a positive or at least neutral way. It can be featured or incidental. Product placement of one product or brand often also involves the exclusion of competitors' products and brands (giving us, for example, movies in which every character drives an Audi).

Australia is the third-largest market for product placement, behind the United States and Brazil, with advertisers annually spending more than $250 million on product placement in Australian television programs, such as *MasterChef*. US advertisers spent an estimated $4 billion on product placement in a recent year.[30] In the case of the *MasterChef* television program in Australia, show sponsor Coles has reported that certain grocery items have had significant sales spikes immediately after featuring in recipes on the show. For example, Coles sales data on key ingredients for beef stroganoff (such as beef fillet steak, parsley and shallots), all increased significantly shortly after the recipe featured on the popular show.[31] This sales trend has been repeated at Coles for numerous other recipes that have aired on *MasterChef*.

Coles sponsors *MasterChef* in the hope that viewers will be inspired to try recipes they see on the show and will choose to buy ingredients from Coles stores.

There are many other examples of product placement:

- In a cross-promotion between the Ten Network and the *Oprah Winfrey Show*, Channel 10 personality Carrie Bickmore promoted McCafés in a segment on Oprah's US television show in which she offered a 'crash course in the Australian way'. 'While you have your diners, we have McCafés. Guys come for business meetings, girls come for a catch-up over coffee. It's all just a little bit fancy', shared Bickmore. The veracity of the comment — particularly the inferred significance of 'McCafés' in Australian culture — was queried by the media. As it turned out, the segment was paid for and sponsored by McDonald's. To reinforce this message, McDonald's food was also served to the studio audience as part of the show.[32]

- James Bond films always feature a car. Traditionally it has been an Aston Martin, but BMW and Lotus vehicles have also featured in some movies. Interestingly, the producers of the James Bond films recently announced that they would continue to accept product placement arrangements, but would not guarantee that the product would actually appear in the final cut of the movie. This did not deter companies from paying for placement.[33]
- Coca Cola paid for more than 3000 mentions on US network television in just six months.[34]
- In a twist on product placement, a brewery tried to start marketing a real version of the Duff beer featured in *The Simpsons* — only to be sued by the producers of the program.

Not every product seen in a movie is the result of product placement. Some products are so commonplace that their absence in certain types of content would be odd; for example, a lot of people eat Kellogg's breakfast cereal or drive Toyota cars. Some media producers invent brands to use. For example, a number of Quentin Tarantino's films include 'Big Kahuna Burgers' and *The Simpsons* creators have invented an entire world of made-up brands, including Krusty Burger, Duff Beer and Kwik-E-Mart.

While product placement offers a way for marketers to have their products presented to their target market, often in a desirable context, there are some disadvantages:
- it can be difficult to measure the effectiveness of a product placement strategy
- they are expensive (e.g. car company Buick paid $1 million for one of its vehicles to be promoted in one episode of *Desperate Housewives*)[35]
- consumers can react negatively to product placement if they feel it is over done or interferes with the integrity of the show (such as the *Sex and the City* movie, which was heavily criticised for featuring several dozen product placements).

Somewhat related to product placement is the plug. A plug is when the media overtly promotes a product within a program rather than as a separate advertisement, such as when a lifestyle program such as *Better Homes & Gardens* recommends a particular brand and type of paint to use for a DIY project. In contrast, Australia's public broadcaster, the ABC, avoids plugs in its shows. For example, *Gardening Australia*, when the presenters are shown using actual products, carefully angles product labels so the brand name is not caught by the camera.

## Guerrilla marketing

Originally coined to refer to highly creative, low-budget marketing efforts,[36] **guerrilla marketing** is now used to describe any aggressive and unconventional marketing approach. It is most commonly used by small businesses that cannot afford large-scale marketing efforts. Its effectiveness relies on its ability to take its target unawares — they don't expect it, so they don't filter it out.

**guerrilla marketing**
The use of an aggressive and unconventional marketing approach.

Even large organisations with substantial budgets may choose to use guerrilla marketing approaches. For example, Land Transport New Zealand promoted safe driving around schools by placing flyers under the windscreen wipers of cars parked near schools in the town of Waikato. When the driver got into their car, they were met with a graphic photograph of a child injured when struck by a car, along with the message 'Please don't speed near schools'.[37] The campaign was cheap and impacting, and generated a lot of publicity. Some of this publicity included criticism due to the graphic nature of the image portrayed. It could certainly be argued, however, that the campaign effectively caught its target audience by surprise — one of the key aspects of guerrilla marketing.

# Viral marketing

**Viral marketing** is the use of electronic social networks to spread a marketing message. Viral marketing gets its name from the idea that the marketing message, once introduced, spreads from one person to another via contact, much the way a virus (such as the flu virus) spreads. It can occur via word-of-mouth, the forwarding of emails or links to websites and so on. For example, a person may email the URL of a campaign that they find interesting to their email address book at the start of a day. The people who receive the email may spend time perusing that website and forward the email to their address book and so on. Some people along the way may add the URL to their Facebook profiles, potentially exposing all of their Facebook friends to the campaign.

Successful viral marketing can reach millions of people very quickly. Because the marketing message is spread by friends and colleagues it has greater credibility — and is more likely to be considered — than marketing messages sent via mass media. Among the most famous and successful examples of viral marketing in recent times was Tourism Queensland's 'Best job in the world' campaign. The campaign generated more than $100 million of free publicity around the world once the online community and the world's media became fascinated by the offer. Tourism Queensland advertised a job that would pay $150 000 for six months 'work' living on a tropical island and writing a blog about the islands of the Great Barrier Reef. At the height of the campaign, the www.islandreefjob.com website was receiving 40 hits per second from interested applicants for the position.[38]

The flipside of viral marketing is that it can go very wrong. Firstly, attempts at viral marketing can fail to get off the ground. If the content or presentation does not grab the attention of the people initially targeted it will not be forwarded and will not spread. Credibility is all that opinion leaders online have, so they are choosy about what they choose to promote. The social nature of viral marketing can backfire on marketing organisations that try to initiate viral marketing messages. Viral marketing campaigns can also be hijacked. Confectionery company Skittles invited people to post their own comments online about Skittles using Twitter; however, when word spread over the internet that Skittles had begun to use its Twitter search feed as its homepage, users began posting crude messages and even links to pornographic material, much to its embarrassment. Skittles has now changed its site to redirect users to its Facebook page, and uses a moderator.[39]

# Permission marketing

**Permission marketing** is the broad term given to activities that are centered around obtaining customer consent to receive information and marketing material from a company.[40] As people have become increasingly concerned about the amount of junk mail, telemarketing and advertising that interrupts programs, permission-based marketing has emerged as an alternate philosophy to traditional forms of 'interruption marketing'. With permission-based marketing, marketers actually ask and gain permission to contact the customer. This reduces waste and may encourage genuine customers who want to 'opt-in' and be informed about new stock or sales.

Permission-based marketing campaigns can utilise traditional media, such as direct marketers sending newsletters or catalogues, as well as e-marketing facilities to send emails and provide relevant links to prospective customers who have agreed to the communication. Customers can opt-in to the communication by ticking a box on a form when buying a product from a company to indicate that they are receptive to being contacted by the company with future information and offers. Pumpkin Patch, for example, provide this service to customers, encouraging them to join their Patch VIP club in order to receive information on exclusive offers, early notice of promotions and sales, and alerts of trends and new collections.[41] Similarly, online stores can offer the ability for consumers to opt-in or opt-out of permission-based marketing campaigns. If they opt-in, consumers are likely to receiving future emails from the company in relation to future products and offers.

# Sponsorship

**Sponsorship** is the paid association of a brand with an event or person. A company develops a sponsorship relationship with a particular event, providing financial support in return for the right to display a brand name, logo or advertising. For example, Holden is the major sponsor of the Australian netball team (The Diamonds) while New World is the sponsor of the New Zealand netball team (The Silver Ferns). Sponsorship can be used in cause-related marketing, positively associating an organisation with the sentimental feelings aroused by certain causes, including charities or other worthwhile endeavours. DHL sponsors surf lifesaving in Australia and Westpac sponsors rescue helicopters in both Australia and New Zealand.[42]

Australasian Sponsorship Marketing Association member Jann Kohlmann has warned potential sponsors to be aware of four emerging issues:
1. media fragmentation
2. consumer cynicism
3. social consciousness
4. environmental awareness.

As media become more and more fragmented with smaller, niche audiences, the pay-off on the extraordinary sums of money required to sponsor events diminishes. Consumers are also becoming more cynical about commercial interests in what to them is a leisure pursuit. Some consumers would rather watch their football without advertisements plastered over the players, venue and television screen. Social consciousness and environmental awareness are prompting consumers to think about the overall activities of marketing organisations, rather than to analyse and accept the promotional message in isolation. A recent study found consumers are rapidly paying less attention to corporate sponsorships. During the global economic downturn, corporate sponsorships of sporting events by US organisations were found to have a negative effect on consumer perceptions if the organisation was known to be accepting some form of government financial assistance. The study found that the most effective sponsorships in terms of raising public opinion were philanthropic sponsorships of not-for-profit organisations (with 41 per cent of survey respondents claiming it would improve their opinion of the organisation).[43]

There does not need to be a direct connection between the products of the sponsor and the event sponsored. For example, eating KFC probably does not help young children play cricket better, but KFC does sponsor youth cricket in Australia. Sometimes there is a direct connection, such as Gatorade sponsoring numerous sporting events and athletes, and Nike sponsoring athletes who wear Nike clothing and shoes while competing. Sponsors need to be careful that there can be no negative association with an event. For example, KFC's sponsorship of youth cricket drew some negative publicity, with the Institute of Nutrition, Obesity and Exercise calling the sponsorship 'unhelpful and irresponsible', given the increasing incidence of childhood obesity in Australia.[44]

**sponsorship** The paid association of a brand with an event or person.

# Spotlight Sport, scandals and sponsorship

Sponsorship of high-profile athletes and successful sporting teams is a part of the marketing budget for many large organisations. It is only natural for companies to want to derive benefits from being

associated with winners who achieve a lot of positive media coverage. However, such sponsorship also comes with the potential risk of the organisation being associated with negative publicity, as two recent examples demonstrate.

In a recent year, the Melbourne Storm NRL club was the centre of a major scandal. It was revealed that the club had kept 'two sets of books' — covertly paying their star players more money to retain them at the club. Over five years, the club had assembled a playing roster that breached the salary cap guidelines in place for clubs competing in the NRL competition by more than $3 million. These were the findings of auditors from Deloitte, who were hired by the NRL to investigate the club's financial dealings.

When the scandal broke, the club was heavily penalised financially, via fines, and stripped of two previous premierships and all competition points for the 2010 season. Some sponsors also sought to swiftly terminate their association with the once high-flying club. ME Bank was one such organisation, abruptly ending their lucrative jersey sponsorship arrangement with the Melbourne Storm team. Their chief executive, Jamie McPhee, said at the time: 'As an organisation, ME Bank believes in the principles of strong governance, transparency, integrity and fairness, and we seek to ensure that all of our corporate and community partnerships uphold these same values.' HOSTPLUS was another sponsor that immediately severed ties with the club, with chief executive officer David Elia stating that 'the club's dishonest behaviour made their relationship untenable'.

Similarly, after news broke internationally regarding the numerous extramarital affairs of the world's number one golfer, Tiger Woods, sponsors quickly began breaking their arrangements with the disgraced sports star. It was estimated that Woods was earning about US$100 million (A$111.7 million) a year in endorsements before his private life unravelled publicly in November 2009. With his image as a clean-cut family man in tatters, major international companies like AT&T and Accenture dropped him almost immediately. Gatorade announced: 'We no longer see a role for Tiger in our marketing efforts and have ended our relationship.' Other long-term sponsors to have kept their distance from Tiger Woods since the news broke are Gillette and Tag Heuer, while Nike and EA Sports have continued their association with him.

Olympic swimming champion Stephanie Rice is another star who experienced a fall from sponsorship grace in controversial circumstances. Rice lost a coveted sponsorship deal with Jaguar in 2010 after posting a careless tweet on Twitter that was perceived as a homophobic slur. While Rice later retracted the tweet and apologised, Jaguar did not reverse its decision to drop the high-profile swimmer as a brand ambassador.[45]

## Question

Imagine you are the marketing manager for an organisation that sponsors a sporting team or individual involved in a scandal. Outline how you would handle the situation from a marketing perspective.

## Concepts and applications check

**Learning objective 7** discuss a range of marketing communication options additional to the traditional promotion mix

7.1 Organisations can spend millions on sponsorship. What are the advantages and disadvantages of using sponsorship?

7.2 What is product placement? How can this type of promotion be effective?

7.3 Explain the differences between ambush, guerrilla and viral marketing.

# SUMMARY

 **Learning objective 1** explain promotion (marketing communication) and its role in the marketing mix

Promotion (or marketing communications) is the creation and maintenance of communication with target markets. In marketing, promotion is usually thought of as comprising a strategic mix of advertising, public relations, sales promotions and personal selling. Promotion is an extremely important part of the marketing mix: it makes consumers aware of and interested in the product on offer. It is crucial that marketers effectively and efficiently communicate their message about their product to the marketplace. Promotion often sends messages about the other parts of the marketing mix: the product, pricing and distribution.

 **Learning objective 2** understand the integrated marketing communications approach to marketing promotion and the major elements of the promotion mix

Integrated marketing communications (IMC) describes the coordination of promotional efforts to maximise their effectiveness. The goal of IMC is to consistently send the most effective possible message to the target market. The four main components of IMC are advertising, public relations, sales promotion and personal selling. With a basic understanding of each component of the promotion mix and some of their relative strengths and weaknesses, a manager can consider how they are chosen and combined. The most effective choice and mix of promotion elements will vary with the specific goals of the marketing effort, individual product characteristics, individual target market characteristics, the nature of the marketing organisation itself, and the resources and budget available to the marketer.

 **Learning objective 3** describe different types of advertising and the steps in creating an advertising campaign

Advertising is the paid promotion of a business, products and brands to a mass audience using traditional mass media such as television, radio and newspapers, signage, and emerging media such as mobile phone networks. Within the IMC strategy, the overall advertising plan is known as the advertising campaign. Any decisions about advertising should be made in the context of an IMC approach. The key steps in creating an advertising campaign are: understand the market environment; know the target market; set specific objectives; create the message strategy; allocate resources; select media; produce the advertisement; place the advertisement; and evaluate the campaign.

 **Learning objective 4** outline the role of public relations in promotion

Public relations describes promotional efforts designed to build and sustain good relations between an organisation and its stakeholders. Stakeholders include customers, employees, neighbours, shareholders, regulators, governments, competitors, the media and society in general. In contrast to advertising, which often promotes products, brands or the organisation through direct paid communications in the media, public relations uses written materials, sponsorships, giveaways, good deeds and other ways to generate positive publicity and goodwill toward the organisation. Public relations is also used reactively to counter poor publicity or as a part of crisis management. The main outcome of public relations is publicity. Publicity is the exposure a marketing organisation receives when it obtains free coverage in the media.

**Learning objective 5** explain how sales promotion activities can be used

Sales promotions are short-term activities designed to encourage consumers to purchase a product or encourage resellers to stock and sell a product. Sales promotions offer some extra benefit or incentive above and beyond the intrinsic value of the product. Sales promotion can be directed at the final consumer (consumer promotions) or to those in the marketing channel (trade promotions). Sales promotion methods aimed at the consumer include: free samples, premiums, loyalty programs, contests, coupons, discounts, refunds, rebates; point of purchase promotions; and event sponsorships. Trade promotions include trade allowances, gifts and premium money, cooperative advertising and dealer listings.

 **Learning objective 6** understand the nature of personal selling

Personal selling is personal communication with consumers to persuade them to buy products. Personal selling is the most expensive form of promotion as it requires the full dedication of a salesperson to a customer, but it does have strong advantages, in particular that the salesperson can tailor the promotion to the customer's needs. Salespeople play a very important role for some companies and are the public face of the business. Many marketing organisations manage the personal selling process by using the INPLCF model, which stands for Information, Needs, Product, Leverage, Commitment/close and Follow-up. In managing the sales force, the sales manager needs to establish sales force objectives and targets; determine the appropriate size and location of the sales force; recruit salespeople; train salespeople; compensate salespeople; and monitor and motivate performance.

 **Learning objective 7** discuss a range of marketing communication options additional to the traditional promotion mix

There are many promotional methods available to an organisation in addition to advertising, public relations, sales promotion and personal selling. Sponsorship is the paid association of a brand with an event or person. A company develops a sponsorship relationship with a particular event, providing financial support in return for the right to display a brand name, logo or advertising. Ambush marketing is the presentation of marketing messages at an event that is sponsored by an unrelated business or even a competitor, and can be extremely successful. Product placement is the paid inclusion of products in movies, television shows, video games, songs and books. Guerrilla marketing refers to highly creative, aggressive and unconventional marketing approaches, most commonly used by small businesses that cannot afford large-scale marketing efforts. Viral marketing is the use of electronic social networks to spread a marketing message from one person to another. Permission marketing is where activities are centered around obtaining customer consent to receive information and marketing material from a company.

# The Resource Super Profits Tax

Political advertising has been playing an increasingly important role in elections in recent times. However, some politics-related campaigns have also been used by political parties, unions, organisations and industry associations outside election time to 'advocate' a particular view on an issue or to set an agenda to ensure a particular issue is being presented and discussed in the public arena. It is argued that political advertising alone cannot actually win elections, as it is only one factor that influences voter behaviour. However, a campaign by the mining industry, particularly the Minerals Council of Australia, against a proposed Resource Super Profits Tax was claimed to be a major force in deposing an Australian prime minister mid term.

In 2010 the federal government announced, as part of a new tax package, a new 40 per cent Resource Super Profits Tax. This angered the mining industry. The Minerals Council of Australia, backed by several key players, began a major advertising and public relations war with the government. The prime minister at the time, Kevin Rudd, said:

> So, I imagine that some within the mining industry will dig deep within their very deep pockets and seek to run a political campaign. We will not be deterred one bit. This is a decision in the long term national interest, good for the economy, good in the long term in broadening the base of the mining industry as well, according to the detail of the tax.

Soon after the announcement of the new tax, several mining companies countered by declaring that they were putting on hold any new projects and preparing for job losses. Rio Tinto claimed that it had shelved an $11 billion expansion of iron ore projects in Western Australia. These announcements were soon followed by a concerted advertising campaign from the Minerals Council of Australia. Ironically, the mining industry campaign was designed by Neil Lawrence, the creative force behind Labor's election-winning 'Kevin07' campaign that was credited as a contributing factor to Kevin Rudd leading Labor to victory and becoming prime minister. The advertisements predicted plummeting shares, job losses and mine closures if the tax went ahead. Word spread that the Minerals Council of Australia was prepared to spend around $100 million on an attack advertising campaign on television, radio, newspapers, and the internet (www.keepminingstrong.com) against the government's planned tax. The final amount actually spent was not made public, but it was believed to be closer to $20 million before what was considered to be an acceptable outcome was achieved.

The industry argued the proposed tax would harm investment in mining projects in Australia, cost jobs and harm the wider economy. Some examples of advertisements that were circulating during the campaign were:

- a print advertisement just before an NRL State of Origin match questioning the commitment of the prime minister at the time, Kevin Rudd, and Treasurer Wayne Swan to their home state of Queensland, organised by the Queensland Resources Council
- a series of advertisements that mocked Kevin Rudd and the tax, organised by the Association of Mining and Exploration Companies. In one radio advertisement, a Russian voice was heard saying: 'I am speaking to you from Kursk Russia, where we are mining 47 billion tonnes of iron ore. Much thanks be to your economic genius Comrade Rudd and new mining tax, now all of Russia is enjoying your prosperity and jobs. Please that you be voting for Kevin Rudd and mining tax in your next democratic elections.'

Despite this adverse reaction from the mining industry, the Rudd government declared it was determined to continue with the tax — and that the miners needed 'to return a fairer share to all Australians'. However, it generally appeared that support for the miners' position was growing in the community as the campaign escalated. The Rudd government countered by accusing the miners of purposely spreading misinformation and began a 'public education campaign' with a proposed budget of $38.5 million over two years, despite Kevin Rudd saying previously that he would not use taxpayer's funds to run such a campaign. This decision further dented the falling popularity of the government in the opinion polls, with the issue becoming a major topic in the news and on radio talkback shows. The government's advertisements stressed that, as part of reforms to make the tax system 'fairer', the proposed tax would help fund an increase to the government superannuation contribution, as well as cuts to the company tax rate.

Also countering the stance of the mining industry were a coalition of unions and environmental, welfare and consumer groups (The Australian Council of Trade Unions, the Australian Council of Social Service, the Australian Conservation Foundation and the Consumers' Federation of Australia), who encouraged the government to hold its nerve on the issue. They accused big mining companies of hijacking the debate about tax reform. ACTU secretary Jeff Lawrence slammed the mining industry's advertising campaign as 'a disgrace'.

A Labor party leadership spill was called while the government was facing criticism for poor handling of a number of issues — including the proposed tax and free-falling opinion polls. Kevin Rudd chose not to contest the leadership ballot, after it became apparent that he did not have the majority support of his colleagues. Julia Gillard became the new Prime Minister and the first woman in Australian history to hold the position. Interestingly, in her first press conference as Prime Minister, Ms Gillard offered to open the door for negotiations on the tax. She said:

To reach a consensus we need to do more than consult, we need to negotiate, and we must end this uncertainty which is not good for the nation . . . Today I will ensure that the mining advertisements paid for by the Government are cancelled and, in return for this, I ask the mining industry to cease their advertising campaign as a sign of good faith and mutual respect . . . Today, I am throwing open the Government's door to the mining industry and I ask that, in return, the mining industry throws open its mind.

In response, BHP Billiton immediately announced:

In response to the new Prime Minister's request, we have immediately asked our agencies to suspend all advertising as a sign of good faith. We look forward to working with the government in this new way to find a solution that is in the national interest.

Later that day, the value of BHP shares increased by 1.5 per cent on the Australian Securities Exchange (ASX). The Minerals Council of Australia and the Association of Mining and Exploration Companies confirmed they would also cease their advertisements on the issue.

Within two weeks, an agreement was reached between the new Gillard government and the largest mining companies, including BHP Billiton and Rio Tinto. This deal paved a way for peace between the government and the mining industry and was a starting point for new negotiations. The result was a Minerals Resource Rent Tax, which will only be placed on companies involved in mining iron ore and coal, with significant changes to other key aspects of the original tax. The tax is due to operate from July 2012. Many commentators claimed that the federal government had backed down in the face of an aggressive advertising and public relations campaign from the mining industry, but this was denied by the government.

The true effect of the rival advertising campaigns will never be known, as in some ways, political advertising is a much weaker form of communication than some other types of communication, such as news articles. Did advertising turn the polls against Kevin Rudd, or did his decisions and personality turn people, and his party, against him? Clearly, political advertising can be an important tool for summarising, emphasising and reinforcing an issue. It can be used to strengthen the reason for a particular attitude on an issue, as well as a tool to influence voting decision during elections. Even though political advertising is perceived as a major form of political communication, there is a sense that its effect may be overly emphasised and simplified. Certainly, with such campaigns, the undisputed winners include advertising agencies and media companies.[46]

## Questions

1. Why would mining companies and associations spend large amounts of money on an advertising and public relations campaign against the Resource Super Profits Tax?
2. What were the messages for the rival groups in this situation?
3. Discuss the advantages and disadvantages of companies using advertising in a risky or potentially controversial politics-related campaign.
4. How effective do you believe the advertising was in making the government change its mind on the original tax?
5. To what extent was advertising involved in the demise of Kevin Rudd as prime minister? Justify your answer from a marketing perspective.

## Advanced activity

Now that you have studied this chapter, look back at the Youi insurance opening case and think about all the issues that relate to the concept of promotion. Imagine you were the marketing manager of Youi and evaluate the strengths and weaknesses of the various promotional methods available from their perspective. Broadly outline an integrated marketing communications strategy that may be appropriate for Youi as it strives to position itself in the competitive Australian insurance market.

## Marketing plan activity

For your marketing plan, think about the promotion (marketing communication) issues that will help you to efficiently communicate a message about your product to the marketplace, and particularly potential customers. Who is best to send the message that will gain the target markets' attention? What is the best message/creative strategy? What are the main media to use? Who is the target audience for the advertisement? Once you have thought about these questions, write down the promotion strategies you have decided will meet the needs of the target market.

A sample marketing plan has been included at the back of this book (see page 523) to give you an idea where this information fits in an overall marketing plan.

## CHAPTER 10

# Distribution (place)

## Learning objectives

After studying this chapter, you should be able to:

- understand the concept of place and how distribution channels connect producers and consumers/organisational buyers

- describe the major activities involved in the distribution of goods

- describe the major activities involved in the distribution of services

- understand the major aspects of retailing

- explain the role of agents and brokers in the distribution channel

- explain the role of wholesalers in marketing distribution.

# Exporting flannel flowers

Flannel flowers (*Actinotus helianthi*) are a native wild flower that is often seen when walking through the Australian bush. While most people would be forgiven for walking past them without a second glance, one grower has found and developed a growing international market for these flowers.

Lana Mitchell established Backcreek Country Enterprises. The company grows Australian native flannel flowers hydroponically in polytunnels near Gundaroo, north of Canberra. The company has won many rural and export awards, and grows more than 7000 plants annually. A yield of up to 30 000 stems go to the Australian east coast, the United States, Austria, Switzerland, Germany and Japan. The flowers are increasing in popularity, and Japanese florists have given them the name 'white velvet'. Native flowers make up 10 per cent of Australia's $170 million cut flower business.

The Australian native flannel flower is growing in popularity in various markets.

However, while there is a large overseas market for the native flowers, they are, unfortunately, very perishable. The industry needs efficient supply chain management to get its product to international customers. The flowers must get from grower to consumer quickly so that they will look appealing in a retail setting, and so that the consumer will be able to enjoy several days of their beauty before they wilt. Air freight to international markets is the obvious distribution choice, but the high costs can be prohibitive, and competition is building from other countries. Sea freight is an alternative as it is around half the price of air freight and modern containers offer more stable humidity and temperature control. Unfortunately, it takes several days for a container ship to get to its destination, which is not suitable for quick orders.

Also, once the flowers arrive at their destination they are subject to a quarantine inspection before reaching the importer and then the retailer. According to Lana: 'They have huge flower auctions over in Holland — almost 90 per cent of all the flowers that go through to Europe go through the Holland auctions. They were looking at my flower and saying there's a huge potential for this and you need to be strategic in how you bring it in and move it around the country'.[1]

> ## Question
> How can marketers attempt to overcome the challenges of distributing a perishable product like a native flannel flower?

# INTRODUCTION

Placing products in the hands of the ultimate consumer is the marketing function known as 'distribution' or 'place'. Distribution requires a chain or network of organisations and individuals. The chain that exists between producers and consumers (or organisational buyers in the case of the business-to-business market) is known as a distribution channel. The key organisations that make up the distribution channel are called intermediaries. The main intermediaries are wholesalers, industrial buyers, agents or brokers, and retailers. Distribution channel intermediaries themselves often rely on a host of specialist service providers. Selling chocolate to overseas consumers, for example, can involve a distribution channel comprising intermediaries and service providers that specialise in trucking, packing, preserving, handling, port operations, sea freight operations, customs, warehousing, wholesaling and retailing.

For a small-scale fruit grower, the distribution channel might involve some boxes, a truck and the delivery bay at the local greengrocer, but for a multinational electronics business, the channel of distribution will be somewhat more complicated. In this chapter we will look at the main components of marketing distribution that are broadly applicable to most businesses: choosing appropriate distribution channels and using marketing intermediaries to move the product to a place of purchase.

## DISTRIBUTION CHANNELS

Many manufacturers and service businesses deal directly with the consumers of their products. For example, if you have bought a loaf of bread from Baker's Delight, flown in a Qantas jet, had an injured limb x-rayed in a hospital or bought software from Adobe's website, you have been a consumer dealing directly with the producer of those goods and services. This approach to marketing is known as direct distribution and it is particularly common for services products, as services are directly tied to the service provider. Conversely, many producers, especially makers of physical products, rely on other organisations and individuals to help them get their product to end users. This approach is known as indirect distribution and the main organisations and individuals who act in the distribution chain between the producer and end user are known as **marketing intermediaries**. The key marketing intermediaries are industrial buyers, wholesalers, agents and brokers, and retailers. The path from the manufacturer or service provider to the end user is known as the **distribution channel** or marketing channel.

Marketing intermediaries are useful and necessary when they can more efficiently connect producers with their customers than can the producers themselves. Perhaps you have bought fruit or vegetables from a roadside stall next to a farmer's driveway. If so, you as the consumer have connected directly with the producer and no intermediaries have been involved. However, most of the farmer's produce only gets to the consumer via a string of intermediaries, such as agents, wholesalers and retailers, before ending with the final consumer. It is obvious that a farmer is not going to be able to sell their million-dollar avocado harvest from a stall at the end of their driveway or even to individual buyers via a website. It is also obvious that you do not want to drive to a farm every time you want to buy an avocado. The same applies to most producers and most consumers. Even if a producer can manage to get their product directly to end users, they are often better off to concentrate on their core abilities (production) and rely on specialist intermediaries who can more efficiently move the product closer to customers. Because they have expertise,

**Learning objective 1**
understand the concept of place and how distribution channels connect producers and consumers/organisational buyers

**marketing intermediaries**
Individuals or organisations that act in the distribution chain between the producer and end user.

**distribution channel** A group of individuals and organisations directing products from producers to end users.

equipment, experience, contacts, skills and scales of economy, intermediaries help producers achieve better results than producers can achieve when acting alone.

When they are well managed, effective intermediaries operating in distribution channels achieve the following benefits. They:

- make products available to the consumer at the time that the consumer wants to purchase them
- make products available in the locations that the consumer wants to purchase them
- customise products to the consumer's particular needs
- make transactions as efficient, simple and cheap as possible for consumers, producers and other intermediaries by establishing and managing efficient exchange processes.

Conversely, when poorly managed, or inappropriately chosen, marketing intermediaries can add to costs, reduce efficiency, create delays and cause frustration. Consumers are often wary of intermediaries, believing they are 'middlemen' who add no value but increase the price they must pay for products. Some producers blame intermediaries for every problem they face and, like consumers, can feel they add little value to the marketing process.

Figure 10.1 shows an example of the simple exchanges required for breakfast. For breakfast, a person may want to consume Sanitarium Weet-Bix cereal, Dairy Farmers milk, Tip Top bread and Mildura orange juice, but if there was no marketing intermediary, the consumer would have to go to each producer and each producer would have to go to each consumer, as shown in figure 10.1(a). The benefit of a well-managed distribution channel compared to marketing without the involvement of marketing intermediaries is shown in figure 10.1(b).

## FIGURE 10.1

The benefits of using distribution channel intermediaries

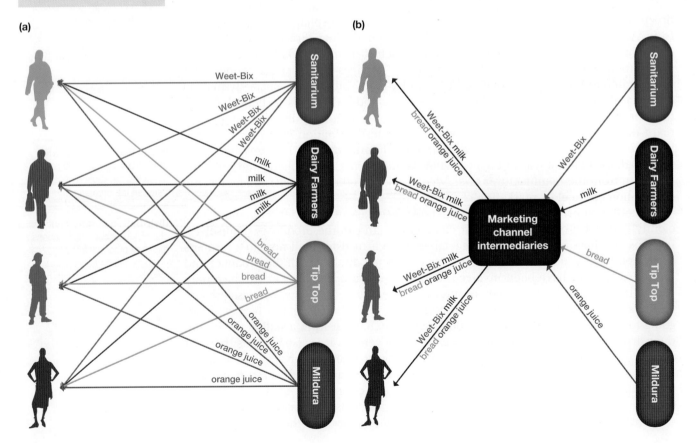

The existence of distribution channel intermediaries reduces the number of inter-actions from 32 to 8 in figure 10.1, as the consumer can go to the one intermediary (e.g. a supermarket) to purchase the products for breakfast. This shows that the exist-ence of an intermediary can make the whole process more efficient for both the producer and the consumer, which can lead to cost savings.

It is clear then that intermediaries can add considerable value to a producer's offering. In choosing a distribution channel, the producer needs to first consider the way in which its product can best be marketed, so that the supply chain from producer to consumer effectively becomes a *value* chain. The market coverage decision takes into account the nature of the product and its target market. Generally, marketers will choose from:

- **intensive distribution**, which distributes products via every suitable intermediary
- **exclusive distribution**, which distributes products through a single intermediary for any given geographic region
- **selective distribution**, which distributes products through intermediaries chosen for some specific reason.

Intensive distribution is an obvious strategy for everyday purchases such as milk. The consumer invests little time in deciding where, when or how much to buy or how much to pay. They make their decision based on convenience, often just purchasing at the closest store, whether that be a corner store, a supermarket, a petrol station or a takeaway food store. In contrast, exclusive distribution is gener-ally used for products that are only purchased after a great deal of deliberation by the consumer or where exclusivity adds to the appeal of the product. Prestige cars and designer furniture are typical examples. Producers and wholesalers can also increase the commitment of retailers in the marketing channel by promising them exclusivity. Selective distribution falls somewhere between intensive and exclusive distribution. It is most appropriate for goods that require some degree of deliberation by the consumer and where the consumer might visit multiple stores to compare prices and products. Selective distribution is often chosen when the intermediary can provide some specific value-adding function to the producer's offering. While it may be good for the consumer, it is not generally beneficial to the parties in the distribution channel to have consumers play suppliers against each other.

In the next two sections we will examine how different intermediaries operate in the consumer products market and the business-to-business products market.

**intensive distribution**
An approach to market coverage that distributes products through every suitable intermediary.

**exclusive distribution**
An approach to market coverage that distributes products through a single intermediary in any given geographic region.

**selective distribution**
An approach to market coverage that distributes products through intermediaries chosen for some specific reason.

## Consumer product distribution channels

For consumer products, the main marketing intermediaries are agents, wholesalers and retailers, which we shall discuss in more detail later in the chapter. A distribu-tion channel can consist of all, some or none of these between the producer and the consumer. Some of the possibilities are now discussed.

**Distribution channel 1**

In distribution channel 1, the producer deals directly with the consumer. This model has increased in use in recent years and is expected to continue to grow as more consumers use the web to research and ultimately purchase products. Exam-ples of this approach include: Dell and Apple, which sell their computers and other goods directly to consumers via their websites; Domino's Pizza, which makes and sells pizzas at its retail outlets; and Just Cuts hairdressing salons, which, like most services businesses, produces and delivers the service at the same time. Because services are consumed as they are produced, there is often little need for intermediaries. Note that it is not always the case though, as we will discuss in a moment. In choosing distribution channel 1, producers must decide that, in addition to making the product, they are able to effectively manage distribution and deal with customers one-on-one. They must also be wary of the reaction of retailers to producers selling directly to customers. For example, when Dell began selling directly to customers, Harvey Norman threatened not to stock Dell computers. In choosing to deal directly with producers, customers need to feel confident that they can get the level of service, including after-sales support, they require. Dealing directly with producers can be attractive to consumers because it can offer greater customisation (generally complete customisation in the case of services) of the product. For example, a consumer dealing directly with Apple can choose to have more memory put in their new computer, software pre-installed or a personal message engraved on an iPod. Consumers also often feel they can get a cheaper price by bypassing retailers. This is often not the case, though, as producers are reluctant to undercut the prices of their retail distributors. Dealing directly with producers will more often than not require the consumer to pay in full for the goods before receiving them, if mail order or online purchasing is involved.

**Distribution channel 2**

```
Producer ──────────────────────▶ Retailer ▶ Consumer
```

In distribution channel 2, producers provide their products directly to retailers for sale to consumers. Both Dell and Apple use this strategy as well as the strategy in distribution channel 1. Many small boutique producers, such as the Byron Bay Cookie Company, use this strategy. Airlines and hotels can also use this strategy, often in combination with distribution channel 1. For example, you can book a motel room directly with the Best Western motel of your choice or use a travel agent or online service such as wotif.com. Similarly, you can book a Qantas flight on the airline's website, or use Flight Centre or some other intermediary. Large retailers often choose strategy 2, preferring to deal directly with producers rather than wholesalers. From the consumer's perspective, many feel that they receive more personal service from a retailer than a producer, including the ability to examine the goods before purchasing them and often to take possession of the goods when paying for them.

**Distribution channel 3**

```
Producer ──────────▶ Wholesaler ▶ Retailer ▶ Consumer
```

In distribution channel 3, producers sell to wholesalers who then sell on to the retailers. This is a common choice for goods that are sold in high volumes through numerous retailers. Examples include grocery items and mass-marketed clothing. The advantage for the producer is in dealing with larger volumes to fewer buyers rather than small volumes to numerous buyers. The advantage for the retailer is the ability to buy a range of different lines from one source (the wholesaler) rather than having to deal with large numbers of producers. In this distribution channel, consumers still deal with a retailer, so their experience is essentially the same as in distribution channel 2. A possible difference is that a retailer that uses wholesalers may carry a wider range of products.

**Distribution channel 4**

Distribution channel 4 is a common choice for exports, where the complexities of dealing with different legal, regulatory and cultural factors suggests an experienced and skilled agent will be able to more effectively deal with intermediaries in the foreign market. It is also used for mass marketed products where the producer believes an agent can more effectively sell the products to wholesalers.

**Distribution channel 5**

Distribution channel 5 is commonly used in the financial services industry. For example, mortgage brokers deal directly with consumers and the banks and other financial institutions that offer loans. For the consumer, they are able to offer a higher level of service than the financial institutions (e.g. home visits after normal office hours) and for the producer (the banks), mortgage brokers can bring new business from otherwise unidentified potential customers. However, the brokers are then paid a trailing commission, which represents a cost to the bank (and therefore the consumer) and, during the housing boom in the early 2000s, mortgage brokers approved loans for people who may not have met banks' own lending criteria.

It should be clear from our discussion that marketing organisations do not always simply choose one strategy. Rather, they might use a combination of strategies for different markets or even the same market. Similarly, consumers might choose different channels. You might buy an iPad or iMac directly from Apple via its website, but you'd be less likely to buy a spare USB cable via the website because the delivery charge would more than offset the convenience of not having to visit a shop. You might also prefer to go to a shop to try out a new mouse or piece of software rather than rely on the description of the product online.

# Business-to-business product distribution channels

In the market for business-to-business products — that is those products that are used in the production of other goods or services or in day-to-day business operations, rather than being sold to end consumers — the main intermediaries are agents and industrial distributors. A distribution channel can consist of both, one or neither of these between the producer and the organisational buyer.

**Distribution channel 1**

The strategy shown in distribution channel 1 accounts for the majority of business-to-business product transactions. Business buyers are usually buying products that are crucial to their own business success and often want to deal directly with the producer so they can be sure of direct access to information and assistance. Sometimes the organisational buyer will need a customised product and so needs to deal directly with the producer. For example, a designer furniture manufacturer would want a foam factory to provide foam cushions in the exact sizes to match their chairs.

**Distribution channel 2**

Distribution channel 2 features an industrial distributor. Industrial distributors play roughly the same role in the business-to-business product channel as retailers do in the consumer product distribution channel. They purchase commonly used goods such as tools and office supplies from producers and resell them to organisational buyers. Corporate Express is a typical industrial distributor. Corporate Express provides stationery, catering, office furniture and other business inputs from 48 locations in Australia and New Zealand.[2]

**Distribution channel 3**

Distribution channel 3 features an agent. An agent in the business-to-business products market is an intermediary who plays matchmaker between producers and organisational buyers and is paid a commission on the sales they bring to the producer.

**Distribution channel 4**

Distribution channel 4 combines channels 2 and 3. The agent takes a commission on sales it secures with industrial distributors. The industrial distributor then sells to organisational buyers, as in channel 2.

## Supply-chain management

It is important not to fall into the trap of thinking that the addition of intermediaries to a marketing channel adds complexity. Indeed, the entire reason intermediaries are used is to allow producers, all of the other intermediaries and consumers to focus on what they are best at and thereby make the path from producer to consumer as efficient as possible. This can be most effectively achieved when the producer and the intermediaries fully understand the goals and needs of the other parties and work together to find efficiencies. This approach is known as **supply-chain management**.

Formally, the supply chain consists of the producer and marketing intermediaries as well as all of the other parties that play direct or indirect roles in getting products to consumers; for example, raw materials suppliers, transport companies, wholesalers, and retailers. Supply-chain management is a complex and crucial task. It does not imply one party managing the role and activities of all the others. Rather, it is based on cooperation and relationship building to the mutual benefit of all parties.

**supply-chain management**
An approach to managing marketing channels based on ongoing partnerships among distribution channel members that create efficiencies and deliver value to customers.

This chapter is concerned with one end of the supply chain — from the producer to the consumer.

## Distribution channel partnerships

Each party in a distribution channel has expectations of and obligations to other parties in the channel. Distribution channels work most effectively when the different parties agree on goals and processes and then cooperate to implement them. Having said that, it is rare that all parties in the distribution channel will reach a consensus on the best approaches, and it is common that the different parties will have different relative amounts of power. When one member of the distribution channel can exert power over the ability of other members of the channel to achieve their goals, that powerful member is known as the channel captain and is said to have channel power. Channel power must be carefully exercised. A distribution channel is only effective when all channel members benefit from their involvement.

An arrangement between Linfox and National Foods' Australia has seen Linfox working hard to optimise National Foods' supply chain, including the construction of a state-of-the-art national distribution centre (NDC) at Laverton, Melbourne. The 28 000 square metre NDC features high-quality chilled warehousing for dairy, cheese and juice products. National Foods' famous brands include Dairy Farmers, South Cape Fine Goods, Yoplait, Berri, King Island and Coon. The warehouse has been divided into two compartments, designed to store approximately 26 500 pallets.[3]

Not all distribution arrangements are successful. Disagreements, misunderstandings and miscommunication all have the potential to create conflict within a marketing channel. The more parties that are involved in a marketing channel, the greater the potential for conflict. The emergence and rise of online selling, in particular, has unsettled many formerly stable marketing channels. The web provides a relatively easy way for producers to sell directly to consumers. For example, US software company Adobe once heavily relied on importers, wholesalers and retailers to make its software available to Australian and New Zealand consumers. Now Adobe maintains its old marketing channels, but also directly competes with those channels by selling its software via its websites, both as packaged products and as downloads.[4] Theoretically, it could abandon its distribution partners and just deal directly with consumers.

## Horizontal and vertical channel integration

In any supply chain, certain functions must be undertaken if a product is to make its way from producer to consumer. We discussed earlier that there are various channels that can be chosen. Within any existing channel it is possible to redistribute particular responsibilities and obligations between different channel members. This is known as channel integration.

**Horizontal channel integration** occurs when organisations at the same level of operation are combined under one management structure. For example, horizontal channel integration occurs when a retailer buys out a competitor. A recent example is the purchase of homewares retailer Bay Swiss by Freedom Furniture. Freedom rebranded the Bay Swiss stores and closed those stores where there were two too close to each other.[5]

**Vertical channel integration** occurs when different stages of the distribution channel are combined under one management structure. For example, vertical channel integration occurs when a wholesaler buys a retailer or a transport business. Vertical integration enables closer cooperation and coordination between the two stages of the marketing channel. At its most extensive, vertical integration brings all stages of the marketing channel under one management structure. The resultant

**horizontal channel integration** Bringing organisations at the same level of operation under a single management structure.

**vertical channel integration** Bringing different stages of the distribution channel under a single management structure.

**vertical marketing system**
A distribution channel in which all stages occur under a single management structure.

structure is known as a **vertical marketing system** or VMS. Australia Post is an example of a VMS. It owns post boxes situated on street corners; post offices that sell envelopes, stamps, boxes and other goods, as well as accept mail; a fleet of delivery vans and bikes; storage and sorting facilities; and so on. Franchises are also a type of VMS in which individual retail outlets are contractually obliged to cooperate closely with the franchisor.

## Franchising

**franchising** An approach to business in which one party (a franchisor) licenses its business model to another party (a franchisee).

**Franchising** is a type of business where the right to sell products or rights to use the main elements of a business model are licensed by one party to another. In franchising, the franchisor:

* licenses the right to use its business model or to sell its products
* provides services such as advertising, business know-how and supplier networks
* stipulates standards and rules by which the franchise business must operate
* sometimes promises exclusive rights to a particular geographic area.

And the franchisee:

* pays the franchisor a fee and/or percentage of sales receipts
* supplies labour and capital
* operates the business in accordance with the conditions of the franchise agreement.

Franchising is growing rapidly in Australia and New Zealand. It offers franchisors a way to expand relatively rapidly, keep some control of the distribution of their products, and to share risk; it offers franchisees a way to start a business without needing to formulate an idea, systems or raise a profile and, statistically, gives them a much higher rate of business success (50 per cent compared to 10 per cent for new independent businesses). According to the Franchise Council of Australia, there are more than 900 franchise systems in Australia with a collective turnover of more than $120 billion.[6]

In Australia, retail franchises operate in the following ways:

* a producer licenses distributors to sell its products to retailers. Coca-Cola operates like this, licensing bottlers to make up its drinks from syrup and then sell the finished beverage to retail stores.
* a franchisor licenses key aspects of its business model to the franchisee. These are among the best known franchises and include stores such as the Domino's pizza stores, Gloria Jean's Coffee and the Jim's Mowing lawn maintenance businesses.
* a manufacturer authorises retail stores to sell its brand name item. Examples include agricultural and lawn care products company John Deere and car companies Ford and Toyota.

## Spotlight  Gelatissimo

Following in their father's footsteps as a gelato maker, Domenico and Marco Lopresti have developed their business to be a fast-growing Australian franchise with stores both locally and overseas, including in the homeland of gelato, Italy. Beginning in 2000, Domenico used a family recipe to make gelato to supply local cafés, retailers and restaurants. Two years later the brothers decided to start a retail store selling their products, presenting them the way gelato is sold in Italy. The success of their first Sydney store encouraged them to adopt a franchising business model in 2005. A mix of company-owned and franchised stores have resulted in the Gelatissimo Group expanding to operations in six countries (Australia, Indonesia, Singapore, Malaysia, the Philippines and Italy). There are 21 locations in Australia and 15 overseas, and more are planned both domestically and internationally.

Gelatissimo serves premium dairy and sorbet flavours that offer a low-fat and creamy alternative to traditional ice-cream. As well as gelato, they sell gelato shakes, Bambino cones and Italian sundaes.

Other products include Italian coffee, traditional Italian biscotti, light meals, chocolates and an affogato (espresso with a scoop of vanilla gelato). The company's slogan is 'The real taste of Italia'.

As a franchisor, it is often looking for new growth opportunities. It costs about $300 000 to purchase a franchise in Australia. New franchisees are required to undergo three weeks of intensive training and to spend time at selected training stores before being placed in their own store. Here, new franchisees can work with ongoing franchisor support.

In a situation like 'selling coal to Newcastle', Gelatissimo opened a store selling its Italian-style gelato next to the Ponte Vecchio in Florence, Italy, in a recent year. The London-based Australian owner of the store in Florence convinced the brothers to sell him the franchise rights for Italy. With Rome and Venice being potential future locations for Gelatissimo, the Aussie-based, Italian-style franchise has an exciting future.[7]

Gelatissimo promotes its products, including a range of premium dairy and sorbet desserts, with the slogan 'The real taste of Italia'.

### Question

**Franchises such as Gelatissimo have been growing in number over the last few years. From a marketing perspective, what are the advantages of franchising for the franchisor, the franchisee and the customer?**

## Concepts and applications check

**Learning objective 1** understand the concept of place and how distribution channels connect producers and consumers/organisational buyers

**1.1** Consumer product distribution channels can vary in the number of intermediaries involved. Choose five organisations and describe their distribution channels.

**1.2** Explain how supply channel management works. What can happen if this system does not run smoothly?

**1.3** From a marketing perspective, what is meant by 'place'? How do marketing intermediaries assist in bringing the product to the customer?

# DISTRIBUTION OF GOODS

Physical products (or 'goods'; see chapter 1) need to be moved from producers to consumers via a number of activities that are collectively known as physical distribution. Service products generally do not require these activities and will be dealt with separately in the next major section of this chapter. Physical distribution involves order processing, inventory management, warehousing and transportation. The physical distribution process is summarised in figure 10.2 (overleaf). You should refer to it as you read through this section.

Physical distribution activities can be performed by any member of the distribution channel. Members may share responsibility for different aspects, one member may take responsibility for all physical distribution activities, or the physical distribution can be outsourced to a specialist provider. Note that outsourcing distribution does not add another party to the marketing channel — the distribution provider does not have any managerial power within the marketing channel; they merely provide

**Learning objective 2**
describe the major activities involved in the distribution of goods

services requested by the producer or marketing channel intermediary. The attraction of outsourcing is that it allows both parties to focus on their core competencies.

Whichever approach is taken, the aim is to minimise costs and the time taken to complete a process and maximise speed, quality, dependability and service.

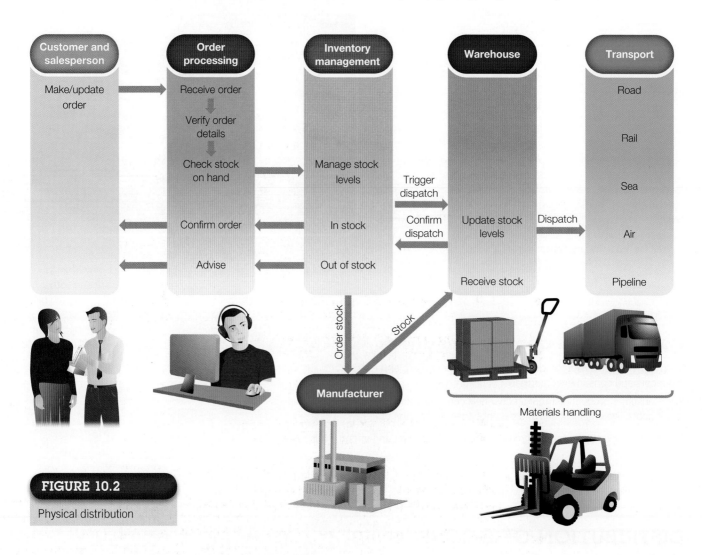

## Order processing

Order processing is the term used to describe all of the activities involved in managing the information required to receive, handle and fill a sales order. Efficient order processing is important to minimise costs and ensure customer satisfaction. Order processing is usually most efficient when computerised systems are involved, but paper-based ordering systems are still common and their relative simplicity and low cost are significant advantages for smaller businesses. Electronic order processing systems are based on electronic data interchange, which uses standardised data formats to share information, often in real time, between all the different functional areas of distribution (order processing, production, inventory, accounting and transportation systems), whether they are performed by the producer, distribution channel intermediaries, outsourced service providers or the consumer.

Order processing begins when a customer or salesperson (on behalf of a customer) places an order. An order usually specifies the products wanted, the price to be paid and how the payment will be made, the time the products are wanted and the location to which the products should be delivered. The next step is order handling, which involves checking that the terms of the purchase are acceptable (price, credit-worthiness of purchaser and so on) and that the product is in stock. If the product is not in stock, it will be ordered and/or the customer will be contacted to see if they will accept a substitute product. When the order details and product availability are verified the order will be assembled and shipped, and the company records will be updated to reflect completion of the purchase.

## Inventory management

Inventory management involves managing stocks of products to ensure availability to customers while minimising holding costs. If a business holds too little stock, it will experience shortages and be unable to meet customer needs, prompting customers to move to other businesses with competing products. Conversely, if a business holds too much stock it will experience higher warehousing, insurance, handling and other costs.

Most businesses have an inventory management system based on:
- *order lead time* — the usual time between placing an order and receiving the stock
- *usage rate* — how much stock is sold during a particular period of time
- *safety stock* — a quantity of stock held to cover unexpectedly high sales and/or unexpectedly long order lead times.

Some businesses try to hold only enough inventory to meet near-term demand; that is, they aim to receive stock just as they are about to use or sell it. Maintaining such low inventory levels requires ordering small quantities frequently. This approach is known as **just-in-time (JIT)**. JIT minimises inventory holding costs, but only works when order lead times and usage rates are predictable and when the supply chain is reliable. This requires a high level of supply chain visibility, which refers to the availability of comprehensive and up-to-date information about all aspects of the supply chain.

**just-in-time (JIT)** An approach to inventory management that involves holding only that stock that is about to be used or sold.

## Warehousing

Warehousing is the use of facilities (generally a building) to store and move goods. Warehousing is an important tool in the inventory management approach of many businesses. Effective warehouse operations enable businesses to hold surplus stock until customers require it and to hold a level of safety stock to ensure unexpected demands can be met. The appropriate type of warehousing facilities is determined by the nature of the products, the location of suppliers and customers, and the types of transportation used.

Many businesses — particularly larger, stable businesses — buy or lease warehouses for their exclusive use. This enables them to set up the warehouse in such a way to most efficiently store and move the business's products. On the other hand, a warehouse represents a substantial cost to a business, including the purchase or rental, plus maintenance, security, insurance and other costs. The increasing incidence of direct links between producers and consumers (brought about by the internet), increasing demand for customised products and the increasing speed of innovation that quickly renders products obsolete are all factors working against the use of company-owned warehouses.

Some businesses specialise in providing warehousing services to other businesses. These public warehouses lease space and distribution and sometimes offer extensive other physical distribution services — if a business wants to, it can, in fact, outsource the entire physical distribution process. Public warehouses are particularly appealing to businesses that have large fluctuations in storage needs, need to maintain inventory at many different locations, require only occasional warehousing or are unsure whether they will have a long-term presence in a particular market. As always, outsourcing enables each party to focus on their core competencies.

A variation on the warehouse is the **distribution centre**, a type of warehouse that focuses on moving rather than storing goods. Distribution centres are designed to efficiently receive goods, assemble them into orders and ship them to customers with a minimum of handling. This practice is known as **cross-docking**. At its best, cross-docking eliminates the storage component of warehousing. As such it is most suited to fast-moving consumer goods — products that are sold quickly and in predictable volumes, and do not require safety stock to be held. For example, perishable products such as milk and bread are well suited to a cross-docking approach. Cross-docking is facilitated by:
- products designed with cross-docking in mind
- protective packaging that reduces or eliminates the need to check the state of the products on receipt
- packaging that is suitable for sale, eliminating the need for repacking
- labelling that can be computer-read and is suitable for retail use
- close cooperation, communication and coordination between the suppliers, distribution centre and customer.[8]

Whether they aim to achieve cross-docking or not, distribution centres are usually highly automated, making extensive use of computer-controlled machinery. They are usually located next to major transport infrastructure (including road, rail, air and sea port facilities).

The effective physical management of goods in a warehouse and on to transport is known as **materials handling**. Effective materials handling minimises time and costs involved in moving physical products. Materials handling strategies include efficient unloading, storing, packing, labelling and loading.

Issues to be considered in materials handling include:
- the use of standard pallets to enable machinery to efficiently move products
- the use of standard containers to hold many small items to enable their efficient transport (the containers you see on the back of trucks, on ships and on trains are all the same size and shape)
- special demands due to the nature of the product such as safety measures that must be taken in handling dangerous chemicals, careful handling of fragile goods such as glassware, and sanitary handling of foods.

# Transportation

Transportation is the process of moving products from their place of manufacture to their place of consumption. The key modes of transportation are road, rail, sea, air and — somewhat less obviously — pipelines. Most distribution channels coordinate multiple modes. This is known as intermodal transportation and relies on the use of standard shipping containers and container handling equipment. Specialist transportation companies known as **freight forwarders** allow businesses with small volumes of freight to combine their products with the products of other businesses so that they can take advantage of containerisation and the efficiencies of larger loads.

### Choosing a mode of transport

Like most marketing decisions, the choice of mode of transport comes down to factors such as availability, cost, speed, flexibility, reliability and environmental impacts. Different transport modes are considered in table 10.1.

**TABLE 10.1** Comparing modes of transport

| Transport mode | Availability | Cost | Speed | Reliability | Environmental impacts |
|---|---|---|---|---|---|
| Road | Extensive road network in most areas, connecting most locations | Mid-range to high | Fast | Highly reliable, but can be affected by accidents, congestion, flooding | Quarrying of materials to build roads<br><br>Destruction of habitat where roads are built<br><br>Production of materials to build trucks<br><br>Exhaust emissions from burning of diesel fuel |
| Rail | Extensive rail network connecting specific points<br><br>Dedicated railroads in mining and agricultural areas | Mid-range | Mid-range | Mid-range<br><br>Infrastructure disruptions can cause severe delays | Mining and smelting of materials to build rails<br><br>Destruction of habitat where railroads are built<br><br>Production of materials to build rolling stock and locomotives<br><br>Exhaust emissions from burning of diesel fuel |
| Sea | Available between specific locations only (coastal with deep water access, or on a major waterway), but reasonably accessible in combination with other modes | Cheapest option | Slow | Mid-range<br><br>Loss at sea is usually catastrophic (complete loss of cargo) or results in a long delay in salvaging cargo<br><br>Sea freighters can spend days or weeks waiting off the coast for port facilities to become available | Mining and smelting of materials to build ships and ports<br><br>Destruction of habitat and pollution of sea around sea ports<br><br>Exhaust emissions from burning of diesel fuel<br><br>Catastrophic environmental damage from oil spills etc. |
| Air | Available between specific locations only, but reasonably accessible in combination with other modes | Very high | Very fast | High<br><br>Loss of aircraft is catastrophic (loss of all cargo) | Mining, smelting and production of materials to build aircraft and airports<br><br>Destruction of habitat around airports<br><br>Exhaust emissions from burning of jet fuel |
| Pipeline | Must be purpose built | Low once constructed | Slow | High | Mining, smelting and production of materials to build pipelines<br><br>Destruction of land and sea habitat around pipelines<br><br>Pollution or contamination caused by leaks |

In the paragraphs that follow, we will look at the key characteristics of each mode of transport and then summarise the issues to be considered when choosing which to use.

Road transport (trucks, vans and so on) offers the most flexibility of all the modes of transport because it has the most extensive infrastructure. You can drive almost anywhere something is produced, almost anywhere something is consumed, and almost everywhere in between. This makes road transport a more attractive option for some businesses, but it is more expensive than rail and more prone to accidents and delays.

Rail transport is best suited to bulky items that need to travel long distances over land. Australia has numerous rail lines built specifically to move mineral ores to processing plants or sea ports. Many of Australia's farming areas are criss-crossed with rail lines designed to move crop harvests to processing centres. Many factories and warehouses have rail yards alongside rail lines to facilitate transportation of their products.

Sea freight takes advantage of the massive cargo capacity of ocean-going vessels and is used for bulky items that do not need to be rushed to their destination. In many countries, including much of Asia, waterways such as rivers are also used for transport. This is less common in Australia and New Zealand where landscapes and regular droughts and flooding make the inland waterways less suitable. More than 95 per cent of international cargo moves via sea freight. Ports are usually serviced by road and rail to facilitate movement of products to and away from the coast.

Air freight is fast but expensive. It is most suitable for perishables, lightweight items, urgent deliveries and high-value items. Like sea freight, it is usually necessary to transfer products to rail or road to complete their journey.

Pipelines are specifically used for water, oil and gas (as well as some items that can be transported in a stream of water, such as some cereal grains) and are usually owned by the businesses that produce the product. Many pipelines are publicly or partly publicly owned. Pipelines can run for thousands of kilometres, carrying raw material to processing plants, or delivering processed materials to customers, as in the case of the water mains into people's houses.

The matrix in table 10.1 offers a convenient way to compare the different transport options. Different businesses will place different weightings on each factor. For example, some businesses will rate environmental impact highly, whereas others — unfortunately — will have little concern for it. Marketing channels may rely on outsourcing some or all of their transportation requirements and there are numerous businesses that offer this service, including some that operate across all modes of transport.

## Technology in physical distribution

The internet and other telecommunications technologies have enabled great advances in the efficiency of physical distribution. The term e-distribution is often used to describe the full implementation of advanced telecommunications technologies in the physical distribution process. E-distribution offers efficiencies internally and externally. For example, internally, scanning technology, databases and reporting software can be combined to keep inventory records. Radio frequency identification (RFID) technology involves attaching small electronic tags to items or containers, enabling their movements within a goods handling facility to be tracked down to a matter of centimetres. Externally, the internet enables two organisations' inventory records to 'talk' to each other, thus automatically generating reorders. Technologies such as these have led to large advances in supply chain visibility.

# Toll marine logistics

The Toll company began in 1888. It was founded by Albert Toll in Newcastle, and starting with hauling coal with horse and cart. Over the years it expanded — focusing on transporting goods associated with diversified mining and manufacturing activities.

The Toll Group (Toll) is now one of the leading providers of integrated distribution and logistics services in the Asian region, generating annual consolidated revenue of $6.5 billion and operating an extensive network of over 1100 sites in more than 50 countries around the world. Toll's distribution and supply chain network includes road, marine and air fleets, as well as warehousing and port facilities. It aims to drive efficiencies in supply chain management for its customers via technology and its extensive operational experience.

The company currently operates in five key business-to-business market sectors:

1. automotive
2. beverage
3. food and retail
4. relocations (for government agencies, the Department of Defence and the corporate market)
5. resources.

Sea freight is one of the distribution services Toll offers via its marine logistics division. Operating a fleet of more than 80 vessels, this division offers customised solutions for bulk handling and transportation (coal, steel, scrap, billets, iron ores and pellets, sand and aggregates) with operations in Indonesia, Malaysia, Cambodia, Vietnam, Philippines, Thailand and Myanmar. As a vessel owner, Toll also provides chartering services to external parties.

In order to improve their sea-based services to customers and remain competitive in the ever-evolving marine sector, Toll recently took delivery of four new tug boats and two new jumbo barges. These vessels are the most powerful the company has ever had in their fleet. They allow Toll's marine logistics division to offer shorter transit times and a faster turnaround for customers.[9]

Toll's jumbo barges allow its marine logistics division to offer shorter transit times and a faster turnaround for customers.

## Questions

1. What sort of products might lend themselves to sea freight distribution over other forms of transportation?
2. What are some other reasons a marketer might choose sea freight distribution over other transportation options?

## Concepts and applications check

**Learning objective 2**  describe the major activities involved in the distribution of goods

2.1  Physical distribution activities can be performed by any member of the marketing channel. Discuss some of these activities and how they can reduce costs and be of benefit to the final consumer.

2.2  Using examples, explain the advantages of using a just-in-time (JIT) approach to inventory management.

2.3  What are the functions of a warehouse? Discuss the different types of warehousing and how they can assist the movement of a product through the marketing channel.

2.4  What is a distribution centre? How is it different to a private warehouse?

2.5  Imagine that you are the marketing manager for Bundaberg Brewed Drinks and you are exporting ginger beer to the United States. What transport issues would you need to plan between the factory and the final consumer?

2.6  There has been a lot of criticism of trucks travelling long distances as a mode of transport for the delivery of goods. Outline the advantages and disadvantages of two potential modes of transport to replace road for the distribution of some non-perishable goods.

# DISTRIBUTION OF SERVICES

**Learning objective 3** describe the major activities involved in the distribution of services

Services products are usually produced at the time of consumption and so the notion of 'service distribution' is quite different to physical distribution. This is discussed in much greater detail in chapter 11, but here we will briefly discuss some key differences and similarities in relation to distribution of services:

- Physical distribution is required for the physical inputs used in producing and delivering the service product.
- Some services are delivered using infrastructure.
- Service businesses must ensure that the labour is available at the right time and in the right quantities to ensure customers can be served.

## Physical inputs

The creation and delivery of most services products requires physical inputs. The service business must ensure that the various physical inputs it needs to deliver the service are available. For example, a potential customer walking into a hairdresser can only receive the blonde dreadlocks they want if the hairdresser has shampoo and bleach on hand, staff to undertake the styling, and chairs, scissors and so on with which to produce the service.

On a grander scale, a state government providing school education to hundreds of thousands of children each year needs to coordinate an array of infrastructure, goods and people. All of the discussion in this chapter about physical distribution applies to the physical inputs required to produce services.

## Delivery infrastructure

Some services are distributed via a physical infrastructure. While you might go to a retailer to purchase a haircut, medical advice or travel advice, some service providers bring the service to you. For example, the electricity supply to your home is delivered via an extensive network of above-ground, underground and under-sea cables. Similarly the gas supply and telephone lines come to you via infrastructure. Mobile phone and internet services themselves are based around satellites and telecommunications towers. The web has expanded the range of services available in this format. Whereas once you would visit a bank branch to make a transaction, technology enabled automatic telling machines and later internet banking.

## Scheduling

Scheduling in service businesses is designed to smooth demand. Just as producers and sellers of physical products must manage inventory to minimise holding costs yet maximise availability to consumers, service businesses must manage their capacity to ensure customers can be served but that there is not excess labour. For example, a restaurant might be able to serve 50 customers a night with three kitchen staff and two waiters. If a 51st customer turns up, the restaurant might be able to cope, but if another ten customers turn up, the restaurant might need to turn them away. On the other hand if only 20 customers go to the restaurant that night, the restaurant still has to pay the three kitchen staff and two waiters. Service businesses go to great lengths to smooth demand. For example, restaurants encourage diners to book well ahead. Diners are told this ensures them a table, but it also helps the restaurant plan to have sufficient staff on hand to cater for the number of customers. Hairdressers have an appointment book for the same reason. Restaurants also often have family nights when children can dine for free or cheap takeaway nights when they offer two-for-one deals or 10 per cent off normal prices to encourage custom on otherwise slow trading days. For example, many cinemas have promotions to encourage more customers on Tuesdays each week.

Some businesses can not so easily control demand for their services. For example, a hospital cannot encourage people to schedule their illnesses and injuries according to a conveniently staggered timeline. Such businesses often face higher costs as they must maintain somewhat higher capacity than will usually be needed to meet demand.

# Video on demand

Free-to-air television networks and pay television services are under threat. Both are experiencing falling advertising rates, and subscriptions to pay television services appear to have flatlined in recent years, with household penetration remaining fairly constant at just 25 per cent. The emergence and increasing popularity of internet video streaming is fragmenting the audience of traditional broadcasters. Their programming content and models of delivery are now challenged by digital channels and internet viewing options that enable consumers to access a diverse range of content — both when and where they want. The increasing bandwidth capabilities offered by internet service providers in recent years has made watching video online a viable alternative.

The traditional broadcasters can no longer even rely on having sole access to unique content that attracts large audiences, such as live sporting events. The popular Indian Premier League 20/20 cricket tournament broke new ground in a recent year when it announced a two-year deal to stream live coverage of games around the world, via a dedicated YouTube channel. Arrangements such as these have been termed 'narrowcasts' (as opposed to broadcasts), in that they deliver niche content to specific audiences.

Advertising and/or subscriptions remain the major revenue streams for online video 'narrowcasters'. For example, such services generally allow advertisers the opportunity to sponsor program downloads, with the consumer getting the video content for free (i.e. paid for by the advertising sponsor) — provided the video content has the sponsor's advertising embedded at the beginning and end of the selected program.

The popular Indian Premier League 20/20 cricket tournament streams live coverage of games around the world via a dedicated YouTube channel.

The Seven Network in Australia and Television New Zealand (New Zealand's largest broadcaster) have responded to the video-on-demand landscape by recently launching a joint venture called Hybrid TV (www.hybridtv.com.au). Hybrid TV's mission statement declares that it aims to 'fundamentally improve the quality of life for our customers through salient services, broadband entertainment and digital television across all screens in the home'.

## Question

**Explain how the concept of 'distribution of services' relates to video-on-demand services.**

## Concepts and applications check

**Learning objective 3** describe the major activities involved in the distribution of services

**3.1** How does the distribution of physical products differ from the distribution of services? Give examples in your answer.

**3.2** Using your own service example, describe how advances in technology have changed the delivery infrastructure of that service over time.

**3.3** Explain the concept of scheduling demand for a service, using an example other than a restaurant.

# RETAILING

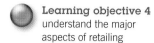
**Learning objective 4**
understand the major
aspects of retailing

From the discussion at the start of this chapter, we know that the main distribution channel intermediaries are retailers, agents and wholesalers in consumer products markets, and agents and industrial buyers in business-to-business products markets. In this section we will discuss the most naturally familiar stage of distribution for most consumers: retailing. We will then work back through the distribution channel to analyse the less familiar roles of agents, brokers and wholesalers, and the important roles each can play in the marketing of goods and services.

**retailing** Any exchange in which the buyer is the ultimate consumer of the product.

**Retailing** describes any exchange in which the buyer is the ultimate consumer of the product. When people think of retailing, many immediately think of department stores, supermarkets and specialist shops such as Myer, Woolworths and Just Jeans. These are examples of businesses whose main concern is retailing. As such they are known as retailers. Retailing excludes transactions in which the buyer intends to resell the product or use it in the making of another product. This activity occurs in business markets.

In addition to the conventional stores, in marketing many other businesses are also, technically, retailers. For example, a passenger airline such as Jetstar sells air transport to consumers and is therefore a retailer. A general practitioner working in a medical clinic primarily sells health care to patients and thus is also a retailer, even though you might not usually think of them as such.

Other businesses may undertake retailing, but their primary focus is on something else. For example, manufacturers often sell their goods to wholesalers or retailers but many also make direct sales to consumers. This has increased massively with the growth of online shopping. For example, the iconic Australian clothing business Driza-bone supplies numerous clothing stores that then sell its clothing and hats to consumers, but Driza-bone also sells its clothing directly to consumers via its website and a small number of company-owned stores.[10] Driza-bone is not a retailer, however, as its primary business is making clothes.

If you think about the operations of the ANZ Bank, you can see that while it has retailing operations (providing savings accounts and loans to individuals), it also provides finance to other businesses, invests money in the stockmarket, lends money to other lenders and so on. It becomes unclear whether you could really classify ANZ as a retailer. You will find this is often the case. Is Apple a computer retailer or computer manufacturer? Or is it a music retailer? What about Optus, which provides landline and mobile phone services to individuals as well as businesses, and sells network access on to other providers, including Virgin Mobile?

Clearly, the concept of retailing is not necessarily straightforward. Many companies may also have a retailing aspect to their business. The important point is that many types of organisations undertake retailing, whether or not they are primarily retailers. The following discussion will focus mainly on retailers, but much of the discussion is also applicable to the retailing operations of other types of organisation.

## Retailing strategy

There are two aspects to retailing strategy:
- the marketing organisation must decide what retailing approach (or approaches) is suitable for its products
- the retailer must decide on location and positioning.

These aspects cross over so much that we will discuss them together.

## Location

Most of the types of retailer that we discuss in this chapter require some type of physical presence, which means they must choose a location. For traditional stores, location is critical. It determines:

- *the natural geographic area from which customers will be drawn.* Retailers should locate their store close to their target customers. For example, an upmarket jeweller will probably do best to locate in the CBD or an exclusive suburb of a major capital city, and not so well in a small town or an industrial area. A convenience store will opt for an area full of residences.
- *proximity to competitors.* Retailers might try to choose to be removed from competitors or to be close to them. For example, in a major shopping centre, a takeaway food store needs to decide whether to locate among its competitors in the food court or away from them in a different part of the mall. Clothing stores will often locate near direct competitors because consumers tend to move from shop to shop trying to find clothes.
- *proximity to complementary retailers.* Groups of stores, if they are the appropriate mix, can draw more customers overall than any of the stores could manage by themselves. For example, a takeaway food store may make a sale to someone whose main purpose was to go to a newsagent. The newsagent might sell a magazine to someone who was mainly concerned with going to the hairdresser. The hairdresser might obtain a customer who wants a new hairdo to go with their new dress from a fashion outlet. Proximity to other stores also enables retailers to share facilities such as car parking, public toilets, signage and security.
- *customer access to public transport and public parking.* With the possible exception of convenience stores, most customers will need to travel to get to a store. Retailers should choose locations that make this convenient for the customer.

The location options tend to be:

- the central business district (CBD), which offers a high density of people and a degree of prestige, but also very high tenancy costs and parking problems
- free-standing structures
- neighbourhood shopping centres, which are in residential areas and comprise a small cluster of convenience and specialty stores
- community centres, which are designed to serve a few suburbs and usually include a department store and a small number of specialty stores
- regional centres, which are located in major metropolitan or regional areas, but which target people from some distance away by offering shops not usually available in smaller centres.

## Positioning

The retail sector is intensely competitive. One response from some retailers has been to develop a retail positioning strategy. Retail positioning refers to the practice of identifying a gap in the market and targeting it by creating some distinguishing feature in the mind of customers. This practice has been adopted by upmarket department store David Jones, whose corporate mission is 'to be Australia's best department store on measures of customer perception and shareholder value and to be an acknowledged worldwide centre of excellence in retailing'.[11]

A store's image is an important factor in attracting customers and positioning the store against competitors. A shop that looks expensive will deter people looking for a budget buy. A shop that looks like a bargain basement will put off shoppers who find status in spending large sums of money and being seen with the right bags. The look, the quality of service and the quality of products on sale all go toward attracting and retaining customers. A lot of mobile phone stores seem to resemble a nightclub and jeans outlets usually feature very loud popular music. By contrast, an upmarket menswear store might have quiet classical music playing and an atmosphere more akin to a library. Store image is particularly important for services businesses, where the store helps to provide the physical evidence (see chapter 11) of the quality of the service on offer.

## Benefits of retailers

As explained earlier, retailers are distribution channel intermediaries that are primarily concerned with retailing (or selling products to end consumers). We saw in the first part of this chapter that marketing intermediaries are useful when they add value to the distribution chain. They add value for customers and producers by creating or providing:

- *time utility*. Vending machines, 24-hour supermarkets, 24-hour service stations and corner shops ensure consumers can buy (and hence producers can sell) a range of basic goods when they need them. Without such retailers it would not be possible to buy a packet of Panadol, nappies or a bar of chocolate in the early hours of the morning.
- *place utility*. Retailers move products closer to the consumer. For example, a corner shop (also known as a convenience store) brings necessities within a short walk or drive of people's homes. More generally, retailers ensure consumers do not need to go directly to producers or wholesalers to make purchases. In the ultimate example of place utility, newsagents can ensure your Saturday morning newspaper is on your front step before you wake up.
- *form utility*. Some retailers can customise products to the consumer's particular needs and preferences. For example, a hi-fi store can put together a stereo system or home theatre system that perfectly suits the customer. A wealthy enthusiast can spend $40 000 on a Classé CD player, stereo receiver and amplifier, $100 000 on a set of Meridian speakers, and a further few thousand dollars on cables to connect it all. A music lover on a more modest budget might leave the same store with $1500 worth of Yamaha gear. A Bunnings customer looking to build a set of shelves can ask the sales assistant to cut the timber to length for them. A tailor will take up the trouser leg of a suit to match the customer's height and style of shoe. Products that are services, discussed in detail in chapter 11, generally involve high levels of form utility.
- *advice and personal service*. Retailers are geared to deal with customers one-on-one, providing advice and personal service. For example, a consumer wanting to buy a new 3D TV television set can speak with a Harvey Norman salesperson about the pros and cons of different models from a variety of manufacturers, as well as actually view the different sets.
- *exchange efficiencies*. Retailers reduce the number of parties that producers and wholesalers must deal with and reduce the number of sellers that consumers must deal with. Retailers can offer consumers a wide range of products from numerous producers all in one place. For example, a David Jones department store in a shopping mall may carry clothing from 50 different designers.[12] In the same shopping mall, there might be half a dozen other clothing stores carrying multiple designers' clothes as well as several specialist clothing stores carrying just one brand. Homemaker centres offer a similar advantage. A consumer looking to buy a new dining suite can often see dozens of options in several stores all under one roof. Supermarkets bring many different types of products into one store, meaning consumers can buy meat, dairy products, fruit and vegetables, canned

foods, cleaning products and many other items with one shopping trip and one transaction. At its extreme, this is known as 'scrambled merchandising'. Even if they choose to visit a butcher, a cheese shop and a greengrocer instead, it is still often much easier for the producer and consumer than having direct exchanges between the producers and consumers for each product.

# Types of retailers

There are many different forms of retailer, each offering relative strengths and weaknesses for the customer and the producer or wholesaler. We will discuss the various forms in this section and also note the 'wheel of retailing' theory, which explains how the overall mix of the retail sector evolves over time.

## Specialty retailers

Specialty retailers usually carry just one or a small number of different types of products, but within that product line, they carry a great deal of variety. The characteristics of the main specialty retailers — specialty stores, category killers and off-price retailers — are outlined in table 10.2.

**TABLE 10.2** Specialty retailers

| Type of store | Description | Characteristics | Examples | |
|---|---|---|---|---|
| Specialty stores | Retailers that carry a relatively narrow range of product types, but offer great variety within those product lines | • Often located in shopping centres<br>• Offer customers variety and personal service by salespeople with a high degree of product knowledge<br>• Higher prices than similar products at department stores or supermarkets<br>• Specialty stores with well-established marketing channels (particularly franchises and chain stores) can obtain substantial discounts from suppliers | Crazy John's<br><br>Sussans<br><br>Michael Hill Jeweller | |
| Category killers | A type of specialty retailer that focuses on a particular product category and attracts customers with low prices and a very wide variety of products within that category | • Operations are big enough that it can buy supplies very cheaply and sell cheaply in enough volume to make a profit<br>• Make it very difficult for smaller-scale specialty stores to compete<br>• Often result in a monopoly or oligopoly | JB Hi-Fi<br><br>Toys 'R' Us | |
| Off-price retailers | Retailers that sell manufacturers' seconds, superseded products, excess supply and returns with little customer service and at very low prices | • Some are collections of manufacturers' stores<br>• Often carry quite similar lines to department stores but at a considerably lower price<br>• Little flexibility in terms of returns<br>• Often locate away from retailers to avoid competing directly on price with partners in the distribution channel | DFO (Direct Factory Outlet) | |

## General-merchandise retail stores

General-merchandise retail stores offer a wide variety of products. The main general-merchandise retail stores are convenience stores, showrooms, department stores, discount stores, supermarkets, superstores and hypermarkets. Most of these will be familiar if you spend much time shopping. Table 10.3 highlights the key characteristics of each of these.

**TABLE 10.3** General-merchandise retail stores

| Type of store | Description | Characteristics | Examples | |
|---|---|---|---|---|
| Convenience stores/ corner shops | Small shops located near residential areas, carrying a small range of basic necessities and opening extended hours | • High operating costs<br>• Low turnover<br>• High prices<br>• Local customers<br>• Source stock from wholesalers or a larger retailer | 7-Eleven<br>BP Select<br>Star Mart | |
| Supermarkets | Self-service retailers that carry a large range of food and non-food grocery items | • Account for about three-quarters of Australia's grocery purchases<br>• Large range of both food (fresh, canned, dried and frozen) and non-food (cleaning products, clothing, storage and hygiene) grocery items<br>• Customers pick items off shelves and pay at central checkouts<br>• Low prices (based on high turnover and efficient supply chain management)<br>• Relatively long opening hours<br>• Often located next to other stores<br>• Face competition from specialty stores | Woolworths<br>Safeway<br>Coles<br>BI-LO<br>IGA<br>Aldi | |
| Discount stores | Self-service stores relying on low prices and high turnover | • Little customer service<br>• Range of products is similar to department stores<br>• Popular with consumers to the detriment of higher-priced department stores | The Warehouse<br>Big W<br>Kmart<br>Target | |
| Department stores | Large stores carrying a wide range of products, often organised into specialist departments, and offering a relatively high level of customer service | • Attentive, personal service<br>• Access to finance<br>• Relatively easy returns<br>• Delivery services<br>• Additional services such as gift wrapping | Myer<br>David Jones<br>Ballantynes (NZ) | |
| Showrooms | Large retail facilities that offer little customer service, handle products in a similar way to warehouses, and base their business on low margins, but high turnover | • Large inventories (stored in warehouse-like facilities in store or off site)<br>• Often present products in simulated real-life settings<br>• High-profile retail locations<br>• Sometimes locate warehouse facilities off site for cost benefits<br>• Often offer a delivery service | IKEA<br>Far Pavilions | |
| Hypermarkets | Retailers that combine the products and characteristics of a supermarket and a discount store | • Relatively unknown in Australia and New Zealand<br>• Common in Europe and Asia<br>• Carry up to 50 000 items ranging from bread and televisions to jewellery and fast food | Tesco Lotus<br>Giant | |

| Type of store | Description | Characteristics | Examples | |
|---|---|---|---|---|
| Superstores | Retailers that carry supermarket lines plus a wide range of other goods more traditionally carried by specialist or department stores | • Relatively unknown in Australia and New Zealand<br>• Common in Europe and Asia<br>• Similar to supermarkets, but carry several times as many products, including whitegoods, hardware and motoring items | Carrefour |  |

## The 'wheel of retailing' theory

The wheel of retailing is a theory about how retailers evolve in the market. It is somewhat similar to the product life cycle concept. According to the **wheel of retailing** theory:

- retailers enter the market using some innovation to achieve low costs and use that to charge low prices
- other new and existing retailers copy the low-cost innovation and compete directly with the new entrants
- to distinguish itself, the retailer adds extra services, improves its location and store image, and so on, which results in higher costs and higher prices
- new retailers enter the market using some new innovation to achieve low costs and then compete with the original, now high-price, retailer.[13]

**wheel of retailing** The theory that retailers enter the market with low costs, low margins and low prices, but move to high costs and high prices as they seek to compete with copiers, only to then have to compete with new low-price entrants.

## Online retailing

Online retailing is a rapidly growing form of retailing. Online retailing (or e-tailing) involves selling to customers via the internet. The most common online purchases are airline tickets, accommodation, DVDs, books and magazines. For customers, online retailing enables purchases without leaving home. This is offset by the inability to examine the product in 'real life', plus the probable postage fees. For the online retailer, catalogue marketing avoids the expense associated with stores and enables them access to customers in any geographic region.

There are generally two types of online retailers: those that exist only online or online in combination with other direct marketing avenues; and those that operate an online 'store' as a complement to their physical store.

In the first category — retailers that operate only through direct marketing approaches — are businesses such as the men's underwear site DUGG (Down Under Guys Gear — www.dugg.com.au) and auction site eBay.

In the second category are retailers such as Officeworks that have stores located in metropolitan areas, but also offer all of their products via their website. This strategy allows Officeworks to sell to customers who do not live anywhere near an Officeworks store, thus competing with local stationery and office supplies outlets, and to sell to those who simply prefer the convenience of buying online. Other examples include Dymocks, ABC, Qantas, and the major banks. Retailers with a physical and an online store need to carefully coordinate the offerings of each. According to Adrian Williams, a senior analyst at retail researcher IGD, the web cannot be seen as a distinct marketing channel; the online price should be available in store and if a consumer buys a product online, that product should be able to be returned to a physical retail outlet.[14]

With the now pervasive nature of the internet, retailers must carefully coordinate their promotional activities. Whereas once consumers might visit five stores and look at dozens of alternative products before making a choice (for major purchases), there is a distinct trend now for consumers to research and shortlist online and then go to just one or two stores and look at only a few products 'in the flesh' before making their choice. Interestingly, many consumers do still prefer to go to a physical store to make the purchase even though they have, or nearly have, chosen which product to buy online.[15]

From the very first days of e-commerce, internet industry strategists and the mass media warned that consumers would be reluctant to buy online because they would have to divulge their credit card and other personal details and/or they did not trust the retailer. With massive media coverage given to cybercrime, a degree of paranoia became entrenched in the early years of online retailing. However, while there are real security risks involved in revealing personal information online, millions of people conduct their transactions online every day. In fact, almost two-thirds of Australians and nearly half of New Zealanders make an online purchase every month. Only a minority of transactions are subject to fraud. Nevertheless, security remains an issue, which stops some customers from using the online purchasing facilities. According to a study by A.C.Nielsen, some 75 per cent of Australians do not feel safe providing credit card information online and only 18 per cent of Australians say they trust online retailers. Over time, however, online shopping has become more pervasive. At the moment, there are still some trends apparent in the profile of online shoppers. While males and females shop in equal numbers, people aged over 55 are under-represented and people with incomes over $95 000 are overrepresented.[16]

Related to online retailing is mobile e-commerce or m-commerce. **Mobile e-commerce** is the use of a mobile phone to make purchases. Given mobile phones are increasingly web-enabled, mobile e-commerce encompasses all of online retailing, plus a number of unique direct selling opportunities. Mobile e-commerce is still very much an emerging field. There should not really be any difference between buying with a mobile and buying with a PC. In fact, it is quite possible already to stand in front of a salesperson in a shop and go online on a mobile to check competitors' prices. So far only 4 per cent of Australians have used their mobile phone to make a purchase, but a further 19 per cent say they might do so. At present, the vast majority of mobile-facilitated purchases are of products for the mobile itself (ringtones, screensavers, applications etc.).[17] Online retailing is discussed further in chapter 12.

### Other forms of retailing

**direct marketing** A type of non-store retailing that promotes and sells products via mail, telephone or the web.

**Direct marketing** is a type of non-store retailing that uses mail, telephone or the web to promote products directly to potential customers and requires the customer to respond in the same way. Direct marketing does not rely on a store, but offers consumers complete flexibility as to the timing of their purchases and the ability to shop without leaving their homes. The main types of direct marketing are online retailing, telemarketing, catalogue marketing, television shopping and direct — response marketing. We will discuss each in turn.

### Telemarketing

Telemarketing is the performance of marketing-related activities over the telephone. Consumers overwhelmingly hate it, but it is successful enough that many businesses invest enormous resources into it. The type of telemarketing that consumers most object to is cold calling at home, whereby a business phones a private residential phone number and tries to sell a product or service to the householder. Sometimes householders are chosen based on an existing relationship with the business (e.g. if you have a savings account with ANZ, they might phone you trying to sell you life insurance); sometimes based on a related interest (e.g. a magazine that you subscribe to sells your details to a business that sells products related to the topic of the magazine); and sometimes there is no pre-selection of the household — the telemarketer is calling you entirely at random. Public resistance to telemarketing reached such a strong point in the early 2000s that the Australian federal government introduced the Do Not Call Register whereby households could opt out of telemarketing offers[18] (except those by charities, religions and businesses with which the householder has an existing business relationship). The New Zealand Marketing Association runs a similar scheme, but it is only applicable to members of the association.[19]

### Catalogue marketing

Catalogue marketing might sound old-fashioned, but it is still an effective direct marketing approach. Avon, Amway and Tupperware are all businesses that use catalogue marketing. In catalogue marketing, the marketing organisation provides a catalogue to customers who then place their orders by mail, telephone or the internet. Catalogue marketing offers customers all the convenience of online shopping. They can peruse the catalogue at their leisure and purchase without leaving their homes. On the other hand, the range of products available via catalogues is fairly limited. For the retailer, catalogue marketing provides access to customers who do not live near stores.

### Direct-response marketing

Similar to catalogue marketing, direct-response marketing requires customers to use the mail, internet or telephone to make a purchase. The difference is that instead of catalogues, direct-response marketing uses advertising, such as a brochure in a mailbox, spam, or a television advertisement. DVDs of old television series are one of the best-known examples. A television advertisement promoting the products ends with a phone number, the instruction to 'call now' and the reassurance that 'our operators are waiting'.

Television home shopping is essentially an enlarged version of direct-response marketing, where a full half-hour program is devoted to promoting a particular product (often in the early hours of the morning) or indeed an entire television channel is dedicated to home shopping. Like the other forms of direct-response marketing, television home shopping promotes a product to viewers and then requires customers to phone in their order details. Television home shopping offers convenience for customers, but as with all direct marketing approaches, the consumer cannot inspect the product before they purchase and may find it does not meet their expectations. Some sellers overcome this by offering to accept the product back if it does not satisfy the customer.

### Door-to-door selling

Door-to-door selling, sometimes known as direct selling, is an approach taking its name from the old practice of a salesperson walking door to door to promote products to people at home. Few companies still use this approach. Today a modified version, whereby potential customers are more strategically selected, is more common. Usually customers are identified through some other means and then an appointment is made for a visit by a salesperson.

A variation on door-to-door selling is the party plan, most commonly associated with Tupperware and Tupperware Parties. In recent years, the party plan concept has expanded to other products, most notably lingerie. The party plan method of direct selling relies on a consumer hosting a party for friends, work colleagues and/or neighbours at which a salesperson leads the group through product demonstrations.

The party plan is generally better accepted by consumers because they opt in to it rather than being targeted by a door-to-door salesperson or someone wandering around a shopping centre.

Successful door-to-door selling relies on a skilful salesperson and a considerable devotion of time and resources to generate sales. As such, it is the most expensive form of retailing. It does, however, offer the marketer exclusive access to the customer and the ability to fully promote the benefits of their products. For consumers, door-to-door selling offers the highest level of customer service and, in the case of a party plan, a degree of entertainment.

### Automatic vending

**Automatic vending** relies on machines to accept payments and then dispense products. Historically, vending machines have involved putting coins in a slot. With increasing prices and for convenience, some now takes notes and some take credit or debit cards. In fact, there are vending machines that accept notes and dispense coins just to provide the coins required for other vending machines! Some vending machines are now being installed that allow payments to be made via the customer's mobile phone — the charge for the product appears on the customer's phone bill. At present these are most common in Japan, but they are gradually being installed in metropolitan areas in other countries, including Australia.

Automatic vending machines are often used to sell the following goods:
- hot and cold beverages (including beer in some countries) and snacks — in workplaces, hospitals, train stations, airports, shopping centres
- lollies — the traditional mechanical gumball machine dispensing a superball, a trinket or a handful of gum
- condoms — particularly in service stations, pubs and clubs
- cigarettes — though this is banned in many countries and declining in others due to anti-smoking regulations and concerns about underage customers
- newspapers — particularly in the USA.

While the type of goods available from vending machines in Australia is fairly limited, in some other countries, most notably Japan, a very wide range of items is available from vending machines. For example, vending machines in Japan sell underwear, toothbrushes, disposable cameras, magazines and iPods.

Some service organisations have made use of vending machines to avoid people queuing to see a customer service officer, when the process does not really require human judgement. Train ticket machines are one example — at some train stations commuters can still choose to buy their ticket from a person; at others they cannot. More recently airlines have adopted similar machines, where passengers can obtain their boarding pass from a vending machine. If they have no luggage to check, it avoids the need to join a long queue at check-in.

The main benefits of automatic vending are that the product can be bought by the customer without any immediate interaction with staff of the marketing organisation. Essentially, vending machines are an 'always open' store. In some cases, like printed tickets and hot drinks, the machine actually does some of the making of the product. While not strictly vending machines, coin-operated laundromats and public toilets work on a similar principle of pay per use without a customer service operator involved.

It is not all good news though. Vending machines are expensive pieces of electronic machinery, which require regular maintenance and restocking (some more sophisticated machines report their inventory back to base). They are subject to vandalism and they are impersonal — not many customers feel loyalty to a vending

**automatic vending** Use of machines to dispense a product; used for small, routinely purchased products.

machine. They often malfunction. Anyone who uses vending machines regularly will have experienced receiving a cup of hot water rather than a cup of hot chocolate, or will have seen the bag of crisps they have paid for dangling from the shelf rather than falling into the dispensing tray.

# Retail versus e-tail

In the early days of the internet in the 1990s, many traditional retailers either feared or hoped they would be swamped by an online retailing revolution, with customers preferring to shop and order products online from the convenience of their own homes. E-commerce websites were hastily erected, particularly during the 'dot com' boom late in that decade.

For many retailers, however, online fears or hopes have proved unfounded as the years have rolled on. While their sites may generate traffic, they generate relatively few sales. The Coles website, for example, is the most frequently accessed website of all traditional local retailers in Australia, yet online sales represent just 1 per cent of its total sales. The pattern is similar across the board in retailing, both locally and globally. In Australia, online sales represent just 2.3 per cent of overall retail sales, slightly behind the rates for the United States (3.3 per cent) and the United Kingdom (6.6 per cent).

Industry analysts, however, believe that looking purely at online sales activity is a misleading representation of the impact of an online retailing presence. The inverse correlation between website traffic and sales for a retailer like Coles suggests that consumers actively use online sites to search for products and prices, and a logical extension of this is that it may influence their choice of which supermarket to shop at in any given week.

Online retail activity in Australia is strongest among products aimed specifically at a younger 'digital native' audience, or for products for which global competition is well established via online retailers such as Amazon (e.g. books and music). Smaller players, however, can find it difficult to establish a presence online, with the manufacturers of some brands being reluctant to deal with less well-known retailers that only have an online presence. Smaller online e-tailers are also limited in their ability to negotiate bulk pricing deals with manufacturers.

Myer recognises the value of an online presence for promoting its brand. It also recognises the value of offering its customers the opportunity to buy online. However, it still firmly believes in the traditional retail shopping experience. Myer's national corporate affairs manager, Mitch Caitlin, explains: 'What differentiates Myer from its competitors in store is that we add an entertainment element to shopping. We have a lot more cosmetics demonstrations and samples, and we make shopping an experience'.

Myer is one company that still firmly believes in the traditional retail experience.

## Question

What might be some distribution implications for retailers such as Coles or Myer if their online sales significantly increase in the future?

## Concepts and applications check

**Learning objective 4** understand the major aspects of retailing

4.1 Think of an example of a product that is exclusively distributed through a specific retailer in your geographic region. Explain why you think the organisation has adopted that distribution strategy for its product.

4.2 Outline the major considerations in choosing a retail location.

**4.3** Choose example stores from two of the types of general merchandise retail stores outlined in table 10.2 (e.g. a discount store such as Kmart versus a department store such as Myer). Outline the advantages that each store has over the other.

**4.4** Imagine you are the marketing manager for a specialty hardware retailer such as Mitre 10. Briefly outline some marketing strategies you may be able to use against a potential 'category killer', such as Bunnings.

**4.5** Explain the 'wheel of retailing' concept in your own words.

**4.6** Discuss three types of non-store retailing. What are the benefits to consumers?

## AGENTS AND BROKERS

Learning objective 5 explain the role of agents and brokers in the distribution channel

Agents and brokers are important intermediaries that connect customers, industrial buyers and other participants with each other in the distribution channel. Agents and brokers earn income from commissions, which are usually calculated on the total size of the sale.

## Agents

**agents** Marketing intermediaries engaged by buyers or sellers on an ongoing basis to represent them in negotiations with other parties in the marketing channel.

**Agents** are engaged by buyers or sellers on an ongoing basis to represent them in negotiations with other marketing channel participants. For example, Max Markson's company Markson Sparks! acts as an agent for a number of well-known celebrities, including TV presenter Catriona Rowntree.[20] The main types of agents are:

- *manufacturers' agents* — agents that act in a similar way to a salesperson for multiple producers, selling specified, non-competing products in a particular region under standard terms and conditions. For the manufacturer, the use of manufacturers' agents can remove the need to employ and manage a sales team. For the retail and wholesale buyers, it is more efficient to deal with a small number of manufacturers' agents than to deal with manufacturers individually.
- *selling agents* — agents commonly used by small producers that cannot afford a salesforce or marketing department. Selling agents usually work for multiple producers, but do not take on competing products. They have a fairly involved role in how the product is promoted and priced.
- *buying agents* — specialist buyers that make purchases and handle goods for long-term partners, such as retailers. Buying, or purchasing, agents generally have extensive knowledge of the products they work with, can advise their partners and are able to obtain beneficial pricing and terms.
- *commission merchants* — agents that receive goods on consignment and negotiate the best possible price in centralised markets. The Tokyo flower markets operate with commission merchants who sell consignments of flowers at a massive flower market by auction each morning.

## Brokers

**brokers** Marketing intermediaries engaged by buyers or sellers on a short-term or one-off basis to represent them in negotiations with other parties in the marketing channel.

**Brokers** are engaged on a short-term or one-off basis to negotiate on behalf of buyers or sellers. They have a more limited role than agents, but their value is in their specialist knowledge and well-established contacts in the industries in which they work. Real estate salespeople (commonly — and rather confusingly — known as real estate agents), insurance brokers, mortgage brokers and stockbrokers are among the better known examples of brokers.

Insurance brokers work to find the most suitable insurance for individuals and organisations and provide expert advice about insurance contracts. Even standard consumer insurance products such as motor vehicle insurance and home and contents insurance can involve long and complex policy documents. For the extensive and often very specific insurance requirements of businesses (including insurance for assets, revenue, liability, personnel and indemnity), an insurance broker can use their industry knowledge and contacts to negotiate a suitable insurance product that adequately covers the business. Insurance brokers can also help insurance providers by handling many of the upfront administrative tasks.

Mortgage broking became a boom industry in the 1990s as many non-bank lenders entered the home loan sector to compete with the traditional banks. As the mortgage market became more competitive and as mortgage products themselves became more complex, offering a bundle of financial services in one integrated package, many consumers turned to mortgage brokers to help them identify the best deal. As discussed earlier in the chapter, mortgage brokers can offer consumers a higher level of service than the financial institutions and offer lenders access to new customers. Mortgage brokers often take responsibility for almost all aspects of the loan application.

The insurance and mortgage broking industries have been widely criticised over the past decade, as it has come to light that some brokers have guided their customers towards products that maximise the broker's income rather than necessarily providing the most suitable product. Mortgage brokers, for example, receive different fees and trailing commissions from different financial institutions, providing an incentive to direct their customers to the loan that will provide the highest payment to the broker. Some, particularly in the United States, have also been criticised for manipulating the loan application process to obtain much larger loans for borrowers than they can realistically afford to repay.

The business of many brokers has changed over the past decade as e-commerce has taken over many of the functions of processing transactions. For example, the broker Commonwealth Securities, better known as Commsec, offers traditional telephone broking of shares and other financial securities, but the vast majority of its business is now done through its low-cost online service (www.comsec.com.au). Traditionally, stockbroking was undertaken by specialist stockbrokers for a small number of investors, but the increasing stockmarket awareness of the general public, combined with the ability to provide cheap broking, has greatly increased the number of people investing in the stockmarket. The budget online services usually provide low-cost access to stockmarket data that investors can analyse, but do not provide specialist advice, which remains a premium add-on product.

## CommSec: breaking the mould for broking     Spotlight

Most people interested in finance would have heard of CommSec, but what is CommSec and what does it do? CommSec (Commonwealth Securities Ltd) is Australia's largest discount online broker. It is a wholly owned, but not guaranteed, subsidiary of the Commonwealth Bank of Australia (CBA). CommSec started operations in 1995, with the aim of making investing 'easy, accessible and affordable for all Australians'. It began with an over-the-phone share trading service in Australian equities, and has expanded to offer online access to Australian and international share trading; investment and super funds; margin loans and online research tools.

In 1997 CommSec launched its share trading website (www.commsec.com.au). The website has become the main platform for communication and business with its customers, as well as one of the most popular and widely used online share trading platforms in Australia. More recently CommSec became the first Australian brokerage firm to offer a brokerage website specifically designed for a portable device. However, it also offers a telephone-based brokerage service and advisory service,

and has created CommSec iPhone Edition for the Apple iPhone, the first home-grown iPhone application in Australia for trading.

Over the years, CommSec's market share in retail broking has increased through acquisition of other Australian broking operations, including TD Waterhouse, AOT, Neville Ward Direct, Sanford and Avcol. CommSec also provides a white label trading platform for AFSL holders and their clients.

CommSec is a major player in business trading. It has also been highly successful as a discount broker by attracting many 'mums and dads' (retail) investors. Continuing the aim of making investing 'easy, accessible and affordable', the minimum buy trade amount is $500, plus a $19.95* brokerage fee charged when buying or selling shares. Trading can be done through a secure website, over the phone or by an iPhone. CommSec continues to be a leader in retail broking.[21]

* Conditions apply

> **Question**
>
> How has stockbroking changed in recent decades? What are the advantages that companies like CommSec bring to the financial industry?

---

## Concepts and applications check

**Learning objective 5** explain the role of agents and brokers in the distribution channel

**5.1** How is a wholesaler different to an agent? What type of industries would use an agent?

**5.2** What is the difference between an agent and a broker? Give examples in your answer.

**5.3** Explain how agents and brokers can assist in bringing about a sale.

---

# WHOLESALING

**Learning objective 6**
explain the role of wholesalers in marketing distribution

**wholesaling** Exchanges in which products are bought for resale, for use as inputs in other products, or for some other use in a business.

**Wholesaling** comprises exchanges in which products are bought for resale, for use as inputs in other products, or for some other use in a business. Wholesaling does not include transactions with end consumers. A wholesaler is simply an organisation primarily engaged in wholesaling. Some organisations do undertake wholesaling and retailing. For example, Sydney Fish Market Pty Ltd is a fresh fish wholesaler, but also has an extensive fresh seafood retail business.

While retailing is familiar to most of us, consumers do not usually deal with wholesalers. Wholesaling differs from retailing in that wholesalers deal with businesses. Their marketing mix is geared towards that, so, for example, they generally do not advertise in the mass media or try to site themselves in a fashionable shopping area. They tend to deal in large volumes of product in each transaction. While some wholesalers do deal directly with end consumers, they are usually not set up to handle numerous small transactions.

## Major wholesaling functions

Wholesalers act as the connection between producers and retailers and offer benefits to both. For the producer, wholesalers:
- act as a salesforce, promoting and selling its products to retailers
- hold and manage inventory, relieving the producer's warehousing and transport burden
- assume the risk when retailers are given products on credit

- provide cashflow by paying for and taking possession of inventory shortly after it is produced
- communicate producer and market issues to retailers.

For many producers, these benefits — and the fact that wholesalers, being specialists, can provide the services more efficiently than the producer can perform them itself — outweigh the financial costs of dealing with wholesalers in the marketing channel.

For the retailer, wholesalers:
- manage distribution
- help choose and source appropriate inventory
- have bulk buying power and the ability to negotiate good deals with producers
- provide access to a wide range of goods through one business partnership
- can provide sophisticated technology solutions to manage ordering
- can provide credit
- communicate market and retail issues to producers.

## Types of wholesalers

Wholesalers are considered to be merchant wholesalers if they are independently owned and manufacturers' wholesalers if they are owned by the producer. Agents also share many of the characteristics of wholesalers, but the fact they do not take ownership of the products at any point in the distribution channel is an important distinction.

### Merchant wholesalers

**Merchant wholesalers** are independently owned (i.e. not owned by the producer). They take ownership of the product from producers and sell it on to retailers. (Industrial distributors are the business market equivalent of merchant wholesalers — selling to producers rather than retailers.) Merchant wholesalers are either full-service wholesalers or limited-service wholesalers.

**merchant wholesalers**
Independently owned wholesaling businesses that take title to products.

### Full-service wholesalers

Full-service wholesalers, as the name suggests, perform the full gamut of wholesaling activities, and retailers and producers rely heavily on them for numerous services. Full-service wholesalers are one of the following:
- *general-merchandise wholesalers* — wholesalers that carry a wide variety of product lines, but relatively little depth within those product lines
- *limited-line wholesalers* — wholesalers that carry only a few different product lines, but have considerable depth in each line
- *specialty-line wholesalers* — wholesalers that carry a single product line and only a few items within that line.

### Limited-service wholesalers

Limited-service wholesalers specialise in a narrow range of wholesaling services, leaving it to producers and retailers to perform for themselves many of the functions provided by full-service wholesalers. For example:
- *cash and carry wholesalers* — wholesalers that supply a limited number of lines of high-turnover products to small businesses, which pay in cash and transport the products themselves.
- *drop shippers* — wholesalers that purchase from producers and sell to retailers, but organise shipment directly between those two parties rather than take possession of the products
- *mail-order wholesalers* — wholesalers that use catalogues and mail or courier services rather than salespeople and their own transport to promote, sell and deliver goods to retailers.

## Manufacturers' wholesalers

**Manufacturers' wholesalers**, also known as manufacturers' sales branches and offices, are similar to merchant wholesalers, but are owned by the producer itself and thus represent a form of vertical integration. A producer will choose to operate its own wholesaler when no existing wholesaler provides the necessary services or when the producer, through some technique, can more efficiently handle wholesale than could a partner.

Manufacturers' wholesalers are either sales branches or sales offices. Sales branches are located close to the manufacturer's major customers and provide credit, transport, promotional and other services. In addition to selling the producer's products to retailers and other intermediaries, sales branches support the producer's salesforce. Sales offices do not carry inventory, but otherwise function in much the same way as sales branches.

## Spotlight  Costco

Costco's store in Docklands, Melbourne, is popular with consumers.

The retail industry was buzzing when Costco, a US wholesaler/retailer, recently began trading in Australia at Docklands, Melbourne — with plans for expansion to Sydney and other cities to cater for the growing wholesale shopping and bulk buying market. The parent company, Costco Wholesale Corporation, operates an international chain of membership warehouses under the 'Costco Wholesale' name. The company opened its first store in Seattle in 1983. It now has stores at 563 locations (and counting) in countries including the United States, Puerto Rico, Canada, Mexico, Taiwan, Korea, Japan and the United Kingdom.

Costco offers an exclusive cash-and-carry style of shopping experience. This means that it is membership-based, with an annual upfront membership fee of $60. Two types of membership are available: Business and Gold Star. Business members qualify by owning or operating a business, while Gold Star membership is available to individuals.

Costco has one of the largest and most exclusive product ranges of any major supermarket or shopping chain. The Docklands store carries 3600 product lines and employs 230 staff, and is expected to increase competition between supermarkets. The products sold at the store include groceries, confectionery, appliances, television and media devices, automotive supplies, tyres, toys, hardware, sporting goods, jewellery, watches, cameras, books, homewares, apparel, health and beauty aids, tobacco, furniture, office supplies and office equipment. It carries top brands such as Vegemite, as well as grocery brands including Huggies, Duracell and Cadbury. It also sells international brands such as Calvin Klein, Sony and Prada.

According to a Costco wholesale regional operations manager, Rick Carlson, the aim is to provide the most competitive prices for consumers: 'We buy globally; our focus of the business is to drive costs down through logistics. We master logistics throughout the world and, doing that, we're able to drive the costs down. Our margins are transparent, we don't mark up anything over 15 per cent margin, which is unique in the retail sector anywhere in the world.'[22]

### Question

Wholesalers such as Costco usually deal with both businesses and consumers. What problems could this cause in the marketing channel?

## Concepts and applications check

**Learning objective 6**  explain the role of wholesalers in marketing distribution

**6.1**  Explain the role of a wholesaler in your own words.

**6.2**  Outline how wholesalers can benefit producers.

**6.3**  Outline how wholesalers can benefit retailers.

**6.4**  Explain the difference between manufacturers' wholesalers and merchant wholesalers.

# SUMMARY

 **Learning objective 1**   understand the concept of place and how distribution channels connect producers and consumers/organisational buyers

The concept of 'place', or distribution, involves the way products can be eventually 'placed' in the hands of the final consumer through a supply chain between producers and consumers (or organisational buyers in the case of business-to-business markets). The chain of distribution is known as a distribution channel. The key organisations in the marketing channel, or intermediaries, include wholesalers, industrial buyers, agents or brokers, and retailers. Marketing intermediaries are useful and necessary when they can more efficiently connect producers with their customers than can the producers themselves. Even if a producer can manage to get their product directly to end users, they are often better off to concentrate on their core abilities (production) and rely on specialist intermediaries who can more efficiently move the product closer to customers. Because they have expertise, equipment, experience, contacts, skills and scales of economy, intermediaries help producers achieve better results than producers can achieve when acting alone.

 **Learning objective 2**   describe the major activities involved in the distribution of goods

Physical distribution is the movement of physical products from the producer to the consumer. It involves order processing, inventory management, warehousing and transportation. Order processing involves receiving and validating orders from customers and salespeople. Inventory management involves ensuring the organisation holds enough stock to fill orders without having so much stock on hand that inventory holding costs become unreasonably high. Warehousing is the use of facilities (generally a building) to store and move goods. Transportation is the process of moving products from their place of manufacture to their place of consumption, principally via road, rail, sea, air and pipelines. Most distribution channels coordinate multiple modes of transport.

 **Learning objective 3**   describe the major activities involved in the distribution of services

Services products are usually produced at the time of consumption and so the notion of 'service distribution' is quite different to physical distribution. However, physical distribution is required for the physical inputs used in producing and delivering the service product, some services are delivered using infrastructure, and service businesses must ensure that the labour is available at the right time and the right quantities to ensure customers can be served.

 **Learning objective 4**   understand the major aspects of retailing

Retailing describes any exchange in which the buyer is the ultimate consumer of the product. Distribution channel intermediaries that are primarily concerned with retailing are called 'retailers'. Retailers provide customers with time utility, place utility, form utility, advice and personal service, and exchange efficiencies. There is an enormous range of retailers, including general-merchandise retail stores, specialty retail stores, online retailers and numerous others.

## Key terms and concepts

agents 374
automatic vending 372
brokers 374
cross-docking 358
direct marketing 370
distribution centre 358
distribution channel 347
exclusive distribution 349
franchising 354
freight forwarders 358
horizontal channel
   integration 353
intensive distribution 349
just-in-time (JIT) 357
manufacturers'
   wholesalers 378
marketing
   intermediaries 347
materials handling 358
merchant wholesalers 377
mobile e-commerce 370
retailing 364
selective distribution 349
supply-chain
   management 352
vertical channel
   integration 353
vertical marketing
   system 354
wheel of retailing 369
wholesaling 376

**Learning objective 5** explain the role of agents and brokers in the distribution channel

Agents and brokers bring together other participants in the distribution channel. Agents are engaged by buyers or sellers on an ongoing basis to represent them in negotiations with other distribution channel participants. The main types of agents are manufacturers' agents, selling agents, buying agents and commission merchants. Brokers, on the other hand, are engaged on a short-term or one-off basis to negotiate on behalf of buyers or sellers. They have a more limited role than agents, but their value is in their specialist knowledge and well-established contacts in the industries in which they work.

 **Learning objective 6** explain the role of wholesalers in marketing distribution

Wholesaling comprises exchanges in which products are bought for resale, for use as inputs in other products, or for some other use in a business. Wholesaling does not include transactions with end consumers. Wholesalers tend to deal in large volumes of product in each transaction. Wholesalers offer benefits to the producer by acting as a sales force, promoting and selling its products to retailers; holding and managing inventory, relieving the producer's warehousing and transport burden; assuming the risk when retailers are given products on credit; providing cashflow by paying for and taking possession of inventory shortly after it is produced; and communicating market issues to the producer and retailers. For the retailer, wholesalers can manage distribution; help choose and source appropriate inventory; have bulk buying power and the ability to negotiate good deals with producers; provide access to a wide range of goods through one business partnership; can provide sophisticated technology solutions to manage ordering; can provide credit; and communicate market and retail issues to producers.

# Foodbank

When discussing the elements of the marketing mix, examples are usually given of tangible products by profit-making organisations. While we have mentioned the distribution of services earlier in the chapter, it should also be noted that many not-for-profit and charitable organisations need skills in distribution and logistics. One such organisation is Foodbank, the largest hunger relief charity in Australia. Foodbank is working with donors, supporters, partners, welfare agencies, volunteers and staff to tackle the hidden problem of hunger. Through efforts to alleviate the extent of this problem in society, Foodbank also indirectly assists other charities by reducing the burdens placed on them. According to Patrick McClure, a former CEO of Mission Australia, 'Foodbank will save Mission Australia $1 million over five years'.

The problem of hunger in Australia and in many other countries around the world is a growing one. Consider the following sobering statistics:

- About 11 per cent of Australian adults and 12 per cent of children live in poverty, and the numbers are growing.
- About 2.2 million Australians don't have enough money to take care of basic needs such as housing, clothing and food.
- About 15 per cent of Australian children live in jobless households.
- Up to a million children don't always get enough to eat in Australia.
- The aged, singles and the working poor have become the new battlers in Australia.
- Hunger is a largely hidden social problem and many victims suffer in silence. The victims could be a child, unemployed or elderly person in your street.
- Each year about two million Australians, half of whom are children, rely on food relief. The children in this situation often go to school without breakfast, or to bed without dinner.

The Australian Foodbank operation is part of an international network of similar organisations around the world. In Australia, Foodbank has distribution centres in New South Wales, Queensland, South Australia, Tasmania, Victoria and Western Australia, as well as in the Northern Territory. The warehouse facility at Wetherill Park, in Sydney's west, is 2900 square metres in size, and houses 1200 pallets of dry goods, 200 pallets of frozen goods and 100 pallets of chilled goods. Foodbank also has satellite warehouses in eight regional centres: Mt Gambier and Whyalla (in South Australia), Bendigo and Dandenong (in Victoria), and Albany, Geraldton, Bunbury and Mandurah (in Western Australia). Foodbank has about 20 000 square metres of warehousing space nationally.

Foodbank delivers more than 19 million kilograms of donated food annually, which is the equivalent of more than 25 million meals — feeding an average of 70 000 people per day. Its goal is to increase its annual delivery to 50 million kilograms by 2015 as, unfortunately, the demand is there. According to the chairman of Foodbank, Enzo Allara, there is still a significant gap between the amount of produce available and what is needed to feed the nation's hungry residents. Hunger is not just an issue that affects the homeless — it also affects the elderly, single-parent families, students, asylum seekers and children, among others.

Foodbank provides the distribution link between the food and grocery industry and more than 2200 welfare agencies around Australia. It views itself as 'the pantry of the welfare sector and the food and grocery industry's chosen distributor of donations'. Each welfare agency must satisfy the following criteria in order to be eligible to receive donations from Foodbank:

- it must be a registered charity
- it must have public liability insurance
- it must have a qualified food safety supervisor
- it cannot trade, sell or barter donated product.

Various food and grocery manufacturers, producers, growers and retailers deliver their donations to Foodbank warehouses. This food is then sorted, collected and distributed to welfare agencies throughout Australia to help feed vulnerable people.

Foodbank also assists people in times of crisis, such as during and after the 2009 Victorian bushfires, when it donated 400 tonnes of food and groceries to victims of the disaster.

Foodbank's warehouses stock a wide variety of fresh and staple foods. The main items that are stocked include:

* fresh fruit and vegetables
* fresh milk, dairy and bread
* breakfast cereal
* pasta and pasta sauce
* canned food including baked beans, meats, fruits, vegetables and fish
* UHT milk (milk manufactured to have a packaged shelf life of up to nine months)
* rice
* noodles
* sugar
* spreads (e.g. jam and peanut butter).

Foodbank is always looking for organisations willing to donate food that may be surplus to commercial demand, slow-moving, short-dated, package-damaged or not suited for sale. Eliminating food waste is a key element of Foodbank's efforts to alleviate hunger.

There are a number of companies that regularly donate staple foods to Foodbank, including:

* Goodman Fielder Baking, which donates daily supplies of fresh bread to Foodbank in every state — averaging 2200 loaves a day for every day of the year.
* Rinoldi Pasta, which donates an average 7 tonnes of pasta every month. Masterfoods, Unilever and Simplot donate pasta sauce to complete the meals.
* Woolworths is a special donor, giving over 2.3 million kilograms of food annually, thanks to a 'reverse logistics' initiative to re-route non-saleable products from its outlets. The initiative brings non-saleable products from 825 metropolitan and country Woolworths outlets by identifying and collecting them at store level and enabling them to be delivered to distribution centres in trucks that would normally return empty. This initiative also diverts surplus food that would otherwise end up as landfill.

Arnott's, Campbell's, Coca Cola Amatil, Coles, Fonterra and Heinz are also significant donors to Foodbank each year. In return, Foodbank takes every opportunity to publicise and acknowledge donors in its promotional material and via media releases. They offer donors the following guarantees:

* a commitment to protect donated brands and product integrity
* the same standard of food safety that applies to the food industry
* best-practice warehouse, handling, stock control, storage and distribution procedures
* an assurance that donations will not be sold, exchanged or bartered
* single access to 2200 member charities who will distribute the donations
* monitoring of welfare agencies that distribute donations to ensure brand protection.

Food distribution to the needy is a major logistical effort that is undertaken by this invaluable not-for-profit organisation. However, in addition to having an ongoing need for more food donations, Foodbank require funding and volunteer time to continue doing this good work. Foodbank operates with only 70 paid employees. Over 2000 volunteers are on its books, and these people are its lifeblood. The volunteers perform a variety of tasks, including:

* sorting mixed grocery donations from supermarkets
* packing Christmas hampers
* packing drought relief or other emergency hampers
* assisting collections at central fruit and vegetable markets
* driving trucks.

Transport expenses are Foodbank's greatest cost. The company has an annual transport bill in excess of one million dollars — one-third of which is related to refrigerated products. Fuel costs for Foodbank vehicles exceed $160 000 each year. In addition, as its distribution operation grows, Foodbank has an ongoing need for enhanced information systems that are capable of handling its planned tripling of food distribution in the next few years.[23]

## Questions

1. Discuss some of the likely similarities and differences between the physical distribution needs of not-for-profit organisations (such as Foodbank) and profit-making organisations (such as their donors).
2. What major distribution issues would Foodbank be likely to encounter?
3. What are some other not-for-profit organisations that might need distribution and logistics skills? List some of the potential challenges these organisations may face, and discuss how these challenges could potentially be overcome.

## Advanced activity

Distribution decisions cannot be made in isolation from the other elements of the marketing mix. Outline how the distribution choices for the Australian wildflower industry might affect the rest of the marketing mix and also how the rest of the marketing mix might affect distribution options.

## Marketing plan activity

For your marketing plan, think about the distribution issues that will help you to efficiently move your product (good or service) through the marketing channel to be placed in the hands of your customer. What is the best distribution strategy? What are the main intermediaries? What is the best retailer for your target market? Once you have thought about these questions, write down the place (distribution) strategies you have decided will meet the needs of the target market.

A sample marketing plan has been included at the back of this book (see page 523) to give you an idea where this information fits in an overall marketing plan.

## CHAPTER 11

# Services marketing

## Learning objectives

After studying this chapter, you should be able to:

 explain the importance of the service sector to the Australian and New Zealand economies, and the difference between services products and service as the delivery of products

 describe how to develop and manage an effective marketing mix based on the unique characteristics of services

 appreciate the major challenges in the marketing of services

 understand the nature of not-for-profit marketing.

# The changing face of Australia Post

When you think of Australia Post, you probably think of a postal delivery service, perhaps accompanied by a retail arm primarily selling envelopes and stamps. However, the growth of courier services, online bill payment facilities and the widespread use of email and social networking sites have resulted in a long-term decline in Australia Post's traditional mail delivery business. In recent times, Australia Post has enhanced its service, enabling consumers to conduct a range of financial transactions within its retail shops, as well as expanding its product mix into new areas, such as insurance.

The general insurance sector is a $24 billion industry, with the average Australian household spending more than $1600 per year on insurance products. Recently, Australia Post announced that it would expand into this market — initially by offering car insurance, but with subsequent plans to offer other insurance products, such as home and contents insurance and travel insurance. The new insurance arm is a joint venture with Auto and General Insurance Services, and is in competition with large insurance companies, such as IAG, Suncorp and QBE Insurance.

Australia Post is owned by the Commonwealth Government and has a giant distribution network, with more than 4400 retail stores nationwide. This is bigger than the combined number of outlets of the four major Australian banks (Westpac, NAB, CBA and ANZ). Approximately one million people visit an Australia Post outlet each working day, conducting more than $80 billion worth of transactions annually, including paying car registrations. As Australia Post spokesperson Andrew Wiseman explains: 'People come in to do transactions with us that are triggers for thinking about insurance. It is no surprise there is a high correlation between when people register their car and when they insure their car'.

Australia Post's expansion into new product areas is not a unique initiative. Postal organisations in several countries around the world (including France, New Zealand, Britain, Japan, Singapore and Ireland) have also expanded their product mix to include an array of financial services and insurance products. In Great Britain, approximately 2 per cent of cars are insured by the country's postal service, while in New Zealand, Kiwibank is owned by New Zealand Post.

Changes in the marketing environment may have pushed part of Australia Post's business into decline. However, along other similar organisations around the world, Australia Post is adjusting its product mix in an attempt to bring about new growth.[1]

## Questions

1. From a marketing perspective, what are some potential advantages Australia Post could exploit in entering the insurance market?
2. What potential obstacles are they likely to encounter in making this foray a success?

# INTRODUCTION

In chapter 7 we learned about the concept of a product and how to manage a product through its life cycle. In our discussion of the marketing mix in chapters 7 to 10, we touched on some of the complexities of marketing products that are services. In this chapter, we will focus on concepts that apply specifically to the marketing mix for services.

The strong growth of the services sector over the past few decades in many ways has been the result of external macro-environmental forces, such as economic, social and technological changes. The needs and wants of consumers have also changed, particularly as they have become more affluent (see the discussion of higher-order needs in chapter 4). Services now account for the major share of total economic activity in developed economies. The vast majority of organisations in any modern economy are in the business of offering services as a central part of the 'product mix'. Such organisations in the for-profit sector include those offering financial (e.g. banks), personal (e.g. hairdressers) and professional (e.g. accounting) services; and in the not-for-profit sector include charities, sporting and social clubs, religious organisations and educational institutions. In addition, the public, or government, sector exists to provide social and community services and accounts for roughly one-third of the national economy.

We will begin this chapter by defining services and outlining the growing importance of the service sector in developed economies. We will then discuss the unique characteristics of services and the marketing opportunities and challenges they provide. This discussion also provides insights into the modified marketing mix for services, taking into account the people, processes and physical evidence aspects that we mentioned in chapters 1 and 7. We will then explore some of the particular challenges in services marketing, including the importance of providing high levels of customer service. The chapter concludes with a discussion of the marketing of not-for-profit services.

## SERVICE-DOMINANT ECONOMIES

Service industries generate about 70 per cent of the national incomes of Australia and New Zealand, and accordingly employ the majority of the workforces of both countries. Similar service-based economies include the United States, Japan and the United Kingdom. Emerging economies such as China and Thailand are still more grounded in manufacturing, with the services sector representing about 40 and 45 per cent of their respective national incomes.[2]

**Learning objective 1**
explain the importance of the service sector to the Australian and New Zealand economies, and the difference between services products and service as the delivery of products

As with most service-dominant economies, private sector organisations in Australia and New Zealand are the primary providers of many services including retail, property and construction, with the government sector being a major provider in the areas of defence, health, education and welfare. The most rapidly growing service industries are communications, education and health, and these areas are expected to provide many opportunities for marketers in the coming decades. Other service industries can be quite volatile, including the finance, tourism and hospitality industries — all of which are more exposed to fluctuations in the global economy, experiencing severe contractions in global economic downturns, and vice versa. However, despite this potential for volatility, these areas are fundamentally sound parts of the services sector and provide numerous opportunities for marketers.

Service industries are expected to provide many opportunities for marketers in coming decades.

**services** Activities, performances or benefits that are offered for sale, but which involve neither an exchange of tangible goods nor a transfer of title.

# 'Services' and 'service'

Before we begin a detailed exploration of the marketing of services, it is important to clearly understand the concepts of *services products* and *service as the delivery of products* (whether goods or services):

- *Services* are products, distinguished from goods by a number of unique characteristics. The most obvious distinguishing feature of services is their intangible nature. Services are not 'things'; rather, they are deeds, activities or performances. More formally, **services** are activities, performances or benefits that are offered for sale, but which involve neither an exchange of tangible goods nor a transfer of title. Much of this chapter will be dedicated to examining the uniqueness of services products and the consequences for marketing strategy.
- *Service* is the act of delivering a product (whether it is a good or services product). Service involves human, intellectual or mechanical activity that adds value to the product.

Services are usually provided through the application of intellectual or physical efforts to a person or physical object; for example, medical services are provided to people, and repairs and maintenance are provided to mechanical objects such as cars and computers. As such, *services* involve a *service* component. Marketers need to be concerned with offering a competitive range of services and ensuring those services are delivered with the highest standards of service.

In reality, most products are a combination of tangible and intangible components. For example, when you have your car maintained by a mechanic, you may pay for new spark plugs, a few litres of oil, a new timing belt and brake pads (all of which are goods) as well as the mechanic's efforts and a fee for environmental disposal of the old engine oil (both of which are services). Depending on exactly what is done to the car, either the good or the service component may make up the majority of the overall product. A purely intangible service is the exception rather than the rule.

Further, a wide variety of services, such as construction and health care, are provided using combinations of equipment and people's intellectual and physical efforts. They are considered services because the intangible inputs into the services comprise the largest proportion of the value delivered by the product. For example, when you are treated by a doctor, they may use cotton swabs, pharmaceuticals and latex gloves, but you are purchasing the service product of medical care.

# Service product classification

In chapter 7 we learned that products generally can be considered consumer products or business-to-business products. **Consumer services** are those services purchased by individual consumers or households for their own private consumption (to provide, for example, functional, sensory or psychological benefits). Common consumer services include airlines, banking, finance, hairdressing, hotel accommodation and restaurants. The drivers of demand for consumer services are similar to the drivers of demand for all consumer products, discussed in chapter 7. Many areas of the service sector are dependent on the health of the economy as a whole. During periods of economic growth, demand for services tends to increase. This provides the opportunity for organisations to sell greater quantities of services, to augment their existing services and to create new services (e.g. in the economic boom of the mid 1990s to the late 2000s, services such as personal fitness coaching and adventure travel were created). During tougher economic times, demand for many services drops away. Some services, however, are counter-cyclical; for example, during periods of higher unemployment, the demand for higher education and training services tends to increase as people seek to 'upskill' to improve their chances of gaining work.

Lifestyle changes over the years have also created demand for new services; for example, the emergence of dual income families in recent decades has increased the need and thus the demand for child care and home maintenance services. Technological change has also created opportunities for service providers, such as eBay and CommSec Securities, which have succeeded in creating new service opportunities that exploit the power, reach and economies of the internet.

The ageing of the population in Australia and New Zealand also represents a major demographic shift in each country's marketing environment. Increasing life expectancies, along with the ageing of the large Baby Boomer generation (born in the 20 years after World War II), mean the older demographic represents a substantial and growing market. In Australia, for example, the number of people over the age of 65 is projected to increase from 13 per cent in 2010 to 23 per cent by 2050.[3] Similar figures exist for New Zealand, where the number of people aged 65 and over is expected to double from 2005 levels by the 2030s.[4] As the Baby Boomers are beginning to reach retirement age, many businesses — particularly in the services sector — are realising the opportunities presented by this growing and relatively affluent market segment. For example, home services such as cleaning, maintenance, pet care and gardening are potential services that can capitalise on this demographic trend. The ageing population can also be expected to create demand for health and aged care services such as physiotherapy and nursing care. Tourism operators also actively target the retiree market, offering various specialist packages to meet the travel expectations and lifestyles of those in their retirement years. A significant number of people in this segment are cashed up and have time on their hands to travel.

consumer services Services purchased by individual consumers or households for their own private consumption.

Older Australians are actively targeted by tourism operators because they generally have both money and time to travel. This market segment, which includes the Baby Boomers, is also driving strong demand for health and aged care services such as physiotherapy and nursing care.

**business-to-business services** Those services purchased by individuals and organisations for use in the production of other products or for use in their daily business operations.

**Business-to-business services** are those services purchased by individuals and organisations for use in the production of other products or for use in their daily business operations. Business-to-business services are also often known as 'professional services'. They include the services provided by lawyers, accountants, engineers and management consultants. Again, the drivers of demand for business-to-business services are similar to the drivers of demand for all business-to-business products, discussed in chapters 5 and 7. The economic boom of the mid 1990s to late 2000s saw strong growth in the importance and variety of business-to-business services, including consulting, installation, equipment leasing and outsourcing. In the case of outsourcing, organisations shift business activities that they consider to be peripheral to their core business to specialist providers. For example, major retailers such as Woolworths may choose to outsource their warehousing logistics and delivery operations to specialist logistics companies, such as Linfox. Similarly, in recent years major banks have outsourced much of their call centre and data processing operations to specialist information technology and computer service providers, such as EDS.

For many organisations, an important question in the delivery of their core service products is whether or not to rely on their permanent full-time workforce or use specialist outside service providers as contractors. Outsourcing tends to go hand in hand with 'downsizing'. Telstra, for example, has regularly made hundreds of permanent employees redundant. It relies on part-time employees and contractors to work on special projects or to cover the workload during periods of peak demand.

For many organisations, especially those operating globally, it makes sense to employ a global workforce, particularly where communications technology creates, effectively, a 'borderless world'. Global businesses such as American Express and Citibank maintain customer service call centres in several locations around the world, to deliver '24/7' service availability. Changes in information and communications technologies have both created the demand for, and enabled the delivery of, such services.

## Spotlight  Ezypay

For many small business owners, managing and collecting regular customer payments is a time-consuming activity. Unlike large corporations, they usually don't have dedicated staff for this activity. But with cashflow being crucial for any business, it is an activity that simply cannot be ignored.

In the 1990s George Holman was running a loss-making fitness centre in Sydney's Pennant Hills. One of the major problems with the fitness centre was people choosing not to renew their annual memberships. Holman set about devising an automated billing system for his club, in the belief that people would be more likely to remain club members if they had the opportunity to pay in automatic monthly installments, rather than all at once.

The results were impressive. In the first year after Holman introduced a self-devised automated monthly billing system at the fitness centre, revenue doubled. The member retention rate increased, and new members were attracted to the club due to the flexible payment option. Holman was even able to charge a premium membership rate using this payment method.

Sensing an opportunity to market the automated billing technology he had developed to other businesses, Holman launched Ezypay, an outsourced direct debit service for businesses. His first customers were other health clubs, childcare centres and educational institutions. The business has been remarkably successful, filling an important niche for small payment collections that are not as attractive for the major banks to target and service. Importantly for small business owners, Ezypay does not charge an ongoing monthly or annual fee to businesses that implement the payment collection system. Instead, Ezypay has a fee per transaction model, meaning if the small business doesn't get paid, neither does Ezypay. The fee is readily identifiable and can be passed on by the business to their customers who choose this payment method.[5]

Ezypay founder George Holman launched a direct debit service for businesses after recognising he was losing customers at a Sydney gym because of a lack of flexibility in membership payment options.

> ## Questions
>
> 1. Using Ezypay as an appropriate example of one or the other, distinguish between the concepts of services products and service as the delivery of products.
> 2. In terms of the broad service product classifications, how would you describe the Ezypay operation?

## Concepts and applications check

**Learning objective 1** explain the importance of the service sector to the Australian and New Zealand economies, and the difference between services products and service as the delivery of products

1.1 Identify at least three factors that may affect the potential consumer and/or business demand for each of the following broad categories of service products:
- health
- education
- retail
- construction
- accommodation
- transport
- finance and insurance
- telecommunications.

1.2 In your own words, explain the distinction between *services as products* and *service as delivery of products*.

1.3 Provide three examples of consumer services and three examples of business-to-business services, other than those outlined in the preceding discussion.

# THE SERVICES MARKETING MIX

From your study of this textbook so far, you may have begun to appreciate some of the underlying characteristics of services that differentiate them from goods. In the first part of this section of the chapter, we will discuss the characteristics that formally distinguish services from goods:
- intangibility
- inseparability
- heterogeneity
- perishability.

**Learning objective 2** describe how to develop and manage an effective marketing mix based on the unique characteristics of services

Each of these characteristics has important consequences for the development of the marketing strategy for service products. They suggest that the marketing of services may be fundamentally different from, and perhaps more complex than, the marketing of tangible goods. Although the marketing mix for services necessarily includes the familiar '4 Ps' — product, pricing, distribution (place) and promotion — the unique characteristics of services suggest an additional range of variables, which need to be considered when formulating the marketing mix. These new variables have been conveniently labelled an additional '3 Ps' — people, process and physical evidence — to make up the '7 Ps' marketing framework. We will discuss the extended services marketing mix in the second half of this section.

## Unique characteristics of services

Much of our discussion in chapters 7 to 10 applies to the marketing of services, but some specific characteristics of services products — intangibility, inseparability, heterogeneity and perishability — necessitate modifications to the marketing mix.

### Intangibility

**intangibility** The characteristic of lacking physical form.

The characteristic of services which most fundamentally distinguishes them from goods is their **intangibility**. Because a pure service is an activity and not an object, it cannot be easily perceived by the five physical senses. You cannot touch financial advice or smell education. As we discussed in the first section of this chapter, however, pure services are very rare. Even with a service such as education, there are tangible elements that form an important part of the value of the product — students do place value on textbooks, printed lecture notes, and access to university computers and equipment. Similarly, pure goods are very rare — even a commodity such as salt must be stored, priced, displayed and delivered, all of which are activities with a service component.

Most products contain elements of goods *and* services and therefore products are better described as sitting on a continuum with purely tangible goods at one end and purely intangible services at the other. In the middle, we find products such as restaurant dining. When a product contains tangible and intangible elements, marketers can add value to the product component of the services marketing mix by:

- adding tangible components to their intangible service — for example, an investment advisor could provide a DVD to further explain their services
- adding intangible service components to their tangible goods — for example, a consumer electronics company could provide installation and an extended warranty.

Of course, an organisation should add only those extra attributes that increase the value of the product to the target market.

Recall from chapters 4 and 5 that as part of the purchasing decision-making process, potential customers evaluate alternatives by examining the products. While this is relatively simple with goods (e.g. a potential customer can try on a skirt for fit and check how it looks in the dressing room mirrors), intangibility makes the evaluation of services prior to purchase difficult, if not impossible. The inability of a customer to examine a service before they purchase it increases their feelings of uncertainty and perception of risk about the purchase. For marketers, intangibility makes it difficult to promote the features and benefits of service attributes. There are two strategies marketers can employ to reduce the uncertainty that potential customers feel:

- Marketers can use *tangible cues*, such as logos, staff uniforms, architecture and décor, to communicate the desired image of the intangible service. This tangible evidence will serve as both a promise and a reminder of the otherwise intangible service. For example, Hilton International went to great lengths in the design of the extensively renovated Hilton Sydney hotel to evoke an ambience of luxury and refinement. The hotel foyer is designed to convey to prospective guests that they will enjoy the finest treatment and the highest quality facilities during their stay — from the uniformed concierge to the combination of limestone floors and walls, natural light, timber and plush fabrics. Similarly, Qantas highlighted the size and comfort of the Airbus A380 when it introduced this model to its Australian fleet. Alternatively, advertising might focus on corporate logos that link the organisation and the benefits of its services; for example, the 'helping hands' of the St. Vincent de Paul Society. Because of the intangible and often complex nature of services, advertising themes should focus on simplifying the service, highlighting the benefits and linking the service to the brand.

- Reduce the level of risk perceived by customers through such techniques as service guarantees, testimonials and positive word-of-mouth. A *service guarantee* offers the potential customer the knowledge they have some course of redress should the service not live up to expectations. *Testimonials* provide potential customers with the confidence that other individuals or organisations have been happy with the service provided. In this way, service providers can emphasise their reputation, qualifications and experience. Advertising agencies, architects and consultants often quote past and existing customers as evidence of their track record. A similar, even more effective, technique is to generate positive *word-of-mouth*, but it remains largely untapped by commercial organisations. Negative word-of-mouth of course can prove swift and destructive, especially when service performance fails to meet customers' expectations. In this sense, word-of-mouth, particularly in internet chat rooms and blogs, can create or destroy corporate reputations more quickly than commercial advertising. When subject to negative word-of-mouth, the best response is likely to be to use public relations to spread more favourable discussion of the brand or service among the population at large.

More generally, the intangible nature of services makes it necessary for service providers to educate their customers as a means of managing — and meeting — their expectations.

Potential customers often look to price as an indicator of the likely quality of the service. In this way, professional service providers such as doctors, lawyers, accountants and management consultants are often able to charge high prices, especially when they have a strongly established brand name and reputation. In these cases, the combination of price and brand name can promote customer confidence in the service provider and the likely outcome of the service.

Intangibility also creates challenges in developing new services, particularly in testing new service concepts through market research. Because consumers find it difficult to imagine new intangible services, it is often necessary to explain new services as a series of brief concepts and value propositions. Even after such explanations, consumers may still not understand or may not believe the value propositions. Because it is difficult to illustrate new services in a model or visual representation, marketers need to spend more time in carefully researching new service concepts.

Marketers can use *tangible cues*, such as logos, staff uniforms, architecture and décor, to communicate the desired image of an intangible service. The Hilton Sydney hotel evokes an ambience of luxury and refinement, and it is no coincidence: the parent company of the hotel has ensured that various tangible cues convey this impression to consumers.

## Inseparability

For most services, it is impossible to separate the production of the service and the consumption of the service. This characteristic is known as **inseparability** or simultaneity. If you think about the services a dentist provides, it quickly becomes

**inseparability** The characteristic of being produced and consumed simultaneously.

evident that the dental service is created at the same time it is consumed and it is created and consumed in the same location. This means that, usually, the service provider and the consumer have close interpersonal interaction. In fact, often the consumer plays a role in the production of the service. This holds true for almost all services. Contrast this with goods, which are produced, stored, transported and consumed sometimes months or even years later (e.g. in the instance of vintage wine). In this case, the producer may never see the consumer, who could live in another part of the world.

The inseparability of services presents a significant challenge in the marketing and delivery of services. Because buyers and sellers of services are frequently 'co-producers' of the service, it can be very difficult to control quality and, hence, customer satisfaction. For example, a dentist with a patient who has a severe fear of dental procedures will find it very difficult to deliver a satisfactory service experience, regardless of his or her skill and chair-side manner. Under such circumstances, managing the quality and delivery of the service and building a happy relationship between the customer and service provider may prove near impossible. At the same time, it is essential that service providers develop their interpersonal skills. This is especially so in the case of medical practitioners, for whom 'bedside manner' has always been regarded as a crucial technique and skill. Their customers (or patients) may find it difficult to evaluate the technical quality of the service provided even after the medical procedure has been successfully concluded. Even for more understandable services such as a haircut, service providers need to be concerned with both their *technical skills* and their *customer service delivery*. Further, the service provider should actively manage their customers' expectations and remind them of their own role in producing the service; for example, a gym should remind its customers 'no pain, no gain'.

In addition to ensuring a high level of customer service delivery, service providers often need to promote their products through *personal selling* (see chapter 9). To a much greater degree than for goods, customers are often unaware of the nature of the service, its benefits and its relevance to their needs. For example, life insurance is a service which, arguably, provides greatest potential benefits to those whose immediate needs make life insurance a low priority — in particular, those entering the workforce. These potential customers, who will benefit most from life insurance in the long term by locking in low premiums when they are young, will often require the most persuasion. This is why all life insurance companies engage a large number of agents who spend the majority of their time in the homes or workplaces of potential customers.

Modern information and communications technologies have somewhat altered the traditional inseparability characteristic of services products. Technology is allowing new distribution and service delivery models for some services. It is still most common for customers to attend service providers' retail outlets to consume the service; for example, to attend a hairdressing salon for a hair cut or a doctor's surgery for a medical check-up. It is also common for service providers to attend the consumer's home or business to provide the service; for example, to provide garden maintenance, plumbing, electrical, air-conditioning and heating repairs and service. Increasingly, however, routine services — especially 'administrative' services that do not require physical contact between customer and service provider — are delivered via telephone, mail or internet. These services include banking transactions, travel bookings and insurance. The ability to transact such business remotely provides increased convenience to the consumer and lower distribution and processing costs to the service provider. While delivering services face-to-face will generally promote trust and confidence, it is important for marketers to consider and explore alternative distribution channels that may provide greater convenience to the customer and/or lower costs to the service provider. When potential customers or clients believe there are few differences among the leading service providers, a low price, based on low-cost delivery, is likely to be necessary to secure market share. This is true of household and car insurance.

It is common for service providers to attend a consumer's home or business — as in the case of a plumber inspecting a tap in a family home — and for consumers to attend a service provider's outlet — as in the case of a patient attending an appointment at a doctor's clinic.

The internet offers the potential to revolutionise traditional distribution channels for services. For example, a university education can be delivered over the internet (although the experience of academic staff and students will not be the same), so it is not necessary for the producer and consumer to be in the same location or to produce and consume at the same time. Generally, though, many services, including dental, medical and other professional services, are likely for the most part to retain the traditional direct channels of distribution. Under such conditions, the need for a close personal relationship between service provider and customer (or client) will usually mean that the industry will be dominated by a large number of small independent professional service providers.

When setting prices based on costs, the largest component is often that of time. Pricing for professional services such as medical, dentistry, accounting, physiotherapy and architectural services will primarily reflect the hours spent by professionals in consulting with the customer, and in resolving the problem. For some services, however, particularly those which are delivered using expensive technology, time and direct labour are less important components of costs. In such cases, the high fixed costs of the technology results in very low transaction costs, and profitability is often dependent upon recovering fixed costs over a very large volume of transactions. Examples include telecommunications and internet-based services. In such cases, flexible pricing, with low joining fees, but which encourages high-volume or frequency of transactions and/or a contractual membership period are common. Service marketers, therefore, need to understand their cost structure, and the balance of fixed and variable costs, upon which their pricing strategy will crucially depend.

## Heterogeneity

**heterogeneity** Inevitable, but minimisable, variations in quality in the delivery of a service product.

Services are provided by humans who, unlike machines, are subject to variations in mood, skill and willingness to provide service of an agreed quality. This makes it unrealistic to promise perfect service every time. The inevitable variations in the service provided give services the characteristic of **heterogeneity**. For service marketers, the challenge is to provide a product with a reasonably consistent level of quality that matches customers' expectations. The key strategies for the marketer are:

- *to develop service delivery systems*. McDonald's and many other fast food outlets provide some of the most obvious examples of how systems can standardise service delivery. Despite having millions of customer service staff around the world, each with their own individual characteristics, a restaurant such as McDonald's has achieved a high level of consistency in the delivery of its meals in thousands of stores by developing and implementing extensive, detailed procedures that cover every aspect of service delivery. Technology and machinery can also reduce heterogeneity; for example, unlike a bank teller, ATMs provide the same service to every user, every time. Similarly, the use of electronic scanners at supermarket checkouts has improved the speed and accuracy of supermarket service.

McDonald's has sophisticated service delivery systems in place to ensure that consumers receive their food orders quickly and reliably. The delivery systems that are in place also help to streamline costs, ensuring that consumers can buy their burgers, fries and drinks at a competitive price.

- *to manage the expectations of customers*. Service providers must work to ensure the service they deliver matches the service they promote. In other words, they must be careful to not 'over promise and under deliver'. Virgin Australia, for example, regularly publishes its 'on-time performance' each month. Cumulatively these figures show that the airline achieves on-time departures and arrivals for approximately 84 per cent of its flights over a calendar year.[6] This approach suggests to customers that they can usually expect their flights to run on time, although there will sometimes be inevitable delays.
- *to invest heavily in staff training*. Staff need to be trained to effectively implement the service delivery systems and to manage the expectations of customers. The first aspect involves developing competence and technical skills. The second involves developing interpersonal communication and personal selling skills.

For service marketers, measuring and managing service quality should be a continuous process, using such techniques as 'mystery shoppers' or customer service surveys.

Combined with the inseparability characteristic, these strategies to manage heterogeneity result in distribution channels that are usually short and direct, with little or no scope for the use of intermediaries. In those service industries where intermediaries are common (e.g. in travel, insurance and mortgage broking) it is usually possible because, as agents, they are selling standardised services in the form of 'packages' on behalf of original service providers who have strong brand names and reputations. The keys to the success of distribution using intermediaries are standardisation of the service and a market that has confidence in the agent and the original service provider.

The heterogeneous nature of services, in addition to presenting marketers with some challenges, creates an opportunity for service providers to add value to the product they offer customers. The service provider can, within reason, tailor the service provided to the individual needs of each customer. For example, gym operators can customise their service to the individual needs of each member by assessing their current health and fitness, enquiring about their fitness goals and recommending an appropriate exercise regimen, including classes and individual instruction. Of course, this customisation comes at a cost to the operator, which must be reflected in the pricing of the service — by building it into the overall prices charged or by adjusting the price to reflect the components of the customised service provided to the individual. Some service providers offer a number of standardised packages, thus providing a midpoint between standardisation and customisation of the service.

As with all pricing, a key consideration is the perceived uniqueness of the product, whether for goods or services. Service providers should therefore seek to differentiate their products as far as possible through such means as respected brand names and through their reputation and customer service. Singapore Airlines, for example, has secured for itself a pre-eminent position among international airlines based upon its strong brand and its reputation for technical excellence and high levels of customer service.

## Perishability

The inseparability of the production and consumption of services leads to a further distinctive characteristic, known as perishability. **Perishability** refers to the inability to store services for use at a later date — they are 'time bound'. For example, the vacant rooms in a motel during the low season cannot be stored and sold to guests in the high season. Similarly, unsold concert tickets and empty seats on an aeroplane are permanently lost. These situations arise when supply exceeds demand. Conversely, if hundreds of people would still like to buy tickets to a sold-out concert, the demand exceeds supply and the potential profit from the people who cannot obtain a ticket is foregone. This is an example of a situation in which it becomes necessary to discourage sales or consumption of services in order to avoid unacceptable levels of crowding, poor service and customer dissatisfaction; for example, at the annual Big Day Out music festival. In such circumstances, service providers need to strictly adhere to their capacity and safety limits, commonly accompanied by pricing and promotional adjustments.

**perishability** The inability to store services for use at a later date.

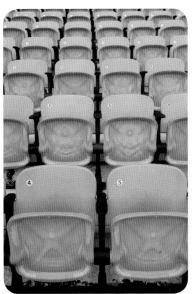  

The vacant rooms in a motel during the low season cannot be stored and sold to guests in the high season. Similarly, unsold concert tickets and empty seats on an aeroplane are permanently lost. These situations arise when supply exceeds demand.

The challenge that perishability presents to marketers is to balance supply and demand in such a way as to maximise profitability. Marketers have a number of strategies at their disposal:

- *stimulate demand*. It is appropriate to stimulate demand when the organisation has excess capacity to deliver services. For example, cinemas tend to experience huge variations in demand for their services. Most people go to the movies at night. This often leaves cinemas playing movies to just a handful of people during the day. To stimulate demand, cinemas often offer cheaper tickets on Tuesday (traditionally the slowest day of the week) and Greater Union cinemas have even introduced a 'Babes in Arms' program that encourages stay-at-home parents to take their young children to screenings on Wednesday mornings, when young children are admitted for free. This both stimulates demand at an otherwise unpopular viewing time and provides extra value to the cinema experience for parents of young children. The program is suspended during school holidays, when cinemas experience a natural increase in demand from school-aged children.[7] Businesses in the accommodation, travel and entertainment sectors have taken advantage of the internet to promote price discounts during slow periods. For example, lastminute.com and Halftix.com offer discount prices for accommodation and entertainment. A danger for marketers is that customers will become accustomed to purchasing services at reduced prices and therefore resist ever paying normal prices.

- *restrict demand*. It seems counterintuitive that an organisation would seek to restrict demand for its services, but it must be remembered that the objective of the services marketer is to smooth demand to level out peaks and troughs in demand. The objective is not so much to reduce demand as to manage when it occurs. For example, popular restaurants use a reservation system that is designed to maximise the number of diners served. Perhaps the most popular time to dine is 7.30 pm, but many people will be prepared to accept a booking for 6.30 pm or 8.30 pm. In this way, the restaurant can accommodate the most possible diners instead of having to turn people away due to a lack of tables. Government traffic and public transport authorities undertake promotional activities to encourage people to travel in off-peak periods to minimise congestion on roads and to make the most efficient use of public transport services. Public transport operators often implement a pricing strategy with different fares for different parts of the day (as do taxi services and airlines). Cheaper fares during off-peak travel times encourage people who are not travelling to work to avoid the busy commuter periods in the morning and afternoon.

- *increase or decrease supply capacity*. Services organisations that experience fluctuations in demand can increase or decrease supply capacity. This is a particularly suitable approach if the periods of high and low demand are reasonably predictable. For example, the hospitality and entertainment industries use casual workforces that can be adjusted with hourly, daily and seasonal changes in demand. The Wet'n'Wild Water World amusement park on the Gold Coast alters its operating times throughout the year to suit demand.

These issues all affect the pricing of services, which is frequently based on the likely level and variation in customer demand. In circumstances where demand would otherwise fluctuate over time, flexible pricing can be employed to ensure that demand and supply are balanced as far as possible. For example, electricity and airline ticket pricing can vary according to the time of day. Cinema pricing varies according to days in the week and hotel accommodation prices are varied according to weeks, months and seasons. The key to the success of such a pricing approach is to ensure that all available capacity is sold at the highest prices that buyers are prepared to pay. In the case of the theatre, hotel and airlines, no revenue is obtained from empty seats and flexible pricing is therefore common. For airlines, the key to the success of this pricing is the instant availability of data on seat vacancies. To meet this need, 'yield management' computer software is essential to ensure accurate and timely changes in pricing to meet hourly fluctuations in customer demand.

# The extended services marketing mix

The intangibility, inseparability, heterogeneity and perishability of services create the following issues for marketers:
- inability for customers to inspect and evaluate a product prior to consumption
- inevitable variability in service quality
- inability to store product.

As we read earlier, marketers can pursue various strategies to deal with these issues:
- create tangible cues
- invest heavily in staff training
- develop and implement standardised service delivery systems
- use customer testimonials
- manage customer expectations
- manage supply and demand.

These strategies clearly involve managing the product, pricing, promotion and distribution of services. It should also be clear from our discussion that there are other elements that need to be carefully managed when marketing services. These elements are *people*, *process* and *physical evidence*, and they are focused upon 'the delivery of the promise'; that is, the service delivery and customer's experience. Combined with the traditional 4 Ps of the marketing mix, they make up the '7 Ps' marketing framework, also known as the extended services marketing mix. We will discuss each of these additional elements in turn.

### People

Our discussion of the inseparability characteristic of services noted that the production and consumption of most services occur at the same time and in the same place. This means, of course, that the customer or client will usually have close contact with the person or *people* creating and delivering the service. Although customers and clients are usually focused on the service outcome, rather than the person (or process) providing the service, it is crucial the marketing organisation understands and manages the role of people in defining the quality of each customer's or client's service experience. The 'people' in the extended services marketing mix are those coming into contact with customers who can affect value for customers: the organisation's staff (particularly the actual service provider and/or its 'front-line' customer service staff; the customer or client being served; and other customers or clients either directly or indirectly involved in the service experience.

The most controllable factor in service delivery is the organisation's staff. It is essential that the organisation chooses staff who are:
- technically competent
- able to deliver high standards of customer service
- able to promote products through personal selling.

To ensure high standards of service delivery, service organisations need to carefully consider the selection, training, outfitting, motivating and rewarding of their staff so that they deliver services effectively, efficiently and to the standard expected by customers and the organisation. In service organisations, a key issue for the delivery of high standards of customer service is the concept of 'empowerment', which enables staff to respond to the particular needs of individual customers. Companies which are renowned for their customer service excellence will typically provide high levels of empowerment and discretion to front-line customer service staff. A further requirement for customer service excellence is the development of a 'customer service culture' (of which 'empowerment' is a common feature), but which also stresses the importance of customer service in the functional management and organisation of the business. Experience across a wide range of industries suggests that the use of 'self-directed work teams' with a dual focus on operational performance and customer service is an increasingly common practice.

Beyond the organisation's staff, the customer or client is, of course, an important factor in service delivery. Not only does the customer or client often play a role as co-producer of the service, but the service provider also needs to manage the customer's expectations and their interaction with the organisation during the service transaction and in their future relationship with the organisation. While the customer or client is not controllable in the manner that staff members are, the service provider must train staff to ensure they can deal with customers effectively through the skills of technical competence, customer service and personal selling. In doing so, customer service staff need to be able to display empathy, flexibility and integrity in meeting customers' particular needs.

Beyond the staff and the customer, other customers within physical proximity of the service delivery can influence the outcome of the service and customer satisfaction. Service organisations need to manage the behaviour of surrounding customers to ensure that they do not intrude on the customer's personal space or on the service process. In this context, crowding and the behaviour of unruly or dissatisfied customers can significantly impact on customer satisfaction. For example, at major sporting events, when spectators are sometimes forced to sit in crowded and cramped conditions for extended periods of time, it is essential that security staff ensure that the behaviour of tired, unruly or intoxicated fans does not impinge on the amenity and experience of others watching the match. Similarly, nightclubs usually employ bouncers to control the behaviour of patrons.

Nightclubs employ bouncers to control the behaviour of patrons and to ensure that patrons meet minimum entry requirements, such as having suitable identification. The presence of bouncers, and the role that they perform, helps to ensure that other customers can enjoy the experience that is on offer at clubs.

**process** The systems used to create, communicate, deliver and exchange an offering.

## Process

In the services context, **process** refers to all of the systems and procedures used to create, communicate, deliver and exchange an offering. An organisation's processes define the manner in which the service is coordinated and delivered. The key concern is that the process delivers the service in a way that at least matches the customer's expectations. Ideally, the performance should exceed the customer's expectation, although this becomes increasingly difficult over the long term of the relationship. It is therefore essential that an organisation understands customers' expectations and, from that understanding, designs and delivers operational systems and procedures that enable staff to match those expectations consistently.

As a generalisation, customers usually have two kinds of expectations:

- *functional expectations*—expectations of the technical delivery of the service transaction
- *customer service expectations*—expectations that relate to the service experience and the social interaction between the customer and service provider.

In this sense, it is generally advisable to be 'efficient first and friendly second'. Service providers should therefore rightly focus their attention primarily on the delivery of effective and efficient service. When this level of technical performance is assured, they should focus additional energies on the customer service experience. Factors that help deliver this level of service include service delivery systems, the management of customer expectations, and staff training. It is important that organisations constantly assess customer service performance and a range of metrics are available to do so. For example, Australia Post constantly measures delivery time and accuracy as key performance measures.

## Physical evidence

The intangibility of services makes it difficult for customers to evaluate the quality and suitability of services, especially when using the service for the first time. As discussed earlier, one strategy marketers can use to manage the uncertainty that intangibility creates is to offer tangible cues as to the quality of the service. Customers look to these cues and other **physical evidence** as a way of evaluating the service prior to purchase.

**physical evidence** Tangible cues that can be used as a means to evaluate service quality prior to purchase.

Service marketers should therefore pay close attention to the physical environment in which the service is delivered and to all the other accompanying physical cues. The physical environment should be designed to inspire confidence in the technical delivery and effectiveness of the service and in the likely service experience. The physical environment includes architectural design, floor layout, furniture, décor, shop or office fittings, colours, background music and even smell. All potentially affect the customer's or client's experience, and need to be carefully 'choreographed'. Similarly, staff uniforms, brochures, service or delivery vehicles and stationery are all potentially influential in the customer's experience.

## 24/7 workout

### Spotlight

Gyms are notoriously fickle businesses, particularly smaller ones. Recently, however, there has been a new franchise entrant to the Australian and New Zealand markets, Jetts Fitness. It has an innovative 'no frills' service offering that has quickly proven popular. Jetts Fitness is open 24 hours, seven days a week, but is only staffed for approximately seven hours per day on weekdays and Saturdays, and not at all on Sundays and public holidays. Members use a swipe card to gain access outside of the hours when the Jetts Fitness centres are actually staffed. The company describes its core target market as being '25 to 45 year-old, time-poor, value-conscious customers'.

Although it has modern gym equipment, it has no additional facilities such as saunas and pools. In the Jetts Fitness franchisors' initial research into their venture, such facilities were revealed as being costly and high maintenance add-ons that were rarely used by members at traditional gyms. In addition, centres are usually located in residential areas of suburbs, meaning they are close to members' homes. Accordingly, there is a reduced need for large and costly change and showering facilities. No group classes are offered at Jetts Fitness clubs. Instead, members train individually at a time that suits them.

All of these factors help Jetts Fitness centres to offer lower prices than traditional gyms. Shift workers and students have helped to drive the growth of the franchise. The company, which was founded in Queensland, now has outlets in all Australian states and is expanding into New Zealand.

Critics in the fitness industry have raised concerns about Jetts Fitness centres being staffed for limited hours, but there is currently no legislation regulating mandatory staffing for gyms in Australia. The managing director of Jetts Fitness has defended the franchise against this criticism — pointing out that all Jetts Fitness centres have emergency systems in place to respond to any injuries, as well as 24-hour video surveillance and wall-mounted distress alarms that are available for members to access.[8]

## Questions

1. Discuss the extended service marketing mix as it applies to the Jetts Fitness franchise.

2. Imagine you are the marketing manager for a rival 'traditional' gym chain, such as Fitness First. How would you respond to the competitive threat posed by a Jetts Fitness franchise opening near a Fitness First gym?

## Concepts and applications check

**Learning objective 2** describe how to develop and manage an effective marketing mix based on the unique characteristics of services

2.1 Explain the major differences between goods and services in your own words.

2.2 Goods and services can be thought of as being on a scale, with a purely intangible service (with no accompanying physical good) being at one end and a purely tangible good (with no accompanying service) at the other. Categorise the following goods and/or services in the likely order they could appear on such a scale:
- restaurants
- soap
- insurance
- cars
- hospitals
- salt
- public transport
- computer software
- holiday resorts
- mobile phones

2.3 Using service examples of your own choosing, outline several ways that marketers can offset potential consumer uncertainty and risk.

2.4 What are some techniques that services marketers can attempt to balance supply and demand?

2.5 What measures can marketers take to ensure service quality?

2.6 In your own words, explain the 'people', 'process' and 'physical evidence' aspects of services marketing.

# SERVICES MARKETING CHALLENGES

The four key differences between goods and services (intangibility, inseparability, heterogeneity and perishability) pose particular challenges in the marketing of services. While there are numerous challenges in the successful marketing of services, there are three key issues which, arguably, make the marketing of intangible services more challenging than the marketing of tangible goods. These are:

**Learning objective 3**
appreciate the major challenges in the marketing of services

1. achieving a sustainable differential advantage in marketing services
2. managing profitable customer relationships
3. delivering consistently high levels of customer service.

## Managing differentiation

Because services are produced by people and not machines, and because it is difficult to protect service innovation from immediate copying by competitors, it is difficult to achieve lasting product differentiation in service industries. Services do not enjoy the protection of legal patents and can be more readily mimicked by competitors. For example, the core products provided by the major banks (cheque and savings accounts, mortgage and personal loans, credit cards and foreign exchange) are generally 'standardised' products with closely comparable — if not identical — benefits, conditions and prices. In such an environment, any service innovations are almost immediately replicated by competitors. Furthermore, in such market conditions, customers also expect their bank to offer closely comparable products to those of the competition, and customers are therefore often reluctant to switch banks, even in the face of short-term product innovation and intense marketing promotion.

Recall that a product can be viewed as a collection, bundle or package of attributes comprising a 'core' service, expected service, augmented service and potential service. The core service is the want or need the product satisfies. The expected service is those attributes that deliver the benefit. For example, in a hotel, the core service is accommodation, provided by the expected service of a room and a bed. In addition to the core and expected service, a range of supplementary services are often included, which add value from the customer's perspective and which may serve to differentiate the service offering from that of competitors' offerings. In the case of a hotel, in addition to the room, a range of augmented services such as use of the swimming pool and gymnasium, complimentary laundry, safekeeping and breakfast are frequently included in the room tariff. It is also important to note that the core and expected service is usually a 'given', from the customer's perspective, and the focus in marketing the service product will therefore usually be on the augmented services. Marketers should therefore explore opportunities to enhance or add value to their core services (or goods) through the provision of supplementary or supporting services, such as guarantees, technical advice, 'help lines', or membership services or privileges (such as Qantas' Frequent Flyers club).

At the same time, there may also be new market opportunities in offering reduced ('no frills') service packages. For example, Jetstar competes with Qantas and Virgin Australia by offering low-price, basic airline services, with the customer paying additional money when they require supplementary services such as meals, in-flight entertainment and additional baggage. Similarly, discount share

Marketers often enhance or add value to core services or goods through the provision of supplementary or support services. Qantas' Frequent Flyers club is an example of this strategy, being a club that has been set up to add value to the company's offering of domestic and international flights.

trading has enjoyed rapid growth in recent years, partly fuelled by the low-cost service and delivery model made possible by the internet.

For service organisations, the sources of sustainable differentiation are relatively few. If products cannot be protected from imitation, then 'service culture' offers an opportunity to create a unique market positioning. This is an approach favoured by luxury hotel chains, such as Ritz Carlton, some airlines such as Emirates, exclusive restaurants and other 'boutique' service providers. Another potential source of differentiation is in distribution coverage or quality. For example, the major retail banks have created a strong market positioning by virtue of the number of their retail outlets. This investment is difficult to match in the short term. Similarly, the quality of distribution provided by retail outlets may prove difficult for competitors to match. For example, Lexus established its position in the luxury car market based, in part, on the quality of its dealer service, the enhanced warranty provision enjoyed by customers, and augmented services such as free parking at the Sydney Opera House. For all service providers, however, the objective of achieving meaningful differentiation in the face of competitive imitation remains a challenge.

## Developing profitable customer relationships

For many service organisations, long-term survival depends upon the ability to create and maintain profitable relationships with target customers or customer segments. *Professional service* providers, such as accountants, lawyers, architects and investment advisers, manage their customers closely as individuals and provide each with a service tailored to their unique circumstances and needs. Professional service providers in this context can be contrasted with *consumer service* providers who typically provide a standardised service offering, such as that provided by the retail banks. For most service providers, it is not enough to attract new clients or customers (even in their thousands), as new customers are generally not profitable in the early stages of their relationships with the service provider. This is because the costs of 'customer acquisition' are high, as are the fixed costs of establishing the relationship, and these costs cannot be recovered in the immediate future.

For many service providers, the problems of high customer turnover (or 'churn') together with low average transaction volumes and values, mean that many customers may never be profitable. In such circumstances, the challenge for services marketers is to develop close relationships with profitable customers. To achieve this implies that the service provider can accurately measure the profitability of individual customer relationships and that the service provider can tailor an offer to meet the requirements of these potentially profitable customers. It also implies that the customer sees value in developing a closer relationship with a service provider.

Developing closer relationships (particularly in the case of large organisations dealing with large numbers of customers) typically requires extensive customer information files, often managed by customer relationship management (CRM) software. Such systems are costly to establish and are not guaranteed to succeed. They are most likely to be effective if accompanied by comprehensive management systems that support the creation and maintenance of customer relationships. The key to successful customer relationship management lies in building the trust and satisfaction of customers such that customers reward the service provider with their long-term loyalty, even in the face of competitors' efforts to persuade the customers to switch providers.

## Delivering consistent customer service quality

The intangible nature of services makes it difficult for customers to evaluate some of the services they receive. More generally, products can be classified according to the different qualities which customers use in evaluating them. Some products can be objectively evaluated prior to purchase via what are known as *search qualities*, which include colour, size and smell. Many services, however, lack search qualities and instead customers rely on other qualities. The quality of most services are most likely to be evaluated during and after service delivery. These are known as *experience qualities* and include a theatre performance or restaurant service. In some circumstances, consumers cannot even assess the quality of the service after they have consumed it. For example, surgery provided under general anaesthetic may leave the medical patient sore and sorry when the effects of the anaesthetic wear off, but the outcome of the procedure will probably be only immediately known by the medical staff. Depending on the type of procedure, the patient may never really know the quality of the service provided. Car servicing is another example, in which the customer usually knows little about the service provided and is limited in their ability to assess the quality of the service. Such services must be evaluated based on *credence qualities*, which are based on an evaluation of the service provider's trustworthiness, integrity and professionalism. Figure 11.1 illustrates the use of search, experience and credence qualities in the evaluation of products.

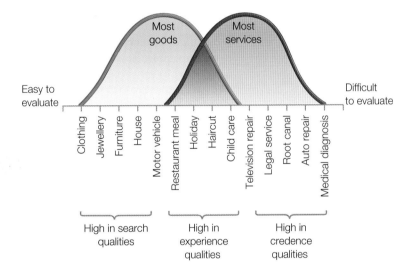

**FIGURE 11.1**

Product evaluation using search, experience and credence qualities

Because services are delivered by humans, rather than machines, it is very difficult to provide perfect service delivery every time. Even 'six-star' hotel chains such as Shangri-La Hotels and Resorts will find it almost impossible to perfectly satisfy every customer, every time. For marketers, the challenge is to match the 'promise' with the 'performance', so that customers are satisfied consistently. Of course, many service marketers will argue that 'mere satisfaction' of customers is not enough. Rather, they argue that superior service providers aim to 'delight' their customers by providing a level of service which exceeds the customer's expectations. This idea is simple in theory, but extremely difficult to execute in practice. The consistent delivery of such a promise requires the highest levels of training, motivation, performance and rewards. This is both difficult and costly to achieve.

For organisations such as banks, government agencies and airlines who serve millions of customers in the broad population every day, it may simply not be practicable to aim to 'delight' customers consistently. Of course, this is no justification for low levels of customer service as customers will quickly switch service providers if they believe they are receiving consistently substandard levels of service. The challenge for service organisations is to set high standards of customer service that can be consistently achieved, and for these customer service standards to form part of the core promise made to customers in the organisation's marketing communications. Delivering such high standards of service is the responsibility of the entire organisation and requires total commitment from senior management, extending all the way to front-line customer service staff.

In delivering high levels of customer service, organisations need to consider four key issues:

1. understand customers' expectations
2. establish service quality standards
3. manage customers' service expectations
4. measure employee performance.

### Understand customers' expectations

In order to deliver high levels of customer service, the organisation must first develop an objective understanding of customers' expectations. This involves identifying the specific *service attributes* that customers use to evaluate and distinguish between service providers. For example, when evaluating a hotel, customers will form opinions about décor, room sizes, cleanliness, friendliness of staff, accuracy of billing, speed of room service and price, to name only a few attributes. While the range of service attributes is potentially limitless, five common dimensions have been identified which customers use to evaluate service quality across a wide range of industries. These dimensions are outlined in table 11.1.[9]

**TABLE 11.1** A checklist of service quality

| Dimension | Explanation | Evaluation criteria |
| --- | --- | --- |
| Reliability | Consistency and dependability | • Began on time<br>• Finished on time<br>• Billed correctly |
| Tangibles | Physical evidence | • Condition of premises<br>• Presentation of service provider<br>• Condition of equipment |
| Responsiveness | Willing and able to provide the service | • Enquiries responded to<br>• Service provided promptly<br>• Accommodated urgent needs |
| Assurance | Trust and confidence in the service provider | • Demonstrated knowledge and skills<br>• Reputation<br>• Personal manner of service provider |
| Empathy | Care and attentiveness | • Listened to needs<br>• Cared about customers' interests<br>• Provided personalised service |

In general, reliability is the most important criterion; that is, the service provider does consistently what it promises. Beyond identifying the service attributes, it is necessary for the marketing organisation to understand the customers' service performance *expectations*; that is, the quality level at which they expect the service to be performed. Customers will have much higher expectations of a five-star hotel than of a three-star hotel, even though they may be evaluating the same service attributes. Understanding service expectations is crucial and customers typically have a range of service expectations ranging from 'ideal' to 'the bare minimum'. It is crucial that the organisation's service at least falls within the 'zone of tolerance', which describes the range of service quality between the minimum 'acceptable' level and the actual 'desired' level. Within this range, customers will generally be satisfied with the customer service. Above the zone of tolerance, customers are said to be 'delighted' and will become 'advocates' for the company. Conversely, below the zone of tolerance, they will be dissatisfied and will be likely to defect and to spread bad word-of-mouth.

To understand both the range of relevant service attributes and the level of customers' expectations, as well as the actual level of customer service performance, organisations will need to conduct thorough market research typically involving qualitative research, such as focus groups, to establish the customer service performance criteria, and regular sample surveys of customers to determine actual levels of customer service delivery. Service organisations such as banks and airlines, and fast food and retail chains should conduct such surveys more or less continuously.

### Establish service quality standards

Once an organisation has determined its customers' service expectations, it can translate them into service standards, which can in turn be built into staff training and evaluation processes. In banking, for instance, customers overwhelmingly expect accuracy and therefore it is necessary for bank management to establish objective standards (e.g. error rates) against which service can be evaluated. In a changing, competitive marketplace, it is likely that customer service expectations will change and it is therefore necessary for management to monitor these changes and to adjust performance specifications to correspond with customers' expectations. Beyond establishing such specifications, it is essential that the organisation demonstrates commitment to the standards. In particular, line managers need to ensure that they have confidence in the staff and the performance standards so that individual customer service staff can appreciate the link between the organisation's service expectations and their own performance and rewards.

### Manage customers' service expectations

Because services are typically intangible and frequently variable in quality, it is important that service marketers actively manage customers' expectations, so that customer service delivery will consistently fall within customers' zone of tolerance. In this context, advertising and other promotional vehicles (e.g. websites and in-store promotions) can play an important role. The temptation for management to over-promise, however, should be resisted. At the same time, customers need to be attracted to visit a service provider, especially for the first time. In this context, there may be an opportunity for a 'special introductory offer', rather than relying upon unsustainable promises. After the first service experience, customers will place less reliance upon advertising and promotion and will overwhelmingly base their service expectations on their experience. Again, it is important to ensure that their experience matches the promise.

Customer service expectations are also shaped by word-of-mouth as customers tend to tell many of their friends when they receive exceptional service, especially exceptionally poor service. In instances of poor service, management needs to give close attention to 'service recovery', ideally ensuring that, as far as reasonably possible, no customer leaves a service provider's premises dissatisfied and in a mood to tell their friends. (Of course, there are some customers who are *not* always right; for example, the abusive, deceitful or intoxicated.)

The adage 'The customer is always right' is reinforced to staff because of the damage that can be caused by unhappy customers. Customer service expectations can be shaped by different factors. If expectations are not met, dissatisfied customers will often not hesitate to share details about their negative experience with others.

## Measure employee performance

Having established service quality specifications and demonstrated management's commitment to such expectations, it is necessary for management to ensure the customer service staff members are able to meet these expectations consistently. In this context, training, equipping, motivating and rewarding staff should recognise the importance of customer service as part of the employees' overall job performance. Difficulties will frequently arise when job efficiency expectations clash with the need to provide high levels of customer service, such as in periods of peak demand. In such circumstances, customers will usually — and quite rationally — expect 'efficiency first and friendliness second', although it is important to note that they *will* expect both. Organisations which are renowned for their customer service recognise the frequent need to juggle these competing expectations and carefully manage their staff training and operations to ensure that customer service is always a high priority. Finally, staff members need to be rewarded for delivering high levels of customer service in addition to their high standards of technical competence. The challenge for organisations in such circumstances is to be able to objectively measure and reward the customer service performance of individual staff members.

## Spotlight Jumping the queue

The time spent queuing up for various thrill rides and attractions can make up a frustratingly significant part of a visit to a theme park. Waiting times in queues of up to half an hour or more for a three-minute thrill ride or a 30-minute show are not uncommon, particularly during peak periods such as weekends and school holidays.

In an attempt to overcome this issue, Dreamworld recently introduced an option for its patrons to purchase a virtual queuing device, called the 'Q4U'. This is a palm-sized gadget that lets up to six people register their place in a thrill ride queue, and then be free to explore restaurants and other attractions of the theme park rather than having to wait in line for their turn. The device is programmed to vibrate approximately five minutes before users are scheduled to reach the front of the queue, allowing them to return just in time for their ride. Q4U users rejoin the queue via a clearly marked lane to avoid any potential for other customers becoming agitated that they are 'queue jumping'. A Q4U device can only be registered in the queue of one thrill ride at a time.

Dreamworld customers wishing to use the Q4U service pay a rental fee of $10, and $7.50 for each person (up to a maximum of six) registered to the device. Critics argue that this expense is just an additional burden for customers in what is already an expensive outing, but Dreamworld spokesperson Shelley Winkel counters that the cost is justified, as it allows customers to 'get more value into their day' by avoiding time spent waiting in queues. Dreamworld also offers visitors the option of entering their venue an hour before the official opening time for an additional $10 fee, in a further attempt to alleviate queuing concerns.[10]

### Question

Explain how the **Q4U** device can differentiate Dreamworld's service offering from those of its competitors, via enhancing service quality expectations and experience.

# Concepts and applications check

**Learning objective 3** appreciate the major challenges in the marketing of services

**3.1** Using your own service example, explain ways in which the service is differentiated from competitive offerings in the market.

**3.2** Outline the key differences between professional, as opposed to consumer, service providers. How would these differences affect marketing strategy?

**3.3** Evaluate a recent service experience you have had in terms of the five dimensions of service quality outlined in table 11.1.

**3.4** What measures can services marketers take to ensure quality?

# NOT-FOR-PROFIT MARKETING

**Not-for-profit marketing** refers to the marketing activities of organisations or individuals intended to achieve objectives other than conventional business goals such as profits. Not-for-profit marketing includes two broad categories of marketing activities:

- the marketing activities of not-for-profit organisations, such as The Smith Family
- 'social marketing', which refers to the marketing of socially desirable causes such as anti-smoking, bowel cancer screening or responsible drinking campaigns.

In general, not-for-profit marketing involves the same processes as those undertaken by commercial organisations. However, most not-for-profit marketing involves marketing of services and, for many not-for-profit marketing organisations, their non-commercial nature arguably makes it more difficult to compete for the attention and support of their target audiences.

Many not-for-profit organisations practise marketing in much the same way as commercial organisations and so their methods, objectives and tools are similar. Fundamentally, many not-for-profit organisations are competing for clients or members and do so by providing desirable products and client satisfaction, while building long-term relationships. Of course, not all not-for-profit organisations are competing for clients. Some government bodies, such as Centrelink and Medicare, are monopoly providers of the services they deliver and as such do not compete.

The core objectives of not-for-profit organisations are, therefore, not related to financial returns. For example, the St Vincent de Paul Society will not measure its success in financial terms, but rather in the number of needy people to whom it can provide assistance. Similarly, the Cancer Council, whose mission is to limit the incidence and impact of cancer in the community through promotion and research of prevention and cures, will not be primarily driven by financial objectives. Government organisations such as Centrelink do not aim to generate a profit, but they do have many financial objectives related to their costs and to the value they obtain from their budgets. Not-for-profit organisations do need to be financially viable and concern themselves with how they derive their revenue (often through membership, subscription, sponsorship or 'fee-for-service'), as well as how they manage their costs (including their often limited promotional budgets). In the case of government organisations, 'revenue' is often a share of the government's total tax revenue, and the organisations need to compete for that funding, as well as demonstrate a return on the government's investment.

 **Learning objective 4** understand the nature of not-for-profit marketing

**not-for-profit marketing** The marketing activities of individuals and organisations designed to achieve objectives other than to generate profits.

Governments also undertake social marketing activities to promote ideas they believe are in the best interests of the public; for example, through anti-smoking and safe-driving campaigns. In this context, state governments and local councils in Australia regularly run advertising and promotional campaigns to warn of bushfire dangers and of appropriate precautionary measures in 'bushfire season', and of water conservation regulations in periods of prolonged water shortages. One particularly prominent campaign was the publicity efforts surrounding the threat of the H1N1 influenza virus (swine flu), which addressed the appropriate measures to take to minimise the risk of infection and highlighted the efforts the government was making to monitor and manage the threat. It is also common for governments to undertake marketing activities on behalf of parts of the economy. For example, government efforts to promote tourism ultimately benefit many for-profit businesses.

Many not-for-profit organisations have primarily social objectives and will frequently limit their income through memberships to the bare minimum so that their members enjoy the social benefits at minimum costs. Many sporting clubs and community groups have very modest marketing objectives. At the same time, large, not-for-profit organisations, including large charities such as Lifeline, which have genuine ambitions to serve the widest possible community audience, still have limited financial resources. They therefore rely on the generosity of the public and of many of their suppliers, including management and marketing professionals who provide their services 'pro bono' (free for the public good).

Charities also enjoy strong community support and their message will often reach a sympathetic audience and achieve remarkable results. The Salvation Army's annual 'Red Shield Appeal' is always well received and financially supported by the community. While not-for-profit organisations often enjoy strong community support, this support also brings with it strong community expectations regarding what is considered appropriate for such not-for-profit organisations. These expectations limit the range of marketing activities which the community will accept. Therefore, not-for-profit organisations may not be able to engage in the same wide range of activities practised by commercial marketing organisations. For example, the use of aggressive telemarketing through commission-based fundraising organisations will not always be widely accepted, especially when such telemarketing practices are seen to be obtrusive, aggressive or ill-timed.

The Salvation Army's 'Red Shield Appeal' is always well received and supported by the community.

Not all not-for-profit organisations have universal community support. Some not-for-profit organisations promote potentially controversial causes and may attract as many opponents as supporters, particularly in local areas. Organisations such as Amnesty International, Greenpeace and many others have their critics and promotional messages need to be carefully tailored to minimise criticism.

Finally, many organisations rely for their existence on volunteer membership and usually volunteer boards. While volunteers are the lifeblood of the organisation, they do not necessarily possess the managerial experience and abilities which may be necessary to ensure the organisation's financial viability. Volunteer trustees or board members of not-for-profit organisations may not have commercial experience to be able to critically evaluate the performance of their professional staff.

More importantly, they may lack the commercial experience or ability to provide the necessary strategic direction and financial guidance to the organisation. Moreover, volunteers who provide their time and energy to support not-for-profit organisations will usually do so because they identify strongly with the traditional ethos, image and practices of the organisation. These people may have a strong bond to the traditions of the organisation and to the 'status quo'. While these traditional values and practices may have proven attractive to members or supporters in the past, such commitment to traditional values may not guarantee the survival of the organisation in the future in the face of changes in social values, technology or demography. For not-for-profit organisations, the marketing challenges in adapting to changes in society may be both more urgent and more difficult. While the use of commercial marketing practices by not-for-profit organisations may not always be possible or appropriate, the fundamental marketing principles still provide important guidance.

# Marketing a preventative cure for cancer — Spotlight

The New Zealand Ministry of Health's National Cervical Screening Programme has delivered impressive results over a sustained period. The aim of the program is to increase both the rates of cervical cancer screening among women (via pap smear tests), as well as the overall awareness of the need for women to have these tests at least every three years. Cervical cancer is largely preventable through regular screening, yet prior to the launch of the Ministry of Health's program in 2007, statistics revealed that:

- screening rates for women with a Maori or Pacific Island background were 47 per cent and 46 per cent respectvely, compared with 80 per cent for other women
- the incidence of cervical cancer among Maori and Pacific Island women was double the rate of other women, and mortality rates due to the disease were three to four times higher.

The Ministry of Health's pre-campaign research identified the major reasons for these discrepancies as being generally higher levels of misunderstanding, misinformation and embarrassment over both screening procedures and the necessity for regular testing among Maori and Pacific Island women.

The Ministry of Health's subsequent National Cervical Cancer Screening Programme set about redressing this imbalance. In addition to regular television, radio and magazine advertisements run throughout the year in both English and Te Reo Maori language, the Programme's major integrated promotional campaign is Cervical Screening Awareness Month, which is held in September each year. During this month, initiatives include:

- the distribution of packages to clinics containing cervical cancer awareness month 'tent' cards and posters, samples of sanitary products, and free hand and body lotion products for women choosing to have smear tests during September
- cervical screening messages being advertised on sanitary products in supermarkets. Metrics indicating the effectiveness of the most recent Cervical Screening Awareness Month's promotional activities included:
- more than 20 000 new visitors to the National Screening Unit's website
- approximately 1000 additional calls to the Programme's toll-free number, compared to the average monthly call rate at other times of the year.

Significantly, since the campaign's inception in 2007, screening rates for all women, including those with Maori and Pacific Island backgrounds, have increased.[11]

Do it for you and your whānau

Haere hei painga mōu, mō tō whanau hoki

Being around for the whanau is so important. You owe it to them and to yourself to stay well. That's why you should have regular smear tests every three years.

A smear test will tell you if there are any changes to the cells on your cervix. These changes are caused by a common sexually transmitted virus called Human Papillomavirus (HPV), that most women have at some stage in their lives. Usually the virus just goes away by itself but in a few cases it can lead to cervical cancer.

A smear test can find the changes before cancer has a chance to develop. It could save your life.

   Don't put it off.

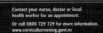
Contact your nurse, doctor or local health worker for an appointment. Or call 0800 729 729 for more information. www.cervicalscreening.govt.nz

## Concepts and applications check

**Learning objective 4**  understand the nature of not-for-profit marketing

**4.1** Explain the major ways in which not-for-profit marketing activities are likely to differ from those of commercial organisations.

**4.2** Choose a major government organisation and use the 7 Ps framework to analyse how it markets its services.

**4.3** Imagine you are the marketing manager for a charity of your own choosing. Briefly outline a marketing strategy you could implement to attract the 'donor dollar'.

# SUMMARY

 **Learning objective 1** explain the importance of the service sector to the Australian and New Zealand economies, and the difference between services products and service as the delivery of products

Service industries generate about 70 per cent of the national incomes of Australia and New Zealand. For-profit businesses comprise the largest part of the service sector, but the government is a substantial service provider, particularly in the areas of health, education, welfare and defence.

Services are activities, performances or benefits that are offered for sale, but do not involve the exchange of goods nor transfer of title. 'Service' is the act of delivering a product. Services involve a significant service component (as do many goods). Consumer services are purchased by individual consumers or households for private consumption. Business-to-business services are purchased by individuals and organisations for use in the production of other products or for use in day-to-day business operations.

 **Learning objective 2** describe how to develop and manage an effective marketing mix based on the unique characteristics of services

Four characteristics fundamentally distinguish services from goods: intangibility, inseparability, heterogeneity and perishability. These distinguishing characteristics have important consequences for how services are marketed. In addition to product, pricing, promotion and distribution, the services marketing mix is usually extended to include the factors of people, process and physical evidence, highlighting the need for the services marketer to focus on the role of people — staff, the customer and other customers — who affect service delivery, the procedures and systems they use to ensure services are reasonably consistent in quality and the tangible cues that services marketers use to reduce the risk or uncertainty that people often feel when considering purchasing a service.

 **Learning objective 3** appreciate the major challenges in the marketing of services

The intangibility, inseparability, heterogeneity and perishability require organisations to focus on achieving a sustainable differential advantage, managing profitable customer relationships and delivering consistently high levels of customer service. Differentiation is difficult in the services sector because services are easily copied by competitors. Establishing a service culture to provide consistently high-quality service is one approach. Many services customers are unprofitable and it can be expensive to attract new customers. The organisation must focus on identifying and building relationships with those customers that offer the most profit potential. To deliver consistently high-quality service, the organisation must understand customers' expectations, establish service quality standards, manage customers' service expectations and measure employee performance.

 **Learning objective 4** understand the nature of not-for-profit marketing

Not-for-profit marketing refers to the marketing activities of organisations or individuals intended to achieve objectives other than profits. Not-for-profit marketing includes the marketing activities of not-for-profit organisations, such as The Smith Family, and 'social marketing', which refers to the marketing of socially desirable

## Key terms and concepts

business-to-business services 390
consumer services 389
heterogeneity 396
inseparability 393
intangibility 392
not-for-profit marketing 409
perishability 397
physical evidence 401
process 400
services 388

causes, such as anti-smoking campaigns. While not trying to generate profits, not-for-profit organisations do need to remain financially viable and do compete with other organisations, including for-profit organisations, for funds, members and clients. Many, though not all, not-for-profit organisations enjoy strong community support, but this is coupled with strong community expectations about how they conduct their activities, including their marketing efforts.

# Four is a crowd

The Virgin Group, founded and chaired by Sir Richard Branson, is a multinational conglomerate with a diverse range of business interests, many of which are in the services sector. In Australia, the organisation has interests in telecommunications (Virgin Mobile), finance (Virgin Money), and health services (Virgin Active), but it is the Virgin Blue (rebranded in 2011 as Virgin Australia) airline for which the organisation is undoubtedly best known. The airline was founded in 2000 and, in its brief history, has provided numerous examples of the challenges of successfully running a contemporary service enterprise. In this case, we will focus on some key events and incidents that highlight key services marketing concepts.

In terms of competitiveness, the Australian aviation market can best be described as 'cut-throat'. The Australian population is currently served domestically by four major players — Qantas, Jetstar (a subsidiary of Qantas), Virgin Australia and the Singapore-owned Tiger Airways. With the exception of Qantas, none of these airlines was operating in Australia prior to 2000. Like Virgin Australia, both the Jetstar and Tiger Airways operations are relative newcomers to the Australian market, commencing operations locally in 2003 and 2006 respectively. Like Virgin Australia, they compete heavily on price. Qantas is still clearly Australia's largest airline, followed by Virgin Australia. Although there have been peaks and troughs in demand (due to a number of factors we will explore in this case) the number of domestic flights available for Australian passengers has risen by almost 80 per cent in the first decade of the 2000s.

Virgin Australia is one contender in the competitive Australian aviation market.

It hasn't always been quite so competitive, and the attraction of operating an airline has fluctuated. The one constant in the local airline market over the past 20 years has been change. Once Australia emerged from recession in the early 1990s, a period of seemingly endless economic growth led to rapid increases in disposable income, giving many people the freedom to travel regularly and extensively by plane — both within Australia and abroad. This was helped along by increased competition in the airline industry that pushed fares lower. A budget airline sector emerged with the establishment of Impulse Airlines and Virgin Blue (as the airline was known for the first decade of the twenty-first century). This lower-priced competition, along with a disastrous takeover by Air New Zealand, saw one of the major established airlines, Ansett, fail. At around the same time, the terrorist attacks on New York and Washington in the United States severely curtailed people's desire to fly, especially internationally. This was a relatively short downturn, but did result in the collapse of a number of overseas airlines that could not ride out the period of lower demand.

Virgin Blue took advantage of the gap created in the Australian market by the failure of Ansett and built a substantial business. It offers cheap fares, charging passengers for their flight only as the standard price. Those passengers who want additional extras such as meals, drinks and in-flight entertainment are charged individually on board the Virgin Blue aircraft.

This is a different strategy to that taken by Qantas, which includes such extras in standard airfares. Qantas was better placed than Ansett to cope with lower margins in the early 2000s, and was able to reduce its fares, in line with Virgin Blue, in order to compete. It also downgraded some aspects of its service to match Virgin Blue's relative 'no frills' offering. At around the same time that Ansett was collapsing, Qantas acquired the budget Impulse Airlines, which would later form the basis of a low-cost offshoot of Qantas, Jetstar.

The much more affordable fares that resulted from the price war between Qantas/Jetstar and Virgin Blue further encouraged many Australians to adopt air travel as a regular part of their lives. Often it was cheaper to fly from Brisbane to Melbourne than to catch a taxi from one side of the city to the other. In response to this much greater demand, the airlines added more routes, scheduled more frequent flights and ordered bigger planes that could carry more people. Virgin Blue also created a subsidiary, Pacific Blue. The subsidiary was based in Christchurch, and the airline began offering flights between Australia and New Zealand. Tiger Airways subsequently also began its foray into the Australian market on limited routes that it would later expand.

The airlines were already coping with lower fares — and, hence, lower margins — but this was being offset by much greater numbers of passengers. The airlines were also facing another challenge to their profitability: wildly fluctuating oil prices. Oil prices are linked to the cost of aviation fuel, which is a significant contributor to airlines' total operational costs. Massive growth in demand for oil in the rapidly industrialising China had pushed oil prices up 400 per cent in just four years. As fuel prices dramatically rose, low-cost airlines such as Virgin Blue were the hardest hit, as soaring fuel prices eroded their profit margin. Like many airlines around the world, Virgin Blue implemented a range of measures in response to the record fuel prices, including introducing baggage fees and increasing fares across many routes.

Ironically, the subsequent event that ultimately triggered oil prices to fall as dramatically as they had rose solved one problem for airlines such as Virgin Blue, but created another. The global financial crisis plunged many of the world's leading economies into recession, and although Australia largely escaped the worst effects of the crisis, it still experienced a subsequent economic downturn. There was a sudden collapse in demand across many sectors of the world economy, and the demand for air travel was particularly hard hit. Globally, more than two dozen low-cost airlines stopped flying or filed for bankruptcy protection. The collapse of many low-cost airlines provided some relief for competitors such as Virgin Blue that were able to ride out the tougher times, though they had to once again reduce their fares to attract passengers. They also reduced the number of flights offered across many routes, to ensure their capacity better reflected demand and that they weren't flying planes with large numbers of empty seats.

In a somewhat ironic move during this time — given the number of domestic flights were being reduced — Virgin Blue launched its V Australia subsidiary, with the initial aim of providing flights for Australians to and from the United States (routes have since expanded to include South Africa and Thailand). The United States route had long been the domain of Qantas, and was a signal that Virgin wanted to even more aggressively compete against its local rival. The international V Australia flights provided considerably more services for passengers than comparable 'no frills' domestic Virgin Blue flights. V Australia further signalled its growing international ambitions by establishing a strategic partnership with United Arab Emirates airline Etihad Airways, allowing V Australia to access Etihad's network of 65 destinations across North America, Europe, Asia and the Middle East.[12]

Domestically, as the economy has recovered, Virgin Blue is now turning its attention to a segment of the market it has rarely attracted — the business traveller. Currently, the airline attracts less than 10 per cent of this market, with Qantas having the lion's share. Positioning is a significant barrier for Virgin Blue in this regard. It has always been perceived as a low-cost, no-frills airline, and has traded very successfully on this basis. Qantas responded to Virgin Blue's entry into the market by creating Jetstar as its subsidiary to compete more directly with it. In terms of the business market, Qantas has invested heavily in its Qantas Club facilities at domestic airports, providing a range of upmarket services for discerning business travellers, including work stations and complimentary food and beverages while passengers wait for flights.

Generally business travellers evaluate an airline on flight frequency and its range of aircraft and airport services. Virgin Blue is likely to find it has to spend money on comparable airport lounges and on-board products to Qantas if the airline is going to appeal to corporate customers. Trying to do this within the existing Virgin Blue brand may be difficult, and, if it is serious, it may be forced to do what Qantas did with its Jetstar subsidiary, but in reverse, so as not to alienate its core market of flying leisure travellers around the country on a no-frills service that is priced accordingly.

Commenting on making Virgin Blue an attractive alternative to discerning business travellers, Paul Fiani, the managing director of fund management group Integrity Investment Management, has observed: 'It's a bit like Kmart trying to take on DJs. Sure, it is possible, but they would have to invest a lot of money and reposition the business to do it properly'.

John Borghetti, Virgin Blue's chief executive, agrees, saying: 'The challenge for Virgin Blue is to keep a low-cost model operating whilst at the same time offering a premium service for the business traveller'. Borghetti is speaking from a position of knowledge, having spent 36 years at Qantas prior to his appointment to the top job at Virgin Blue. He believes that Virgin Blue must aggressively pursue the Qantas-dominated business travel market, with the company having been too reliant on the leisure market alone in its first decade of existence. This market is traditionally more volatile and less lucrative. Speaking at the company's annual general meeting in 2010, Borghetti told shareholders that Virgin Blue's goal is to increase its share of the business travel market to 20 per cent within two years, while maintaining its already strong position in the leisure market.[13]

Such aims will not be helped by the recent ticketing fiasco experienced by the airline. In 2010 its check-in system crashed, stopping the airline's activities for a day and a half. The malfunction affected the flight plans of at least 50 000 passengers. A back-up system could not be put in place for 21 hours. The end result was a lot of bad publicity for the airline, and a costly bill as it was forced to hastily arrange and pay for the overnight accommodation arrangements of stranded interstate passengers.[14] Although the IT failure may not have been avoidable, it is clear from this example that contemporary organisations need to ensure adequate information technology back-up systems are in place in the event of emergencies. In a society that is increasingly dependent on computers for automated processes, such back-up systems are a worthwhile investment.

A highly publicised technological glitch like the one Virgin Blue experienced can offset a lot of confidence and goodwill that has taken years to develop in the marketplace. It is safe to assume that many of its affected passengers will long remember this incident, even if they are aware of a statistic mentioned earlier in this chapter — that on average, Virgin Blue currently achieves on-time departures and arrivals for approximately 84 per cent of its flights over a calendar year.[15]

In 2011, Virgin Blue Holdings Ltd launched the Virgin Australia brand to replace the existing three brands it had developed during its first decade of operation — Virgin Blue, V Australia and Pacific Blue. The rebranding move was expected to cost $30–$35 million, including the costs of new colour schemes for its planes (all white with red trim), new uniforms for staff, and new services offered primarily to attract business customers. The announcement came amidst the company declaring that it would likely post a pre-tax financial year loss of $30–$80 million. Factors such as rising fuel prices, the Christchurch earthquake, south-east Queensland flooding and north Queensland cyclones were all mentioned by Sir Richard Branson and CEO John Borghetti as having an adverse effect on operations and/or the travel plans of many people during that period.[16]

## Questions

1. Outline the major drivers of demand for air services.
2. Using examples, explain how an airline like Virgin Australia can manage the service characteristic of perishability in its product offering.
3. Using examples, explain how the extended marketing mix applies to the services of an airline like Virgin Australia.
4. Virgin Blue struggled to capture a slice of the domestic business traveller market. In terms of viewing service products as a bundle of core, augmented and potential attributes, explain how Qantas is better positioned to currently service this market's needs.
5. Imagine you are the marketing manager for Virgin Australia. How would you attempt to differentiate your service offering further in
   (a) the domestic flight market
   (b) the international flight market.

## Advanced activity

Refer back to the opening case about Australia Post entering the insurance market. Now that you have read the chapter, outline how you believe they could:
(a) create a sustainable differential advantage in marketing insurance products
(b) enhance profitable customer relationships
(c) deliver consistently high levels of customer service across their range of services, using the extended services marketing mix.

## Marketing plan activity

If you have chosen a service organisation for your marketing plan, analyse that service in relation to the additional 3 Ps of the services marketing mix, as outlined in this chapter (people, process and physical evidence). Outline potential marketing strategies to achieve sustainable competitive advantages in each of these three areas.

If you have chosen a good rather than a service for your marketing plan, analyse the good in terms of potential customer services (human, intellectual or mechanical activities) that can add value to it. For example, as outlined in the chapter, the provision of a warranty can add value to the purchase of a car or a home entertainment system. Can you identify any sustainable customer service competitive advantages for your good?

A sample marketing plan has been included at the back of this book (see page 523) to give you an idea where this information fits in an overall marketing plan.

## CHAPTER 12

# Electronic marketing

## Learning objectives

After studying this chapter, you should be able to:

- identify electronic marketing activities

- explain the unique characteristics of e-marketing

- explain specific e-marketing methods

- appreciate ethical and legal issues relating to e-marketing

- discuss the role of e-marketing in an overall marketing strategy.

# Cradle rock

Online store Cradle Rock specialises in a large range of baby and childrens' clothing, toys, gifts, footwear and accessories with a touch of 1950s style. Cradle Rock was

founded by Julie Lemmon and her husband Greg in 2004. The company prides itself on its customer service, stating that 'Cradle Rock is a 21st century business with 1950s style-service; our aim is to exceed your expectations'.

From small beginnings, the website now has a stocklist comparable in size to some larger retailers' online outlets. The range of labels includes Oobi Baby, Little Horn, Boo Foo Woo, Itch Design, Rock Your Baby and Gaia Organics. Further, there are brands that recreate a 1950s style, such as Tin Toys, Wee Gallery Smart Art and Fish Lilly.

Unlike many online stores, Cradle Rock decided to open a 'bricks and mortar' store with their showroom at Port Melbourne, Victoria, after having success in the online market. In an interview with the ABC's *Inside Business* program, Ms Lemmon explained:

> We found a site. I sort of thought well this is something that we could probably run the business out of, but even have a sort of showroom/retail space so that the people who did want to touch and feel could actually come, or the people that wanted to try on something because they weren't sure if their child would fit a size four or five.

But did opening a store negatively affect the online sales? In the interview, Ms Lemmon discussed the implications of opening the store on the company's overall success, commenting:

> I would say that by having the store it's increased my online business by probably 20 per cent. I was creating new customers. I think that they know they're more accessible to you; that you are a person. That you're not just going to hide behind an email.

If you can't get to the store, you can always go online to www.cradlerock.com.au, 24 hours a day, so that you can 'shop when the stars are out'.[1]

---

## Questions

1. Why do you think Cradle Rock's products are (or are not) suited to being sold online? Justify your answer.
2. Why might establishing a physical store have increased Cradle Rock's online sales?

# INTRODUCTION

From time to time throughout history, a technological change has come along that has fundamentally changed the way humans live. The internet and mobile telecommunication technology represent such a technological shift. In Australia and New Zealand — and all developed countries — these technologies have transformed the way individuals communicate and consume, the way organisations do business, and the way government, businesses and citizens interact with each other. Businesses such as Castle Rock have been established, with their main presence being on the internet.

According to government figures, 72 per cent of Australian households have home internet access and 78 per cent of households have access to a computer.[2] Much of this access is shared, be it at home, work or school. Virtually all businesses are online in some capacity, ranging from having a simple email address and conducting internet banking transactions through to multinational corporations conducting virtually all aspects of their businesses online.

Although mobile phones, the internet and all the associated technologies that are gradually converging into one have been with us for a couple of decades now, many of the marketing approaches are still very much in the exploratory and evolving stages. Of course, there have been some spectacularly successful business and marketing models, such as Amazon and Google, and some equally spectacular failures, including Boo.com, GeoCities and eToys — all victims of the 'dot.com' meltdown at the end of the 1990s.

It is important to remember that the availability and nature of technology is quite different around the world. Many rural areas in developing countries have virtually no telecommunications infrastructure. In parts of rural India, for example, advertisers place television screens on the side of vans and park them in town centres for people to watch (including the advertising messages, of course). In Africa, internet access is more commonly achieved via mobile phone than via a computer, with the Central African Republic being the most expensive place to get a fixed broadband connection, costing nearly 40 times the average monthly income there.[3]

This chapter focuses on the use of electronic marketing (or e-marketing). In this chapter we will define e-marketing and explain its unique characteristics, including profiling, interaction and community, control, accessibility and comparability, and digitalisation. Then we will explain specific electronic marketing methods, such as e-commerce, digital products, banner and pop-up ads, viral marketing and search engine optimisation. Any organisation wishing to participate in e-marketing must be aware of the relevant legal and ethical issues. We will examine legislation, ethics and how the rules of e-marketing are still developing. Finally, we discuss the role of e-marketing in an overall marketing strategy. It is important to remember that e-marketing is just one part of a broader marketing strategy and that e-marketing efforts must be consistent and coordinated with the overall marketing plan.

## ELECTRONIC MARKETING

**Learning objective 1**
identify electronic marketing activities

**Electronic marketing** refers to all of the activities involved in planning and implementing marketing in the electronic environment, including the internet and web, mobile phones and other information and telecommunications technologies. Examples of e-marketing include:

**electronic marketing** The activities involved in planning and implementing marketing in the electronic environment.

- the sale of products via an e-commerce website (at its most basic, the e-marketing equivalent of a mail order service)

- the texting of potential customers about a new offer or sale (an example of e-promotion)
- an email sent to an existing customer asking them to click a link to participate in a survey for the opportunity to win a prize (a promotion and customer relationship management technique)
- the use of magazine advertising to encourage consumers to subscribe to an SMS horoscope service (an example involving a product and distribution method unique to e-marketing)
- the inclusion of discount vouchers on takeaway food websites that encourage people to visit the website, knowing they will be able to access a lower price as a result (an example involving promotion, pricing and the active involvement of the purchaser, contrasting with the delivery of pizza discount vouchers via mail that entail no active engagement by the consumer).

It is clear then that the internet and other technologies offer numerous opportunities for e-marketing. These opportunities are only likely to increase in the future with the younger generation, often referred to as 'digital natives' or the 'net generation',[4] not surprisingly being the most prolific users. As figure 12.1[5] shows, younger consumers are spending an enormous amount of time using the internet compared to other generations. According to this Roy Morgan study, even though Australians in general spend more time viewing television than consuming other media, observing TV and internet viewing across different generations, the time spent on the internet for both Generation Y and Z is now at a level that is comparable to television. Older users, sometimes referred to as 'digital immigrants', are also increasing their hours a week online and there has been a slight decrease in TV watching. A marketing organisation that fails to engage with e-marketing is clearly setting itself up for failure. The key purchasing decision makers of the future are definitely 'online'.[6]

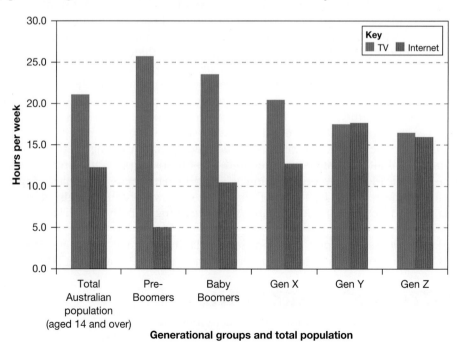

**FIGURE 12.1**

Average hours spent on TV or the internet by generation (per week)

Roy Morgan generation definitions: Pre-Boomers — Pre 1946; Baby Boomers — 1946–1960; Generation X — 1961–1975; Generation Y — 1976–1990; Generation Z — 1991–2005.

No doubt you will have engaged with many examples of e-marketing and found various advantages and disadvantages. One of the main advantages to you might be convenience, as you can access websites 24 hours a day, 7 days a week, from just about anywhere, to obtain information that will assist in making the final purchase decision — and in many cases you can make the purchase. You are not limited by the usual store opening hours, the location of the store or having to wait while other customers are served. Of course, among the disadvantages for the consumer are the inability to physically examine the product before making the purchase and the risk of credit card fraud.

Marketing organisations also find pros and cons in e-marketing. For example, they are potentially exposed to much greater competition (as geography has little meaning online), but they also have access to the entire global market (something that cannot be easily achieved in the bricks and mortar world). Additionally, not everyone has access to the internet, and some specific target markets in particular (e.g. the elderly, those living in remote areas and those with low socioeconomic status) have low rates of access. Payment can also give rise to issues, with consumers concerned about security and the possibility of online fraud or deception (not everyone has a credit card or wants to give credit card details online).

E-marketing allows consumers to interact deeply with the marketing organisation without the need for dealing with an actual person. Banking is one of the most obvious examples. Only a few decades ago, to withdraw cash from a bank required the customer to take a passbook to a teller during opening hours and be handed cash over the counter, with the transaction handwritten and stamped in the passbook. Today, customers can withdraw cash from an automatic teller machine 24 hours a day or move their money around using credit cards, EFTPOS and internet banking more or less as they please. There are quite clear advantages in terms of convenience for the consumer, although some consumers, particularly some older people, prefer personal service rather than dealing with technology. There are also very big advantages for the banks. For example, a banking transaction performed by a consumer using internet banking costs about 20 cents. The same transaction performed in a bank branch costs $3.[7] Considering banks conduct millions of transactions a day, this is a very significant saving. The banks found though that consumers still generally prefer to deal with bank personnel when it comes to more complex matters such as discussing investments, loans and insurance. Some of the larger banks experienced a consumer backlash when they began closing branches in rural and regional centres, forcing consumers to use technology or to travel if they wanted personal service.

# Socially mobile                                      Spotlight

Consider the following statistics from a recent social media report that analysed the online social network behaviour of Australians over a year. During this time:
- nine million users used social media to connect to other people
- nine million users watched an online video about services or products they were thinking of buying
- eight million users went online to read a blog
- seven million users created a profile on a social network site
- five million users used the internet to interact with a brand or organisation
- more than four million users discussed products or services online.

More than a quarter of social networkers access social networks via their mobile phones. This trend has coincided with the uptake of smartphones (now owned by 43 per cent of online Australians) and more affordable data download plans. More than 65 per cent of these mobile social networkers are under 35 years of age.

Although Facebook is currently the most popular social network by far, Twitter is the fastest growing social network. According to the report, Twitter's annual usage grew by more than 400 per cent, with

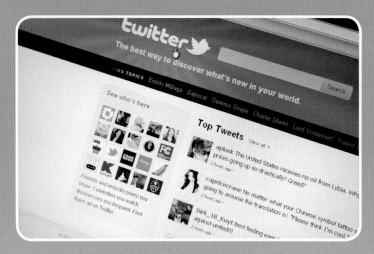

34 per cent of online Australians stating that they have visited the site. In comparison, 75 per cent of the online Australians that participated in the survey said that they had visited Facebook at one time or another.

Melanie Ingrey, a research director for the company that conducted the survey, Nielsen, predicts:

> The opportunities for brands and companies to tap into the social media phenomenon are really just beginning to emerge, and to date, we've only seen the tip of the iceberg. Incredibly, nearly nine in ten Australian internet users (86 per cent) are looking to their fellow internet users for opinions and information about products, services and brands, and Australians' engagement with online word-of-mouth communication is going to increase in coming years as social media plays an increasingly important role in consumer decision making.[8]

## Questions

1. Outline the types of e-marketing activities that may be most effective in reaching you and your friends.

2. Imagine you are the marketing manager for a product that is being 'slammed' (criticised) in an online forum. From a marketing perspective, briefly outline how you would address the situation.

## Concepts and applications check

**Learning objective 1** identify electronic marketing activities

1.1 What is meant by the term 'e-marketing'?

1.2 Outline the advantages and disadvantages of e-marketing activities, both from a consumer's and a marketer's perspective.

1.3 Describe some e-marketing activities that you have experienced. Have these been successful in making you aware of a particular product or prompted you to purchase it?

# CHARACTERISTICS OF ELECTRONIC MARKETING

**Learning objective 2**
explain the unique characteristics of e-marketing

A number of key characteristics of e-marketing differentiate it from other forms of marketing. To truly harness the potential of online marketing, it is important to understand these characteristics and their consequences for any marketing approach. The key characteristics we will examine are profiling, interactivity and community, control, accessibility and comparability, and digitalisation.

## Profiling

**profiling** The process of getting to know about potential customers before they make a purchase and to find out more about existing customers.

**Profiling** refers to the process of getting to know about potential customers before they make a purchase and to find out more about existing customers. In a sense it takes the place of the information and needs stages of the INPLCF sales model that we discussed in chapter 9. The more the organisation knows about the customer and their needs and preferences, the better it can present a product that will offer value to the customer. Marketing organisations can gather information about their customers in the e-marketing environment through:

- *requiring registration.* Registration may be required to access a website, parts of a website or some other electronic service (such as email newsletters, RSS feeds or SMS services). Registration usually requires the visitor to provide such information as their name, age, occupation, income level and address.
- *the use of cookies on websites.* Cookies are small pieces of software written to a user's computer when they visit a website. They send information back to the website operator about how often a user visits, what pages they visit, when they visit and how much time they spend on the site. The cookie can also respond to the user's preferences to tailor their experience on the website (e.g. if an online newspaper reader often clicks on sports stories, the website can present more links to sports stories as well as more advertising related to sports).
- *competitions.* Many organisations operate online competitions that require users to provide personal information in return for an entry into the competition. Some competitions may actually involve games or skill, but they all require the user to provide information that the marketing organisation can analyse and use to gain a view of both its overall market and each member of the market.

Once the organisation has collected all of this qualitative and quantitative information from customers and potential customers, it needs to be able to organise, analyse and apply its new wealth of knowledge. Information is usually stored in a structured database or data warehouse, which will contain profiles of individual customers and their transaction records. This data is analysed and used to ensure marketing offerings to each customer provide the maximum possible value to that customer. For example, the surf wear chain City Beach ran a campaign that would build a customer database while generating revenue at the same time. The campaign, Shopping Surfari, saw City Beach deliver 1.3 million catalogues tagged with a premium SMS number to targeted areas across Australia. Customers were asked to send their name (so future communications may be personalised) and postcode (to track the effectiveness of the catalogues) to a premium SMS number. At the close of the campaign, City Beach had over 11 000 entries in the competition and was left with a database of 5464 highly profiled customers.[9]

In the e-marketing environment, this can be done in real time, with the software underlying the website drawing on the data store to make informed responses to the customer's actions. As discussed in chapter 3, data is only useful if it is structured, organised and accessible, so this must be planned into any e-marketing efforts that aim to gather data.

## Interaction and community

Other than an in-person interaction with a salesperson or other customer service officer, e-marketing offers the most opportunity for **interaction** between the marketer and the customer. In many ways, this type of interactivity can surpass even that offered by a one-on-one marketing experience (e.g. if the salesperson does not have a good knowledge of the product) and it is certainly a cheaper option that can reach far more people than one-on-one in-person contact. Interactive technologies such as smartphones and websites offer customers an avenue by which to tell the marketer who they are and want they want. This can be as direct as posting a suggestion in a 'feedback' form on an organisation's website, or as indirect as long-term

**interaction** The ongoing exchange of information between marketer and customer (or potential customer).

profiling of preferences and characteristics, as described above. Interactivity can occur in many ways, including:

- *a virtual customer service officer.* Websites, particularly those driven by Web 2.0 technologies, can respond to customers' enquiries and comments with tailored answers.
- *a real customer service officer.* Telstra's website offers a chat facility that allows customers, or potential customers, to ask questions and have basic changes made to their service, or apply for a new service. An actual customer service officer responds to the website visitor in real time to answer their queries and respond to their comments. The service only operates to a certain level of complexity, with more challenging or out of the ordinary questions being referred to a specialist customer service officer. Essentially the website visitor is directed to a phone number.
- *email newsletters and RSS feeds.* Sending a weekly, monthly, quarterly or ad hoc newsletter or other information via email or RSS feed (with consent) helps maintain brand awareness in a customer's mind. While the organisation must strike a careful balance between regular contact and respecting the customer's privacy (and peace), well-timed information, particularly if it includes some special offer, can be very effective.
- *survey participation.* Surveys are an important market research tool that help marketers find out more about their target market. Surveys can be emailed to customers or can appear as a pop-up on websites. To be effective, online surveys need to be completed, and so they should usually be kept short and relevant to maximise the likelihood the user will fill in the survey. Survey participation can be improved by offering some incentive, such as entry into a prize draw, to respondents.
- *online communities.* Hosting an online community (discussed in more detail later in the chapter) provides a virtual meeting place for customers and potential customers. The marketing organisation can observe their comments and their interests, and can seed ideas in the community to gauge responses to proposed marketing or product campaigns. An active online community centred around a brand or organisation can help build very strong long-term relationships and brand associations. Marketing organisations need to be aware, however, that online communities can also generate and sustain negative commentary about a business, forcing the organisation to weather the criticism, intervene in the community (a move itself guaranteed to generate more negativity), close the community down, or try to make some positive response to the criticism.

## Control

Individuals exercise varying degrees of control over their interaction with marketing. For example, the driver of a car may pay no attention to roadside billboards; their passenger might only glance at them, or might read their detail if they are of interest. A television viewer may watch an advertisement or channel surf during commercial breaks. A web surfer might block advertising, ignore advertising, glance at it or in fact click through to the website it links to. As you can see, the e-marketing mode offers the customer many more options to control how they relate to the marketing message. The formal marketing terms used to distinguish these different modes are *push* and *pull*. **Push advertising** refers to advertising sent from the marketer to the customer (it is pushed to them). **Pull advertising** refers to advertising that the customer actively seeks out (they pull it from the marketing organisation). Some e-marketing is push marketing (e.g. banner advertisements on websites), but much of the more sophisticated e-marketing uses pull marketing

**push advertising** Advertising sent from the marketer to the customer.

**pull advertising** Advertising that the customer actively seeks out.

(e.g. subscription SMS services). Control, formally defined, is the ability of the customer to determine how they interact with the marketing message and to influence the presentation and content of the marketing message. This can involve permission marketing, which was discussed in the 'Promotion' chapter, where there are activities aimed at obtaining customer consent to receive information and marketing material from a company. For example, online stores can offer the ability to opt-in or opt-out of receiving further emails, catalogues, announcements of promotional offers, and so on.

As customers have more — sometimes complete — control in the e-marketing environment, marketing organisations have to go to greater lengths to attract the attention of customers. They have to make them actively want to engage with marketing messages that many customers have learnt to actively avoid.

## Accessibility and comparability

The web provides individuals with more ability than ever before to research products, compare products and seek the opinions of others about products. In the past, a prospective customer may have visited a few stores to look at and ask questions about a few different models of a product they were considering purchasing. Today, using the web, customers can easily research numerous different options, as well as read independent product reviews online. Their research is conducted outside the influence of a salesperson and it is not rare for a customer to know as much or more about their desired product than a salesperson does by the time the customer goes to a store (assuming they do not complete their transaction online).

Some online services actually prepare detailed comparisons for customers. For example, iSelect chooses the most appropriate private health insurance plans for clients based on the information they fill out in an online form. Realestate.com.au enables web users to get information like 'local sales' of recently purchased properties in the same area that you are searching.

Hence, customers are far more informed about products and competing products than ever before. The online environment also offers them the choice of completing a transaction online, which opens them up to a choice of many more retailers than they can access in the real world. Online, the only real difference between buying from a local store and buying from a warehouse on the other side of the globe is the freight charge and delivery time (though even that does not always vary).

> Realestate.com.au enables users to find out the sold prices for properties in different areas. This service is a benefit designed to enhance the overall appeal of the site for users.

## Digitalisation

**Digitalisation** is the ability to deliver a product as information or to present information about a product digitally. For example, an MP3 or MPEG4 file downloaded from the iTunes store is a product delivered as information; a Flash presentation on a website that offers a 3D walkthrough of an art gallery presents information about the product, but does not deliver the product (a visit to the art gallery) itself.

Some products can be completely digitalised. Music is one such example. Since the advent of the CD (and other similar digital recording media), music recordings have

> **digitalisation** The ability to deliver a product as information or to present information about a product digitally.

been just bits of information, so the move to distributing music via telecommunications technologies was not much of a technological leap. The appropriate business model for doing so, however, has proved quite a challenge. For example, Apple created the best-known online music store, iTunes Store, but restricted playback of purchased music to its own devices and software (iPods, iPhone and iPad) and prevented the music being further copied. Some established and emerging performing artists have offered their recorded music to fans for free (including Paul Kelly, the Arctic Monkeys and Radiohead). While not making any money from the recordings, they served as a strong incentive for fans to purchase other merchandise and to attend very lucrative live performances. This approach was partly a response to the pervasive copying/pirating of music. This had always occurred, with friends making cassette copies of records or CDs for other friends, but the internet and peer-to-peer sharing technologies ensured that once an illegal copy of a song was online, virtually everyone could obtain an illegal copy. Torrenting technologies have similarly facilitated the piracy of movies in recent years.

As outlined in the chapter 2 Spotlight feature 'Let's get digital', file sharing is a major issue for the recorded music industry. According to ARIA (the Australian Recording Industry Association), approximately 3.4 million Australians have illegally downloaded music files via file sharing services[10], while globally a report by the IFPI (International Federation of the Phonographic Industry) suggested 40 billion music files are illegally shared annually.[11] This represents 95 per cent of all music downloads. Interestingly though, the other 5 per cent represents millions of people still choosing to purchase legal music.[12] A further consequence is for record companies, which traditionally have profited most from recorded music. Home recording technology that matches that used in multi-million dollar recording studios, combined with the internet, has enabled emerging and well-established recording artists to work without record companies. Of course, one of the key functions of record companies has been to gain radio play for new songs and new artists as well as other types of promotion. It is interesting to note that most of the artists who have given away their music for free are either completely unknown (and without a recording contract) or very well known (and thus not needing further publicity to their established fan base). Music is not the only industry affected by digital downloads. The television and film industries are similarly affected. Market research into the apparent reasons for this consumer behaviour is outlined in the 'Illegal downloads' Spotlight that follows shortly.

Other products cannot be completely digitalised, but part of the service can. For example, various grocery retailers have experimented — with mixed success — with offering online grocery stores in which consumers shop at an online store using a virtual shopping trolley and then pay a fee to have the full order delivered to their homes. The benefits to the consumer are convenience, traded off against the fee charged for delivery (around $15). Some of the disincentives are the requirement to plan grocery needs (including meals) a week ahead and to be sufficiently organised that running out of something does not force a trip to the grocery store anyway. It appears many consumers, however, find the benefits insufficient motivation. Take-up has been slow and as a result retailers have been very slow to expand their offerings. Most online grocery services currently operate only in the inner areas of the major capital cities. The service has mainly appealed to young families who are stretched for time, and people who are older or have a disability that makes it more difficult to go to and shop in a grocery store.[13]

The next Spotlight looks at illegal downloads, and includes figure 12.2.[14]

# Illegal downloads

Illegal downloading of online material is a constant problem in the music, TV and film industries. Many Australians who downloaded pirated media were asked why they did it in a recent survey. The survey was conducted by news.com.au and the market research company CoreData. The findings provide some interesting information for online marketers.

The online survey was completed by 7324 respondents who said they had illegally downloaded or streamed TV shows, movies or music in the 12 months before completing the questionnaire. The respondents were asked to choose the most applicable reasons, from a list of about 12 possible choices, for illegally downloading or streaming media. The respondents needed to choose the most applicable reasons for each type of media — TV shows, movies and music. The main survey findings were interesting.

- According to the respondents, convenience is as much of a motivating factor in downloading media illegally as is money.
- More than two-thirds of the respondents said they would be prepared to pay for a similar legal service if it existed.
- The findings showed Gen Y is prepared to pay more for legal downloads of TV shows and movies than any other age group, while people between 31 and 50 are more likely to pay top dollar for music.
- The findings suggested the young (under 20) and the elderly (61 and over) are least likely to say they would pay for legal content.
- According to the survey results, TV shows are illegally downloaded more regularly, and by more people, than movies or music.

Regarding the specific media of TV shows, movies and music:

- 6694 respondents said they had illegally downloaded or streamed a TV show in the past 12 months. Of these, 86.8 per cent said they did so regularly.
- 5902 respondents said they had illegally downloaded or streamed a movie in the past 12 months. Of these, 72.7 per cent said they did so regularly.
- 5712 respondents said they had illegally downloaded or streamed music in the past 12 months. Of these, 69.5 per cent said they did so regularly.

The main reasons given by respondents as to why they downloaded material illegally for each media are found in the diagram with this feature. Interestingly, most of the respondents said that they would pay for media downloads if there was a cheap and legal service available.[15]

## FIGURE 12.2

Why Australians say they choose illegal downloads

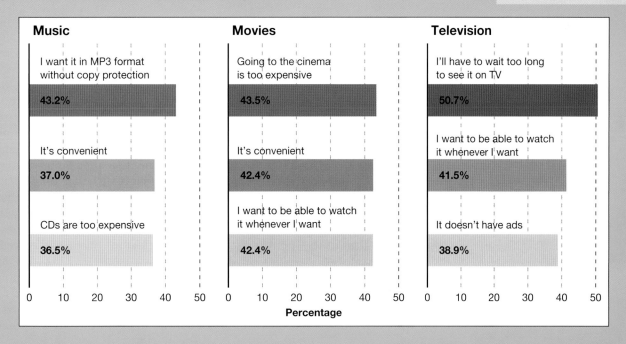

| Music | |
|---|---|
| I want it in MP3 format without copy protection | 43.2% |
| It's convenient | 37.0% |
| CDs are too expensive | 36.5% |

| Movies | |
|---|---|
| Going to the cinema is too expensive | 43.5% |
| It's convenient | 42.4% |
| I want to be able to watch it whenever I want | 42.4% |

| Television | |
|---|---|
| I'll have to wait too long to see it on TV | 50.7% |
| I want to be able to watch it whenever I want | 41.5% |
| It doesn't have ads | 38.9% |

Percentage

## Concepts and applications check

**Learning objective 2**  explain the unique characteristics of e-marketing

**2.1** Using your own examples, briefly describe the unique characteristics of e-marketing that differentiate it from traditional marketing.

**2.2** Describe some of the ways marketing organisations can 'profile' their customers in an electronic environment.

**2.3** Prepare an argument for and against the following statement: 'Electronic marketing provides greater opportunity for interaction between a marketer and a customer than a one-on-one marketing experience.'

**2.4** Provide your own examples of 'push' and 'pull' e-marketing activities.

**2.5** Assume that you are going to purchase a new piece of clothing. Compare and contrast the steps you would take if you were looking to purchase online as opposed to purchasing in a traditional retail environment.

# ELECTRONIC MARKETING METHODS

**Learning objective 3**
explain specific
e-marketing methods

There are numerous specific methods used in e-marketing. We will describe the key features of these in this section. Bear in mind as you read this that any one method may be just one part of a complete e-marketing approach, and that the e-marketing approach is often just one part of the organisation's complete marketing strategy.

## Banner and pop-up advertisements

Two popular forms of online advertising are:

- *banner advertisements*. Banner advertisements appear on websites, much like newspaper advertisements. They are relatively cheap on most websites, but sites that can prove they have high visitor numbers or desirable niche audiences can charge significant sums for advertising space. One of the key issues confronting organisations considering using banner advertising is to assess how effective it will be. Just like advertising in traditional media, many website visitors simply ignore advertisements. Organisations have come up with various ways to measure the effectiveness of advertising and charge the advertiser accordingly. For example, the Adwords advertising service offered by the Google search engine only charges advertisers if the user actually clicks on the advertisement (and hence travels to the advertiser's site). Variations on this include advertising that only incurs a charge if the website visitor completes a purchase or registration transaction. Facebook gives advertisers the option of paying by the 'click' like Google, or by the number of 'impressions' (i.e. the number of times the advertisement is shown on a webpage, regardless of the number of times it is 'clicked').[16] In the earlier years of the internet, software to block advertising was commonplace, but this has declined in popularity as internet connection speeds have increased to the point that advertising no longer noticeably affects the speed with which a page loads.
- *pop-up advertisements*. Pop-ups are advertisements that open in a new web browser window. While this means that the user is not confronted with the advertisement

on the page they have visited, many users react negatively to the manner of pop-up advertisements and many actually disable them in their browser software. Pop-ups are popular among survey companies that ask users to participate in a survey, and among gambling and adult entertainment providers.

A variation on banner and pop-up advertising involves banner advertisements that temporarily enlarge to cover the main part of the website, thus drawing the user's attention (and often requiring them to manually close the advertisement before they can see the actual content of the page). A similar device is the inclusion of a static or video advertisement before granting access to an article, photo gallery or other feature of the website. To avoid a customer backlash, most such advertisements provide the option of allowing the user to close them without watching them. Other forms of online advertising include brochure sites and search engine marketing (both of which are discussed in the next few pages).

## Brochure sites

Brochure sites are websites that are essentially an online advertisement for the organisation. They usually present product and contact details, but offer little other functionality. They rely on users finding the site through more traditional advertising or through a search engine or link from another site. They are particularly useful for presenting a portfolio of work. For example, a cabinetmaker can post extensive photos of completed work in a variety of styles so interested potential customers can examine their work.

## Web 2.0

**Web 2.0** is a term used to describe the various technologies (e.g. wikis and Ajax) and experiences that involve online communities where members contribute to and build the community and content, and where users can substantially control their own online experience through customisation and interactivity. Therefore, Web 2.0 websites do not just allow users to retrieve information but encourage interactive information sharing and user-generated content. This means that content on particular websites, or a part of a website, is made available to the general public and is produced or generated by the end-users in a virtual community. This is in contrast to websites where users can only passively view information. Examples of user-generated content can take the form of news, research, reviews, and gossip, which can be positive or negative towards a company or a brand.

Examples of Web 2.0 include social networking, podcasting and video/photo sharing sites, as well as those that facilitate blogs, wikis, and question-answer databases. Web 2.0 is also sometimes referred to as the *social web*, with the websites being examples of *social media*. There are several types of social media depending on the primary focus of the website. *Social networking* provides an interactive platform where people can add friends, comment on profiles, join groups and have discussions. Facebook, Twitter, MySpace, Hi5, and LinkedIn are some examples of widely used social networks. YouTube and Flickr are examples of *social photo and video sharing* sites, where photos and videos are shared and comments can be posted. A *wiki* is the term given to websites that allow for the creation and editing of web pages, such as when articles can be posted and subsequently edited by users or a community. Wikipedia and Wikia are examples of this.

Many businesses have tried to capitalise on Web 2.0, particularly its social nature, to try to build communities based around their products and to generate positive associations with their products.[17] This has included rock bands, artists and products aimed at younger audience, who have been the main users of social networking sites. A New Zealand outdoor clothing company, Icebreaker, uses Web 2.0 approaches on its website.

**Web 2.0** The various technologies and experiences that involve online communities where members contribute to and build the community and the content, and where users can substantially control their own online experience through customisation and interactivity.

On its website you can view the most recent media releases; watch videos about the company's philosophy, history and supply chain; download detailed product images; and read a blog and then leave a comment. There is also an opportunity to add your name to the opt-in email news list. This helps cement customer loyalty as it allows outdoor enthusiasts to build a relationship with the company. It also enables potential customers to read about the experiences of people who have tried Icebreaker products.

Telstra, in Australia, is another company attempting to harness social media, particularly the interactive communication element. It has an active presence on YouTube, with videos showcasing its own products and services, as well as associated technologies. The channel also features videos on how to solve a range of technical issues that customers may experience with technology in general. Like any YouTube channel, Telstra's channel has a blogging capability, which the company actively monitors for feedback. It responds to blogs on the channel when necessary and appropriate. Telstra also utilises Twitter for such things as new product reviews. In 2010, via Twitter, it invited members of the public to review a new mobile phone alongside 'tech' journalists. Over 2000 applications were received for the 25 trial phones on offer, and the successful applicants ultimately produced more than 360 blogs about their experiences with the phones. Kristen Boschma, Telstra's head of online communications and social media, explains:

Telstra's YouTube channel uses a variety of Web 2.0 tools, as part of a social media pull strategy.

Traditional advertising involves a sort of broadcast to the masses, which is all about a push strategy whereas with social media you're looking at a pull strategy. Where you're engaging with your customers and inviting them to come to you.[18]

There is an important caveat, however, for organisations considering putting so much control in the hands of their actual and potential customers. Not all customer experiences are positive ones and the online complaints of a few disgruntled customers can cause more damage to a brand than can hundreds of positive comments from happy customers.

## Viral marketing

**viral marketing** The use of social networks to spread a marketing message.

**Viral marketing** is the use of social networks to spread a marketing message. As we read in chapter 9, it gets its name from the idea that a marketing message can spread from one person to another, in much the same way as a virus spreads. Online, it generally relies on the forwarding of email messages, links to websites or word-of-mouth in online discussion groups and other communities. Because viral marketing messages are spread by friends and colleagues, they have a much greater chance of being considered than traditional advertising.

One of the most successful viral marketing efforts of all time in recent times was the 'Best job in the world' campaign created by Tourism Queensland. The campaign comprised an advertisement for a job that involved, principally, spending six months on tropical islands in the Great Barrier Reef. Word-of-mouth saw the $2 million campaign gain $150 million worth of publicity around the world, highlighting Queensland as an ideal holiday destination during the Northern Hemisphere winter. Later figures revealed that visits to Queensland by young travellers from the United Kingdom,

Germany, France and the Netherlands all increased at a higher rate than the national average, which was taken as a metric that the highly awarded campaign worked.[19]

Viral marketing online is very much controlled by the online community and some businesses have paid a heavy price for trying to manipulate online word-of-mouth or use social networking sites for commercial purposes. For example, when the women's clothing label Witchery launched a line of men's clothing, it posted a video on YouTube that featured a woman asking for help to find a mysterious man she had met in a café and who had left without his jacket. The video attracted 60 000 viewers in just four days, but the campaign unravelled when people noticed that the woman also appeared as a model on Witchery's website and that the jacket was suspiciously over-emphasised in the video. The campaign, designed to generate exposure for the new line of menswear, suffered an extreme backlash from viewers who had engaged with the woman's romantic story, only to find they were being manipulated. Eventually a 'confession' video was posted trying to defend the campaign. The advertising company behind the campaign also felt compelled to post a justification of the approach taken.[20]

## Portals

Web portals were very popular in the 1990s when the web first became widely used. A **portal** is a website that is designed to act as a gateway to other related sites. It carries news stories or other information relevant to the topic of the portal and includes links to other sites with related information. The portal itself either carries advertising or is intended to serve as an advertising tool for the portal business itself. The popularity of the portal has declined as search engines have become more powerful and as users have realised they can often better find content themselves. Most portals now feature a search engine. Portals are still widely used by government where the intention is to provide citizens with a starting point from which to access all government services; for example, the New Zealand Government maintains the http://newzealand.govt.nz website as an entry point for all online government information and services. Ninemsn is one of the better known Australian portals and features Microsoft's Bing search engine.

**portal** A website that is designed to act as a gateway to other related sites.

## Search engine optimisation

**Search engine optimisation (SEO)** means tailoring certain features of a website to try to achieve the best possible ranking in search results returned by a search engine. The theory behind this approach is that consumers will be most likely to click through to the first sites listed among the search results. An enormous industry has developed around SEO and numerous businesses exist that specialise in providing SEO services to other businesses.

**search engine optimisation (SEO)** Tailoring features of a website to try to achieve the best possible ranking in search results returned by a search engine.

Search engines themselves have taken steps to try to prevent or at least restrict the commercial manipulation of search results, in a bid to preserve the integrity of their service and the usefulness of their service to their customers. For example, Google continually reinvents its search algorithms to prevent organisations manipulating their own websites to appear at the top of Google search results. Traditionally search engines used metadata to find websites that were most relevant to users' searches. Metadata is a series of words or phrases included in the data underlying a website. More sophisticated approaches are often now used, including Google's approach which bases search results on the actual content of the sites and on how many other sites include links to the site.

The effectiveness of SEO has also declined as users have become knowledgeable and cynical about how businesses work to appear among the top hits on search engines. The inclusion of paid advertising — that looks very similar to search results — at the top of lists of search results has also decreased the effectiveness of SEO. Nevertheless it is still a common approach to ensuring visibility online.

# Search engine marketing

As mentioned above, many search engines now seek paid advertising to place on search results pages. This approach is known as **search engine marketing**. These are usually presented slightly differently or separately to the actual search results. The advertisements that appear at the top of search results are known as sponsored links. Sponsored links are appealing to businesses because they are only returned for searches that are relevant to the advertised product, effectively ensuring the link is placed more prominently than links that are returned purely due to SEO efforts. There has been somewhat of a user backlash, particularly against Google and Yahoo!, in response to the use of sponsored links on search pages, but they have proved popular with business. Even some Australian government departments now advertise using Google's sponsored links feature. Figure 12.3 outlines the basic method of operation of Google's Adwords advertising product.

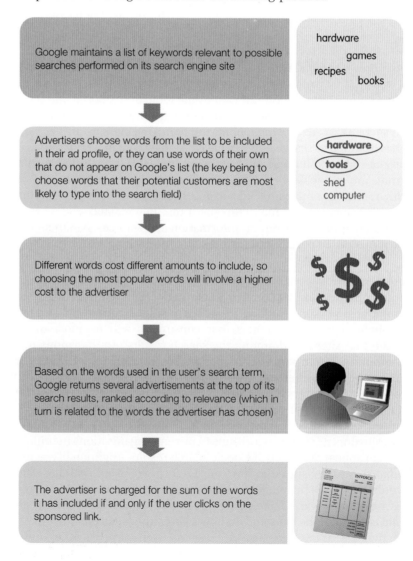

Google maintains a list of keywords relevant to possible searches performed on its search engine site

hardware
games
recipes
books

Advertisers choose words from the list to be included in their ad profile, or they can use words of their own that do not appear on Google's list (the key being to choose words that their potential customers are most likely to type into the search field)

hardware
tools
shed
computer

Different words cost different amounts to include, so choosing the most popular words will involve a higher cost to the advertiser

Based on the words used in the user's search term, Google returns several advertisements at the top of its search results, ranked according to relevance (which in turn is related to the words the advertiser has chosen)

The advertiser is charged for the sum of the words it has included if and only if the user clicks on the sponsored link.

**FIGURE 12.3**

How Google Adwords works

Yahoo!'s online advertising system works in a similar way. Advertisers choose key words, each of which has a price based on its desirability, and put money into an account that is then debited when someone clicks on their advertisement. Smaller advertisers can find their accounts run down quickly and their advertisements are then hidden until they top up their account. It is therefore crucial that advertisers ensure that a reasonable percentage of click throughs on their search engine marketing advertisements are converted to sales.

Google recently extended the Adwords concept to YouTube, a company it purchased in 2006. Advertisers wishing to utilise the 'Promoted videos' facility on YouTube can bid for priority listings related to particular video searches. The advertisements appear when YouTube viewers arrive on particular video pages, and advertisers are charged on a similar cost-per-click basis as that utilised on the advertisements related to Google's search engine.[21]

## Email, SMS and MMS marketing

While spam is an unwelcome and illegal approach to marketing, legitimate email and SMS marketing can be an effective way to build customer relationships. For example, when a business makes a sale, a well-timed follow-up email can help reduce purchase dissonance and can prompt a further purchase. For example, a consumer who has purchased a home theatre system online might welcome an email or SMS text a week later offering a discount on DVDs. In contemporary society, many people carry their mobile phones permanently with them, enabling them to virtually be reached anywhere, anytime. The chances are that an SMS will be read (and perhaps responded to) within minutes of receipt. Mobile phones are also personal items, allowing for direct communication with the intended recipient of messages.

The capabilities of contemporary smartphones also provide additional opportunities for marketers via multimedia message services (MMS). Such messages can contain audio, images and video, as well as text. Brewer Lion Nathan in New Zealand recently ran an MMS campaign whereby for a limited time consumers could receive free Beck's beer at selected bars by registering to receive vouchers to download onto their mobile phones via MMS. The benefit for Lion Nathan was publicity, as well as the creation of a 'Beck's community' (database) for future marketing campaigns. The metrics for the Beck's MMS campaign were impressive. Over six weeks, there were more than 16 700 requests for free beer, and 41 per cent of text coupons were redeemed by consumers within seven days.[22]

## 'Apps'

A phenomenon that has coincided with the increased availability, affordability and consumer uptake of smartphones has been the development of application software (or 'apps') to run on these mobile devices. Within a few years, a bewildering array of 'apps' has become available for consumers to download onto their phones. Some 'apps' are purely entertainment-based, such as games; some are information-based, such as news services; and others still are designed to solve problems and/or improve user productivity. 'Apps' are generally priced cheaply (or are even free in some cases), with software developers hoping to achieve volume sales and/or publicity. Once downloaded, 'apps' appear as visual icons on the user's smartphone — being ready for them to access at any time.

Marketers are increasingly recognising the potential for 'apps' to enable brands to be displayed permanently on consumers' mobile phones. Pizza Hut is an example of an organisation that has embraced the concept. Owners of smartphones can download a free Pizza Hut ordering application that enables them to order and pay for their pizza meal online, for either pick-up or delivery, thereby avoiding queues. Customers can use the 'app' to customise their pizza toppings, and save their favourite menu combinations on their smartphone for 'one click' ordering in the future. The 'app' also helps to locate the direction and distance to their nearest Pizza Hut, no matter where the person with the 'app' on their phone may be located. The ease and convenience of this mobile ordering solution benefits consumers. The benefit for Pizza Hut is constant reinforcement of their brand and logo in consumers' minds, via the visual icon on the user's smartphone. Not to be outdone, Pizza Hut's competitors such as Domino's also offer a similar 'app' for their stores.

## E-commerce

Of course, all of the approaches we have described above are designed to result in a marketing exchange. When the marketing exchange occurs via the internet, mobile phone or other telecommunications technology, it is known as e-commerce. For example, most local council websites allow residents to renew and pay the licence for their pet dog. Online stores such as Cradle Rock, profiled at the start of this chapter, enable customers to examine, order and pay for products online. E-commerce is particularly attractive to small, niche businesses. The web enables them to reach consumers across the globe, potentially making a business viable that would not be able to generate adequate turnover just through local customers.

## Spotlight  The devil in the eTail

Despite the 'dot.com' bubble that spectacularly burst in the late 1990s, there is still a belief by some people that in today's e-business world, all you have to do is create a website and, like the 'better mousetrap', the world will beat a path to your door.

This idealistic view continually amazes web-preneur Tim Nieuwenhuis, who, with Scott Wotherspoon, is managing director of Down Under Guys Gear (www.dugg.com.au). The company was established in 2004 and is now Australia's largest online store for men's underwear, socks, T-shirts and swimwear. He explains that the company's success has been hard earned:

It is not easy to attract people to the website. DUGG, for example, has advertised in print media and on Google Adwords, a newsletter, sales promotions, a loyalty club and is on Facebook. Sometimes it is a case of hit or miss when it comes to which media gets increased traffic and sales. But clearly, if someone doesn't know about a website, they are not going to buy from that site.

DUGG ships its underwear worldwide, and its labels include designer brands Calvin Klein, Bjorn Borg, Lonsdale, Van Heusen, Trent Nathan and Macpherson Men. Orders are normally dispatched the next working day. Australian customers who order over $75 worth of product receive free delivery.

Nieuwenhuis continues:

There are still many similarities between traditional and online retailers. If you want a good position, or web address, it will cost you money. Further, if you want a good domain name, design, development and maintenance, it can cost thousands — even more than renting a store. And like a traditional store, you will have a lot of passing traffic with potential customers having a look, checking prices, even asking questions, and leave without buying anything.[23]

### Questions

1. Identify the electronic marketing methods DUGG currently uses and how it can potentially make best use of these methods.
2. What additional electronic marketing methods could DUGG consider implementing?

# Concepts and applications check

**Learning objective 3** explain specific e-marketing methods

**3.1** Compare and contrast banner advertisements and pop-up advertisements. What are the advantages and disadvantages of each of these forms of online advertising?

**3.2** Provide an example of a product for which a marketer could effectively utilise the capabilities of Web 2.0, and explain how they could do this.

**3.3** Differentiate between search engine optimisation and search engine marketing.

**3.4** Provide examples of e-marketing methods whose popularity has changed over the years, and explain why this has occurred.

**3.5** Visit a website for a newspaper and observe the types of advertising that appear when you click on different pages. Do the advertisements seem related to the topic of the news stories you are viewing? Is it appropriate having so much advertising on a news site? Justify your answer.

# ETHICAL AND LEGAL ISSUES

Just as in the wider field of marketing, e-marketing raises many ethical and legal issues, questions and responsibilities. Some of these need particular attention when related to e-marketing because of:

**Learning objective 4** appreciate ethical and legal issues relating to e-marketing

- the pervasive, always-on nature of modern information and telecommunications technologies
- the personalised and interactive nature of e-marketing
- the international, cross-border nature of modern information and telecommunications technologies
- the failure of laws and international agreements to keep pace with technological change and the innovative use of new technologies.

These particular features are central to the main themes in ethics and law surrounding e-marketing: privacy, misleading or deceptive conduct, spam, intellectual property rights, consumer protection and technology burnout.

## Privacy

One of the main focuses of e-marketing has been gathering information about customers and potential customers for profiling to use in formulating marketing strategy and in delivering optimum marketing experiences to help build and sustain relationships.

Virtually everything an individual does in the online world leaves a digital footprint:

- cookies that send information about what an individual has done on a website they have visited, how long they were there, what site they were on before and which site they went to when they left (people can tell their computers not to accept cookies, but they lose functionality as a result)
- transaction records that detail where and when an individual has used EFTPOS or a credit card to spend money and how much they have spent — and in many cases exactly what they have purchased
- subscribing to or registering for any online (or offline) service requires the provision of a lot of personal information, usually including full name, date of birth, address, email address, phone numbers and often other details such as gender, occupation and income.

For many people, collection of the information itself is not a problem (although privacy advocates oppose it). What most people are concerned with is how the information is used. No-one takes issue with a bank issuing a credit card statement that shows a transaction's time, place and amount. Few people mind that the bank might include an advertising brochure with the statement. Many people, however, are unhappy when they receive marketing approaches from businesses they have no existing connection with. Often such approaches are based on information that can be traced back to some online activity. Many businesses and other organisations now specify what they will and will not do with information collected from customers. For example, consider this extract from Bholu, an online homewares store, www.bholu.com:

> We aim to provide all of our customers with a safe online shopping experience. Our system encodes your credit card and contact details to ensure its safe transfer to us. We respect your privacy and personal information, and will not share it with anyone else. We may use your email address to send our email newsletters and other announcements regarding promotions, new products and special features. Should you wish to be removed from our mailing list at any time, please let us know via email, phone or fax.

Similar statements are published on many other websites.

Visiting a few websites across a range of different types of organisation reveals that the level of detail and the specifics of privacy policies vary considerably (the privacy policy details usually appear as a link at the bottom of the home page). In particular, privacy laws and privacy policies differ across national boundaries. In Australia and New Zealand, the common themes found in most privacy policies relate to the type of personal information that may be collected, the user's right to access that information, whether that information will be used to market products to you, if and how that information will be shared with related and unrelated organisations, and how to contact the organisation should the user need to. In some isolated cases, the security of the records of online organisations has been compromised, resulting in personal details of their customers or clients falling into the hands of others.

A related problem is people misappropriating the identity of others, or 'identity theft'. While this can lead to credit card fraud and other serious crimes, there are also simpler invasions of privacy that can occur, such as someone registering or subscribing to a web service under someone else's identity. To overcome this, many online organisations now require registrants to respond to a confirmation email sent to the nominated address and, for purchases, will not deliver to an address other than the registered residential address.

With the exception of spam laws (discussed later in this section) and the *Privacy Act 1988* (enacted before the widespread public adoption of the internet), there are few laws or rules aimed directly at regulating privacy protection online. However, the Australian Law Reform Commission has recommended a series of updates to the legislation in order to bring it into the internet era, and these proposals are currently being considered by the Australian federal government. Among the recommendations is a steep increase in fines for organisations found to be breaching the privacy of individuals.[24] However, many marketing organisations have now voluntarily curtailed their use of data, in contrast to the loose practices that emerged in the early days of the internet. They have imposed restrictions on themselves in an attempt to not only avoid the imposition of formal regulations, but to avoid the risk of an online consumer campaign against them and all of the associated negative publicity.

# Misleading or deceptive conduct

Just as in the 'real' world, business activities in the online realm are governed by the Competition and Consumer Act in Australia and the Fair Trading Act and the Commerce Act in New Zealand, which prohibit misleading or deceptive conduct. Companies must be honest and truthful in all their business dealings and, if they are not, they are liable to be punished by the law. Specifically, the Competition and Consumer Act, the Fair Trading Act and the Commerce Act prohibit:

- anti-competitive behaviours (such as colluding with competitors on pricing)
- unconscionable conduct
- unsafe products and practices
- some aspects of trade mark infringement
- making false or misleading statements
- misrepresentation of product characteristics.

Unfortunately the internet is used by some people to fraudulently obtain money from others. While some scams are well known, people still regularly get caught. Online fraud has grown to be a multi-million dollar global industry. Common scams include:

- *phishing.* Phishing involves the use of an official-looking email, often purporting to be from a bank, online retailer or credit card company. These emails direct recipients to a website that looks like the real website of a retailer or financial institution and then tries to elicit the visitor's financial details such as credit card numbers, account names and passwords or other personal information.
- *pharmaceutical scams.* Usually distributed by email, these scams offer for sale products that supposedly boost health, appearance or virility.
- *Nigerian scams.* These scams — many of which have originated in the African nation of Nigeria, hence the name — involve an email which asks the target to send money in return for a much larger lump sum being transferred to their bank account at a later date.
- *work-at-home schemes, lottery wins and prizes.* These scams all involve the target making some type of financial 'investment' before being sent money they have 'won'.
- *pump 'n' dump stock scams.* These scams involve creating massive demand for a particular stock and then selling that stock while the price is pumped up.[25]

As people have become more at home online, some of the less sophisticated scams have become ineffective, leading to increasingly sophisticated approaches. One of the outcomes of the long history of online scams, the increasing sophistication of some fraudsters and the regular media coverage of online dangers, is that some consumers have been reluctant to fully engage with businesses and other organisations online, particularly in terms of actually completing a financial transaction. In their most recent report into 'scam' activity, the Australian Competition and Consumer Commission (ACCC) revealed that fraudsters currently swindle a reported $70 million from Australians each year, much of it online. However, the report also revealed that the ACCC estimates the figure would most likely be closer to $1 billion annually, as some consumers are loathe to report becoming victims of fraud due to embarrassment.[26]

# Spam

As most users of email know, the amount of **spam** (unsolicited commercial) email sent and received is mind-boggling — estimated at more than 183 billion messages a day.[27] Spam is a financially attractive way to advertise because millions of emails

**spam** Unsolicited commercial electronic messages.

can be sent for just a few cents. It only takes a few recipients to respond to make the exercise profitable. This is in contrast to more traditional advertising that can cost tens of thousands of dollars and needs to generate significant business to create an acceptable return on the investment.

The impact of spam on individuals (wasted time, invasion of privacy, sometimes exposure to obscene content, usage of paid download allowance), businesses (similar to individuals) and internet service providers (it is common for spammers to hijack the servers of internet service providers and businesses to send spam), however, has prompted the Australian and New Zealand governments to introduce legislation to regulate how commercial electronic messages can be sent. In Australia, the relevant legislation is the *Spam Act 2003*. In New Zealand, it is the Unsolicited Electronic Messages Act 2007, which applies to email, instant messaging, SMS and MMS, but does not apply to fax, pop-up advertising on websites, or telephone telemarketing. While most of us think about spam as specific to email, the legislation in both countries covers most unsolicited commercial electronic messages (except traditional phone and fax).

The key points of each piece of legislation are outlined in figure 12.4.[28]

**SPAM ACT 2003 (AUSTRALIA)**
- Commercial electronic messages should only be sent with the recipient's consent (whether explicit or inferred from the fact they are an existing customer).
- Commercial electronic messages must include information about who sent the message.
- Commercial electronic messages must include an unsubscribe facility.

**UNSOLICITED ELECTRONIC MESSAGES ACT 2007 (NEW ZEALAND)**
- It is illegal to send spam to and from New Zealand and within New Zealand.
- Commercial electronic messages must include details of who sent the message.
- Commercial electronic messages must include an unsubscribe facility by which the recipient may opt out of future messages.
- It is illegal to use software to 'harvest' email addresses to create lists for targeting with spam.
- In principle, people should not misuse information and communications technology.
- In principle, businesses should only send commercial electronic messages to customers and others who have consented to receive it.

**FIGURE 12.4**

Regulation of spam

In a bid to encourage compliance with the Spam Act and to ensure that e-marketing does not attract extensive and restrictive regulation, the Australian Direct Marketing Association has developed the eMarketing Code of Practice[29] to govern the e-marketing efforts of its members. This Code of Practice as it applies to mobile e-marketing is discussed in more detail in the next Spotlight feature later in the chapter.

Governments and industry bodies have also recommended consumers take steps to protect themselves from spam, including simple measures such as:
- protecting email addresses and mobile phone numbers online
- deleting suspicious emails without opening or replying to them
- reading the terms and conditions attached to any online offer or service
- using spam filtering software
- implementing appropriate security measures to ensure that spammers cannot hijack a personal or business computer to send spam
- using internet resources designed to protect children and young people online
- learning more about email scams and fraud.[30]

# Intellectual property

Intellectual property theft has long been a crime in most Western countries. It has also been one of the more difficult areas of the law to enforce, but modern information and communication technologies have greatly increased the problem. For example, it has always been illegal to copy movies. However, it has also always been very simple to do so by merely hooking two video recorders together, or more recently copying DVD files to computer and burning back to DVD. Pirated movies represent an enormous industry, particularly in parts of Asia. The anonymous interconnected nature of the internet has increased the problem a thousandfold. Now high-quality digital copies of films can be posted online for all to download. This has significant ramifications for the rightful copyright owners, as it denies them sales. The same principle applies to music and text. While many people who download copies of music, movies, software or books do not see themselves as criminals, they are actually committing a crime, with potential to be punished with very large fines and imprisonment.

Of broader relevance to business is the potential theft of intellectual property assets such as trade marks or the misuse of trade marks. Online, it is quite simple to copy logos, designs and other corporate branding materials and essentially recreate an online facsimile of a real business.

A practice that was common in the earlier days of the internet was for someone to buy a domain name that closely relates to an existing business and then force the business to pay huge sums of money to buy the domain name. Litigation has since made this more difficult to do. A number of celebrities have also been forced to litigate or pay to buy their own names online. One of the highest profile examples was Madonna, who sued to gain control of the madonna.com domain. Julia Roberts has also been involved in such litigation. Corporations that have litigated to take over domains from 'cybersquatters' include Christian Dior, Deutsche Bank, Microsoft, Nike and Australia's own Southcorp Wines. Southcorp took legal action against a cybersquatter who had registered a domain in the name of the wine group's Lindemans brand and then tried to sell it to Southcorp.[31]

Pirated movies are a serious problem that authorities are trying to get under control, particularly in some parts of Asia. Intellectual property breaches can also involve the misuse of trade marks and the theft of such assets.

# Consumer protection

Despite some relatively clear ethical guidelines for businesses and, increasingly, laws aimed at regulating online behaviour, consumers are well served by taking their own steps to manage their online experience. The simplest yet most effective methods consumers can take to protect themselves online include:

- use a secondary email address (such as Gmail or Hotmail) when registering for online services
- install anti-virus software and keep it up to date
- install a firewall
- use email filters to automatically delete spam (junk emails)
- never respond to unsolicited email messages
- never give personal details, particularly banking information, to strangers online

- read the privacy policy of any organisation you deal with online
- use information and communication technologies appropriately and moderately.

## Technology burnout

An interesting counter-trend has emerged in the aftermath of the technological revolution in recent times — that of professionals seeking to literally 'switch off' or 'unplug'. The incredible business and personal adoption of technologies such as laptop computers, BlackBerry devices, mobile phones and mobile internet has led to a situation in which many people feel they cannot have time to themselves. Those working 9 to 5 (or perhaps longer — 8 to late) suddenly found they would be reading and replying to work emails from their bedroom at midnight or from an island beach during their summer holidays with their family — connected to work (and other commitments) virtually 24 hours a day, 7 days a week. As individuals and organisations increasingly began to realise the damage this was doing to wellbeing, a move began to encourage people to take time out from technology; to ensure their holidays were holidays; and to make time with their families.[32]

## Legal enforcement

There can be significant legal consequences for organisations and individuals that breach laws related to their conduct online. These include fines that can run into the hundreds of thousands of dollars as well as significant prison time for officeholders within organisations. The borderless, international nature of the online world, however, makes it complicated to determine which laws apply and who can or should enforce them. This has resulted in some interesting defamation suits, including the case Dow Jones & Company Inc v Gutnick [2002] HCA 56. In this case, mining magnate Joe Gutnick claimed that an article published in the US magazine *Barron's* defamed him. He began proceedings against the US publisher Dow Jones & Company Inc in a Victorian court, arguing that he had been defamed in Victoria because a number of Victorian residents subscribed to the internet version of *Barron's*. The publisher argued that the article was published in the United States (its website is hosted on servers in New Jersey). The court had to decide whether it had jurisdiction to hear the case and which law should be applied. The court decided that it could hear the case because the article was in fact 'published' in Victoria whenever it was downloaded and read.

The matter of jurisdiction has also led to some complex international business arrangements in the online gambling industry, as well as some inconsistencies of approach. For example, Australia's *Interactive Gambling Act 2001* makes it illegal to provide an interactive gambling service to someone in Australia, but it is not illegal for someone in Australia to gamble online. Gambling in that sense refers to traditional casino games such as poker. By contrast, gambling on sport events is legal with high-profile sports gambling operations Centrebet and Sportingbet licensed by the government. Centrebet's business arrangements hint at the complexity of online law and how businesses use them to establish the best possible organisational structure. Centrebet is an Australian company licensed to operate betting operations under Northern Territory law. To comply with the various laws of different countries, Centrebet:
- offers sport and horse-race betting through a licensed Australian bookmaker
- offers sport and horse-race betting through a licensed UK bookmaker
- operates gaming services through a licensed Netherlands Antilles company
- prohibits access to online gaming (poker and casino games) to residents of Australia, Netherlands Antilles, Estonia, Israel, Cyprus and Antigua and Barbuda
- prohibits access to all sites and services to people from the United States and Turkey.[33]

# Mobile marketing code of practice

The Australian Direct Marketing Association (ADMA) is a national non-profit organisation that was founded in 1966. It provides numerous benefits for its nearly 500 member organisations, including advocacy on collective issues facing direct marketers (i.e. those promoting or selling products via the mail, telephone or the web), educational seminars and events. A condition of ADMA membership is that organisations must comply with the ADMA Code of Practice relating to direct marketing activities. According to ADMA, its Code of Practice was developed 'to set standards of conduct for direct marketers, minimise the risk of breaching legislation, promote a culture of best practice, serve as a benchmark in settling disputes and increase business and consumer confidence in doing business with ADMA members who are bound to the provisions of the Code'.

Over the years, the ADMA Code of Practice has had to be revised as new technologies and capabilities have emerged that have further facilitated the potential for direct marketing activities (such as email, e-commerce and mobile phones). One of the most significant recent updates was the incorporation into the Code of a set of standards relating to mobile marketing (i.e. marketing via mobile wireless technology, such as sending messages via SMS and MMS).

Many of the provisions relating to mobile marketing in ADMA's Code of Practice are similar to those for other more traditional forms of direct marketing, and are aimed at helping to reduce the incidence of consumer complaint over unsolicited and unwanted contacts. The Code restricts the sending of messages to a consumer unless the following conditions apply:

- The recipient has requested the message or has an established business/ contractual relationship with the marketer.
- The recipient has provided the marketer with prior consent to send such marketing messages.

The Code also notes that:

- Anyone marketing their products or services via SMS is required to include symbols or text which allows the recipient to easily identify the advertiser, and a contact number to opt out of receiving further messages.[34]

## Question

Imagine you are the marketing manager for an organisation/product of your own choosing that would potentially be suited to a mobile marketing campaign. Broadly describe what this mobile campaign would be, including its target audience and how it would be implemented to ensure it was compliant with the key provisions of the ADMA Code that has been outlined.

## Concepts and applications check

**Learning objective 4**  appreciate ethical and legal issues relating to e-marketing

4.1  Compare and contrast privacy issues in relation to e-marketing with those in the traditional marketing environment.

4.2  Describe some measures an organisation can take to enhance consumer privacy in an e-marketing environment.

4.3  How is the legal enforcement of business laws made more complicated in an electronic environment?

4.4  One of the most popular websites for selling is the online auction site eBay. Visit the eBay site and analyse what measures they use to ensure ethical behaviour, as well as their legal warnings.

# ELECTRONIC MARKETING AND MARKETING STRATEGY

**Learning objective 5** discuss the role of e-marketing in an overall marketing strategy

An organisation's marketing strategy should be a cohesive whole designed to achieve the organisation's overall goals. While we are looking specifically at e-marketing approaches in this chapter, any e-marketing strategy will be part of — and consistent with — a broader organisational marketing strategy. It will come as no surprise then that many of the issues to be considered in an e-marketing strategy are the same as those considered in formulating the overall marketing strategy and marketing plan. In this section we will examine target markets, customer relationship management, the marketing mix and evaluating effectiveness, as well as briefly overview electronic business.

## Target markets

Just as in the physical world, the total of online users can be divided into different segments or niches based on particular characteristics. As discussed earlier in the chapter, the potential for gathering information about potential customers in the online environment can provide the marketing organisation with a powerful tool with which to identify and profile target markets.

Identifying target markets is an important step. Organisations should generally avoid assuming that all online users are their target market. In the early days of the web, particular types of people were more likely to be online (i.e. male, professional, relatively young), but today the online community is extremely diverse. Over one-third of Australians who have access to the internet have made online purchases, with many more doing research online prior to making a purchase at a physical store. In New Zealand, almost half (45 per cent) of internet users make regular online purchases. According to one study, people who shop online are more likely to be high-income earners who prefer quality over bargains.[35]

The pull nature of online marketing means some of the target market will actively seek out the marketing organisation, but this is not a sufficient plan in itself. The organisation must generate awareness of its existence and its offerings.

## Customer relationship management

The earlier parts of the chapter have examined how the online marketing environment provides marketing organisations with many opportunities to gather extensive data on individuals and how the online experience for customers and potential customers can be tailored to make use of that knowledge and so deliver the best possible product offering. This of course is part of the broader approach of 'customer relationship management', which we have discussed from time to time through this book.

**customer relationship management (CRM)**
The processes and practices put in place to identify, track and use customer information and preferences to provide superior customer service and sustain long-term relationships.

In e-marketing, **customer relationship management (CRM)** focuses on using information about customers to produce e-marketing experiences that create, build and sustain long-term relationships. As discussed earlier, the online environment provides the opportunity to address customer needs at the individual level, which is the concept at the heart of CRM. When done well, CRM can build strong customer loyalty, lead to positive word-of-mouth, and create in the customer a sense that it will be difficult or costly for them to change to another provider.

Marketing organisations need to be aware that the public is becoming more aware of customer relationship technologies and approaches, and that individuals have simultaneously developed a degree of cynicism about them *and* a high level of expectation about what the organisation should already know about them. Unfortunately, many CRM software packages suffer from clumsy interfaces and numerous screens. It is all too easy to overlook notes and information that has been recorded earlier when dealing with a customer, which is likely to lead to frustration — just the opposite of what a CRM system is intended to do. The tool is merely there to record and present information and make it available to whomever in the organisation is dealing with the customer — it parallels the long-term personal relationship and knowledge that would once have been built between a customer and a salesperson.

Another pitfall of CRM tools is the tendency for organisations to over-rely on them. Some organisations can fall in to the trap of expecting customers to serve themselves based on interactions with the organisation's technology.

## The marketing mix

Developing a marketing mix for the online environment is based on the same principles as developing the overall marketing mix, but the specific details and approaches can be quite different. The following sections look at various marketing mix considerations.

### Product

Some products have characteristics that better lend themselves to online purchase than others. Those that can be completely digitalised are particularly attractive propositions, followed by products that can be partly digitalised. Products that cannot be digitalised may seem inappropriate for online purchase, but this is not necessarily so. While it may be difficult to promote and impossible to deliver such a product online (e.g. a haircut or a car tyre), some aspects of the transaction can still be undertaken online. For example, a person may be able to book a haircut appointment online and a trucking company may be able to order 100 tyres from their supplier using an extranet. In fact, at present, business-to-business transactions make up the vast majority of online purchases.

The most popularly purchased consumer products bought online are airline and concert tickets, books/magazines and clothing/shoes/accessories, as well as technology-related products, such as computers and downloadable products (e.g. software, ringtones, MP3s, MPEG4s). Some online products are actually a result of the online environment itself. For example, various internet service providers and other technology businesses offer online services such as secure, backed-up data storage and 'cloud' computing services that enable customers to synchronise their mobile phones, iPods, laptops, home computers and other devices. BigPond offers such a service to its web customers and Apple offers a similar MobileMe service for subscribers.

### Pricing

As mentioned earlier, the online environment enables consumers to easily compare the offerings of numerous online businesses. One particular feature that can be compared is price. In fact, many websites have been developed that aggregate prices from other sites, enabling potential customers to identify the cheapest vendor without needing to do any actual comparison work themselves. Combined with the fact that the purchase and delivery experience can be very similar — even indistinguishable — between competing online vendors, online marketers must find ways to offer more value, rather than necessarily engaging in a price war.

Additionally, as discussed in chapter 10, online vendors need to ensure that the prices they offer online are consistent with the prices offered in their physical stores. More expensive prices online (or additional costs due to delivery) or more expensive prices in-store will both lead to confusion or annoyance among customers.[36]

### Promotion

The amount of information on the internet has empowered consumers with more product and price knowledge than ever before. A couple of decades ago, a business like bookseller Dymocks only really had to worry about the offerings of their competitor in the same or surrounding suburbs — perhaps an ABC or Angus and Robertson store. Today, a regional Dymocks store is competing with businesses all over the world, including the formidable Amazon.com. It is not uncommon for bookstore customers to tell bookstore staff that they can get books from Amazon faster than the bookstore can get them in from their suppliers. So while the internet provides opportunities for promotion, those opportunities are also available to all competitors. The challenge for the marketer is to offer a better value proposition than competitors. Many businesses perform an environment scan (an examination and analysis of online competitors) to inform them better about the offerings of competitors in the online realm.

The pull nature of online marketing suggests that website visitors have an existing interest in the product — otherwise they would not be on the website. Their interest in the website may have been generated by search results, word-of-mouth, or a URL printed in some other medium (e.g. in a print advertisement, a television advertisement or on product packaging). Some of the more innovative television advertisements include links to websites (for viewers with interactive television devices such as TiVo). These, for example, enable television viewers to go to the Domino's Pizza website to order a pizza in response to a television advertisement. Similar features are being built into Blu-ray discs, enabling movie watchers to engage with the story online, beyond the actual movie presentation.

### Distribution (place)

The internet and other telecommunications technologies, such as mobile phones, can themselves act as a distribution platform. For example, a ringtone is delivered via the mobile phone network to the mobile phone device. Another example is the downloading of software directly to the user's computer rather than the user purchasing a software package on a boxed set of disks.

The ability of the internet to transfer data in real time between individuals and organisations has led to greater efficiencies in distribution. For example, a customer can place an order on a website, knowing that it is in stock, be given an estimated (or guaranteed, depending on the vendor) delivery date, and so on. The organisation itself can have systems in place that automatically order a freight delivery company in response to an online order and trigger their suppliers to send more stock. The customer can track the progress of their order online and the organisation can follow up with the customer after delivery via email.

One important challenge for online businesses is to control the cost of delivery. Most online stores display a sale price. Some include delivery in that price, whereas others add a delivery fee. The need to send the product to the customer (as opposed to many retail arrangements where the customer collects the product) can create pricing disadvantages. On the other hand, savings should be made in inventory management and holding costs.

## Evaluating e-marketing effectiveness

Practitioners actively engaged in e-marketing know that it is notoriously difficult to measure the effectiveness of e-marketing campaigns. There are some technical tools that do offer very specific data on the success of some types of online activities, but many of the difficulties experienced in evaluating 'real world' marketing also apply online. It can also be difficult to decide exactly what success is. For example, it has been found that one in two Australians plan their holidays online, but less than one in seven then books and pays for the holiday online.[37] Should the travel agent consider that a success? It depends on whether the agent the customer books through is the same one they used to plan their trip.

Some online marketing efforts are much easier to evaluate. For example, websites that offer an e-commerce facility get direct feedback through purchase volumes. Big Brown Box, for instance, is a subsidiary of Radio Rentals that wanted to expand its operations to include selling online. With an advertising campaign and viral competition, the new online store established a solid brand identity quickly and in its first year the site attracted in excess of 800 000 visits.[38] Another online success story is Old Spice's 'The Man Your Man Could Smell Like' campaign in the United States that became a worldwide sensation. It has been reported that on the first day of the campaign it received almost 6 million views; by day three it had over 20 million views; and over the first six months, sales had increased by 27 per cent.[39]

Online advertising is one area that offers further potential for marketers to assess effectiveness. If a customer visits a store after seeing a newspaper or television advertisement for the store, the business may never know that it was the advertisement that prompted the store visit. Online, however, as discussed earlier in the chapter, the consumer will 'visit the store' by clicking on the advertisement. Hence, there is direct feedback as to the effectiveness of the advertisement. The business may never know how many people ignored the advertisement, but they will know exactly how many people clicked on it (and, therefore, click-through rate) and exactly how many people went on to complete a transaction (conversion rate). Deciding on a particular metric that quantifies as aspect of marketing performance can be invaluable information for the online marketer to know how successful a marketing activity is. For example, if an online promotion can generate a high click-through rate and conversion rate, the marketer may continue with similar promotions. However, if there is a high click-through rate but also a low number of unique visitors or conversion rate, or a high customer acquisition cost, then the marketer may reconsider such an activity and try something more effective. Table 12.1[40] provides an overview of some of the metrics commonly used by marketers to evaluate the effectiveness of online marketing campaigns, particularly online advertising.

**TABLE 12.1** Online advertising marketing metrics

| Metric | Description |
| --- | --- |
| Cost per thousand views | The cost of an online advertisement in terms of how many thousands of people see it. |
| | The cost is known and the number of people visiting a web page on which the advertisement appears is easy to measure. It is impossible, however, to know how many of those visitors saw or paid attention to the advertisement. |
| Click-through rate | The percentage of people who visited a web page on which the advertisement appears that actually clicked on the advertisement. |
| | This can be accurately measured and can give an indication of the effectiveness of an advertisement relative to other advertisements. It is still impossible to tell how many people who visited the web page actually saw the advertisement. |
| Cost per click | This is determined by dividing the total cost by the total number of people who click through. |

*(continued)*

**TABLE 12.1** (continued)

| Metric | Description |
|---|---|
| Conversion rate | This is determined by how many people who clicked through actually completed a marketing transaction. This is the most effective marketing metric in determining the overall outcomes of the advertisement, but does not necessarily allow us to determine why the marketing effort was successful for each customer. |
| Customer acquisition cost | This is the cost associated with acquiring a new customer. It can be calculated by dividing the total acquisition expenses by the total of new customers. |
| Unique visitors | This is the number of individuals who have visited the website at least once over a given period of time. Calculations can be based on the IP address and viewed over a 30-day period, or during the campaign. |

The interactive nature of the online environment also offers opportunities for detailed qualitative information from consumers. Feedback forms, chat services, forums and online communities all encourage consumers to communicate directly with the business. Marketing organisations are also well advised to look beyond their own online presence. There is a proliferation of online communities dedicated to consumer reviews and these can provide valuable information and feedback to businesses.

# Electronic business

The focus of this textbook is marketing, rather than the broader topic of business, but, as we have stressed throughout this textbook, marketing is all about creating maximum customer value. We will therefore devote a little space to discussing some aspects of electronic business that can help the organisation's overall service delivery.

## Supply chain management

Technology plays a crucial role in managing the supply chain (the process of getting raw materials made into products and then getting them to the retailer and the consumer). Because the web provides comprehensive, secure and real-time data exchange (known as electronic data interchange, or EDI), organisations can remain connected with partners, ensuring stock is managed in real time. Well set up supply chain management systems can remove many manual tasks involved in managing inventory levels. They can also monitor and confirm dispatch processes. For example, if a customer purchases a product from Apple's online store, they are sent a confirmation email which includes a link to freight company TNT Express's parcel tracking site, and they can watch the progress of their goods (e.g. notification of pick-up, arrived at distribution centre, arrived at destination city, on board van for delivery, delivered in full).

Another example of supply chain management is when a salesperson at a Bay Leather Republic furniture store uses an intranet to access stock levels in the company's Sydney warehouse to let the customer know when their desired stock will be available in the local store or delivered to their residence. This is a simple system, almost universally used in businesses with multiple outlets.

Businesses that make extensive use of barcode scanning can build stock management into their checkout procedures. For example, when a checkout operator scans the barcode on a jar of Vegemite, not only does the price add to the customer's bill, the stock record for that particular sized jar of Vegemite is reduced by one. An automated process such as this can help ensure stock is managed correctly, without the need for a manual stocktake, and can help inventory managers identify purchase patterns (from the obvious, such as selling more ice cream in summer, to the obscure, such as selling more pork sausages on Thursdays).

## Intranets and extranets

Just as the web offers consumers many opportunities to access information, it can be used to provide information to (and gather information from) members of the marketing organisation. For example, many organisations maintain an **intranet** that hosts detailed product information, training materials and an online community for staff members.

Many organisations also have extranets, which are private networks among a number of member organisations. For example, a furniture retailer may be part of an **extranet** with a trucking company so the two businesses can share information on deliveries.

**intranet** An internal website for the use of staff.

**extranet** A private website for sharing information securely between different organisations.

## The virtual organisation

A further consequence is that virtual organisations can come together easily and cheaply. Whereas traditionally many organisations kept many functions within the organisation, telecommunications technologies and the internet have enabled organisations to come together based on skills to complete a particular task or project and then dissolve again. It has become cheaper and more efficient to bring together specialist teams or individuals than to maintain different functional areas within one organisation.

# Hidden Pizza

A new restaurant needs publicity to get its name out into the marketplace. A new pizza restaurant that launched in Melbourne managed to do this with no traditional advertising or promotion. Instead, it created a lot of 'buzz' in the social media scene, which resulted in a lot of online chatter, word-of-mouth, and big lines stretching down the street within days of it opening. In a unique experiment, the location of the restaurant was largely kept a secret, but the pizzas were free (!) and the restaurant was only open for two weeks. This is what happened with the 'Hidden Pizza' restaurant, a creative promotion run by the Yellow Pages directory service.

Clearly, 'Hidden Pizza' was not like every other restaurant. It was a central part of a campaign to 'highlight the value of Yellow Pages to small businesses'. Yellow Pages derives revenue via attracting businesses to advertise their products and services in its print and online directories. The challenge for people in the 'Hidden Pizza' campaign was to find the phone number of the restaurant in order to be able to call, find out its location and visit to get free pizza. The only place the phone number and address of the 'Hidden Pizza' restaurant was officially published was on the Yellow Pages website.

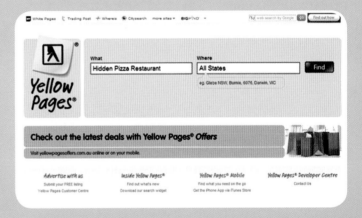

Metrics for the campaign were very favourable for the Yellow Pages. During the two weeks of the promotion, the 'Hidden Pizza' restaurant received over 8000 calls. Each caller was asked where they had found the restaurant's phone number, and the results were as follows:

- 6079 callers found the number online via the Yellow Pages website (more than 70 per cent)
- 2167 callers found the number in other ways (word-of-mouth, email, blogs, texts and so on).

To maintain the integrity of the 'Hidden Pizza' promotional experiment, Yellow Pages hid any involvement with the restaurant while the campaign was operating. This ensured that the campaign metrics were not compromised.

During the two weeks the restaurant was operational, pictures and video footage were taken in-store. This material was then featured in the next phase of the Yellow Pages campaign. After the restaurant closed, a follow-up campaign using both traditional and online media was launched to highlight the effectiveness of the Yellow Pages in promoting the 'Hidden Pizza' restaurant.[41]

## Concepts and applications check

**Learning objective 5** discuss the role of e-marketing in an overall marketing strategy

5.1 Briefly outline the major considerations in developing an e-marketing strategy, and how an e-marketing strategy should relate to an organisation's overall marketing strategy.

5.2 Describe the type of products most suited to online purchase.

5.3 Explain how e-marketing activities can facilitate customer relationship management and the potential benefits for both marketers and customers.

5.4 Several CRM software packages are available to help companies interface with their customers. Do a search for 'CRM software' and analyse what the companies have on offer. As a marketer, what elements would encourage you to purchase a particular package?

5.5 Describe some ways in which the effectiveness of e-marketing activities can be measured and evaluated.

5.6 Provide examples of how marketers can utilise supply chain technology to create customer value and enhance service delivery.

# SUMMARY

 **Learning objective 1** identify electronic marketing activities

Electronic marketing (e-marketing) refers to all of the activities involved in planning and implementing marketing in the electronic environment, including the internet and web, mobile phones and other information and telecommunications technologies. Examples of e-marketing include the sale of products or providing marketing information via a website, texting and email. A key consumer advantage is convenience: they are not limited by the usual store opening hours, the location of the store or having to wait while other customers are served. Among the disadvantages are the inability to physically examine the product before making the purchase and the risk of credit card fraud. Marketing organisations are potentially exposed to much greater competition online, but they also have access to the entire global market. E-marketing allows consumers to interact deeply with the marketing organisation without the need for dealing with an actual person.

 **Learning objective 2** explain the unique characteristics of e-marketing

A number of key characteristics of e-marketing differentiate it from other forms of marketing: profiling, interactivity and community, control, accessibility and comparability, and digitalisation. Profiling is the process of getting to know about potential customers before they make a purchase and to find out more about existing customers. Interaction is the ongoing exchange of information between marketer and customer (or potential customer); an online community provides a virtual meeting place for customers and potential customers. Control is the ability of the customer to determine how they interact with the marketing message and to influence the presentation and content of the marketing message. Accessibility is shown by the web providing individuals with information 24/7, while comparability means that access to a variety of websites enables the individual to compare products, brands, and options, and seek the opinions of others. Digitalisation is the ability to deliver a product as information or to present information about a product digitally.

 **Learning objective 3** explain specific e-marketing methods

A popular e-marketing approach is online advertising, which includes banner advertisements appearing on websites and pop-up advertisements that open in a new web browser window. Brochure sites are websites that are essentially an online advertisement for the organisation which present product and contact details, but offer little other functionality. Web 2.0 describes the various technologies and experiences that involve online communities where members contribute to and build the community and content, and where users can substantially control their own online experience through customisation and interactivity. Viral marketing is the use of social networks to spread a marketing message from one person to another. A web portal is designed to act as a gateway to other related sites. Search engine optimisation (SEO) means tailoring certain features of a website to achieve the best possible ranking in search results returned by a search engine. Search engine marketing is paid advertising that appears similarly to a search result on a search engine page. E-commerce involves marketing exchanges that take place online.

 **Learning objective 4** appreciate ethical and legal issues relating to e-marketing

E-marketing raises many ethical and legal issues due to the pervasive nature of telecommunications technologies, the personalised and interactive nature of

## Key terms and concepts

customer relationship management (CRM) 444
digitalisation 427
electronic marketing 421
extranet 449
interaction 425
intranet 449
portal 433
profiling 424
pull advertising 426
push advertising 426
search engine marketing 434
search engine optimisation (SEO) 433
spam 439
viral marketing 432
Web 2.0 431

e-marketing, the international, cross-border nature of telecommunications, and the failure of laws and international agreements to keep pace with technological change and the innovative use of new technologies. The main themes in ethics and law surrounding e-marketing are privacy, misleading or deceptive conduct, spam, intellectual property rights, consumer protection and technology burnout.

 **Learning objective 5** discuss the role of e-marketing in an overall marketing strategy

An organisation's marketing strategy should be a cohesive whole designed to achieve the organisation's overall goals. Therefore, any e-marketing strategy will be part of, and consistent with, a broader organisational marketing strategy. Many of the issues to be considered in an e-marketing strategy are the same as those considered in formulating the overall marketing strategy and marketing plan. In formulating an e-marketing strategy, consideration must be given to how e-activities affect target markets, the marketing mix (product, price, promotion, distribution), and evaluating campaign effectiveness. In particular, customer relationship management (CRM) focuses on using information about customers to produce e-marketing experiences that create, build and sustain long-term relationships.

# Tiger Beer — online and standing out from the crowd

While there are many brands competing in the highly competitive international beer market, Tiger Beer, a key brand of the Singapore based Asia-Pacific Breweries, has been very successful in building its market share worldwide over many decades. First brewed in 1932, it is now sold in more than 60 countries worldwide, including in Australia, New Zealand, Europe, the United States, Canada and Latin America. Tiger Beer's original slogan, 'It's time for a Tiger', was used for many years; however, in recent times, Tiger has been involved in a number of innovative and award-winning campaigns. One of the most interesting campaigns was by Tiger Beer in Malaysia, where the brand is produced and marketed under license by Guinness Anchor Berhad (GAB). The campaign combined traditional and online social media, and was called 'Stand out with Tiger Beer'.

Like many beer markets around the world, the Malaysian market is over-saturated and highly competitive, with opposition brands offering relatively generic products. Big budget marketing efforts focusing on branding and sponsorships of sporting and music events are common. However, there are restrictions that prohibit alcohol advertising on broadcast media (television and radio), but not print.

There are many global beer brands in Malaysia with no unique positioning. Tiger Beer faced a challenge in differentiating itself from the clutter. They needed a campaign that would enable them to connect with consumers on a deeper level. Its target audience is 21–30 year olds.

Market research conducted in Malaysia revealed that most consumers are not particularly loyal to beer brands, with most readily switching between the different varieties available. However, the research did identify a need that Tiger's target audience wanted to consume and be associated with 'cool' and trendy brands and products that offer them a differentiated image. The challenge for the Tiger Beer brand in Malaysia was to position itself so as to 'stand out' as a unique, 'cool' and contemporary beer for these young adults.

In response to this market research, Tiger Beer came up with a three-phase positioning plan to allow their target market to 'stand out with Tiger Beer'. The campaign involved innovative packaging as well as promotions via social and traditional media.

A 'cool' limited-edition bottle design was pivotal to phase one of Tiger Beer's positioning plan for its brand.

## Phase 1: Producing limited-edition Tiger Beer bottles

To excite their target market, Tiger launched three different limited-edition designer bottles based on elements from internationally acclaimed artists. Both the bottles themselves and their labels were more stylised and artistic than any of their competitors. These unique, 'cool' and contemporary designs allowed Tiger Beer bottles to stand out from the typical green glass bottles in the Malaysian beer market.

## Phase 2: Establishing a community platform

The next phase aimed to promote the repackaged product in the digital social space appropriate for their target market. To do this a community platform was established on Facebook (www.facebook.com/tigerbeer) for 'fans' to congregate and interact, both with the Tiger brand and each other. A community of over 18 000 people grew in just two months — one of the fastest growing online communities ever in Malaysia. Via a 'mystery photographer' program, members of this Facebook community were encouraged to post photos on the site, showing themselves and their friends in social situations enjoying Tiger Beer from the special limited edition bottles. This generated a lot of site traffic and comments among the target audience, who were also regularly given notifications on Tiger Beer promotional activities that were occurring.

This online promotion was supported by traditional media advertising in the nation's top English and Chinese daily newspapers (*The Star* and the *Sinchew*) and in lifestyle magazines (e.g. *JUICE, Mint, Clive*). The advertisements invited people to join Tiger Beer's Malaysian Facebook community. Web banner advertisements were also placed on Facebook and on MSN's Hotmail and Messenger services.

### Phase 3: Partnering with bloggers

Phase 3 saw Tiger partner with Nuffnang (Malaysia's largest online blog advertising company) to organise and promote a 'Stand out' party. Announcements were made through emails and advertisements on the blog sites of key opinion leaders, in order to generate awareness of the forthcoming Tiger party. A blog-based contest was launched titled, 'Tell us on your blog, why you're a STAND OUT in life with Tiger Beer'.

The party was very appealing to Tiger Beer's identified target market, and was hosted by Malaysian celebrity artists Liang and Jojo. Blogger attendees were asked to come to the party dressed in a costume that would make them 'Stand out'. The night was well attended, with the best dressed for 'Stand out' King and Queen being crowned and pictures of the winners and other partygoers subsequently uploaded onto Facebook — further driving site traffic.

After the party, Tiger Beer benefited with substantial coverage of the festivities on blogs, Facebook profiles and Twitter accounts. It is estimated that the party generated public relations worth approximately US$150 000. Party pictures were posted on Flickr and Twitpic and videos were uploaded to YouTube. The hype from the event also carried over to mainstream news sites (e.g. *The Star Online*), key web portals and leading national dailies and lifestyle magazines in Malaysia.

The 'Stand out with Tiger Beer' campaign was extremely effective. Subsequent analysis revealed the following key metrics:
- Facebook fan page — recruited over 18 000 'fans' within two months
- banner advertisements placed on websites — click-through rate 0.22 per cent (just over one in five viewers)
- print and magazine advertisements — reached 74.78 per cent of the target market.

A subsequent survey revealed that Tiger Beer's brand image among its target market had been reinforced as being 'cool', modern and contemporary across five key tracking scores:
1. Tiger Beer is the right drink with friends — plus 3 per cent
2. Tiger Beer is young & trendy — plus 7 per cent
3. Tiger Beer is for people like me — plus 8 per cent
4. Tiger Beer is for good times and fun — plus 14 per cent
5. my friends approve of Tiger Beer — plus 12 per cent.

Most importantly for the Tiger Beer brand, the survey revealed that brand loyalty among their target audience had increased by 6.25 per cent and consumption by 6 per cent.

Not only was the 'Stand out with Tiger Beer campaign' effective in the marketplace, but it also won a number of awards, including an 'Effie' in 2009 (an international award recognising the effectiveness of marketing communications), and an Asian Marketing Effectiveness Award in 2010 for its product design and packaging.

Asia is not the only market for Tiger Beer's innovative marketing activities. It also recently ran a 'Know the not known' campaign in the United Kingdom. This campaign again had a Facebook page at its core (www.facebook.com/tigerbeeruk), and was supported by an iPhone 'app', a Twitter feed and a YouTube channel. Clearly, Tiger Beer views online promotion and the use of social media as an important way to contact and build a relationship with their target audience.[42]

## Questions

1. How has the use of online media changed how companies such as Tiger Beer can communicate effectively to their target audience?
2. Discuss the Tiger Beer campaign in Malaysia and the use of web tools. What are the advantages of using Facebook, YouTube, and blogs to connect with a target audience?
3. How can Web 2.0 tools potentially be used for future marketing campaigns?

## Advanced activity

Now that you have read this chapter, look back at the Cradle Rock case and think about all the issues that relate to the concept of e-marketing. What issues should Cradle Rock take into account in determining an e-marketing strategy and what e-marketing methods could the company consider implementing? How can they develop an integrated marketing campaign for both their online and physical retail store?

## Marketing plan activity

For your marketing plan, think about how the electronic environment will affect how you market your product to your target audience. Go back through the elements that relate to your marketing strategy and think about what will be influenced by an e-marketing strategy. How could the electronic environment affect decisions on the target market, the marketing mix and campaign evaluation? Once you have thought about these questions, add to the relevant sections in the marketing plan.

A sample marketing plan has been included at the back of this book (see page 523) to give you an idea where this information fits in an overall marketing plan.

## CHAPTER 13

# International marketing

## Learning objectives

After studying this chapter, you should be able to:

 understand the concept of 'globalisation' and its consequences for organisations seeking to engage in international marketing

 discuss the political, economic, sociocultural, technological and legal forces at play in international markets

 understand why and how organisations internationalise

 explain how marketers create, communicate and deliver a product of value in an international market.

# Boosting sales

Fruit juice queen Janine Allis still has to pinch herself when she contemplates her success. Boost was one of the first Australian franchises to recognise the demand for healthy fast food and drinks. While accompanying her husband Jeff on a trip to the United States, Janine Allis saw a hole in the Australian market for a healthy fast food alternative. As a consumer, she had always struggled to find anything healthy to eat and drink when she was short on time, particularly for her children. Upon returning to Australia, Janine developed a business plan and raised $250 000 to get her venture underway. She consulted with nutritionists and naturopaths to create a menu of healthy juices and smoothies that were free of preservatives, artificial flavours and colours. She is passionate about creating products that are as healthy as possible, and continues to research new ways to make the products better.

The first store opened in Adelaide in 2000, selling a broad range of fruit juices, smoothies and drink supplements. Since launching the initial store, Janine and her husband have expanded nationally and internationally. Today Boost Juices are sold in more than 180 stores throughout Australia and in several other countries throughout the world — including Chile, Kuwait, Indonesia, South Africa, Portugal, the United Kingdom, Singapore, Hong Kong, Macau and Estonia. The company has a multi-million dollar turnover. However, international expansion has not been without its pitfalls. Boost now has competitors who have copied the Boost brand in Turkey, due to a failure to trade mark. Learning from its mistake, Boost now ensures that it registers trade marks in each country that it enters to protect the Boost brand.[1]

## Question

From a marketing perspective, what factors do you think Boost would need to consider before expanding to various international markets?

# INTRODUCTION

The increasing political, economic, social, cultural and technological interconnectedness of countries throughout the world has given rise to the concept that we are living in a 'global village' and that we are becoming 'global citizens'. If there was ever any doubt that these flows of money and products connect us all in a web of interdependence, it was dispelled with the onset of the global financial crisis in the late 2000s. The crisis subsequently damaged almost every economy and highlighted just how much all of our lives are tied together.

While countries are connected through trade, and trends are being followed the world over, those that have travelled and spent a lot of time overseas will know there are still very substantial differences between the peoples of different countries and regions. We remain more different than we are the same. For marketers charged with the responsibility of marketing across borders, this poses some unique challenges. International marketers need to understand the similarities and differences that exist in the marketplaces and marketing environments in which they operate.

International marketing — the application of marketing principles beyond the home country — has, over the past couple of decades, presented both huge opportunities and threats for organisations. Even those businesses that do not choose to actively participate in international marketing may find themselves competing with businesses and products from overseas.

It is therefore imperative that marketers understand the international marketplace and individual foreign markets, how to choose appropriate target markets, and ultimately how to create, communicate and deliver products of value in the international market. The fundamental approach to marketing remains the same — understand, create, communicate and deliver — and this is represented in figure 13.1.

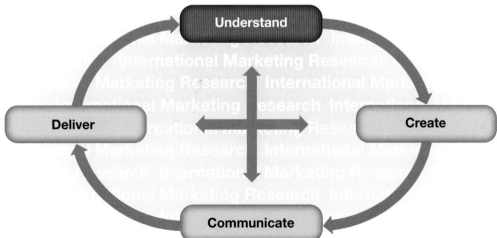

The challenge for marketers is to understand the similarities and differences in the markets and their environments. Marketers need to consider whether what works at home will work abroad or whether an alternative offering needs to be created, communicated and delivered to better meet the needs of the international market.

# INTERNATIONAL MARKETING FUNDAMENTALS

**Learning objective 1** understand the concept of 'globalisation' and its consequences for organisations seeking to engage in international marketing

For most of history, communities have been isolated and self-sufficient. Contact and exchange with other communities was difficult if not impossible until the advent of efficient transport and communications technologies. While some forms of transport have been with us for thousands of years — horse-drawn carriages and sailing vessels — their impracticality, lack of speed and lack of size meant that until the last few hundred years trade was largely restricted to precious and non-perishable commodities such as gold, textiles and spices. These were so highly valued that kings would send their best captains on treacherous year-long sea journeys to obtain them.

With the leaps in technology that began with the Industrial Revolution in the 1700s, the world started becoming a smaller place. Just a couple of hundred years ago, the journey from England to Australia took eight months and even the well travelled would make such a journey just once in a lifetime (often in close quarters with convicts); today the flight takes 24 hours and business travellers can travel up to a dozen times a year. Undoubtedly the world is now a smaller place. We can travel quickly and easily between almost any country we choose, exchanging products and ideas as we go. We have communications technologies that enable us to exchange information instantaneously with people on the opposite side of the world, whether one-to-one via email or phone, or to a billion people tuning into an Olympic Games broadcast or to watch the US presidential election. In recent years, as the benefits of a relatively free exchange of products and ideas have become increasingly accepted and desired, political, social, cultural, language and economic barriers have diminished, facilitating ever greater interconnections between different countries and their different peoples. This close interconnection has produced a close interdependence in terms of trade, finance, living standards and security — and many people now say we live in a truly global village.

## A global village?

The global village/global citizen/global market concept is derived from the process of globalisation. Globalisation has been occurring since the first time someone travelled beyond their home territory. They would be influenced by what they would experience and they, in turn, would influence the country and people they came into contact with. The process of globalisation has increased rapidly over the past few hundred years and in the past 50 years has become the subject of much research in the business and academic worlds.

**globalisation** The process through which individuals, organisations and governments become increasingly interconnected and similar.

Formally defined, **globalisation** is the process through which individuals, organisations and governments become increasingly interconnected, with consequences for national identity, national sovereignty, economic activities, laws and culture. Almost every aspect of our lives is touched by globalisation. While it is not our intention to deliver a lesson on world history, it is important to recognise that globalisation has been going on throughout much of modern history. In the 1500s, England, Spain, Portugal and France were building colonial empires around the world. Parts of Asia and the Pacific islands were colonised by Portugal and France. Later, the United States, Australia and New Zealand were colonies of England, with early settlers taking land from the Indigenous peoples.

For many years the United States has been the dominant world power. The United States has used its economic power, mass media dominance and technological infrastructure to 'export' its culture, ideals, products and way of life to the world. This has given rise to the notions of 'Americanisation' and 'CocaColonisation', in which people equate the blending of cultural, social, economic and political characteristics that arises from globalisation with countries 'becoming like America'. It is easy to see why such perceptions arise — think about Australian or New Zealand teen boys wearing baseball caps backwards (or indeed wearing *baseball caps* at all); think about how close you are to the nearest McDonald's takeaway food outlet; think about where your favourite five movies were made, the nationality of the stars, and where the stories were set; think about the global financial crisis and how it all began with American corporations granting home loans to people without incomes, without jobs, without assets — without the ability to repay the loans (these were subsequently called 'Ninja' loans). There is no doubt that the USA has more pervasively influenced the other cultures of the world than any other country in modern times and that some countries have actively opposed this, but globalisation is more complex than a simple one-way transfer of values.

It is a fascinating, though exhausting, exercise to spend a day analysing the origins of each thing you engage with. You will most probably find yourself immersed in products and ideas from all through Asia, Europe and the United States, and to a lesser degree South America and Africa. Cheaper air travel, the increasing internationalisation of business activities and the greater openness of most countries to foreign visitors has also led to greatly increased international travel compared to just 20 years ago. This travel can broaden people's conception of their world and blur the historical national frontiers that have defined much of history. In fact, international travel and work experience can be a valuable asset for people seeking work and other opportunities in many spheres of business. Multinational businesses and universities often offer top-performing employees and students the chance to undertake exchange programs to gain international experience and exposure to different cultures, societies and politico-legal systems. Some organisations even *require* their senior managers to have international experience, and executives in some multinational companies spend significant time abroad each year. Increasingly, school leavers and university graduates take it upon themselves to travel overseas for a period of time before embarking on a career. During these travels, they experience both the similarities and many differences across national borders. It is an understanding of those similarities and differences that can help create a competitive advantage and a successful marketing approach in business (both internationally and domestically, considering the multicultural nature of Australian and New Zealand societies).

While many of us do not have the opportunity to travel extensively for work or pleasure, much can still be learned about the rich diversity of the world's peoples by research and engaging with people from diverse cultural backgrounds.

## Standardisation versus customisation

There are thousands of businesses across the country engaging with the world through their marketing activities. To do so requires a sound understanding of the different forces at play in different countries, how to select potential target markets and how to implement a marketing mix for them. This could be as simple as selling products designed for the home market to businesses or consumers based in another country or as complex as creating an entire marketing mix aimed specifically at the unique needs of customers abroad.

In this section of the chapter, we will look at one of the biggest decisions the international marketer must make and one of biggest areas of academic debate: the extent to which an international marketer should maintain one marketing mix across international markets (standardisation) versus the extent to which the international marketer should tailor the marketing mix to the specific characteristics of various target markets (customisation).

Regardless of the products offered, the currency they are priced in, how they are transported and whether the packaging and advertising is in English, Spanish or Japanese, the marketing organisation has at some point made a decision about whether to:

- make one standardised offering across international markets
- customise offerings for each market
- strike some balance between the two extremes.

International marketers must understand the commonalities and differences between the markets.

A key decision faced by international marketers is whether to standardise or customise their offerings. **Standardisation** refers to applying a uniform marketing mix across international markets, with only minor modifications to meet local conditions (e.g. printing packaging or instructions in the local language or choosing a different price point to suit local incomes). **Customisation** refers to carefully tailoring the marketing mix to the specific characteristics and wants of each market. For some marketers their offering is a mix of the two strategies. Think about Google. It has essentially the same search engine interface for every country (a simple interface that can load quickly regardless of the speed of the user's internet connection) and the same set of algorithms underlying the indexing and search functions, but provides the interface in the local language. Australian beer companies tend to sell the same product around the world, but position it differently. For example, Foster's lager is an everyday beer in Australia but is considered a premium beer in Europe, just as Heineken is considered an everyday beer in the USA but is marketed as a boutique beer to Australians.

On the other hand, some companies find that the very characteristics that give them a competitive advantage in their home market also provide an advantage offshore and thus little customisation is required. For example, Australian based company Splatter (www.splatter.biz) have built a strong reputation, both locally and globally in recent years, and have become a leader in products designed with children and families in mind. Splatter markets paintings for children's rooms and baby nurseries using an online gallery and exhibitions in key geographic markets.[2]

Figure 13.2 summarises the main aspects of standardisation and customisation. Keep these in mind as you study the rest of this chapter, as the marketer's decision about the appropriate degree of standardisation or customisation must be based on a sound understanding of the factors that we discuss in the following pages.

**standardisation** Applying a uniform marketing mix across international markets, with only minor modifications to meet local conditions.

**customisation** Carefully tailoring the marketing mix to the specific characteristics and wants of each market.

| STANDARDISATION | CUSTOMISATION |
| --- | --- |
| • Similarities between different countries/convergence | • Social, cultural, economic, political and legal differences between countries |
| • Economies in research and development | • Creation of competitive advantage |
| • Economies of scale in production | • Competition from local marketers in the foreign market |
| • Economies in marketing | • Facilitation of innovation in the foreign market |
| • Uniformity and ease of control of marketing approach | |

**FIGURE 13.2**

Standardisation versus customisation

# Global trade

There is no doubting that global trade connects the world in a complex web of exchanges. Table 13.1 summarises the extent and overall nature of Australia's and New Zealand's trade. It is clear that a large proportion of total production and consumption is sent overseas or sourced from overseas. For example, a local university student may work on a laptop made by Lenovo, a Chinese company, under licence from IBM, a US company, running software by Microsoft, a US company, but sold in Australia.

**TABLE 13.1** The flow of products and services

| Australia | Exports[3] (type) | | Merchandise Imports (type)[4] | |
|---|---|---|---|---|
| GDP: $1.2 trillion | Agricultural | 4% | Manufacturing | $147 billion |
| | Mining | 39% | Agricultural | $12 billion |
| | Manufacturing | 32% | Minerals and fuels | $26 billion |
| | Services | 21% | Other goods | $15 billion |
| | Total | $253 billion | Total | $200 billion |
| | **Exports (destination)** | | **Imports (source)** | |
| | China | $46 billion | China | $36 billion |
| | Japan | $37 billion | USA | $21 billion |
| | Korea | $17 billion | Japan | $18 billion |
| | India | $16 billion | Thailand | $12 billion |
| | USA | $9 billion | Singapore | $10 billion |
| **New Zealand**[5] | **Exports (type)** | | **Imports (type)** | |
| GDP: $119 billion | Merchandise | $40 billion | Merchandise | $40 billion |
| | Services | $13 billion | Services | $12 billion |
| | Total | $53 billion | Total | $52 billion |
| | **Exports (destination)** | | **Imports (source)** | |
| | Australia | $9 billion | Australia | $7 billion |
| | United States | $4 billion | China | $6 billion |
| | China | $4 billion | USA | $4 billion |
| | Japan | $3 billion | Japan | $3 billion |

The contaminated milk powder crisis in China demonstrates how not only finished products are traded around the world, but how the components of those products may cross borders several times before ending up in the hands of consumers. The Chinese dairy group Sanlu, part-owned by New Zealand dairy group Fonterra, recalled its infant milk formula after reports of hundreds of children in a number of Chinese districts developing kidney stones. It was suspected the milk powder was contaminated with the industrial chemical melamine (used in plastic production and in the production of cheap furniture and cabinetry). The milk powder was also exported to Burma, Bangladesh, Yemen, Gabon and Burundi. Some 21 other businesses had to recall products because they used the milk powder in their production. Taiwan was forced to remove thousands of products from stores that had the milk powder as an ingredient and South Korea was also investigating whether products had included the powder during processing. This incident highlights the extent to which products and the parts that go into their production travel freely across national borders.

Although the volume of international trade is enormous, an organisation contemplating moving into the international markets faces numerous decisions and risks. Many governments have established export promotion programs to help domestic organisations enter and succeed in international markets. Further, most governments provide some degree of direct assistance to organisations undertaking international marketing. Assistance may take several forms:

- information and advice
- production support
- marketing support
- finance.

The Australian Trade Commission (Austrade) is a government agency established to provide advice, marketing intelligence and support to organisations to help them reduce the cost, time and risk involved in their international marketing efforts. Austrade also helps domestic organisations identify potential overseas joint venture and investment opportunities. The New Zealand Trade and Enterprise agency performs a similar role for New Zealand organisations, as do SPRING Singapore, the Hong Kong Trade Development Council and the Malaysia External Trade Development Corporation, in their respective countries.[6]

## Spotlight  East meets West

Across the world, tapioca pearl tea (also called boba tea but most commonly known as bubble tea), is gaining in popularity. Bubble tea originated in Taiwan in the early 1980s as a sweet, milky, ice cold tea

with chewy black tapioca pearl balls at the bottom. It is these balls that give the drink its 'bubble' nickname. Bubble tea is served in clear plastic drinking cups with a straw wide enough to enable the numerous tapioca balls to be 'slurped', and is considered healthier than coffee as the tapioca content has iron and calcium.

The popularity of bubble tea soon spread from Taiwan to Hong Kong and Japan. Over time, it also gained favour in China, Thailand, Malaysia, Singapore, Indonesia and the Philippines. With the success of bubble tea in both East and South-East Asia, international marketers began to consider the potential for the product among Western countries that were known to typically spend billions of dollars on coffee and other out-of-home beverages each year. One potentially lucrative market was the United States, and businesses began distributing bubble tea through Chinatowns and other Asian community hubs in the United States and Canada in the 1990s. 'Made-in-Asia trends' in both food and drinks in the late 1990s also helped to catapult bubble tea into non-Asian areas. Franchises for bubble tea in the region soon emerged.

From its origins as a sweet milky tea, the bubble tea menu has broadened to fit both Western and Eastern taste buds. While Asians tend to prefer flavours such as lychee, coconut and honey melon, Westerners favour flavours such as strawberry, vanilla and chocolate. The tea is now also available in both hot and cold varieties. The colourful drinks with tapioca pearls, drunk through fat straws, have even been described as the next 'sushi of the West', with an increasing amount of Asian food and drink being incorporated into Western diets.[7]

## Concepts and applications check

**Learning objective 1** understand the concept of 'globalisation' and its consequences for organisations seeking to engage in international marketing

1.1 Are fundamental domestic and international marketing principles the same? Explain your answer.

1.2 Prepare an argument for and against the following statement: 'The world is a global village.'

1.3 Using a product of your own choosing as an example, briefly outline the main arguments for and against a standardised marketing strategy for it in international markets.

1.4 A significant trend in consumer culture is the global spread of brands. List five global brands that readily come to mind. Why do you believe each of these brands is successful in international markets?

# THE INTERNATIONAL MARKETING ENVIRONMENT

In chapter 2 we examined the marketing environment in relation to the marketing organisation, its internal environment, micro environment and macro environment. In the macro environment, we identified several forces at play — political, economic, sociocultural, technological and legal (commonly referred to as the PESTL model). A similar set of forces is at play in the international marketing environment, both within individual target foreign markets and in the organisations, arrangements and other circumstances between countries. These factors are outlined in figure 13.3 (overleaf).

**Learning objective 2** discuss the political, economic, sociocultural, technological and legal forces at play in international markets

Marketing organisations that engage in international marketing need to develop a strong understanding of how these forces differ from the more familiar forces in their home countries in order to select appropriate target markets and to amend their marketing approach appropriately. Ideally, international marketers should understand the international market in the same ways they would understand their local market. This is no small ask. This part of the chapter is designed to introduce you to the issues that international marketers need to consider. We cannot possibly teach you all you will need to know. For those who seek to work in international marketing, we encourage you to:

- travel — recreationally, for study and for work
- read — guide books, magazines, international newspapers
- learn — a second (or third or fourth) language
- watch — movies and television shows on foreign channels to broaden your horizons
- experience — different foods and beverages
- work — with students from a foreign background
- overcome — a home-country bias in your view of the world. It is a somewhat natural tendency to favour the familiar, but it is of little help in the world of international marketing.

**Political**

International marketers must consider:

1. Alliances and agreements:
   - bilateral trade agreements
   - free trade areas
   - the World Trade Organization

2. Market-specific political factors:
   - View on private ownership and business activity
   - The influence of government policy
   - The stability of the political environment

**Economic**

International marketers need to understand the economy in both the short and long term. They must consider:

1. the overall state of the global economy
2. country-specific conditions such as levels of income and wealth, exchange rates, the availability of credit, employment levels and the quality of national infrastructure.

**Sociocultural**

Social and cultural influences have a large effect on businesses. For each country in which they wish to operate, international marketers must understand:

1. religion, culture, subcultures, values, attitudes and beliefs
2. population trends including age, household size and composition, marriage and divorce trends, places lived, ethnicity and health.

**Technological**

International marketers must consider:

1. the role of technology in their marketing mix
2. the differing technological infrastructure in different countries
3. the different levels of access to information and communications technologies among citizens of different countries.

**Legal**

International marketers need to understand legal and regulatory influences such as:

1. international 'law', agreements and regulatory bodies (e.g. the World Trade Organization)
2. the specific laws of international markets in which they wish to operate
3. trade barriers

**FIGURE 13.3**

The international marketing environment

More information can be accessed from various government sources, including Austrade and New Zealand Trade and Enterprise, both of which exist to promote the participation of businesses in the international marketplace. Austrade's overview of the Chinese market includes details such as its political and economic conditions and statistics about its trade relations. It shows, for example, that Australia's trade with China has increased massively over the past decade, thanks mainly to the booming construction sector in China, which has driven strong demand for Australia's mineral ore exports. Today China is Australia's largest export partner, having overtaken the United States. The corresponding page on New Zealand Trade and Enterprise's website includes information about China and links to specific market research conducted into sectors relevant to the New Zealand business sector, including wine and education exports. For example, a New Zealand business thinking about establishing a subsidiary in Shanghai can find out important details such as office rental costs, average salaries and appropriate methods for recruiting local staff.[8]

Following, we will examine each of the major environmental factors in turn and then look at the key international organisations that govern aspects of international trade in order to give you a taste of the complexity of the international marketing environment.

# Political forces

Political forces may be broadly categorised as:
- political alliances and agreements between countries
- political factors within a target market country.

## Alliances and agreements

It is important for international marketers to understand political alliances. Some alliances favour trade between countries, enhancing the chances of success, while others can work against international marketing goals. Some countries align in regional trading arrangements. International trade agreements are formal arrangements between countries to encourage and facilitate trade between them. They aim to:
- streamline paperwork
- reduce or eliminate trade barriers (e.g. tariffs)
- create preferred zones of trade among their member countries (often, incidentally, to the detriment of non-members).

Such arrangements can be bilateral or multilateral. *Bilateral trade arrangements* involve two countries, whereas multilateral arrangements involve more than two countries, often located within a region. Table 13.2 shows some of the bilateral agreements in place involving Australia and New Zealand.[9]

**TABLE 13.2** Australia and New Zealand bilateral trade agreements

| Party 1 | Party 2 | Date of commencement |
| --- | --- | --- |
| Australia | New Zealand | 1983 |
| New Zealand | Singapore | 2001 |
| Australia | Chile | 2008 |
| Australia | Thailand | 2005 |
| New Zealand | Thailand | 2005 |
| Australia | USA | 2005 |
| New Zealand | China | 2008 |
| New Zealand | Hong Kong | 2009 |
| New Zealand | Malaysia | 2009 |

Table 13.3 (see overleaf) shows some of the *regional trade areas* that are of the most direct relevance to Australian and New Zealand marketers.

For Australia and New Zealand, arguably the most important free trade agreements are ASEAN and APEC, illustrated in figures 13.4 and 13.5 over the following pages. In 2010 Australia and New Zealand entered into what is for both countries their largest ever trade agreement when the ASEAN–Australia–New Zealand Free Trade Agreement came into force.[10]

**TABLE 13.3** Regional trade areas

| Trade area | Parties |
| --- | --- |
| Asia–Pacific Economic Cooperation (APEC) | Australia, Brunei, Canada, Chile, China, Hong Kong, Indonesia, Japan, South Korea, Malaysia, Mexico, New Zealand, Papua New Guinea, Peru, Philippines, Russia, Singapore, Taiwan, Thailand, USA, Vietnam |
| Association of South-East Asian Nations (ASEAN) | Brunei, Cambodia, Indonesia, Laos, Malaysia, Myanmar, Philippines, Singapore, Thailand, Vietnam |
| Association of South-East Asian Nations (ASEAN)–Australia–New Zealand Free Trade Area (AANZFTA) | ASEAN (above) plus Australia, New Zealand |
| European Union (EU) | Austria, Belgium, Bulgaria, Cyprus, Czech Republic, Denmark, Estonia, Finland, France, Germany, Greece, Hungary, Ireland, Italy, Latvia, Lithuania, Luxembourg, Malta, the Netherlands, Poland, Portugal, Romania, Slovakia, Slovenia, Spain, Sweden, UK |
| North American Free Trade Agreement (NAFTA) | Canada, Mexico, USA |
| South Asian Association for Regional Cooperation (SAARC) | Bangladesh, Bhutan, India, Maldives, Nepal, Pakistan, Sri Lanka, Afghanistan |

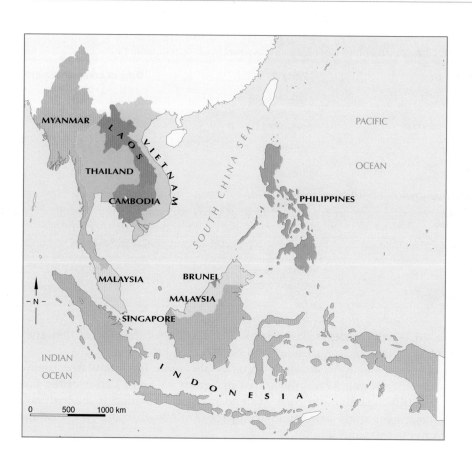

**FIGURE 13.4**

ASEAN countries

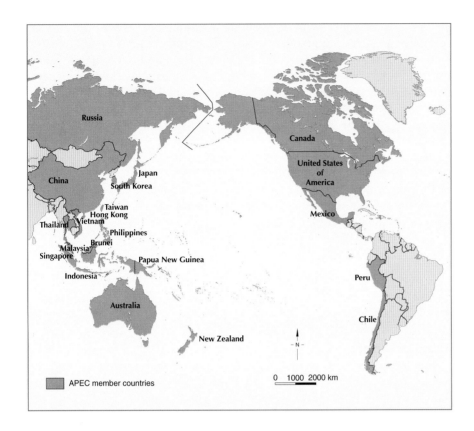

**FIGURE 13.5**

APEC countries

A number of global organisations exist to encourage trade. The General Agreement on Tariffs and Trade (GATT) was established after World War II to help settle trade disputes and encourage the involvement of developing countries in the global economy. GATT aimed to reduce tariffs and other barriers to trade and asked member countries to treat other member countries equally in terms of trade arrangements. GATT created the World Trade Organization in 1995 with the aim of further liberalising trade between nations, while at the same time establishing and enforcing rules to govern e-commerce and outlaw, or at least discourage, some unhelpful trade practices.

## Country-specific political factors

Political systems vary greatly between countries. Marketers need to understand the political system of each target country and understand its influence on business and commerce. Democratic political systems tend to see reasonably regular changes of government, which result in changes of policies, some of which can have significant effects on business. Dictatorships tend to see infrequent changes in rule, but when those changes happen they often fundamentally alter the state of the country. Multi-party systems, while offering representation of a broad range of interests, often suffer an inability to actually implement policy, which means governmental change can be slow.

Political factors can determine the degree to which private ownership and business activity is allowed. For example, capitalist countries such as the United States give great scope for private sector business activity with relatively little regulation; socialist countries such as Cuba greatly restrict private-sector activity, particularly of foreign businesses. Many countries fall somewhere on a continuum between the two classic economic/political models.

Marketers need to understand the stability of the political system in the countries in which they operate, as instability can severely impact on business performance. In particularly unstable countries, the degree of risk may be too high to accept (this risk may be to the safety and security of employees and physical assets; the value of the country's currency; or in the possibility of nationalisation of assets).

The political forces in different countries also combine to create an international environment that can be more or less conducive to international marketing. Another important international effect is the overall stability of the world economy. In the first decade of this century, there was a gradual destabilising of the global community prompted by factors such as the 9/11 terrorist attacks on the United States and the US invasion of Afghanistan and Iraq, the increasing economic and military might of China and India, the threat of nuclear proliferation, and the virtual collapse of the global financial system.

# Economic forces

International marketers' understanding of the economic forces in the international marketplace must encompass:

- the global economy
- the economies of the specific countries of interest to them.

## The global economy

As we emphasised in the first part of this chapter, communications and transport technologies have led to unprecedented levels of interconnectedness and interdependency between countries. This means that the economic conditions within any specific country are likely to be significantly influenced by the global economy. Conversely, the global economy can be significantly influenced by economic conditions within one or a few economies if those economies are big enough.

The global financial crisis that began with a liquidity crisis in the United States led to the worst economic crash since the Great Depression and clearly demonstrated just how interconnected the world's economies are. Consider that the seeds of the crisis were planted in the early 2000s when funds flowed freely from Asia and the Middle East into the United States, facilitating cheap and easy credit. The massive growth in borrowing led to the invention of complicated financial instruments that enabled investors around the world to use credit to speculate. US and European lenders reduced their loan criteria to the point that many of the loans were irresponsible, with little prospect of being paid in a negative growth environment. The realisation that many organisations around the world were owed money that could never be repaid triggered a loss of confidence among lenders, resulting in an unwillingness to lend and hence an abrupt halt to business investment. Business and consumer confidence collapsed, resulting in corporate collapses, plummeting profits and job losses. It is intriguing — though not really difficult — to contemplate that the massive wealth generated by oil and manufacturing in Asia, Europe and the Middle East over the past decade led — eventually, through a convoluted path — to Australian or New Zealand retirees who had to return to work because superannuation was no longer sufficient to fund a long retirement.

Overall, the worldwide losses caused by the global economic crisis totalled in the trillions of dollars and few economies escaped unscathed. Some economies, most notably in the United States and Europe, are still struggling to recover. It is clear then that international marketers must be aware of global economic conditions and alert for the sudden and substantial effect any changes can have, not only on each international market, but also on the home market conditions.

## Country-specific economic factors

The economic environment in a particular country will to some degree determine the relative attractiveness of that country as a potential target market. Levels of income and wealth, exchange rates, the availability of credit and the quality of national infrastructure will all affect the suitability of a business's product and overall marketing mix to a particular international market. A business may target those markets with similar characteristics to the home market, or other characteristics that suggest their products may succeed. Alternatively, the business, upon discovering the different economic conditions may decide to customise their marketing mix to suit those conditions. It is important to avoid the assumption that the wealthiest countries are the best potential foreign markets. They will be countries already well served by domestic business and a host of other international businesses. While they may offer attractive opportunities, less developed countries can also offer great market potential. In particular, India and China are enormous emerging markets in which many consumers are keen to pursue the opportunities afforded by growing affluence.

Exchange rates are one of the most important economic factors for international marketers. As the economic conditions in countries change or there is a shift in overall global economic conditions, the value of a country's currency relative to others may change. International marketers need to be aware that in international currency dealings, there is potential for misunderstanding due to so many currencies sharing the dollar name and symbol ($) — Australia, New Zealand, Singapore, Hong Kong and the United States, to name a few. Usage of International Standard currency codes avoids this problem, as each currency has its own unique three-letter code as its symbol (e.g. Australian dollar AUD, New Zealand dollar NZD, Singapore dollar SGD, Hong Kong dollar HKD, United States dollar USD). In international transactions, these codes should always be quoted.

While it is often assumed that exchange rate changes will be gradual and foreseeable, that is often not the reality. For example, just after the onset of the global economic crisis, over a period of about four months the Australian dollar fell from being worth USD 0.98 to USD 0.60. For the international marketer, currency fluctuations have serious consequences, for example:

- an Australian importer paying USD 20 million a month for supplies from a United States firm suddenly found themselves with a USD 33 million a month bill for the same quantity of supplies
- an Australian exporter receiving AUD 10 million a month for goods suddenly found themselves asked to supply nearly half as much again as it was now costing the US company only AUD 6 million for the same quantity and so they could afford more of it.

Of course, the situation is reversed when the Australian dollar appreciates against other currencies. In 2010 the Australian dollar appreciated by 20 per cent versus the US dollar, making it very difficult for Australian exporters to remain competitive in key export markets. At the same time, imports became cheaper, affecting the local market.

Many businesses enter into complex financial arrangements to insure themselves against such currency movements (using a technique known as foreign exchange hedging), but changes in exchange rates can fundamentally affect the supply and demand of various products across national borders, particularly for the traditional agricultural and mining industries that account for such a large part of Australia's foreign trade.

# Sociocultural forces

Sociocultural forces are among the most important factors at play in the international marketing environment. They are often also the forces that display the most subtlety and complexity, and international marketers will find themselves needing to pay a great deal of attention to understanding the sociocultural characteristics of the markets that they wish to enter. To complicate matters further, each international market is likely to have sociocultural variations within it.

As we have learned throughout this book, at the heart of marketing is the creation of value for customers. Because that value is determined by individuals' beliefs, attitudes, experiences and so on, and the major forces at play in their society, value is intimately connected with the culture and society in which those consumers live. For example, ANZ Bank has been pushing into Asia over the past decade in a bid to establish itself as a major financial services institution ahead of the expected emergence of a new level of affluence within parts of Asia. It has, however, not chosen countries that are predominantly Muslim as Muslim religious law forbids traditional Western financial arrangements — the charging of interest on borrowings. While there are ways to provide such services without breaking the Muslim laws, it is a degree of complexity that banks have chosen to avoid in the initial efforts to enter Asian markets. With the growing affluence of some predominantly Muslim countries, however, there is an increasingly attractive opportunity for a financial services firm willing to adapt to the different needs of Islamic investors.

On a simpler level, marketers need to be aware of the different cultural meanings of symbols, such as colour, in different countries. For example, PepsiCola lost its dominant market share to Coca-Cola in South-East Asia when Pepsi changed the colour of its vending machines and coolers from deep 'regal' blue to light 'ice' blue — light blue is associated with death and mourning in South-East Asia. The colours red and yellow have specific (and sometimes very different) symbolic meanings in many Asian countries. Table 13.4 summarises some of the meanings of colours in different cultures.[11]

**TABLE 13.4** The different meanings of colour

| | Cultural group | | | | | |
| --- | --- | --- | --- | --- | --- | --- |
| | Anglo-Saxon | Germanic | Chinese | Japanese | Korean | Slavic |
| **BLUE** | High quality Corporate Masculine | Warm Feminine | High quality Trustworthy | High quality Trustworthy | High quality Trustworthy | |
| **GREEN** | Envy Good taste | | Pure Reliable | Love Happy | Pure Adventure | |
| **YELLOW** | Happy Jealousy | Envy Jealousy | Pure Good taste Royal Authority | Envy Good taste | Happiness Good taste | Envy |
| **RED** | Masculine Love Lust Fear Anger | Fear Anger Jealousy | Love Happiness Lucky | Love Anger Jealousy | Love Adventure Good taste | Fear Anger Jealousy |
| **BLACK** | Expensive Fear Grief | Fear Anger Grief | Expensive Powerful | Expensive Powerful | Expensive Powerful | Fear Anger |

In Australia or New Zealand, when presented with a business card, you might poke it in to your notebook or top pocket, but this is considered disrespectful in Japan, where you should receive the card with both hands, read the details and then neatly file the card. Cultural differences can greatly complicate business negotiations and this has important consequences for sales people. For example, some cultures, particularly in the Middle East, expect to haggle over price, whereas in Japan it is considered offensive to deal with price during negotiations. In some parts of Asia, facilitating payments are expected in the course of doing business. In Australia and New Zealand, such payments would usually be considered a bribe, but in other countries, business people may find it difficult to win any business with another organisation or to seal a deal with a partner in the absence of such payments. Each year, Transparency International issues an index of the level of 'corruption' of different countries. See figure 13.6 (bearing in mind that a map produced by the countries labelled highly corrupt might look somewhat different!).

**FIGURE 13.6**

The Corruption Perception Index map

*Source:* Transparency International, Corruption Perception Index.

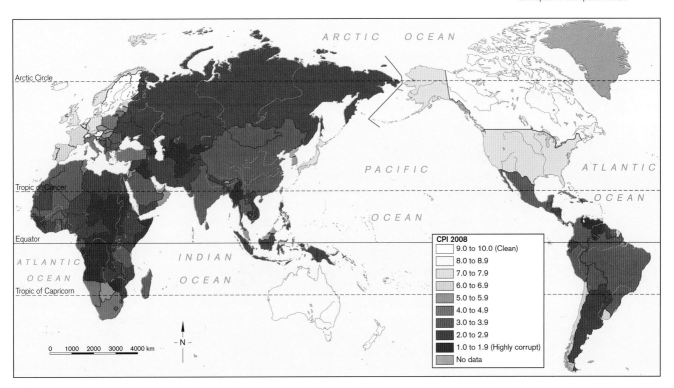

## Technological forces

Technology has become a great enabling force in international marketing over the past 20 years with the advent and relatively cheap price of communications technologies that enable easy transfer of information between different countries in moments. Technology has also created, revolutionised and destroyed entire industries. For example, traditional full-service stock brokers struggle to compete with online brokers that offer enormous quantities of information and cut-price broking services to people who can manage their own stock trades from home. The introduction of digital television is predicted to cause the video rental market to decline. The internet has also revolutionised the newspaper industry, with newspaper publishers increasingly reliant on advertising sales as they are forced to offer most of their content for free online, and this content is accessible to anywhere around the world, to anyone with an internet connection. While their content is more accessible and open to a potentially wider audience, the challenge for newspaper publishers in the internet era is how to monetise their content, with the number of consumers paying for it in its traditional paper format declining. Alternative revenue streams are being explored; for example, with various tabloids launching paid iPad applications. However, newspapers such as *The Times* in the United Kingdom that have moved to lock their internet content behind 'paywalls' have seen their online readership figures plummet (which subsequently impacts upon advertising revenue). Significantly though, Rupert Murdoch, the chairman and chief executive officer of News Corporation, which publishes numerous newspapers around the world, has committed his organisation to exploring paid online content models for the future.[12] Exactly what these models will be remains uncertain.

The other great influence of technology in the sphere of international marketing is the infrastructure available in different foreign markets. Marketers cannot assume that potential target markets will have a similar technological infrastructure as the home market. For example, many metropolitan businesses in Australia assume that most households have broadband internet connections, but in fact only about half do, with many regional and remote areas poorly served by service providers. Some developing countries have few phone lines and hence little telephone or internet access, and some countries have few mass media outlets, making advertising difficult. In countries suffering political or civil instability, technological infrastructure is regularly targeted in war.

## Legal forces

The laws in force in different countries can be vastly different. For example, in Australia and New Zealand, intellectual property is legally protected by copyright, patent and trade mark legislation and a host of case law, whereas many Asian countries have cultures that do not even recognise the concept of intellectual property (it is a Western idea) and thus do not protect copyright. This means goods as wide ranging as DVDs, software, drugs, fashion clothing and books are regularly counterfeited or pirated — sometimes poorly, but sometimes at a standard little different, at least on the surface, to the original — and sold at a significant discount to the genuine product. Some consider this practice undermines sales, profits and the prestige and brand image of the creator of the original product. Marketers with products particularly susceptible to imitation must take other steps to protect themselves, such as tightly controlling distribution channels.

Marketing organisations must be aware of the laws in force in the markets in which they operate to ensure their marketing mix complies with all legal requirements. In addition, most multinational businesses seek to base various parts of their operations in countries that have the most conducive mix of environmental factors, legal forces being one. Sometimes this raises ethical dilemmas; for example, is it reasonable for an extremely successful US company to engage child labour in a developing country in order to minimise production costs, in turn to maximise profits, while at the same time reducing employment opportunities in its home country? Many countries also base their head offices in 'tax havens', countries that charge little or no corporate tax.

Some countries restrict trade practices through laws and regulations. It is important for international marketers to be aware of trade barriers such as:

- **tariffs** a duty charged on imports that has the effect of increasing the price of imported goods relative to domestically made goods (e.g. Australia charges a tariff on cars in a bid to protect the local car industry from cheaper imports; New Zealand charges a 10 per cent tariff on clothing, footwear and carpets)[13]

**tariffs** Duties charged on imports that effectively increase the price of imports relative to domestically made products.

- **quotas** limits on the amount of particular types of goods that are allowed to be imported per year (quotas, combined with tariffs, have often presented barriers to Australian exports to Japan)
- **embargoes** and sanctions — a ban or other restriction on the import of a particular product or a ban on products from a particular country, often due to political motivations (e.g. South Africa was subject to trade embargoes during the apartheid era; and Iraq was subject to trade embargoes relating to oil exports while under the rule of Saddam Hussein)
- limits or bans on foreign ownership — for example, Australia imposes limits on the amount of Australian assets that can be foreign owned, with larger acquisitions subject to approval from the Foreign Investment Review Board; New Zealand similarly requires government approval for large foreign purchases of land.

The World Trade Organization has worked for many years to promote free trade by the reduction and eventual elimination of restrictive trade practices.

Finally, the degree and types of regulation imposed on marketing activities need to be understood. More developed countries tend to have more laws and rules in place to ensure marketing activities are in the overall interest of the public (e.g. bans on cigarette advertising and bans on dangerous goods). Less-developed countries often have fewer regulations.

> **quotas** Annual limits on the amount of particular types of goods that can be imported.
>
> **embargoes** Bans or restrictions on imports from a particular country.

# Westfield — an international retail empire    Spotlight

In July 1959 John Saunders and Frank Lowy opened their first shopping centre — Westfield Plaza in Blacktown. With 12 shops, two department stores and a supermarket, people flocked to see the plaza. Newspapers of the day described the Westfield Plaza as 'the most modern American-type combined retail centre'. By the end of that year Westfield Plaza was established as the commercial hub of Blacktown's 100 or so shops, and people from all over the area were drawn to the 'progressive shopping centre'. Westfield was incorporated in June of 1960, and shortly afterwards, Saunders and Lowy issued a prospectus for its listing on the Sydney Stock Exchange. In September Westfield Development Corporation Ltd was floated with the issue of 300 000 ordinary shares at a price of five shillings each. The first purpose-built centre, funded by the recent float, opened at Hornsby at a cost of £345 000. With 22 stores, it played a major role in attracting residents to the area. Three more centres opened in Sydney by 1962. In 1966 the first branded centre opened at Burwood with the now familiar red Westfield logo.

Westfield Plaza — Blacktown, NSW, 1959.

Westfield London shopping centre, 2011.

The Westfield Group is now the world's largest listed retail property group by equity market capitalisation. It has interests in and operates a global portfolio of 119 regional shopping centres in Australia, New Zealand, the United Kingdom and the United States. Westfield's portfolio is valued at more than $61 billion. It is a vertically integrated organisation, managing all aspects of shopping centre development — from design and construction through to leasing, management and marketing. Westfield works with over 23 700 retailers across more than ten million square metres of retail space. It has an extensive marketing arm with the core aim of attracting shoppers to Westfield shopping centres.

## Concepts and applications check

**Learning objective 2** discuss the political, economic, sociocultural, technological and legal forces at play in international markets

**2.1** Explain how aspects of culture in certain Asian countries would influence marketing practices.

**2.2** Consumers around the world display both similarities and differences depending on their cultural backgrounds, values, motives and demographics. Prepare an argument for and against the following statement: 'Consumers around the world are becoming more homogeneous.'

**2.3** In your opinion, are countries economically independent? Justify your answer.

**2.4** From an international marketing perspective, conduct research to compare and contrast two countries of your choice on political, technological and legal macro-environmental factors.

**2.5** Research and collect data on China that will help you prepare a brief profile of the types of foods and beverages that could be marketed in China by Australian or New Zealand firms.

# WHY AND HOW ORGANISATIONS GO INTERNATIONAL

**Learning objective 3** understand why and how organisations internationalise

In many ways, the imperative for international marketing is straightforward:

- the world holds many more potential customers than does the home market, thus offering a way to increase revenues and profits
- communication and transport technologies make international marketing a realistic option, even for smaller businesses
- the increasingly free trading environment makes international marketing easier and at the same time increases competition within the domestic market (few businesses can escape competition from marketing organisations entering their home market from abroad)
- faced with increasing competition at home, a marketer may be able to find a market that does not currently have access to its product
- greater economies can be achieved by increasing the scale of overall operations.

Internationalising can be a profitable way of expanding a business. Austrade research shows that, on average, exporting companies are more profitable than their non-exporting counterparts.[14] Due to the comparatively small populations of both countries in world terms, for Australian and New Zealand marketers more than 98 per cent of potential consumers live overseas. Businesses choosing to focus their efforts on domestic markets restrict their market potential, while businesses choosing to internationalise broaden their market potential considerably. For example, a decision by an Australian business to export to Thailand increases their market potential three-fold.

Internationalisation can also help businesses to become more efficient. In producing a greater volume, the cost of production per unit should decrease. Tapping international markets can therefore assist businesses to lower their per unit production costs and increase profitability.

Businesses that internationalise also increase their potential to gain new knowledge. They may be forced to adapt to best practice or new forms of technology in order to effectively compete in the global market. Their experiences in international markets can be used by a business to improve both its domestic and foreign operations. International business, like any new experience, exposes businesses and their managers to new ideas, management practices, marketing techniques, and ways of competing that may not have been thought of prior to internationalising.

Diversifying risks is a further potential advantage of internationalising. With an organisation's expansion into other countries, risks such as economic downfall and market changes are more evenly distributed. While domestic companies may be wholly affected by misfortune in the domestic market, a company with foreign interests may not necessarily suffer to the same extent in other markets.

In addition to the many benefits that accrue to businesses that choose to internationalise, benefits also accrue in the wider community. Internationalisation activities such as exporting can help the wider community by creating jobs and wealth for all partners in the business activity. Additional jobs and work help put more money into local communities and businesses that support that community, which raises living standards and supports publicly funded services. Of course, branching out into international markets can be a risky and complex venture. Most organisations naturally have far less knowledge of international markets and the issues that can arise.

## Selecting overseas markets

There are 230 national markets in the world and some are easier to enter than others. The 'easiest' (i.e. lowest risk) international markets to enter are those which share similar cultural and business practices and a common language with the domestic market, and that are geographically close. The process of selecting foreign markets for export, sales or manufacturing is complex and time consuming, requiring much research. Selecting an international market involves a two-step approach (see figure 13.7).[15]

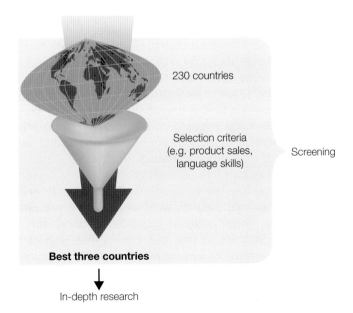

230 countries

Selection criteria
(e.g. product sales,
language skills)

Screening

**Best three countries**

↓

In-depth research

### FIGURE 13.7

A two-step process for researching international markets: screening followed by in-depth research

First, marketers should screen markets using secondary data to generate a short list of countries to consider. A range of factors can be used in this market screening stage (see stage 1 of table 13.5). The second step in the process involves more detailed primary research to permit a thorough examination of short-listed markets prior to selecting the preferred country or countries to enter. This stage must consider the opportunities and risks in each market (see stage 2 of table 13.5).

**TABLE 13.5** Two stages of international market research: screening followed by in-depth

| Stage 1: screening | Screening research should consider broad market selection criteria such as: <br> 1. Population <br> 2. Income <br> 3. Demographic information (e.g. population age) <br> 4. The business environment <br> 5. Competitors in the market <br> 6. Government stability <br> 7. Market access |
|---|---|
| | To narrow the search further, consider more specific criteria including: <br> 1. Sales potential <br> 2. Market growth rates <br> 3. Gross margin potential <br> 4. Forecast market development expenditure |
| Stage 2: in-depth research | Shortlisted international markets need to match business strengths. The second phase involves detailed market research to assess: <br> 1. Required product positioning <br> 2. Required marketing mix, including service support to enable cost implications and appropriate mode of entry to be identified. |

# Methods of market entry

Once the decision has been made to enter one or more international markets, the marketing organisation must choose from among the available entry modes. Choosing a market entry mode is a management function more than a marketing one, but the marketer must understand the implications of each mode of entry in order to devise the best marketing plan. This section will outline the many ways that companies can enter foreign markets.

It is inevitable that a decision to internationalise (and how this will be achieved) will affect an organisation's departmental structure in many areas, not just marketing. As such it is important to note that any decision to internationalise has resource implications for the head/home office and thought needs to be given to company structure following a decision to enter international markets. Different entry modes will require different structures and it is important the company be structured in a way that allows the business to be resourced and managed appropriately. In terms of the marketing department, examples of such decisions would include whether to structure the department and appoint managers or staff for each region and/or product line, and where those staff will be located.

The mode of international market entry depends on a wide array of environmental and organisational factors. Factors such as risk, government control, local infrastructure, competition, organisational objectives, need for control, flexibility and organisational resources, assets and capabilities impact the way products are marketed. It is important to understand that there is no one ideal way to internationalise.

For most organisations, however, exporting is their first experience of international marketing. It requires relatively little commitment and there are many intermediaries that can handle the more complex or resource-intensive aspects of exporting. As organisations become more experienced with international marketing, increase the scale of their international involvement or — through greater knowledge — identify more opportunities, they often evolve through increasingly direct means of international marketing. In the following sections we will briefly describe the various market entry choices, bearing in mind that the marketing organisation will often evolve from the simpler approaches to the more complex ones.

## Exporting

**Exporting** is an approach to international marketing involving the sale of products into foreign markets while remaining based in the home market. Exporting can occur directly (where the company is responsible for exporting activities) or indirectly. **Direct exporting** is an approach to exporting in which the marketing organisation deals directly with the international market. The complexities of exporting will usually prompt the marketing organisation to establish an internal department to focus on exporting activities, including developing knowledge of the target markets to inform the marketing mix. Depending on the product, some direct exporters may be able to deal with specialist buyers from foreign governments or businesses that are specifically looking to import particular products and to encourage trade generally. This last approach tends to suit smaller companies. They often rely on some transferrable aspect of their home product and put little or no effort into understanding or directly marketing to the international market.

**exporting** The sale of products into foreign markets from a home market base.

**direct exporting** An approach to exporting in which the marketing organisation deals directly with the international market.

**Indirect exporting** allows marketing organisations to access the international market without having to develop the expertise and contacts required to successfully place products into what is often a relatively unfamiliar market. It also lets them avoid many of the upfront costs and minimise the risks that can be involved with moving into exporting. The main types of export intermediaries are:

**indirect exporting** An approach to exporting that relies on the use of specialist marketing intermediaries.

- export agents, which bring together buyers and sellers from different countries and charge a commission on the sale
- trading companies, export houses and export merchants, which purchase products from businesses and then sell them into international markets.

## Contractual arrangements

**Licensing** is an arrangement in which a business (the licensee) in a foreign country undertakes to manufacture and sell the products of the home country company (the licensor) and pays a commission on the sales it makes. Licensing enables the international marketer to access an international market and have its products marketed in a manner suited to the target market without having to make a direct investment there. Coca-Cola is one of the best known examples. The next time you or a friend has a bottle or can of Coke, check the label. It will acknowledge this approach to international marketing with the words 'Bottled in Australia under licence by...' Many beers are treated the same way.

**licensing** An agreement in which a brand owner permits another party to use the brand on its products.

In a **franchising** arrangement, a business (the franchisee) pays the franchisor a fee in return for the right to market the franchisor's product using the franchisor's overall marketing and business plan. Such arrangements are familiar in the domestic market — for example, Boost Juice, Red Rooster, Snooze and Baker's Delight are all franchises. Franchising offers businesses a way to enter an international market without making a large upfront investment, transfer much of the risk to the franchisee, and yet maintain considerable control over the product, way it is promoted, standards and so on. For the franchisee, franchising offers a ready-made business plan. This is complicated of course by the need to ensure the plan will work in different markets.

**franchising** An approach to business in which one party (a franchisor) licenses its business model to another party (a franchisee).

**contract manufacturing**
An approach to international marketing in which a business pays a foreign business to manufacture its product and market it in the foreign country under the domestic business's name.

**international strategic alliance** A cooperative arrangement between a business and another business in a foreign market.

**international joint venture** An approach to international marketing in which a marketing organisation forms a new business with an existing business in the target foreign market.

**foreign direct investment** Outright ownership of a foreign operation.

**Contract manufacturing** in contrast to licensing and franchising, is an approach to international marketing in which a domestic business pays a foreign business to manufacture its product and market it in that foreign country under the domestic company's name.

## Strategic alliances and joint ventures

A business that does not wish to or cannot make a direct investment in a foreign market may choose instead to form an **international strategic alliance** with a business based in that country. This requires both businesses to be confident in the abilities and products of the other. Strategic alliances only make sense and can only succeed when each partner brings value to the alliance and each partner stands to benefit. The international airline industry is a prime example of strategic alliances. For an airline to compete with every other airline offering trips on the same route would be disastrously expensive. Instead, three global alliances have emerged in the airline industry: the Star Alliance (with 28 member airlines, including Air New Zealand, Lufthansa, Continental Airlines and Singapore Airlines), SkyTeam (13 members including Air France and Korean Air) and OneWorld (11 members including Qantas, Cathay Pacific and Japan Airlines). These alliances allow the bigger airlines to penetrate smaller markets by code-sharing with smaller operations. Under code-sharing arrangements, the passenger experience is virtually seamless when moving from one carrier to another — it is as if both flights are on the same line.

A related approach is the **international joint venture**. In a joint venture arrangement, rather than form an alliance, the two businesses actually form a new business together in the target market and forge a new identity for it, distinct from the parent businesses. Some joint ventures are balanced, while others will have a clear senior partner and clear junior partner. Joint ventures can help foreign businesses get around restrictions that might be imposed by some countries and can help the foreign business achieve some level of official and public acceptance in the target market.

## Direct investment

**Foreign direct investment**, as the name suggests, involves outright ownership of a foreign operation. Direct ownership involves a long-term commitment, considerable investment and acceptance of risk, and would usually only be pursued by an international marketer who was highly confident of success. Most marketers would only consider direct ownership once they have experience and success using the other approaches to international marketing. They may make a direct investment by establishing a greenfields operation (a new business from the ground up), buying out a strategic ally or even a competitor or buying a business somewhere up or down the supply chain (e.g. a manufacturing plant or a retailer). Businesses that develop extensive directly owned assets in numerous foreign countries are known as multinational corporations.

Directly owned subsidiaries may operate with little or considerable autonomy depending on the nature of the foreign market and the business's products. If the target international market is dissimilar to the parent business's market, the subsidiary may be given wide-ranging freedom to customise its products, marketing mix and business operations, taking advantage of the local know-how of its management. Success will then lead to greater autonomy. Such businesses also need to maximise cooperation and standardisation where possible though, to ensure they benefit from economies of scale and cumulative wisdom.

The inconsistencies and vagaries of laws around the world make direct ownership approaches to international marketing very complex, but also potentially very lucrative. Entire industries are built around finding the best countries to undertake different functions. For example, diamond companies have, naturally, subsidiaries in countries with rich deposits; while it may be an interesting ethical debate, the reality is that many businesses are headquartered in tiny island nations that do not charge corporate tax; and many manufacturing operations are located in countries with few laws to protect workers.

## Born global

The preceding sections have discussed the various ways that a business may enter a foreign market or evolve its foreign marketing operations to ever-greater levels of commitment. Before leaving this discussion we will briefly consider the phenomenon of businesses that are 'born global'. A **born global** business is one that views the whole world as it's market from day one. It will source materials from the most efficient country to source them, locate manufacturing operations in the country that provides the optimum conditions, manage itself from wherever it pleases and sell to anyone who wants it's products anywhere in the world. Clearly such a business model is not suitable to all industries or products. Those that can most successfully pursue global markets from day one are businesses that offer intellectual property or data services (where transport is irrelevant), that offer very high-end products where price is of little consequence, and those that have a unique, desirable product (such as a new pharmaceutical). The emergence of e-commerce has been an important facilitator of born global business and most born global marketing organisations are internet-based. Online auction site eBay is a prime example.

**born global** A business that views the whole world as its market from the outset.

# I still call Australia home?

## Spotlight

The Gloria Jean's story began in 1979 in the United States, where the company's namesake Gloria Jean Kvetko opened a shop offering a warm and friendly atmosphere and speciality coffee. The concept was a success, and in 1993 Gloria Jean sold the franchise for an estimated US$40 million. In 1995, following a visit to the United States, Nabi Saleh bought the master franchise for Gloria Jean's in Australia. The first Australian store was opened in 1996 in Sydney. By the end of 2004 Gloria Jean's had opened more than 200 coffee houses across Australia and owned the international branding and roasting rights for all countries outside of the United States.

Since that time Gloria Jean's has experienced significant growth, entering numerous new international markets, including China and India. In 2009 Gloria Jean's Coffees International also acquired Gloria Jean's Coffees USA, comprising 102 locations across the United States and making the Gloria Jean's brand Australian-owned and operated in all global markets. The acquisition also included a separate US coffee house brand — the 'It's a Grind' specialty coffee franchise — incorporating a further 103 stores across the United States.

There are now more than 1000 Gloria Jean's coffee houses in 38 countries around the world. More than 600 of these are in the 14 markets that comprise the Asia–Pacific region, including Australia, China, Fiji, India, Indonesia, Japan, Korea, Macau, Malaysia, Pakistan, the Philippines, Singapore, Thailand and Vietnam.

Today Gloria Jean's is an award-winning company that is still fully Australian-owned and locally operated, as well as being recognised for business excellence. It has won the annual high-profile International Franchise of the Year award at the Australian Excellence in Franchising Awards, and has been named as an 'Export Hero' by the Australian Institute of Export. It was also the first Australian company to win the Rainforest Alliance Green Globe Award for commitment to sustainable agriculture.[16]

### Question

Referring to the major methods of market entry outlined in the preceding section of the text, explain how Gloria Jean's has expanded internationally.

## Concepts and applications check

**Learning objective 3**  understand why and how organisations internationalise

**3.1**  Explain the major reasons organisations would consider internationalisation.

**3.2**  Identify one organisation in your local region or state that has successfully internationalised. How did it internationalise and what benefits have arisen for the local community as a result?

**3.3**  For *each* of the internationalisation options discussed in this section of the chapter, identify and outline an organisation that has internationalised using that particular method.

## THE INTERNATIONAL MARKETING MIX

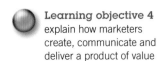

**Learning objective 4** explain how marketers create, communicate and deliver a product of value in an international market

So far, we have discussed the process of globalisation and how it is leading to greater similarities across markets as well as greater openness of markets to people and businesses from abroad. We have also examined the imperative for marketing organisations to take a world view and how they can select a target market and decide on varying degrees of standardisation and customisation of their marketing mix. Once the decision to internationalise is made, a marketing organisation must choose an entry mode. Most businesses start with the relatively simple approach of exporting and rely on specialist intermediaries. As they gain experience, success and ambition they may evolve to more direct means of international marketing.

As we have reiterated throughout this chapter, the aim of the international marketer is to gather the knowledge and skills necessary to develop, implement and evaluate marketing strategies in their target international markets. With such knowledge and skills, the marketer can make decisions that properly respond to the uncontrollable environmental variables in the marketplace. Because the environmental forces are not controllable, they must be continuously monitored so that the international marketing strategy can be modified to deal with change. This will sound familiar — it is essentially the same process used for domestic marketing, which we have dealt with throughout this book. We gather information to learn about the market. We analyse the information so that we can formulate sound options for action. Then we choose among the options.

At the heart of this is the four-step process that we outlined at the beginning of the chapter: while building knowledge of the international marketplace may involve special challenges, marketers must develop such an understanding in order to create, communicate, deliver and exchange offerings that have value for customers, clients, partners and society at large.

Consider Tourism Australia. The campaigns implemented over the past few decades by Tourism Australia to lure international visitors to Australia for holidays offer an interesting case study in the complexities of understanding international markets. Tourism Australia's approach has changed over time. In the 1980s, comedian, television and soon-to-be movie star, and quintessential 'Aussie bloke' Paul Hogan or 'Hoges' featured in a long-running series of advertisements that invited foreigners to come to Australia. Hoges promised he would 'slip an extra shrimp on the barbie for you'. The tagline of the campaign was 'Come and say G'day'. The overall theme was that Australia was a country of relaxed, laid-back, generous and welcoming people. The campaign — aimed mainly at the USA — was an enormous success, with overseas visitor numbers to Australia doubling in just five years and the country becoming one of the preferred destinations of US tourists. The tagline of the campaign itself reveals a careful consideration of the target market. Australians cook *prawns* on the barbie (barbecue), not shrimp, but the advertisements were not aimed at Australians (use of the word 'barbie' spawned a wave of parodies in which prawns were hurled at the famous plastic Barbie doll toy). Nevertheless, so popular were the ads and so well-loved was the Australian persona they portrayed that the line — modified to 'throw another shrimp on the barbie' — has became part of the Australian lexicon.

In the years after the shrimp on the barbie campaign, tourism from Asia grew strongly. Once growth began to weaken, a new, major overseas tourism push began, featuring the presentation of some of Australia's best known attractions, particularly the beaches, and concluding with model Lara Bingle standing on a picturesque beach asking potential visitors 'So where the bloody hell are you?' The $180 million campaign sought to continue the theme that Australians are a relaxed and welcoming people. Unfortunately the translations of the taglines in Asian countries (which in most cases omitted 'bloody hell') were interpreted as a demand, rather than an invitation, to visit Australia; Britain banned the ads because of the use of the words 'bloody hell'; and Canada banned the ads because of the opening line 'We've poured you a beer' which contravened Canada's rules on alcohol advertising. It appears the campaign badly misjudged the cultural and social values of their target markets (various countries in North America, Asia and Europe). The campaign was widely regarded as arrogant and offensive (and somewhat embarrassing to Australians).[17]

Not surprisingly Tourism Australia has changed their approach, evolving to an online platform. In 2010 the 'There's nothing like Australia' campaign involved Australians sharing their favourite Australian holiday stories online. The campaign was developed in two phases. The first phase invited Australians to share their personal stories of where they live and holiday in Australia — to show the world why they should visit. For two months, Australians were given the chance as part of a competition to upload their thoughts and photos online, explaining why 'There's nothing like Australia'. Australian holiday prizes valued at $5000 were offered for the photo judged to be the best entry in each state and territory, and an Australian holiday valued at $25 000 was offered for the best entry nationally. Tourism Australia subsequently used the entries to create an interactive map of Australia that was made up of the things Australians think are special about their country. This map is available online (www.nothinglikeaustralia.com) and is searchable by experience type, location and keywords.

Tourism Australia's various campaigns to promote the country as an attractive destination for international tourists provides an example of the complexities of adjusting the promotional message in the marketing mix to cater to different international markets. Similar issues arise in formulating product, pricing and distribution strategies, and, in the case of services products, people, process and physical evidence strategies. In contrast to the variety of themes delivered by Tourism Australia's international marketing campaigns in recent years, Tourism New Zealand has promoted a consistent message for more than a decade. Its award winning "100% Pure New Zealand" marketing message focuses on the country's natural beauty, culture and people, its food and wine, vibrant cities and extreme adventure tourism. However, despite this consistent message, in a clear sign that Tourism New Zealand understands that it must target

Tourism New Zealand's '100% Pure New Zealand' marketing campaign has been highly successful in attracting tourists to the region.

particular foreign markets in appropriately customised ways, it maintains different websites for different country markets: Australia, Belgium, Holland, the Netherlands, Canada, India, UK-Ireland, Italy, France, Switzerland, USA, Germany, Japan, Korea, China and Singapore.

The *product* mix needs to respond to customer preferences. For example, while it is popular for women to bleach their hair blonde in Australia and New Zealand, there is little market for hair-colouring products in Asia and so the marketers of hair styling products are better advised to target that market with hair care rather than hair-colouring products. The different levels of disposable income and wealth encountered across the world also may require product quality, size and packaging modifications for different markets. Nestlé's ice-cream line in China, for example, includes treat-sized products that sell for as little as 15 cents.[18] Competitive pressures may also necessitate product changes. Coca-Cola, in a bid to offer greater value than its competitors, sells a wide range of 'functional' drinks (e.g. Shpla, a citrus drink designed to overcome mental stress) that are specific to the Japanese market.

Once operating in different markets, the marketing organisation is likely to learn more about each market and can then further refine its product mix to best service its target customers. Branding is also an important consideration. Many organisations aim to establish a consistent global brand, but this can give rise to some difficulties. For example, many motoring industry commentators blame Nissan's decision to rebadge its Pulsar model 'Tiida' (the global model name) as a contributing factor in the declining popularity of the car in Australia. Toyota's Australian marketers successfully campaigned for the company to retain the Corolla badge in Australia, despite it renaming the model 'Auris' in every other market.

Services products present some additional challenges. The inseparability characteristic of services (see chapter 11) means most service delivery requires close interpersonal interaction between the customer and the service provider (or *people* in the extended services marketing mix). This poses a host of challenges even in the domestic market, but the numerous sociocultural differences between the people of different countries can require changes — sometimes subtle, sometimes substantial — to the way the service is delivered. The *process* by which the service is delivered may also require changes due to different technological and legal factors. Similarly, the tangible cues (or *physical evidence*) that support the service provider may need to be tailored to suit the different meanings of symbols in different cultures. It can also be difficult to elicit feedback from customers in some cultures that are reluctant to provide criticism.

In addition to the *promotion* issues highlighted by our discussion of the Tourism Australia campaigns, international marketers must also confront language barriers, advertising regulations, differing media infrastructure and differences in market maturity. These factors can require significant changes to promotional efforts in different markets.

International marketing, by definition, introduces an enormous range of *distribution* challenges that do not necessarily confront the domestic marketing organisation. The factors to be considered include:

- the need to transport products over much larger distances
- exchange rate fluctuations that substantially and quickly affect costs
- the appropriate use of marketing intermediaries who may facilitate distribution into foreign markets (or can make distribution difficult if not handled properly) — essentially, the international marketer can choose to sell directly to international

customers using its local sales force or via e-commerce, or it can use independent intermediaries within the foreign market.

*Pricing* is one of the most complex issues facing international marketers. Not only must pricing be sensitive to the local conditions in each market, but it must also reflect the costs involved in the international marketing effort. Importantly, prices need to display some consistency across markets — if not, the marketer may find that an unrelated business independently imports products from a 'cheap' market to resell in an 'expensive' market, undermining the legitimate marketer's business. Pricing is also influenced by exchange rates, trade barriers, government regulations, the level of competition and the organisation's specific marketing goals for each international market.

It should be clear then that international marketing *is* difficult. International marketers have made many very newsworthy mistakes and it is from these mistakes that we can all learn. Advertisers that failed to translate (e.g. English to Chinese) and then back translate (e.g. Chinese to English) found out the hard way, as did marketers who did not rely on market research to thoroughly test their offerings prior to introduction. Consider this often-quoted example: Scandinavian vacuum manufacturer Electrolux used the slogan 'Nothing sucks like an Electrolux' in its campaign, perhaps overlooking the less literal meaning of the word 'sucks', or perhaps deliberately trying to draw attention.[19]

So far we have learnt that successful marketing requires the marketer to know their market. Successful organisations put their customers' wants and needs at the heart of marketing and business decisions. International marketers with limited or no experience in the market must rely on market research to understand their target international market. To put it simply, in order to create, communicate, deliver and exchange offerings that have value for customers, clients, partners and society at large, marketers need to first understand what is of value. Market research is an essential component of *understanding* the market. As we learned in chapter 3, without market research international marketers would be left in the dark and decisions would be an educated guess at best. International marketers need to rely on market research to identify problems, uncover emerging trends, generate ideas on how greater value can be offered to customers, determine how to create offerings, understand how to communicate and, finally, evaluate the effectiveness of marketing initiatives. Market research needs to be used by international marketers to stay in tune with their customers, clients, partners and society at large.

## Internationalising: a smart way to go? Spotlight

Ginger and Smart was founded in 2002 by Sydney-based sisters Alexandra and Genevieve Smart. The inspiration to establish this clothing design business came from the desire to combine family talent to build a strong fashion-lifestyle brand. Alexandra had a creative business background as an editor and publisher for luxury lifestyle magazines, books and the internet. Genevieve had spent years at the helm of some of Australia's most successful fashion businesses. Their united industry knowledge, it would seem, put the sisters in a great position to launch a successful and exciting fashion business.

Ginger and Smart's core target market is women aged between 25–49 years, but they also sell to girls as young as 13 and women as old as 65 — suggesting their designs have broad appeal. Their range is designed to project an image of 'cool confidence'. With garments priced around $500, Ginger and Smart is positioned somewhere between the middle and upper end of the Australian fashion market, which is known to be fiercely competitive.

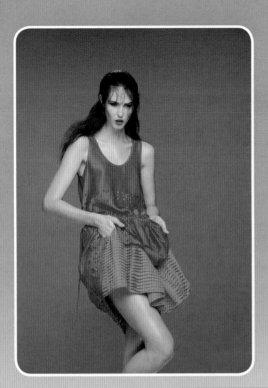

Fashion design has the lowest growth of any design industry nationally, and The Design Institute of Australia estimates there are about 2700 working fashion designers in Australia. These statistics mean many Australian designers must look internationally to broaden their potential market, though fashion is also a very competitive industry globally. Ginger and Smart aspire to be an international brand and have been selling in international markets for more than six years — including in Russia, the United Kingdom, the United States, Japan, Hong Kong, Denmark and New Zealand.

As business owners, sisters Alexandra and Genevieve acknowledge that internationalising is not an easy process. They recognise that it is important to have people 'on the ground' in international markets. Their approach to internationalisation has been to employ sales agents who promote their range to selected stockists in each country.[20]

## Question

Outline some of the key considerations for a clothing design business such as Ginger and Smart in developing an international marketing mix.

## Concepts and applications check

**Learning objective 4**  explain how marketers create, communicate and deliver a product of value in an international market

4.1 Ideas about international penetration often revolve around going to geographically and/or culturally close countries. How does this approach relate to the beer market?

4.2 Using a product and international market of your own choosing as an example, briefly outline the importance of market research in international marketing.

4.3 Choose a product that you are quite familiar with from your local market. Now choose an international market that you think could welcome your chosen product. Research the international market to discover what changes you might need to make to the marketing mix to give your product the best chance of success.

# SUMMARY

 **Learning objective 1** understand the concept of 'globalisation' and its consequences for organisations seeking to engage in international marketing

Through the process of globalisation, individuals, organisations and governments have become increasingly interconnected. This has greatly increased the number of businesses engaging with the world through their marketing activities and the flow of international trade is astounding: in the time it takes to read this chapter, more than $1.5 billion of goods and services was exchanged across national borders. One of the biggest decisions the international marketer must make is the extent to which it should maintain one marketing mix across international markets (standardisation) versus the extent to which it should tailor the marketing mix to the specific characteristics of various target markets (customisation).

 **Learning objective 2** discuss the political, economic, sociocultural, technological and legal forces at play in international markets

Political, economic, sociocultural, technological and legal forces are at play in the international marketing environment, both within individual target foreign markets and in the organisations, arrangements and other circumstances between countries. International marketers need to develop a strong understanding of how these forces differ from the more familiar forces in their home countries in order to select appropriate target markets and to amend their marketing approach appropriately. Most governments have established specialist organisations to help organisations interested in expanding into the international market; for example, Austrade and New Zealand Trade and Enterprise.

 **Learning objective 3** understand why and how organisations internationalise

The imperatives for international marketing include access to many more customers than exist in the home market, the increasingly free trading environment, increasing levels of competition within the domestic market, the identification of unserviced foreign markets and the pursuit of greater economies of scale. Organisations have a number of market entry modes available, including direct and indirect exporting, licensing, franchising, contract manufacturing, strategic alliances, joint ventures and direct investment. Some businesses are 'born global', treating the entire world as their market from the outset.

 **Learning objective 4** explain how marketers create, communicate and deliver a product of value in an international market

In common with domestic marketing, at the heart of international marketing is the need to build an understanding of markets and customers in order to create, communicate, deliver and exchange offerings that have value. To help build this knowledge, they will often rely on marketing intermediaries, extensive market research and their own experiences. Once armed with such knowledge, the marketer can make decisions that properly respond to the uncontrollable environmental variables in the international marketplace. These variables must be continuously monitored so that the international marketing strategy can be modified when necessary to deal with changing circumstances.

## Key terms and concepts

**born global** 481
**contract manufacturing** 480
**customisation** 462
**direct exporting** 479
**embargoes** 475
**exporting** 479
**foreign direct investment** 480
**franchising** 479
**globalisation** 460
**indirect exporting** 479
**international joint venture** 480
**international strategic alliance** 480
**licensing** 479
**quotas** 475
**standardisation** 462
**tariffs** 474

# Subway in Japan

Subway began in the United States in 1965 as a single sandwich store called 'Pete's Super Submarines'. It was founded by Fred DeLuca, who remains Subway's president and CEO today. The company started franchise operations in 1974, and its stores sell sandwiches and salads that are made to order in front of the customer. Subway markets itself as a healthier fast-food option than stores such as McDonald's and KFC.

Subway has over 23 000 franchised stores in the United States. Significantly, it surpassed the number of McDonald's stores in the United States in 2002. By 2005 the company had also overtaken the number of stores McDonald's operated in Australia, Canada and Northern Ireland. Despite already having 10 000 stores internationally in more than 90 countries, Subway is committed to the further expansion of its business in overseas markets in the coming years, via the franchising model. It focuses on what it calls 'high potential' markets, where several factors are favourable for their operation. These factors include:

- population density
- political and economic stability
- target customers' levels of disposable income
- the culture's general receptiveness to fast-food style restaurants.

However, one broad market that has proved difficult for Subway is Asia. CEO Fred De Luca has acknowledged that the company's growth in Asia in general has been slow, and that stores there have not been as profitable as in other markets. He has suggested that food cultures in many parts of Asia that revolve around rice may be part of the reason for this lacklustre performance. Japan is a case in point, being a country that Subway decided to enter in 2002. However, out of the first 200 stores that Subway franchisees opened in the country, more than half failed, with the average survival rate for a store being less than three years.

In order to analyse Subway in the context of this market, it is necessary to understand Japan and its food culture. Walk the streets of downtown Tokyo or Osaka or any other Japanese city at lunchtime and you will likely see office workers heading out to udon (Japanese flour noodle) and donburi (rice bowl dish) restaurants for something to eat. However, you will also likely see McDonald's franchises filled with high school students who are chatting and sending e-mails and tweets on their mobile phones over milkshakes and small-sized bags of French fries. Office employees often head to Italian cafes for pasta lunch sets, and those too busy to head out of the office may grab a bento (Japanese lunch box) or onigiri (rice balls) from convenience stores on their way to work. There are also ramen (noodle) and takoyaki (Japanese dumpling) shops. The food choices for consumers are seemingly endless. Japan is truly a gourmet paradise, and not simply at the 'high end' of sushi or kaiseki (multi-course traditional Japanese style) restaurants.

Subway competes in the fast food market, which is heavily saturated in Japan. While the market has been growing in volume every year in recent times, the growth rate in the number of fast food restaurants has exceeded the growth rate in total sales. In Japan, Subway has several direct competitors. These competitors are now discussed.

- **McDonald's.** The market leader, McDonald's has had a presence in Japan since 1971, and now has more than 3000 stores in the country. It operates with a low-price, set-menu strategy, designed to increase sales per customer (a basic set menu is just JPY 500, for a burger, French fries and a drink — approximately AUD 6). McDonald's advertises heavily; for example, on TV and by use of discount vouchers regularly handed out by staff in urban centres. The company launches seasonal products (such as the 'Tsukimi' burger in autumn — a teriyaki burger with an egg on top — to celebrate the Japanese 'moon viewing' season). It targets a wide cross-section of the market, and is popular with children, offering them the traditional 'Happy Meal' that is popular around the world. McDonald's has a high number of loyal, repeat customers.
- **Mos Burger.** Established in 1972, this Japanese burger chain has 1300 stores across the country. Mos Burger's menu has similarities to McDonald's, but its prices are a little higher (burger sets are around JPY 600; approximately AUD 7.20). However, Mos Burger cooks burgers to order, and the company stresses fresh ingredients, including the use of seasonal vegetables. Its advertising heavily features salad, vegetables and wholesome ingredients. It offers original Japanese

adaptations to the burger format, such as the rice burger — a burger with two rice cakes used instead of a split bun that features Japanese-style fillings. Mos Burger targets women aged in their twenties and thirties, and is the second-most successful burger chain in Japan, behind McDonald's.

- **Yoshinoya.** With a history dating back to 1899, Yoshinoya is a long-established fast food restaurant and could best be described as offering traditional Japanese fast food. The company mainly sells gyudon, a Japanese dish of simmered beef and onions served on a bowl of rice. It targets male students and workers, offering very cheap dishes (from JPY 300 — approximately AUD 3.60) and fast service. Yoshinoya has more than 1000 branches in Japan. Its food is fast, inexpensive and convenient, as well as being healthier than a burger.
- **Starbucks.** Starbucks has made inroads into the Japanese market over the last ten years. Prices of its sandwiches start from around JPY 380 (approximately AUD 4.50), and its coffee costs from JPY 250 to 330 (AUD 3 to 4). Starbucks targets young people, especially women (and in particular, Japanese 'OLs', or 'office ladies'). They have been successful due to their convenience for breakfast, lunch and also 'coffee break' times, as well as the relaxing atmosphere of their stores. Starbucks operates more than 700 stores in Japan.
- **Kentucky Fried Chicken (KFC).** KFC has proved to be a very popular franchise in Japan, and targets the family market. Its prices tend to be higher than McDonald's or Subway. It offers set menu items for around JPY 750 (approximately AUD 9). KFC operates more than 1100 stores in Japan and promotes heavily using TV advertising.
- **Mister Donut.** Mister Donut, owned by Duskin Corporation, has operated in Japan since 1971, and has approximately 1300 stores in the country. Mister Donut offers doughnuts at very low prices, as well as dishes such as ramen noodles and Chinese steamed pork buns. Its main customers are young people, including students and office workers. The company advertises on TV and via discount vouchers handed out on the street. Mister Donut's TV commercials have been very popular in Japan, featuring famous Japanese TV personalities, and even members of the Spanish football team Real Madrid. The company regularly holds campaigns offering all doughnuts for sale at JPY 100 (approximately AUD 1.20), which prove massively popular, especially with high school and university students.

In addition to these large fast food companies, there are a plethora of local restaurants in Japan that serve fast and cheap meals. For example, ramen noodle shops can be found everywhere. Prices for a bowl of noodles are around JPY 500 to 700 (approximately AUD 6 to 8.40), but some chains are cheaper. Other restaurants can be seen around the country specialising in dishes such as soba and udon noodles, pork cutlets, curries and omelettes, as well as Japanese 'fast food' like okonomiyaki or takoyaki.

As they do in other countries, Subway in Japan promotes its sandwiches as fresh, healthy and made-to-order. They use their internationally familiar slogan 'Eat Fresh', and the price of a six-inch 'Sub', plus a drink, is around JPY 480 to 580 (approximately AUD 5.80 to 7). On their Japanese website, Subway has also promoted the story of US customer Jared Fogle, who famously lost approximately 112 kilograms on a diet of Subway sandwiches. Like their international counterparts, Subway customers in Japan can choose between six- or 12-inch rolls for their sandwiches, with different types of bread, several kinds of toppings, and lots of salad and dressings. Every menu item has a calorie count next to the price; some products even display a fat count. Calories listed on its six-inch menu items range from about 200 to 400 kilocalories.

However, the average weight for a Japanese man aged 20 to 24 is 65.4 kilograms. For women in the same age group, the average weight is 55.4 kilograms. While obesity exists in Japan, it is not on the same scale as in many Western countries, and Subway's advertising revolving around the concept of health and beating obesity does not carry the same resonance there as it does in other countries. Concepts of 'healthy' food are not necessarily the same in Japan as in many Western nations. While, of course, there are many people watching their calorie intake, many Japanese think of healthy food more in terms of quality — for example, how fresh, pure or organic the ingredients are — rather than in terms of calorie or fat content. This is how a chain such as Mos Burger, selling fried burgers and deep fried chicken and potatoes, can successfully market a wholesome image in Japan. They use good quality ingredients, which are likewise reflected in the chain's higher prices.

Fast food aside, many other common restaurant food items in Japan would not be considered healthy by Western standards. For example, deep-fried dishes such as tempura or kushi-katsu (skewered meat or vegetables, dipped in breadcrumbs and then deep fried) are common, as are deep-fried pork cutlets. Another food consideration in Japan, however, is portion size. Typically, people will have this kind of food in smaller amounts, and often accompanied with side dishes such as rice, miso soup and pickled vegetables. Even ice-cream chain Cold Stone Creamery downsized its servings when it entered the Japanese market.

Subway has largely moved into the Japanese market without significantly adjusting its product or marketing for local tastes. One concession to their model that it has made, however, is reducing the amount of filling in sandwiches. 'Subs' purchased in Japan are not filled with the same amount of ingredients as elsewhere, though the bread dimensions are the same. This alteration was made as a result of criticism from Japanese customers when Subway first entered the market that their large sandwiches were difficult to eat.

Subway Japan Inc. is 100 per cent owned by Japanese company Suntory Ltd, who negotiated the master franchise agreement for Japan with Subway in the United States. Originally a brewery, Suntory has diversified its holdings into a range of different industries, including food and other non-alcoholic beverages. According to its franchise application guide book, Subway Japan focuses on opening stores where there are demographic centres — for example, in downtown, office and amusement areas, as well as in front of railway stations.[21]

## Questions

1. Identify the various macro-environmental challenges Subway faces in the Japanese market.
2. How does Subway's positioning compare with that of its competitors?
3. Should Subway pursue a customisation strategy for its marketing mix in Japan, rather than its largely standardised strategy that has been successful in other international markets? Justify your answer.

## Advanced activity

Visit the Boost website (www.boostjuice.com.au) and compare and contrast how Boost creates, communicates and delivers their product in two different countries of your choice. In particular, outline the following:

(a) To what extent is Boost following a standardised or customised strategy? Justify your answer.
(b) What environmental factors could potentially impact on Boost's success in the international markets you have chosen to analyse?
(c) How has Boost chosen to go international and why do you think it would have chosen the foreign countries you are analysing?
(d) How does (or might) Boost's international marketing mix differ between countries?

## Marketing plan activity

Now that you have read this chapter, think about which parts of your plan you would need to adjust to cater for an international market. Choose one country as a potential international market for your product. Research and adjust one of the following components of your marketing plan accordingly with information relating to that international market's potential for your product:

(a) situation analysis
(b) SWOT analysis
(c) target market(s).

A sample marketing plan has been included at the back of this book (page 523) to give you an idea where this information fits in an overall marketing plan.

## CHAPTER 14

# Marketing planning, implementation and evaluation

## Learning objectives

After studying this chapter, you should be able to:

 explain the relationship between the marketing cycle and marketing management

 understand the importance of effective marketing planning in achieving organisational and marketing objectives

 describe how to manage the implementation of a marketing strategy

 explain the role of marketing metrics and the ongoing evaluation of marketing performance in the marketing cycle.

# Bank bashing via Twitter

Australians have long been frustrated with their banks. Consider the following statement posted on Twitter in October 2010:

NAB $4.58 billion. ANZ $5.02 billion. Commonwealth Bank $6.1 billion. All profit. How many homeless could be housed for that money?

A study of five months' worth of tweets about Australia's big four banks has found that people dislike all banks about the same, but find different reasons to be fed up with each one. The Alliance Strategic Research study analysed more than 5000 tweets in a recent year. Findings from the study were presented at the 2010 Australian Marketing & Social Research Society conference in Melbourne. The issue most commented upon for all banks was service, followed by issues related to social media, brand image, branch locations and bank staff. Internet banking services and bank websites attracted a lot of criticism, with numerous complaints over log-in issues and sites being down or running slowly. About 85 per cent of tweets about ANZ were negative, compared to an average of 71 per cent for the other three banks (Westpac, the CBA and the NAB).

The Alliance Strategic Research study found important differences between what kind of messages people put on Twitter. People were more strongly negative and more likely to swear in their banking tweets if the message was not addressed to anyone specific. Significantly, at the time of the study, Westpac was the only one of the four banks actively monitoring and responding to tweets.

Twitter has grown in popularity to become one of the largest social networking sites. In contrast to Facebook and MySpace, Twitter pages are viewable to anyone online, making them an ideal data source for marketers seeking unsolicited feedback on their brand. A simple keyword search can reveal all online tweets where they have been mentioned.

The Alliance Strategic Research study highlights how marketing managers can use Twitter to track word-of-mouth feedback about their brand and how they can monitor consumer incidents to understand how service improvements can be delivered across their business.[1]

---

## Question

How could the big four banks in Australia use Twitter to inform their marketing planning and improve their businesses?

# INTRODUCTION

Throughout this book we have emphasised the need for organisations to adopt a marketing orientation. A market-oriented approach to business simply means that decisions are made to maximise customer value, based on knowledge of the market and the marketing environment. In this chapter we consider the marketing cycle. The marketing cycle commences with understanding the market in order to create, communicate and deliver value to customers. This process of creating, communicating and delivering is then evaluated by marketers to understand the impact made, if any. Once marketers understand the impact of their marketing program, they make adjustments to their program based on the feedback obtained. The marketing cycle is best considered as an ongoing loop where marketing programs and plans are constantly revised and refined. It is evaluation, throughout and after marketing efforts, that makes the marketing process cyclical in nature. It is also evaluation that truly enables a marketing organisation to know, understand and respond to changes in the market.

## THE MARKETING CYCLE

We have emphasised throughout this book that marketing is not a linear process that begins with an idea, proceeds to a plan and ends with successful implementation of the plan. Rather, marketing is an ongoing and interrelated process of understanding, creating, communicating and delivering offerings. This can be represented in a simplified fashion as shown in figure 14.1. We call this the **marketing cycle**. It emphasises that:

- understanding the customer results in the ability to create, communicate and deliver value
- evaluation of marketing performance builds further understanding that enables the marketing program to be refined to improve future performance.

**Learning objective 1** explain the relationship between the marketing cycle and marketing management

**marketing cycle** The cyclical and interrelated process of understanding, creating, communicating and delivering value, refined by continuous evaluation.

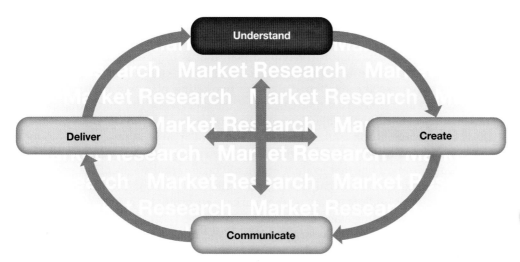

**FIGURE 14.1**

The marketing cycle

Remember that feedback mechanisms work between each part of the process represented in figure 14.1. For example, a marketer uses market research to create a new product variant for breakfast cereal. Market research is once again used to test if the new breakfast cereal variant appeals to the market.

# Understanding, planning, implementation and evaluation

The main activities an organisation must undertake in relation to marketing are:

- develop a detailed understanding of the market
- plan how to achieve the organisation's goals
- implement the plan
- continuously evaluate marketing performance.

It is important to remember that this is not a linear process; in practice, marketers continually refine and adapt each and every aspect of their offering based on the changing marketing environment and evaluation of their marketing program to date. The management task of understanding the market, and planning, implementing and evaluating marketing activities is known as **marketing management**. Marketing management aims to ensure that the organisation achieves its marketing objectives by maximising the value obtained from the marketing exchange — for the organisation itself and its customers, clients, partners and society at large.

**marketing management**
The management task of understanding the market, and planning, implementing and evaluating marketing activities.

The first six chapters of this textbook provided the foundations for building an *understanding* of the market. Chapter 1 outlined the marketing concept and the importance of adopting a market orientation. Chapter 2 introduced the marketing environment and how a marketing plan can be developed from such an understanding. Chapter 3 discussed the role of market research in building market understanding. Chapters 4 and 5 explained the decision-making processes and behaviours of consumers and business purchasers respectively. Chapter 6 described approaches to understanding the composition of the market in such a way that plans can be made to specifically target appropriate market segments.

Based on a sound understanding of the fundamental concepts related to the market and marketing, the organisation can formulate a marketing *plan* to achieve the organisation's marketing objectives. This plan will incorporate the components and issues discussed in chapters 7 to 13. A marketing plan communicates to all how the marketing team plans to get to where it needs or wants to be. It details how to create value, communicate the offering to potential customers and deliver the offering to the market.

Putting the plan into action is the *implementation* part of marketing. Just as implementation requires a marketing plan, a plan cannot ignore the realities of implementation. There is little point in having a plan that is impossible to implement or goals that are impossible to achieve. This chapter discusses steps the organisation can take to maximise the likelihood that the marketing plan will be implemented effectively. We also note risks that can affect the success of the marketing plan in achieving the organisation's objectives and how these can be managed.

During implementation and at the conclusion of a marketing campaign, marketing metrics and other systems can be used to *evaluate* marketing performance. It is important to remember that evaluation should occur at all stages of the marketing cycle so that the organisation can quickly and effectively respond to changing conditions or some new understanding of the market. Accordingly, at this point you are back to the understanding stage of the marketing cycle.

To better understand the marketing cycle and the role of marketing management, let's consider some examples.

Ezibuy is a mail order company that targets women in Australia and New Zealand. Despite Ezibuy being the number one website in its category, customers were generally opting to place orders by phone. The challenge was to change customer behaviour to encourage people to purchase online without harming the emotional relationship they had with the brand. Ezibuy undertook customer analytics and delivered a one-to-one message tailored to each customer's range preferences and geographic area, together with a tailored incentive as a call to action. The campaign resulted in readership of 27 per cent, click through of 11 per cent and sales conversions rates of 30 per cent when an offer was used and 10 per cent with no offer. Ezibuy refined and adapted their offering based on the changing marketing environment and evaluation.[2]

Not-for-profit organisations also use marketing to improve performance. As is the case with many Australian charities, the Heart Foundation needs to stay on its toes to maintain a large donor base in a competitive market. The charity recently implemented a new donor acquisition strategy and introduced a promotional pack aimed at recruiting new donors. The Heart Foundation aimed to find people to add to their mailing list and wanted these people to share the characteristics of their current donors. Some of those characteristics included people aged over 65, who were retired, owned their own home, enjoyed reading, gardening and walking and knew that the Heart Foundation funds and conducts research. Working with First Direct Solutions, a division of Australia Post, the Heart Foundation was able to access prospective 'lookalike' donors from First Direct Solutions' lifestyle database, which comprises considerable name and address records. Using a powerful profiling database tool, First Direct Solutions is able to identify individuals who match the Heart Foundation's donor profile — and then supply personalised contact details (including telephone and email when available) for use in the Heart Foundations direct marketing campaigns.[3]

Now that we have explored the nature of the marketing cycle, we will dedicate the rest of the chapter to discussing marketing planning (including marketing objectives), implementation and evaluation in more detail.

# Keeping Cloncurry waterwise

Like most regional areas of Australia, the Cloncurry Shire, near Mount Isa in far north Queensland, is prone to extreme weather conditions. It has experienced both a flood and a drought in recent years. During their most recent severe drought and consequent water shortages in mid 2008, an urgent and unique demand management program needed to be implemented. An award-winning social marketing partnership between the state government, the local government and private enterprise was born — one that continues to benefit the shire in non-drought periods.

Qualitative and secondary market research identified that while the Cloncurry community had developed ways to cope with their long-term water situation, they generally continued to adopt inefficient water usage behaviours. Cloncurry residents understood what behaviours generated unnecessary high water use, and they understood the community was continually at risk of water shortages; yet, they had not significantly changed their behaviours. Behavioural change could only be achieved if Cloncurry residents could be motivated to participate.

The Cloncurry Waterwise Service was created and a campaign implemented for residents of the shire over a short and intense six-week period. During this time, business and households were entitled to a visit by a licensed plumber to receive the following free services:
• have all inefficient showerheads replaced with high-quality water-efficient ones
• have all minor leaks fixed anywhere inside and outdoors
• have aerators installed on inside taps to help stop water waste.

The key marketing communication message of the campaign was 'Help us make Cloncurry even more waterwise'. Awareness raising and 'call to action' press and radio advertising were utilised, as well as direct mail. Community-based and direct response channels, such as community group bulk bookings, mobile kiosks, plumber referrals and door-to-door visits, contributed to the majority of residential bookings.

Satisfaction with the service provided and subsequent water and energy savings were independently evaluated by specialist external agencies, and the metrics were impressive. The service achieved a residential take up rate of 85 per cent, with an overall satisfaction rating of 93 per cent. The water savings to residences as a direct result of the Waterwise program were estimated to be 37.4 megalitres per annum, representing a 4.6 per cent saving in total residential water use. Importantly, this is a long-term water saving measure for the drought-prone region.[4]

## Concepts and applications check

**Learning objective 1**  explain the relationship between the marketing cycle and marketing management

1.1  Market research is only required once in the marketing cycle. Discuss this statement.

1.2  Prepare an argument for and against the following statement: '*Understanding* is the key phase of the marketing cycle.'

1.3  Imagine you have just been employed in your first marketing role for a civil engineering company with four employees, all of whom have a specialist engineering backgrounds. The business will specialise in car parks, roads and other infrastructure. The entire marketing 'department' initially will consist only of you. How would you explain the marketing cycle to your colleagues, and their place in it, in your own words?

# MARKETING PLANNING

**Learning objective 2** understand the importance of effective marketing planning in achieving organisational and marketing objectives

In chapter 2 it was outlined that a thorough situational analysis, together with an organisation's objectives, forms the basis for marketing planning. Organisations that operate with a marketing philosophy put customers at the centre of their thinking. Research shows that organisations with a marketing philosophy perform better for their stakeholders — they offer more value to customers and clients, better financial returns to partners and owners, and more benefits for society at large.[5] Let's consider how this occurs in practice. Organisations state their purpose using mission statements, values and organisational goals. Let's take a look at some examples:

• *Fuji Xerox* — To help people find better ways to do great work — by constantly leading in document technologies, products and services that improve our customers' work processes and business results.[6]

• *Facebook* — Facebook's mission is to give people the power to share and make the world more open and connected.[7]

• *Woolworths* — Woolworths mission statement is to deliver to customers the right shopping experience each and every time.[8]

• *Singapore Airlines* — Singapore Airlines is a global company dedicated to providing air transportation services of the highest quality and to maximising returns for the benefit of its shareholders and employees.[9]

Organisation goals, missions and values vary considerably and can serve to distinguish one organisation from another. Recall our discussion in chapter 2 that organisations need to distinguish themselves from competition. Mission statements represent the starting point as they communicate to both internal stakeholders (e.g. employees) and external stakeholders (e.g. customers, investors and media).

All of the examples above sound like reasonable — in some cases noble — objectives. Read the examples again and imagine you are the marketing director of each organisation. Consider how you would go about achieving the objectives. You might have some ideas, but you will have found that the statements do not in themselves tell you much about how to go about achieving the objectives or indeed exactly how you might know/measure if you have achieved the goals. While top management establishes **mission statements** and overarching organisational goals, it is up to senior and middle managers to plan and implement respectively to achieve those goals. To fulfil the mission statement, organisational goals and values must be translated and disseminated throughout the entire organisation. Organisational objectives must be carefully interpreted into objectives for each single business unit. Business unit objectives then get translated into functional or area objectives.

Consider the following vision, which belongs to Tourism Queensland as stated in its 2008–2012 Corporate Plan:

> As a global leader in destination management, our vision is to be the champion of world's best practice in sustainable tourism.

Tourism Queensland has a formal corporate plan that outlines the organisation's strategic direction for four years. It is formulated through a process of business and financial planning and is updated annually. The main function of Tourism Queensland's corporate plan is to outline primary responsibilities and to specify how key challenges will be achieved and measured. Its current plan outlines five key challenges it faces as an organisation. These are:
1. Capitalise on our global reputation as a must see part of an Australian holiday.
2. Mitigate the shocks on the industry through sustainable development.
3. Facilitate investment to meet the needs of the consumers and the growing Queensland population.
4. Counter the increasing overseas travel by Australians.
5. Minimise the impact to Queensland of the global contraction of air services.

Key result areas outline how Tourism Queensland will seek to overcome the challenges it faces. For illustrative purposes, selected projects and outcomes appear in table 14.1.[10] The categories shown in the left column represent the matters of concern for the Tourism Queensland's **corporate strategy** and the desired broad outcomes in the right column guide Tourism Queensland's decision-makers in formulating the details of their corporate strategy (essentially what to do and how to allocate resources to achieve those outcomes). Specific performance metrics for these desired outcomes are contained in Tourism Queensland's internal organisational documents and these are tracked regularly and reported upon annually.

**mission statements**
A summary statement of the overarching goals of the organisation.

**corporate strategy** A specific, but high-level plan to achieve objectives that reflect the overall mission of the organisation.

**TABLE 14.1** Tourism Queensland major projects and outcomes

| Major projects | Outcomes |
| --- | --- |
| • Better understand the needs of our key target markets | • Adoption of TQ international and domestic segments by all stakeholders |
| • Market the Queensland brands internationally and domestically, in line with the Global Brand Strategy | • Global Brand Strategy initiatives are implemented as agreed |
| • Increase advertising sales revenue from advertising with TQ | • Broaden the partnership between TQ and tourism and non-tourism organisations |
| • Website enhancements to match consumer requirements | • Best practice in innovation and user-friendly online information delivery |
| • Targeting youth, increase interest of tourism as a career opportunity | • National Tourism Careers Portal is progressed and agreed by all stakeholders |
| • Support a skilled, motivated team in Australia and overseas | • Maintain the staff average overall satisfaction with TQ above 75 per cent |

**business-unit strategy**
Strategies for the various business areas within an organisation to guide their contribution to achieving the overall corporate objectives.

From this broad corporate strategy, objectives at the business unit level would be set and used to develop a **business-unit strategy**, which will guide the resources allocated to each business unit within Tourism Queensland. Strategies for each functional area within each business unit would then be developed to assist the business unit to achieve its objectives. Functional area strategies are then translated into functional area objectives. By breaking the organisational mission, goals and values into business units and, later, functional objectives, organisations can assist each area in an organisation to understand what needs to be done, when and by whom. Given that 'what is measured gets done', this translation of organisational mission into functional area objectives ensures that each and every person in the organisation understands the organisation's mission and the part that they need to play to achieve the mission. This is represented in figure 14.2.

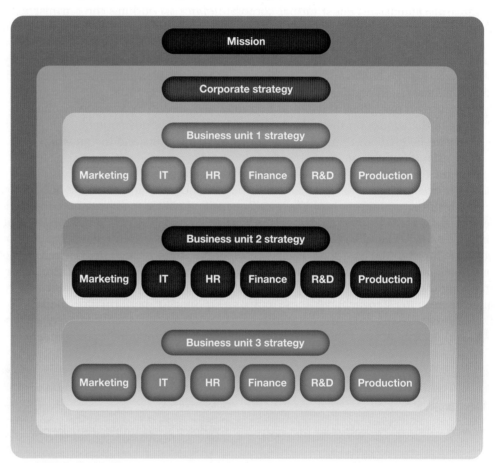

**FIGURE 14.2**

Hierarchy of strategic planning

All areas of an organisation should be working to meet the same organisational goals. While each functional area may have its own objectives, they are still working together to meet one common goal. It is important to understand the relationship between marketing and other organisational functions:

- *human resources and marketing*. The marketing and human resources functions need to work together to recruit the 'right' people to project the required image.
- *finance and marketing*. The marketing and finance functions need to work together to ensure that funding is available to create, communicate and deliver the organisation's products and to ensure that marketing activities operate within the financial resources of the organisation.

- *accounting and marketing.* The accounting and marketing functions need to work together to ensure marketing has comprehensive, timely and structured data on sales and past marketing performance, and that the marketing function is providing the accounting function with the necessary information to ensure mandatory business and legal accounting obligations are fulfilled.
- *information systems and marketing.* Information systems and marketing work together to cnsurc marketing has the necessary tools to communicate and deliver the product to customers. For technology-based organisations or organisations that deliver technology-based products, the information systems area, if it incorporates information technology, can be crucial in ensuring the product is delivered at a satisfactory level of customer service. For example, for a bank such as Westpac that offers customers the convenience of internet banking, the information systems area must ensure that the service is working correctly virtually all of the time. Similarly, businesses that use e-commerce rely heavily on their information systems area to ensure the communication and delivery aspects of marketing are reliably carried out.
- *research and development and marketing.* Research and development has an important role in keeping marketing up to date with new technologies and innovations and in responding to market needs and wants as advised by the marketing area. It is crucial that the research and development area focus its activities on the current and anticipated needs of the market and this can only be achieved by close communication and cooperation with those most in touch with the market — the marketing department.
- *production and marketing.* Marketing and production must communicate and cooperate to ensure that products are produced in the appropriate quantities, at the appropriate quality and at the right time. Historically, many organisations have had a bias toward production, where products are created based on the capabilities of the organisation's production department, but organisations with a market orientation try to focus the production department on delivering products demanded by the market.
- *logistics and marketing.* Delivery of products to customers when and where they are wanted is a crucial part of marketing and the marketing and logistics departments (such as warehousing and transport) must work together to ensure this aspect is completed well. Marketing is able to provide details as to likely levels and locations of demand and can also undertake actions (such as discounts or advertising) to affect demand at particular points in time.

# Marketing objectives

The concept of marketing objectives will be familiar from your studies of this textbook. Most for-profit marketing organisations share the goals of profit, market share growth and customer retention. We will dedicate some discussion to these objectives now and then look at a model for creating effective objectives.

### Profit

Business organisations exist ultimately to generate wealth for the business owners. Hence a particular level of profit will be an objective of all business organisations. Not-for-profit organisations do not have this as an objective, but they will usually have some financial objectives (e.g. to generate enough funds to be self-supporting or to generate funds in order to carry out charity or other philanthropic work).

The generation of profit is the culmination of virtually all of the processes that take place within an organisation. Hence the objective of profit is like to exist at the corporate mission level and a particular level of profit is likely to be detailed in the corporate strategy. This in turn will be broken down into targets and methods for achieving those targets in particular business units and functional areas.

### Market share growth

Market share growth is linked with profit, but it should not be mistaken for the same thing. Successful business organisations are long-term entities and operate with a view to sustainable operation. Hence organisations may be willing to sacrifice profit to establish market share. This is often seen when a business enters a new market — it will undercut the prices of existing competitors to attract trial customers and win market share. Once a degree of customer loyalty is established, it will gradually increase prices to ensure long-term profitability. Similarly, some businesses offer free trials of services to hook customers who then must pay once the free trial expires if they wish to maintain the service. Apple did this with its online Mac and MobileMe services.

### Customer retention

To ensure profitability and achieve market share growth, the business must not only win new customers, but also retain the loyalty of its existing customers. It does this by putting customers at the centre of its decision making. Attracting new customers is difficult, so once a customer has engaged with a business, the aim should be to generate customer loyalty and repeat business. This can occur by providing outstanding service, acting quickly on problems or disputes and undertaking customer relationship management. **Customer relationship management** (often abbreviated to CRM) refers to the processes and practices put in place to identify, track and use customer information and preferences to provide superior customer service and sustain long-term relationships. A simple example of customer relationship management is a bank sending an income insurance brochure to a customer who has just taken out a loan. Another example is a hairdresser knowing which shampoo a customer favours, and yet another is a customer being able to ask for 'their usual table' at a restaurant or 'the usual' drink at a bar. The 'cookies' used by websites to 'remember' a visitor's preferences or habits are an example of an automated CRM process.

Customer relationship management can be a very important tool in retaining customers and in generating additional business from existing customers. The increasing use of phone and other technologies to communicate with customers has led to substantial growth in customer relationship management approaches. Businesses must be aware though that this practice has also led to much higher expectations from customers. Customers expect the business to know more about them and to tailor their offerings in response to that. Businesses that fail to know much about long-term customers are at significant risk of losing that customer. Another thing businesses need to beware of in adopting a customer relationship management approach is that they can be complex and demand buy-in from all employees who will work with the system. For them to be effective, every contact with the customer needs to be logged.

### Societal objectives

In addition to the commonplace organisational objectives, many businesses have objectives aimed at the good of society. These have been developed out of a sense of obligation to the society in which the business operates and the increasing importance placed on social responsibility by growing numbers of potential customers. For example, McHappy Day is one of Australia's longest standing charity fundraisers. However, by 2008, McHappy Day was stagnating and people were donating less to the cause than in previous years. McDonald's was faced with a tough task and set out to improve donations for McHappy Day at a time when the economy was performing poorly due to the ramifications of the global financial crisis. McDonald's

**customer relationship management (CRM)** The processes and practices put in place to identify, track and use customer information and preferences to provide superior customer service and sustain long-term relationships.

subsequently made heavier use of emotion in its marketing communications, enabling people to feel they were collectively making a significant contribution to the lives of sick children. The following year, McHappy Day reached a 19-year record high of $2.4 million in donations.[11]

**Corporate social responsibility** is the notion that corporations are obliged to act in the interests of the society in which they operate; for example, by protecting the natural environment and creating employment.

**corporate social responsibility** The obligation of businesses to act in the interests of the societies that sustain them.

### The SMART model

We will use the SMART model to consider the characteristics of effective marketing objectives, which we first explored when we looked at defining the marketing challenge and developing a marketing plan. According to the **SMART model**, objectives must be:

- Specific
- Measurable
- Actionable
- Reasonable
- Timetabled.

**SMART model** An approach to determining effective marketing objectives that requires they be Specific, Measurable, Actionable, Reasonable and Timetabled.

#### Specific

Objectives need to be clearly defined so that it is easy to understand what is to be achieved and what will be considered successful. For example, 'increase revenue' is not a specific objective; 'increase revenue by 10 per cent while containing cost growth to 4 per cent' is. Another example of a specific objective is 'increase brand awareness (measured by unaided recall) by 10 per cent'. By stating the measure of brand recall, managers know what needs to be achieved.

#### Measurable

The exact measure must be stated and the objective must be able to be measured through some means. Look back at the two examples above. It is relatively straightforward to measure whether a marketing campaign has managed to 'increase revenue by 10 per cent while containing cost growth to 4 per cent' by referring to the business's financial records. The second example above involves an objective that can also be measured. Determining whether brand awareness had increased by 10 per cent would require a validly constructed survey before and after the campaign. Even less specific objectives can be measured. For example, the objective of a retailer to improve in-store service could be measured by an exit survey of customers conducted before and after the improvement program. If you refer back to table 14.1, you will see, for example, that Tourism Queensland measures the level of employee satisfaction within its organisation.

#### Actionable

The organisation needs to ensure that its business-unit managers, such as marketing managers, have the authority and resources to take the actions necessary to achieve the objectives that are set. If the necessary actions cannot be taken to achieve the objectives, the objectives should not be set. For example, an objective for a sales agent for a clothing designer may be to make presentations to 50 retail chains. This objective would be actionable as long as the agent's manager ensures that the necessary time, materials and other resources are available to the agent.

#### Reasonable

There is little point setting unrealistic objectives for a marketing objective. An organisation may well harbour grand ambitions and is entitled to do so, but it must set objectives that are realistic. Unreasonable objectives can act as a disincentive for managers and their employees. For a new industry entrant in a stable, mature market, a reasonable objective might be to achieve a 5 per cent market share in five years. An unreasonable objective would be to secure a 50 per cent market share in five years (although it can happen in particular circumstances).

For an established business, a reasonable objective might be to grow 1 or 2 per cent faster than the industry growth rate, but it would be unreasonable to expect a business to achieve year-on-year double-digit growth in a mature industry that is growing at only a few per cent each year.

### Timetabled

Marketing is an ongoing effort, though marketing campaigns may occur over a particular period of time. Moreover, marketing is an ongoing process that changes in response to the marketing environment. To ensure consistent progress, and to ensure that progress can be measured, objectives should have milestone dates set. For example, if a company such as SleepMaster that manufactures quilts, blankets and pillows wants to achieve 10 per cent sales growth over a financial year, it would set that as an objective, but would also have intra-year objectives. For example, it might have an objective to implement an extensive advertising campaign in April as the weather starts to cool down, combined with specific sales objectives for the peak winter season of May, June and July. If the sales increase is not achieved during winter, it may have to introduce a new objective to increase sales in spring by offering aggressive price discounts. Objectives need to be timetabled to assist managers to understand when to measure to assess performance.

### Objectives and marketing metrics

Marketing objectives can take a variety of forms including profit related, sales and market share related, customer related and societal objectives. Specific measures of marketing performance are referred to as **marketing metrics**. As outlined in chapter 2, the Australian Marketing Institute offers a framework for marketing metrics. This framework's underlying principles are that metrics should be linked to strategy, and should include as a minimum four key elements:

* return on investment
* customer satisfaction
* market share
* brand equity.

However, there is no one set of measures that marketers use to measure and communicate performance. Managers must choose and use metrics that are most relevant to their organisation's mission and the specific objectives that have been set. For example, a marketer whose objective was to gain unaided brand recall of 15 per cent would have achieved their objective if a 16 per cent unaided brand recall was reached. Managers must choose and use metrics that are most relevant to their organisation's mission and objectives. For this reason one measure cannot be recommended for all marketers, nor is there one set of metrics that all marketers can use to measure and communicate performance. Marketers need to choose the metrics that best meet the activities they are undertaking. The use of marketing metrics is discussed in depth later in this chapter, including more detailed measures, but to see how they work in tandem with objectives, consider the following discussion.

Take a moment to think about your university studies. How do you decide which lectures to attend or which concepts to focus your efforts on? The assessment for the course dictates how you choose to study. You are likely to focus on the concepts that are being assessed in more detail than concepts which are not directly assessed.

You are likely to attend lectures that are relevant to the assessment that you are required to undertake. You are more likely to attend a lecture if it is known the lecturer is likely to present exam hints. These behaviours demonstrate the clear link between objectives, performance and measurement: what is measured gets done.

On a personal level, setting objectives and measuring achievements are important for a number of reasons. For example, you can gain a sense of accomplishment from achieving set goals. By exceeding goals set you can communicate your effectiveness as an individual to others, including employers. Many marketing salaries contain significant bonus components and by achieving your objectives you may receive a higher salary as you qualify for available bonus amounts. Table 14.2 outlines contemporary bonus incentives for marketing professionals. For example, a marketing manager paid an annual salary of $80 000 may earn an additional $50 000 in bonuses if all their objectives are met. Of course, the organisation must ensure that achievement of the set objectives generates sufficient revenue and other benefits to justify such a bonus.[12]

**TABLE 14.2** Professional marketer bonus incentives

| Role | Average bonus (percentage of salary) |
| --- | --- |
| Marketing assistant | 17% |
| Marketing executive | 43% |
| Marketing services manager | 53% |
| Product/brand manager | 72% |
| Marketing manager | 63% |
| Marketing director/General manager, marketing | 55% |
| Managing/Deputy managing director | 41% |

It is important for you to understand what your personal and professional objectives are. You need to review these objectives from time to time to reflect on your performance and you need to ensure that you have high-quality objectives.

# Marketing sustainability                    Spotlight

Australia is one of the world's largest greenhouse gas emitters. The most recent estimate is that Australia generates an estimated 537 million tonnes of greenhouse gases annually — the largest amount per person of any developed country. Three-quarters of these emissions come from the energy sector. Australia has pledged, however, to cut its emissions by between 5 and 25 per cent over the next ten years, and government-funded programs are underway to meet these targets. The Townsville Queensland Solar City program is part of the Australian government's leading-edge Solar Cities program that is being implemented in various regions across Australia. The Solar Cities program is trialling energy options now so that we have information to manage energy into the future, reduce greenhouse gases and protect Australia's environment. Ergon Energy leads the Townsville Queensland Solar City consortium, comprising all levels of government and several local developers. The program aims to

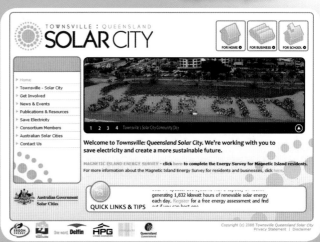

reduce wasteful energy usage, increase solar energy usage and cut greenhouse gas emissions by more than 50000 tonnes in Townsville annually.

A marketing program was needed that would go beyond awareness and short-term product acceptance to deliver deep Magnetic Island community engagement with the issue, and a lasting change to community behaviour. A systematic approach was used to first identify customer perceptions and roadblocks to reduce energy usage; then to address these perceptions and deliver a measurable long-term reduction in energy consumption. The Townsville Queensland Solar City program is providing a model of how solar energy and energy efficiency can deliver both environmental and economic benefits. Reducing 'peak' demand and electricity usage not only helps to reduce greenhouse emissions, but also saves money for individuals and businesses.

Major initiatives of the Townsville Queensland Solar City program include:
- providing advice to consumers (and businesses) about how they can make their homes (and premises/operations) more energy efficient
- promoting and arranging trials and demonstrations of energy efficient products
- running educational programs for schools highlighting the benefits of responsible energy use and the sustainability concept.

Metrics for the Townsville Queensland Solar City program have so far been encouraging. Among the results achieved were an average 8 per cent reduction in Magnetic Island's overall energy consumption within 12 months of the program's launch, with one in five residents reducing their household electricity consumption by 30 per cent within six months.[13]

> ## Question
>
> Imagine you are the marketing manager for the Townsville Queensland Solar City program. Write a marketing objective for each of the three major initiatives outlined in the Spotlight, ensuring that each satisfies the SMART model criteria for effective objectives.

## Concepts and applications check

**Learning objective 2**  understand the importance of effective marketing planning in achieving organisational and marketing objectives

2.1 Evaluate the organisational mission statements presented earlier in the chapter for Fuji Xerox, Facebook, Woolworths and Singapore Airlines. Which mission statements demonstrate a marketing philosophy?

2.2 Explain the relationship between organisational, business-unit and functional objectives.

2.3 Why should managers use objectives?

2.4 Explain the characteristics of effective objectives.

2.5 Using the SMART principles, make improvements to the following marketing objectives:
  (a) improve reputation
  (b) increase brand awareness by 2 per cent in the next 12 months
  (c) increase website traffic to 10000 impressions a day
  (d) increase sales of Heinz Baked Beans by 100 per cent in the next 12 months.

# MARKETING IMPLEMENTATION

**Learning objective 3**
describe how to manage the implementation of a marketing strategy

It is tempting to assume that once the marketing plan is formulated, implementation will proceed in a straightforward manner. There are, however, numerous complexities that make implementing marketing problematic. Additionally, new information is likely to come to light that requires constant refinements of the marketing plan.

By understanding some of the problems that arise in implementing marketing plans, organisations can work to minimise their occurrence. Many of the problems arise from the organisation's internal environment. The first part of this section looks at some of the complexities that can from time to time make implementing the marketing concept a true challenge. If it was a simple matter of putting the marketing plan into action, marketing would not be the diverse and interesting field that it is. In the second part of this section, we will consider some of the things that marketers can do to maximise the likelihood that the marketing plan will be successfully implemented.

# Potential internal barriers

Some of the most common barriers to effectively implementing the marketing concept can be internal: inertia (including resistance to change), a lack of coordination and/ or cooperation, a lack of a clear message or the presence of mixed leadership signals, and focusing too much on the short term at the expense of broader objectives. All are complex problems, which are introduced for your consideration here.

### Inertia

Implementing a change as fundamental and far-reaching as a shift from an internal orientation to a market orientation is difficult, time-consuming and expensive. Many people are resistant to change. Marketers seeking to change the way their company does business can encounter resistance from those uncomfortable with change and those with vested interests in preserving the status quo. Change management is an industry in itself and meaningful change in a large and complex organisation can take many years to accomplish. At each stage, but principally in the early days, there is a risk of falling back into an internal orientation. For example, it is common and natural for people who work in production to favour products and processes that make their task easier, whereas the characteristics of easily produced products may not be the ones valued by customers. Hence there is a conflict. Each time such a conflict arises the market orientation is at risk. To counter such problems, marketers seeking change must implement strong change leadership. To achieve successful change, marketers must be champions for change, and this requires them to develop a powerful and convincing argument for the need for change.

As mentioned, many people are fearful of change; it can be challenging, tiring and threatening. In addition, in any change there is a shift of power that is usually resisted by those who may be required to give up some power. For example, in adopting a market orientation, a research and development division within an organisation may lose some autonomy as customers (via salespeople, the marketing division or actual sales) provide guidance as to the types of product characteristics that the market wants. In addition to resistance to the initial change process, a market orientation is likely to require more organisational flexibility. The market changes, competitors change and customers change as macro and micro-environmental forces work. This means that businesses with a market orientation more often than not need to be agile so that they can move with the market.

### Poor coordination and cooperation

Politics, the quest for power, self-interest and professional ego can result in a lack of coordination and cooperation between different functional areas. For example, a human resources department may try to moderate recruitment, working hours, salary and other issues to the hindrance of a sales department that feels it needs to offer large incentive payments and require salespeople to work long hours during peak seasons. Similarly, a sales department may keep the human resources department ill-informed about some of its practices so that it can bend the rules (possibly even laws). As another example, a production department may be reluctant to change a simple product feature such as colour because it adds complexity to the production line, but the marketing department may consider colour a crucial selling tool. For example, while it would have been easier for Apple to sell just one colour of iPod Nano, it in fact created nine. To achieve organisational goals, missions and values, functional areas must cooperate and coordinate.

### Lack of strong leadership

A market orientation requires strong leadership. Given many people's general resistance to change, any blurring of messages, mixed signals or signs of uncertainty from those leading the change will reinforce this resistance to change. It is crucial that the need for a market orientation be clear and that the organisation's culture, processes and other characteristics are all consistent with a market orientation. For example, there is little point in professing a market orientation if the production division and marketing division only meet once a year.

### A short-term outlook

Many people working in organisations are most concerned with dealing with immediate challenges and completing the work at hand, but ongoing business success is dependent on long-term planning and actions based on sustainable competitive advantage. Compounding most people's concern with the here and now is the fact that many remuneration and performance indicators are tied to short-term results. Salespeople are bonused on monthly or annual sales figures; managers are assessed against annual expense budgets and annual staff turnover numbers; and chief executives are rewarded for annual increases in share prices. Some of the corporate matters that came to light during the global economic crisis clearly demonstrated that bonuses offered on short-term results easily lead to people making business decisions with little regard to the effects on the business and other stakeholders in the longer term.

The high-profile failure of Australian child care company ABC Learning Centres and its founder Eddy Groves in recent times provides a classic example of the damage that a short-term outlook can do. So much focus was put on corporate growth and signing up new child care outlets internationally that insufficient attention was paid to whether the total business would in fact prove profitable — it wasn't. Its share price ultimately crashed, it was placed into receivership and required a $22 million dollar government bailout to stay afloat.[14] Moreover, a short-term focus tends to lead to an inward approach, with cost cutting and productivity increases championed, whereas a market orientation requires an external focus and responsiveness to the market. Key features of a long-term market-oriented approach include building customer loyalty, reputation and goodwill. Most business advisers recommended that organisations try to avoid short-term measures during the onset of the global economic crisis in order to preserve the integrity and competitiveness of their business to take best advantage of the economic recovery.

## Environmental factors

In addition to the internal factors described above, external environmental factors affect the ability of an organisation to implement the marketing concept. One important factor is the increasing **saturation** of the market in terms of all aspects of the marketing mix. It is becoming more and more difficult for marketing organisations to create and sustain a competitive advantage or indeed to differentiate their offerings at all in the midst of extensive competition. Think about mobile phone companies. What are the differences between the offerings of Telstra, Virgin Mobile, Optus and Vodafone? They mostly sell the same handsets and offer phone calls,

**saturation** The existence of so many competitive offerings in the marketplace that it becomes virtually impossible to differentiate an offering or create a competitive advantage.

SMS, and web browsing. Virgin tries to portray its products as somehow more fun than the others while all try to present lower prices than Telstra, while Telstra has a slight advantage in coverage in rural areas. Overall, however, it is difficult to say one is a clear choice over any other for most of us.

Another factor is the **fragmentation** of the market. The market increasingly comprises smaller and smaller niches with specific needs. Consider the mobile phone example again. Between the few companies offering services there are thousands upon thousands of plans and options to choose from, each trying to provide an ideal combination of price and services for a small number of potential customers.

Now that we have considered some of the problems that can arise when implementing a marketing orientation and marketing plan, we will outline the many things that marketers and managers can do to enhance their chances of success.

## Maximising success

Successfully implementing the marketing concept is crucial to sustainable competitive advantage and hence ongoing business success. We will now discuss some of the processes that can maximise the chance of the marketing concept being successfully applied.

### Planning

There is an old adage that 'those who fail to plan, plan to fail'. This recognises the importance of planning ahead of implementation. Research shows that organisations that plan perform better than organisations that do not plan. Think about your own studies. Do you take time out to plan before commencing studies each semester? If so, does this mean you have a plan that allows you to focus on getting the work done to meet deadlines? If not, are you constantly spending time checking what is due and when? Could this time be better spent on studying, working or enjoying some personal time?

Plans that effectively communicate strategies and objectives are documents that outline what needs to done, by whom and when, to achieve agreed upon objectives. Marketing plans typically contain **action plans** to be implemented by departmental and line managers. Ideally, marketing plans will include schedules and specific actions to be taken so that managers who are responsible for implementation (but not involved directly with strategic planning) have a clear plan forward, and a clear idea of what is expected, and of whom.

Organisations do not always completely adhere to their written plans due to changes that may arise in the marketing environment. An **emergent approach** relies on developing strategy in response to changing market conditions. An emergent approach allows marketers to operate in highly competitive and changing markets. It is important, though, not to confuse the absence of planning for an emergent approach.

Plans can help marketers focus on the longer term. Rather than focusing on the next week or month, planning requires marketers to think about this year and the next few years. The planning process requires marketers to monitor their competition. When trying to think about the competition, marketers use their market intelligence to think about the possible ways that competitors may act. Marketers often develop contingencies to identify the different ways that competitors may act. **Contingency planning** requires managers and others to think ahead to things that might not go to plan and to have strategies in place to deal with them. Proper contingency planning helps organisations both identify possible problems (and opportunities) and respond quickly and appropriately to them.

Plans help marketers to develop priorities and focus efforts on achieving specific goals and objectives. The planning process requires marketers to think about their

**fragmentation** The increasing division of the market into ever smaller niches with increasingly specific needs.

**action plans** Implementable plans with specific actions, schedules and goals that direct managers and staff that are not directly involved in strategic decisions.

**emergent approach** The development of marketing strategy in response to changing market conditions.

**contingency planning** The process of putting in place plans for unforeseen or uncertain eventualities to ensure managers think ahead and can respond to emerging problems and opportunities.

customers and this often means that marketers focus on targeting their primary customer. The planning process helps marketers to understand which marketing approaches work and which do not work for their organisations.

### Motivation and incentives

People join organisations for a wide range of reasons. While pay is probably the first thing that comes to most people's minds, most employees (and especially volunteers) also have other motivations such as job satisfaction, the desire to help others, the desire to achieve, the desire for social companionship, intellectual or physical challenges, and so on. Organisations can use these various motivations to encourage marketing implementation. An obvious example is to pay bonuses based on sales results or the provision of quality service, but there are many other opportunities. For example, an employee who values intellectual challenges may be given the opportunity to participate on a team charged with finding more efficient ways to provide call centre services to customers.

It is important that incentives align well with overall organisational objectives. For example, while most salespeople have a bonus component in their overall remuneration, it does tend to encourage a short-term view rather than sustainable competitive advantage.

### Empowerment

**empowerment** Enabling employees to make decisions to do their job properly and ensuring they have the necessary resources to make effective use of their power to make decisions.

**Empowerment** — enabling employees to make the decisions they need to make to properly do their job — is crucial to enabling the organisation to respond to customer needs and wants. Empowerment allows employees to deal with customer queries and complaints quickly and efficiently. An important aspect of empowerment is ensuring that employees have the knowledge, contacts, confidence and support they require to make effective use of their decision-making power.

As we have emphasised throughout our discussion, marketing is a dynamic activity that takes place in an ever-changing environment. While the marketing plan should guide all marketing activities, it cannot possibly come close to covering every possible situation. In addition, opportunities that arise often demand quick action if they are to be taken advantage of. To cope with these inevitabilities, managers and employees in organisations need to be appropriately empowered to make decisions that accord with the objectives of the organisation but that may not be specifically covered in the marketing plan. For example, BigPond Internet has empowered its call centre managers to offer a discount to unhappy customers who have been let down by some aspect of the organisation's service. A call centre operator dealing with a customer who is complaining about a late delivery of an installation package has the authority to compensate the customer by waiving the first month's subscription fee. Google perhaps represents the ultimate expression of employee empowerment, with employees free to use a portion of their time each work day on their own projects and to allocate themselves to various Google projects according to their interest. Of course, they also need to produce results for Google.

### Structure for cooperation and coordination

**organisational structure** The formal arrangement of business functions within an organisation.

The **organisational structure** itself can be an important factor in the success or otherwise of implementing the marketing concept. Organisations that are structured to encourage cooperation, coordination and communication between different functional areas are more likely to achieve a consistent market orientation across the business. Organisations with discrete functional areas, often located in different sites, or with a silo mentality — each area concerned with its own agenda — may struggle to achieve cooperation and coordination across the various functions and so it is likely that they will be characterised by a production department with a production focus, a finance department with a budget focus, a human resources department with a bureaucratic focus and so on.

On a smaller scale than the structure of the organisation is the structure of the marketing department itself. The structure of the marketing department defines responsibilities, authority and expectations. It can have a significant impact on the success of the organisation. The main options for structuring the marketing department are:

- *customer structure.* Organisations with distinctly different groups of customers may organise the marketing department by customer type. For example, most car dealers have separate sales people for fleet sales and personal sales.
- *product structure.* In a business with a diverse array of products, it may make more sense to have separate units dedicated to particular products or product lines. It would not really make sense for the marketing department at Wesfarmers to adopt a functional structure which would see its advertising team responsible for advertising clothes to Kmart shoppers and fertilisers to farmers.
- *functional structure.* In a marketing department organised along functional lines, there will be separate units dedicated to functions such as market research, sales and advertising. This structure is most suited to large organisations with established and relatively homogeneous customers.
- *regional structure.* Organisations that operate across dispersed geographic regions may be best to structure their marketing department along regional lines so that each marketing team can be located close to their target market and cater for regional differences.

### Organisational culture

The factors above all contribute to the **organisational culture** — the organisation's shared values and behaviours. It is crucial that organisational culture be aligned with the marketing concept. This is not the case in many organisations and, to make matters worse, cultural change is one of the most difficult things to achieve in an organisation. It requires considerable effort, years of commitment and eternal vigilance. In organisations with a market-focused culture, all employees and managers will make all decisions and act in accordance with the ideal of delivering maximum customer value.

**organisational culture** The values and behaviours shared throughout the organisation.

# A well-deserved break

## Spotlight

CSC is one of the world's leading consulting and information technology services firms, having been in business since 1959 delivering business results to clients. CSC develops and manages solutions that help organisations in many industries achieve their business goals. Headquartered in the United States, CSC is now registered to do business in more than 90 countries, and has 94 000 employees around the world. Its annual revenues exceed US$17.1 billion. CSC's Australian operation was established in 1970 and it is now a $1.1 billion company in its own right.

However, during the recent global financial crisis, CSC Australia needed to reduce its costs. Two of the most significant of these were costs associated with both annual and long service leave. A significant proportion of their workforce had been with the company for many years, meaning that CSC Australia faced significant long service leave liabilities.

CSC Australia subsequently initiated an internal marketing campaign to provide its staff with an incentive to take leave. The broad aims of the campaign were to deliver the following three benefits to the organisation and its employees:
1. reduce the organisation's financial leave liability
2. ensure those employees who had accrued a significant amount of leave took a well-deserved break
3. boost morale during a tough business period.

The 'Life beyond the laptop' program was launched by CSC Australia, with its employees each being given a reduced leave target to reach within six months. The incentive provided for employees to take leave was a chance to win one of five overseas holidays for two people, each to the value of $12 000. The success of the program was reflected in CSC Australia subsequently winning an Australian Marketing Institute Marketing Excellence Award for internal marketing.[15]

**Question**

Identify potential barriers that CSC would have had to consider and manage in implementing this internal marketing campaign within their organisation.

## Concepts and applications check

**Learning objective 3**  describe how to manage the implementation of a marketing strategy

**3.1**  Outline some of the potential barriers to effective marketing implementation.

**3.2**  How can an organisation (and its marketing manager) attempt to eliminate or minimise the barriers identified in question 3.1?

**3.3**  Marketing includes activities performed across the entire organisation; it is not limited to the subset of activities that have been assigned to the marketing department. Explain some different ways that marketing can be implemented in practice.

# EVALUATING MARKETING PERFORMANCE

**Learning objective 4** explain the role of marketing metrics and the ongoing evaluation of marketing performance in the marketing cycle

The marketing cycle is best considered as an ongoing loop where marketing programs are constantly revised and refined. It is evaluation, throughout and after marketing efforts, that makes the marketing process cyclical in nature. It is also evaluation that truly enables a marketing organisation to know, understand and respond to changes in the market. In the many examples presented in this textbook, we have demonstrated some of the many ways that marketers have evaluated their performance. It is important that we conclude with evaluation, as evaluation is the means by which marketers can assess the performance of their marketing programs.

As we read in chapter 13, it is quite possible for a large organisation such as Tourism Australia to spend an enormous amount of money and other resources on a complex and extensive marketing campaign without having clearly determined exactly what it is the campaign is meant to achieve. This is a mistake. Only with clearly defined and understood objectives can the marketing organisation:
• properly plan and implement an effective marketing campaign
• evaluate the extent to which the objectives have been achieved (and therefore identify what, if anything, needs to change).

While we are presenting this section on evaluation towards the end of your course, we have mentioned evaluation and marketing metrics throughout the book and we reiterate that marketing is not a simple linear process, or even simply a cyclical process. Rather it is a complex web of plans, actions, feedback, modifications and so on. A formal evaluation should certainly occur at the conclusion of a marketing campaign, but evaluative actions should also occur periodically during the campaign and ideally as an ongoing process from day one that enables the marketing organisation to properly respond to the successes or otherwise of the campaign, alter the campaign to cater for changing environmental conditions and so on.

# Measuring performance

As mentioned earlier in this chapter, in order to evaluate how well objectives have been achieved, a marketing organisation must use metrics. Marketing metrics are the various measures that marketers use to understand how their marketing program has performed. In the absence of marketing objectives and metrics it is difficult, if not impossible, to evaluate the achievement of goals.

The performance of every student is measured for each course they undertake at university. Course grades indicate the student's performance. The Grade Point Average (GPA) indicates their overall performance at university and it can assist employers to understand if a job candidate is an average or high performer. Similarly, performance is measured in the workforce. Individual performance is measured for promotion purposes; areas are measured to determine how effective managers are; and company initiatives are measured to understand their impact on the business. Marketing programs are assessed both to understand how they performed to improve for the future and to communicate the contribution of the program to the overall business.

Performance is measured by comparing the performance achieved against the objectives that were set. Consider Pizza Hut, which implemented a \$4 million marketing communications campaign to promote its new Pasta Hut brand and range of pasta meals. Pizza Hut's objective is for pasta to account for 20 per cent of the business by 2013. In order to understand its performance against this objective, Pizza Hut will monitor the contribution of its pasta products to the business. If pasta accounts for 20 per cent or more of the business by 2013, then Pizza Hut will report that it met its objective.

In order to be effective, the metrics used to assess performance must be relevant to the organisation's strategy. Marketing metrics should be chosen carefully to ensure they are suitable and they should be applied fairly and objectively. To illustrate the potential complexity of using marketing metrics, consider how the Hong Kong Department of Health's 'EatSmart' Restaurant Campaign[16] encouraged restaurants to supply healthier food options for patrons. Eating out is a way of life for Hong Kong people with over 50 per cent of Hong Kong adults eating out of home at least five times per week. Unhealthy diet is a known major risk factor for chronic diseases. Based on the understanding that more than 90 per cent of Hong Kong adults wanted to be offered healthier dishes when eating out, the Hong Kong Department of Health collaborated with local restaurants in launching the 'EatSmart@restaurant.hk Campaign'. The EatSmart Campaign offers labeling at point of purchase when restaurants offer five or more dishes, which are made up primarily of 'fruit and vegetables' and/or are 'low in salt, sugar and oil'. To qualify as an EatSmart Restaurant, staff training and changes in business practice are required. The EatSmart@restaurant.hk Campaign was branded as a trendy, healthy eating movement, driven by socially responsible restaurants.

A pilot study was initially undertaken in 50 EatSmart Restaurants, involving 200 staff and 500 customers. The results of the pilot study found an increase in the demand and sales of EatSmart Dishes. Nearly all staff (98 per cent) interviewed considered the EatSmart@restaurant.hk Campaign a feasible mode of operation. Among customers who had ordered EatSmart Dishes:

- 99 per cent supported the notion that restaurants should offer healthier choices
- 95 per cent indicated satisfaction with the dish served
- 75 per cent said they would patronise the restaurant again for healthy dishes.

After the pilot phase, the program was rolled out. Within a year, over 580 restaurants were involved in the EatSmart Restaurant program. Overall, 897 restaurateurs and chefs have received nutrition training.

Consider how the Hong Kong Department of Health has implemented and measured the effectiveness of its social marketing campaign in changing restaurant serving practices and customer ordering behaviour. The Hong Kong Department of Health introduced the campaign initially in 50 restaurants to understand restaurant owner/employee and customer perceptions. Once it understood that the social marketing campaign did assist in providing healthy meal options, it then rolled the campaign out territory wide. If no effect had been noted in the pilot study involving 50 Hong Kong EatSmart Restaurants, the Hong Kong Department of Health could have focused on building an alternative marketing program to improve customer food choices. This example shows how marketers can evaluate performance. This knowledge also allows marketers to adjust their programs as required to improve performance in the future.

Marketing objectives can take a variety of forms including profit related, sales and market share related, customer related and societal objectives. *Marketing metrics* are used to both set objectives and to evaluate marketing performance against marketing objectives. The Australian Marketing Institute has developed a list of more than 160 marketing metrics, and some of the more common of these are defined in table 14.3.

**TABLE 14.3** Marketing metrics

| Metric | Description |
| --- | --- |
| Acquisition cost | Total acquisition spending divided by the number of new customers acquired. |
| Ad awareness | Percent of total population that is aware of the advertising by a brand. |
| Brand awareness | Percent of total population that is aware of a brand. Awareness may be prompted (a list of ads or brands is shown), unprompted or total (prompted unprompted). Prompted awareness is also called recognition. |
| Brand valuation | The financial net worth of the brand (equity) asset. Clearly crucial when buying or selling brands but of limited value for marketing planning or evaluation. |
| Churn | A measure of customer attrition. It refers to the percent of customers a business loses over a specific period of time. Churn (%) = 100% − Retention (%) |
| Click through rates | Measures user response to online advertising. |
| Complaints | Recorded number of communicated complaints. |
| Contribution margin | Mean contribution per unit as a percent of unit price. |
| Conversions | In the hierarchy of people in the target market progressively becoming customers, conversion is the percent of targets graduating from one level to the next; e.g. leads becoming prospects. |
| Cost per call | The cost of handling a telephone call; e.g. in a call centre. |
| Cost per thousand impressions | Cost of advertising/Impressions generated (in thousands). |
| Customer lifetime value | Expected net cash flow to company from a customer. This formula assumes a constant customer defection rate, a constant net margin and a discount rate. CLTV = m / (k + d) where m = constant net margins (profits − retention costs); k = discount rate; d = constant defection rate. |
| Customer profit | The difference between the revenues earned from and the cost associated with the customer relationship during a specified period. Note singular customer. When the metric is for all customers then that is the same as business profitability. |

**TABLE 14.3** Marketing metrics *(continued)*

| Metric | Description |
|---|---|
| Customer satisfaction | The degree to which the expectations of a consumer are fulfilled or surpassed by a product. |
| Customer traffic | The total number of buyers during a specific period of time; e.g. per hour. |
| Impressions | Opportunities to see (OTS) or exposures. |
| Knowledge | Should not be confused with awareness, namely knowing of the brand. Knowledge is an index of the extent to which the average user understands the brand and product characteristics and capabilities. |
| Leads | Number of individually identified potential customers. |
| Likeability | Used for advertising, an index of how agreeable the advertisement is to view or hear. |
| Marketing cost per unit | Total marketing cost per unit divided by total units sold in time period. |
| Market penetration | The number of purchasers of the category as a percent of total population or target market. |
| Market share | Describes a company's sales as a percentage of total sales volume in a specific industry, market or product area. |
| Preference ratio | Percent of target market who claim to prefer the brand (used by BA). |
| Purchase intention | Percent of people who respond to a survey indicating that they expect/intend to purchase the brand in future. |
| Reach | The number of people who see/hear/receive at least an impression of an advertisement (usually expressed as a percent of target market) within a fixed period of time. |
| Recall | May be aided or unaided. Percent of people mentioning ad or brand name when suitably prompted. |
| Retention rate | The number of active customers at the end of a time period divided by the number of active customers at the start of that time period. |
| Revenue | Total income from sales of products and services. |
| Sales volume | Sales expressed as units or quantities. |
| Share of requirements | Brand purchases as a percent of total category purchases by buyers of that brand. Unit Share of Requirements (%) = Brand purchased (X) ÷ Total category purchases by brand buyers (X). |
| Top-of-mind awareness | First brand mentioned when questioned about the category by researchers. |
| Willingness to recommend | Percent of surveyed customers who say they would recommend the brand to a friend. Should correlate with top box satisfaction but may not. The Reichheld question: How likely is it that you would recommend [company X] to a friend or colleague? |
| Willingness to search | Willingness to Search (%) = Percent of customers willing to delay purchases, change stores, or reduce purchase quantities to avoid switching brands. |

*Source:* Australian Marketing Institute

The Australian Marketing Institute also offers calculators to assist in the calculation of additional marketing metrics, including **customer lifetime value**. Customer lifetime value (CLV) is the dollar value of a customer relationship based on the present value of the projected future cash flows from the business/customer relationship. CLV provides a basis for quantifying the long-term health of the customer relationships. CLV can be computed for an individual customer, segments of customers, and

**customer lifetime value**
a metric of the dollar value of a customer relationship based on the present value of the projected future cash flows from the business/customer relationship

the total customer base. Computing CLV by segments can be useful when different segments have different retention rates and/or margins.

Alternative tools, such as the direct mail return on investment calculator, are also offered by the Australian Marketing Institute.[17] A direct mail investment should not be made unless there is an expectation of a sufficiently high positive return on investment using reasonable assumptions (ideally based on past performance). Marketing metrics such as direct mail return on investment calculator can be used to evaluate the return on investment (ROI) of alternative direct mail options and as such provides a good basis for choosing between alternative direct mail methods.

Marketing metrics enable marketers to refine their marketing approach based on performance achieved and they also help marketers to demonstrate the important, central contribution that marketing makes to the overall success of the organisation. As we have stressed throughout this chapter, and indeed this book, evaluation of marketing plans, actions and outcomes is an ongoing process that should continuously inform marketing strategy.

# Spotlight  Drug driving

While the focus of many government social marketing campaigns over recent decades has been on the dangers of drink driving, drug driving is also emerging as a prevalent issue in society. Driving under the influence of drugs is just as dangerous. It affects driving ability, with similar side effects to alcohol including slower reaction times, distorted perceptions of speed and distance and reduced concentration and coordination. In South Australia, for example, an analysis of road toll statistics revealed that 24 per cent of drivers or riders killed in South Australia tested positive to drugs such as ecstasy and methylamphetamine (meth) over a recent five-year period. In South Australia, police detection rates for drug driving now exceed drink driving.

South Australia's Motor Accident Commission needed a social marketing campaign to change driver behaviour. They undertook market research to understand how a creative message could be developed in a way that would resonate with their target audience.

This market research revealed that part of the underlying problem is that 16–39 year old males who take recreational drugs believe that drug driving is not dangerous. Beliefs included ideas that marijuana makes people more cautious, 'speed' makes people more alert and that the effects of ecstasy wear off quickly. These insights were used by the Motor Accident Commission to develop an integrated communications campaign featuring images of drugged people in various occupations (such as pilots, surgeons and bus drivers), in order to bust these myths. After the implementation of the campaign, follow-up research was used to assess the impact on attitudes and self-reported driver behaviours.[18]

The results indicated the campaign had a significant impact on attitudes, with drug users feeding back positive changes in their views towards drugs and the effect of drugs on their driving. More importantly, changes in behaviour were evident, with sharp decreases in self-reported incidents of drug driving recorded.

## Questions

1. Referring to table 14.3, what additional marketing metrics might be suitable to assist the Motor Accident Commission's evaluation of their campaign?

2. Explain how the Motor Accident Commission has demonstrated their understanding of the marketing process.

# Concepts and applications check

**Learning objective 4** explain the role of marketing metrics and the ongoing evaluation of marketing performance in the marketing cycle

**4.1** Explain how to evaluate marketing performance.

**4.2** Pizza Hut recently launched a $4 million marketing communications campaign to promote its new Pasta Hut brand and range of pastas. Pizza Hut's objective is for pasta to account for 20 per cent of the revenue of its business by 2013. How can Pizza Hut assess its performance?

**4.3** Explain the role of marketing metrics.

# SUMMARY

 **Learning objective 1** explain the relationship between the marketing cycle and marketing management

The marketing cycle is the cyclical process of understanding, creating, communicating and delivering value, refined by continuous evaluation. The management task of building market understanding, and planning, implementing and evaluating marketing activities is known as marketing management. Marketing management aims to ensure that the organisation achieves its marketing objectives by maximising the value obtained from the marketing exchange — for the organisation itself and its customers, client, partners and society at large.

 **Learning objective 2** understand the importance of effective marketing planning in achieving organisational and marketing objectives

Organisations with a marketing philosophy perform better for their stakeholders — they offer more value to customers and clients, better financial returns to partners and owners, and more benefits for society at large. Top management establishes mission statements and overarching organisational goals; senior and middle managers plan and implement, respectively, to achieve those goals. Organisational objectives must be carefully interpreted into objectives for each business unit. Business unit objectives then get translated into functional or area objectives. Effective objectives should display the characteristics described by the SMART model; they should be: specific, measurable, actionable, reasonable and timetabled.

 **Learning objective 3** describe how to manage the implementation of a marketing plan

Implementing a marketing plan involves numerous complexities. Some of the most common internal complications in implementing marketing are: inertia, a lack of coordination and/or cooperation, a lack of a clear message or the presence of mixed signals, and focusing too much on the short term at the expense of broader objectives. Characteristics of the micro and macro environment also pose possible problems. They include increasing saturation of the market and fragmentation of the market. To minimise problems and build a platform for marketing success, marketers should plan, provide motivation and incentives for organisational members, empower staff, structure the organisation to support a market orientation and build a customer-focused organisational culture.

 **Learning objective 4** explain the role of marketing metrics and the ongoing evaluation of marketing performance in the marketing cycle

The marketing cycle is an ongoing loop where marketing programs are constantly revised and refined in response to evaluation, both throughout and after marketing efforts. Evaluation enables a marketing organisation to know, understand and respond to changes in the market. Marketing metrics are the measures that marketers use to understand how their marketing program has performed against the objectives set for it. This enables marketers to not only refine their marketing approach, but also to demonstrate the important, central contribution that marketing makes to the overall success of the organisation.

# Flight Centre — tracking customer experience and store performance

Marketers need to understand a customer's experience, which encompasses a broad range of issues. To understand a customer's experience, marketers should monitor a wide range of factors, including:

- customer satisfaction
- a customer's perception of the quality delivered and value
- a customer's loyalty, advocacy (e.g. willingness to recommend to friends and family)
- other customer perceptions (e.g. reputation, trust, image and awareness and knowledge relating to the brand).

Flight Centre Limited, a travel and associated travel services company, trades in more than 20 different brand names. It continues to diversify and grow, pursuing a strong international growth strategy. The company has about 2000 stores in Australia, the United Kingdom, the United States, Canada, New Zealand, China, South Africa, Dubai and Singapore. The flagship Flight Centre brand is Flight Centre Limited's best-known travel business, and is regarded as one of Australia's most valuable brand names. In Australia, Flight Centre Limited employs over 4000 travel consultants that have day-to-day interactions with tens of thousands of customers looking to purchase travel products such as flights, cruises, accommodation, car hire and organised tours. Flight Centre's customer experience program aims to ensure that the experience of each customer is optimised across the entire transacting and service delivery process.

To assist in the monitoring and improvement of customer experience, Flight Centre recently undertook market research with Colmar Brunton. The customer experience tracking study utilised a 15-minute questionnaire, which was administered to all transacting customers at any one of Australia's travel agent stores across Australia. The web link to the questionnaire was emailed to customers at the end of every month for six months. A total of 18 004 customer surveys were collected during one six-month period, and analysis was conducted at an individual store level.

The survey contained a range of questions relating to the customer's experience with the Flight Centre outlet and its transaction processes. Data was collected relating to customer preferences, priorities and behaviours.

It was then aggregated into 12 satisfaction, loyalty value perception and advocacy metrics at an individual store level (these are summarised in table 14.4). For analysis purposes, stores were split into high, average and low performers on each of the metrics. High performers were defined as the top 25 per cent of stores for that metric, while low performers were the bottom 25 per cent of stores for that metric.

**TABLE 14.4** Marketing metrics — Flight Centre customer experience

| | Customer experience survey measure | Bottom stores (25%) | Top stores (25%) |
|---|---|---|---|
| **Overall experience** | Rate your overall experience with Flight Centre for your last service encounter<br><br>Ten point scale (10 is excellent and 1 is very poor)<br><br>Proportion scoring 9 or 10 | 69 | 81 |
| **Service quality** | How does Flight Centre perform on quality of service received?<br><br>Five point scale (5 is excellent and 1 is poor)<br><br>Proportion scoring 4 or 5 | 54 | 69 |
| **Willingness to recommend** | How likely is it that you would refer friends or family to Flight Centre?<br><br>Ten point scale (1 is very unlikely and 10 is very likely)<br><br>Proportion scoring 9 or 10 | 64 | 76 |
| **Net promoter score** | A separate calculation is made using the 'Willingness to recommend' measure.<br><br>The net of the proportion responding 9 or 10 minus the proportion responding 1 to 6 | 51 | 70 |
| **Repurchase likelihood** | How likely is it that you would use Flight Centre the next time you book travel?<br><br>Ten point scale (1 is very unlikely and 10 is very likely)<br><br>Proportion scoring 9 or 10 | 71 | 82 |
| **Likelihood to change** | How likely is it that you will consult with travel companies other than Flight Centre when booking travel in the future?<br><br>Ten point scale (10 is very likely and 1 is very unlikely)<br><br>Proportion scoring 9 or 10 | 13 | 24 |
| **Share of wallet** | In the past 12 months, how many times have you booked travel at any travel agent? How many of these bookings were made at Flight Centre? | 55 | 67 |
| **Value for money** | How does Flight Centre perform on price or value for money?<br><br>Five point scale (1 is poor and 5 is excellent)<br><br>Proportion rating the store as excellent | 37 | 51 |
| **Reputation** | How does Flight Centre perform in terms of reputation?<br><br>Five point scale (1 is poor and 5 is excellent)<br><br>Proportion rating the store as excellent | 35 | 48 |
| **Knowledge and expertise** | How does Flight Centre perform on travel knowledge & expertise?<br><br>Five point scale (1 is poor and 5 is excellent)<br><br>Proportion rating the store as excellent | 39 | 53 |
| **Trustworthiness** | How does Flight Centre perform on trustworthiness?<br><br>Five point scale (1 is poor and 5 is excellent)<br><br>Proportion rating the store as excellent | 44 | 59 |

Table 14.5 provides an index of revenue growth over the six-month period of the study. For the six-month period presented in this case study, data was available for 219 stores. Stores that were not open for the full period of analysis (six months) were excluded. Stores where survey results contained less than 30 customer responses for that store were also excluded. The total customer sample across these 219 stores was 9058, representing an average of 41 customers per store. The overall revenue growth for all 219 stores for the six-month period of the research study was compared to the previous six-month period. Average revenue growth for all 219 stores was 8.47 per cent — an index score of 0.66. Stores with an index above 0.66 grew at an above average rate. Stores were grouped into high, average and low performers on each of the metrics to understand relative revenue growth performance (see table 14.5).

**TABLE 14.5** Marketing metrics and revenue growth

| Marketing metric | Lowest 25% of stores | Mid 50% of scores | Highest 25% of stores |
|---|---|---|---|
| Willingness to recommend | 0.21 | 0.62 | 1.17 |
| Net promoter score | 0.21 | 0.65 | 1.12 |
| Repurchase likelihood | 0.33 | 0.68 | 0.92 |
| Service quality | 0.49 | 0.54 | 1.07 |
| Overall experience | 0.44 | 0.62 | 0.96 |
| Reputation | 0.48 | 0.61 | 0.92 |
| Trustworthiness | 0.54 | 0.58 | 0.92 |
| Knowledge and expertise | 0.50 | 0.67 | 0.77 |
| Share of wallet | 0.60 | 0.57 | 0.87 |
| Value for money perception | 0.62 | 0.57 | 0.86 |
| Likelihood to shop around | 0.85 | 0.60 | 0.58 |

To aid interpretation of table 2, stores with the greatest proportion of customers who indicated they were very likely to recommend their travel agent achieved the highest revenue growth, almost doubling the revenue growth achieved in the average Flight Centre store. This would equate to store revenue growth of 15 per cent in six months. Looking at the revenue performance of stores using the 'Willingness to recommend' metric, revenue growth over the six-month period for stores in the top 25 per cent was twice the average, and six times greater than stores in the bottom 25 per cent. Stores with the highest proportion of customers who were very likely to shop around achieved the lowest revenue growth (below the average of 0.66).[19*]

*This case study was co-authored by Steven Cierpicki, director, Colmar Brunton Research, and Sharyn Rundle-Thiele, one of the authors for the text.

# Question

Imagine you are a member of the corporate marketing team for Flight Centre and have just been presented with these Colmar Brunton market research findings. Outline how you would plan, implement and evaluate a marketing campaign to improve Flight Centre's revenue performance in the next six months.

## Advanced activity

Revisit the 'Bank bashing via Twitter' case at the start of the chapter and imagine you are a marketing manager at one of the big four banks. In response to this research, outline a marketing campaign that you could plan and implement in order to improve customer satisfaction. Ensure that you set SMART objectives for your campaign, and explain what metrics you would use in order to evaluate the effectiveness of your campaign.

## Marketing plan activity

Use some of the marketing metrics displayed in table 14.3 (see pages 514–515) to refine the marketing objectives for your marketing plan. Then check that each of your objectives satisfies each of the criteria in the SMART model outlined in the chapter.

Finally, develop a guide for the measurement of marketing performance for your marketing plan. Your plan must clearly show how marketing performance will be assessed.

Upon completing the above tasks — and if you have been working steadily through the marketing plan activities in each chapter of the book — you should have enough information to assemble your organisation's marketing plan. The appendix to this book (see page 523) provides a sample of a marketing plan for an organisation (adidas eyewear), that you can use as a guide in terms of the structure, layout and content of the marketing plan that you are preparing for your own chosen organisation.

# Marketing plan

The following is an example of an actual marketing plan, which shows how the marketing planning process could be implemented. This model is a useful guide if you have to prepare a marketing plan.

*This marketing plan is based on a plan prepared by Brent and Carl Doherty and Cassandra Mow for adidas eyewear. Note that due to corporate confidentiality, some of the financial figures are not disclosed or have been changed. The authors would like to thank Brent, Carl and Cassandra for their permission to use the plan.*

# Marketing plan
# adidas eyewear

## Executive summary

The following report is the marketing plan for adidas eyewear in Australia for the 2011–2012 financial year.

The adidas brand continues to grow in popularity in Australia after many years of under-performance. This has been helped by the adidas sponsorship of the Australian cricket team, Collingwood and Adelaide Australian Football League teams and the St. George Illawarra National Rugby League team.

In Australia, more than 20 million pairs of sunglasses are sold each year, with the sunglasses industry worth approximately $200 million annually (Everitt 2010). adidas eyewear is a functional performance sports eyewear product that is manufactured under license by Silhouette International, which is one of the world's leading manufacturers of quality eyewear. The eyewear range was launched in 1993 and is an extension of the adidas brand, being a global sports brand which was launched in 1949 by Adolf (Adi) Dassler (Das).

The company's mission statement is:

> The adidas Group strives to be the global leader in the sporting goods industry with sports brands built on a passion for sports and a sporting lifestyle.
> - **We are dedicated** to consistently delivering outstanding financial results.
> - **We are innovation and design leaders** who seek to help athletes of all skill levels achieve peak performance with every product we bring to market.
> - **We are consumer focused** and therefore we continuously improve the quality, look, feel and image of our products and our organisational structures to match and exceed consumer expectations and to provide them with the highest value.
> - **We are a global organisation** that is socially and environmentally responsible, creative and financially rewarding for our employees and shareholders.
> - **We are committed** to continuously strengthening our brands and products to improve our competitive position.

This marketing plan will focus on the eyewear market and initially analyse the market in Australia, analysing the relevant factors within a company, competitor, customer and SWOT analysis.

The target market consists of two market segments. This report will explain the primary (15–25-year-olds with a male skew) and secondary (25–40-year-olds with an interest in sport) target markets, as well as the positioning of the product.

The sales objective is to achieve sales of 20 000 units and net sales of $2 000 000. The total marketing budget is 10 per cent of sales.

Recommendations for the marketing strategy are explored. This includes an overall marketing strategy for the company as well as more specific tactics for each of the marketing mix areas. An evaluation is conducted, followed by an action plan outlining how to achieve the marketing objective.

# Introduction

adidas is one of the world's leading sports brands. It is the largest sportswear manufacturer in Europe and the second largest in the world, after Nike. Founded by Adolf Dassler, it started out as a shoe brand, specifically for playing sports. Over the years it has developed other products in its range, including bags, shirts, watches and eyewear. The adidas slogan is: 'Impossible is nothing'.

adidas has divided the brand into three main brand categories, each with a separate focus:
- **adidas Performance**, designed to focus on sports and the athlete
- **adidas Originals**, designed to focus on fashion and life-style
- **adidas Casuals**, with the main group within this one being Y-3.

The eyewear range was launched in 1993. The vision for the eyewear range is:

> No matter whether it's a world record or your personal best — sport and vision belong together. Yet in order to reach your goal, you not only need to know it but must discern it clearly as well. Sports frames by adidas eyewear offer an unobstructed view of clear objectives.

> They are developed around and with athletes, whose visions are the power that drives us. Supporting them is our task. Thus vision, protection, fit and durability are the central concepts that help you to keep sight of your personal vision.

> adidas eyewear — support your vision.

The eyewear range comprises sunglasses and ophthalmic frames. While the adidas brand in general continues to grow in popularity, this marketing plan will focus on the marketing of the sunglasses within the adidas eyewear range within Australia.

# Situation analysis

## Company analysis

The decision makers in Australia for the adidas eyewear marketing activities are the brand manager, marketing director and CEO. The company has recently employed a couple of additional marketing staff to implement the plans, due to the scale of activities being far greater than required prior to taking on the distribution contract. There is a person who handles training materials. Then there is a newly appointed marketing manager, who handles marketing and PR activities for all the company's brands and supports the brand manager with sports marketing for adidas eyewear.

There have not been consistent promotional activities for adidas Originals eyewear to date. Mostly the activities have centred around new collections being launched, but the lack of retail distribution has impacted on the success of the sales. The most likely reason for the lack of successful campaigns is the lack of resources dedicated to designing and implementing the campaigns, due to small sales of this line. This has been contributed to by a lack of planning for this part of the brand. All the focus has been on the sport performance eyewear, which makes up 90 per cent of the sales volume. The company is perceived well in the marketplace as a distributor of quality eyewear and is relatively easy to do business with.

# Environmental analysis

## Political and legal

In 1971 Australia developed the world's first national standards for sunglasses. The current standards have been revised to incorporate the European standard *EN 1836 Personal Eye Protection*. The standards that regulate sunglasses have been revised after much consultation with the industry. *Australian Standard, AS 1067: Sunglasses and fashion spectacles* is a mandatory standard under the *Competition and Consumer Act* (Everitt 2010). For example, the standard requires manufacturers to substantiate claims that they make about UV protection, and incorporates a new category 5 rating system for lens. The most recent version of the standard is *AS/NZS 1067:2003/Amdt 1:2009 Sunglasses and fashion spectacles*.

Intellectual property (IP) laws also impact on the product. By registering IP in the form of a patent, trade mark or copyright, a business is given the legal rights of ownership and has exclusive rights to use, license or sell it (WIPO 2008). This is relevant for adidas eyewear as its competitive advantage comes from the unique brand and IP.

## Economic conditions

While the global economic downturn has affected a number of industries, the local economy has remained relatively strong with per capita gross domestic product (GDP) of $40 000 (CIA 2010). Despite this, consumers have cut back on spending, specifically on items such as food, clothing, furniture, entertainment, cars and mobile phones, and sales in the retail sector have decreased (Uren 2008). Therefore, with the economy in general slowing down and consumers not spending money, this will mean that sales of sunglasses will slow, as consumers save money and not be as quick in buying replacement glasses.

Also, another economic factor is the licence agreement with adidas International in Germany and the manufacturer of adidas eyewear, an Austrian company, in which the local company makes payment in euros. The exchange rate of the Australian dollar to the euro can vary and has dropped as low as 0.49 and risen to 0.71. Changes in the exchange rate will affect the margin that the local company makes. Insurance and freight are 13 per cent of the cost price, which is added onto the cost price.

## Social and cultural factors

Sunglasses are an accepted form of eyewear. The main purpose of sunglasses is to protect the eyes and the skin around the eyes from ultraviolet (UV) rays. Sun damage includes 'disorders such as corneal, lenticular and retinal damage, leading to pterygium (overgrowth of tissue on the eye), cataracts, cancer of the eyelid, photo keratitis (sunburn of the cornea) and corneal degeneration' (Everitt 2004). Macular degeneration is also linked to exposure to the sun's UV rays. Sunglasses should eliminate glare, reduce UV transmission, and allow clearer vision and contrast, reducing eye fatigue, while protecting from wind, dust and water. Another important factor in purchasing sunglasses is fashion. While there are important health factors, the wearer also wants to look good when wearing a pair of sunglasses. A fashionable brand is also important to the wearer, and for some this is more important than the UV protection.

## Technology

In recent years there have been a number of technological advances in the materials used in the frames and lenses of sunglasses, such as tinting, optical power and the weight of frames. However, suppliers and retailers of sunglasses must provide safe products and ensure their products comply with the mandatory safety requirements. Apart from the actual product, technological advances in communication have resulted in increased usage of the internet as an information source and retail outlet. This has resulted in adidas eyewear expanding into a new channel, offering information and selling products over the internet.

## Competitor analysis

There are sunglasses for almost every consumer fashion brand in the world. Therefore the sunglasses market is very competitive, but the majority of sunglasses retail for under $150. This means the retail segment for adidas eyewear is even more limited, being in the mid to upper segment combined with being in the main fashion segment, competing with all the big fashion and lifestyle brands. The biggest competitor as a brand is Oakley.

A selection of the primary target market competitors is found in table 1. A secondary group of target market competitors for Originals eyewear include: Black Flys, Dirty Dog, Ugly Fish, Rip Curl and Fish. They are secondary only because they are in a much lower price and quality segment.

**Table 1: Primary target market competitors for two adidas eyewear brand categories**

| Sport Performance | Originals |
| --- | --- |
| Nike | Smith |
| Oakley | Von Zipper |
| Rudy Project | Rayban |
| Bolle | Arnette |
| Carrera | Oliver Peoples |
| Uvex | Police |
| Mako | Vuarnet |
| Tag Hauer | Oakley |
| Maui Jim | Diesel |
| Serengeti | Persol |
| Revo | |
| Porsche Design | |

### Competitive advantages
- The adidas brand is in a current global resurgence and is one of the most widely recognised brands in the world.
- adidas eyewear has innovative designs and materials, which are appealing to the target market.
- adidas eyewear is competitively priced at retail against its direct competitors.
- adidas eyewear is a high-quality product made in Austria.
- High-profile sportsman Ricky Ponting will be wearing adidas eyewear sunglasses as part of an adidas international sponsorship.

## Customer analysis

Even though the product is a sports/casual item, price is still a major factor for the Australian consumer. The consumer is primarily younger in age, and demands value for money at a competitive price. The other factors that are important to the consumer are quality, comfort, function, style, image and status.

## SWOT analysis

### Strengths

- adidas is one of the most well-known and reputable brands in the world.
- adidas is experiencing a global resurgence.
- adidas Australia has invested in key assets in Australian sport (e.g. Australian Cricket team, all Australian State cricket teams, Australian Olympic and Commonwealth Games teams, St. George rugby league team, Collingwood and Adelaide Australian Rules Football teams).
- adidas Australia is investing in own retail outlets with stores opened in Melbourne, Sydney, Brisbane and Surfers Paradise.
- There is an existing distribution network established with optical, sports and sunglass accounts, which gives the company a good base from which to expand the distribution network.
- The product is produced by one of the world's best manufacturers of eyewear, Silhouette International. The designs are innovative, feature-rich and generally suit the Australian market.

### Weaknesses

- Little control over production of product and designs that suit the market.
- The optical range does not have enough new releases each year.
- Time delays in production when product is out of stock.
- The adidas brand is not strong in the United States and United Kingdom. These markets can have a flow-on effect in Australia.
- Australia has a surf culture and adidas is not regarded as a surfing brand. The biggest sports brand in Australia is Billabong. This makes it difficult to connect with the '17'-year-old consumers who are style and opinion leaders in the surf and youth scene.
- No control over foreign exchange rates between the Australian dollar and the euro.
- Currently do not supply to some major retail or optical chain stores.
- The Australian sunglass and optical frame market is very competitive.
- Increased prices from Silhouette International for adidas eyewear make it hard to compete with other suppliers as some wholesale prices are regarded as high for the product category.

### Opportunities

- To increase the distribution network of optical and non-optical accounts (especially with golf and cycling stores).
- To increase existing business with accounts in all channels.
- To continue to produce local content promotional material.
- To continue to improve in-store promotion in an effort to increase brand awareness in-store.
- To continue to intensify the sales of adidas Originals sunglasses to the market with introduction of more sunglass models.
- To become a supplier to more retailers for sunglasses.

### Threats

- Chain stores not wanting to stock adidas eyewear.
- Independent stores not wanting to stock adidas eyewear.
- Independent stores converting to become part of the chain retailers (i.e. losing customer base).

- Retail stores wanting bigger discounts and having preferred suppliers.
- Competitor's products.
- Bad weather, which will affect sunglass sales.
- The euro getting stronger against the Australian dollar.

# Objectives

## Mission statement

adidas International's mission statement is:

The adidas Group strives to be the global leader in the sporting goods industry with sports brands built on a passion for sports and a sporting lifestyle.

- **We are dedicated** to consistently delivering outstanding financial results.
- **We are innovation and design leaders** who seek to help athletes of all skill levels achieve peak performance with every product we bring to market.
- **We are consumer focused** and therefore we continuously improve the quality, look, feel and image of our products and our organisational structures to match and exceed consumer expectations and to provide them with the highest value.
- **We are a global organisation** that is socially and environmentally responsible, creative and financially rewarding for our employees and shareholders.
- **We are committed** to continuously strengthening our brands and products to improve our competitive position.

## Corporate objectives

- To continue to develop adidas eyewear as a reputable brand of eyewear to the primary target market.
- To make a profit after tax.
- To improve business relationships with customers, especially independent optical customers and chains/buying groups.

## Marketing objectives

- Experience an increase in new customers who develop into long-term customers.
- Increase adidas market share by 10 per cent by the first year from the launch of campaign.
- To improve the total number of ABC customers from 36 to 65 (A-C).

## Communication objectives

- To increase the brand awareness of adidas eyewear so that 65 per cent of the target market knows that it exists and that 50 per cent of the population between the ages 15–50 know it exists.
- Highlight the brand message of unique functional features to suit different sports.
- Alter the existing perception that adidas Originals is only related to clothing.

## Sales objective

- To achieve sales of 20 000 units and net sales of $2 000 000. The total marketing budget is 10 per cent of sales.

# Target market

## Primary target market

15–25-year-old males and females, with a male skew. With focus around the adidas target market profile of '17'. They are: Cutting-edge opinion leaders. Educated and ambitious. Socially aware. Fashion conscious. Informed, interested and indeed interesting. Enjoy music and sport. Enjoy a high level of disposable income. Spend heavily on clothes, accessories, entertainment and lifestyle. Comfortable with new technologies and will be first to try a new product or idea. Like to be an individual. Considers him/herself young.

## Secondary target market

25–40-year-old males (70 per cent) and females (30 per cent). They are involved in or interested in sport. They: are sports enthusiasts and watch a lot of sporting events; enjoy a high disposable income; and spend a portion of their disposable income on sporting products for use in sport and/or everyday life.

## General market

To expand the customer base slightly with selected stores that could sell adidas Originals eyewear. Target the mainstream market in a way so the product is seen as a quality functional performance sports eyewear.

## Positioning strategy

Desired positioning:
- **Optical** — A quality product with a young sporting image.
- **Sunglasses** — Functional sports sunglasses of high quality used by top Australian and international athletes.
- **Originals Sunglasses** — Fashionable sunglasses with a streetwear/fashion edge that are original in design.

# Marketing mix strategy

## Product

To have an extensive range of quality ophthalmic glasses and sunglasses, which carry the adidas brand name. The designs of the frames will appeal to the target market.

### Sunglasses

The sunglass range is broken down into three segments:
- **Performance Sport** — Sunglasses with high functionality to be used primarily for sport. These sunglasses have innovative functional designs to enhance athletic performance.
- **Originals Sunglasses** — Original designs with a fashion/streetwear appeal. These sunglasses are more about the way they look rather than functionality.
- **Casuals** — Sunglasses made of SPX plastic with radical designs, that push the current boundaries and set new trends and also some more conservative models. More conservative metal sunglasses for the mainstream market and also a rimless range. Included in the casual range are two youth/kids sunglasses.

## Branding

All optical frames and sunglasses have some form of adidas branding, which is placed in strategic locations on the frames and is subtle. The most common branding is the word 'adidas' or the adidas logo on the temples.

## Packaging

All sunglasses come with a micro-fibre cleaning bag, a small adidas eyewear logo sticker and a product information booklet. Some models come with a complimentary hard plastic competition case. These are packaged inside a cardboard adidas eyewear box.

## Price

Prices are set against direct competitors. The retail prices range from $119.95 to $429.95, which puts the collection in the middle to upper price segment in the eyewear industry. The lower priced items have been introduced within the last year and have proven to be popular, which indicates a demand for the product.

The wholesale mark-up ranges from 50 per cent to 100 per cent. Best reference sunglass models have higher mark-ups. These are all plastic frames. Metal frames have smaller mark-ups as their costs are higher.

## Distribution (Place)

Sunglasses will be sold through optometrists, dispensing opticians, adidas' own retail outlets, specialist sunglasses stores, sports stores, cycling stores, golf retail stores, snow and outdoor stores, department stores, fashion and streetwear stores, and ski/snowboard stores. The opportunity exists to expand the distribution network in all areas. The main outlets to target are optical outlets, specialist sunglass stores, and non-optical accounts concentrating on sunglass retail, golf and cycling stores throughout Australia.

A selective distribution policy will be undertaken for the adidas Originals sunglass range. The main focus will be on the non-optical customer base. The priority will be given to current adidas Australia customers who stock adidas Originals clothing.

## Promotion

Promotion of the sunglasses will be focused on the different product categories, like Performance Sport and Originals. The local campaign will feature sunglasses and optical frames following the International 'Support your vision' campaign. This will add to adidas eyewear's credibility in Australia.

The main method of promotion for sunglasses will be magazine and radio advertising/competitions and sponsorship. This gives the product exposure and credibility. Along with sponsorship, point of sale material will be the main focus for promotion. A special Gift with Purchase promotion will be run for the adidas performance optical frames. This will revolve around an adidas youth cap being given away free with every sports frame sold. Promotion will be cool and innovative just like the product. In addition to this, the following activities will be undertaken: event sponsorship and exhibitions; incentive programs with stockists and key account staff sell-through incentives. The use of local athletes in promotional material will be a key component in the marketing mix. Promotion of optical frames will focus on in-store promotion and staff incentive programs.

It is very important that adidas eyewear is still promoted and seen by the target market as being cutting edge, new, functional, cool, innovative and fashionable.

# Budget

The tables that follow outline the sales and promotion budget for adidas eyewear.

**Table 2: Sales budget**

| Category | Units | % of sales | Net value ($) |
|---|---|---|---|
| Performance Sport | 12 700 | 63 | 1 270 000 |
| Performance Casual | 5 000 | 25 | 500 000 |
| Originals Sunglasses | 2 300 | 10 | 230 000 |
| Total | 20 000 | 98 | 2 000 000 |

NOTE: The above figures have been changed for privacy reasons.

**Table 3: Promotion budget for 2011**

| Media | Dollars ($) |
|---|---|
| **Print** | |
| Magazine advertisements | 45 000 |
| Magazine competitions | 25 000 |
| **Radio** | |
| Radio advertisements | 10 000 |
| **Sponsorship** | |
| Athlete | 20 000 |
| Event | 25 000 |
| **Point of sale** | |
| Display | 35 000 |
| Catalogue | 15 000 |
| Incentives | 10 000 |
| **Trade shows** | |
| Mobile stand | 15 000 |
| **Total** | **200 000** |

NOTE: The above figures have been changed for privacy reasons.

# Implementation

| Tactic | Jan | Feb | Mar | Apr | May | Jun | Jul | Aug | Sep | Oct | Nov | Dec |
|---|---|---|---|---|---|---|---|---|---|---|---|---|
| **Print** | | | | | | | | | | | | |
| Magazine advertisements | ■ | ■ | | | | | | ■ | ■ | ■ | ■ | ■ |
| Magazine competitions | ▨ | ▨ | | | | ▨ | ▨ | | | | ▨ | ▨ |
| **Radio** | | | | | | | | | | | | |
| Radio advertisements | ▨ | ▨ | | | | ▨ | | | | | | ▨ |
| **Sponsorship** | | | | | | | | | | | | |
| Athlete | ▨ | ▨ | ▨ | ▨ | ▨ | ▨ | ▨ | ▨ | ▨ | ▨ | ▨ | ▨ |
| Event | | ▨ | ▨ | ▨ | | ▨ | ▨ | ▨ | ▨ | ▨ | | |
| **Point of sale** | | | | | | | | | | | | |
| Display | ■ | ■ | ■ | ■ | ■ | ■ | ■ | ■ | ■ | ■ | ■ | ■ |
| Catalogue | | | | | | ■ | | | | | | ■ |
| Incentives | ▨ | ▨ | | | | ▨ | ▨ | | | | ▨ | ▨ |
| **Trade shows** | | | | | | | | | | | | |
| Mobile stand | | | ▨ | ▨ | | | | | | | | |

# Evaluation

Campaign evaluation is a critical component of the plan as it is utilised to measure the overall effectiveness of the campaign in key areas such as the marketing environment, sales, consumer attitudes and promotions effectiveness. There are a range of measuring facilities and research procedures that can be used to aid the evaluation process, which will be assigned to a person who will be responsible for the success of each issue.

| Issue | Responsibility | Review date |
|---|---|---|
| 1. Review marketing environment factors | Management team | Fortnightly |
| 2. Review company objectives | CEO | Monthly |
| 3. Sales review | Marketing manager | Weekly |
| 4. Consumer attitudes | Brand manager | Fortnightly |
| 5. Test promotions activities | Marketing manager | Quarterly |
| 6. Review marketing mix | Brand manager | Monthly |
| 7. Review promotions activities | Management team | Fortnightly |

## Conclusion

This report sets out the marketing plan for adidas eyewear in Australia. As outlined in the report, the target market consists of two market segments: the primary (15–25-year-olds with a male skew) and secondary (25–40-year-olds with an interest in sport) target markets. The sales objective is to achieve sales of 20 000 units and net sales of $2 000 000, and the total marketing budget is 10 per cent of sales. Promotion activities will include magazine and radio advertising, sponsorship, point of sale material and trade shows. By the end of this campaign the objective is to increase adidas eyewear's market share by 10 per cent and develop positive brand attitude towards adidas sunglasses.

It is believed that there is an opportunity for adidas eyewear to expand its position in the sunglasses market. It is, therefore, recommended that this marketing plan be accepted by adidas eyewear management to assist in continuing this growth in the marketplace.

## References

Adidas website, www.adidas.com.au.

Adidas website, 'Eyewear', www.adidas.com/eyewear.

Adidas, 2008, 'Corporate Mission Statement', *Annual Report 2008*, www.adidas-group.com.

All About Vision website, 'Macular degeneration: frequently asked questions', www.allaboutvision.com.

AMD Alliance International website, 'Prevention and early detection', www.amdalliance.org.

Central Intelligence Agency (CIA), 2010, *The World Factbook: Australia*, Central Intelligence Agency, www.cia.gov.

Everitt, Terry, 2004, 'Good vision for now and the future', Association of Professional Aestheticians of Australia, www.apaa.com.au.

SAI Global Infostore website, http://infostore.saiglobal.com.

Standards Australia website, www.standards.org.au.

Uren, David, 2008, 'Growth defies RBA and government predictions', *The Australian*, 4 September, www.theaustralian.news.com.au.

World Intellectual Property Organisation (WIPO), 2008, 'Intellectual property and small- and medium-sized enterprises', www.wipo.int.

# Glossary

**action plans** Implementable plans with specific actions, schedules and goals that direct managers and staff that are not directly involved in strategic decisions. 509

**advertising** Paid promotion of a business, product or brand to a mass audience. 311

**agents** Marketing intermediaries engaged by buyers or sellers on an ongoing basis to represent them in negotiations with other parties in the marketing channel. 374

**ambush marketing** The presentation of marketing messages at an event that is sponsored by an unrelated business or a competitor. 332

**aspirational reference groups** Groups to which the individual would like to belong. 120

**automatic vending** Use of machines to dispense a product; used for small, routinely purchased products. 372

**behavioural segmentation** Market segmentation based on actual purchase and/or consumption behaviours. 193

**born global** A business that views the whole world as its market from the outset. 481

**brand** A collection of symbols such as a name, logo, slogan and design intended to create an image in the customer's mind that differentiates a product from competitors' products. 21, 232

**brand equity** The added value that a brand gives a product. 233

**brand extension** Giving an existing brand name to new product in a different category. 235

**brand image** The set of beliefs that a consumer has regarding a particular brand. 232

**brand loyalty** A customer's highly favourable attitude and purchasing behaviour towards a certain brand. 233

**break-even analysis** An analysis designed to estimate the volume of unit sales required to cover total costs. 268

**brokers** Marketing intermediaries engaged by buyers or sellers on a short-term or one-off basis to represent them in negotiations with other parties in the marketing channel. 374

**bundle of attributes** The features and functions of a product that benefit the customer. 21

**business markets** Individuals or organisations that purchase products for resale, use in the production of other products, or for use in their daily business operations. 147

**business-to-business products** Those products purchased by individuals and organisations for use in the production of other products or for use in their daily business operations. 218

**business-to-business services** Those services purchased by individuals and organisations for use in the production of other products or for use in their daily business operations. 390

**business-unit strategy** Strategies for the various business areas within an organisation to guide their contribution to achieving the overall corporate objectives. 500

**buying centre** The groups and structures within an organisation that make business buying decisions. 162

**causal research** Research that assumes that a particular variable causes a specific outcome and then, by holding everything else constant, tests whether the variable does indeed effect that outcome. 86

**cause-related marketing** Philanthropic activities tied to the purchase of a product. 303

**clients** 'Customers' of the products of not-for-profit organisations. 12

**co-branding** The use of two or more brand names on the same product. 236

**cognitive dissonance** A purchaser's second thoughts or doubts about the wisdom of a purchase they have made. 138

**competition-based pricing** An approach to pricing based on the prices charged by competitors or on the likely response of competitors to the organisation's prices. 273

**consumer behaviour** The analysis of the behaviour of individuals and households who buy goods and services for personal consumption. 113

**consumer decision-making process** The process of need/want recognition, information search, evaluation of options, purchase and post-purchase evaluation that are common to most consumer buying decisions. 135

**consumer products** Those products purchased by households and individuals for their own private consumption. 218

**consumer services** Services purchased by individual consumers or households for their own private consumption. 389

**consumers** People who use the good or service. 12

**contingency planning** The process of putting in place plans for unforeseen or uncertain eventualities to ensure managers think ahead and can respond to emerging problems and opportunities. 509

**contract manufacturing** An approach to international marketing in which a business pays a foreign business to manufacture its product and market it in the foreign country under the domestic business's name. 480

**convenience products (fast-moving consumer goods)** Inexpensive, frequently purchased consumer products that are bought with little engagement with the decision-making process. 219

**corporate social responsibility** The obligation of businesses to act in the interests of the societies that sustain them. 16, 503

**corporate strategy** A specific, but high-level plan to achieve objectives that reflect the overall mission of the organisation. 499

**cost-based pricing** An approach to pricing in which a percentage or dollar amount is added to the cost of the product in order to determine its selling price. 271

**cross-docking** The practice of expediting the movement of goods from receipt to shipping. 358

**culture** The system of knowledge, beliefs, values, rituals and artefacts by which a society or other large group defines itself. 116

**customer lifetime value** a metric of the dollar value of a customer relationship based on the present value of the projected future cash flows from the business/customer relationship 515

**customer relationship management (CRM)** The processes and practices put in place to identify, track and use customer information and preferences to provide superior customer service and sustain long-term relationships. 444, 502

**customers** People who purchase goods and services for their own or other people's use. 12

**customisation** Carefully tailoring the marketing mix to the specific characteristics and wants of each market. 462

**demand** A want that a consumer has the ability to satisfy. 22, 262

**demand curve** A graph showing the relationship between price and volume sold. 263

**demand schedule** A table showing quantity demanded for a particular good at particular prices. 263

**demand-based pricing** The influence of demand on pricing decisions. 263

**demographic factors** The vital and social characteristics of populations, such as age, education and income. 125

**demographic segmentation** Market segmentation based on demographic variables, which are the vital and social characteristics of populations, such as age, education and income. 189

**derived demand** Demand in business markets that is due to demand in consumer markets. 158

**descriptive research** Research used to solve a particular and well-defined problem by clarifying the characteristics of certain phenomena. 86

**differential pricing** The practice of charging different buyers different prices for the same product. 285

**differentiated targeting strategy** A marketing approach that involves developing a different marketing mix for each target market segment. 184

**diffusion of innovations** The theory that social groups influence the decisions made by individuals in such a way that innovations are adopted by the market in a predictable pattern over time. 226

**digitalisation** The ability to deliver a product as information or to present information about a product digitally. 427

**direct exporting** An approach to exporting in which the marketing organisation deals directly with the international market. 479

**direct marketing** A type of non-store retailing that promotes and sells products via mail, telephone or the web. 370

**dissociative reference groups** Groups with which the individual does not wish to be associated or which the individual may wish to leave. 120

**distribution (or place)** The means of making the offering available to the customer at the right time and place. 24

**distribution centre** A warehouse focused on moving rather than storing products. 358

**distribution channel** A group of individuals and organisations directing products from producers to end users. 347

**economic forces** Those factors that affect how much people and organisations can spend and how they choose to spend it. 53

**electronic marketing** The activities involved in planning and implementing marketing in the electronic environment. 421

**embargoes** Bans or restrictions on imports from a particular country. 475

**emergent approach** The development of marketing strategy in response to changing market conditions. 509

**empowerment** Enabling employees to make decisions to do their job properly and ensuring they have the necessary resources to make effective use of their power to make decisions. 510

**environmental analysis** A process that involves breaking the marketing environment into smaller parts in order to gain a better understanding of it. 41

**equipment** Capital equipment and accessory equipment used in the production of the business's products. 220

**ethics** A set of moral principles that guide attitudes and behaviour. 14

**exchange** The mutually beneficial transfer of offerings of value between the buyer and seller. 10

**exclusive distribution** An approach to market coverage that distributes products through a single intermediary in any given geographic region. 349

**exploratory research** Research intended to gather more information about a loosely defined problem. 86

**exporting** The sale of products into foreign markets from a home market base. 479

**extended decision making** High-involvement purchasing decisions involving high-price, high-risk and/or infrequent, unfamiliar products. 135

**external environment** The people and processes that are outside the organisation and cannot be directly controlled. 45

**external reference price** A price comparison provided by the manufacturer or retailer. 283

**extranet** A private website for sharing information securely between different organisations. 449

**family branding** A branding approach that uses the same brand on several of the organisation's products. 234

**family life cycle** A series of characteristic stages through which most families pass. 122

**foreign direct investment** Outright ownership of a foreign operation. 480

**fragmentation** The increasing division of the market into ever smaller niches with increasingly specific needs. 509

**franchising** An approach to business in which one party (a franchisor) licenses its business model to another party (a franchisee). 354, 479

**freight forwarders** Specialist transportation businesses that combine cargo from different businesses in order to achieve efficient load sizes. 358

**frequency** The number of times each target market member is exposed to the advertisement. 317

**generic brands** Products that only indicate the product category. 235

**geographic pricing** A pricing strategy that includes price differentials based on those costs that vary with distance between the buyer and seller. 280

**geographic segmentation** Market segmentation based on variables related to geography, such as climate and region. 188

**globalisation** The process through which individuals, organisations and governments become increasingly interconnected and similar. 460

**good** A physical (tangible) offering capable of being delivered to a customer. 22

**government markets** The market for selling products to national (Commonwealth), state (provincial) and local (municipal) governments for use in providing services for citizens. 150

**green marketing** The marketing of environmentally safe or beneficial products. 17

**greenwashing** The dissemination of questionable or potentially misleading information by an organisation in relation to its products, in order for the organisation and its products to be perceived as environmentally friendly. 19

**guerrilla marketing** The use of an aggressive and unconventional marketing approach. 335

**habitual decision making** Low-involvement purchasing decisions, usually involving small, routine, low-risk products. 135

**heterogeneity** Inevitable, but minimisable, variations in quality in the delivery of a service product. 396

**horizontal channel integration** Bringing organisations at the same level of operation under a single management structure. 353

**hypothesis** A tentative explanation that can be tested. 86

**indirect exporting** An approach to exporting that relies on the use of specialist marketing intermediaries. 479

**individual branding** A branding approach in which each product is branded separately. 234

**individualism** The extent to which people focus on their own goals over those of the group. 117

**inelastic demand** Demand that is relatively independent of price, a common characteristic of demand within industries in business markets. 159

**inseparability** The characteristic of being produced and consumed simultaneously. 393

**institutional markets** Business markets in which non-public, not-for-profit organisations buy and sell products. 151

**intangibility** The characteristic of lacking physical form. 392

**integrated marketing communications (IMC)** The coordination of promotional efforts to maximise the communication effect. 305

**intensive distribution** An approach to market coverage that distributes products through every suitable intermediary. 349

**interaction** The ongoing exchange of information between marketer and customer (or potential customer). 425

**internal environment** The parts of the organisation, the people and the processes used to create, communicate, deliver and exchange offerings that have value. The organisation can directly control its internal environment. 43

**internal reference price** The price expected by consumers, largely based upon their actual experience with the product. 283

**international joint venture** An approach to international marketing in which a marketing organisation forms a new business with an existing business in the target foreign market. 480

**international strategic alliance** A cooperative arrangement between a business and another business in a foreign market. 480

**intranet** An internal website for the use of staff. 449

**joint demand** Interdependent demand for products that are used together in the production of another product. 159

**just-in-time (JIT)** An approach to inventory management that involves holding only that stock that is about to be used or sold. 357

**laws** Legislation enacted by elected officials. 55

**licensing** An agreement in which a brand owner permits another party to use the brand on its products. 236, 479

**limited decision making** Limited-involvement purchasing decisions, usually involving infrequently bought, but familiar, products. 135

**line extension** A new product that is closely related to an existing product in a product line. 243

**logistics** That part of the marketing process concerned with supply and transport. 24

**long-term orientation** The extent to which a pragmatic, long-term orientation is valued over a short-term focus. 117

**loss leader** A high-volume product priced below cost to attract customers into the store, where it is expected they will buy other, normally priced, products. 268

**loyalty programs** Schemes that reward customers based on the amount they spend. 326

**macro environment** The factors outside of the industry that influence the survival of the company; these factors are not directly controllable by the organisation. 51

**manufacturer brands** Brands owned by producers and clearly identified with the product at the point of sale. 235

**manufacturers' wholesalers** Wholesalers owned by the producer. 378

**marginal analysis** An analysis designed to determine the effect on costs and revenue when an organisation produces and sells one more unit of product. 270

**market** A group of customers with heterogeneous needs and wants. 11, 179

**market potential** The total sales of a product category that all organisations in an industry are expected to sell in a specified period of time assuming a specific level of marketing activity. 198

**market research brief** A set of instructions and requirements that generally states the research problem and the information required, and specifies the timeframe, budget and other conditions of the project. 82

**market research** A business activity that discovers information of use in making marketing decisions. 75

**market segment profile** A description of the typical potential customer in the market segment; that is, a description of the common variables shared by members of market segments and how the variables differ between market segments. 196

**market segments** Subgroups within the total market that are relatively similar in regards to certain characteristics. 181

**market share** The proportion of the total market held by the organisation. 198

**market specialisation** A target marketing strategy in which all marketing efforts are focused on meeting a wide range of needs within a particular market segment. 184

**marketing** The activity, set of institutions and processes for creating, communicating, delivering and exchanging offerings that have value for customers, clients, partners and society at large. 3

**marketing cycle** The cyclical and interrelated process of understanding, creating, communicating and delivering value, refined by continuous evaluation. 495

**marketing environment** All of the internal and external forces that affect a marketer's ability to create, communicate, deliver and exchange offerings of value. 40

**marketing information system (MIS)** The structure put in place to manage information gathered during the usual operations of the organisation. 77

**marketing intermediaries** Individuals or organisations that act in the distribution chain between the producer and end user. 347

**marketing management** The management task of understanding the market, and planning, implementing and evaluating marketing activities. 496

**marketing metrics** Measures that are used to assess marketing performance. 61, 504

**marketing mix** A set of variables that a marketer can exercise control over in creating an offering for exchange. 21

**marketing planning** An ongoing process that combines organisational objectives and situation analyses to formulate and maintain a marketing plan that moves the organisation from where it currently is to where it wants to be. 57

**marketing process** A process that involves understanding the market to create, communicate and deliver an offering for exchange. 7

**masculinity** The extent to which traditionally masculine values are valued over traditionally feminine values within a culture in Hofstede's cultural dimensions. 117

**Maslow's hierarchy of needs** A theory of motivation that suggests that people seek to satisfy needs according to a hierarchy that places lower order needs before higher order needs. 128

**materials handling** The physical handling of goods. 358

**membership reference groups** Groups to which the individual belongs. 120

**merchant wholesalers** Independently owned wholesaling businesses that take title to products. 377

**micro environment** The forces within an organisation's industry that affect its ability to serve its customers and clients — target markets, partners and competitors. 47

**mission statements** A summary statement of the overarching goals of the organisation. 499

**mobile e-commerce** The use of a mobile phone to make purchases. 370

**modified rebuy** The purchase of a product that is similar, but not identical, to one a business has previously purchased, after evaluating a small range of alternatives. 161

**motivation** An individual's internal drive to satisfy unfulfilled needs or achieve goals. 128

**multiculturalism** The existence of diverse cultures within a society. 117

**need** A day-to-day survival requirement: food, shelter and clothing. 22

**new task purchase** A first purchase in a product category in response to a new problem, process or product. 161

**non-probability sampling** A sampling approach that provides no way of knowing the chance of a particular member of the population being chosen as part of the sample that will be studied. 93

**not-for-profit marketing** The marketing activities of individuals and organisations designed to achieve objectives other than to generate profits. 409

**opinion leader** A reference group member who provides relevant and influential advice about a specific topic of interest to group members. 121

**opportunities** Factors that are potentially helpful to achieving the organisation's objectives. 64

**organisational culture** The values and behaviours shared throughout the organisation. 511

**organisational structure** The formal arrangement of business functions within an organisation. 510

**partners** Organisations or individuals who are involved in the activities and processes for creating, communicating and delivering offerings for exchange. 12

**parts and materials** Business-to-business products that form part of the purchasing business's products. 220

**penetration pricing** A pricing tactic based on setting a low price in order to gain rapid market share and turnover for a new product. 284

**perception** The psychological process that filters, organises and attributes meaning to external stimuli. 130

**perishability** The inability to store services for use at a later date. 397

**permission marketing** Marketing that aims to build an ongoing relationship with customers. 336

**pester power** The influence of children on their parents' purchasing decisions. 123

**physical evidence** Tangible cues that can be used as a means to evaluate service quality prior to purchase. 25, 401

**political forces** The influence of politics on marketing decisions. 53

**population** All of the things (often people) of interest to the researcher in the particular research project. 92

**portal** A website that is designed to act as a gateway to other related sites. 433

**positioning** The way in which the market perceives an organisation, its products and its brands in relation to competing offerings. 202

**power distance** The degree of inequality among people that is acceptable within a culture. 117

**premium offers** Bonus products given for free or sold at a heavily discounted price when another product is purchased. 326

**price elastic** Demand for which price elasticity is greater than 1 (i.e. the percentage change in quantity demanded exceeds the percentage change in price). 265

**price elasticity of demand** The sensitivity of quantity demanded to changes in price. 264

**price floor** A minimum price that must be charged to cover costs. 268

**price inelastic** Demand for which price elasticity is less than 1 (i.e. the percentage change in quantity demanded is less than the percentage change in price). 265

**price leader** A high-volume product priced near cost to attract customers into the store, where it is expected they will buy other, normally priced, products. 268

**price skimming** Charging the highest price that customers who most desire the product are willing to pay, and then later lowering the price to bring in larger numbers of buyers. 284

**primary data** Data collected specifically for the current market research project. 87

**private label brands** Brands owned by resellers, such as wholesalers or retailers, and not identified with the manufacturer. 235

**probability sampling** A sampling approach in which every member of the population has a known chance of being selected in the sample that will be studied. 93

**process** The systems used to create, communicate, deliver and exchange an offering. 24, 400

**producer markets** The markets in which business organisations and professionals purchase products for use in the production of other products or in their daily business operations. 149

**product** A good, service or idea offered to the market for exchange. 21, 215

**product adoption process** The sequential process of awareness, interest, evaluation, trial, and adoption through which a consumer decides to purchase a new product. 225

**product deletion** The process of removing a product from the product mix. 244

**product differentiation** The creation of products and product attributes that distinguish one product from another. 229

**product item** A particular version of a product. 218

**product life cycle** The typical stages a product progresses through: new product development, introduction, growth, maturity and decline. 223

**product line** A set of product items related by characteristics such as end use, target market, technology or raw materials. 218

**product mix** The set of all products that an organisation makes available to customers. 218

**product placement** The paid inclusion of products in movies, television shows, video games, songs and books. 334

**product positioning** The way in which the market perceives a product in relation to competing offerings. 243

**product specialisation** A target marketing strategy in which all marketing efforts are concentrated on offering a single product range to a number of market segments. 184

**product–market specialisation** A target marketing strategy in which marketing efforts are concentrated on offering a single product to a single market segment. 184

**product-line pricing** An approach to pricing that sets prices for groups of products in a product line rather than for individual products. 284

**profiling** The process of getting to know about potential customers before they make a purchase and to find out more about existing customers. 424

**promotion** The marketing activities that make potential customers, partners and society aware of and attracted to the business's offerings. 23, 299

**promotional pricing** The combination of a pricing approach with a promotional campaign. 285

**psychographic segmentation** Market segmentation based on the psychographic variables of lifestyle, motives and personality attributes. 190

**psychological characteristics** Internal factors, independent of situational and social circumstances, that shape the thinking, aspirations, expectations and behaviours of the individual. 128

**public relations** Promotional efforts designed to build and sustain good relations between an organisation and its stakeholders. 322

**publicity** Unpaid exposure in the media. 322

**pull advertising** Advertising that the customer actively seeks out. 426

**pull policy** An approach in which a product is promoted to consumers to create demand upward through the marketing distribution channel. 309

**push advertising** Advertising sent from the marketer to the customer. 426

**push policy** An approach in which a product is promoted to the next organisation down the marketing distribution channel. 309

**qualitative research** Research intended to obtain rich, deep and detailed information about the attitudes and emotions that underlie the behaviours that quantitative research identifies. 90

**quantitative research** Research that collects information that can be represented numerically. 88

**quotas** Annual limits on the amount of particular types of goods that can be imported. 475

**reach** The proportion of the target audience exposed to the advertisement at least once. 317

**reference group** Any group to which an individual looks for guidance. 119

**regulations** Rules made under authority delegated by legislation. 55

**research design** The detailed methodology created to guide the research project and answer the research question. 85

**research problem** The question that the market research project is intended to answer. 81

**reseller markets** The market of retailers, wholesalers and other intermediaries that buy products in order to sell or lease them to another party for profit. 148

**retailing** Any exchange in which the buyer is the ultimate consumer of the product. 364

**sales promotions** Short-term incentives to encourage purchase of a product by either resellers or consumers. 325

**sales revenue** Total volume of sales multiplied by the average selling price. 198

**sample** The group chosen for the study. 92

**sampling error** A measure of the extent to which the results from the sample differ from the results that would be obtained from the entire population. 93

**saturation** The existence of so many competitive offerings in the marketplace that it becomes virtually impossible to differentiate an offering or create a competitive advantage. 508

**search engine marketing** Paid advertising that appears similarly to a search result on a search engine page. 434

**search engine optimisation (SEO)** Tailoring features of a website to try to achieve the best possible ranking in search results returned by a search engine. 433

**secondary data** Data originally gathered or recorded for some purpose other than to address the current market research problem. 87

**segmentation variables** Characteristics that buyers have in common and that might be closely related to their purchasing behaviour. 187

**selective distribution** An approach to market coverage that distributes products through intermediaries chosen for some specific reason. 349

**service** An intangible offering that does not involve ownership. 22

**services** Activities, performances or benefits that are offered for sale, but which involve neither an exchange of tangible goods nor a transfer of title. 388

**services and supplies** Business-to-business products that are essential to business operations, but do not directly form part of the production process. 220

**shopping products** Consumer products that involve moderate to high engagement in the decision-making process, in the purchase decision being based on consideration of features, quality and price. 218

**situation analysis** An analysis that involves identifying the key factors that will be used as a basis for the development of marketing strategy. 57

**situational influences** The circumstances a consumer finds themself in when making purchasing decisions. 114

**SMART model** An approach to determining effective marketing objectives that requires they be Specific, Measurable, Actionable, Reasonable and Timetabled. 503

**social class** A group comprising individuals of similar rank within the social hierarchy. 119

**social marketing** A process that uses marketing principles and techniques to influence target audience behaviours that will benefit society, as well as the individual. 28

**sociocultural forces** The social and cultural factors that affect people's attitudes, beliefs, behaviours, preferences, customs and lifestyles. 53

**spam** Unsolicited commercial electronic messages. 439

**specialty products** Highly desired consumer products with unique characteristics that consumers will make considerable effort to obtain. 219

**sponsorship** The paid association of a brand with an event or person. 337

**stakeholders** Individuals, organisations and other groups that have a rightful interest in the activities of a business. 16

**standardisation** Applying a uniform marketing mix across international markets, with only minor modifications to meet local conditions. 462

**straight rebuy** The low-engagement purchase of the same products as previously purchased from established vendors under established terms. 161

**strengths** Those attributes of the organisation that help it achieve its objectives. 64

**subculture** A group of individuals who share common attitudes, values and behaviours that distinguish them from the broader culture in which they are immersed. 117

**supply chain** The parties involved in providing all of the raw materials and services that go in to getting a product to the market. 24

**supply-chain management** An approach to managing marketing channels based on ongoing partnerships among distribution channel members that create efficiencies and deliver value to customers. 352

**SWOT analysis** An analysis that identifies the strengths and weaknesses and the opportunities and threats in relation to an organisation. 63

**target market** A group of customers with similar needs and wants. 21

**target marketing** An approach to marketing based on identifying, understanding and developing an offering for those segments of the total market that the organisation can best serve. 182

**tariffs** Duties charged on imports that effectively increase the price of imports relative to domestically made products. 474

**threats** Factors that are potentially harmful to the organisation's efforts to achieve its objectives. 64

**total product concept** A view of the product that describes the core product, expected product, augmented product and potential product in order to analyse how the product creates value for the customer. 216

**trade mark** A brand name or brand mark that has been legally registered so as to secure exclusive use of the brand. 232

**uncertainty avoidance** The extent to which people in a culture feel threatened by uncertainty and rely on mechanisms to reduce it. 117

**unsought products** Goods or services that a consumer either knows about but doesn't normally consider purchasing, or doesn't even know about. 219

**value** A customer's overall assessment of the utility of an offering based on perceptions of what is received and what is given. 11

**vertical channel integration** Bringing different stages of the distribution channel under a single management structure. 353

**vertical marketing system** A distribution channel in which all stages occur under a single management structure. 354

**viral marketing** The use of social networks to spread a marketing message. 432, 336

**want** A desire, but not necessary for day-to-day survival. 22

**weaknesses** Those attributes of the organisation that hinder it in trying to achieve its objectives. 64

**Web 2.0** The various technologies and experiences that involve online communities where members contribute to and build the community and the content, and where users can substantially control their own online experience through customisation and interactivity. 431

**wheel of retailing** The theory that retailers enter the market with low costs, low margins and low prices, but move to high costs and high prices as they seek to compete with copiers, only to then have to compete with new low-price entrants. 369

**wholesaling** Exchanges in which products are bought for resale, for use as inputs in other products, or for some other use in a business. 376

# References and notes

## Chapter 1

1. This definition was adopted by the American Marketing Association in October 2007.
2. American Marketing Association, October 2007. The AMA reviews the definition every few years to ensure it reflects current marketing practice. See L.M. Keefe (2008), 'Marketing defined', *Marketing News*, 15 January, pp. 28–29.
3. I. Maignan and O.C. Ferrell (2004), 'Corporate social responsibility and marketing: an integrative framework', *Journal of the Academy of Marketing Science*, 32(1), pp. 3–19.
4. L.M. Keefe (2008), 'Marketing defined', *Marketing News*, 15 January, pp. 28–29.
5. Febfast website, www.febfast.com.au.
6. Tourism Australia website, www.australia.com.
7. N. Stone (2010), 'Legacy embarks on branding mission', *Professional Marketing*, July–September.
8. Market Data (2010), 'Battle of the bottle: Aussies love of NZ wines continues', *Professional Marketing*, pp. 38–9.
9. Amway website, www.amway.com.au; Brand Profile (2010), 'Direct hit', *Professional Marketing*, pp. 36–7.
10. V.A. Zeithaml (1988), 'Consumer perceptions of price, quality and value: A means end model and synthesis of evidence', *Journal of Marketing*, 52(July), pp. 2–22.
11. K. Miller (2007), 'Investigating the idiosyncratic nature of brand value', *Australasian Marketing Journal*, 15(2), pp. 81–96.
12. J.C. Sweeney and G. Soutar (2001), 'Consumer perceived value: the development of a multi-item scale', *Journal of Retailing*, 77, pp. 203–220.
13. X. Luo and C.B. Bhattacharya (2006), Corporate social responsibility, customer satisfaction and market value, *Journal of Marketing*, 70(4), pp. 1–18.
14. National Centre for HIV Epidemiology and Clinical Research, 2009, *Annual Surveillance Report*, University of New South Wales.
15. Department of Health and Ageing (2010), 'National notifiable diseases surveillance system', www.health.gov.au; A. Smith, P. Agius, A. Mitchell, C. Barrett and M. Pitts (2009), *Secondary students and sexual health 2008*, Australian Research Centre in Sex, Health & Society, La Trobe University, www.latrobe.edu.au;

S. Smith and M. Sanderson (2010), 'Txt 4 safe sex', *Proceedings of the International Nonprofit and Social Marketing Conference*, www.icebergevents.com.
16. Marketing and Sales Standards Setting Body (2006), Functional Map.
17. Business New Zealand Government Information Site (2009), www.business.govt.nz.
18. Ministry of Economic Development (2009), *Competition policy*, www.med.govt.nz.
19. Queensland Government (2011), 'Premier's Disaster Relief Appeal major donors', www.thepremier.qld.gov.au; Commonwealth Bank (2011), 'Support for customers living in flood or cyclone affected areas', www.commbank.com.au.
20. Dietitians Association of Australia (2008), *Food advertising to children*, www.daa.asn.au; Advertising Federation of Australia (2009), *Ad ban plans will dampen the economic recovery*, media release, 28 January 2009, www.afa.org.au; P. Lavelle (2004), 'Ban junk food ads from kids' TV?', *ABC Health and Wellbeing*, www.abc.net.au.
21. The Chartered Institute of Marketing (2007), 'Shape the agenda: the good, the bad and the indifferent — marketing and the Triple Bottom Line', 11, www.cim.co.uk.
22. A. Main, 'CBA chief executive Ralph Norris sees pay packet soar to $16.2 million', *The Australian*, www.theaustralian.com.au; G. Lekakis, 'Westpac boss Gail Kelly banks $10.6m salary', *The Courier Mail*, www.couriermail.com.au.
23. A. Joseph (2010), 'Sustainable marketing and CSR: Just do it', *Professional Marketing*, April–June, p. 31; Nike Biz, 'Nike responsibility', www.nikebiz.com.
24. S. Colothan (2007), 'Exclusive: Radiohead sell 1.2 million copies of "In Rainbows"', *Gigwise*, www.gigwise.com; Digital Journal (2007), 'The end of record labels: Radiohead clears an estimated $8 million in first week', 16 October, www.digitaljournal.com.
25. J. Oxenbridge (2010), 'Gold Coast Business News Young Entrepreneur 2009', *Gold Coast Business News*, Nov 2009–Jan 2010, pp. 12–27; Wealthfarm website, www.wealthfarm.com.au.
26. T. Levitt (1960), 'Marketing myopia', *Harvard Business Review*, 38(4), (July/August), pp. 45–56.

27. J.C. Narver and S.F. Slater (1990), 'The effect of a market orientation on business profitability', *Journal of Marketing*, 54(4), (October), pp. 20–35.

28. R. Cooper, C. Easingwood, S. Edgett and E. Kleinschmidt (1996), 'What distinguishes the top performing products in financial services?', *Journal of Product Innovation*, (September), pp. 281–299; B. Gosh, K. Meng and L. Meng (1993), 'Factors contributing to the success of local SMEs: an insight from Singapore', *Journal of Small Business and Entrepreneurship*, 10(3), pp. 33–45; J. Huck and T. McEwen (1991), 'Competencies needed for small business success: perception of Jamaican entrepreneurs', *Journal of Small Business Management*, 3, pp. 90–93.

29. R. Brooksbank and D. Taylor (2002), 'The adoption of strategic marketing and its contribution to the competitive success of New Zealand companies', *Marketing Intelligence and Planning*, 20(7), MCB UP Limited, pp. 452–461.

30. ACCORD (2010), 'The nonprofit sector in Australia: a fact sheet', www.accord.org.au.

31. HAYS (2010), *The 2010 Hays salary guide: sharing our expertise*, Hays, Sydney, NSW, www.hays.com.au.

32. G. Medcalf (2008), 'Gaulter Russell salary survey: tightening the screws', *NZMarketing Magazine*, www.marketingmag.co.nz.

33. My Career, 'Australian marketing', http://mycareer.com.au.

34. Michael Page International (2009), *New Zealand 08/09: sales and marketing salary survey*, www.michaelpage.co.nz.

35. C. Hamilton (2005), 'Affluenza: The new illness in Australia?', *Online Opinion*, www.onlineopinion.com.au; C. Hamilton and R. Denniss (2005), *Affluenza: when too much is never enough*, Allen & Unwin, Australia.

36. D. Niven (2000), 'The 100 simple secrets of happy people: what scientists have learned and how you can use it', Harper Collins Publishers, New York.

## Chapter 2

1. AAP (2010), 'Diet group under fire over Maccas deal', *news.com.au*, www.news.com.au.

2. Weight Watchers website, www.weightwatchers.com.au.

3. Ministry of Health (n.d.), 'Obesity in New Zealand', www.moh.govt.nz/obesity.

4. Eating Disorders Foundation Incorporated (2008), 'Obesity Epidemic Exaggerated: Report', www.edf.org.au; J. Mile (2007), 'Tick the Marketing', *Courier Mail*, 10 February, p. 64; S. Rundle-Thiele (2007), *Student views on corporate social responsibility in an Australian fast food context*, 4th International Nonprofit and Social Marketing Conference: Social Entrepreneurship, Social Change and Sustainability, 27–28 Sept 2007, Brisbane, Australia.

5. J. Mile (2007), 'Tick the marketing', *Courier Mail*, 10 February, p. 64.

6. American Marketing Association (2007).

7. M. Ketchell (2010), 'Cycling hits top gear as Aussie riders help propel economic cycle', *The Courier Mail*, 8 January.

8. K. Walters (2010), 'Wheels of fortune', *BRW*, 29 July–1 September, p. 59.

9. M. Bingemannand and M. Sainsbury (2009), 'Telstra pulls $32m deal with Satyam', *Australian IT*, 26 March, www.australianit.news.com.au.

10. L. Cutcher (2008), 'Service sells: exploring connections between customer service strategy and psychological contract', *Journal of Management and Organization*, 14(2), pp. 116–126.

11. N. Shoebridge (2009), 'Marketing's moment of truth', *BRW*, 26 March–29 April, p. 76.

12. J. Stensholt (2009), 'Sky's the limit', *BRW*, 8–14 October, pp. 26–7.

13. ARIA (2010), 'ARIA releases 2009 wholesale sales figures', 3 February, press release, www.aria.com.au.

14. Music Industry Piracy Investigations (2009), 'Internet piracy', www.mipi.com.au.

15. A. Moses (2008), 'Please don't rip off our music', *The Age*, 29 April, www.theage.com.au; N. Shoebridge (2008), 'Marketers face the music', *BRW*, 8–14 May.

16. Music Industry Piracy Investigations (2009), 'Internet piracy', www.mipi.com.au.

17. Tanya Nolan (2011), 'Big retailers wage war on web', *The 7.30 Report*, 5 January, www.abc.net.au.

18. Carbon Planet, 'Greenhouse gas emissions by country', www.carbonplanet.com;

19. ABCDiamond, 'House sizes in Australia', www.abcdiamond.com; J.V. Douglas (2010), 'Backyard bount', *BRW*, 4 January, pp. 28–9.

20. J. Summers and B. Smith (2010), *Communication skills handbook*, third edition, John Wiley & Sons, Milton, Queensland, p. 72.

21. Tourism Alliance Victoria (2003), 'Drought & regional tourism', issues paper, www.vtoa.asn.au; Australian Marketing Institute (2004), 'What value marketing: a position paper on marketing metrics in Australia', discussion paper, www.ami.org.au; Victorian Employers Chamber of Commerce (2007), 'VECCI survey shows drought impacts disproportionately on regional tourism businesses', www.vecci.org.au.

22. Australian Marketing Institute (2004), 'What value marketing: a position paper on marketing metrics in Australia', discussion paper, www.ami.org.au.

23. Earth Hour website, www.earthhour.org; Bureau of Meteorology website, www.bom.gov.au.

24. Australian Bureau of Statistics (2009), *Not-for-profit organisations, Australia, 2006–07* (re-issue), cat. no. 8106.0, Australian Bureau of Statistics, Canberra; ACCORD, 'The nonprofit sector in Australia: a fact sheet', www.accord.org.au; Youngcare website, www.youngcare.com.au; P. McGill, A. Lye and S.R. Rundle-Thiele, (2009), 'Lack of early engagement: a pre-eminent barrier to Australian university bequest giving?' *International Journal of Non-profit and Voluntary Sector Marketing*, vol. 14, pp. 271–83; Department of Family and Community Services (2005), *Giving Australia: research on philanthropy in Australia*, October, report, Commonwealth of Australia, Canberra.

## Chapter 3

1. Nielsen website, 'Radio ratings research', http://au.nielsen.com.

2. This is the formal definition of the American Marketing Association, adopted in October 2004, www.marketingpower.com.

3. This list is derived from D.A. Aaker, V. Kumar, G.S. Day, M. Lawley and D. Stewart (2007), *Marketing research*, 2nd edn, John Wiley & Sons Australia, Brisbane.

4. K. Romanin and S. Cierpicki (2010), 'Drawing insights from 2.0 & traditional market research approaches: how Virgin Blue do it', Australian Marketing Institute Annual Conference and Awards for Marketing Excellence, October, www.ami.org.au.

5. Australia Post, 'Enter the Australian Lifestyle Survey', www.australianlifestylesurvey.com.au.

6. B&T Today website, www.bandt.com.au.

7. D.A. Aaker, V. Kumar and G.S. Day (2007), *Marketing research*, 9th edn, John Wiley & Sons, Hoboken.

8. Colmar Brunton, 'Our brand tracking experience', www.colmarbrunton.com; S. Cierpicki, pers. comm., 22 October 2008.

9. The World Association of Opinion and Marketing Professionals' code of conduct is commonly known as the ICC-ESOMAR code. It was formulated by the then European Society for Opinion and Marketing Research in 1948, revised with the International Chamber of Commerce in 1976, and has been revised since. The ICC-ESOMAR code is available at www.esomar.org.

10. Australian Marketing Institute (2010), 'Winner — brand revitalisation', AMI Awards for Excellence, p. 24; IBIS World (2010), *Bread and cake retailing in Australia*, report summary, www.ibisworld.com.au; La Famiglia website, www.lafamiglia.com.au; T. Addington (2007), 'Whybin/TBWA wins garlic bread brief', *B&T*, 31 August, www.bandt.com.au.

11. This is part of the formal definition of the American Marketing Association, adopted in October 2004, www.marketingpower.com.

12. RAC website, 'Public transport', www.rac.com.au.

13. M. Larbalestier, 'The history of market research in Australia', AMSRS, 2004, www.amsrs.com.au; 'About the industry', www.amsrs.com.au; Australian Bureau of Statistics (ABS), *Market research services, Australia*, cat. no. 8556.0, 2004, www.abs.gov.au.

14. M.S. Gazzaaniga and T.F. Hetherton (2006), *Psychological Science*, 2nd ed., W.W. Norton & Company, New York.

15. A. Sharp and M. Tustin, 'Benefits of observational research', *Proceedings of ANZMAC*, Adelaide, 1–3 December 2003, pp. 2590–2595.

16. Such a study is known as a census.

17. Complete the Picture Consulting Pty Ltd (2010), *Mobile data survey — a global snapshot!*, sample findings of PowerPoint presentation co-published by Griffith University, Complete the Picture Consulting and mNet Group, Brisbane; Dr Marissa Maio Mackay (2010), pers. comm., May.

18. Colmar Brunton Research, Online Poll Feedback on Billabong Brand, June 2006.

19. S. Coakes and L. Steed (2010), *SPSS: Analysis without anguish, version 17*, John Wiley & Sons Australia, Brisbane.

20. R. Arnold, B. Burke, C. James, B. Martin and D. Thomas (2001), *Educating for a change*, Doris Marshall Institute for Education and Action Between the Line, Toronto.

21. Adapted from Complete the Picture Consulting Pty Ltd (2010), *Mobile data survey — a global snapshot!*, sample findings of PowerPoint presentation co-published by Griffith University, Complete the Picture Consulting and mNet Group, Brisbane, p. 12.

22. First Direct Solutions (n.d), 'Leading QLD based children's charity: data co-operative strategy', www.fdsolutions.com.au.

23. M. Fynes-Clinton (2010), 'Queensland tourism is out of ideas', *The Australian*, www.theaustralian.com.au; Tourism Queensland (2007), *Destination Management Plan highlights for tourism in the Fraser Coast*: 2007–2010, www.tq.com.au; Queensland

Government (2009), *Bundaberg — Fraser Coast Tourism Opportunity Plan: 2009–2010,* www.tq.com.au; A. Tkaczynski, S.R. Rundle-Thiele and N. Beaumont, (2010), 'Destination segmentation: a recommended two-step approach', *Journal of Travel Research,* vol. 49, no. 2, pp. 139–52.

## Chapter 4

1. Different publications and researchers use a range of years to define Generation Z. Generally, it refers to those born after 2001, but, for example, it can also refer to those born between 1996 and 2009. Similarly, different publications and researchers use a range of years to define Generation Y. Generally, this cohort refers to those born between 1982 and 2000, but, for example, it can also refer to those born between 1980 and 1994.

2. 'Are you ready for Gen Z?' (2009), *New Zealand Marketing,* November–December, p. 70.

3. Different publications and researchers use different age spans to describe the tween market, with some research suggesting that it describes children aged eight to 12, or nine to 13, years of age.

4. ABC News (2010), 'Bieber's Oz show axed after crowd crush', *ABC News online,* 26 April, www.abc.net.au; Forbes.com (2009), 'Number 29: Miley Cyrus', *The Celebrity 100,* 6 March, www.forbes.com; Justin Bieber website, www.justinbiebermusic.com; Miley Cyrus website, www.mileycyrus.com.

5. G. Hofstede (1994), 'Management scientists are human', *Management Science,* vol. 40, no. 1, January, pp. 4–13.

6. M. Kotabe, A. Riege, K. Griffiths, G. Noble, S.H. Ang, A. Pecotich and K. Helsen (2008), *International Marketing,* 2nd edn, John Wiley & Sons Australia, Brisbane, pp. 140–141.

7. Data from Geert Hofstede — Cultural dimensions, www.geert-hofstede.com; Note: The vertical placement in figure 4.2 is not meaningful; it is for clarity only.

8. See, for example, Australian Bureau of Statistics (2008), *Australian Social Trends 2008,* cat no. 4102.0, www.abs.gov.au.

9. E.M. Rogers (2003), *Diffusion of innovations,* 5th edn, The Free Press.

10. 'Marketers plug into pester power to target parents' (2002), *B&T,* www.bandt.com.au.

11. Tourism New Zealand (2010), 'Fans flock to RWC 2011 on Facebook', 16 February, media release, www.tourismnewzealand.com.

12. Nielsen Panorama: Survey 7 September 2007–1 March 2008–February 2009, 12 month database.

13. A.H. Maslow (1943), 'A theory of human motivation', *Psychological Review,* vol. 50, no. 4, pp. 370–96; A. Maslow (1954), *Motivation and Personality,* Harper, New York.

14. The Sydney Morning Herald (2009), 'And the winner is . . . a happy little Vegemite', 27 September, www.smh.com.au.

15. Kraft Foods (2009), 'The vote is in: Vegemite Cheesybite is the people's choice', 7 October, media release, www.kraft.com.au; J. Lee (2009), 'Unhappy little Vegemites vent their fury over iSnack 2.0', 29 September, *The Sydney Morning Herald,* www.smh.com.au.

16. Petnet website (2010), 'Pet statistics', www.petnet.com.au; Australian Companion Animal Council Inc. (2006), *Contribution of the pet care industry to the Australian economy,* 6th edn, www.acac.org.au; L. Allen (2009), 'Capital canines', *BRW,* 1–7 October, www.brw.com.au.

17. R. Le Pla (2005), 'Too Slow? Are Your Customers Leaving You Behind?', *NZMarketing Magazine,* February.

18. A. King (2009), 'Crying out for more', *BRW,* 22–28 October, p. 21–2; Kimberley-Clark website, www.kca.com.au; Huggies Australia website, 'Huggies club benefits', www.huggies.com.au.

19. L. Allen (2009), 'Tourism's rising tide', *BRW,* 2–8 July, www.brw.com.au; Tourism Australia website (2010), 'Campaigns', www.tourism.australia.com; The Steering Committee (2009), *The Jackson report: informing the national long-term tourism strategy,* Commonwealth of Australia, www.ret.gov.au; Australian Government Department of Resources, Energy and Tourism website 2010, 'Department', www.ret.gov.au; ABC News (2010), 'Australians rack up $33b in untaken leave', 6 July, www.abc.net.au.

## Chapter 5

1. M. Kaplan (2009), 'Global vision of eye health and prosperity', *The Australian,* 10 October, www.theaustralian.com.au; Opto website, www.opto-global.com.

2. Australia Times (2010), 'Telstra signs National Broadband Network agreement', 20 June, www.australia-times.com.au.

3. AAP and S. Tindal, 'Telstra signs on to the NBN for $11bn', ZDNet, www.zdnet.com.au.

4. Coles, 'Our national charity partners', www.coles.com.au.

5. ICIS (2010), 'The ICIS top 100 chemical companies: analysis', 13 September, www.icis.com.

6. BASF, 'Chemicals', www.basf.com.

7. International Council of Chemical Associations (n.d.), *Innovations for greenhouse gas reductions: questions and answers*, www.icca-chem.org.

8. ECN Group website, www.ecngroup.com.au.

9. Australian Competition and Consumer Commission website, www.accc.gov.au; Commerce Commission website, www.comcom.govt.nz.

10. Commerce Commission (2009), 'Commerce Commission issues warning to Real Estate Network', 31 March, www.comcom.govt.nz.

11. Bloomberg (2009), 'Airbus, Boeing duel to save plane orders', *The Age*, 16 June, www.theage.com.au; S. Lannin (2009), 'Crisis forces Qantas to cancel Boeing deal', *ABC News*, 26 June, www.abc.net.au; S. Creedy (2010), 'Emirates ups Airbus double-decker order by 32', *The Australian*, 10 June, www.theaustralian.com.au; C.S. Ling (2010), 'Qantas, Singapore Airlines, Lufthansa may need A380 engine fix', *Bloomberg*, 16 November, www.bloomberg.com.

12. Australian Bureau of Statistics (2007), *Business Use of Information Technology, 2005–06*, cat. no. 8129.0, Australian Bureau of Statistics, Canberra.

13. V. Carson (2009), 'Packer's US ambitions thwarted again', *Business Today*, 13 March, www.businesstoday.com; B. Trembath (2010), 'Industry angered by scrapped Sydney Metro plans', *ABC News*, 23 February, www.abc.net.au.

14. Interbrand, 'Best global brands 2010', www.interbrand.com.

15. IMS Health cited in Reuters (2010), 'Factbox: the 20 largest pharmaceutical companies', 26 March, www.reuters.com.

16. Medicines Australia (2010), *Facts Book*, second edition, October, Medicines Australia, Deakin, ACT, p. 54.

17. IMS (2010), 'IMS forecasts global pharmaceutical market growth of 5–8% annually through 2014; maintains expectations of 4–6% growth in 2010', 20 April, press release, www.imshealth.com;. Tufts Center for the Study of Drug Development (2006), 'Research milestones', http://csdd.tufts.edu;.M. Metherell (2010), 'Medicare extended to nurses, midwives', *The Age*, 1 November, www.theage.com.au; Medicines Australia (2010), *Facts Book*, second edition, October, Medicines Australia, Deakin, ACT; Medicines Australia (2009), *Facts Book*, first edition, December, Medicines Australia, Deakin, ACT; Medicines Australia (2010), *Code of Conduct Guidelines*, version 1

(January 2010), Medicines Australia, Deakin, ACT; Nursing Careers Allied Health (2010), 'Nurses brace for marketing onslaught', 10 May, www.ncah.com.au.

**Chapter 6**

1. N. McDonald (2010), 'On the road again', *The Herald Sun*, 29 January.

2. A. Sibillin (2009), 'New money market', *BRW*, 15–21 January, www.brw.com.au; HSBC website, www.hsbc.com.au.

3. M. Buchanan and L. McKenny (2010), 'Mambo launches range in Big W', *The Sydney Morning Herald*, 11 August, www.smh.com.au; Mambo (2000), 'Mambo design Australian uniforms for Olympic opening ceremony', 24 July, http://mambosurfdeluxe.com.

4. Roy Morgan Research.

5. SRI Consulting Business Intelligence (SRIC-BI), www.sric-bi.com/VALS; C.L. Hallenberg, personal communication, 27 May 2009.

6. Intrepid website, www.intrepidtravel.com; J. Lindhe (2009), 'Trip to bountiful', 27 August–30 September, *BRW*, www.brw.com.au.

7. Gold Coast City Council, 'Facts and figures', www.goldcoast.qld.gov.au; J. Tovey and K. Munro (2010), 'Boom town: Sydney tops 4.5 m', *The Sydney Morning Herald*, 31 March, www.smh.com.au; Auskick website, www.aflauskick.com.au; G. Chambers and N. Keene, 'Copping a kicking in battle of codes', *The Daily Telegraph*, 2 July, www.dailytelegraph.com.au.

8. The Sydney Morning Herald (2010), '30 000 quit Facebook in protest', 1 June, www.smh.com.au; The Sydney Morning Herald (2010), 'Social networking face-off as over-55s catch up and teenagers log off', 14 February, www.smh.com.au.

**Chapter 7**

1. L. Plunkett (2010), '*Guitar Hero 6* is a warrior of rock, apparently', *Kotaku*, 26 May, www.kotaku.com.au; G. Tim (2010), 'Guitar Hero: warriors of rock to feature 'rock and roll adventure'', *Lazygamer*, 28 May, www.lazygamer.net; G. Tim (2010), '*Guitar Hero 6* gets detailed', *Lazygamer*, 17 May, www.lazygamer.com.au; T. Walker (2009), 'Short way to the top' *QW*, pp. 24–8; and K. Stuart (2011), 'Guitar Hero axed: five reasons why music games are dying', Games Blog, 10 February, www.guardian.co.uk.

2. Developed from T. Levitt (1983), *The marketing imagination*, The Free Press: New York.

3. Bonds website, www.bonds.com.au.

4. Toyota website, www.toyota.com.au; Toyota, 'Hybrid Camry', www.toyota.com.au; Toyota (2009),

'The benefits of Toyota's local manufacturing — up close and personal', *Hybrid Synergy Drive — News*, press release, 29 June, www.toyota.com.au; Toyota (2010), 'Hybrid Camry gets maximum five-star rating', *Toyota Newsroom*, press release, 3 May, www.toyota.com.au.

5. 'Special report: New products' (1998), *Ad Age International*, 13 April.

6. News.com.au (2010), 'PlayStation 3 announces movie service', 18 May, www.news.com.au; M. Starr (2010), 'Sony announces video delivery service through PlayStation network', 18 May, *cnet australia*, www.cnet.com.au; Bigpond (2010), 'Sony PlayStation announces movie service', 19 May, http://bigpondnews.com.

7. E.M. Rogers (1983), *Diffusion of innovations*, Free Press: New York.

8. Hungry Jack's website, www.hungryjacks.com.au; S. Cusick (2009), 'Hungry Jack's enters Angus burger war', *Ninemsn*, 17 November, www.news.ninemsn.com.au; A. Harris (2009), 'Hamburgers hit the high life', *news.com.au*, 31 October, www.news.com.au.

9. L. Hearn (2009), 'iPhone 4 plans: the experts' choice', *The Sydney Morning Herald*, 29 July, www.smh.com.au; P. Smith (2009), 'Telcos look for ways to entertain', *The Australian Financial Review*, 7 April, p. 28.

10. A.C. Nielsen (2008), 'Top brands special report', The Nielsen Company, http://au.nielsen.com.

11. IP Australia, www.ipaustralia.gov.au; Intellectual Property Office of New Zealand, www.iponz.govt.nz.

12. Interbrand (2010), 'Best Australian brands 2009: ranked by brand value', Interbrand, www.interbrand.com.

13. PepsiCo corporate website, www.pepsico.com.

14. G. Medcalf (2006), 'Marketing Magazine marketing awards 2006: A slice of High Country', *NZMarketing*, August.

15. Redheads website, www.redheads.com.au.

16. Franchising (2010), 'Domino's links with The Biggest Loser to meet growing demand for healthy meals', 1 February, www.franchise.net.au.

17. J. Lee (2009), 'Unhappy little Vegemites vent their fury over iSnack 2.0', *The Age*, 29 September, www.theage.com.au; R. Lamperd (2009), 'Vegemite product renamed Vegemite Cheesybite after iSnack 2.0 was dumped', *The Herald Sun*, 7 October, www.heraldsun.com.au; C. Kellett (2009), 'Don't blame Dean: iSnack 2.0 creator cops it', *The Brisbane Times*, 1 October, www.brisbanetimes.com.au.

18. G. Medcalf (2006), 'Marketing Magazine marketing awards 2006: a slice of High Country', *NZMarketing*, August.

19. S. Sacharow (1982), *The package as a marketing tool*, Chilton Book Company: Radnor, Pennsylvania.

20. A.C. Nielsen (2008), 'Packaging and the environment: a global Nielsen consumer report', The Nielsen Company, www2.acnielsen.com.

21. S. Balogh (2010), 'Last gasp', *The Courier Mail*, p. 1; 'Doubt cast over plain cigarette packaging', *ABC News*, 30 April, www.abc.net.au; J. Kelly, S. Maher and AAP (2010), 'Big tobacco to fight Rudd's cigarette plain packaging plan', *The Australian*, 29 April. www.theaustralian.com.au.

22. Pauls Zymil website, www.zymil.com.au.

23. A. Harris (2009), 'Hamburgers hit the high life', news.com.au, 31 October.

24. K. Courtney (2008), 'Adidas: walk this way', *Marketing*, August.

25. T. Huynh (2008), 'JVC shuts down VHS players production, still produces DVD/VHS hybrids', Techgeek, www.techgeek.com.au.

26. A. Moses (2010), '3D TV price gouge: $150 for glasses alone', *The Brisbane Times*, 10 March, www.brisbanetimes.com.au; A. Ramadge (2010), '3D TV is here, but you should read the rules', news.com.au, 12 April, www.news.com.au.

27. Staff writers (2011), 'Thinner, lighter, more powerful than ever. Then there's the iPad 2 . . .', 3 March, www.news.com.au; S. Hutcheon (2011), 'Steve Jobs unveils iPad 2', *The Age*, 3 March, www.theage.com.au; Ninemsn staff (2011), 'Apple's iPad 2 sells out worldwide', 29 March, http://news.ninemsn.com.au; NewsCore (2011), 'Tablet market falls ahead of iPad 2', 12 March, www.news.com.au; Apple, 'iPad', www.apple.com; A. Moses and L. Hearn (2010), 'Crowds flock to shop as iPad goes on sale', *The Sydney Morning Herald*, 28 May, www.smh.com.au; S. Kennedy (2010), 'Putting iPad through its paces', *The Australian*, 1 June, www.theaustralian.com.au; S. Fenech (2010), 'Chinese copycats pouncing on the iPad with their iPed', *The Daily Telegraph*, 3 June, www.dailytelegraph.com.au; S. Fenech (2010), 'Business pushing iPad's boundaries', *The Courier-Mail*, 9 June, www.dailytelegraph.com.au; A.Colley (2010), 'iPad sales hit 250,000 in Australia', *The Australian*, 19 October, www.theaustralian.com.au; The Sydney Morning Herald (2010), 'iPad feeds menu makeover', 21 October, www.smh.com.au; E. Veiszadeh (2010), 'Man aims to be first Aussie with iPad', *The Sydney Morning Herald*, 27 May, www.smh.com.au; ABC News (2010), 'Aussie geeks get their hands on iPads', 28 May, www.abc.net.au.

## Chapter 8

1. J. Lindhe (2009), 'Hits & misses', *BRW*, 12–18 Nov, pp. 26–7; N.T. Koha (2010), 'Band U2 are coming to Melbourne in December for the 360 Degrees tour', *Sunday Herald Sun*, 22 August, www.heraldsun.com.au

2. Volkswagen (2010), 'The Golf', www.volkswagen.com.au.

3. D. Palmer (2009), 'Unit pricing code to be implemented by year's end', *Australian Food News*, 24 March, www.ausfoodnews.com.au; Aldi website, www.aldi.com.au.

4. R. Blackburn (2009), 'Numbers game: why advertised car prices are going up', *The Sydney Morning Herald*, 16 May, www.smh.com.au; Mercedes Benz website, www.mercedesbenz.com.au.

5. Great Wall website, www.greatwallmotors.com.au; B.T. Patchford and G.T. Ford (1976), 'A study of prices and market shares in the computer mainframe industry', *Journal of Business*, April, in Martin Christopher (1993), Value in use pricing', *European Journal of Marketing*, vol. 16, no. 5, pp. 35–46.

6. Australian Institute of Health and Welfare (2010), *Australia's health 2010*, 23 June, www.aihw.com.au. Department of Health and Ageing (2010), *Taking preventative action — a response to Australia: the healthiest country by 2020 — the report of the National Preventative Health Taskforce*, Australian Government, Canberra, www.yourhealth.gov.au; Cancer Council Western Australia (2010), *Make smoking history*, September, www.cancerwa.asn.au; Australian Institute of Health and Welfare (2008), *Australia's health 2008*, 24 June, www.aihw.com.au.

7. RiverCity Motorway Group (2011), 'Clem7 tolls from 4 April 2011', press release, 18 March, www.clem7.com.au; Annie Guest (2011), 'Clem7 operator placed in receivership', *ABC News*, 28 February, www.abc.news.com.au; 'Robyn Ironside (2011), 'Add another dollar to your Clem7 trip', *The Courier Mail*, 18 March 2011; Leanne Edmistone, 'RiverCity Motorways says sorry, but Clem7 tolls have to rise', *The Courier Mail*, 5 November, www.couriermail.com.au; S. Parnell (2010), 'Clem7 operator slashes road toll', *The Australian*, 29 June, www.theaustralian.com.au; Ursula Heger (2010), 'Clem7 tunnel team knew of risk', *The Courier Mail*, 11 June, www.couriermail.com.au; T. Grant-Taylor (2010), 'Clem7 tunnel owner RiverCity Motorway in financial black hole after $1.67 billion loss', *The Courier Mail*, 31 August, www.couriermail.com.au.

8. Edmunds Inside Line (2010), '2011 Hyundai Sonata Hybrid revealed: 2010 New York Auto show, 31 March, www.insideline.com; Hyundai website (2011), www.hyundai.com.au.

9. Homeloans website, 'What will my repayments be?', www.homeloans.com.au.

10. Mars snackfood Australia (n.d.), 'Mars lifts the bar on price', press release, www.makingchocolatebetter.com.au; C. Peper (2009), 'Mars Bars size slashed but price to stay the same', *The Courier Mail*, 7 December, www.couriermail.com.au.

11. AAP (2011), 'Foster's halts beer to Coles and Woolies', 23 March, http://au.news.yahoo.com; Clancy Yeates (2011), 'Senators suggest breaking up big supermarkets', *The Sydney Morning Herald*, 30 March, www.smh.com.au; Rhys Haynes (2011), 'Milk wars: Coles pushing up petrol prices to pay for cheap milk', *Herald Sun*, 30 March, www.heraldsun.com.au; (2011), Nick Hartgerink (2011), 'Retail giants milking farmers', *Ilawarra Mercury*, 14 February, blog, www.illawarramercury.com.au; Clancy Yeates (2011), 'Rationale for milk wars gets heated reception', *The Sydney Morning Herald*, 30 March, www.smh.com.au; Eli Greenblat and Mark Hawthorne (2011), 'Coles takes the battle to Woolies', *The Age*, 12 February, www.theage.com.au; P.B. Ellickson and S. Misra (2008), 'Supermarket pricing strategies', *Marketing Science*, vol. 27, no. 5, pp. 811–28; CHOICE (2009), 'Supermarket price survey 2009', www.choice.com.au; Parliament of Australia (2009), *Trade Practices Amendment (Guaranteed Lowest Prices — Blacktown Amendment) Bill 2009*, 24 November, Commonwealth of Australia, Canberra, www.aph.gov.au; A.L. Montgomery (1997), 'Creating micro-marketing pricing strategies using supermarket scanner data', *Marketing Science*, vol. 16, no. 4, pp. 315–37; M. Janda and staff (2009), 'Supermarket giants in petrol price war', *ABC News*, 13 July, www.abc.net.au; N. Boyes (2010), 'Grocery giant Aldi eyes NZ market', *Waikato Times*, 9 January, www.stuff.co.nz; B. Atkinson (2010), 'Coles dons the price uniform', *Inside Retailing*, 29 January.

## Chapter 9

1. Youi website, www.youi.com.au; George Lekakis (2009), 'Locals feel heat from big insurers', *The Herald Sun*, 9 December, www.heraldsun.com.au; J. Livesley (2010), 'Breaking campaign: Youi highlights Melbourne Storm response', *B&T Weekly*, 18 March, www.bandt.com.au; V. Papandrea (2010),

'Insurers connect with generational mindset', *Investor Daily*, 18 May, www.investordaily.com.

2. C.E. Shannon and W. Weaver (1999) [1949], *The mathematical theory of communication*, University of Illinois Press, Chicago, IL; W. Schramm (1961), 'How communication works', *The Process and Effects of Mass Communication*, University of Illinois Press, Urbana, IL.

3. Gina McColl (2009), 'Cause & effect', *BRW*, 5 October, pp. 40–41.

4. The Daily Telegraph, 24 June 2010; The Daily Telegraph, 23 September 2009.

5. AdNews, 4 April 2008/CEASA, industry estimates.

6. Advertising Standards Authority.

7. McHappy Day website, www.mchappyday.com.au.

8. Volkswagen website, www.volkswagen.com.au; Jez Spinks (2010) 'VW takes pop at girly cars', *Drive*, 12 May, news.drive.com.au; 'Volkswagen and DDB Sydney launch integrated campaign for the all new Polo', Campaign Brief, 10 May 2010, www.campaignbrief.com.

9. Dr J. Durante, J. Greig, M. Morrison and Dr J. Ward (2008), 'Encouraging participation in market based instruments and incentive programs', *Land & Water Australia*.

10. 'Green media fails online' (2008), *BRW*, 14–20 August, p. 14.

11. A. Sibillin (2009), 'Don't believe it', *BRW*, 19–25 March, p. 45.

12. M. Russell (2010), 'Slap on the wrist for power balance', *The Sydney Morning Herald*, 21 November, www.smh.com.au.

13. Georgina Robinson (2010), 'Power balance wristbands a sham: ACCC', *The Sydney Morning Herald*, 23 December, www.smh.com.au.

14. Australian Association of National Advertisers, 'AANA Code of Ethics', www.aana.com.au.

15. Advertising Standards Authority (2009), 'Advertising code of ethics', www.asa.co.nz.

16. A. Sharp (2009), 'Anger at lack of action on obesity', *The Age*, 3 June, www.theage.com.au; *The Courier Mail* (2009), 'Fast food giants sign children's code', 26 June.

17. 'Subliminal advertising in Network Ten's ARIA Awards telecast', *The Courier Mail*, 8 October 2008.

18. Complaint # 425/09 'Advertiser Nautilus Marine Boat Insurance', ASB, 14 October 2009.

19. 'Shine Lawyers: Erin Brockovich visit and launch', www.bbspr.com.au.

20. BP website, www.bp.com.

21. C. Beaumont (2010), 'Apple "knew about iPhone 4 antenna problems"', *The Telegraph,* 16 July, www.telegraph.co.uk; M. Helft (2010), 'Apple goes on the offensive', *The New York Times*, 16 July, www.nytimes.com.

22. 'Public relations office' (2009), MyFuture, www.myfuture.edu.au.

23. Julian Lee (2010), 'Handling bad PR turns sticky for Nestle', *The Age*, 26 March, www.theage.com.au; J. Dunn (2010), 'Nestle makes palm oil pledge', Australian Food News, 19 May, www.ausfoodnews.com.au; Greenpeace website, www.greenpeace.org; E. Fox (2010), 'Nestle hit by Facebook "anti-social" media surge', *The Guardian,* 19 May, www.guardian.co.uk; C. McCarthy (2010), 'After Facebook backlash, Nestle steps up sustainability', CNET, 17 May, www.news.cnet.com; S. Washington (2010), 'Greenpeave claims sweet victory over Nestle', *The Sydney Morning Herald,* 17 May, www.smh.com.au.

24. Sports for Schools, Coles website, http://sportsforschools.coles.com.au; J. Tovey (2010), 'It's not docket science — but parents are learning new ways of being a good sport', *The Sydney Morning Herald*, 7 October, www.smh.com.au.

25. 'The job guide — sales representative' (2009), Department of Education, Employment and Workplace Relations, www.jobguide.thegoodguides.com.au.

26. S. Canning (2007), 'Careful, that brand-name bag could incur a fine', *The Australian*, 22 February; Media Watch (2000), transcript 2 October, www.abc.net.au.

27. Jon Kelly (2010) 'How ambush marketing ambushed sport', *BBC News*, 17 June, www.news.bbc.co.uk.

28. A. Harris (2007), 'Have an opinion on . . . ambush marketing', *Intheblack*, March, p. 15.

29. F. Balfour (2008), 'Ambush in Beijing', *BRW*, 20–26 March.

30. A. Meade and L. Sinclair (2010), 'When Oprah Winfrey educates Yanks on our "hip" McCafes, it's the dollar talking', *The Australian*, 6 December, www.news.com.au.

31. J. Lee (2008), 'James Bond reins in his licence to sell', *The Sydney Morning Herald*, 23 October.

32. PQ Media and Nielsen cited in R. Browne, 'Ads' 30 seconds of fame under threat', *The Sydney Morning Herald*, 24 August 2008.

33. PQ Media and Nielsen cited in R. Browne (2008), 'Ads' 30 seconds of fame under threat', *The Sydney Morning Herald*, 24 August.

34. H. Ife and G. Jones (2010), 'MasterChef drives fresh produce sales', *The Herald Sun*, 2 July www.heraldsun.com.au.

35. R. Browne (2008), 'Ads' 30 seconds of fame under threat', *The Sydney Morning Herald*, 24 August.

36. The term was first used by Jay Conrad Levinson in his 1984 book, *Guerrilla Marketing*.

37. 'NZ Road Safety — Windscreen Flyer', The Gruen Transfer, www.abc.net.au.

38. S. Molloy (2009), 'Rush for "best job in the world" crashes website', *The Sydney Morning Herald*, 14 January, www.smh.com.au; K. Schneider (2009), 'Ben Southall wins Tourism Queensland's "dream job"', 6 May, www.news.com.au.

39. Patrick Stafford (2009), 'Skittles Twitter stunt backfires spectacularly... or does it?' Smart Company, 5 March, www.smartcompany.com.au.

40. Seth Godin (1999), 'Permission Marketing: turning strangers into friends, and friends into customers', Simon & Schuster, New York.

41. PumpkinPatch VIP website, www.pumpkinpatch.com.au.

42. G. Medcalf (2008), 'Building invincible brands', *NZMarketing*, February.

43. BRW (2009), 'Sports sponsors fail to sway consumers', 19–25 March, p. 13.

44. AAP (2008), 'KFC sponsorship of cricket must end: obesity experts', *The Sydney Morning Herald*, 5 October, www.smh.com.au.

45. The Daily Telegraph (2010), 'ME Bank withdraws sponsorship of Melbourne Storm', 23 April, www.couriermail.com.au; Peter Dixon (2010), 'PepsiCo brand Gatorade drops Tiger Woods from sponsorship deal', *The Times*, 27 February, www.theaustralian.com.au; G. Whateley (2010), 'Storm's magnificent four and football's great lie', *ABC News*, 16 July, www.abc.net.au; J. Robertson (2010), 'Stephanie Rice loses sponsor Jaguar after anti-gay tweet', *The Courier Mail*, 7 September, www.thecouriermail.com.au.

46. Phillip Coorey (2010), 'Miners step up campaign against super profits tax', *The Sydney Morning Herald*, 7 May, www.smh.com.au; D. Hurst, M. Levy and A. Sharp (2010), 'Gillard cancels mining tax ad campaign', *The Age*, 24 June, www.theage.com.au; Daniel Hurst (2010), 'Super-profits tax: Digging into the PR war', *The Brisbane Times*, 16 June, www.brisbanetimes.com.au; news.com.au (2010), 'Prime Minister Julia Gillard caves in to mining industry and cuts resources tax rate', 2 July, www.news.com.au; M. Janda (2010), 'Gillard, BHP can ads in mining tax truce', *ABC News*, 24 June, www.abc.net.au; Kevin Rudd (2010), 'Delivering macroeconomic stability and laying the foundations for long-term prosperity', speech, Melbourne Press Club, 6 May, http://pmrudd.archive.dpmc.gov.au; Kevin Rudd (2010), Transcript of joint doorstop interview, Whittlesea, 6 May, http://pmrudd.archive.dpmc.gov.au.

## Chapter 10

1. Debra Jopson (2010), 'Forget Tinseltown, flannel stole her heart', *The Sydney Morning Herald*, 25 February, www.smh.com.au; Sarina Locke (2007), 'Native Flannel flowers for export, *ABC*, 13 December, www.abc.net.au; J. Ekman, J. Eyre and D. Joyce (2008), 'Flowers by sea: improving market access for Australian wildflowers', *RIRDC*, January 2008, RIRDC publication no. 07/181.

2. Corporate Express website, www.ce.com.au.

3. Solutions Asia Pacific (2010), 'Innovation at National Foods', June; Linfox website, www.linfox.com.au.

4. Adobe website, www.adobe.com.au.

5. B&T Weekly (2003), 'Bayswiss is power brand for freedom', 19 February.

6. Franchise Council of Australia (2008), 'What every franchisor must know', *Franchise Business*, www.franchisebusiness.com.au.

7. Gelatissimo (2010), 'Gelatissimo brings gelato back to the Italians!'; Mark Fenton-Jones, 'Sweet spot for Aussie gelato', *Australian Financial Review*, 22 June, www.afr.com; Gelatissimo website, www.gelatissimo.com.au.

8. M. Napolitano (2007), 'Warehouse management: how to be a lean, mean cross-docking machine', *Logistics Management*, www.logisticsmgt.com.

9. Tollgroup website, www.tollgroup.com; Tollgroup website www.tollgroup.com; Toll Today (2010), 'Toll Marine Logistics takes delivery of new tugs and barges', June–August, p. 8.

10. Driza-bone website, www.drizabone.com.au.

11. David Jones website, www.davidjones.com.au.

12. David Jones website, www.davidjones.com.au.

13. R.F. Hartley (1985), *Retailing: challenge and opportunity*, 3rd edn, Houghton Mifflin.

14. IGD senior analyst Adrian Williams, cited in *BRW*, 24–30 July 2008, p. 41.

15. Google Australia retail marketing manager Ross McDonald, cited in *BRW*, 24–30 July 2008, p. 41.

16. The Nielsen Company (2009), 'New Zealanders embracing online consumer generated activity', media release, 18 May, www.nielsen-online.com; The Nielsen Company (2009), 'Online shopping hits record levels: Nielsen online', media release, 18 March, www.nielsen-online.com; *BRW* (2008),

'Two-thirds shop online', 24–30 July, p. 41; M. Freitas (2007), 'The New Zealand online market under the microscope', *Entrepreneurship*, 29 March, www.geekzone.co.nz.

17. 'Two-thirds shop online' (2008), *BRW*, 24–30 July, p. 41.
18. The Australian Government body is at www.donotcall.gov.au.
19. New Zealand Marketing Association, 'Do not call service' www.marketing.org.nz.
20. Markson Sparks website, www.marksonsparks.com.
21. CommSec website, www.commsec.com.au.
22. Costco website, www.costco.com.au; ABC News (2010), 'US retailer Costco gets Sydney green light', 15 April, www.abc.net.au; The Herald Sun (2009), 'Discounts at Docklands in Melbourne as Costco opens', news.com.au, 17 August, www.news.com.au.
23. Foodbank website, www.foodbank.com.au; Nicole Eckersley (2010), 'Woolies helps Foodbank net record donations', Ausfoodnews, 20 July, www.ausfoodnews. com.au; Ryan Witcombe (2010), '"Pasta Fix" brings corporate, community and government together', Pro Bono Australia, www.probonoaustralia.com.au.

### Chapter 11

1. Anthony Sibillin (2009), 'Australia Post's move into insurance may herald an eventual assault on the big banks', *BRW*, 10–16 September, p. 43; Richard Gluyas (2009), 'Australia Post pushes into insurance', *The Australian*, 2 September.
2. The data is drawn from the respective country entries of the Central Intelligence Agency's *The World Factbook*, www.cia.gov.
3. Australian Government, Treasury website, www.treasury.gov.au
4. Kim Dunstan and Nicholas Thomson (2006), 'Demographic aspects of New Zealand's ageing population', Statistics New Zealand, www.stats.govt.nz.
5. Anthony Sibillin (2009), 'Direct approach', *BRW*, 23–29 April, www.ezypay.com.au.
6. Virgin Blue (2009), 'On-time monthly performance', www.virginblue.com.au; Virgin Blue website, www.virginblue.com.au.
7. Greater Union Birch Carroll & Coyle website, www.greaterunion.com.au.
8. Jetts Australia website, www.jetts.com.au; Jetts New Zealand website, www.jetts.co.nz; Mitch Gaynor (2009), 'Power play goes 24/7', *The Sunday Mail*, 28 June; John Lyons (2009), 'Fit for the customer', *BRW*, 6–12 August.
9. L.L. Berry and A. Parasuraman (1991), *Marketing services: competing through quality*, The Free Press, New York; A. Parasuraman, L.L. Berry and V.A. Zeithaml (1988), 'SERVQUAL: a multiple-item scale for measuring consumer perceptions of service quality', Journal of Retailing, vol. 64, pp. 12–37.
10. Jennifer Dudley-Nicholson (2009), 'Gadget beats queues', *The Courier Mail*, 4 April; Dreamworld website, www.dreamworld.com.au.
11. New Zealand Marketing (2010), 'Life savers', 1 January, www.marketingmag.co.nz; National Screening Unit website, www.nsu.govt.nz.
12. Virgin Blue, 'Virgin Blue Group announces major new partnership with Etihad', press release, www.virginblue.com.au.
13. Courtney Trenwith (2010), 'Budget roots won't be forgotten: Virgin Blue boss', *The Sydney Morning Herald*, 24 November, www.smh.com.au.
14. ABC (2010), 'Virgin ill-prepared for system crash, experts say', 27 September, www.abc.net.au
15. Matt O'sullivan (2010), 'Discount dogfight in the skies', *The Sydney Morning Herald*, 18 September, www.smh.com.au; Virgin Blue (2008), 'ASX statement — new fuel mitigation measures', media release, 18 July, www.virginblue.com.au.
16. AAP (2011), 'Virgin Australia targets business market', *Sydney Morning Herald*, 4 May, http://news.smh.com.au.

### Chapter 12

1. Cradle Rock website, www.cradlerock.com.au; Rebecca Nash (2010), 'Shops open for online operators', transcript, *Inside Business*, 3 October, www.abc.net.au.
2. Australian Bureau of Statistics (2010), 'Household Use of Information Technology, Australia, 2008–09', cat. no. 8146.0, ABS, Canberra.
3. A. King (2008), 'Click go the cheers', *BRW*, 9–15 October, p. 26; Andrea Petrou (2010), 'Internet as a human right in developing countries', *TechEye. net*, 3 September, www.techeye.net.
4. Don Tapscott (2008), *Grown up digital: how the net generation is changing your world*, McGraw-Hill, New York.
5. Roy Morgan Research (2009), 'More than two million Australians use their mobile phone to access the internet'.
6. Roy Morgan Report (2009), 'Report on time spent with media trends visit online store', www.roymorganonlinestore.com.
7. A. King (2008), 'Click go the cheers', *BRW*, 9–15 October, p. 25.

8. Nielsen (2010), 'Nine million Australins now interacting via social networking sites', 15 March, www.asiadigitalmap.com; Jeanne-Vida Dougals (2010), 'Plugged in and profiting', *BRW*, 12–25 August.

9. Impactdata website, www.impactdata.com.au.

10. ARIA (2003), 'Impact of internet music file sharing & CD burning', 16 July, www.aria.com.au.

11. *The Sydney Morning Herald* (2009), 'Almost all music downloads illegal: report', 19 January, www.smh.com.au.

12. A. King (2008), 'Click go the cheers', *BRW*, 9–15 October, p. 25.

13. P. Hintz (2009), 'Coles sparks online battle for shopping dollars', *The Courier Mail*, 22 January, www.news.com.au.

14. Magic Formula Marketing (2010), 'Top three reasons we choose illegal downloads', 7 May, http://magicformulamarketing.com.

15. Andrew Ramadge (2010), 'Top three reasons we choose illegal downloads', www.news.com.au, 7 May, www.news.com.au; Andrew Ramadge (2010), 'Most pirates say they'd pay for legal downloads', www.news.com.au, 6 May.

16. Facebook website, www.facebook.com.

17. Daniel Nation, 'What is Social Media?', About.com, www.webtrends.about.com.

18. Jeanne-Vida Douglas (2010), 'Big business made personal', *BRW*, 19–25 August.

19. AAP (2010), '"Best Job" campaign is working', *The Sydney Morning Herald*, 9 June, www.smh.com.au.

20. 'YouTube's "Man in the jacket" Heidi admits love story a campaign for Witchery Man' (2009), *The Australian*, 21 January, www.news.com.au; YouTube, various.

21. Liz Tay (2009), 'Google launches AdWords for YouTube', itnews, 28 October, www.itnews.com.au.

22. Alex Erasmus (2010), 'The third screen', *NZ Marketing*, Jan–Feb, p. 28.

23. Tim Nieuwenhuis, personal communication, October 2010; Down Under Guys Gear website, www.dugg.com.au.

24. Natasha Bita (2010), 'Australia's 22-year-old Privacy Act gets internet-era update', *The Australian*, 21 July, www.news.com.au.

25. Australian Communications and Media Authority website, www.acma.gov.au.

26. Australian Competition and Consumer Commission (2010), 'Targeting scams: Report of the ACCC on scam activity 2009', www.accc.gov.au.

27. Commtouch Software Ltd. (2010), 'Q1 2010 internet threats trend report', press release, www.commtouch.com.

28. National Office for the Information Economy and Australian Communications Authority (2004), 'Spam Act 2003: A practical guide for business', Australian Government; New Zealand Department of Internal Affairs (2008), 'services: Anti-spam', www.antispam.govt.nz.

29. Australian Direct Marketing Association website, www.adma.org.au.

30. Australian Communications and Media Authority website, www.acma.gov.au.

31. IP Australia (nd), 'Tales of cybersquatting — Southcorp', IP Toobox, IP Australia; Reuters (2000), 'Madonna wins domain name battle', *CNN*, 16 October, http://cnn.com.

32. A. King (2008), 'Click go the cheers', *BRW*, 9–15 October, p. 25.

33. Centrebet Administration (2009), 'About us', http://centrebet.com.

34. Australian Direct Marketing website, www.adma.com.au.

35. P. Hintz 2009, 'Coles sparks online battle for shopping dollars', *The Courier Mail*, 22 January, www.news.com.au; The Nielsen Company (2009), 'New Zealanders embracing online consumer generated activity', media release, 18 May, www.nielsen-online.com; The Nielsen Company (2009), 'Online shopping hits record levels: Nielsen online', media release, 18 March, www.nielsen-online.com; 'Two-thirds shop online' (2008), *BRW*, 24–30 July, p. 41.

36. IGD senior analyst Adrian Williams, cited in *BRW*, 24–30 July 2008, p. 41.

37. Federal Minister for Broadband, Communications and the Digital Economy, Senator Stephen Conroy cited in A. King (2008), 'Click go the cheers', *BRW*, 9–15 October, p. 26.

38. Big Brown Box website, www.bigbrownbox.com.au; Internet Retailing (2010), 'What's in the big brown box?', 19 January, www.internetretailing.com.au.

39. Old Spice website, www.oldspice.com; Matty Soccio (2010), 'Are you on a horse', *Marketing*, October, p. 43.

40. T. Court (2007), 'Web metrics', *Fuel4arts.com*, Australia Council, www.australiacouncil.gov.au; I. Lurie (2007), '7 internet marketing metrics you must track (and how)', *Conversation Marketing*, 21 September, www.conversationmarketing.com; Marketing terms website, www.marketingterms.com.

41. Hidden Pizza website, www.hiddenpizza.com.au; Lachy Wharton (2010), 'Hidden Pizza Restaurant reveals not-so-hidden flaws in Yellow Pages' digital strategy', *Australian Anthill*, 16 April, http://anthillonline.com; Stephen Ronchi (2010),

'Hiding pizzas and proving value', *Australian Anthill*, http://anthillonline.com.

42. Tiger Beer website, www.tigerbeer.com.my; Mindi Chahal (2010), 'Tiger Beer's "know the not known" campaign', www.promomarketing.info, 5 October; Adoi Magazine (2010), 'Winning case history: Tiger Beer wins bronze at AME 2010', www.adoimagazine.com; Kim Shyan Fam and David Waller, 'Cultural values and advertising in Malaysia: views from the industry', *Asia Pacific Journal of Marketing and Logistics,* apmforum.com.

## Chapter 13

1. J. Lindhe, (2009), 'Boost bears fruit', *BRW*, 16–19 April; Boost Juice Bars Australia website, www.boostjuicebars.com.au.
2. Splatter website, www.splatter.biz/Home.aspx.
3. Department of Innovation, Industry, Science and Research website, www.innovation.gov.au.
4. Department of Foreign Affairs and Trade website, www.dfat.gov.au.
5. Doing Business with New Zealand website, http://business.newzealand.com.
6. M.R. Czinkota, I.R. Ronkainen, M.H. Moffett, S.H. Ang, D. Shanker, A. Ahmad and P. Lock (2009), *Fundamentals of international business*, 1st Asia–Pacific edition, John Wiley & Sons Australia, Brisbane.
7. Feature adapted from M.R. Czinkota et al., *Fundamentals of international business*, 1st Asia–Pacific edition, John Wiley & Sons, Brisbane, pp. 42–3.
8. Austrade (2009), 'China', www.austrade.gov.au; New Zealand Trade and Enterprise (2009), 'China', www.nzte.govt.nz.
9. New Zealand Trade and Enterprise website, www.nzte.govt.nz; New Zealand Trade and Enterprise website, www.nzte.govt.nz.
10. Department of Foreign Affairs and Trade website, www.dfat.gov.au.
11. H. Assael, N. Pope, L. Brennan and K. Voges (2007), *Consumer behaviour*, 1st Asia–Pacific edition, John Wiley & Sons, Brisbane.
12. Mark Colvin (2010), 'News Corp defends paid online content', transcript, *PM,* 19 November, www.abc.net.au.
13. New Zealand Ministry of Economic Development (2009), 'Tariffs level held until 30 June 2011', www.med.govt.nz.
14. Austrade website, www.austrade.gov.au.
15. International Market Selection website, 'screening in context', www.intlms.com.au.
16. Gloria Jean's (2010), 'Gloria Jean's executive chairman honoured with top retail award', media release, 15 February, www.gloriajeanscoffees.com.au; Gloria Jean's website, www.gloriajeans.com.au, Austrade (2009), 'Gloria Jean's Coffees — coffee franchise', *Journey to International Business*, July, pp. 74–6.
17. J. Drape (2008), 'Tourism Australia has 'no bloody idea how it's doing', *The Australian*, 26 November.
18. 'Nestlé hits mainland with cheap ice-cream' (2005), *Advertising Age*, 7 March, p. 12.
19. B. Henderson (2008), 'Top ten biggest international marketing mistakes', Ezine articles, http://ezinearticles.com.
20. M. Ross (2010), 'Ginger and Smart', *Professional Marketing*, October–December, pp. 19–23, http://gingerandsmart.com.
21. Subway website, www.subway.com; Mos Burger website, www.mos.co.jp/english/; Yoshinoya website, www.yoshinoya.com; Starbucks website, www.starbucks.com; KFC website. www.kfc.com; Mister Donut website, www.misterdonut.com; case study partially adapted from a case prepared by Daryl Johnson, Kentaro Oku and Shigeru Tamiya of Kwansei-Gakuin University, under the supervision of Professor Masaaki Kotabe.

## Chapter 14

1. Christine Walker (2010), 'A little birdie told me: Twitter unearths surprising brand insights', Australian Market & Social Research Society conference, Melbourne, 9-10 September, www.amsrs.com.au.
2. Australian Marketing Institute (2008) '2008 Awards for Marketing Excellence', www.ami.org.au.
3. Anonymous (2007) 'Data for donors', *Proximity*, Oct–Nov, p. 39.
4. A. Coates and T. Davis (2010), 'The Cloncurry Waterwise Service: motivating behaviour change through a service offering', International NonProfit and Social Marketing Conference, Brisbane, July, p. 242.
5. T.S. Gruca and L.L. Rego (2005), 'Customer satisfaction, cash flow and shareholder value', *Journal of Marketing*, vol. 69, pp. 115–30; N.A. Morgan and L.L Rego (2006), 'The value of different customer satisfaction and loyalty metrics in predicting business performance', *Marketing Science*, vol. 25, no. 2, pp. 426–39; L. Aksoy, B. Cooil, C. Groening, T.L. Keiningham and A. Yalcin (2008), 'The long-term stock market valuation of customer satisfaction', *Journal of Marketing*, vol. 72, pp. 105–22.
6. Fuji Xerox website, www.fujixeroxprinters.co.nz.
7. G. Regan (2009), 'The evolution of Facebook's mission statement', *The New York Observer,* 13 July, www.observer.com.

8. Woolworths website, www.woolworths.com.au.

9. Singapore Airlines website, www.singaporeair.com.

10. Tourism Queensland website, www.tq.com.au.

11. Australian Marketing Institute (2010), 'Winner — corporate social responsibility', Awards for Marketing Excellence, p. 18.

12. G. Medcalf (2009), 'Tightening the screws', *NZ Marketing*, Dec–Jan, pp. 26–31.

13. Australian Marketing Institute (2010), 'Winner — green marketing', Awards for Marketing Excellence, p. 21; Solar City website, www.townsvillesolarcity.com.au; B. Cubby (2010), 'Our greenhouse gas emissions back on the rise', *The Sydney Morning Herald*, 28 May, www.smh.com.au.

14. Alexandra Kirk (2008), 'Govt injects $22m bailout into ABC Learning', transcript, *PM,* 7 November, www.abc.net.au.

15. CSC website, www.csc.com.au; Australian Marketing Institute (2010), 'Winner — internal marketing', Awards for Marketing Excellence, p. 23.

16. R. Ching (2010), 'EatSmart restaurants: create health when people eat out', International Nonprofit and Social Marketing Conference Proceedings, Brisbane, July, p. 234.

17. These are available on the Australian Marketing Institute website for institute members (see www.ami.org.au).

18. Transport and Main Roads website, www.tmr.qld.gov.au; Australian Marketing Institute (2010), 'Winner — social marketing', Awards for Marketing Excellence; Drug and Alcohol Services South Australia website, www.dassa.sa.gov.au.

19. Andrew Flannery (2010) 'Flight Centre Limited 2010 half year results', 25 February, www.flightcentre.com.au; S. Cierpicki and T. Moffat (2009), 'Demonstrating the ROI of customer experience', AMSRS 2009 National Conference, Sep–Oct; S. Cierpicki and S.R. Rundle-Thiele (2009), 'Store revenue growth and customer experience metrics', 18th Annual Frontiers in Services Conference, Hawaii, 29 Oct–1 Nov.

# Index